CHILDREN
WITH
SPECIAL NEEDS

Children With Special Needs

Edited by

Katharine T. Bartlett

and

Judith Welch Wegner

Transaction Books

New Brunswick (U.S.A.) and Oxford (U.K.)

Library of Congress Catalog Number: 87-10907
ISBN: 088738-690-3
Printed in the United States of America

Library of Congress Cataloging in Publication Data

Children with special needs.

  Published also as v. 48, nos. 1-2, winter-spring 1985, of Law and contemporary problems.
    1. Handicapped children—Education—Law and legislation—United States. 2. Handicapped children—Education—Law and legislation. I. Bartlett, Katharine T.   II. Wegner, Judith Welch.
KF4210.A75C47 1987   344.73′0791   87-10907
ISBN 0-88738-690-3   347.304791

CONTENTS

FOREWORD

The presence of children with special needs in the public schools has been the source of diverse and shifting tensions. In the early and middle decades of this century, educators were uncertain of the capabilities of exceptional children, concerned about their possible adverse effect on other youngsters, and hesitant to modify standard curricula to respond to the unique requirements of such children. Placement in segregated classrooms and exclusion from public schools altogether was a common response. During the 1970's, parents and advocates sought to remove existing barriers and secure greater educational opportunity for handicapped children in public education, insisting that all children can learn and that even nonhandicapped children suffer adverse effects from the exclusion of the handicapped from public schools. The legislation that was the product of their efforts, Public Law 94-142, The Education for All Handicapped Children Act of 1975 (EAHCA), has become central to the continuing debate over the role of public schools in educating children with special needs.

The authors of the essays included in this volume, together with others who participated in a conference on children with special needs in the public schools held at the Duke University School of Law in 1984, contribute to that debate in two ways. First, they evaluate the success of the EAHCA and other legal mechanisms designed to ensure that the requirements of children with special needs are adequately met from a variety of historical, empirical, analytical, and comparative perspectives. In doing so, they have assumed a general familiarity with that legislation, discussing its terms in detail only where needed to advance the course of argument. Second, they suggest steps that might be taken to improve the efficacy with which such legal strategems attain their goals. These suggestions respond to many tensions that will continue to shape the response of educators, parents, and the legal system to children with special needs during the years to come.

The volume begins with William Clune and Mark Van Pelt's discussion of the tension between the formal goals of special education legislation and the reality of statutory implementation. Professor Clune and Mr. Van Pelt argue that evaluation of such legislation should not proceed by simple comparison of legislative goals and actual implementation. Instead, they argue that evaluation requires a three-step process: (1) positive political analysis that identifies and explains adjustments that have been made in practice during implementation of the legislative scheme; (2) normative evaluation of each adjustment from the point of view of influential political interests affected; and (3) formulation of a new agenda for public policy development based on an understanding of these political adjustments.

Using this scheme, Clune and Van Pelt examine three major facets of the EAHCA: its procedures for referral and assessment of children who may be eligible for special education services; its requirements for development of individualized educational programs (IEPs); and its provision for due process hearings and associated procedural protections. They conclude that federal legislation has resulted both in notable successes, such as the end of exclusionary practices, the implementation of special programs, and the introduction of beneficial organizational routines within the public schools, and in certain failures, such as the routinization rather than individualization of educational programming and the limited efficacy of parental participation. Clune and Van Pelt suggest that, although statutory provisions for development of IEPs and for due process procedures may have failed to provide all benefits originally foreseen, they have had other beneficial consequences that justify their retention. The authors suggest that additional efforts are needed to address other serious problems that have been identified during the first ten years of the Act's existence, such as the use of educable mentally retarded and learning disabled classifications.

The next two chapters, by scholars with a longstanding interest in special education, focus upon the tensions associated with the due process requirements of EAHCA. The chapter by David Neal and David Kirp explores the dynamics of adopting a "legalization" model, rather than either a "professional" or a "bureaucratic" model, as a means of giving substance to the public policy objectives underlying the Act. The legalization model focuses on the individual as bearer of rights, with attendant use of legal concepts and reasoning and legal techniques of enforcement. In comparison, the professional model emphasizes professional discretion, while the bureaucratic model relies upon governmental departments to administer public programs under specific criteria.

After tracing the historical roots of the legalization model in the special education context, Neal and Kirp assess its appropriateness on the basis of empirical evidence and their evaluation of the wider context of the education system. They conclude that due process procedures have had mixed success at best, in view of the formalistic compliance that characterizes some schools' implementation of the Act's IEP requirements and the limited use made of the Act's hearing opportunities. While the legalization model empowers actors who have previously lacked access to resources and allows for principled decisionmaking, the authors argue that the model has several more troublesome features, such as its inability to address questions of quality and substance in special education, its failure to deal with questions of resource allocation, and its tendency to promote distrust between parents and teachers and to inhibit the discretion of professionals whose judgment should be used on behalf of children. These features lead Neal and Kirp to suggest that as the education system comes to accept the presence of handicapped children and recognizes the legitimacy of their claims, less reliance will be placed on some aspects of the legalized structure of special education.

The chapter by Peter Kuriloff focuses more specifically upon competing factors which influence outcomes in the process hearings. Acknowledging that there is no real way to establish the "accuracy" of special education hearings, he attempts to measure how well these hearings serve "justice," which he defines in terms of the ability of parents to affect hearing outcomes. In his empirical examination of the results of due process hearings involving mentally retarded children in Pennsylvania during 1972-76, Professor Kuriloff addresses several questions. Of those who use due process hearings, who wins? Does winning depend on the quality of use of procedural safeguards by parents and by schools? Do hearing officers' biases affect hearing outcomes? Do other variables, such as the age and gender of the child or the size of the district, which should be irrelevant to outcome in most or all cases, operate to skew the results while undermining any conclusions that can be drawn from the due process variables themselves?

Professor Kuriloff concludes that outcomes in due process hearings reflect a combination of substantive factors and, although perhaps to a lesser extent, adversarial techniques. He reports that parents with severely handicapped children are more likely to prevail in due process hearings than those whose children are less substantially impaired. But, he points out that parents of severely handicapped children tend to present their cases most effectively. Not surprisingly, these parents, as well as other parents, who present their cases better, also tend to prevail more frequently. In contrast, Kuriloff reports that schools' use of lawyers in due process hearings tends to correlate negatively with the quality of presentation and with compliance; however, this correlation may suggest that schools use lawyers more when they know they have a weak case. Kuriloff also indicates that, for a number of possible reasons, parents tend to win more frequently in larger districts than in smaller ones.

William Buss brings a comparative perspective to the role of both procedural protections and substantive attributes of legal schemes in ensuring the responsiveness of public schools to children with special needs. After noting fundamental differences in the structure of American and British legal rights, the nature of the federal system, and the role of the judiciary, Professor Buss focuses on the 1981 British Education Act, which governs the provision of special education in England and Wales. Using the provisions of the EAHCA as a foil, he highlights a variety of tensions which underlie both statutes. He first describes the narrower class of children protected under the new British statutory scheme and discusses the substantive guarantee of beneficial, individualized educational programming it creates. He contrasts the Education Act's mainstreaming provisions with those included in the EAHCA, stressing distinctions in the degree of integration required and the conditions controlling the duty to integrate under each of these statutory schemes. Finally, Professor Buss discusses the extensive procedural protection afforded parents under the British legislation and the more limited administrative and judicial review available under that system. In doing so, he highlights recurrent questions of the deference to be accorded professional decisions and the role of the judiciary, which are evident in both the American and British legal schemes.

Next, Judith Wegner and Kate Bartlett address major tensions which have influenced interpretation of the EAHCA's substantive requirements. Professor Wegner argues that tensions resulting from the Act's attempt to afford handicapped children educational opportunities "equal" to those enjoyed by their nonhandicapped peers have subtly, but significantly, complicated the courts' interpretation of statutory educational programming mandates. She suggests that recent debates concerning the level and extent of services to be provided handicapped children, the scope of needs to be addressed, and the availability of certain non-educational "medical" services reflect competing approaches to the application of the notion of "equal educational opportunity." Professor Wegner concludes that no single definition of equal opportunity can successfully resolve all these questions; rather, careful assessment of competing equality-based interpretations, in light of each particular context in which the definition of equality is sought, can significantly aid the process of statutory interpretation.

Kate Bartlett explores the challenge to legal reform posed by the high cost of special education. She first traces the diverse judicial efforts to resolve the question of whether cost should be taken into account in defining school district responsibility under the EAHCA. She then identifies several areas of tensions between the EAHCA and the institutional context in which that legislation must be implemented that have exacerbated the fundamental problem of allocating scarce resources between handicapped and non-handicapped children in the public schools. These include the tension between individualized and collective decisionmaking, between need and merit, and between federal and state/local decisionmaking. Professor Bartlett then proposes an approach to taking cost into account in educational decisionmaking for the handicapped that she argues would mediate these underlying tensions more adequately than current approaches and would better resolve the cost issue. The model she develops, which would require parity between the quality of educational programs offered to handicapped children and those offered to nonhandicapped children in a particular school district, would allow decisionmakers to take the cost of particular programs into account but would protect handicapped children from absorbing more than their fair share of the effects of resource scarcity.

Rounding out the discussion of the Act's substantive requirements are two contributions by student authors and a chapter by a practicing attorney with substantial special education casework experience. The first of the student contributions explores the difficulties associated with defining education for purposes of the EAHCA where unconventional goals and programs are substituted for more standard objectives and offerings. It advocates a broad definition of education under the Act to reflect that broad range of handicaps possessed by individuals intended to benefit from the legislation. The second student contribution discusses the additional problems raised by demands for placements that are age-appropriate and concludes that the age of the surrounding peer group should be a factor to be taken into account in determining whether a program is educationally appropriate for a given student.

The chapter written by Karen Sindelar, an attorney with the North Carolina Governor's Advocacy Council for Persons with Disabilities, offers an analysis of the causes of the gap between the substantive requirements of the EAHCA and its implementation. Ms. Sindelar discusses services to retarded children to illustrate her arguments that the EAHCA has not resulted in the substantive improvements in education for handicapped children envisioned by its framers and that policymakers must analyze areas of noncompliance and failed implementation individually in order to better target efforts to achieve change. She examines the reasons that services for retarded children continue to be unnecessarily segregated and inferior despite legal mandates. She discusses, in particular, attitudes of local administrators and parents, lack of state leadership, state fiscal incentives that promote segregated placements, and funding patterns and bureaucratic relationships that make it difficult for retarded students to gain access to "mainstream" educational services. She also analyzes the role that some of the same factors have played in promoting change. Ms. Sindelar concludes by proposing a multi-faceted strategy designed to bring about greater equalization of services to, and integration of, retarded students. Her proposal includes suggestions for training at the local level as well as federal regulatory revision heightened federal monitoring, and a federal incentive program that would encourage states to abandon fiscal subsidies for segregated educational placements.

The volume concludes with chapters discussing two universal tensions that arise not only in the context of special education, but also in other cases where the traditional practices of public schools are reshaped to respond to children with special needs. Martha Minow argues that a common dilemma–the "dilemma of difference"–

underlies efforts to develop satisfactory programs of special and bilingual education. She suggests that both types of programs confront a single, fundamental question: How can schools deal with children defined as "different" without, on the one hand, recreating opportunities for discrimination which come with separate treatment, or, on the other hand, leaving intact a neutral system that advances the dominant group while it simultaneously hinders others? Professor Minow considers efforts to redesign programs or constrain power as possible ways out of the dilemma. She concludes, however, that the dilemma reappears despite these efforts. She recommends that future reform should begin with the recognition that the dilemma is one shared by the entire student group, and that solutions should seek to reconstruct the relationships that associate difference with stigma.

Betsy Levin addresses the problems of designing educational programs for children with special needs within the context of a federal system of government. In a comparative study of the Australian and American legal and educational systems, Dean Levin explores the tensions created by federal educational activism designed to provide equal opportunity to special pupil populations whose needs cannot be fully addressed by local authorities. After tracing the historical role of the Australian Commonwealth in setting educational policy, she considers the constitutional basis for federal intervention within the Australian system. She then describes current Australian grant-in-aid programs designed to serve language-minority, handicapped, and economically disadvantaged populations and notes a number of differences in the ways that the tension between federal and local interests has been mediated in the Australian and American systems.

Further understanding of the dimension of federalism in the American systems is provided by a student-prepared analysis of state special education laws. It compares the federal law framework of the EAHCA and other federal legislation, with the state law network that complements and in some cases imposes stricter duties upon school districts than does federal law.

This important collection tackles many of the most important legal and policy issues concerning children with special needs in public education. While these efforts do not resolve forevermore the issues, they continue and enlarge a debate upon which sensible solutions depend.

PART I

PART I

1

A POLITICAL METHOD OF EVALUATING THE EDUCATION FOR ALL HANDICAPPED CHILDREN ACT OF 1975 AND THE SEVERAL GAPS OF GAP ANALYSIS

WILLIAM H. CLUNE*

AND

MARK H. VAN PELT†

I

INTRODUCTION

This article argues that an evaluation of Public Law No. 94-142, the Education for All Handicapped Children Act (EAHCA)[1] (and by analogy any other social program), should consist of six elements discussed in the following pages: a synthesis of empirical research on the implementation of EAHCA relative to reformist objectives (what happened?); a political explanation of the implementation "gap" revealed in these empirical studies (whose interests were served?); an assessment of how the policy instrument chosen for the EAHCA ("legalization") contributed to the implementation gap (what were the realistic limits of change?); a discussion of the standards appropriate as normative yardsticks against which to evaluate the law (reformist versus politically realistic standards); an overall evaluation of the EAHCA in light of the standards developed in the preceding section; and some recommendations about what should be done now. As a connected whole, these topics comprise a "political method" of social program evaluation,[2] a method with two essential components: a descriptive idea that implementation is a process of political adjustment among competing interests, and a normative idea that the political interests revealed during implementation must be given some nor-

---

* Professor, University of Wisconsin Law School.

† J.D. and Ph.D. (Educational Policy Studies) candidate, University of Wisconsin-Madison.

The research for this article was supported by Grant Nos. NIE-G-81-0009 and NIE-G-84-0008 to the Wisconsin Center for Education Research. Helpful comments were received from Jack Coons and most if not all of the participants at the Children With Special Needs Symposium, held at Duke Law School, February 1984. Such support, assistance or approval does not imply agreement with the conclusions of this research.

1. 20 U.S.C. §§ 1400-1461 (1982) (codifying Pub. L. No. 94-142, 89 Stat. 773 (1975) and subsequent amendments).

2. The basic political model and approach to evaluation used in this article may be found in Clune, *A Political Model of Implementation and Implications of the Model for Public Policy, Research, and the Changing Roles of Law and Lawyers*, 69 IOWA L. REV. 47, 86-95 (1983).

mative significance. Evaluations which ignore the descriptive fact of political adjustments are usually formalistic, concerning themselves with the meaning of legal language rather than the fates of affected individuals and organizations.[3] Evaluations which ignore the normative significance of political adjustments fall into either of two antithetical fallacies: the ideological fallacy (or "gap analysis"), which assumes the ethical primacy of reformist objectives, ignoring the ethical claims of competing interests,[4] or the sociological fallacy, which assumes the ethical primacy of actual behavior.[5] Evaluations also must be pragmatic. Before judging what has occurred, and before recommending reform, one must develop a theory of the possible. For this reason, the limits of social change through legalization will be discussed in section II B.

The two major parts of this article correspond to the two major components of a political evaluation: a descriptive political analysis of the implementation of the EAHCA (provided in part II) and a normative discussion of success, failure, and the need for reform (provided in part III). Part II offers a description and explanation of what happened during the implementation of the EAHCA (what program adjustments occurred and which political interests were responsible for them). The product of that effort is a picture of implementation as a mosaic of human interests and intentions, a dynamic equilibrium struck from the ethical, economic, political, and organizational goals and resources of the people and organizations concerned with special education.[6] Part III begins with this political analysis and evaluates what happened in light of it. Looking at special education implementation as a human interaction, the questions are whether it was a constructive interaction and how future intervention should try to change the interaction.

---

3. Formalistic evaluations may overestimate program success (e.g., by assuming that due process provides a realistic opportunity to be heard simply because there is a legal right), or underestimate program success (e.g., by assuming that a right to a minimum of education is unimportant when in practice advocates can use such a right quite effectively). See discussion of Board of Educ. v. Rowley, 458 U.S. 176 (1982), *infra* note 188 and accompanying text.

4. Gap studies were the subject of an unpublished speech by Austin Sarat at the annual meeting of the Law and Society Association, June 1983. *See* Abel, *Law as Lag: Inertia as a Social Theory of Law*, 80 MICH. L. REV. 785, 786, 795 (1982).

This gap is significant in three ways. *See infra* notes 189-218 and accompanying text (gap explained descriptively in terms of political adjustments during implementation; examination of role of legalization as policy instrument in producing gap); *infra* notes 219-230 and accompanying text (uniform negative evaluation implied from gap disputed because of failure to recognize normative significance of competing interests revealed during implementation); *infra* part III (gap a necessary part of ongoing democratic evaluations because of the need for and inevitability of a counterfactual idealistic perspective, for example, in arguments over the practical meaning of reformist legal language in statutes, court decrees, and administrative rules). In addition, all of section I A, *infra*, is an empirically grounded description and explanation of the EAHCA implementation gap.

5. *See* Etzioni, *Two Approaches to Organizational Analysis: A Critique and a Suggestion*, 5 AD. SCI. Q. 257 (1960).

6. The set of those affected by a law and concerned enough to make responses and adjustments has been called the "social field." *See* S. Macaulay, Private Government (Working Paper No. 1983-6, Disputes Processing Research Program, University of Wisconsin Law School) (also forthcoming in the Social Science Research Council Handbook of Law and Social Science); Moore, *Law and Social Change: The Semi-Autonomous Social Field As An Appropriate Subject of Study*, 7 LAW & SOC'Y REV. 719 (1973).

II

THE POLITICS OF EAHCA IMPLEMENTATION—WHAT HAPPENED AND WHY?

This part proposes a description and political explanation of EAHCA implementation. In section A, empirical studies of EAHCA implementation are summarized according to outcomes, chronological stages, and procedural mechanisms in the process of special education decisionmaking. It is illustrative of the indelible normativity of law, that one cannot describe the process of implementation without measuring it against some standard, expectation, or norm.[7]

Section A also begins the political explanation of implementation patterns by suggesting specific, contextual reasons for the adjustments which seem to have occurred at each stage of the process. Section B generalizes on those particularized observations by suggesting a general model of social change through social program implementation (legislation or institutional litigation).[8] According to this model, change occurs because the law provides a variety of new resources, but change is limited because of the intrinsic limitations of these resources and a variety of countervailing forces. Section B also considers specific strengths and weaknesses of the particular form of legal intervention chosen by the EAHCA: legalization, or proceduralism.[9] Even under the optimum conditions represented by the EAHCA, that method is found to produce change which is fast and widespread but also shallow and uneven.

A. EAHCA Implementation Summarized: Successes, Failures and Reasons

Summarizing the implementation of a law centers on a few deceptively simple inquiries. First, what are the requirements set forth by the law? Second, what would the law achieve if it were perfectly implemented according to the standards and expectations of its reformist sponsors? Third, how did outcomes of the implementation process compare with these goals? Finally, to what extent can outcomes of implementation be linked to the chronological sequence of procedures established by the law as a means of achieving the ultimate goals?

---

7. On the sociological normativity of legal facts, see Clune & Lindquist, *What "Implementation" Isn't: Toward a General Framework for Implementation Research,* 1981 WIS. L. REV. 1044, 1114; Clune, *Courts and Legislators As Arbitrators of Social Change* (Book Review), 93 YALE L.J. 763, 770-71 (1984).

8. Some authorities implicitly or explicitly distinguish social program implementation from regulation. *Compare* E. BARDACH, THE IMPLEMENTATION GAME: WHAT HAPPENS AFTER A BILL BECOMES A LAW (1977), *with* E. BARDACH & R. KAGAN, GOING BY THE BOOK (1982). *See also* SOCIAL PROGRAM IMPLEMENTATION (W. Williams & R. Elmore eds. 1976) (implementation seemingly defined as laws involving financial aid or program development). Clune has defined implementation functionally as resources, assistance, and regulation seeking to change preferred behavior, especially of complex organizations. Clune & Lindquist, *supra* note 7, at 1072-83; Clune, *supra* note 2, at 50-51.

9. Proceduralism in education has been a concern of Professors Kirp and Yudof for some time. *See* Kirp, *Proceduralism and Bureaucracy: Due Process in the School Setting,* 28 STAN. L. REV. 841, 859-76 (1976); Yudof, *Legalization of Dispute Resolution, Distrust of Authority, and Organization Theory: Implementing Due Process for Students in the Public Schools,* 1981 WIS. L. REV. 891; *see also infra* note 215.

Answers to the third and fourth questions in this sequence suggest that the research has established what usually are problematic causal links between social actions. The data base for this article is not so strong. No randomized experiments have been performed, and there is really no practical way to separate the influence of the EAHCA from other forces in the environment moving in the same direction (state laws, popular attitudes, etc.). Further, the existing studies leave unanswered many questions pertinent to causation issues. For example, not much is known about the reasons for teacher referral decisions, although teachers are the principal decisionmakers in the referral process. Nonetheless, the causation problem is not especially troublesome. The conclusions reached in this section represent a synthesis of a score of extensive, well-constructed implementation studies. The data base cannot be much improved, and any gaps do not prevent the studies from establishing reliable general patterns of implementation.

One final point: keep in mind that, throughout the synthesis of implementation research, the political explanations of the observed patterns are a major concern. In every section dealing with implementation results, questions will be asked about whose interests were served by the particular adjustments discussed. The implementation case studies examined all seem to rely on this form of explanation. Major organizational adjustments are seen as satisfying some set of organizational needs. As will be seen in the case of organizations like schools, which are under a great deal of pressure to do various things, the idea of politically adaptive organizational adjustments is not a bold assumption.

1. *The EAHCA Process.* The EAHCA requires each state and, in turn, each local education agency (LEA), to identify, locate, and evaluate all handicapped children in all public and private agencies and institutions[10] and provide them with a free appropriate public education. An LEA must provide written notice to parents in each of the following situations: if it identifies their child as handicapped, evaluates the child for determination of a handicapping condition, proposes to change the child's identification or evaluation, refuses to initially identify and evaluate, or subsequently refuses to reidentify and reevaluate the child.[11] The LEA must receive the parents' consent for a preplacement evaluation.[12]

Children who are referred[13] must be evaluated before they are placed in any special education program.[14] The evaluation must be administered by a multidisciplinary team (M-Team) in the child's native language or mode of communication using at least two valid, correctly administered procedures,

---

10. 20 U.S.C. §§ 1412(2)(C), 1414(a)(1)(A) (1982).

11. *Id.* § 1415(b)(1)(C) (1982).

12. 34 C.F.R. § 300.504(b)(1)(i) (1984).

13. EAHCA and its implementing regulations do not provide explicit guidelines regarding the initial referral.

14. 20 U.S.C. § 1412(5)(C) (1982); 34 C.F.R. §§ 300.531 - .532 (1984).

including at least one procedure that is not a general IQ test.[15] Assessments must cover all areas of suspected disability[16] and may not be racially or culturally discriminatory.[17] Placement decisions should not be based on tests alone, but should include at least one other evaluation source, such as a teacher's observation of the child's classroom performance.[18] Children who are placed after the M-Team determines that they have a special education need must be reevaluated at least every three years to insure that they are receiving the appropriate education resources.[19] Each state's annual program plan must include a comprehensive system of personnel development which insures that education agency personnel, as well as parents and volunteers, receive inservice training which will, among other things, assist them in identifying and evaluating children with special educational needs.[20]

Once an education agency determines that a child has a handicapping condition within the meaning of the EAHCA, it must develop an individualized education program (IEP)[21] for that child. The IEP should be developed at a meeting which includes a representative of the education agency who is qualified to provide or supervise special education, the child's teacher, the parents or guardian of the child, and, where appropriate, the child.[22] The education agency must provide adequate notice of the meeting to insure that the parents have the opportunity to attend and the meeting must occur at a convenient time and place.[23] The child's IEP must be implemented in the least restrictive environment for that child; that is, the child should be mainstreamed to the fullest possible extent.[24]

In the event that parents are dissatisfied with this process, they may present complaints to the LEA "with respect to any matter relating to the identification, evaluation, or educational placement of the child, or the provision of a free appropriate public education to such child."[25] Whenever the LEA receives such a complaint, the parents (or guardian) of the child shall receive the opportunity to have an impartial due process hearing conducted either by the State Education Agency (SEA), LEA, or another state authority, as determined by the state.[26] The parents are accorded specific hearing

---

15. 20 U.S.C. § 1412(5)(C) (1982); 34 C.F.R. § 300.532(a)-(e) (1984).
16. 34 C.F.R. § 300.532(f) (1984).
17. *Id.* § 300.530(b) (1984).
18. 34 C.F.R. § 300.533(a)(1)-(3) (1984). The regulations contain additional detailed requirements for M-Teams with respect to evaluating a child suspected of having a specific learning disability, including provisions for additional M-Team members, classroom observations, a special written report, and a specific finding that the child's disability is not actually another type of disability. *See id.* §§ 300.540-.543 (1983).
19. *Id.* § 300.534(b) (1984).
20. 20 U.S.C. § 1413(a)(3) (1982); 34 C.F.R. § 300.382 (1984).
21. 20 U.S.C. § 1401(19) (1982).
22. *Id.*
23. 34 C.F.R. § 300.345(a)-(b) (1984).
24. 20 U.S.C. § 1412(5)(B) (1982).
25. *Id.* § 1415(b)(1)(E) (1982). This right extends to the child's parents or guardian. LEA's may initiate the hearing process in the event that, for whatever reason, no parental consent is provided for the child's evaluation or initial placement. 34 C.F.R. § 300.504(c) (1984).
26. 20 U.S.C. § 1415(b)(2) (1982).

rights,[27] a timely response to their complaint,[28] and an impartial and independent review of the hearing at the state level if the original hearing was conducted below the state agency level.[29] When these administrative procedures are exhausted,[30] any aggrieved party has the right to a civil action with respect to the original complaint and may bring that action in any state court of competent jurisdiction or in a U.S. district court. The court 1) reviews the administrative record, 2) hears additional evidence at the request of either party, and 3) on the preponderance of the evidence, "grant[s] such relief as the court determines is appropriate."[31] In addition to establishing this elaborate procedural mechanism designed to ensure that each handicapped child receives an appropriate free public education, the EAHCA also establishes a funding mechanism to help states cope with the new costs of special education.

2. *Implementational Assumptions and Reformist Purposes.* Congress had to make many assumptions about how this sequence of elaborate procedural mechanisms could fully achieve the ambitious, even monumental, reformist objective that *all* handicapped children were to receive a free, appropriate education (and that no nonhandicapped children were to accidentally end up in a special education program). First, Congress assumed an operational environment in which relatively few referral and assessment errors would occur either as a result of inadequate knowledge within the system or as a result of inherently inadequate testing mechanisms. Although Congress knew that teachers were not entirely prepared to implement the Act,[32] it assumed that the evaluation process, through better trained personnel and nondiscriminatory multiple assessment procedures, would screen the errors generated through teacher referral. Gradually, teacher inservice programs would increase referring teachers' knowledge of special education needs, thereby increasing the accuracy of the referrals and reducing the need for such screening and the workload on the assessment staff.[33]

---

27. *Id.* § 1415(d) (1982). The parties involved in such a hearing may: 1) be accompanied and advised by counsel; 2) be accompanied by persons with special knowledge or training with respect to special education; 3) present evidence; 4) confront, cross-examine, and compel attendance of witnesses; 5) have a written or electronic verbatim record of the hearing; and 6) have the right to written findings of facts and a copy of the decision. A final due process hearing regarding the complaint must be conducted within forty-five days of receipt of request of the hearing. In the event that the initial hearing was conducted below the SEA level, "any party aggrieved by the findings and decision rendered in such a hearing may appeal to the State educational agency which shall conduct an impartial review of such hearing. The officer conducting such review shall make an independent decision upon completion of such review." *Id.* § 1415(c) (1982). The same rights apply to the parties if the original hearing occurred at a level below the SEA and one of the parties appeals the result of the hearing to the SEA.

28. 34 C.F.R. § 300.512(a) (1984).

29. 20 U.S.C. § 1415(c) (1982).

30. *Id.* § 1415(e)(1) (1982).

31. *Id.* § 1415(e)(2) (1982).

32. S. REP. No. 168, 94th Cong., 1st Sess. 33, reprinted in 1975 U.S. CODE CONG. & AD. NEWS 1425, 1457.

33. 20 U.S.C. § 1400(b)(7) (1982).

Second, Congress believed the IEP procedure was "a way to provide parent involvement and protection to assure that appropriate services are provided to a handicapped child."[34] Although it did not explicitly so state, Congress clearly assumed that educators would not on their own maximize the educational potential of each child. While Congress saw the IEP conference as the culmination of the identification and evaluation process, it simultaneously expected that parents would utilize it "as an extension of the procedural protections guaranteed under existing law to parents of handicapped children. . . ."[35]

Third, Congress assumed that the due process provisions would make it easier for parents to take successful action against uncooperative districts. In contrast to court procedures, the EAHCA's due process provisions were assumed to be relatively informal, inexpensive, quick, and substantively oriented.[36] A procedural mechanism with these characteristics supposedly would lead to more systematic pressure on school systems, put handicapped children on an educational par with nonhandicapped students, and lead to uniformity of treatment among handicapped children.[37] Further, advocates

---

34. S. REP. No. 168, 94th Cong., 1st Sess. 12 (1975), *reprinted in* 1975 U.S. CODE CONG. & AD. NEWS 1425, 1436; *see also* H.R. REP. No. 332, 94th Cong., 1st Sess. 13 (1975); S. REP. No. 168, 94th Cong., 1st Sess. 11 (1975), *reprinted in* 1975 U.S. CODE CONG. & AD. NEWS 1425, 1435 (adequate involvement).

35. S. REP. No. 168, 94th Cong., 1st Sess. 11 (1975), *reprinted in* 1975 U.S. CODE CONG. & AD. NEWS 1425, 1435.

36. The Act's legislative history contains numerous statements assuming that the due process provisions would make life easier for parents and schools. *See, e.g.,* S. REP. No. 168, 94th Cong., 1st Sess. 9 (1975), *reprinted in* 1975 U.S. CODE CONG. & AD. NEWS 1425, 1433 ("It should not . . . be necessary for parents throughout the country to continue utilizing the courts to assure themselves a remedy."). Several senators sponsoring the EAHCA expressed views that the due process requirements would remove the difficulties that the court system presented to most parents trying to get an appropriate education for their children. "It is part of the rhythm of life in this country, an unconscious assumption, that our children will be educated. So should it be for the handicapped child and his parents. It must not be, for them, a court battle." 121 CONG. REC. 37,411 (1975) (remarks of Senator Stafford); *see also* 121 CONG. REC. 37,416 (1975) (remarks by Senator Williams) (stressing the importance of a prompt hearing process in order to avoid setbacks to the child's education). Indeed, the classic, pre-EAHCA federal court decisions implemented due process requirements because the courts also thought that due process would provide a more facilitative shadow under which to bargain than that presented by the courts. *See* Pennsylvania Ass'n for Retarded Citizens v. Pennsylvania, 334 F. Supp. 1257 (E.D. Pa. 1971), *enforced,* 343 F. Supp. 279 (E.D. Pa. 1972); Mills v. Board of Educ., 348 F. Supp. 866 (D.D.C. 1972). The EAHCA, it should be noted, does not provide substantive standards to decide placement disputes. Indeed, one congressional report specifically noted that inasmuch as each handicapped child is unique, the Act was meant to give local school districts a certain degree of flexibility in balancing state, local, and parental interests while providing the child with an appropriate education. H.R. REP. No. 332, 94th Cong., 1st Sess. 16 (1975). In this respect, it is clear that Congress—if not the handicapped advocacy community—wanted to leave education agencies with a certain amount of discretion to determine what was an appropriate education for each child. However, there are also many statements in the reports and the Congressional Record indicating that the Congressional goal was to assure the maximization of each handicapped child's potential, thus implying that Congress did have a significant scale in mind against which substantive standards should be measured. *See, e.g.,* H.R. REP. No. 332, 94th Cong., 1st Sess. 19 (1975); *see also* Neal & Kirp, *The Allure of Legalization Reconsidered: The Case of Special Education,* LAW & CONTEMP. PROBS., Winter 1985, at 63.

37. *See* L. Lynn, The Emerging System for Educating Handicapped Children 30-31 (Oct. 29, 1981) (unpublished manuscript) (proponents of the EAHCA hoped that the law would provide the handicapped with the same level of services and the same respect from teachers and administrators

hoped that results in individual cases would be followed across the board, producing a general pattern of compliance.

Finally, Congress knew that the EAHCA created an expensive compliance burden for the states.[38] Some of the changes, such as changes in organizational routines and attitudes, would entail nonmonetary costs. Others, such as individualized education, the development of new programs, and adequate and timely evaluations, would require an infusion of new financial resources. As to these increased costs, the EAHCA assumed that Congress would fulfill the financial side of the bargain it had made in seeking state support for the legislation.[39]

3. *EAHCA Implementation Synopsis.* Having laid out the essentials of the formal EAHCA process and the operational assumptions implicit in its reformist objectives, the next step is an examination of EAHCA implementation developments and the reasons for them.

a. *Reformist objectives and the bottom line.* Special education reformists expected the EAHCA to fulfill four broad objectives. First, they wanted to ensure that each child with a handicapping condition received an appropriate education. Second, the reformists wanted to increase the resources available for special education, particularly resources coming from the federal government. Third, reformists wanted each handicapped child, in the progressive education tradition,[40] to have individualized educational services. Finally, the special education advocates wanted handicapped children mainstreamed to the maximum extent possible. The following briefly summarizes what is known about EAHCA implementation in light of these objectives.[41]

---

that regular education students received). For example, two child advocacy groups who led the way in passage of the EAHCA, the Children's Defense Fund and the California Rural Legal Assistance Foundation, were heavily involved in litigation activities and did not believe that the LEAs were likely to comply with the law without the due process legalism. One advocate involved in the process said: "We felt we couldn't trust the professionals so we wanted a procedure whereby the parents could say, I don't want my child classified as mentally retarded. . . . We knew that was the only way that the power of the school districts could be offset . . . . We knew that just the presence of such a [due process] system would force the district to play more honestly." *See, e.g.,* Neal & Kirp, *supra* note 36, at 74.

38. *See, e.g.,* H.R. REP. No. 332, 94th Cong., 1st Sess. 7, 23 (1975); S. REP. No. 168, 94th Cong., 1st Sess. 7 (1975), *reprinted in* 1975 U.S CODE CONG. & AD. NEWS 1425, 1431; *see also* Tweedie, *The Politics of Legalization in Special Education Reform,* in SPECIAL EDUCATION POLICIES: THEIR HISTORY, IMPLEMENTATION, AND FINANCE 48, 59 (1983).

39. The Act's language indicates that, as of 1982, Congress expected to fund a significant proportion of the total excess cost of special education. 20 U.S.C. § 1411(a)(1)(B)(v) (1982). However, federal funding never has risen to more than fifteen percent of the total cost of special education, and appropriations always have been far less than authorizations under the Act. *See* Magnetti, *Some Potential Incentives of Special Education Funding Practices,* in PLACING CHILDREN IN SPECIAL EDUCATION: A STRATEGY FOR EQUITY 300, 315 (1982); Neal & Kirp, *supra* note 36, at 80-81 (noting the growing gap between authorizations and appropriations for the EAHCA).

40. For a discussion of the progressive tradition in American education and its individualized approach to education, see L. CREMIN, THE TRANSFORMATION OF THE SCHOOL (1961).

41. This analysis relies on the best available data. Despite the many studies of EAHCA implementation, a great deal remains unknown. Some of the gap in our knowledge is the result of unasked questions; the rest is the result of questions which were asked at only one point in the Act's implementation cycle. In the latter case, the data do not provide a dynamic picture of the implementation

(i) *Appropriate education.* Prior to the passage of the EAHCA, many handicapped children were excluded from school because the services they required were too costly and too institutionally difficult for public schools to provide,[42] even though the children could benefit from educational services.[43] Estimates of the number of children denied educational services in the 1970's ranged from one to two million children.[44] Congress accepted the one million figure in justifying passage of the EAHCA in 1975.[45] Congress required LEA's and SEA's to develop Child Find procedures to rectify this problem. Although it appears that these estimates of excluded children were too high,[46] school districts and SEA's rapidly implemented Child Find procedures under the impetus of the EAHCA. In 1976 the Department of Health, Education and Welfare's (HEW) Office of Civil Rights (OCR) estimated that 463,000 children remained excluded from school;[47] by 1980 OCR estimated that the number of unserved children had dropped to 22,600.[48] Other agencies, while

---

process. It is unlikely, however, that there will be many more detailed studies of EAHCA implementation. What we have now is all that we are likely to have (at least sponsored by the government) for some time to come. *See* EDUCATION OF THE HANDICAPPED ACT AMENDMENTS OF 1983, H.R. REP. NO. 410, 98th Cong., 1st Sess. 24, *reprinted in* 1984 U.S. CODE CONG. & AD. NEWS 2088, 2111 (noting that emphasis in EAHCA research should shift away from implementation studies to studies of new technologies for improving special education methodologies, instructional environments, and curricula).

42. *See generally* T. COTTLE, BARRED FROM SCHOOL 50-69 (1976) (describing inadequate public resources and institutional response to handicapped children); S. SARASON & J. DORIS, EDUCATIONAL HANDICAP, PUBLIC POLICY, AND SOCIAL HISTORY 360-63 (1979) (on institutional barriers to mainstreaming retarded children). On the additional costs of special education, see J. KAKALIK, W. FURRY, M. THOMAS & M. CARNEY, THE COST OF SPECIAL EDUCATION 5 (1981) (Rand Note N-1792-ED), and Hartman, *Projecting Special Education Costs,* in SPECIAL EDUCATION POLICIES: THEIR HISTORY, IMPLEMENTATION AND FINANCE 241 (1983).

43. Educators consider as educable virtually all handicapped children. *See e.g.,* D. HALLAHAN & J. KAUFFMAN, EXCEPTIONAL CHILDREN 413-15 (1978); Baer, *A Hung Jury and a Scottish Verdict: "Not Proven,"* 1 ANALYSIS & INTERVENTION IN DEVELOPMENTAL DISABILITIES 91 (1981); Favell, Risley, Wolfe, Riddle & Rassmussen, *Limits of Habilitation: How Can We Identify Them and How Can We Change Them?,* 1 ANALYSIS & INTERVENTION IN DEVELOPMENTAL DISABILITIES 37 (1981).

44. *See* Neal & Kirp, *supra* note 36, at 67 (citing 1970 estimate of two million excluded handicapped children).

45. 20 U.S.C. § 1400(b)(4) (1982).

46. *See* Kirp, Buss & Kuriloff, *Legal Reform of Special Education: Empirical Studies and Procedural Proposals,* 62 CALIF. L. REV. 40, 63 (1974) (child find activities as a result of the consent decree in Pennsylvania Ass'n for Retarded Citizens v. Pennsylvania, 343 F. Supp. 279 (E.D. Pa. 1972), turn up "far fewer" excluded children in Pennsylvania than advocates or the state expected); C. Brown, Special Education for Minority and Low Income Children 3 (1983) (unpublished manuscript) (a 1976 Office of Civil Rights (OCR) survey estimated that 463,000 handicapped were excluded from school nationwide, less than half of what Congress had estimated). The fact that only fourteen states had special education legislation in 1970, but forty-six had some form of special education legislation by 1974, as well as the fact that state funding of special education more than doubled between 1972 and 1974 indicates that the overestimates of excluded handicapped children may have resulted from data lagging behind state action. *See* GOV'T ACCOUNTING OFFICE, DISPARITIES STILL EXIST IN WHO GETS SPECIAL EDUCATION 3 (Sept. 30, 1981) (GA 1.13 IPE-81-1).

47. *See* Brown, *supra* note 46, at 3.

48. *Id.*. The Government Accounting Office also has concluded that there are essentially no handicapped children excluded from public schools. GOV'T ACCOUNTING OFFICE, *supra* note 46, at 77. However, some caution should be observed in working with these estimates of excluded and unserved children. Though states uniformly indicate that they have identified all excluded children (that is, all first priority children under the EAHCA), the states also privately acknowledge that their EAHCA compliance is pro forma, and that they do not really know how many children remain excluded. M. THOMAS, STATE ALLOCATION AND MANAGEMENT OF PL 94-142 FUNDS 21-22 (Sept. 1980)

unwilling or unable to make such a precise estimate, concurred in the finding that, by 1980, few children in need of special education services remained out of school.[49] At the same time that the number of unserved children plummeted, the number of children classified as handicapped and served by the schools grew sharply. In 1966, approximately 2.1 million children received special education services.[50] By 1981-82, that number had risen to 4.2 million.[51]

The evidence on the number of children receiving an appropriate placement is not as clear as the evidence on complete exclusion.[52] If all handicapped children were appropriately placed, there would be no appreciable differences in the rates at which various ethnic groups are placed in special education programs.[53] Yet black children are placed differently than white children.[54] Disproportional placement is especially noticeable in the educable mentally retarded (EMR) and learning disabled (LD) categories.[55] Differential classification into EMR and LD is seen as a problem because of the self-

---

(Rand Note N-1561-ED). Indeed, some states statutorily exclude children under age six and over age eighteen who, if excluded in other states, would be illegally excluded.

49. GOV'T ACCOUNTING OFFICE, *supra* note 46, at 43; *see also* A. WRIGHT, R. COOPERSTEIN, E. RENNEKER & C. PADILLA, LOCAL IMPLEMENTATION OF PL 94-142: FINAL REPORT OF A LONGITUDINAL STUDY 17 (1982) (SRI International, Menlo Park, Calif., Project No. 7124) (a longitudinal case study consisting of interviews of parents, special education teachers, special and regular education administrators, principals, psychologists, vocational educational personnel, and representatives of human service agencies conducted over a four-year period at sixteen local education agencies of varying sizes in nine states finding few excluded children over a four-year period of Child Find activities, despite complete implementation of the Child Find legalism) [hereinafter cited as SRI FINAL].

50. R. MACKIE, SPECIAL EDUCATION IN THE UNITED STATES: STATISTICS 1948-1966, 36 (1969).

51. UNITED STATES DEPARTMENT OF EDUCATION, FIFTH ANNUAL REPORT TO CONGRESS ON THE IMPLEMENTATION OF PUBLIC LAW 94-142: THE EDUCATION FOR ALL HANDICAPPED CHILDREN ACT 2 (1983) [hereinafter cited as FIFTH ANNUAL REPORT].

52. Inasmuch as it is difficult to get professional agreement on what "appropriate" education means, we note that we are using the term simply in the sense that a child receiving an appropriate education is getting a reasonably fair share of resources which are used to educate the child in a reasonable way.

53. *See* DESIGNS FOR CHANGE, CAUGHT IN THE WEB: MISPLACED CHILDREN IN CHICAGO'S CLASSES FOR THE MENTALLY RETARDED 34 & n.110 (1982) (no more than 1.25 percent of any ethnic group should be considered mentally retarded) [hereinafter cited as DESIGNS FOR CHANGE]; D. HALLAHAN & J. KAUFFMAN, *supra* note 43, at 44 (some experts believe only about one percent of the population would be considered mentally retarded if adaptive behavior is considered).

54. GOV'T ACCOUNTING OFFICE, *supra* note 46, at 33-34 (data from an OCR Special Education Survey indicate that in 1978, 5.9 percent of white children, 5.8 percent of Hispanic children, and 8.4 percent of black children participated in educable mentally retarded (EMR), trainable mentally retarded, severely emotionally disturbed, learning disabled (LD), and speech impaired programs).

55. *See id.* at 61-62 (disproportional EMR placements for black children; overclassified as EMR and underclassified as LD); DESIGNS FOR CHANGE, *supra* note 53, at 58 (black children are disproportionately placed in EMR programs in the principal U.S. urban areas, such as New York, Chicago, Los Angeles, Philadelphia, Detroit, and Houston); Finn, *Patterns in Special Education Placement as Revealed by the OCR Surveys,* in PLACING CHILDREN IN SPECIAL EDUCATION: A STRATEGY FOR EQUITY 322, 364-66 (1982) (indicating that, for example, in 1978-79, an OCR survey found 1.17 percent of the nonminority students in New York were in EMR programs, compared to 7.13 percent of the black student population; in Alabama, the percentages were 2.07 percent nonminority, 9.48 percent black; in Indiana, 1.5 percent nonminority, 12.04 percent black; in Kentucky, 2.55 percent nonminority, 7.60 percent black).

Finn's analysis also found that the 1978-79 OCR survey indicated great variation in learning disabilities placement rates, as the table below indicates.

fulfilling effect of the global EMR label versus the "specific problem" connotation associated with LD.

Although these data at least raise the possibility that racial discrimination is a factor in placing children, they also may be explained by etiology, regional variation, or an effort on the part of schools to provide children with more resources and attention.[56] Although local instances of racial discrimination in special education placement occur,[57] many uncertainties remain in determining either the extent to which racial discrimination skews local placement rates or the system's potential for systematic misplacement on the basis of race.[58]

Even so, it would be surprising if there were not some measure of racial disproportion in special education. Special education has been historically identified with cultural bias; it began as a means of ridding schools of "lockstep laggards," who usually came from among the poor immigrant population.[59] To some extent special education still performs this institutional function. Nonetheless, despite the uncertainties in the data, there is at least some

---

Average Percent of Enrollment Classified As Learning Disabled

State	Minority	White
N.Y.	1.79	1.16
Pa.	3.93	1.40
Mo.	3.90	3.47
Texas	8.31	3.76
Iowa	15.53	4.18
Kansas	18.08	2.28
Minn.	4.82	3.48
Ohio	2.21	1.96
Wis.	1.77	2.23
Calif.	3.01	2.93

Id. at 358-60.

56. GOV'T ACCOUNTING OFFICE, *supra* note 46, at 63.

57. *See, e.g.,* DESIGNS FOR CHANGE, *supra* note 53, at ix-x (noting lawsuits involving Chicago school system); Larry P. v. Riles, 495 F. Supp. 926 (N.D. Cal. 1979) (action in California challenging classification system as discriminatory).

58. *See* APPLIED MANAGEMENT SCIENCES, A STUDY TO EVALUATE PROCEDURES UNDERTAKEN TO PREVENT ERRONEOUS CLASSIFICATION OF HANDICAPPED CHILDREN: EXECUTIVE SUMMARY ll (1983) (Dept. of Educ. Contract No. 300-79-0669) (study involving a 1980 representative sample of 100 school districts including a random sample of over 400 schools and 7,000 school personnel which produced analysis of administrative records, self-administered questionnaire responses, and personal interviews and noted that while the aggregate result tends to show equality of treatment and outcomes, many factors, including subjective evaluations by teachers, race of the teachers, variations in testing instruments, and the like have a significant impact at the local level) [hereinafter APPLIED MANAGEMENT SCIENCES]. All of these studies provide us with many more questions than answers. For example, we have been unable to find any studies which correlate by ethnic background the incidence of placement of children and the staff persons who refer, assess, and place them. For another example, we do not know if black children are more likely to be referred for special education by white teachers than black teachers, or what effect the race of the assessing professionals has on assessment results. The APPLIED MANAGEMENT SCIENCES study has indicated that teachers may view minority students as more likely to require special educational services than nonminority students, but that minorities are proportionally overrepresented among special education teachers. The study, however, does not indicate in what direction the racial considerations may work at the various stages of referral, assessment, and placement. *See id.* at 10-11.

59. *See, e.g.,* Lazerson, *The Origins of Special Education,* in SPECIAL EDUCATION POLICIES: THEIR HISTORY, IMPLEMENTATION AND FINANCE 15, 16-21 (J. Chambers & W. Hartman eds. 1983).

indication that disproportional placement rates are improving.[60]

Apart from variance along ethnic lines, the overall improvement in the provision of appropriate special education services is tempered by significant local variations in the rate of special education placements. For example, a May 1979 report by the Inspector General for HEW stated that diagnostic practices vary enough that "children classified as handicapped in one district may be regarded as 'behavior problems' in another."[61] Some districts with high educational standards reportedly identified children as handicapped who would not even be considered to have learning problems in other districts.[62] The Government Accounting Office (GAO) in early 1980 found significant variability in how states determined that children were speech impaired.[63] At least in the early years of implementation, it appeared that state eligibility criteria, which in fact determine whether a child is "handicapped" under federal law, varied in their degree of ambiguity and comprehensiveness. For example, in 1977, thirty states had definitions of mental retardation inconsistent with the EAHCA definition.[64] In 1979-80 the ranges of children identified at the state level as mentally retarded, emotionally disturbed, or learning disabled were 0.63 to 4 percent, 0.10 to 3 percent, and 0.83 to 5.2 percent respectively.[65] The range of variation had changed little by 1981-82.[66]

In sum, there has been a sharp rise in the number of children who are receiving an appropriate, or at least a more appropriate, education. Within that rising trend, however, there is a wide band of variation in placement outcomes which may be the result of ethnic, geographic, and resource factors.

(ii)   *Resources.*   Just as there has been a dramatic improvement in the reach of special education, there has been a significant increase in the resources available for special education services. For example, in 1966, the total expenditures for the "excess cost" of special education programs was $680 million.[67] In 1972, the excess cost expenditures had risen to $2.7 billion.[68] By 1978, that figure had grown to an estimated $7 billion,[69] and a comparable figure today may well be in excess of $10 billion.[70] The number of special education teachers and other staff employed to serve handicapped

---

60. *See* APPLIED MANAGEMENT SCIENCES, *supra* note 58, at 10.
61. GOV'T ACCOUNTING OFFICE, *supra* note 46, at 69.
62. *Id.*
63. *Id.* at 69-70.
64. *Id.* at 72.
65. *Id.* at 71.
66. *See* FIFTH ANNUAL REPORT, *supra* note 51, at 70-71 (consider in particular the 1981-82/1979-80 "percent change in number served" column in the tables that appear therein).
67. 2 ISSUES IN THE CLASSIFICATION OF CHILDREN 442 (N. Hobbs ed. 1975).
68. G. BREWER & J. KAKALIK, HANDICAPPED CHILDREN: STRATEGIES FOR IMPROVING SERVICES 392-93 (1979).
69. J. KAKALIK, W. FURRY, M. THOMAS & M. CARNEY, *supra* note 42, at 5.
70. FIFTH ANNUAL REPORT, *supra* note 51, at xvi, 90 (the $10 billion figure is estimated by multiplying the total number of handicapped 6-year-old children currently served times the average excess cost figure provided in the text for special education services, and then making a conservative adjustment for inflation); *see also* Hartman, *Projecting Special Education Costs*, in SPECIAL EDUCATION POLICIES: THEIR HISTORY, IMPLEMENTATION, AND FINANCE 241, 283 (1983) (1980-81 cost estimate for special education services was $9 billion, with range of probable costs from $7.3 to $12.4 billion).

students has also grown sharply. In 1976-77, there were 179,804 special education teachers and 151,649 school staff employed to serve handicapped children. By 1980-81 those numbers had increased to 232,627 and 207,384 respectively.[71] Of course, the availability of funds and staff, just as the availability of special education services generally, varies significantly at the local level.[72]

(iii) *Individualized education.* While the EAHCA also sought to ensure that each handicapped child received an individualized education program, it is not at all clear that this objective has been met. Educators have achieved almost total compliance with the procedural mechanism designed to produce individualized programs, the Act's IEP requirement.[73] In achieving paperwork compliance, however, educators have reduced the paperwork burden by such devices as standardized educational objectives and standardized IEP checklists. Although such methods technically violate the law[74] and undermine the ideal of individualization, they save time and may permit the staff to devote more time to more important requirements, such as the IEP conference.[75] In general, LEA's have refined and streamlined their IEP process, particularly by broadening the short term objectives they write into each IEP.[76] Thus, LEA's have reached full compliance by reacting pragmatically to

---

71. FIFTH ANNUAL REPORT, *supra* note 51, at 100-01.

72. *See, e.g., id.* at 112-13 (showing wide variation among states in pupil teacher ratios for various handicapping conditions); M. THOMAS, *supra* note 48, at 5-22 (noting variability in special education funding at local level); Magnetti, *supra* note 39, at 300 (noting variability in local funding pattern). One study has stressed that it is impossible to overemphasize the importance of funding to the provision of appropriate educational services for the handicapped. SRI FINAL, *supra* note 49, at 157; *see also* Stark, *Tragic Choices in Special Education: The Effect of Scarce Resources on the Implementation of Pub. L. No. 94-142,* 14 CONN. L. REV. 477 (1982) (discussing the triage decisions states must make in allocating services to children under conditions of insufficient resources).

73. J. PYECHA, J. COX, L. CONAWAY, D. DeWITT, D. DRUMMOND, A. HOCUTT, J. JAFFE, M. KALT, C. LANE, J. PELOSI & R. WEIGERINK, A NATIONAL SURVEY OF INDIVIDUALIZED EDUCATION PROGRAMS (IEPs) FOR HANDICAPPED CHILDREN: VOLUME I, EXECUTIVE SUMMARY OF METHODOLOGY AND MAJOR FINDINGS 6 (1980) (Research Triangle Institute, Durham, N.C.; ERIC Doc. No. ED 199 970) (a study of IEPs created in 1978-79 for 2,657 students from 507 public schools in 208 school districts in 42 states) [hereinafter cited as A NATIONAL SURVEY OF IEPs: VOL. I]. Yet, there are some groups for whom initial IEP's frequently are not generated. J. PYECHA, J. PALMOUR & L. WARD, A STUDY OF THE IMPLEMENTATION OF P.L. 94-142 FOR HANDICAPPED MIGRANT CHILDREN: FINAL REPORT 20-21 (1980) (Research Triangle Institute, Durham, N.C., ERIC Doc. No. ED 199976) (data not good enough to draw conclusive findings but does indicate that classification and IEP generation varies a great deal for migrant children as they move from one school to the next; IEP's generated less frequently for migrant children). It would not be surprising to find similar problems of IEP generation to be especially acute for inner city children, who tend to move a great deal within school districts and are likely, as a result, to slip through the cracks more easily than children who are less frequently mobile.

74. The IEP must be developed at the IEP meeting. 20 U.S.C. § 1401 (19) (1982). To the extent that teachers pre-form the IEP, they violate the technical mandate of the EAHCA.

75. *See* M. KNAPP, M. STEARNS, B. TURNBULL, J. DAVID & S. PETERSON, CUMULATIVE EFFECTS OF FEDERAL EDUCATION POLICIES ON SCHOOLS AND DISTRICTS 62 (1983) (SRI International, Menlo Park, Calif., SRI Project 3590) (1982 interview case study of 900 school staff members in 20 school districts in 8 states, involving 81 elementary schools and 25 high schools) [hereinafter referred to as CUMULATIVE EFFECTS].

76. SRI FINAL, *supra* note 49, at 34-37. Apparently, some education agencies tried streamlining to the extent that they did not bother to develop IEP's for some children before they placed those children. In January 1981, the Secretary of Education reiterated that IEP objectives had to be written before placement occurred. The move toward permissibly broader short term objectives may be a tacit recognition by the Department of Education that near-perfect IEP compliance will not occur

the paperwork burden, but it is not clear that the IEP process has led to an increase in the amount of individualized instruction.[77]

(iv) *Mainstreaming.* Before the EAHCA, it was a common practice to permit handicapped children to participate in regular classrooms for nonacademic activities and social exposure. The EAHCA has institutionalized mainstreaming.[78] For mild handicaps, the shift has been from self-contained class placements to a resource room model. Nonetheless, the extent of mainstreaming still is heavily dependent on attitudes of the staff and administrators.[79] Indeed, available data and qualitative judgments indicate little overall impact on the extent to which handicapped children are mainstreamed.[80]

On the other hand, the slight impact may simply be the result of a limited objective. At least one commentator has observed that the mainstreaming concept was aimed largely at the practice of "dumping" handicapped children into inadequate special education programs.[81] And, unlike placing children who are completely excluded from school, or writing IEP's where none existed before, mainstreaming is not so much a specific, concrete objective as a value, a "moral triumph."[82] More than any other aspect of special education law, mainstreaming is a subtle, subjective concept that cannot be easily measured.

b. *The Contribution of EAHCA legalisms to the bottom line.* Some of the chronologically sequenced procedures established by Congress correspond more or less directly to one of the objectives described above, while others are aimed at a broad spectrum of objectives. This section examines some of the key procedures and evaluates what is known about their role in realizing EAHCA objectives. While it is clear that the EAHCA is not the sole mechanism contributing to the progress of handicapped children in receiving special educational services, and thus cannot take either full credit or blame in that

---

without concessions to the IEP workload volume. By stressing that the IEP is *not* an instructional plan, but merely a set of benchmarks, the Department reinforces the view that it recognizes the need for streamlining the IEP process. It is not clear, however, that streamlining IEP terms helps better insure education agencies against adverse due process hearing results or whether it may ease the workload at the cost of a higher risk of loss in the event parents file complaints. *Id.* at 38.

77. Although we know that IEP's are, by and large, not really individualized, we do not know how much individualization there is in practice. That is, students may be slotted into programs, nonetheless there may be a considerable amount of individualized instruction that occurs as a matter of course within the classroom. Further, comparatively speaking, children in special education may receive more individualized attention than they ordinarily would receive as students in regular classrooms.

78. SRI FINAL, *supra* note 49, at 50-56.

79. *Id.* at 105-13.

80. FIFTH ANNUAL REPORT, *supra* note 51, at 15 (little change between 1977-78 and 1980-81 in percent of children mainstreamed); *see also* Turnbull, Brotherson, Czyzewski, Esquith, Otis, Summers, Van Reusen & DePazza-Conway, *A Policy Analysis of "Least Restrictive" Education of Handicapped Children,* 14 RUTGERS L.J. 489, 530-31 (1983) (qualitative assessment of least restrictive environment policy implementation indicates little movement toward greater adherence to policy as result of the EAHCA).

81. Note, *Enforcing the Right to an "Appropriate" Education: The Education for All Handicapped Children Act of 1975,* 92 HARV. L. REV. 1103, 1121 (1979).

82. L. Lynn, *supra* note 37, at 41-42.

regard, it is the most important and the most heavily studied.[83]

(i) *Child Find.* Child Find has been the principal means of identifying handicapped children entirely excluded from public education. There are at least four reasons for its considerable success. First, field level advocacy groups monitored LEA and SEA Child Find efforts and actively assisted school officials in locating excluded children.[84] Second, school officials have no discretion with regard to excluded children; they may not be excluded under any circumstances. Discretion arises only in regard to the nature of the services these children will receive. Third, although Child Find activities were initially burdensome, the burden was mediated by several factors. Child Find activities did not require LEA's to develop new programs or new record-keeping procedures. LEA's normally conduct school censuses, run systematic screening programs, and notify their communities of important matters (such as immunization requirements) through the media. Child Find requirements fit within this administrative framework and therefore required little adjustment by the system.[85] The fact that most LEA's easily systematized and implemented Child Find activities suggests a manageable administrative impact.[86] In addition, advocacy groups helped alleviate the need for LEA's to develop new avenues of community contact, thus compensating for whatever organizational weaknesses did exist. Fourth, LEA's usually receive special education funds from outside sources on the basis of the *number* of children they have identified as requiring special educational services.[87] Therefore, LEA's generally have a financial incentive to find previously excluded children, even though they may not have a similar incentive to provide appropriate services.[88] The only real question is why the anticipated cost of special education services did not restrict the success of Child Find. Lack of discretion under the law and excellent local "enforcement resources" are probably adequate answers to this question.[89]

(ii) *Referral mechanisms.* The success of referral mechanisms designed to ensure that children already in the system are provided special education services appropriate to their handicapping condition[90] is not as uniform or clear

---

83. *See, e.g.,* SRI FINAL, *supra* note 49, at 133-56 (on major impact and central importance of the EAHCA to special education reform).

84. *See, e.g.,* Kirp, Buss & Kuriloff, *supra* note 46, at 71 (effective child find activities require advocacy group vigilance); Lazerson, *supra* note 59, at 38-39 (on importance generally of advocacy groups in getting attention for excluded children).

85. While school districts that responded poorly to Child Find requirements, such as Philadelphia, may simply have been intransigent in opposition to handicap rights, they may also simply have been bureaucratically inept and disorganized.

86. *See, e.g.,* SRI FINAL, *supra* note 49, at 16-17; Kirp, Buss & Kuriloff, *supra* note 46, at 61.

87. The EAHCA allocates funds to states on the basis of the number of children each state counts as handicapped. 20 U.S.C. § 1411(a) (1982).

88. For a discussion of the complex incentive structure created by the EAHCA, see M. THOMAS, *supra* note 48; Magnetti, *supra* note 39.

89. It may be that LEA's can exert discretionary powers successfully at later stages in the service process. *See, e.g., In re* Kanawha County School Dist., 3 [§ 504 Rulings] EDUC. HANDICAPPED L. REP. (CRR) 257:439 (Sept. 28, 1983) (children identified as handicapped were placed on a waiting list instead of being provided with special education services).

90. It is difficult to know how many children might fall into this group. Part of the problem is

as the success of Child Find. Referral to a school's evaluation process begins each handicapped child's participation in special education programs. Regular classroom teachers are the principal source of special education referrals,[91] although referrals come from a variety of other sources, including parents, health and special education professionals, and supplementary service teachers.[92] Consequently, regular classroom teachers have potentially enormous discretion in determining whether children needing special education services will receive them, particularly because the EAHCA does not provide any specific guidelines for teacher referral practices.

Teachers exercise this discretion both to underrefer and overrefer children they suspect of having handicapping conditions. Sometimes teachers do not refer children whom they believe are handicapped.[93] Underreferrals are the product of assessment backlogs,[94] program availability,[95] and nonuniform standards for handicap evaluation.[96] While it is clear that more in-school

---

the lack of a solid baseline indicating the total number of handicapped children. Estimates made around 1970 of the number of children having handicapping conditions varied from 4 percent to 24 percent of the total youth population. G. BREWER & J. KAKALIK, *supra* note 68, at 80. Congress estimated in 1975 that one-half of this handicapped population, or something on the order of 4 million children, received inappropriate educational services. 20 U.S.C. § 1400(b)(1), (3) (1982). But inasmuch as few children are now totally excluded from the schools and only about 4 million children receive special education services, it appears that the congressional estimate was excessive. A 1968 estimate indicated that 38 percent of all handicapped children were enrolled in special education programs. Lazerson, *supra* note 59, at 38. Congress concluded that many children did not receive the service most appropriate for their individual needs. 20 U.S.C. § 1400(b)(2), (3) (1982). Of course, children may properly be referred, and yet receive inadequate services due to evaluation and placement decisions. *See infra* notes 112-13 and accompanying text.

91.   *See* Bickel, *Classifying Mentally Retarded Students: A Review of Placement Practices in Special Education*, in PLACING CHILDREN IN SPECIAL EDUCATION: A STRATEGY FOR EQUITY 182, 187 (1982) (teachers are the most important source of referrals); APPLIED MANAGEMENT SCIENCES, *supra* note 58, at 5 (study of a 1980 representative sample of 100 school districts, including a random sample of over 400 schools and 7,000 school personnel, analyzing administrative records, self-administered questionnaire responses, and personal interviews, showed that regular education teachers referred 68 percent of the newly identified and placed handicapped students for the 1980-1981 school year).

92.   Bickel, *supra* note 91, at 187; APPLIED MANAGEMENT SCIENCES, *supra* note 58, at 4.

93.   Bickel, *supra* note 91, at 188 (teachers withhold referrals because assessment backlogs frustrate their efforts to get special education services to children who need them). Of course, many teachers may not exercise their referral discretion at all in some cases because they do not feel they know enough to be sure that the child should be referred in the first place. *See* L. McDONNELL & M. McLAUGHLIN, EDUCATION POLICY AND THE ROLE OF THE STATES 130-31 (1982) (in a study of a large urban school system, one-third of elementary and two-thirds of secondary teachers said they felt unprepared to identify handicapped children).

94.   *See* C. BLASCHKE, CASE STUDY OF THE IMPLEMENTATION OF P.L. 94-142—STATE A: FINAL REPORT 57 (1979) (ERIC Doc. No. ED 175233) [hereinafter cited as C. BLASCHKE, STATE A]; C. BLASCHKE, CASE STUDY OF THE IMPLEMENTATION OF P.L. 94-142—STATE B: FINAL REPORT 44 (1979) (ERIC Doc. No. ED 175234) (three state case studies, each examining three school districts, revealed that teachers become frustrated because referred children often wait up to two years for assessment services) [hereinafter cited as C. BLASCHKE, STATE B].

95.   *See* Weatherly & Lipsky, *Street Level Bureaucrats and Institutional Innovation: Implementing Special Education Reform*, 47 HARV. EDUC. REV. 171, 187 (1977) (administrators in a studied school district told principals to curtail evaluations because placements are too costly; referrals in another district done on basis of program availability); SRI FINAL, *supra* note 49, at 48-49 (districts only recommend services they already can provide); Bickel, *supra* note 91, at 188 (program availability can severely influence identification of handicapping conditions).

96.   *See* Bickel, *supra* note 91, at 188-89 (a child's special education program may be determined by the referring teacher in some places, rather than by evaluation staff; ambiguity in program eligi-

youth are underreferred than children who are excluded altogether, the precise number is uncertain.[97]

It is likely that underreferral stems from a child's personality traits.[98] For example, children who are marginally in need of special education services, or children whose need, in the teacher's judgment, is too slight to warrant labeling the child or disrupting the child's class schedule, are commonly underreferred.[99] The underreferral problem may be remedied through non-school referrals, improved teacher training in special education, and increased resources to eliminate conditions which make teachers hesitant to make bona fide referrals;[100] however, underreferral is a boundary problem the extent of which will probably remain indeterminate and problematic due to the nature of any system which requires an eligibility cutoff. In a system of limited resources, teachers quite understandably will attempt to make adjustments to the system as a means of insuring that children with the most serious problems receive the first attention.[101] Indeed, without that discretion to underrefer, teachers could seriously overload the system's ability to meet its legal mandate in other respects.

The more problematic use of teacher discretion lies in overreferral of children for evaluation.[102] Some teachers discovered that they could use their referral power to rid themselves of troublesome and disruptive, if not handicapped, children.[103] Early in EAHCA implementation, teachers could purposefully misrefer because assessments frequently were hastily conducted[104] and because school districts frequently employed inappropriate assessment tools.[105] However, as the referral and assessment process has stabilized and

---

bility criteria may create wide variation in referral decisions); GOV'T ACCOUNTING OFFICE, *supra* note 46, at 43-46 (states set specific priorities for numbers of students to be served, for example, in secondary education, which causes variation in referrals).

97. The Government Accounting Office (GAO) observes that there is an uncertain number of children underreferred (that is, handicapped children in school but not receiving services), with the lowest estimate—derived from education agency service delivery claims—being perhaps as few as 100,000 children. The worst case estimate is that 2 million children are not receiving services. The GAO strongly questions this latter figure, but is unable to determine what a reasonable figure would be. GOV'T ACCOUNTING OFFICE, *supra* note 46, at 46.

98. *See* APPLIED MANAGEMENT SERVICES, *supra* note 58, at 5 (only about one-half of 2.8 million students for whom regular education teachers requested special education were found eligible and were provided special education services).

99. *See* Bickel, *supra* note 91, at 189 (children with emotional problems or who were quiet and well-behaved were likely to be underreferred).

100. CUMULATIVE EFFECTS, *supra* note 75, at 62 (teachers and special educators report ambivalence about usefulness of labeling in providing educational services).

101. *Id.* at 108 (assessment backlogs persist as a source of teacher frustration and still produce decisions not to refer because delays are so long that referral does not seem worth it).

102. The EAHCA mandates a triage system. *See* 20 U.S.C. § 1412(3) (1982) (states must give first priority to handicapped children who are receiving no education at all, and second priority to the children with the most severe handicaps within each disability who are receiving an inadequate education).

103. Brown, *supra* note 46, at 22-24 (explaining how some teachers have used the special education system to rid themselves of difficult children).

104. Bickel, *supra* note 91, at 194 (referral backlogs affect quality of assessments as school systems attempt to catch up on work load).

105. *See id.* at 196-97 (suggesting that, regardless of apparent assessment practices, education agencies frequently relied exclusively on IQ tests, despite directive of the EAHCA to do otherwise,

assessment techniques have improved, teachers are finding it more difficult to "dump" children into special education.[106] Special education personnel have used mandated assessment procedures (tests, M-teams, etc.) to prevent regular classroom teachers from dumping nonhandicapped children.[107] Hence, the system has adjusted successfully to prevent the more gross and conscious special education misplacements.

Most referrals, however, are made in good faith, and good faith has led teachers to err on the side of caution, thus resulting in significant overreferral. The EAHCA did anticipate that it would be difficult for teachers accurately to assess which of their students were handicapped, and established inservice training requirements as a method of insuring the development of increasingly accurate referral.[108] To date, however, inservice training largely has failed to provide the level of training which is needed to prevent mistaken referrals.

Although most special education teachers have received preservice training in assessment,[109] regular classroom teachers have not received much assessment training, even at the inservice level.[110] Much LEA-based inservice training has focused on formal compliance (special education procedures and orientation to special education laws), though some districts have offered more substantive training.[111] Some problems are due to teacher resistance to additional inservice programs and the lack of programs which teachers consider useful,[112] but the biggest obstacle to improved training is low budgetary priority.[113] When LEA's are faced with the immediacies of evaluation and placement and the possibility of expensive court action from failing to follow the requirements of due process, inservice training receives a low priority because it has a distant and imprecise payoff and little direct relation to reducing risks or immediate staff workloads. Teacher layoffs may also be a problem, because they tend to eliminate teachers with the most preservice

---

thereby leading many education agencies to place children in inappropriate programs); P. KURILOFF, D. KIRP & W. BUSS, WHEN HANDICAPPED CHILDREN GO TO COURT: ASSESSING THE IMPACT OF THE LEGAL REFORM OF SPECIAL EDUCATION IN PENNSYLVANIA 163 (1979) (National Institute of Educ. Project No. Neg.-003-0192) (school districts tend to equate retardation with performance on I.Q. tests); cf. SRI FINAL, supra note 49, at 33 (children are more likely to be better assessed now than in the past).

106. See, e.g., CUMULATIVE EFFECTS, supra note 75, at 96 (it is becoming more difficult to dump children who merely are difficult to handle); APPLIED MANAGEMENT SERVICES, supra note 58, at 10 (suggesting that use of more complete range of assessment instruments has helped prevent teachers and diagnosticians from placing minority students as frequently in special education programs as their intuitive judgments indicate).

107. See CUMULATIVE EFFECTS, supra note 75, at 130 (special education teachers are making sure troublesome students are not being inappropriately "dumped" into special education programs).

108. See 20 U.S.C. §§ 1400(b)(7), 1413 (a)(3) (1982); S. REP. No. 168, 94th Cong., 1st Sess. 33 (1975), reprinted in 1975 U.S. CODE CONG. & AD. NEWS 1425, 1456-57.

109. APPLIED MANAGEMENT SCIENCES, supra note 58, at 6-7.

110. See SRI FINAL, supra note 49, at 61 (in-service training has not received much emphasis in school districts); L. McDONNELL & M. McLAUGHLIN, supra note 93, at 128-30 (observing slow pace of inservice program development).

111. SRI FINAL, supra note 49, at 62-63.

112. Id. at 64-66.

113. Id. at 65.

training.[114]

Many school districts have recognized that mistaken referral places an unnecessary burden on special education staff because complete and accurate assessments can be extremely time-consuming, and have responded by developing formal or informal prereferral screening procedures to produce more accurate referrals.[115] These procedures are organizational innovations not required by the EAHCA. Prereferral activities vary from intervention documentation by classroom teachers to formal prescreening teams who consult with teachers regarding potential referrals.[116] It appears that prereferral does ease evaluation backlogs.[117]

Since prereferral screening is not aimed at increasing the system's base of substantive special education knowledge, it may simply permit financial and other nonsubstantive considerations to be factored into placement judgments before the system is ever legally committed to notify parents of a decision to evaluate the child. On the whole, it is difficult to know which way prereferral screening cuts with respect to ensuring accuracy in special education placements.

(iii) *Testing and evaluation.* The EAHCA requires multiple-testing and bias-free test instruments to assure appropriate, individualized placement of children with special educational needs. As schools have accommodated themselves to the various demands of the law, they have increasingly used more neutral, balanced, and time-consuming testing approaches.[118] Indeed, on the average, diagnosticians now use about six assessment instruments for each child.[119] It is thought that the quality of evaluations has improved over the years and that errors in the evaluation process are less likely now than during initial EAHCA implementation.[120] Without necessarily creating any

---

114. The most recently trained teachers are the first to be laid off, and these teachers, whether in regular or special education, are more likely to have had the best preservice training in both substantive concerns and in EAHCA requirements.

115. SRI FINAL, *supra* note 49, at 17; A. ALTMAN, J. MILLER & M. BRANDIS, VERIFICATION OF PROCEDURES TO SERVE HANDICAPPED CHILDREN: FINAL REPORT—ASSESSMENT COMPONENT (1980) (ERIC Doc. No. ED 201 114). School districts have adopted these prereferral screening techniques in part because teachers do not have the needed special education identification skills. *See* U.S. DEPT. OF EDUCATION, FOURTH ANNUAL REPORT TO CONGRESS ON THE IMPLEMENTATION OF PUBLIC LAW 94-142: THE EDUCATION FOR ALL HANDICAPPED CHILDREN ACT xiii-xiv (1982) (estimating that 25 percent of elementary teachers had had training in identification of handicaps) [hereinafter cited as FOURTH ANNUAL REPORT]; *cf.* L. MCDONNELL & M. MCLAUGHLIN, *supra* note 93, at 130 (survey of over 700 teachers in large metropolitan area revealed that 40 percent of elementary teachers and 57 percent of secondary teachers had had no training in implementing the EAHCA).

116. SRI FINAL, *supra* note 49, at 18-19.

117. *Id.* at 21; Mehan, *Identifying Handicapped Students*, in ORGANIZATIONAL BEHAVIOR IN SCHOOLS AND SCHOOL DISTRICTS 391 (1981).

118. SRI FINAL, *supra* note 49, at 32-33.

119. APPLIED MANAGEMENT SCIENCES, *supra* note 58, at 9. However, the use of a large number of assessment instruments still does not demonstrate that the IQ test or some other aspect of the referral and assessment process is not the single determinative factor in the final assessment disposition. *See* Bickel, *supra* note 91, at 196-97. Nonetheless, at least superficially, compliance with the letter of the law has improved.

120. SRI FINAL, *supra* note 49, at 27-33.

new placement opportunities, testing practices have, on the whole, contributed to assuring more appropriate, individualized placements in whatever programs are available. This improvement has occurred for several reasons. Administrators have lent support to the referral-assessment continuum because they have found it has contributed generally to their school systems' ability to identify and place children.[121] The assessment legalisms have thus helped schools more ably perform their traditional sorting function.[122] In many districts, the assessment procedure became less burdensome because districts increased special education funding. LEA's also have moved from an ad hoc approach to a more systematic compliance approach, which permits them to do assessments in less time.

Finally, the specialization of the work force has had a significant impact. Special education staff members now in the schools come out of college trained to deal with EAHCA requirements. They see as natural what older staff members considered novel and burdensome. The younger staff may also have a greater commitment to the handicapped than the older staff members and a greater commitment to the system because the EAHCA has given them an esteem and power that they did not have before Congress passed the law.[123] In essence, they have a professional investment in a quality evaluation program.

On the other hand, the EAHCA's testing mechanism does not unequivocally contribute to a more appropriate, individualized assessment for the handicapped. For example, minorities are assessed with essentially the same techniques used for nonminorities; few school districts use culturally fair techniques.[124] Hence, the Act's testing legalism may not be adequately addressing the problem of disproportionate minority placements.

In addition, overreliance on the IQ test, which has been thought to lead to many inappropriate placements, may not be eliminated by multiple testing. Multiple testing may simply "mask" continued use of the IQ test as the critical assessment tool. Other factors reducing our understanding of and confidence in the effect of multiple testing are the unreliability of test results (for example, IQ test results become less reliable as the results move further from the norm) and variations in the skill levels of the test givers. Conceivably, more accurate placements could come simply from multiple application of a single test, or a few comparable tests.

Local variations in testing and evaluation also tend to affect the positive impact of the procedure. For example, eligibility criteria vary enough that a given child could be classified as handicapped in some school district in the

---

121. *See* CUMULATIVE EFFECTS, *supra* note 75, at 65-66, 79.

122. *See generally* R. CALLAHAN, EDUCATION AND THE CULT OF EFFICIENCY (1962); J. SPRING, THE SORTING MACHINE (1976); D. TYACK, THE ONE BEST SYSTEM: A HISTORY OF AMERICAN URBAN EDUCATION (1974).

123. CUMULATIVE EFFECTS, *supra* note 75, at 116.

124. *Cf.* APPLIED MANAGEMENT SCIENCES, *supra* note 58, at 11 (minorities are assessed with test batteries virtually identical to those used with white children).

state but as *not* handicapped in another district in the same state[125] In addition, the EAHCA leaves the choice of testing instruments completely to the discretion of educators at the field level, thus creating variability through test choice. Assessment rates may also be affected by assessment styles favored by the evaluation staff.[126] For example, evaluators inclined to take a behavioral approach to evaluation will follow the results of assessment instruments closely. On the other hand, professional staff who favor an informal intuitional approach are likely to make pro forma use of assessment instruments and distrust the results of those tests.[127] Differences in diagnostic criteria have been a problem, but their current importance is unknown.

The costs of existing testing methods also must be considered since giving special educators so much discretion may be expensive and may detract from the day-to-day quality of the assessment process. For example, one urban LEA faced with vague eligibility criteria and shrinking resources had to spend a large amount of staff time in creating and revising its special learning disabilities guidelines.[128] Special education assessments are time-consuming and generate a lot of paperwork.[129] In the early stages of EAHCA implementation, evaluators often were overwhelmed by the number of referrals and serious evaluation backlogs occurred.[130] Consequently, school districts initially responded to their increased evaluation workload by increasing evaluation staff, making less than thorough evaluations, and relying heavily on IQ tests for handicap evaluation purposes.[131] Evaluation backlogs have been reduced by many districts, but some particularly large urban districts continue to be plagued by these backlogs.[132] School districts are under pressure to

---

125. *Id.* at 70, 92-95.

126. Special education professionals have considerable problems in achieving diagnostic congruence. That is, given a particular child, professionals are likely to provide a variety of diagnoses for that child. Inconsistencies in these diagnoses may derive from the use of different diagnostic criteria, different theoretical frameworks, variance in the weighting of diagnostic data, incorporation of nondiagnostic biasing of the information, and changes in diagnostic style by a single professional within and across cases. Professionals also may make consistent errors in diagnosis which depend on nonverifiable diagnostic techniques or on the assumption that it is always the child, and not something else, which is the source of the child's problem. *See, e.g.,* McDermott, *Sources of Error in the Psychoeducational Diagnosis of Children,* 19 J. SCH. PSYCHOLOGY 31 (1981).

127. CUMULATIVE EFFECTS, *supra* note 75, at 105-08.

128. SRI FINAL, *supra* note 49, at 32.

129. *See, e.g.,* SRI FINAL, *supra* note 49, at 32-33 (evaluation process is time-consuming and generates much paper work); CUMULATIVE EFFECTS, *supra* note 75, at 114 (counselors and special education teachers hit hard by administrative paperwork associated with EAHCA).

130. SRI FINAL, *supra* note 49, at 28; C. BLASCHKE, STATE B, *supra* note 94, at 44; C. BLASCHKE, STATE A, *supra* note 94 at 56-57.

131. SRI FINAL, *supra* note 49, at 25.

132. Parents must receive written notice whenever an education agency initiates the identification and preplacement evaluation of a child. 34 C.F.R. § 300.504(a)(1) (1984). Parents who object to the identification or evaluation may initiate a due process hearing at any time after they have received the written notice. *Id.* § 300.506(a) (1984). Education agencies must hold, within thirty calendar days, meetings with the parents of any child for whom a determination has been made that the child needs special education and related services. *Id.* § 300.343(c) (1984). The IEP developed out of this meeting must be "implemented as soon as possible" after the meeting. *Id.* § 300.342(b)(2) (1984). State laws paralleling the EAHCA may have similar or more stringent timelines.

process referrals quickly[133] because evaluation delays create due process compliance problems for school districts.[134] Therefore, though the Act has encouraged complex, sensitive evaluation mechanisms, it frequently has failed to significantly change old practices precisely because the evaluation mechanism is complex and sensitive.

Finally, although assessments for handicapping conditions are objective in theory, in practice, the LEA's resources influence eligibility criteria and placement recommendations.[135] A strong tendency exists for LEA's to assess a child only if the child's disability fits a preexisting special education program, or to find that the child's assessment happens to fit the child into an existing program.[136] The most objective and accurate testing program cannot overcome inadequate resources. Unless the testing mechanism is given an independent financial role, it is unlikely to have the impact that the special education reformers hoped it would have.[137]

(iv)   *IEP's: substance.*   The basic question of whether the substance of IEP's leads to more appropriate educational placements logically entails two subordinate questions: whether the plans are any good (do they follow the content requirements of the Act?); and whether the plans are complied with or followed in practice. The literature reveals different answers to the two questions. Good paper compliance suggests that the IEP's are good but some

---

133.   *See infra* note 185 and accompanying text. In most if not all federal courts, school districts will not become liable for damages for violation of the EAHCA unless it appears that they have seriously violated the Act's due process provisions. *See, e.g.,* Anderson v. Thompson, 658 F.2d 1205, 1214 (7th Cir. 1981). Therefore, school districts have an incentive to follow the formal procedures established by the Act in order to avoid financial liability for substantive evaluation errors.

134.   Bickel, *supra* note 91, at 193-97; SRI FINAL, *supra* note 49, at 28-29. Of course, taking shortcuts may occasionally cause districts to alienate a parent whom a more careful procedure might have assuaged. Taking shortcuts therefore can also cause districts to end up in a due process hearing. But clearly the resource tradeoff, at least in the early stages of implementation when the process is largely ad hoc and unsystematized and the staff is on a relatively more inefficient point of its learning curve, favors shortcuts in required procedures. The risk is a potentially greater (but unlikely) expense in the event that the shortcutting leads to time-consuming compliance efforts by resource and staff stemming from an adverse result in an administrative hearing.

135.   SRI FINAL, *supra* note 49, at 26, 48-49; GOV'T ACCOUNTING OFFICE, *supra* note 46, at 72-73.

136.   CUMULATIVE EFFECTS, *supra* note 75, at 61-62, 92; Brown, *supra* note 46, at 32.

137.   The interplay of resources and commitment is further demonstrated by the implementation of reassessment procedures for children already placed in special education programs. LEA's usually place little emphasis on reassessment, even though it is a kind of safety net for a child who is erroneously placed and whose parents fail to object to the placement. SRI FINAL, *supra* note 49, at 27; CUMULATIVE EFFECTS, *supra* note 75, at 105-06. The LEA's give reassessment attention equal to that of initial assessment only when SEA monitoring or court cases push them to do so. SRI FINAL, *supra* note 49, at 27; DESIGNS FOR CHANGE, *supra* note 53, at 2. (Of course reassessment may not be of much use if it is done hastily, without reforms in referral practices, and without adequate testing instruments.) Resources are not the only problem, however. For example, school psychologists traditionally have not been involved in reassessment functions, and because they are the ones usually burdened with reassessment duties, they have given reassessment a low priority. Without external pressures, they responded to the demands of the EAHCA by conforming to the traditional school psychologist function. P. KURILOFF, D. KIRP & W. BUSS, *supra* note 105, at 92-107. Court actions sometimes have led to significant changes in testing because they compelled shifts in financial resources. *See, e.g.,* Larry P. v. Riles, 495 F. Supp 926 (N.D. Cal. 1979); United States v. Board of Educ., 80 F.R.D. 679 (N.D. Ill. 1980) (consent decree).

evidence shows a loose correspondence between the IEP's and actual programs. How did the pattern of formal compliance develop?

IEP provisions initially imposed a significant burden on LEA's.[138]
Although most education agencies created IEP's for children who needed special education services,[139] these initial IEP's frequently omitted EAHCA-man-
dated information and often contained useless provisions.[140] As time went
on, rather than shedding the IEP, education agencies brought the plans into a
high degree of compliance with the Act without a corresponding change in
actual educational programs. This differential evolution might be explained
as a classic pattern of formal compliance, or goal displacement, in which more
strenuous compliance efforts are directed toward the activity monitored by
regulatory inspectors than toward the activity with substantive significance. A
second appealing explanation is the loose coupling literature as explicated by
the sociologist John Meyer. The "institutional" aspects of schools, such as
grades, diplomas, and IEP plans are relatively easy to conform to environmental demands, as compared with the "technical" aspects, like what actually
goes on in classrooms. An IEP plan could say all sorts of good things about
how classroom teachers should help a particular child. Changing the behavior
of classroom teachers, who are bombarded by conflicting demands in a fluid,
shifting environment, is not so easy. The plans may or may not be doing *some*
good, as a "model" to be emulated, for example. But in the best of all possible worlds, goals will be easier to manage than actual behavior.[141]

There are several reasons to believe that the classic pattern is operative in
this case. First, well-formulated IEP's serve the local education agency as documentation of procedural compliance in the event a child's parent or guardian
files a formal complaint and the education agency ends up in an administrative or judicial proceeding.[142] IEP's are the essential audit track for litigation.
Second, many state education agencies monitor IEP's only for paper compliance and do not apply effective sanctions for noncompliance. Only about
one-third of state education agencies examine IEP documents for their substantive correctness during site visits to local education agencies. Even these

---

138. SRI FINAL, *supra* note 49, at 34.

139. A NATIONAL SURVEY OF IEPs: VOL. I, *supra* note 73, at 4 (approximately 95 percent of the
children identified as requiring special education had IEP's on file); SRI FINAL, *supra* note 49, at 34
(most children in 1978-79 in districts studied had IEP's); CUMULATIVE EFFECTS, *supra* note 75, at 105
(initial IEP's generated in most instances).

140. A NATIONAL SURVEY OF IEPs: VOL. I, *supra* note 73, at 7, 11 (only 40 percent of the IEP's
were "informative and internally consistent"; only 5 percent of the IEP's were judged "exceptionally
informative and internally consistent").

141. On paper compliance, see SRI FINAL, *supra* note 49, at 34-49 (IEP's are routine practice and
more technically complete, while their substantive use is declining); A NATIONAL SURVEY OF IEPs:
Vol. I, *supra* note 73, at 13 (IEP's have become more internally consistent). On goal avoidance, see
infra note 194 and accompanying text. For John Meyer's work, see *infra* note 218. On the different
constraints which operate on goals as an ideological system versus actual behavior, *see* Etzioni, *supra*
note 5.

142. *See Proposals to Amend Pub. L. 94-142*, 1981-82 EDUC. HANDICAPPED L. REP. (CRR) AC125,
126 (Supp. 71, April 30, 1982) (criticism of proposed amendments to the EAHCA on grounds that
they would eliminate documentation which school boards need in establishing the appropriateness of
their educational plan in the face of a parental challenge).

relatively few diligent states usually restrict themselves to inspection of the plans. California may be alone in attempting to use independent classroom observations to determine whether the actual instructional programs conform to each child's IEP.[143] Even when the states have seriously monitored LEA's and discovered problems, they usually have not applied permissible legal sanctions. Instead, states have chosen less coercive and more informal means of obtaining compliance.[144]

Third, paper compliance was easier than expected. Educators are complaining less about the IEP burden because it literally has become less burdensome; they have not shed IEP's because they can live with them. Some studies suggest that burden is primarily subjective and that, after educators accepted the legitimacy of the Act and understood the purpose behind the paperwork, the burden did not seem so great.[145] After the initial shock, the unreasonable tends to become routine.

Finally, local education agencies continue to develop IEP's because the IEP process has had a positive impact on schools as a whole. The IEP procedures have led LEA's generally to develop better staff program planning skills, better diagnostic and evaluation techniques for all students, and better training programs for teachers.[146] Indeed, one study indicated that each studied district stated that it would retain the IEP process in some form even if the EAHCA were abolished.[147] The administratively burdensome IEP process also turned out to be a positive educational innovation. Programs may not correspond closely to plans, but the educational effects are positive anyway (e.g., better placement into whatever programs are available). Thus, the paper compliance is not really only paper compliance, although the substantive changes were not the ones anticipated by the legislation. (The interesting phenomenon of unanticipated positive consequences also occurs in connection with due process and is characteristic of the substantive educational innovations developed by educators in response to "legalization"—the

---

143. *Cf.* FOURTH ANNUAL REPORT, *supra* note 115, at 65-68. The lax monitoring data come from an unpublished 1981 survey of nineteen states conducted by the National Association of State Directors of Special Education (NASDSE Study). The monitoring process varies significantly among and within states. Several states apparently believe they have no legal authority for their monitoring function. There is some indication that state monitoring is gradually becoming more rigorous with respect to substantive aspects of IEP's. But the federal Office of Special Education Programs found in 1980-81 that "none of the 21 states visited were effectively identifying and determining all actual or potential problems in educating handicapped children in accordance with PL 94-142," and that the states were not taking effective steps to remedy the deficiencies they did find.

144. *Id.* at 66-68. Frequently, states offer education agencies technical assistance if they are having problems complying with EAHCA requirements.

145. CUMULATIVE EFFECTS, *supra* note 75, at 113; SRI FINAL, *supra* note 49, at 45.

146. CUMULATIVE EFFECTS, *supra* note 75, at 79; SRI FINAL, *supra* note 49, at 46-47.

147. FOURTH ANNUAL REPORT, *supra* note 115, at 28. Eighteen of the twenty local education agencies in an unpublished study conducted in 1981 by the National Association of State Directors of Special Education (NASDSE) strongly supported the IEP process. Sixteen agencies said they would retain the IEP conference and fifteen said they would document IEP's just as they did presently even if federal and state mandates were discontinued. All local education agencies said they would use the IEP in some form even if the federal and state requirements were abolished. It is possible, however, that a strong bias exists in the result of this study because of the small sample and the perspective of the group performing the study.

substantively empty proceduralisms typical of the EAHCA. Both are discussed below.)

(v) *IEP's: parental participation.* Congress enacted the IEP requirement as a means of ensuring that education agencies would provide all handicapped children with an appropriate education. At one level, the law required SEA's to monitor IEP's largely by verifying paperwork. The state role, however, is after the fact. Congress believed that immediate parental input in IEP conferences was a crucial means of catching potentially erroneous placements which had escaped detection in the referral and evaluation stages.

Initially, the IEP did increase parental participation in creating programs for their handicapped children, although the degree of participation varied from school district to school district.[148] However, the initial upsurge in parental participation quickly leveled.[149] The typical pattern now is that significant numbers of parents do not appear at all for IEP conferences, while those who do attend do not provide significant input.[150] There appear to be two reasons for this rather low rate of active participation.

First, quite frequently the school district's evaluation and placement recommendations do not propose so significant a change that parents are willing to object.[151] Therefore, while significant numbers of parents may not be

---

148. *See* SRI FINAL, *supra* note 49, at 39-40 (noting initial upsurge and variability of participation); C. BLASCHKE, CASE STUDY OF THE IMPLEMENTATION OF PL 94-142: EXECUTIVE SUMMARY 20 (1979) (ERIC Doc. No. ED 175 232) (summarizing study of nine local education agencies in three states between 1977 and 1979; noting no dramatic increase in parent participation in placement decisionmaking).

149. SRI FINAL, *supra* note 49, at 39-40.

150. One recent study of parents attending IEP meetings in a western school district indicates both the problems that parents have in using the IEP to their advantage and the problems in gauging exactly how well parents understand what is going on in the IEP process. In that survey, most parents—three-quarters—felt actively involved in the IEP process. When they were asked for specifics, however, parents included listening, understanding, and working with staff as active involvement; only 15 percent indicated that they ever expressed any opinion or made suggestions regarding the plan itself. Most parents claimed they understood the educational objectives, rights, and the IEP procedures; however, the survey did not make any objective determination of parent knowledge, so it is impossible to know if parents in fact understood sufficiently to participate. Their understanding is particularly cast in doubt because the survey data indicate that large percentages of parents had procedural and qualitative grounds for challenging the school's conduct. For instance, 5 percent of the parents did not receive an IEP to sign, 22 percent were not contacted prior to their child's assessment, 19 percent claimed the schools did not try to set a convenient meeting time, and 31 percent of the parents felt that their child was not receiving the appropriate training. Lynch & Stein, *Perspectives on Parent Participation in Special Education,* 3 EXCEPTIONAL EDUC. Q. 56, 60 (1981).

A broader national study of IEP procedures indicated that parents only participate in creating the IEP about two-thirds of the time (though about three-quarters indicated that they had discussed IEP's with school personnel) and only one-half of the parents claimed that they provided "input" to IEP committees during the development of the IEP. Again, despite relatively large numbers of parents who did not participate in the IEP process at all or only marginally (only about one-half of the nationwide survey of IEP's indicated that the parents had even signed the document), less than 1 percent of the parents in the survey had refused to approve their child's IEP. *See* A NATIONAL SURVEY OF IEPs: VOL. I, *supra* note 73, at 8-9. Perhaps the principal point to be made is that very little systematic knowledge exists regarding the nature of parent participation in the IEP process. *See, e.g.,* Morgan, *Parent Participation in the IEP Process: Does It Enhance Appropriate Education?,* 3 EXCEPTIONAL EDUC. Q. 33, 34 (1982).

151. For example, one study comparing a small set of parents of learning disabled (LD) children—a frequently rather mild, if variable, form of handicapping condition—with parents of regular

entirely happy with their child's IEP,[152] the program the school proposes may not raise parents' concerns enough for them to ask the school district to modify its proposal.[153]

Second, parents have a low rate of participation in conferences because the structure of parent-professional relations,[154] the context of IEP confer-

education children found little difference between the groups in terms of parent involvement with their children's education. McKinney & Hocutt, *Public School Involvement of Parents of Learning-Disabled Children and Average Achievers*, 3 EXCEPTIONAL EDUC. Q. 64, 68 (1981). Another study observed that parents were much more likely to participate in the IEP if the education agency recommended that the child be decertified. Parents became concerned that their child would be entirely cut off from needed services. *See* SRI FINAL, *supra* note 49, at 40.

152.   There are no national studies which purport to question directly parents' satisfaction with their child's IEP. A study which surveyed four and one-half counties in the northwest corner of Iowa in 1979 found, on the basis of a 39.4 percent questionnaire response rate, that 3 percent of the families in that predominantly upper middle class area were dissatisfied with their child's special education program. *See* Polifka, *Compliance with Public Law 94-142 and Consumer Satisfaction*, 48 EXCEPTIONAL CHILDREN 250 (1981). Another study, conducted under the sponsorship of the California State Department of Education, took a random sample of 400 parents from a school district in Southern California which enrolled over 11,000 children in special education programs. Of those 400, 328 were directly interviewed. The interviewers found that 31 percent of the parents to whom the question was applicable (71 of 229) felt that their child was not receiving appropriate life planning skills training. *See* Lynch & Stein, *supra* note 150, at 56.

153.   With procedural violations a commonplace, many more parents probably could get satisfaction from the due process proceedings than those who actually have complained about their child's placement. Undoubtedly for many parents the complaint does not seem worth the trouble. *See supra* note 151. On the other hand, many parents may not know they have a right to complain. *See* Lynch & Stein, *supra* note 150, at 60 (15 percent not informed of rights); Polifka, *supra* note 152, at 252 (13 percent not informed of rights). The studies do not indicate if parents who tend to disagree with the placements are more likely not to know of their hearing rights than those who do agree with the placements. It may be that, in many circumstances, parents become motivated to challenge IEP's not so much because they are unhappy with the substantive program, but because they dislike the label the education agency attaches to it. Although in many instances educational activities for learning disabled (LD), mentally retarded (MR) and emotionally disturbed (ED) are nearly identical, parents frequently resist the idea that their child is retarded. *Cf.* FOURTH ANNUAL REPORT, *supra* note 115, at 106, 108-09 (between 1976-77 and 1980-81, the number of children classified as LD increased from 797,214 to 1,468,014; the number classified as ED rose from 283,072 to 348,954; while those classified as MR dropped from 969,597 to 844,180).

Studies of the issues raised at due process hearings also suggest that labels are often the principal sore point, though this conclusion also varies a great deal. *Compare* Kirst & Bertken, *Due Process Hearings in Special Education: Some Early Findings from California*, in SPECIAL EDUCATION POLICIES: THEIR HISTORY, IMPLEMENTATION AND FINANCE 136, 143 (1983) (study of hearings in California during 1978-79 shows only a few—less than 3 percent—of the hearings revolved around classification issues) *with* P. KURILOFF, D. KIRP & W. BUSS, *supra* note 105, at 160-62 (of the 168 due process hearings in Pennsylvania held between 1975 and 1979, 64 involved parental resistance to a school proposal to classify their child as retarded or to remove the child from mainstream school activities; parents favored LD and normal classifications, while schools favored educable mentally retarded (EMR) classifications). For a classic labeling disagreement, see Anderson v. Thompson, 658 F.2d 1205, 1207 (7th Cir. 1981) (school district, after identifying child with exceptional educational needs in speech and language and further undifferentiated exceptional educational needs, recommended placement in an EMR classroom, while parents' independent evaluation found speech, language, LD, and ED problems; hearing examiner found no LD, EMR, or ED problem, but determined that speech and language disability existed, and approved moving child from a private school program to the school district's EMR classroom "because it offered all of the components necessary for the development of a program meeting [the child's] individual needs.").

154.   *See generally* S. LIGHTFOOT, WORLDS APART: RELATIONSHIPS BETWEEN FAMILIES AND SCHOOL 20-42 (1978) (discussing the tensions in parent-teacher relations); D. LORTIE, SCHOOLTEACHER: A SOCIOLOGICAL STUDY (1975) (discussing need of teachers to control degree of parent input); M. Miles, Common Properties of Schools in Context: The Backdrop for Knowledge Utilization and "School Improvement" 82-84 (1980) (Center for Policy Research, New York, N.Y.) (professionalism

ences in the EAHCA regulatory scheme, and the structure of the IEP conferences themselves weigh against parent participation. Despite education professionals' long history of neglecting handicapped children and misusing special education services,[155] parents nonetheless "tend to trust the placement and services recommended by the schools."[156] This residual trust comes in part from parents' traditional willingness to defer to professional educational judgment,[157] reinforced by many educators' studied resistance to any parental input.[158] Professional resistance may explain why IEP conferences frequently are highly formal, noninteractive, and replete with educational jargon.[159] Professional resistance to parental input may also explain why one limited study found that IEP's were "always developed after the placement decision was made . . . ."[160] In a word, most educators are unac-

---

and the structure of the school bureaucracy buffer teachers and administrators from parental efforts to have input in school decisionmaking processes).

155. *See, e.g.*, Lazerson, *supra* note 59.

156. SRI FINAL, *supra* note 49, at 41.

157. *See id.*; Note, *supra* note 81, at 1110-11.

158. *See* Gilliam & Coleman, *Who Influences IEP Committee Decisions?*, 47 EXCEPTIONAL CHILDREN 642 (1981) (parents not perceived as equal partners); Goldstein, Strickland, Turnbull & Curry, *An Observational Analysis of the IEP Conference*, 46 EXCEPTIONAL CHILDREN 278 (1980) (same); Yoshida, Fenton, Kaufman & Maxwell, *Parental Involvement in the Special Education Pupil Planning Process: The School's Perspective*, 44 EXCEPTIONAL CHILDREN 531 (1978) (most professionals do not think parents should be directly involved in planning special education); CUMULATIVE EFFECTS, *supra* note 75, at 143 (educators disturbed by parental veto of program proposals not so much because of potential financial burden on school system but because parents are permitted to question successfully educators' professional judgment). Some school principals so resist any parent participation that many parents never even have an IEP conference. *See* C. BLASCHKE, STATE A, *supra* note 94, at 53-55 (in 1977, one district studied so entirely excluded parents that the Office of Civil Rights had to intervene). School principals seem less likely now to exclude completely parents from the IEP process than they did before the EAHCA, but significant proportions of parents may continue to be excluded altogether. For an example of professional educator resistance to lay input in England, see S. TOMLINSON, A SOCIOLOGY OF SPECIAL EDUCATION (1982).

159. *See* Kirp, Buss & Kuriloff, *supra* note 46, at 105-06 (pre-EAHCA study observed that educators break down parent resistance to program with overload of child's test results); SRI FINAL, *supra* note 49, at 22 (IEP conferences generally formal, not interactive); R. WEATHERLY, REFORMING SPECIAL EDUCATION: POLICY IMPLEMENTATION FROM STATE LEVEL TO STREET LEVEL 52-55 (1979) (conferences filled with "jargon"). At least one study has observed, however, that educators may just as well use "informal" or "interpretive" conferences as a method for successfully excluding parents from placement decisionmaking. S. THOUVENELLE, J. RADER & L. MADER, STUDY OF PROCEDURES FOR DETERMINING THE LEAST RESTRICTIVE ENVIRONMENT (LRE) PLACEMENT OF HANDICAPPED CHILDREN: FINAL PROJECT REPORT 7.3 (1980) (ERIC Doc. No. 199981) (study of 134 placement meetings in 15 school districts located in 5 states) [hereinafter referred to as STUDY OF PROCEDURES].

160. STUDY OF PROCEDURES, *supra* note 159, at 7.5. Of course, some parents may find this summary treatment insulting enough to prompt them to push the education agency into a hearing. One study of Massachusetts parents who pursued administrative remedies after unsatisfactory IEP conferences explained the parents' reactions to education agency behavior at IEP conferences. One parent called the conference a "kangaroo court." Another said that, "At the end of it, they handed me a blank piece of paper and said, 'Sign.' There wasn't anything on the paper. It was just a blank form. So I said, 'I would like to go home and discuss it with my husband.' And they became very angry and said I would be preventing the child from getting what he needed. They try and make the parents guilty for not signing a blank piece of paper." M. BUDOFF, A. ORENSTEIN & C. KERVICK, DUE PROCESS IN SPECIAL EDUCATION: ON GOING TO A HEARING 59 (1982) (longitudinal study of 80 families who participated in Massachusetts due process hearings between 1975 and 1977). Less blunt tactics left one parent feeling that "[T]hey listened, but they didn't listen, if you know what I mean. They listened, but they had their minds made up. The meeting is just really a pretense of listening, and then they write the plan they want." *Id.* at 61. In this respect, education agencies that try so hard to

customed to permitting parents an equal voice in educational decisions, and they have adapted the IEP conference legalism to perpetuate this customary relationship.

Beyond the structure of parent-professional relations, realistic organizational constraints made it necessary for LEA's to restrict parental participation. The first priority for school districts after passage of the Act was to identify and place previously neglected children. Since this requirement usually overburdened agency personnel, each step in the placement process had to be conducted as quickly as possible. Quick IEP meetings were expedient.[161] Although hurried IEP meetings may simply have been, as noted above, another method intentionally applied to thwart parental input, in many instances educators simply were reacting to time pressures.[162] The pressure to meet evaluation deadlines, the burden of handling due process hearings, and the large amount of paperwork and time commitments generated by the IEP process itself all motivated LEA's to rush IEP conferences and discourage parental participation. Parental participation was not bureaucratically efficient.

Finally, the structure of the IEP conferences themselves discourages parental participation. Parents are almost always outnumbered at IEP conferences.[163] The dynamic of small groups usually prevents a minority viewpoint from exerting any real influence, even if the placement decision is not, as it usually is, predetermined.[164] In fact, one study indicated that, even if parents assert themselves at IEP conferences, they implicitly follow the agenda set by the educators around the table. According to this study, educators do not raise the touchy issues, such as placement options, potential social stigma, or possible harmful effects of proposed placements.[165] Further, as educators rarely organize their evaluation findings in a manner designed to create a coherent whole for the parent, parents find it difficult to reconstruct these

---

defuse parental input that they unilaterally end communication between themselves and parents may end up facing the very problem they sought to avoid. It might also be that these high-handed school tactics have been motivated by the belief that the IEP, which is supposed to be signed by the education agency and parents, is a contract to which the school could be bound. If the IEP were viewed as a contract, the education agencies would naturally have wanted parents to sign a blank piece of paper, since undoubtedly the financial burdens of special education frequently put school districts in the position where they do not feel they can afford to negotiate. The legislative history makes it clear, however, that the IEP is not a contract. *See* 121 CONG. REC. 19,492 (1975) (statement by Senator Williams, a principal sponsor of the EAHCA that the IEP conference does not create a "contractual relationship"). Inasmuch as only about one-half of the IEPs have parental signatures, it is apparent that many school districts do not strictly view the IEP as a type of contract. *See* A NATIONAL SURVEY OF IEPs: VOL. I, *supra* note 73, at 8.

161. C. BLASCHKE, STATE B, *supra* note 94, at 44; R. WEATHERLY, *supra* note 159, at 87.

162. *See* R. WEATHERLY, *supra* note 159, at 56 (school officials were often willing and able to provide inquiring parents with useful explanations of what was going on, but school officials rarely volunteered those explanations because it took much longer to convey them).

163. For example, in the NASDSE study, described *supra* note 143, 11 of the 20 districts sampled indicated a median of 6 participants, with a range of 5 to 8, for a mildly handicapped eighth grader. Fourteen of the 20 districts indicated a median of 6 participants, with a range of 5 to 10, for a severely handicapped elementary school student. FOURTH ANNUAL REPORT, *supra* note 115, at 29.

164. M. BUDOFF, A. ORENSTEIN & C. KERVICK, *supra* note 160, at 62.

165. STUDY OF PROCEDURES, *supra* note 159, at 7.7-7.9.

findings in the form of an alternative proposal.[166]

In sum, the IEP provisions of the EAHCA have increased parental participation somewhat, but probably not nearly to the extent that Congress originally contemplated. In the end, the IEP legalism seems ill-suited to significantly alter preexisting patterns of parent-school relations.[167] If the IEP process has improved the rate at which children are appropriately placed in special education programs, it apparently does so not because of the specific contours of the process, or even because of the content of the IEP itself, but simply because some kind of process exists.

(vi) *Due process.* At the end of the chronological line of procedural mechanisms stands the EAHCA due process requirement, an administrative hearing designed to further none of the Act's objectives specifically and all of them generally. Because the requirement is designed in part as a deterrent whose effect is detectable only if parents insist on compliance, the role due process plays in the decisionmaking framework is difficult, if not impossible, to evaluate in situations when the process is not pursued ultimately to a hearing.[168] However, the effectiveness of due process as a deterrent may be assessed in part by analyzing the cases where due process is used to see how frequently it is used, who "succeeds" in using it, how difficult it is to use, and whether it triggers the development of extra-legal mechanisms for solving the problems it was intended to solve.

Parents appear to win, and thus obtain desirable services and placements for their children, in slightly more than one-third of EAHCA hearings;[169] however, they must first get to a hearing. Few parents, as observed earlier, participate effectively enough in the IEP process even to raise a complaint.[170] Even if parents have the skill and knowledge to raise complaints at the IEP

---

166. *Id.* at 7.6-7.9. One innovative school district—Madison, Wisconsin—has recognized the inevitable temptations and dynamic consequences of the IEP conferences format, and actively encourages parents to bring an advocate with them to an IEP conference. *See* J. Handler, The Discretionary Decision (1984) (unpublished manuscript).

167. *See generally* H. BROUDY, THE REAL WORLD OF THE PUBLIC SCHOOLS 20-38 (1972) (explaining why schools are unresponsive to externally initiated change); M. Miles, *supra* note 154, at 73-96 (on mechanisms used by school systems to deflect and defuse forces attempting to compel change in the schools).

168. *See generally* Hawkins & Thomas, *The Enforcement Process in Regulatory Bureaucracies,* in ENFORCING REGULATION 3 (1984) (effectiveness of statute like the EAHCA significantly affected by enforcement practices from the top level of the hierarchy to the field level, and effectiveness is influenced by the complexity of the enforcement environment); Scholz, *Cooperation, Deterrence, and the Ecology of Regulatory Enforcement,* 18 L. & SOC'Y REV. 179 (1984) (describing the difficulty in predicting how deterrent structures will work in an organizational framework).

169. D. KIRP & D. JENSEN, WHAT DOES DUE PROCESS DO? PARC v. COMMONWEALTH OF PENNSYLVANIA RECONSIDERED 15 (1983) (ERIC Doc. No. ED 229 878) (parents not likely to succeed on appeal); P. KURILOFF, D. KIRP & W. BUSS, *supra* note 105, at 168 (parents won 35 percent of 168 hearings in Pennsylvania from 1974-78; Kirst & Bertken, *supra* note 153, at 136, 139-45 (study of 145 due process hearings in California held in 1978-79 indicates that parents achieved at least partial grants of their claims in 49 percent of the local decisions and state appeals); Smith, *Status of Due Process Hearings,* 48 EXCEPTIONAL CHILDREN 232 (1981) (741 of 2,006 hearings won by parents in 38 states sampled up to 1980). A cautionary note: all of these data are quite old. It is not clear that parents have been as successful in recent years.

170. *See supra* note 150.

conference, they may not have enough to succeed at a hearing.[171] The relative handful of parents who do make it to a hearing[172] must increasingly face the education agencies' winning documentation and procedural compliance strategy.[173] Thus, a relentless attrition quells threats to the professional decisions of educators.

Even favorable results frequently have been of little comfort to parents. Some education agencies complied with the hearing officer's directives immediately; others waited until a few adverse decisions accumulated. On the other hand, there were many opportunities for procedural gamesmanship and noncompliance. Even if schools lost at the hearing level, they might appeal to the state level for relief from the hearing officer's decision.[174] If the appeal process was not too discouraging, schools could still frustrate the parents by resubmitting the same plan that they originally gave to the parents,[175] or by simply refusing to comply. In many instances, nothing compelled schools to provide the program the hearing system required.[176] If these devices were too crude, districts also learned that they could temporarily comply, but then reevaluate the child at the legally mandated point (three years after the initial evaluation) and resubmit that original plan on the basis of their reevaluation.[177]

Of course, if hearing results sorted themselves out in a triage-like process based on the substantive worthiness of the claims and a precedent-based system, then the high rates of attrition would not be so troublesome. The due process system still would be systematically providing an appropriate education for all similarly situated children in an order corresponding to the severity of their needs. Due process could encourage all meritorious claims, however, only if it functioned informally enough that it would be easily, inexpensively, and equally accessible to each potential complainant.

---

171. M. BUDOFF, A. ORENSTEIN & C. KERVICK, *supra* note 160, at 117-18 (discussing extremely extensive preparation parents must undergo before the hearings); *cf.* P. KURILOFF, D. KIRP & W. BUSS, *supra* note 105, at 210-12 (parent success at hearings is strongly related to the depth of their preparation).

172. In 1979-80, only 0.065 percent of all children receiving special education services challenged any aspect of their special education program, while only 0.007 percent actually filed a complaint in any court. Children's Defense Fund, Comments of the Children's Defense Fund on the Department of Education's Proposed Regulations Implementing Pub. L. 94-142, at 5 (Dec 3, 1982) (formal comments).

173. P. KURILOFF, D. KIRP & W. BUSS, *supra* note 105, at 205-06 (school districts tend to do better in hearings if they show they have complied with procedural requirements of law); L. McDONNELL & M. McLAUGHLIN, *supra* note 93, at 124 (state education agencies emphasize correct EAHCA procedures in their monitoring of local education agencies, rather than insure that there is an appropriate match between the child's diagnosis and the educational services the child receives).

174. *See* M. BUDOFF, A. ORENSTEIN & C. KERVICK, *supra* note 160, at 144 (in a study of Massachusetts hearings, several parents gave up because they could not afford to appeal, or simply did not want to continue in the process); P. KURILOFF, D. KIRP & W. BUSS, *supra* note 105, at 238-39 (noting that administrative appeals process in Pennsylvania between 1972 and 1975 distinctly favored school districts).

175. M. BUDOFF, A. ORENSTEIN & C. KERVICK, *supra* note 160, at 139.

176. *Id.* at 121-22, 141, 149; *cf.* FOURTH ANNUAL REPORT, *supra* note 115, at 65-68 (on gentle enforcement monitoring practices of state education agencies).

177. M. BUDOFF, A. ORENSTEIN & C. KERVICK, *supra* note 160, at 142.

Instead, the due process system increasingly has moved away from such informality. The financial cost of hearings may be substantial for both sides, although these costs may vary considerably depending on factors such as the extent of legal assistance the parties employ.[178] The high costs associated with these procedures probably skew hearings toward the more financially consequential handicaps, since parents who have much to gain from a favorable decision presumably will be more willing to accept high litigation costs. Even more important, far from being unintimidating, the hearings process exerts a terrible toll on the participants. Parents, teachers, and administrators all become very frustrated by the process because it demands so much of their time, because it challenges their personal and professional integrity, and because it represents an utter breakdown in communication.[179] Breakdowns in communication may be so severe that the substantive issues between the parties cannot be resolved until either the family or the school administrator moves out of the school district.[180] Not surprisingly, the hearings have become less like informal dispute resolution and have taken on characteristics of judicial procedures.[181]

At the same time that effectively limited access to the system has cut into the range of substantive complaints addressed by the due process procedures, the hearing system has failed to generate the necessary precedential value.[182] Each due process hearing depends on an ad hoc analysis that, at least formally, ignores past solutions to similar problems.

Despite the apparent failure of the due process procedures to address the imbalance of power between individual parents and education agencies, there

---

178. See M. BUDOFF, A. ORENSTEIN & C. KERVICK, supra note 160, at 113-14, 139 (describing wide variation in hearings cost for parents, ranging from a few hundred to thousands of dollars); STATE OF MINNESOTA DEPARTMENT OF EDUCATION, THE IMPACT OF CONCILIATION CONFERENCES AND DUE PROCESS HEARINGS, 1981-1982 (1983) (some parents' hearing costs in the hundreds of dollars range; hearings costs for school districts in the several thousands of dollars range) [hereinafter cited as MINNESOTA MEDIATION]; FOURTH ANNUAL REPORT, supra note 115, at 46 (average hearings may cost state education agencies thousands of dollars); Bickel, supra note 91, at 211 (attorney fees and time necessary to follow due process hearings for both parents and schools may depress use of hearing process); Kirst & Bertken, supra note 153, at 141-42 (noting hearing costs for school districts ranging from several hundred to a few thousand dollars).

179. See M. BUDOFF, A. ORENSTEIN & C. KERVICK, supra note 160, at 56-63, 69-72, 77-83, 101-18, 127-30, 203-04, 208-11 (poor parent-school communication and very heavy workloads take toll on parents and educators in terms of energy, morale, sense of integrity, and professional competence).

180. Id. at 210.

181. See id. at 202, 324-26; D. KIRP & D. JENSEN, supra note 169, at 30; FOURTH ANNUAL REPORT, supra note 115, at 47-48.

182. See M. BUDOFF, A. ORENSTEIN & C. KERVICK, supra note 160, at 125, 195-96 (hearing officers' actions, by not precisely specifying the educational program, often lead to a further hearing aimed at clarifying the original hearing decision; school administrators tend to see hearing process as substantively unpredictable); id. at 333 (unique case facts prevent precedents from being established); D. KIRP & D. JENSEN, supra note 169, at 20-30 (hearing appeals decisions permit divergent diagnosis of the handicap of a given child to withstand review, and restrict authority of hearing officers to solve educational problems); id. at 15 (noting that the use of individualized education may so affect hearing process that hearing officers may refuse to follow precedent because each case is too individualized); P. KURILOFF, D. KIRP & W. BUSS, supra note 105 (noting that hearings officers in Pennsylvania frequently were prevented or discouraged from making specific substantive placement recommendations).

nonetheless are indications that due process gives parents leverage against education agencies. The unpleasant qualities of due process hearings have led a number of states to develop prehearing mediation procedures. These mediations are not part of the special education law; at least one state (Pennsylvania) has run into difficulties with the Department of Education because the federal authorities felt that the mediation process was used by the state to circumvent the hearings process.[183] It is clear, however, that the mediation process is significantly supplanting the need for due process hearings in several states.[184] For example, in 1981-82, only five of Minnesota's eighty-four conciliation cases ended up at a formal hearing.[185] In 1981, sixty-four of Connecticut's eighty-three mediations reached agreement. Only twelve of the remaining cases resulted in a hearing.[186] Thus, perhaps because it better preserves the long term cooperative relationship between parents and schools,[187] mediation may be a more effective mechanism than the due process hearing for ensuring that more children receive an appropriate, individualized education in the least restrictive environment. Mediation, rather than the due process hearing, seems to achieve the informality which encourages meritorious claims.

In sum, the due process hearing probably has increased the proportion of handicapped children receiving an appropriate education, though the magnitude of the increase is unknown. While we suspect that due process has had a small impact on the delivery of special education services,[188] that impact undoubtedly varies significantly among states and among districts within states. As in the case of every other part of the procedure, variables outside the system, such as the presence of active parent groups, financial status of the education agency, and administrative style of the local educators, are critical determinants of procedural effectiveness.

---

    183.   D. KIRP & D. JENSEN, supra note 169, at 16. Minnesota had to arrange a special agreement with the Department of Education to keep its mediation process. See MINNESOTA MEDIATION, supra note 178, at 10.
    184.   See FOURTH ANNUAL REPORT, supra note 115, at 47-48.
    185.   MINNESOTA MEDIATION, supra note 178, at 4.
    186.   DIVISION OF ELEMENTARY AND SECONDARY EDUCATION, CONNECTICUT STATE DEPARTMENT OF EDUCATION ANALYSIS OF 1981 SPECIAL EDUCATION MEDIATIONS 1 (1982).
    187.   See Macaulay, Non-Contractual Relations in Business: A Preliminary Study, 28 AM. SOC. REV. 55-67 (1963).
    188.   Perhaps one reason for the failure of due process requirements to have a larger impact on the delivery of special education services is that the courts have, by and large, not pushed hard to create a remedial framework which will weigh rather heavily on the minds of educators. One reason for this, of course, is that it is difficult, if not impossible, to decide whether the parents or educators will have the better substantive arguments because the state of knowledge is often rather primitive. See, e.g., Board of Educ. v. Rowley, 458 U.S. 176 (1982) (Court concluded that it cannot determine who has the better substantive position). In any case, courts have been unwilling to provide remedies which have enough bite to be influential at the field level of decisionmaking. Few courts will give damages, attorney fees, or compensatory educational service remedies under the EAHCA. For policy arguments against broad-stroke damage remedies, see Hyatt, Litigating the Rights of Handicapped Children to an Appropriate Education: Procedures and Remedies, 29 U.C.L.A. L. REV. 1 (1981). For a general analysis which suggests why the structure of school-parent relationships embodied in the EAHCA precludes much better results for due process, see J. Handler, supra note 166. See generally Galanter, Why the "Haves" Come Out Ahead: Speculations on the Limits of Legal Change, 9 L. & SOC'Y REV. 95 (1975).

B. What Causes the Implementation Gap? Political Adjustments and the Limits of Legalization

After comparing reformist objectives with implementation realities and briefly exploring organizational/political reasons for the difference, it is time to focus more sharply on the organizational/political explanations. We need to collect and collate the various kinds of interpretations we have already made and transpose them into a more systematic framework.

The gap between reformist objectives and implementation is often explained in passive terms, like inertia or complexity. Explanation is sometimes avoided by referring to unexpected consequences. In contrast, a political explanation presupposes political activity. Gaps occur because the priorities represented by the law enter a world with many other priorities. What is sometimes referred to as a unilateral process of enforcement and impact actually is an interactive process of mutual adjustment. Legal objectives are compromised so that other objectives do not need to be compromised, or compromised so much. One person's gap is another person's gain.[189]

This section of the article attempts to demonstrate the essentially political character of EAHCA implementation more systematically than the densely factual narrative of the preceding section. To show the interactive nature of the process, the law is represented as a set of initiatives or resources, which the active environment of law answers with initiatives and resources of its own.

1. *Law as Resources and Limitations on Those Resources.* Why does a law such as the EAHCA cause any social change at all? Why is it not simply ignored? Literally speaking, enactment of legislation consists of putting words on paper. How and why do those words change behavior?

One way to answer these questions is to conceive of law as a set of initiatives and resources. To a certain extent, law itself acts as an initiative because of the general law-abiding nature of people. A complex law like the EAHCA probably does not create much automatic compliance, however. For such a law, compliance occurs because people are encouraged or allowed to request or demand compliance from regulated organizations. A law like the EAHCA is a "demand entitlement," a resource for those inclined to ask for change.

Those requesting change include state and local education agencies, either undertaking a process of voluntary compliance or seeking information about legal requirements from federal agencies and service organizations. Federal agencies engage in both formal and informal enforcement and assistance.

---

189. This description is especially appropriate for what has been called the "compliance relationship" (as opposed to the "deterrence relationship"). In the compliance relationship, both parties have a high degree of social legitimacy and the emphasis is on preventing rather than punishing harms. *See* Clune, *supra* note 2, at 65-66; Hawkins & Thomas, *The Enforcement Process in Regulatory Bureaucracies*, in ENFORCING REGULATION 3, 8-9 (1984); Reis, *Selecting Strategies of Social Control Over Organizational Life*, in ENFORCING REGULATION 23 (1984).

Outside the government, advocacy groups, individual advocates, and individual parents make demands on schools, request hearings, complain to enforcement agencies, and bring court actions. All of these people use four basic kinds of resources: new financial resources (federal aid); a new source of moral authority (the idea that handicapped children have a right to more educational resources); the substantive right provided by the law (an appropriate education, as defined by regulations and courts); and, most important in the case of the EAHCA, the right to demand a whole set of new organizational procedures (child finds, referrals, new tests, M-team assessments, IEP's, due process hearings).

Change is limited because the resources used by these groups and individuals are limited. Federal aid was limited, especially as initial commitments were compromised under fiscal pressure. The EAHCA's direct service requirements were a relatively efficient means of requiring that money be spent for the purpose intended.[190] Even so, the availability of financial aid for intended beneficiaries is always problematic.[191] New moral authority is offset by countervailing moral authority (e.g., the claim of resources, such as teacher and psychologist time, for the handicapped versus other uses).[192] The substantive right to an appropriate education was vague. Although it suggested some content, its essential definition was procedural; appropriate education became the education defined by key decisionmakers during implementation. Enforcement agencies, hearing officers, school officials, and courts determined the meaning of appropriate education, and all were more or less responsive to competing claims for resources. Practically speaking, implementation is a process of compromise, in which legal scholars as well as courts take part. Several of the articles in this volume, for example, contain carefully developed doctrinal methods for balancing the needs of the handicapped against other claims.[193]

Limitations on procedure as a resource are especially significant because of the importance of procedure under the legislation. Two kinds of procedures established by the Act should be distinguished for analytical purposes: the organizational routines, such as IEP's, required of all schools for all chil-

---

190. For a discussion of the direct service requirements of the EAHCA compared with other types of grant mechanisms, see Barro, *Federal Education Goals and Policy Instruments: An Assessment of the "Strings" Attached to Categorical Grants in Education,* in THE FEDERAL INTEREST IN FINANCING SCHOOLING 229 (M. Timpane ed. 1978).

191. The basic problem with financial aid is additivity—aid recipients reduce their own expenditures on the aided activity and save the difference or spend it on something else. *See* Barro, *supra* note 190; Clune, Serrano & Robinson: *Studies in the Implementation of Fiscal Equity and Effective Education in State Public Law Litigation,* in SCHOOLS AND COURTS 67-120 (P. Piele ed. 1979). *See also supra* note 39 and accompanying text.

192. *See supra* note 189 and accompanying text.

193. *See, e.g.,* Bartlett, *The Role of Cost in Educational Decisionmaking for the Handicapped Child,* LAW & CONTEMP. PROBS., Spring 1985, at 7; Wegner, *Variations on a Theme—The Concept of Equal Educational Opportunity and Programming Decisions Under the Education for All Handicapped Children Act of 1975,* LAW & CONTEMP. PROBS., Winter 1985, at 169. On the lack of substance and procedural quality of the EAHCA, see *supra* note 36; Buss, *Special Education in England and Wales,* LAW & CONTEMP. PROBS., Winter 1985, at 119; Yudof, *Education for the Handicapped: Rowley in Perspective,* 92 AM. J. EDUC. 163 (1984).

dren; and litigation entitlements, which establish the right to complain on the part of enforcement agencies and parents. Organizational routines are subject to the problem of formal compliance.[194] Organizations lacking a clear substantive direction or strong commitment to the protected group can reach any preferred result following proper procedures. M-teams using broadly based tests can produce properly drafted IEP's to justify almost anything short of complete exclusion. The effectiveness of the procedures depends upon the skill and motivation of various people involved, but the degree of skill and the commitment of school personnel toward the handicapped varies greatly. Model communities may exist side by side with communities that lag far behind in implementing the Act.[195] Among those motivated to use the new procedures constructively, formal compliance presents a different problem. Resources used to meet formal requirements detract from actions that are more efficient in particular contexts.[196]

Litigation entitlements are subject to similar limitations. Federal and state enforcement agencies have limited resources and other responsibilities. Political pressures and divided loyalties may prevent the use of available enforcement resources. Enforcement also tends to gravitate toward formal compliance. Formal compliance is more easily monitored than substantive compliance (especially when the substantive right is vague and invites compromise), but formal compliance also is tempting politically. In choosing a high standard of procedural compliance coupled with a low standard of substantive compliance, and a high degree of deference to professional decisionmakers,[197] courts have adopted a relatively nonintrusive, nonactivist role.

The plasticity of substantive rights, organizational routines, and administrative enforcement partially explains the relative ineffectiveness of parental entitlements. If parents had a clear entitlement (for example, a right to $500 upon determination of a handicapping condition), backed up by a strict enforcement agency, things might be different.[198] Of course, all litigation entitlements (complaint-triggered liability systems)[199] are constrained by the cost of litigation, both financial and personal, and by the many advantages to

---

194. In formal compliance, rules are followed technically, but the underlying purpose of the rule is frustrated. Such means/end conflict has been called "goal avoidance." See E. BARDACH, supra note 8, at 85-95; P. BLAU, THE DYNAMICS OF BUREAUCRACY—A STUDY OF INTERPERSONAL RELATIONS IN TWO GOVERNMENT AGENCIES 231-65 (2d ed. 1963); J. PRESSMAN & A. WILDAVSKY, IMPLEMENTATION 1 passim (2d ed. 1979); P. SELZNICK, LAW, SOCIETY, AND INDUSTRIAL JUSTICE 13 (1969); P. SELZNICK, TVA AND THE GRASS ROOTS—A STUDY IN THE SOCIOLOGY OF FORMAL ORGANIZATION 259 (1949) ("deflection of goals"); Barro, supra note 190, at 229.

195. Paul Berman emphasizes the importance of matching implementation strategies to the type of regulated enterprise and situation. See P. BERMAN, FROM COMPLIANCE TO LEARNING: IMPLEMENTING LEGALLY-INDUCED REFORM 27-28 (1981) (Institute for Research on Educational Finance and Governance, Stanford University, Project Report No. 81-A20).

196. The idea that field-level inspectors and regulated enterprises can often find a more efficient way to meet regulatory goals than the way specified in the law is at the heart of E. BARDACH & R. KAGAN, supra note 8, at 99-104.

197. Board of Educ. v. Rowley, 458 U.S. 176 (1982).

198. See Rebell, Educational Voucher Reform: Empirical Insights from the Experience of New York's Schools for the Handicapped, 14 URB. LAW. 441 (1982).

199. See Clune & Lindquist, supra note 7, at 1083-88.

institutional repeat players.[200] Parents' effectiveness in the school setting is further reduced by their special relationship with schools—not simply a continuing relationship based upon trust but a highly dependent one as well.[201] Professor Handler aptly identifies the class of problems as dependent relationships and discretionary decisions.[202]

2. *Reprise: Strengths and Weaknesses of Legalization as a Source of Social Change.* A process of political adjustment during implementation takes place regardless of the type of legal intervention. Policy instruments very unlike the EAHCA evoke similar processes of adjustment (vouchers, categorical grants, teacher training, mental health and employment programs, and the Tennessee Valley Authority (TVA), for example).[203] One way to sharpen the discussion of the limits of change under the EAHCA is to focus on the specific policy instrument used in that law and many others.

Choosing a word for this kind of policy instrument is not easy because of the typical problem of terminology in the social sciences; a variety of words with overlapping but also inconsistent meanings are used to describe approximately the same things. The word adopted in this article is "legalization." "Legalism" was an earlier choice,[204] but that term may have pejorative connotations. A term permitting both positive and negative elements is preferable. Legalization also has serious disadvantages. Professor Kirp restricts the term to judicial interventions establishing individual rights and relying heavily on due process.[205]

Our usage is much broader. Legalization is most usefully defined broadly and functionally as a mechanism of social control (or influence) characterized by *externally observable routinized behavior.*[206] The essence of legalization, whether ordered by a legislature, court, or administrative agency, is the requirement of standardized organizational behavior (routines) designed to be observed, audited, and monitored from other social locations (e.g., enforcement agencies).[207] So defined, legalization reaches into every area of organizational life, including categorical financial aid (involving monitoring of the use of money), planning (e.g., programmed budgeting, school improvement plans), client influence (e.g., due process rights), and routine administration (e.g., audits, record keeping, reports).

---

200. *See* Galanter, *supra* note 188 (advantages of "repeat players").
201. In this respect, the difficulties in using legal remedies in the school situation are greater than those in the continuing business relationships described by Macaulay, *supra* note 187.
202. J. Handler, *supra* note 166.
203. *See, e.g., supra* notes 191 & 194.
204. Clune, Rationalistic and Political Interpretations of Legalism: A Review Essay on Bardach & Kagan's *Going By The Book* (unpublished paper presented at the annual meeting of the Law & Society Association, June 1983).
205. *See* Kirp, *supra* note 9.
206. This was how "legalism" was defined in Clune, *supra* note 204.
207. The "monitorability" aspect of legalization is sometimes the source of efficiency (when individualized decisions are too expensive), sometimes the source of inefficiency (when only individualized decisions will do), and sometimes the source of political oppression (when monitoring is done for the sake of domination or disruption). *See* Clune, *supra* note 204.

Formally, that is, ignoring important patterns of informal influence and communication,[208] the EAHCA is entirely composed of legalizations. Various procedures are imposed to implement accurate referral, assessment, and placement, such as Child Find census operations, multiple-testing instruments, interdisciplinary evaluation teams, and IEP's. Parental influence is routinized by veto power over evaluation[209] and placement, participation in the IEP conference, and due process rights or litigation entitlements which compel school authorities to go through certain legal routines on parental demand. Financial aid, in the manner typical of federal programs, is targeted on districts with high concentrations of the protected class of children.[210]

Such a functional definition makes it easy to see the strengths and weaknesses of legalization as a source of social change. Widespread change can be produced quickly for two different reasons. As a matter of bureaucratic enforcement, organizational routines are easily monitored and relatively easily adopted. Second, the availability of substantive rights and litigation entitlements instantly authorizes a potentially large class of well-motivated private enforcers, especially when, as in the case of special education, private complainants are numerous, well-informed, and organized at the grassroots.

The weaknesses of legalization as a method of social change are the three great weaknesses of proceduralism: resistance, lack of substance, and cost.

a. *Resistance.* The formal goals of legalization represent the aspirations of the group seeking compensation through legal reform (or, more narrowly, social movement activists), and do not take account of opposing interests whose preexisting priorities must be altered in order to provide compensation. That is, formal goals represent ideals without resistance.[211] Procedures and new organizational routines are enacted for the benefit of the protected class, but they are equally available to other interests even though such interests usually benefit from advantages outside the statutory framework. Apart from the relationship between the parties, schools have several important

---

208. Legalization requirements are just words on paper until someone decides to do something with them. From the enforcement side, "using" legalisms may consist of actual use, as in lawsuits, threats of use, and informal sanctions, such as paperwork. *See* M. FEELEY, THE PROCESS IS THE PUNISHMENT: HANDLING CASES IN A LOWER CRIMINAL COURT (1979); P. HILL, ENFORCEMENT AND INFORMAL PRESSURE IN THE MANAGEMENT OF FEDERAL CATEGORICAL PROGRAMS IN EDUCATION 14-29 (1979) (Rand Note No. N-1232-HEW). Beyond all of these, however, enforcement agencies often try to assist regulated organizations with compliance through such devices as consultation and professionalization of staff. *See* P. BERMAN, *supra* note 195; M. DERTHICK, THE INFLUENCE OF FEDERAL GRANTS 158-218 (1970).

209. 34 C.F.R. § 300.504(c)(2)(i) (1984) (public agency may use hearing procedures to override parental veto of evaluation or initial provision of special education and related services).

210. *See* Magnetti, *Some Potential Incentives of Special Education Funding Practices,* in PLACING CHILDREN IN SPECIAL EDUCATION: A STRATEGY FOR EQUITY 300, 315-16 (1982). The EAHCA funding formula is located in 20 U.S.C. § 1411 (1982).

211. This is the great irony of the Reagan Administration attack on affirmative action. Such things as goals and timetables start out compromised (by such things as good faith exceptions, *see* Clune, *supra* note 2, at 59-60, and are further compromised in practice. Thus the "rigidity" of affirmative action is purely rhetorical, absolute demands being necessary as a bargaining chip, *see infra* part III; and the attacks against it, if successful, will destroy or cripple a program that is already discounted just short of the point of being completely ineffective.

advantages in the adversary process, such as money, time, expertise, and social power. The special relationship between parties which is characteristic of regulatory law increases that advantage. Regulation usually takes the form of the "compliance relationship,"[212] a somewhat contradictory relationship in which the regulated institution is distrusted to the extent that voluntary compliance is considered unlikely, yet trusted at least in the sense that fundamental social legitimacy and continued existence is presumed. This trust may extend even to a sense that a continuing mutually satisfactory relationship is the object of the distrust-motivated system of regulation. All such procedures thus have a difficult dual mission: encouraging complaints against the system, and creating a cooperative relationship between system and challenger. Very often the indispensable quality of the cooperative relationship negates the realistic possibility of challenge—or limits challenging to special cases as, for example, in the case of relatively wealthy parents seeking very large financial benefits from private placements.

b. *Lack of substance.*   Lack of educational substance is the next great weakness of a legalistic solution. Legalization is a crude device sometimes useful as a means of obtaining resources but hardly ever useful in suggesting educational solutions. An organizational routine such as the IEP can capture the attention of an organization, but it cannot provide a good education. Bureaucratic rigidity and technical ignorance remain untouched by due process. Budgeting implications of the right to an appropriate education were left vague, to be hammered out in various procedural forums. Organizational planning and staffing were also underemphasized. The result of all this is a rather strange, but in some ways admirable, process in which the educational content of rights is developed improvisationally in response to sporadic pressure. Schools must develop new programs, personnel skills, and organizational routines in order to meet all demands impinging on the system. Special education cannot have an infinite budget either in dollars or in educational programs. In the best case, schools must "fit" a group of programs with what seems to be the overall mix of demands and needs. In the worst case, schools are frozen in resistance or technical incompetence, subjected to the aimless pressure of legalization or to no pressure at all.

Thus, a system of proceduralization like the EAHCA creates a substantive underground of educational practice consisting of educational solutions created in response to the law but nowhere specified in it. Advocates, schools, researchers, and government agencies cooperate in devising new solutions.[213] But the solutions bear the mark of improvisation. They are erratic and incom-

---

212. *See supra* note 189.

213. On the EAHCA as both a civil rights statute and education initiative, see Yudof, *supra* note 193. Examples of efficient, humanizing, organizational innovations in special education are: having other children in the class help push wheelchairs, and finding out which teachers do not really mind or can easily adapt to catherization. *See generally* Kimbrough & Hill, The Aggregate Effects of Federal Education Programs (Sept. 1981) (Rand Working Paper No. R-2638-Ed.).

plete because the law provided for demands, rather than responses to demands.

c. *Cost.* Cost is the last weakness of legalization. Organizational routines are expensive, especially when they require the participation of specially trained personnel. Because of the pressure of enforcement, formal compliance automatically becomes a high priority even if it is substantively unproductive.[214] Even more important is the stress and confusion produced by the substantively empty procedural solution. Schools are told to do *something* under penalty of the law, but they are not told what to do or how to do it. Meeting the demands of each parent is not sufficient. There must be some overall organizational planning and development.

3. *Summary.* Seasoned observers of legalization are rarely pleased by it.[215] Much happens quickly, partly because of a lot of wasted motion. Benefits are widespread, but they are also uneven and unpredictable. Resources are mobilized, but the educational practice needed to use those resources is left hanging, improvised by school people confused and agitated by an urgent yet strangely uninformative law.[216] Given this ambivalence, whether to like or dislike legalization is partly a function of perspective and expectations.[217] Anti-legalists become preoccupied with costs and the formal, symbolic character of compliance.[218] As a general matter, we are on the pro-legalistic side of neutrality because of what seems to be a potentially dangerous bias in the

---

214. *See supra* note 194.

215. *See supra* note 9; D. KIRP & D. JENSEN *supra* note 169; D. KIRP & D. JUNG, SCHOOLS AND RULES: UNDERSTANDING LEGALIZATION IN COMPARATIVE PERSPECTIVE (1983) (Institute for Research on Educational Finance and Governance, Stanford, Project Report No. 83-B5); Kirp, *Professionalization as a Policy Choice: British Special Education in Comparative Perspective,* 34 WORLD POL. 137 (1982); Neal & Kirp, *supra* note 36. Ambivalence in a situation of considerable benefits and considerable costs is understandable. Professor Kirp's work on legalization may suffer from a certain unwillingness to strike a final balance.

216. Much research on the effect of educational resources, whether dollars, teacher qualifications, learning and teaching time, library books, etc., fails to show any strong educational effects, because the research failed to investigate how resources were transformed at the school level into educational outputs. R. BARR & R. DREEBEN, HOW SCHOOLS WORK 1-4 (1983); H. Levin, About Time for Educational Reform (Aug. 1983) (Institute for Research on Educational Finance and Governance, Stanford University Project Report No. 83-A19); MacKenzie, Educational Productivity and School Effectiveness 30-35 (1983) (unpublished manuscript) (Research Synthesis and Policy Analysis, Southwest Educational Development Laboratory, NIE Contract No. 400-83-0007).

217. For example, one's perceptions of whether the costs of legalization are worthwhile is extraordinarily sensitive to one's evaluation of the substantive right in question. *See* Clune, *supra* note 2, at 90; Clune, *supra* note 7, at 765 n.12.

218. Anti-legalism (the idea that regulation does not produce much useful behavior change) comes from rather different directions: a rationalizing, cost-conscious impulse, *e.g.,* E. BARDACH & R. KAGAN, *supra* note 8; a radical, unmasking impulse, *e.g.,* J. EDELMAN, POLITICAL LANGUAGE: WORDS THAT SUCCEED AND POLICIES THAT FAIL (1977); and a symbol-concious sociological impulse, *e.g.,* Meyer, *Strategies for Further Research: Varieties of Environmental Variation,* in ENVIRONMENTS AND ORGANIZATION 352, 355-57 (1978); Meyer & Rowan, *Institutionalized Organizations: Formal Structure as Myth and Ceremony,* 83 AM. J. SOC. 340, 346-48 (1977); Meyer & Rowan, *The Structure of Educational Organizations* in ENVIRONMENTS AND ORGANIZATION 78, 79-81 (1978); Meyer, Scott, Cole & Intili, *Instructional Dissensus and Institutional Consensus in Schools,* in ENVIRONMENTS AND ORGANIZATION 233, 256-63; J. Meyer, W. Scott & T. Deal, Institutional and Technical Sources of Organizational Structure Explaining the Structure of Educational Organizations (May 1980) (unpublished manuscript on file with the author).

anti-legalist position. The ultimate advantage of legalization is the production of rapid change through substantively empty demand entitlements. The thin, formal quality of these entitlements can produce a serious underestimation of their value in the minds of those demanding an unrealistic degree of intellectual coherence in social life. The empty entitlements can work surprisingly well as the structure for legally unspecified but practically effective social action. In organizations with a high degree of cooperation and skill, the legal rules may provide a stable structure within which to conduct preferred interactions. In highly resistant organizations, the entitlements eventually may provide the key which unlocks the door for progressive change. All sorts of social action benefitting children flows both around and through established procedures. For example, parents may not participate effectively in the IEP conference, but they might have had a useful conversation with school personnel in anticipation of the conference.

In one sense, the value of legalization in the abstract is much too general a question to be useful. Legalization works better or worse across a wide range depending on context. Precisely how well this disorderly and unpredictable process of change turned out in special education is the subject of the next part of the article. As will be seen, because of the characteristic grass roots social activism of parents and special education advocates, special education is a very good—perhaps the best—case for legalization. Other factors, such as the dependent relationship between school and parent, cut in the opposite direction. Before getting to such pragmatic issues, however, a difficult normative question about the proper standards of evaluation must be unravelled.

III

THE SPECIAL EDUCATION GAP EVALUATED: WHAT SHOULD BE DONE NOW?

Preceding sections have described the special education implementation gap and explained how political adjustments between various interested parties are responsible for it. This part of the article is concerned with evaluation. Does the gap indicate failure? What can and should be done to narrow it?

Three aspects of evaluation are problematic and require discussion: the problem of standards (by what measure is success evaluated?); the overall evaluative assessment (given some standard, how can the success of the law be summarized in some meaningful way?); and the related issue of reform (what is worth trying to change?).

A. The Problem of Standards: Success for Whom, and How Much is Enough

Difficulties in measuring the effects of law are serious enough without additional complications, but the problem of choosing standards for evaluation is almost as difficult. Different people and groups evaluate government policy from different perspectives.[219] An abject failure from one perspective may be a satisfactory result from another, and divergent perspectives may use similar or completely different criteria.

Three basic perspectives seem to compete for priority in most discussions. First, there is the purely political perspective, which looks to the real attitudes of political participants and certainly includes what are sometimes referred to as "latent" purposes, or "motivations," instead of legislative intent.[220] Real political standards include the goals of reformers but also include those of legislators who pass legislation as a payoff for campaign contributions or to prevent an electoral threat, such as the opposition of special education advocacy groups. Interests opposing the reform are important parts of the real political perspective, whether the opposition is on account of financial and/or personal cost or principle (lack of sympathy for the protected class). Welfare interests are real political purposes, especially the ever-present rationale of creating jobs through government programs.

Reformist goals are a special class of the real political goals, normally those identified as legislative purpose or intent. When advocacy groups or moral entrepreneurs sponsor legislation, the legislation as a whole probably will be justified in terms of some underlying need, and each major policy instrument contained in the legislation (e.g., financial aid, due process) likewise will have some formal justification. As compared with the full range of political goals, reformist goals are formal (highly rationalized), moralistic, and technical (the work of lawyers, policy analysts, legislative staff, and other experts). Notwithstanding this narrow point of view, evaluation is commonly measured against reformist goals.[221] Due process is "supposed to" create parental participation rather than jobs for hearing officers although the latter is also a real political goal.

The third common evaluative perspective lies somewhere between the first two: the reformist perspective as modified by worthy competing considerations, often called "costs." Worthy competing considerations may be revealed by the legislative process, by public commentary, or during the process of implementation as, for instance, in arguments before courts. Many people who would not be willing to admit the propriety of all real political purposes would insist on counterbalancing reformist objectives with costs of reform. Thus, in our terms, the garden variety "cost-benefit" analysis of government policy probably represents a balancing of reformist objectives against socially legitimate competing considerations. (The omission of socially improper real political purposes from the benefits side of the equation

---

219. *See supra* note 217.

220. *See* Ely, *Legislative and Administrative Motivation in Constitutional Law*, 79 YALE L.J. 1205 (1970).

221. Sunstein, *Public Values, Private Interests, And The Equal Protection Clause*, 1982 SUP. CT. REV. 127. Sunstein is correct that statutory interpretation (whether as part of judicial review or not) necessarily and properly involves a search for genuine and good public (collective) purposes. The specific suggestion of the article that pure redistribution should be the only unacceptable public purpose under the equal protection clause requires an extended response not appropriate here.

is probably one reason why government policy is so frequently considered a failure.)

The "political method" recommended in this article is a version of the third alternative—reformist objectives as modified or discounted by socially important competing considerations. Each of the alternatives has arguments in its favor, however, and it is important to understand what is gained and lost by each possible choice.

Evaluating programs according to real political purposes has the advantage of social realism. Any subset of real political goals, such as reformist goals, has a problem of justification. For any operating social program, the political process has already registered and weighed the complete set of competing goals. By what authority can reformers, policymakers, and policy experts relitigate the same program giving stronger priority to a subset of the goals? The answer to this important and difficult question is not like preferred values and higher moral principles in constitutional law.[222] However, while it is easy enough to disparage empty moralism, the alternative of cynical political realism seems equally unattractive. The most serious problem with real political evaluation is the "sociological fallacy," a brand of ethical postivism according to which everything that happens is not only good but *equally* good. Even in this disenchanted age, no amount of cynicism will convince anyone that all social programs are equally good. In a fundamental sense, evaluation is impossible without reformist standards. Evaluation implies the possibility of counterfactual conclusions. How is it possible to escape this radical swing from empty idealism to sterile realism, from opinion to fact?

Whatever the answer may be at the level of the individual, the social answer is relatively easy: democracy itself.[223] Instead of contradicting democracy, reform-oriented (counterfactual) evaluation hopes to begin a new cycle of democratic action. Evaluation is not above politics; evaluation *is* politics. And, notwithstanding a prior political equilibrium, all sorts of reasons exist why reformist evaluation can be politically effective. At the social level, many people in the political process may be honestly ignorant or confused about what is going on. Some of the patterns revealed by implementation studies may be harmful to just about everyone and thus amenable to a statesmanlike remedy. Also, part of the preexisting political equilibrium may have required secrecy to be effective. "Latent" political purposes, such as pork barrel and symbolic politics, are not less *real* than manifest purposes, but they may be a great deal more difficult to defend in a public forum. The reformist purposes of law tend to be publicly acceptable and legally authorized purposes. If research shows that these purposes are not satisfied, the public may well demand an accounting through courts, legislatures, or administrative agencies. Of course, nothing guarantees the success of reformist research. The

---

222. In a liberal democracy, the preferred value of one group may be regarded by another group as simply a strong preference. *See* Komesar, *Taking Institutions Seriously: Introduction to a Strategy for Constitutional Analysis,* 51 U. CHI. L. REV. 366 (1984).

223. Clune, *supra* note 2, at 91-93.

old political equilibrium may be unperturbed. The point here is philosophical and political coherence rather than political power. Reformist evaluation makes political and ethical sense, even if it gets nowhere.

Because of its counterfactual potential, reformist evaluation has been a mainstay of the sociology of law in the form of the paradigmatic gap study.[224] The word "gap" faithfully describes the entire genre of research because the finding of gap studies is always that laws fail to achieve their reformist purposes—there is always a gap between reformist goals and real implementation. Under a political model of implementation, a gap is also to be expected, because implementation is conceived of as a long process of adjustment between reformist goals and competing interests. If, as just argued, reformist goals supply the requisite counterfactual component of evaluation, a gap study must be a part of every evaluation. An abbreviated gap study of the EAHCA is found in section II A of this article. The problem is what to conclude from the existence of a gap.

Gap studies usually conclude that government programs were failures. This uniform negative finding established the sociology of law as a force to be reckoned with; but, in the end, more questions were raised than answered. Theoretically and pragmatically, the idea of uniform, invariable programmatic failure seems implausible. Normatively and politically, the gap was catastrophic. Proposed initially by left-center social reformers as a justification for intensified government effort, the apparent inevitability of the gap eventually fostered the current mood of fatalistic neo-conservatism.

The problem with gap analysis is an incomplete normative argument—the gap in gap analysis. Evaluating empirical reality against reformist goals is a useful first step, but there are two other normative questions: a qualitative question about which goals *other than* reformist goals should be recognized, and a quantitative question about how much success is enough. A shortfall or deficit in reformist goals that occurs as a necessary result of promoting other socially worthwhile goals may be acceptable. On the quantitative side, the question is how much reformist success is enough to justify the intervention. Thus, gap analysis suffers from an idealogical fallacy, which is the antithesis of its counterpart discussed earlier, the sociological fallacy. While the sociological fallacy, which is the product of purely political evaluation, assumes the normative superiority of actual behavior, the ideological fallacy, which is an intrinsic part of gap analysis, assumes the primacy of reformist goals.

In ethically modified gap analysis, a question arises immediately about *which* nonreformist goals should be recognized. In theory, almost anything could qualify. Practically, the interests which compete for recognition are those revealed during implementation. (Some who receive benefits or bear costs may not be involved in implementation, or may not be well represented. This is a problem beyond the scope of this article.) Interests revealed during implementation have a pragmatic validity of the case or controversy variety.

---

224. *See supra* note 4.

Those interests also have presumptive legal significance.[225] In many social programs—and certainly in the EAHCA—much of the process of adjusting reformist goals against competing considerations had been delegated or deferred to the stage of implementation with all its various participants (including courts).[226] Thus the normative significance of the adjustments is a question unexplored at the time of legislative enactment or judicial decree. Just as a judicial decision applying a statute or constitution is influenced by the concrete facts before the court, so the adjustments of implementation are influenced by newly acquired knowledge about specific program implications.[227] Perhaps a competing consideration was not given sufficient weight (the disruptions of mainstreaming?). Perhaps there were unforseen budgetary implications (the impossibility of complete individualization of instruction and complete remediation?). Perhaps some of the reformist ideals were not as important as others, or, in the light of pragmatics, seem patently unrealistic (parental power?).

The use of the term "a political method of evaluation" in this article refers to an inquiry into the normative significance of the interests revealed by implementation. How much to recognize competing interests is an open question depending on context. Governors blocking the doors of universities protecting white students from the unpleasant experience of black company is one thing. Nonhandicapped students wanting a good education, school teachers wanting to teach effectively, taxpayers wanting to save money, and school psychologists wanting normal working hours are different from racism and different from each other. In other words, interests competing with reformist goals in special education, as revealed by implementation, have a facial normative validity. They seem to be interests which should be taken seriously.

Recognizing the possible normative significance of counter-reformist implementation interests means evaluating them, not necessarily accepting them. Nothing about a political analysis compels adoption of the sociological fallacy which totally dismisses formal goals by concluding that all adjustments are necessarily good just because they happened. Some adjustments may seem clearly undesirable when viewed from almost any perspective other than that of the particular interest responsible for the adjustment.[228] Furthermore, there is no reason to assume that all adjustments are inevitable. Based upon an understanding of the politics of what occurred, new political forces may be able to change the law itself or change the leverage of the existing law, for

---

225. The pervasive role of costs in judicial interpretations is evidence of this significance. *See supra* note 193 and accompanying text.

226. The main deferral mechanism of the EAHCA is the purely procedural definition of the substantive right. An appropriate education is that education which results from appropriate procedures. *See supra* notes 36 & 193.

227. *See* Wellington, *History and Morals in Constitutional Adjudication* (Book Review), 97 HARV. L. REV. 326, 328-39 (1983) (judges interpreting complex statutes are engaged in particularistic lawmaking).

228. In a sense, evaluation may consist of advocates convincing a sympathetic but disinterested observer (e.g., a judge) or, in democratic terms, the "mainstream." Clune, *supra* note 2, at 91-93.

example, by introducing new resources.[229] Fatalism is no more the child of sociology than ethical nihilism.

Thus, this article is intended to offer a method of evaluation which steers a middle course between the ideological fallacy, which assumes the normative hegemony of reformist goals, and the sociological fallacy, which assumes the normative legitimacy of actual behavior. No formula or scientific procedure exists for the distinctly normative phase of this "method." Evaluation remains an ethical and democratic exercise, resting on normative argument and persuasion. Also, although the method steers a middle course between the two types of fallacy, the right conclusion is not necessarily a compromise lying precisely between reformist goals and political adjustments. Perhaps one side or the other has the better of the argument, in spite of the "normative fact" that both sides have socially legitimate positions.[230]

All the constituent elements of a political evaluation have now been discussed: a summary of the EAHCA implementation gap, an explanation of which political interests are responsible for the gap, a discussion of the limits of legalization as a policy instrument in a politicized environment, and an argument for reformist evaluation which is normatively sensitive to opposing political interests. The next two sections will use this method of evaluation to make some recommendations for further reform of the EAHCA. The evaluative mindset with which this task is approached might be called "pragmatic idealism." Compromises of the reformist goals are acceptable if they are made on behalf of the important competing considerations revealed by implementation and if they are not too extensive. Compromises made on behalf of unimportant or disreputable interests should be renounced. Very large compromises made on behalf of significant interests could theoretically require repeal of the legislation. In addition to these normative issues, there is also the problem of feasibility; many things disapproved of cannot be changed. Sometimes law must give way to power regardless of right. While public education is not renowned for its tyrants or moral monsters, rigid bureaucratic attitudes may frustrate reform.[231]

---

229. The improved effectiveness of Title I is traced in Kirst & Jung, *The Utility of a Longitudinal Approach in Assessing Implementation: A Thirteen Year View of Title I, ESEA*, 3 ED. EVAL. & POL. ANAL. 17-34 (1980); *see also* M. MCLAUGHLIN, EVALUATION AND REFORM: THE ELEMENTARY AND SECONDARY EDUCATION ACT OF 1965, TITLE I (1975).

230. The possibility of recognizing socially legitimate competing values while also exercising some independent judgment could be questioned. The problem is similar to the problem of individual consciousness and autonomy in structuralism and the relative autonomy of law in Marxism. *See* Heller, *Structuralism and Critique*, 36 STAN. L. REV. 127 (1984); A. Hunt, The Theory, Method and Politics of Critical Legal Theory (Apr. 1984) (unpublished paper); *see also supra* note 7. Perhaps a more direct analogy is the difficulty of democratic institutions recognizing some emerging, marginalized interest which is incompatible with existing distributions of political rights, economic rights, and consciousness (especially given that all distributions of political rights are also distributions of economic rights, and vice versa). *See* Clune, *supra* note 7, at 764 n.7, 777-79; Tushnet, *Talking to Each Other: Reflections on Yudof's When Government Speaks* (Book Review), 1984 WIS. L. REV. 129. Practically speaking, evaluators can bring to bear some new combination of general knowledge, experience, new facts, and new values.

231. *See* P. BERMAN, *supra* note 195; *see also* the different regulatory issues raised by "bad apples vs. good apples" in E. BARDACH & R. KAGAN, *supra* note 8, at 64-66.

B.   EAHCA Evaluated: Is There Success After Implementation?

An adequate foundation has now been established for EAHCA evaluation. The following discussion will attempt a summary of the successes and failures of the Act, looking not just at reformist legal purposes, but at the welfare of handicapped children generally and the legitimate interests of schools as revealed by implementation behavior. An attempt will be made to reach an overall evaluative position—which is intended to be realistic and sensitive— on the basis of this ledger sheet of successes and failures. Finally, section C discusses what remains to be done.

1. *Summary of Successes and Failures.*   The EAHCA has achieved a number of notable successes. As is frequently true with social reform legislation, the most obvious and shocking problem with which the legislation was concerned—the complete exclusion of handicapped children from schools—was the most completely solved. There have also been successes in more subtle areas. Special education programs have been implemented on a massive scale, whether measured in terms of special classes, teacher aides, or new testing procedures.[232] There also has been widespread use of the IEP; a new and rather expensive educational routine has been adopted almost everywhere. While formal compliance is better than substantive compliance (the IEP's are better than the programs they recommend) and parental effectiveness in the IEP process is questionable, schools seem to approve of the IEP as a pedagogical innovation. Some benefits are likely derived merely from improved organizational planning independent of effective parental participation or detailed compliance. Due process has not been a success in terms of informalist goals, but it has brought schools to a high degree of compliance at least in readily measurable legal requirements. The implementation of special education is also an impressive example of organizational adaptability and innovation. New organizational routines have been developed to cope with and make more effective each of the main types of legalism discussed in this article (pre-referral screening, IEP checklists, and due process mediation). Another triumph is the legion of mostly invisible adaptive educational innovations not specified in the law but developed in response to it by school people, parents, and advocates. Beyond all of these programs and procedures lies a

---

232.   The special education system has grown dramatically over the past decade. In 1966, the total expenditures for "excess cost" on special education programs was $680 million. Lynn, *supra* note 37, at 14. In 1972, the excess cost expenditures had risen to $2.7 billion. G. BREWER & J. KAKALIK, *supra* note 68, at 392-93. By 1978, that figure had grown to an estimated $7 billion, and a comparable figure today may well be in excess of $10 billion. *See supra* note 70 (the $10 billion figure is estimated by multiplying the total number of currently served handicapped children by inflation-adjusted cost figures for special education services). Similarly, the number of handicapped children served has grown. In 1966, approximately 2.1 million children received special education services. Lynn, *supra* note 37, at 14. By 1981-82, that number had risen to 4.2 million. FIFTH ANNUAL REPORT, *supra* note 51, at 90. Finally, the number of special education teachers and other staff employed to serve handicapped students has grown sharply. In 1976-77, there were 179,804 special education teachers and 151,649 school staff employed to serve handicapped children. By 1980-81, those numbers had increased to 232,627 and 207,384, respectively. *Id.* at 100-01.

new era for handicapped children and their parents, an era of new opportunities, changed attitudes, and heightened responsiveness.

One of the conspicuous failures of the Act was the ideal of an individually appropriate education. What occurred instead was the establishment of routinized special programs.[233] Individualized programs fell victim to lack of technical knowledge, budgetary constraints, and the needs of schools for routinized procedures. As organizations with many functions, schools must be able to plan for special education within a finite budget. The idea of a customized education for every handicapped child violated these fundamental organizational precepts.

Another casualty was the ideal of effective participation by individual parents. Individual effectiveness fell victim to a powerful quartet of forces: the continuing and paternalistic nature of the relationship between schools and families, an imbalance of litigation resources between the schools and parents, a lack of technical knowledge about the proper treatment for various handicaps, and a lack of program choices. The tiny number of parents who break through the bureaucratic, economic, and psychic barriers against litigation and actually get to an administrative hearing do respectably well. But if litigation succeeds, it does so through deterrence, not because it is a regular part of the process.

In addition to these two principal shortcomings, there have been many garden variety implementation problems, such as pockets of resistance, areas with especially poor programs, and so forth.

2. *Evaluation of the Successes and Failures.* By any comparative standard, the successes achieved in the implementation of special education have been truly impressive. Universal field level implementation of anything is quite rare. Most unsuccessful social reform programs either fail to get past the stage of symbolic politics, or fail to achieve any meaningful change of activity in the regulated organization.[234] By comparison, special education laws have brought about a great deal of field level activity almost everywhere. The fact that this activity has not achieved some desirable goals should not detract from the fundamental picture of special education as a widely implemented program.

A stronger case can be made—that special education has approached the limits of realistic achievement. Looking at the pattern of implementation as a whole, one can ask how much more can be done for handicapped children given any fair claim on resources and existing state of knowledge about what can be done. Of course, a great many specific things need to be improved.

---

233. *Cf.* E. KRUG, 2 THE SHAPING OF THE AMERICAN HIGH SCHOOL 168, 196 (1972) (progressive, individualized education concept, when translated into use by the masses, led to standardized workbook, rather than individualized instruction); C. WASHBURN & S. MARLAND, WINNETKA: THE HISTORY AND SIGNIFICANCE OF AN EDUCATIONAL EXPERIMENT 21-25, 155 (1963) (describing standardization of efforts to individualize self-instruction in arithmetic in Winnetka, Illinois public schools in the 1920s, resulting in what are now known as workbooks).

234. On the typical range of implementation success, see Clune, *supra* note 2, at 87-89.

But from a more global perspective, it appears that special education has obtained a significant amount of new resources for its clients, and that these resources have been used in reasonably efficient ways, given the limited knowledge base and what is reasonable to expect out of large scale bureaucratic organizations. What is reasonable to expect is, of course, partly a normative judgment. But the normative position is not strictly subjective. As discussed earlier, one of the salient features of the environment of special education is the high degree of moral legitimacy of many of the considerations competing with special education needs.

The impression of relative success is fortified by reference to implementation theory. Viewing the politics of implementation, special education seems to be a prototype of the successful implementation profile: a powerful constituency group well organized at both the national and local levels, with membership cutting across all economic classes.[235] Discussion with education officials at almost any level of government confirms that the special education lobby is renowned for its political clout. Moreover, by and large, the EAHCA is an effectively devised law. IEP's and M-teams represented genuinely progressive educational innovations. Due process rights provided an important source of leverage, especially for advocacy groups bringing institutional litigation and for those individual families with enough motivation, skill, and resources to become litigants.

How then should the conspicuous failures of the Act be evaluated? The argument can be made that not only was the ideal of an individually appropriate education unrealistic, it was implicitly recognized as such in the legislation.[236] For both budgetary and organizational reasons, school systems cannot operate on a truly individual basis, offering each student a separate program of instruction. Tutorial programs for every child would be exorbitantly expensive and parents' expectations of such an enormous shift of societal resources toward their handicapped children must be considered unrealistic. Even if the resources were available, existing technical knowledge does not allow precisely tailored programs for each child. Coarse programmatic categories are probably all that can be managed. Tutorial programs would be nice for handicapped children, but they would be nice for other children, too.

---

235. According to Sabatier and Mazmanian, conditions for an effective implementation include the following: clear standards, sufficient enforcement resources, a supportive regulatory agency, a limited number of parties whose consent is needed or who may veto, skillful leaders, active support by strong constituency groups, and lack of conflict with other programs or socioeconomic conditions. Sabatier & Mazmanian, *The Conditions of Effective Implementation: A Guide to Accomplishing Policy Objectives,* 5 POL'Y ANALYSIS 481, 484-500 (1979).

Michael Pertschuk suggests that six factors are responsible for successful public interest lobbying in Washington, D.C.: (1) a grass roots organization outside Washington; (2) involvement of public and private authorities to confirm the facts; (3) involvement of experienced Washington lobbyists and experts with networks of information; (4) help from political entrepreneurs in Congress; (5) help from a sympathetic and supportive corps of journalists; and (6) overreaching by the opposition (lies, outrageous conduct, etc.). Hesselberg, *'Lobbying Without Money': It's a Tough Job,* Wis. St. J., July 8, 1983, § 3, at 1.

236. *See supra* notes 36 & 193.

The lost ideal of effective parental participation evokes an equally ambivalent response. Perhaps it is possible to increase parental efficacy by providing all parents with more legal services. Exactly what good would be accomplished by such a large investment of resources is less clear. Most of the factors that limit parental control over results are substantive rather than procedural and therefore seem difficult to remedy. If schools must have relatively few rather routinized programs and organizational responses, the most that parents could do is choose between existing programs. If planning and budgeting of special education must be integrated with the rest of the functions of the school, parents cannot expect to be allowed to demand a totally new process of organizational planning at every stage of educational development. In other words, once all the necessary concessions are made to school functions, exactly what is left for parental control? Looming over all these questions is the nature of the school-parent relationship, which must be continuing, trusting, cooperative, and fundamentally paternalistic. Perhaps parental satisfaction could be markedly improved with increased legal services. Whether this is a goal appropriate for special education or worth the cost is debatable.

Overall, the failures of the Act seem to have occurred in areas relating to the individualistic ideal of liberal legalism, while the successes have been examples of collective and organizational problem solving. Indeed, the most forceful question which emerges from the implementation studies is whether those legalisms based on the ideal of individual parent participation—the IEP and due process rights—simply should be abandoned. They seem to produce little parental participation at considerable cost. Why not repeal these provisions, leaving such internal organizational routines as testing requirements and multi-disciplinary evaluation teams?

Although it is worth thinking about, the evidence does not support such a drastic change. Due process rights are not costly unless they are used, and they are used to good advantage by some parents and by advocacy groups seeking structural reform. Also, due process rights seem to have encouraged the widespread practice of informal mediation, thereby accomplishing indirectly the informalist goals intended for the administrative hearings themselves. Since IEP's are used all the time, even when parents do not participate, the case for dropping IEP's seems to be stronger. However, in our view, the IEP is the procedural keystone holding together all of the other requirements of the Act. The IEP serves as the prospective focus of the whole initial internal process of referral, assessment, and placement. It is the written expression of the entire set of organizational decisions that determine a child's treatment. Retrospectively, the IEP serves as the audit track for administrative hearings and government monitoring. Therefore, while all sorts of improvements in IEP's—even though making them burdensome and more substantive—may be welcome, abolishing the requirement of any written record of agency planning does not seem to be good idea. Moreover, regardless of how little most parents participate in organizational planning, the idea of abolishing the right to participate altogether seems somehow to be going in the wrong direction. If parents were not given the right to participate in something called an IEP conference, they would have to be given some other structural opportunity.

It does seem that the case for the IEP has the tenuous quality of the case for many legalisms; it seems sufficiently related to something important that, on balance, it is probably a good idea. There are really three justifications for the IEP: as a matter of internal organizational routine, the IEP forces schools to pay attention to the needs of the individual child; the IEP allows parent participation; and the IEP permits monitoring agencies to determine what has occurred. Each of these justifications is subject to the usual criticism of legalisms that it does not achieve the justifying objective either very directly or very well. Individual attention by the organization is diminished by limitations on available programs and routinization of referral and assessment. Parental participation is reduced by the relational factors discussed often and at length earlier in this article. Monitoring is not really a goal in itself (why monitor if the monitored activity is not doing any good in the first place?). Also, the effectiveness of monitoring in changing organizational behavior is in doubt because of the formalistic quality of administrative and judicial supervision.

Optimism about the IEP must rest ultimately on a somewhat intuitive set of judgments: in this sense, the scientific-sounding goal of an "appropriate education" is misleading. The best case for IEP's is probably that the needs of handicapped children are not well served by customary organizational routines and that even a small amount of special consideration can go a long way in a bureaucratic setting like schools. The benefits are surely spotty, and they come at considerable cost, but there is a net profit. However, collective discussion of such judgment calls is essential. Complex, normative/factual judgments are not scientific and are most valid when they reflect a variety of life experiences and normative perspectives. Positive evaluations can simply be the product of a gullible personality. Regardless of what the answer might be, inevitably there will be serious doubts.

C.   What Should Be Done Now: Is There Reform After Pragmatism?

This is the last of the six elements specified in the introduction as parts of the political method of evaluation, and it is now possible to see the cumulative nature of those elements. The present discussion of reform rests on the five preceding discussions. Having struck a final balance and pondered feasible options, it is time to consider possible reforms.

A logical question emerging from the foregoing is the extent and nature of reforms which might be expected. Has there been such tolerance about system adjustments that there is no basis on which to demand change? On the contrary, concessions to the needs of bureaucratic rationality should not be interpreted as complacency or carte blanche approval of school behavior. The conclusion that the reform program has produced an overall justifiable equilibrium of various legitimately competing forces is perfectly consistent with a position that there are also many serious problems which should be and can be remedied. The key question answered by approval of system adjustments is whether to spend time trying to remedy what are seen as massive structural failures from the perspective of the original reformist purposes, or to concede that some of those failures were the consequence of unrealistic expectations and proceed to other, second generation problems revealed by a study of the actual implementation of the law.

The choice, in other words, is the familiar one between radical and reformist change.[237] Since the EAHCA is, in its domain, a bold piece of progressive legislation, and since the opposing interests are valuable and legitimate, this article comes down firmly on the side of reformism. It seems that attention should be placed not on unrealized and unrealistic goals of the original legislation but rather on selected serious problems which have been uncovered by experience with the law, and for which there are known remedies. This kind of remedy is usually based on systematic knowledge about program implementation and is also structural in form, that is, the problem usually requires either legislation or institutional litigation. Not enough is known about special education to suggest either a complete list of such problems or a sense of priorities. Such knowledge typically must come from the community of researchers, experienced professionals, and advocates whose participation in research funding therefore becomes essential.[238]

Our own evaluation does suggest a number of possible reforms worth serious consideration, and these will serve as examples of the kind of remedy justified by the political evaluation just completed. Such reforms can be usefully divided into two categories: ways of improving the effectiveness of existing legal mechanisms, and means of providing for educational development and assistance. Attention should be paid, in other words, both to the legally institutionalized structure of interaction and the informal "underground" of educational practice.

In the first category, improvements in legal instruments, we suggest reforms of M-teams, IEP's, due process, and diagnostic categories. In many districts, M-teams do not function as they should. Instead of an interdisciplinary group of decisionmakers, special subsets of people participate in or control the team.[239] Even in pragmatic terms, this is substandard. A properly

---

237. *See* Levin, Education and Work (Project Report 82B-8, Institute for Research on Educational Finance and Governance, Stanford University, 1982) (education contains a variety of both progressive and regressive aspects).

238. In an earlier draft, we referred to "structural remedies based on systemic knowledge." Although similar sounding, this is much different than Lindblom and Cohen's "professional social inquiry." C. LINDBLOM & D. COHEN, USABLE KNOWLEDGE 7 *passim* (1979). The core of knowledge about legal reform must come from participants (or those who talk with participants) and really is nothing more than collected, analytically ordered craft knowledge. Thus, we are talking about knowledge which is disciplined and systematic but is also "ordinary."

239. STUDY OF PROCEDURES, *supra* note 159, at 7.7 (it is often difficult to determine who makes a placement decision or when the placement decision is made; decision often reached by one or two staff members rather than team); A NATIONAL SURVEY OF IEPs: VOL. I, *supra* note 73, at 8-9 (Of the three mandated categories of participants in the IEP meetings—teachers, administrators, and parents—about one-third of all IEP meetings had all three classes of participants, although the study

constituted M-team can at least provide the intended expert participation in the larger decisionmaking process. Excluding careful evaluation almost certainly conceals the availability of productive, pragmatic options. As for IEP's, the system also seems to have gone too far in the direction of formal compliance.[240] Experimentation on ways to make IEP's conform better to actual programs, and vice versa, seems well worthwhile. More substantive review at the state level is a possible answer. (Of course, the prevalence of essentially illegal M-teams suggests that even formal compliance with the IEP process is far from perfect.) In the area of due process, a hard look at the use of parent advocates and the "communicative use of conflict" is surely justified. Claims have been made that such improved representation leads to better results, greater satisfaction, and a lower cost.[241] What about reforming special education classifications? Some have urged abolishing the distinction between the learning disabled (LD) and educable mentally retarded (EMR) classifications.[242] The success of special education programs is tied to high expectations for the children. Because the label EMR suggests a "retarded" child who cannot learn, EMR programs can become a dumping ground for all students, especially minority students. Abolishing the EMR category deserves serious consideration.[243]

Of the two avenues for reform, improving educational practice is probably the more important because it has been the more neglected. We suggest three promising areas: the perennial problem of the "bad apple" district or school, the dissemination of successful and unsuccessful educational tech-

---

notes that this is probably an underestimate of the actual rate of participation by all concerned parties. By category, the study found that teachers participated about three-fourths of the time, parents two-thirds of the time, school administrators three-fifths of the time, and school counselors or psychologists about one-fourth of the time.); Bickel, *supra* note 91, at 194 (placement team meetings tend to be dominated by administrative personnel or psychologists); Panel on Selection and Placement of Students in Programs for the Mentally Retarded, *Placement in Special Education: Historical Developments and Current Procedures*, in PLACING CHILDREN IN SPECIAL EDUCATION: A STRATEGY FOR EQUITY 23, 39 (1982) ("Occasionally, school personnel meet in advance to iron out disagreements and present a united front to parents.") [hereinafter cited as *Panel on Selection and Placement*].

240. *See supra* notes 125-41 and accompanying text.

241. *See* J. Handler, *supra* note 166.

242. For example, some experts have observed that:

On the basis of documented effective practice in schools to date, it appears that basically the same kind of instructional processes may be needed for LD children as for mildly mentally retarded children. It should be noted that there is at least one other large group of children with academic difficulties who do not acquire special education labels but who . . . by reason of low family income and poor performance on achievement tests are assigned to various compensatory education programs—usually in particular academic subjects for a part of each school day. The accumulating evidence about these children also suggests that the same features of direct, externally paced, and formally monitored instruction in academic content that have been noted for mentally retarded children produce the best learning results.

If these three theoretically distinct groups of children in academic difficulty seem to prosper best under the same kind of instruction, there is good reason for calling into question the traditional system of categorical labeling within special education. At the very least, the burden of proof seems now to lie with those who would defend the traditional divisions within special education.

See Panel on Selection and Placement, supra note 239, at 86-87.

243. By 1981, California had phased out EMR classes. *Court Backs Ban of IQ Tests for Placing Mentally Retarded Children*, 12 SCH. L. NEWS 1 (Capitol Public. Jan. 27, 1984).

niques, and the design of structures for participation by advocates in educational planning. In the theory of regulatory compliance, the bad apple is the regulated enterprise which will not cooperate with regulatory incentives—the stonewaller.[244] Such enterprises are typically characterized by lack of willingness to comply or capacity to comply or both.[245] Bad apples exist in the area of special education; there are districts and schools that do not accept the fundamental premises of the EAHCA and that respond to requests for change with obstinance. Resistant districts and schools are probably isolated from effective local advocacy groups and staffed with unenlightened leadership. In other words, they lack effective political pressure and leadership from either the community or school. How to identify and reform such organizations is unclear but well worth some serious thinking and research. One possibility which comes to mind is a special staff in state education agencies responsible for organizational development in the area of special education.

A second reform in the category of improved educational practice is the further dissemination of effective and ineffective educational techniques. Consistent with both the underground quality of educational practice and the extremely decentralized quality of organizational responses, compliance with the EAHCA is characterized by a great range of variety in responses. Some districts and schools do very well; others do poorly. Techniques of both effective and ineffective compliance also differ greatly. In this environment of low visibility information, recording and disseminating organizational responses is an important service. Funding by the National Institute of Education of this kind of research has produced encouraging results.[246] Finally, research and development resources should be directed to the question of participation by special education advocates in educational planning. The perspective of implementation offered by this article strongly supports suggestions of greater participation, such as those made in another article in this volume.[247] Implementation is *primarily* regarded as a process of integrating reformist objectives with organizational imperatives. In such a perspective, exclusion of advocates from the planning process reduces the efficiency of their participation. Advocates must react to existing policy as well as making creative suggestions in the formation of new policy.[248]

Expectations for the entire package of recommended reforms should be

---

244. See *supra* note 156.
245. See *supra* note 195.
246. See Kimbrough & Hill, *supra* note 213.
247. See Sindelar, *How and Why the Law Has Failed: An Historical Analysis of Services for the Retarded in North Carolina and a Prescription for Change*, LAW & CONTEMP. PROBS., Spring 1985, at 125.
248. The twin hazards blocking effective representation of outside interests within a bureaucracy are cooptation and selling out. The trick, therefore, is to institutionalize access while protecting new values. See C. STONE, WHERE THE LAW ENDS: THE SOCIAL CONTROL OF CORPORATE BEHAVIOR 120 (1975); S. TAYLOR, MAKING BUREAUCRACIES THINK: THE ENVIRONMENTAL IMPACT STATEMENT STRATEGY OF ADMINISTRATIVE REFORM (1984). In the proper circumstances, this combination of power and priority, access and clout, may be provided by a legislator well connected with the bureaucracy, someone whom Eugene Bardach calls the implementation "fixer." E. BARDACH, *supra* note 8, at 273-78. A judge in institutional litigation may function in much the same way as this legislative "angel." See Clune, *supra* note 191, at 70.

kept modest, even in the unlikely event that they all are successfully enacted and implemented. Unlike Professor Handler, for example, we do not regard any of these reforms as resolving fundamental contradictions between individual participation and organizational imperatives.[249] Handler's recommendations might result in a favorable shift in that balance toward the individual. But the process will still be one of compromise, with results heavily weighted toward the more powerful collective interests. Regardless of how effective a role parents can be given in administrative hearings, for example, very few will challenge organizational decisions. The same obstacles that limit effectiveness now would limit effectiveness then: the trusting, ignorant, dependent relationship; lack of litigation resources and financial incentives for victory; and recognition by hearing officers and judges of organizational interests in the substance of their decisions. Changes might be valuable, but they are certain to be marginal.

IV

CONCLUSION: EVALUATION AS A CONTINUING,
DEMOCRATIC PROCESS

The method of social program evaluation recommended in this article urges that the political adjustments of implementation be taken seriously as normative events. Instead of looking at reformist goals alone, consideration should also be given to the organizational and financial costs of those goals and their feasibility, as revealed by the process of implementation. Following this method one discovers not a law that has failed, but a law that has been the subject of any number of compromises and adjustments, some reasonable, some not.

Do reformist goals therefore become completely outmoded, to be replaced by the more sophisticated political analysis? Interestingly enough, the answer is clearly no, because of the aspirational function of reformist goals. Even sophisticated reformers who understand that a literal realization of program goals would be impossible, and perhaps undesirable, need to maintain the credibility of the goals as ideals. The ideal of an "appropriate education" for every child, while literally impossible, is nevertheless important as a means of pushing systems incrementally closer to the ideal. Appropriate education must retain the *form* of a legal requirement if it is to have any use as an entitlement in negotiations.[250] In order to ask for progress,

---

249. Handler accurately exposes the helplessness of the dependent individual as the adversary of the group; but, in the end, he must concede the dangers of cooptation which are implicit in the group as protector of the individual. *See* J. HANDLER, *supra* note 166, at ch. 6. Thus, contradictions within the liberal legalist paradigm of adversarial individualism can be softened but not completely transcended.

250. The precise role for formalism in all of this is elusive. Advocates are likely to make the formalistic argument that the law *means* an absolute right (which the advocate is entitled to compromise on behalf of the good of the client), rather than the more overtly sociological argument that the law gives the advocate de facto capacity to pester the school on the authority of a vague requirement which could produce adverse results in court. Actually, such sharp distinction is not so apparent.

reformers *must* characterize systems as failing to meet their ideals, even if, on the whole, the systems have been reasonable. Absolutism is an essential component of effective advocacy; advocates have no choice but to reject compromise, at least as an opening position in bargaining ("this child has an absolute right to an appropriate education, but we'll take the best you can do"). Legal rights must be absolute in form in order to be compromised in practice.

If sociological analysis cannot replace ideological advocacy, the question arises how to combine both in practice, or which one to follow if a choice is necessary. The two systems of evaluation are bound to reach different evaluative conclusions. So which is right? In the abstract, both positions are right in the sense that we always need both sides of a basic argument. The overall question of evaluation can never be finally settled. Advocates and realists will inevitably clash over what is right and what is feasible. Neither position can be awarded a final victory because both represent legitimate goals competing for scarce resources. But double vision is not required in judging particular controversies. After listening to both sides, a decisionmaker, such as a judge or a scholar, must decide which side has the better of the argument.

In this article, one of the things that we have done is reached a judgment about the overall success of the Act, implicitly rejecting what may prudentially be regarded as a partisan advocacy perspective—the idea of the EAHCA as a "total failure." By the logic of our own analysis, we are bound to differ with at least some advocates in this respect. However, the political method of evaluation does not automatically legitimate the status quo. Sometimes it cuts in exactly the opposite direction. An examination of implementation patterns may well reveal that regulated institutions in fact have not been doing their best. Some "adjustments," such as stonewalling on compliance with an administrative or judicial order, to take only the most obvious example, do not look good upon closer examination. Implementation studies may well prove so shocking that they galvanize a whole new round of legal reform.[251] Judges who are timid in granting legal rights might well be more bold if they understood the practical limits of implementing rights.[252] Far from diminishing and relativizing a legal right, sociological analysis may strengthen it.

In a sense, an amendment to recent literature on statutory interpretation is being recommended. When a statute is vague on a disputed point, it has been suggested that judges take into account community values, the conflicting political positions of statutory structure and legislative history, and the dictates of good public policy.[253] This article suggests inclusion of implementa-

---

The words "appropriate education" have an idealistic and inchoate element as part of their meaning. Advocates make idealistic normative arguments as part of the contest over what the words should mean in practice. Prior to judicial interpretation, the meaning of the law is indeterminate, and each side must consider the risk of this uncertainty as part of litigation strategy.

251. The improved effectiveness of Title I is traced in Kirst & Jung, *supra* note 229.

252. *See* Comment, *Compensatory Educational Services and the Education for All Handicapped Children Act*, 1984 WIS. L. REV. 1469, 1514-26 (compensatory services not an excessive threat to school authorities because of practical imbalances in the legalized bargaining positions of schools and parents).

253. *See* G. CALABRESI, A COMMON LAW FOR THE AGE OF STATUTES (1982); Posner, *Statutory Inter-*

tion politics on this list. Adjustments hammered out in the real world of budgets, organizational constraints, and precious self-interests may tell a great deal more about competing value positions than the abstracted purposes of laws.

Judges in fact seem to behave in the manner recommended. Judicial decisions during implementation about the meaning of a statute, constitution, or administrative rule are best seen as implementation compromises of the same sort as made by the bureaucracy. Notwithstanding the apparently independent cognitive process of seeking the "true meaning of the law," courts are actors in the democratic process of implementation, rather than transcendental forces above or outside it. Judges inherit the ordinary disputes of implementation with all the social legitimacy possessed by participants in such controversies. Discretion allowed by vagueness in doctrine is adjusted so as to produce politically sensible results. For the sake of true democracy, one hopes that judges respond to idealism as well as expediency.

Thus, for three reasons, no evaluation can ever be final or objective: first, evaluative standards are debatable and depend upon political location; second, perceptions of implementation facts shift with new information and new interpretive mindsets; third, evaluation is a democratic process rather than a scientific exercise.[254] We certainly hope that this article has been a contribution to the democratic evaluation of the EAHCA; but, again, no evaluation can be the last word.

---

pretation—in the Classroom and in the Courtroom, 50 U. CHI. L. REV. 800, 817 (1983); Wellington, supra note 227, at 328-29.

254.   Courts are part of the democratic process in two senses: applying legislative acts in specific situations, and making their own democratic decisions overruling an undemocratic legislature. See Clune, supra note 7; Wellington, supra note 227.

2

THE ALLURE OF LEGALIZATION RECONSIDERED: THE CASE OF SPECIAL EDUCATION*

DAVID NEAL†

AND

DAVID L. KIRP**

SUMMARY

Legalization has been called a major trend in American public life. Yet it is a phenomenon that is conceptually unclear and little understood in the way it affects the institutions on which it comes to operate.

This paper concerns special education, the subject of the Education for All Handicapped Children Act (EAHCA),[1] which was passed in 1975. It will proceed in three steps. Initially, the legislation and the process leading to its passage and implementation will be examined as a case study in legalization. Next, the concept of legalization and its motivations will be outlined and ana-

* Jack Tweedie, our co-researcher in a broader study of special education policy, made invaluable contributions to this paper. Richard Abel, Jack Goldring, Sheldon Messinger, Philip Selznick, Martin Shapiro, and Julius Stone read and commented on earlier drafts of the paper.

A major portion of this research is based on interviews with the principal congressional staff people and lobbyists involved in the passage of the Education for All Handicapped Children Act of 1975 (EAHCA). Interviews were conducted in Washington in July and August 1980, and tape recorded. Interviewees agreed to the interview on the basis that their views were not for attribution. Hence where a quotation appears in the text, only the most general reference to the source is given. It should be appreciated that these people were reporting events that had occurred up to eleven years prior to the interview. Some interviewees referred to documents and memoranda, although most did not. We sought to ensure accuracy by cross-checking one report against another where possible and against whatever records were available. By exercising what we trust was a healthy skepticism, we hope to have minimized inaccuracy. Nevertheless, most of the people we interviewed still work closely with and have discussed the events among one another. There is a need then, to remain cautious about the data. Finally, we submitted a copy of our draft to two of the principal policymakers for comments and suggested revisions. This methodology has yielded a richer account of the policymaking process leading to the EAHCA than reliance on the records could have done. We want to thank the following persons and organizations who generously made large amounts of their time available to us: Michael Francis, Staff Member for Senator Robert Stafford; James Galloway, National Association of State Directors of Special Education; Thomas Gilhool, Attorney for Pennsylvania Association for Retarded Citizens; Robert Herman, Bureau of Educationally Handicapped; Ronald Howard, National Association of State Boards of Education; John Martin, Council of Chief State Schools Officers; Roy Millenson, Staff Member for Senator Jacob Javits; John Morris, Department of Education; Marilyn Roth, American Federation of Teachers; Gus Steinhilber, National School Boards Association; Lisa Walker, Staff Member for Senator Harrison Williams; Fred Weintraub, Council for Exceptional Children; James Wilson, Pennsylvania Association for Retarded Citizens; Daniel Yohalem, Children's Defense Fund.

† Lecturer, Faculty of Law, University of New South Wales, Australia.

** Professor, Graduate School of Public Policy, and Lecturer, School of Law, University of California at Berkeley.

1. Pub. L. No. 94-142, 89 Stat. 773 (codified as amended at 20 U.S.C. §§ 1400-1461 (1982)).

lyzed with respect to how legalization shaped special education policy. Finally, the article will discuss the effects of legalization on the institutions into which it is introduced. Within this context, the article will look at both the use of the due process procedures and the wider setting of legalization in the education sphere.

I

INTRODUCTION

American public policy has recently witnessed the legalization of a host of issues previously left to political or professional solution.[2] The declaration of substantive rights coupled with reliance on law-like procedures has become a characteristic way of framing policy. While legalization has been studied in a number of contexts—industry,[3] regulation,[4] education,[5] and race relations[6]— there is no precise understanding of how legalization comes to dominate policy or its effect upon implementation.[7]

This article will try to improve understanding of these issues by focusing on special education policy. Special education is an ideal case from which to mount a study of legalization. From the first articulated claims, to recognition that handicapped children have a right to education, to the development of special education, policy at the federal level and the implementation of that policy in schools, the evolution of legalization can be traced and its appropriateness analyzed.

The ramifications of this case study go beyond special education and raise general questions about legalization. At the time special education was being legalized, researchers were beginning to express reservations about legalization. Studies of delegalization, alternative forms of dispute resolution, and the nature of disputing counselled a greater sensitivity to legalization's limitations and pathologies.[8] Special education demands particular attention because, unlike the other examples referred to, its legalization has been imposed on schools, which have previously relied on other bases for decision-

---

2. For a discussion of these policy frameworks, see Kirp, *Professionalization as a Policy Choice: British Special Education in Comparative Perspective*, 34 WORLD POLITICS 137 (1982).

3. P. SELZNICK, LAW, SOCIETY, AND INDUSTRIAL JUSTICE (1969).

4. R. KAGAN, REGULATORY JUSTICE (1978).

5. Kirp, *Proceduralism and Bureaucracy: Due Process in the School Setting*, 28 STAN. L. REV. 841 (1976).

6. L. MAYHEW, LAW AND EQUAL OPPORTUNITY (1968).

7. *See* Abel, *Delegalization: A Critical Review of Its Ideology, Manifestations and Social Consequences*, in ALTERNATIVE RECHTSFORMEN UND ALTERNATIVEN ZUM RECHT: JAHRBUCH FUR RECHTSSOZIOLOGIE UND RECHTSTHEORIE, band 6.29 (E. Blankenburg, E. Klausa, and H. Rottleuthneer eds. 1980) [hereinafter cited as ALTERNATIVES].

8. The clearest statement about limitations came from the seminal article by Galanter, *Why the "Haves" Come Out Ahead: Speculations on the Limits of Legal Change*, 9 LAW & SOC'Y REV. 95 (1974). He has also written insightfully on delegalization in *Legality and Its Discontents: A Preliminary Assessment of Current Theories of Legalization and Delegalization*, in ALTERNATIVES, *supra* note 7, at 11 and on the background effect of formal adjudication on dispute resolution in *Justice in Many Rooms*, 19 J. LEGAL PLURALISM 1 (1981). *See also, e.g.*, Abel, *supra* note 7; R. ABEL, THE POLITICS OF INFORMAL JUSTICE (1982); THE DISPUTING PROCESS IN TEN SOCIETIES (Nader & Todd eds. 1972). On the nature of disputes, see Fitzgerald and Dickins, *Disputing in Legal and Nonlegal Contexts: Some Questions for Sociologists of Law*, 15 LAW & SOC'Y REV. 681 (1980).

making.[9] Before addressing these concerns, however, a more complete treatment of the process of legalization is in order.

II

LEGALIZATION

Legalization is only one way to give substance to a policy objective,[10] and one which, at least in its fully developed form under the EAHCA, is fairly new to policymaking in the United States. It is nonetheless a style close to the mainstream of American social and political culture.

The characteristic features of legalization include a focus on the individual as the bearer of rights, the use of legal concepts and modes of reasoning, and the employment of legal techniques such as written agreements and court-like procedures to enforce and protect rights. The EAHCA is filled with legal concepts and procedures: the notion of right or entitlement, the quasi-contractual individualized education program (IEP) meeting in which the right is elaborated, the provision of due process guarantees and appeal procedures, and implicitly, the development of principles through the mechanism of precedent.

A preference for legalization is premised on the classically liberal belief that individuals, and not the organization charged with delivering a good or service, can best safeguard their own interests. Paradoxically, the very fact that the individual has not been an effective self-guardian is the rationale for offering him or her the resources of the state, thus empowering the individual to pursue this interest. Individuals cannot attain the policy goal unaided, either because of ill will on the part of the service provider, or because of an absence of consensus between the individuals and the service deliverer with respect to the goal to be achieved.

Legalization betokens a mistrust of other forms of accountability, particularly accountability based on bureaucratic norms of fairness using statistical tests across classes of affected people. It defines accountability in individual terms; that is, a person polices his or her own interests. Individual accountability also implies singling out a party responsible for malfeasance in a way that group compliance procedures do not.

The aspirations underlying legalization include a desire for principled decisionmaking, minimization of arbitrariness, and a concern for the rights of the individual. In an extreme case, where an organization is frozen into traditional methods, legalization may be needed to bring about a reorientation of goals and priorities. This may entail changes in the power relations between

---

9. By contrast Kagan, Mayhew, and Selznick focus on the spontaneous appearance of legalization as a response to an organization's own perceived needs. *See* R. KAGAN, *supra* note 4; L. MAYHEW, *supra* note 6; P. SELZNICK, *supra* note 3.

10. In a sense, any time Congress makes a law one can say the policy area has been "legalized." That is not the sense we intend to convey here. Rather, we attempt to identify and characterize a particular method or style of policymaking and distinguish it from other ways of achieving policy objectives.

clients and service providers and, as in the case of special education, may involve rearrangement of status positions *within* the hierarchy of the delivery agency. At the same time, the dangers of the approach should not be minimized. One danger is that professionals in key positions may be alienated. More generally, legalization may degenerate into legalism: a narrow approach in which law and procedures become ends in themselves and substantive goals are lost in mechanical adherence to form.[11]

The distinctive features of legalization become clearer if one compares this apprach to other modes of government policymaking. Under a professional model, experts administer and enforce a policy mandate. The beneficiary occupies a passive role, deferring to the professionals' expertise. This model is widely prevalent: it is exemplified in the Federal Vocational Education Program[12] and, outside the education field, in the Legal Services Program.[13] This type of service provision leaves little or no room for the recipient to define the nature and extent of the benefit. Instead, the benefit is defined in the legislation itself or by professionals administering the program. Nor does the recipient play any significant role in maintaining accountability in the system; that function is carried out bureaucratically, through agency review focusing on regularity of systems and procedures. Such agency review relies on policy which impacts on classes of people using probabilistic statistical testing, rather than on a case-by-case review. Indeed, the very notion of an individual right is foreign to this approach.

Compared to the legalization model, the professional model places much more responsibility on the experts' exercise of discretion. Results rather than principles, discretion rather than rules, and groups rather than individuals are emphasized. The individual has little say about the nature or extent of the benefit and the narrower avenues of redress. This is in marked contrast to a legalized model, particularly one using contractual forms treating the individual as a definer and enforcer of the right in question.

Programs providing money payments—welfare, social security and the like —constitute a second variant of government policymaking. These bureaucratic models give less discretion to program administrators than the professional model. Legislation specifies the type of benefit and eligibility criteria and the program is administered by a government department. The notion of

---

11. Selznick described the problem of legalism in this way:
> But legal correctness has its own costs. Like any other technology, it is vulnerable to the divorce of means and ends. When this occurs, legality degenerates into legalism. Substantive justice is undone when there is too great a commitment to upholding the autonomy and integrity of the legal process.

P. SELZNICK, *supra* note 3, at 13. Distinguish this usage of legalism from that of Judith Shklar who means something synonymous with the rule of law. J. SHKLAR, LEGALISM 12 (1964).

12. We are indebted to Martin Shapiro for this example. For a history of federal vocational education policy see C. Benson, *Centralization and Legalization in Vocational Education: Limits and Possibilities,* in SCHOOL DAYS, RULE DAYS: THE LEGALIZATION AND REGULATION OF EDUCATION (D. Kirp ed. 1984) [hereinafter cited as D. KIRP].

13. *See* J. HANDLER, E. HOLLINGWORTH & H. ERLANGER, LAWYERS AND THE PURSUIT OF LEGAL RIGHTS 29-39 (1978).

an individual right has more relevance in this model than in the professional model because greater emphasis is placed on safeguards built into the legislative apparatus. The right, however, is a very limited one in comparison to the legalization model. Unless the claimant can show that the exercise of administrative discretion was either "outrageous or stupid,"[14] the best that can be hoped for is that the court will ask the agency to review the matter. By contrast, in the legalized model for special education, a due process hearing passing on a contract-like document, the IEP, is not limited to a *review* of administrative discretion; the individual may rely on a written agreement to provide substance for a ruling on the merits of the case. The existence of a written IEP, possibly some sort of record of the negotiations, and the opportunity to have input on the substance of the right gives the claimant much more scope for enforcing that right than the narrow bureaucratic model.[15]

The history of the handicapped reveals that choice among styles of policy implementation—legal, professional and bureaucratic—affects the services that are provided. The choice determines the type of service offered, who receives it, and on what terms. It limits the degree of variation and affects the stakes the client group has in the service. It also fixes the extent of regulatory control and the means of redress available to the client group.[16]

III

EVOLUTION OF A RIGHT

Two million handicapped children between 7 and 17 years of age were not enrolled in school in 1970.[17] Many were excluded by state laws, like the Pennsylvania statutes attacked in the *PARC* case,[18] which designated them as ineducable or untrainable. Other handicapped children were consigned to institutions offering only custodial care. By the late 1960's, the wretchedness of the treatment meted out to the handicapped at institutions such as Willowbrook and Pennhurst[19] and the specious nature of the rationale for excluding handicapped children from schools[20] led reformers to demand a radical change in the way handicapped people generally, and handicapped children in particular, were treated. The means adopted for effecting this change were

---

14.   On this and other problems of welfare beneficiaries in suing government officials, see Handler, *Controlling Official Behaviour in Welfare Administration*, in THE LAW OF THE POOR 155, 160-61, 170-76 (J. ten Broeck ed. 1966).

15.   *Id.*

16.   Kirp, *supra* note 2, at 138-39.

17.   CHILDREN'S DEFENSE FUND, CHILDREN OUT OF SCHOOL (1974). Other sources state that there were some 7 million handicapped children of whom only 40 percent were receiving an adequate education. *See, e.g.,* H.R. REP. No. 805, 93d Cong., 2d Sess. 53, *reprinted in* 1974 U.S. CODE CONG. & AD. NEWS 4093, 4138.

18.   Pennsylvania Ass'n for Retarded Children v. Pennsylvania, 343 F. Supp. 279 (E.D. Pa. 1972).

19.   The Pennhurst State School and Hospital, the object of the PARC litigation, enjoyed some notoriety for overcrowding, lack of staff, and inadequate treatment. One commentator described it as "a Dachau without ovens." L. LIPPMAN & I. GOLDBERG, THE RIGHT TO EDUCATION 17 (1973).

20.   The evidence of the experts brought to testify in the *PARC* case on the educability of the handicapped was so overwhelming that after one day of testimony the defendants conceded that all children could benefit from education. *Id.* at 29.

distinctively legal. The language of rights and the mechanisms of due process were introduced into an area that had previously relied on the professional discretion of teachers, psychologists, and school administrators.[21]

A.   From Proclamations to Courts

The civil rights movement and the War on Poverty provided the key ideas and context for the movement on behalf of handicapped people. Both movements heavily emphasized legal rights and focused the idealism of a generation of policymakers whose interests brought them in contact with powerless groups. The emphasis on rights and the active participation of those previously regarded as dependents in decisions affecting their lives, as well as more direct analogies from the emphasis on due process in the student rights movement,[22] suggested strategies to activists in the area of special education. The position of the retarded could be and was analogized to that of blacks, Native Americans, and the poor. For many of these groups the courts were the only effective point of entry into the political system. The courts gave power to groups which otherwise had none, groups which could not attract the attention of legislatures at the state or federal level.

The way in which a claim is defined, and the orchestration of the campaign to have it ratified, are crucial in determining whether it will be recognized at all, and, if recognized, the level of such recognition. The transformation of the political perception about the claims of the handicapped from charity to right began in the 1950's. The formation of associations for retarded citizens at national and state levels was a significant step. The most influential of these organizations was the National Association for Retarded Children.[23] Key figures in this movement carried out research establishing the educability of all children and publicized their findings through an extended national network. The associations became active not only on the political level, but also as service deliverers. For example, the Pennsylvania Association for Retarded Children (PARC) developed and ran state agency-funded programs for handicapped children.

Two crucial research findings became widely accepted in the education community. The first, that all children could benefit from education[24] undermined the rationale that retarded children should be excluded from public schools because they were ineducable. Research also suggested that testing procedures for the assignment of children to classes for the retarded were racially discriminatory,[25] thus strengthening the analogy between the retarded

---

21. On the use of rights as a political resource, see S. SCHEINGOLD, THE POLITICS OF RIGHTS: LAWYERS, PUBLIC POLICY AND POLITICAL CHANGE 8-9 (1974).

22. See Goss v. Lopez, 419 U.S. 565, 576 n.8 (1975). See generally Kirp, supra note 5.

23. L. LIPPMAN & I. GOLDBERG, supra note 19, at 10.

24. Id. at 29.

25. Id. at 8-9. See also Larry P. v. Riles, 343 F. Supp. 1306 (N.D. Cal. 1972), aff'd, 502 F.2d 963 (9th Cir. 1974) (The court found that, while blacks formed 28.5 percent of the school district's population, black children comprised 66 percent of classes for educable mentally retarded as a result of IQ testing. The court enjoined the use of the then current IQ test as racially discriminatory.); Hobsen v. Hansen, 269 F. Supp. 401 (D.D.C. 1967).

and racial minorities. The issue of educating handicapped children had undoubted appeal. Once it became arguable that such children were capable of being educated, it became virtually impossible to mount a politically palatable argument denying handicapped children's claim to education. While educating handicapped youngsters might be expensive, how could costs be weighed against reclaimed lives?

The handicapped rights movement had gained considerable momentum by the late 1960's. While organizations representing the interests of the handicapped had been formed, they had been able to extract only expressions of good intent from the states. One such group, PARC, decided that court action was the only means to break the impasse. The initial focus of PARC's attention was the Pennhurst State School and Hospital, the subject of considerable press and political attention for inhumane treatment of its patients.[26] PARC had engaged in a long battle with Pennsylvania authorities about the conditions at Pennhurst, but to little avail, and so turned to legal counsel. The influence of legal modes of thought in framing and defining the issues, even at this early stage, is noteworthy. PARC's attorney, Thomas Gilhool, advised that the most promising strategy for attacking the Pennhurst situation was to insist on handicapped youngsters' legal right to education.

The case that Gilhool mounted was formidable. He was able to assemble a group of witnesses with overwhelming expertise in the field of special education[27] and to forge a link with the Council for Exceptional Children (CEC), a group which had already demonstrated its effectiveness at the state level and which was to become the major federal lobbyist for handicapped children.[28] The plaintiff's monopoly of expertise and weight of evidence swamped the defense. After one day of testimony the Commonwealth withdrew its opposition to the complaint.[29]

The final court order, which was handed down in May 1972,[30] enjoined the defendants from applying statutes excluding mentally retarded children from public education. It required them "to provide every retarded child access to a free public program of education and training appropriate to his or her learning capacities."[31]

The order also included a detailed stipulation to the procedures that had to be followed in classifying mentally retarded children. It specified a full range of due process procedures, including: parents' or guardians' right to written notice of changes in educational status; the opportunity for a due pro-

---

26. L. LIPPMAN & I. GOLDBERG, *supra*, note 19, at 16-17.
27. For a list, see *id.* at 28-29.
28. The CEC is a national professional organization with 90 percent of its membership composed of special education teachers. Unlike teacher unions, it has no responsibility to its membership for wages and employment conditions. Its purpose is to develop policy in the field of special education. This policy is formulated very broadly by a national convention which enunciated a statement of handicapped children's rights in 1969 along with drafting a model statute for state legislatures.
29. L. LIPPMAN & I. GOLDBERG, *supra* note 19, at 29.
30. Pennsylvania Ass'n for Retarded Children v. Pennsylvania, 343 F. Supp. 279 (E.D. Pa. 1972).
31. *Id.* at 302.

cess hearing where the parents may be represented by counsel, may call and cross-examine witnesses, and may examine records relating to the child; and the right to a verbatim record of the proceedings.

The consent agreement in *PARC* was the culmination of the first stage of the legalization of special education. Political pronouncements about the rights of the retarded were translated into legal arguments and formally recognized in a court of law as protected by the United States Constitution. The federal district court judgment in *Mills*,[32] issued the following August, reiterated the rights established in *PARC* and extended them to all handicapped children. There was more to come. *PARC* and *Mills* precipitated a rash of litigation across the country, both inspired and orchestrated by lobby groups on behalf of the handicapped in order to pressure state governments into action. Some thirty-six cases were filed in twenty-one jurisdictions.[33]

The commitment of a policy area to the hands of attorneys has significant policy ramifications. Rights take on a life of their own in the hands of lawyers, who bring a particular conceptual framework to the problems with which they deal. Analogizing the claims of the retarded to the legally cognizable right to education preempts other potential ways of framing the issues. To cast a claim in terms of a Fourteenth Amendment right also implies creating a set of procedures to protect the right. In the consent agreement drawn up between the lawyers for the parties in *PARC*, which was relied upon in subsequent cases, a detailed set of due process procedures figures prominently. Similar provisions were incorporated in the model statute drafted by CEC. Using the threat of litigation as leverage, organizations such as CEC lobbied successfully for new state legislation. By 1974, twenty-five states required due process procedures.[34]

B. From Test Case to Federal Legislation

Publicity about the treatment of the handicapped led to the introduction of bills adding the handicapped to Title VI of the Civil Rights Act.[35] Discrimination against the handicapped in education was specifically mentioned as one reason for the proposed amendment.[36] The emergence of these issues prompted formation of the Senate Sub-Committee on the Handicapped early in 1972. These developments spurred lobby groups for the handicapped to respond and groups which had traditionally focused their efforts at state and local level were drawn into the Washington orbit.

---

32. Mills v. Board of Educ., 348 F. Supp. 866 (D.D.C. 1972).

33. R. MARTIN, EDUCATING HANDICAPPED CHILDREN: THE LEGAL MANDATE 15 (1979).

34. Abeson, Bolick & Hass, *Due Process of Law: Background and Intent*, in PUBLIC POLICY AND THE EDUCATION OF EXCEPTIONAL CHILDREN 30 (1976).

35. The House Bill was introduced by Congressman Charles Vanik of Ohio on December 9, 1971. 117 CONG. REC. 45,974-75. Senator Hubert Humphrey introduced a similar bill into the Senate on January 20, 1972. 118 CONG. REC. 106-07. These bills later became § 504 of the Rehabilitation Act of 1973, Pub. L. No. 93-112, 87 Stat. 355 (1973) (currently codified at 29 U.S.C. § 794 (1976)).

36. R. MARTIN, *supra* note 33, at 16-17.

Issues involving the handicapped were tentatively placed on the federal agenda. The court cases, however, proved to be the decisive factor because they created a more expensive standard for the school systems to meet. This financial pressure forced the states to turn to Washington for assistance and convinced policymakers in Washington of the need for federal initiatives.

The court opinions also led lobby groups for the handicapped to focus on Washington. The CEC, which had played an influential role in orchestrating the litigation and using it to force states to enact special education legislation, had doubts about the constitutional firmness of the court decisions because none of the cases had been appealed. A federal statute would establish an authoritative national standard which would not have resulted if some of the other cases were lost. While maintaining pressure by continuing to bring suits, the primary focus of the lobby groups for the handicapped changed from seeking substantive change at state level to forcing states to accept— even to promote—federal legislation. The strategy dictated that states be obliged to accept conditions to be imposed by new federal legislation in order to obtain the funds necessary to comply with court orders.

The courts were thus a crucial factor in the combination of events which put special education on the federal agenda. The influence of the courts, however, went beyond this by shaping the substance of policy at the federal level.

C.   The Individualized Education Program (IEP)

The courts approached special education by determining whether handicapped children possessed a right to education. Since courts often deal with individuals as bearers of rights, this format made special education legally cognizable because one's right to it could be protected by due process procedures.

This emphasis on individual needs suited the professional concerns of the CEC as well as the procedural biases of the legalized model. That congruence in turn predisposed policymakers to deal with further policy questions in a legalized mode. Individualism was also critical to the next step in the process of legalization.

The courts had declared the right of handicapped children to a free and appropriate public education, with a presumption that a student be placed in the least restrictive school environment (the environment as similar to the regular classroom as possible). Beyond that, though, the substance of the right was unspecified. Once the idea of an individual right to an appropriate education was accepted, it became nearly impossible to define the substance of the right to education in general terms, for the needs of individuals varied so greatly. Moreover, even if a categorical definition could have been produced, it would have been politically difficult. Since education was still regarded as essentially a local responsibility, even in this interventionist era, federal substantive mandates seemed excessive.

The device settled on to elaborate the right to education, as it appeared in the first Senate bill, was the IEP: "a written educational plan for a child developed and agreed upon jointly by the local educational agency, the parents or guardians of the child and the child when appropriate . . . ."[37] The program was to contain a statement of the child's level of educational performance, long-range educational goals, intermediate objectives, the specific services to be provided, the date of commencement and the duration of the services, and objective criteria and evaluation procedures to determine whether the goals were being achieved.[38]

The character of the IEP process is legal and not administrative. Rather than empowering an administrator to exercise discretion in delivering preordained services to a recipient, the Act recognizes that the handicapped child has a right. This right entitles the child or the parents to negotiate as parties with school officials and involves them in the task of defining the nature and extent of the services to be delivered. This quasi-contractual process is a logical extension of the right to education already established by that stage of the policymaking process.[39]

The IEP is also an ingenious device in terms of political acceptability. It avoids attempting to mandate specific services; it recognizes the rights of recipients, empowers them, and involves them in the process. It avoids encroaching on the professional discretion of teachers and potentially enhances their influence over placement decisions. It provides a means of holding local administrators accountable while paying some deference to the belief that the federal government should not interfere too much with local autonomy in education. Finally, it appeals to local school officials by fixing the upper limit of the liabilities with respect to each child.[40]

D. Compliance: Legalization Begets More Legalization

For the IEP to be a meaningful contract, a means of enforcing its provisions and of assuring compliance with the aims of the law had to be found. A way for parents to express dissatisfaction with the IEP procedure or the performance of local officials was therefore required, as was an assurance that

---

37. S. 6, 93d Cong., 1st Sess. § 3(9) (1973). (The teacher's participation in development of the IEP was added in 1975. S. 6, 94th Cong., 1st Sess. (1975)).

38. *Id.*

39. The term quasi-contractual is used advisedly. The National School Boards Association was at pains to ensure that the IEP not be seen as a contract from which specific performance and other court remedies would flow. CEC agreed to this. *House Select Education Subcommittee Hearings,* 10 April, 1975, 76. The Senate Labor and Education Committee expressed a similar concern. S. REP. No. 168, 94th Cong., 1st Sess. 11, *reprinted in* 1975 U.S. CODE CONG. & AD. NEWS 1425, 1435. One of the first expressions of the idea of a contract was in Gallagher, *The Special Education Contract for Mildly Handicapped Children,* 38 EXCEPTIONAL CHILDREN 527 (1972). As one of the policymakers we interviewed summed it up:

> We intended to strengthen the hands of parents . . . . It was a way of individualizing and contractualizing the relationships and involving parents in the process . . . . It's a way of enforcing what should be delivered to kids. While it's said not to be a contract, it is a contract for service.

Note the commitment to the involvement and empowerment of the recipient. The interviewee alluded to the 1960's and the War on Poverty explicitly later in the interview.

40. One of our respondents informed us that this last item was a selling point for the IEP to local boards.

federal funds were being spent in accordance with the objectives of the legislation.

Early legislative drafts emphasized agency review, a bureaucratic mode of accountability. As the legislation took final form, however, due process guarantees and not administrative monitoring became the primary compliance mechanism.[41] This outcome is a further extension of the legalization process, building on the established theme of individual entitlement and the quasi-contractual IEP. Due process procedures, a natural concomitant of the legalized model, would not only serve as a means of redress for parents but also as a device for policing the expenditure of federal funds by local officials.

The history of this aspect of the legislation begins in the 1973 Senate bill[42] with the monstrously impractical notion of forwarding all IEP's to the U.S. Commissioner of Education for review. The idea of detailed central oversight was abandoned when it was realized that the requirement entailed sending some eight million IEP's to Washington each year. The Senate's alternative was a state-level independent complaint agency called "the entity,"[43] which would conduct periodic evaluations of State and local compliance, receive complaints from individuals, provide opportunity for hearings, notify the state or local agency of a violation and take steps to correct it. The House bill, by contrast, had developed a grievance procedure to be established by the local school district to receive complaints from the handicapped and carry out investigations.[44]

Neither bill entitled any individual to enforce his rights, thus creating a tension between the entitlement provisions of the IEP on the one hand and the enforcement provisions on the other. Advocacy groups, disenchanted with agency review procedures such as those employed by the Office of Civil Rights, put their opposition strongly: "We could have had a complaints, civil rights type procedure and done a study. We didn't want that. This was based on individuals, not group statistic things."

Conflict in the House-Senate conference committee over due process versus administrative review became acute when the decision was made to fund local school districts directly rather than give the states discretion to distribute the federal money. Administrative oversight could not assure accountability from some 16,000 school districts. Congressmen did not want to see "federal money being poured down the same old rat holes," as one policymaker put it, referring to the misuse of funds under earlier federal educa-

---

41. The first bill proposed in January 1973 contained a number of due process measures which looked almost identical to those contained in the *PARC* consent agreement. That bill did not, however, contain the full range of due process provisions ordered by the court in *PARC*. From our interviews it seems that there was little discussion of the due process procedures until the conference committee stage, when there was heated debate due to the pressure to secure a compromise between the House and Senate bills. These bills contained agency review bodies, called "the entity" in the Senate bill, while the House bill included a set of "grievance procedures." These were at odds with one another and with the legalized concepts already implanted in the early drafts.

42. S. 6, 93d Cong., 1st Sess. § 7(a) (1973).

43. *Id.* at § 614(8).

44. H.R. 7217, 93d Cong., 1st Sess. § 617 (1973).

tion legislation. Additionally, the advocacy and civil rights groups did not trust local school administrators and teachers and pushed for due process protections. The Children's Defense Fund (CDF) and the California Rural Legal Assistance Foundation (CRLA), both of which played a key role at this stage as advisors to the congressional conferees, were heavily involved in civil rights and poverty law litigation. Their experience in these fields produced a belief in rights, courts and court-like procedures, and a profound mistrust of bureaucratic accountability.

Quite apart from the inconsistency of agency review with individual entitlement, political factors militated against agency examination. Any watchdog agency large enough to police 16,000 school districts would have resulted in too much violence to traditions of local governance in education. The due process provisions fit perfectly into the federal legislative scheme. They carried through the notion of individual entitlement developed in the IEP. They also enabled client and advocacy groups to undertake their own enforcement initiatives. Enlightened self-interest would obviate the need for a large watchdog agency and reassure advocacy groups like the CDF, which believed that courts and court-like procedures were the only way to counteract the power of local school boards. The due process provisions offered a means of resolving the deadlock between the House and the Senate over compliance mechanisms that were consistent with the legalized model. The conferees could embrace a solution that both embodied a logically coherent development of all that had gone before and solved their more pragmatic political problems. Although the states remained legally obliged to monitor local behavior, the due process procedures assumed primary importance as a means of ensuring compliance and providing a forum for individual grievances.

IV

THE APPROPRIATENESS OF THE LEGALIZED MODEL:
THE EMPIRICAL EVIDENCE

A. Introduction

The evolutionary nature of legalization in special education policy precluded any detailed consideration of whether the legalized model was appropriate. Now that some of the major abuses that led to judicial and legislative intervention have been corrected, this question can be raised.[45]

This appraisal poses serious issues of policy. Does it make sense to impose a policy on education which places little faith in the professional discretion of the service provider?[46] The implications of this shift are not lost on educators

---

45. Atkin, *The Government in the Classroom,* 109 DAEDALUS 85 (1980); Pittenger & Kuriloff, *Educating the Handicapped: Reforming a Radical Law,* 66 PUBLIC INTEREST 72 (Winter, 1982); C. Hassell, A Study of the Consequences of Excessive Legal Intervention on the Local Implementation of PL 94-142 (1981) (Ph.D. Thesis, University of California, Berkeley & San Francisco State University).

46. Of course professionals are coming under a great deal of fire in a number of fields. E. GOFFMAN, ASYLUMS (1961) (the medical profession); I. ILLICH, TOOLS FOR CONVIVIALITY (1973)

who may resent the implicit loss of confidence. More generally, does legalization fit the needs and demands of schools or children? The imposition of legalization schemes onto ongoing complex organizations, such as schools, also creates particular problems.[47] Studies of the implementation history speak less of the promise of legalization and more of its pathology. These studies reveal compliance with the letter rather than the spirit of the law: preparation of standard form IEP's, resentment over handicapped children gaining a priority that may get them more than their fair share of the education dollar, and defensive strategies, such as the tape recording of IEP meetings to protect the interests of the school district and teachers.

Yet the story is more complex than this. While implementation studies view the due process procedures as a separate and severable part of the federal legislation, these procedures are an integral part of a legislative scheme which adopts a legalized policy style. The appropriateness of this policy style must be judged with reference to the place of special education in the school system, not by ignoring this overall context and focusing only on the due process hearings. To be sure, the benefits to special education flowing from the federal presence, more money, more initiatives and the like, must be offset by the costs of the due process hearings. Yet the question is whether these gains could have been achieved without the legalized policy style of the EAHCA.

A radical reorientation of priorities in special education was needed, and those who shaped the EAHCA determined that legalization was the only method to bring it about. In certain situations shock treatment is necessary to convince service deliverers in an ongoing institution that established patterns and values must be changed. Legalization was not the first but the last in a series of approaches taken by educators of the handicapped. Years of campaigning had not convinced the education community of the justice of the claims made on behalf of the handicapped.

Legalization was a plausible approach. Law may not be the only way to reorder priorities or legitimize claims; the availability of a great deal of new money for special education or the operation of a competitive market, for example, might have brought about the same result. But law and legal sanctions offered a surer and more direct means of institutionalizing the values promoted by the proponents of change. The embodiment of values in law and the possibility of sanctions offer powerful reference points to those implementing a reform, thereby serving as a rallying point for claims on the system and a powerful resource for responding to arguments from competing value positions. The law also provides a framework within which values can be translated into services and new values and services can emerge, for it requires the adjustment of power positions of the various groups within a

---

(professions generally); Wasserstrom, *Lawyers as Professionals: Some Moral Issues,* 5 HUMAN RIGHTS 1 (1975) (the legal profession).

47. L. MAYHEW, *supra* note 6, at 1-30, 258-84 (especially at 23). On implementation in special education see R. WEATHERLEY, REFORMING SPECIAL EDUCATION: POLICY IMPLEMENTATION FROM STATE LEVEL TO STREET LEVEL (1979) and on implementation generally, see E. BARDACH, THE IMPLEMENTATION GAME (1977).

system. Proponents of the new values gain power in the institution and can introduce further changes on behalf of their interests.

In short, legalization is neither so cost-free as its proponents suggest nor so defective as subsequent analyses contend. In what follows, this article will explore the effects of legalization by examining the implementation of the EAHCA with particular emphasis on its due process mechanisms.

B.   Implementation: The Due Process Procedures

Studies of the implementation of the due process aspects of the EAHCA are the best available indicators of the effects of legalization, but they need to be evaluated with caution.[48] These studies report a fairly short experience of the legislation and necessarily do not deal with the possibility that implementation improves over time.[49] They are also flawed in a variety of ways. For example, the research typically relies on small, non-random samples of individuals involved in the hearings. While valid as a guide to the experience of those who undertake a hearing, these cases focus on the deficiencies of the process. They do not speak to the appropriateness of the due process procedures generally, nor to the general level of satisfaction with the Act experienced by parents of handicapped children. This research approach shortchanges the systemic effect of the procedural reforms. Moreover, since the studies only report the post-legislation experience, the ill effects attributed to the due process procedures may simply be old problems transferred from other forums or made more visible by the existence of the hearings.

1. *The IEP Meeting.* The notification and procedural requirements necessary to draw up the IEP and hold the meeting are generally in place.[50] Despite some early hearings in which schools failed to comply with notice deadlines and the like, the mechanics of the IEP procedure seem to be operating.

The qualitative picture is not as clear. Two types of IEP meetings have been identified: a legalistic form in which half the time is devoted to narrow procedural requirements, and a child-oriented form, faithful to the spirit of the law.[51] IEP sessions in which the parents are overwhelmed with professional jargon and other strategies used by schools to minimize the portion of

---

48.   They are: M. BUDOFF & A. ORENSTEIN, SPECIAL EDUCATION APPEALS HEARINGS: THEIR FORM, AND THE RESPONSE OF PARTICIPANTS (1979); R. WEATHERLEY, *supra* note 47; Benveniste, *Implementation and Intervention Strategies: The Case of P.L. 94-142,* in D. KIRP, *supra* note 12; Hassell, *supra* note 45; Kirst & Bertken, *Due Process Hearings in Special Education: Some Early Findings from California,* in SPECIAL EDUCATION POLICIES 136 (Chambers & Hartman eds. 1983); Stearns, Green & David, Local Implementation of P.L. 94-142 (1979) (Discussion Draft: SRI International). The studies by Weatherley and Budoff and Orenstein are of the equivalent Massachusetts legislation, the Comprehensive Special Education Law of 1972. 1972 Mass. Acts 766 (codified as amended in scattered sections of MASS. ANN. LAWS chs. 69, 71B (Law Co-op. 1978).

49.   *See* Kirp & Jensen, *Law, Professionalism and Politics: The Administrative Appeals Procedure Under PARC v. Commonwealth of Pennsylvania,* in D. KIRP, *supra* note 12.

50.   Stearns, Green & David, *supra* note 48, at 81.

51.   Hassell, *supra* note 45, at 52.

their resources devoted to meetings have been reported in two states.[52] There are also hearsay accounts of IEP's prepared in advance where the parent is pressured to sign on the dotted line, but there is little evidence to indicate how widespread this practice is.

Reactions to the IEP process are mixed. Parents generally seem satisfied, even enthusiastic, about the development of the IEP. However, in some districts, one-third of the parents describe the meetings as formalistic.[53] Teachers generally regard the IEP as useful, but reports differ as to whether there is a high degree of actual use of the IEP as an instructional tool[54] or whether instructional use is really the exception.[55] Even this more pessimistic accounting acknowledges that the IEP has the force of law and serves as new found leverage both within the school and the district and provides a basis for a due process hearing.[56]

2. Due Process Hearings.

a. *Number of hearings.* The total number of due process hearings held pursuant to the EAHCA is not known. Scattered reports suggest wide variations from state to state. In California, 278 hearings were held in 1978-1979, the first year of uniform state regulations, and one-third of these were held in two school districts. That number represents just .08 percent of California's special education population.[57] A nationwide study of twenty-two sites found that half had experienced hearings, of which seven had only one hearing.[58] Massachusetts had 350 hearings between 1974 and 1977.[59]

As with litigation generally, it is difficult to determine whether those figures represent a large number of hearings compared to the number of people with grievances or whether hearings are highly unusual phenomena in relation to the number of people or even the number of complaints in a given area.[60] Right to education hearings are not atypical in this regard.

The impact of hearings, however, cannot be measured simply in terms of the number of hearings held.[61] The prospect of a hearing and estimations of its likely outcome shape the behavior of participants, both in the formulation of their basic relationships and in the way they handle their disputes. The "shadow of the law"[62] extends well beyond the formally affected parties.

---

52. *Id.* at 60; R. WEATHERLY, *supra* note 47.
53. Hassell, *supra* note 45, at 113.
54. *Id.* at 104.
55. Stearns, Green & David, *supra* note 48, at 79-82.
56. *Id.*
57. Kirst & Bertken, *supra* note 48, at 141.
58. Stearns, Green & David, *supra* note 48, at 98.
59. M. BUDOFF & A. ORENSTEIN, *supra* note 48, at 5-1.
60. See data cited in H. ROSS, SETTLED OUT OF COURT 5 (1970). The figures he uses were for 1963 and taken from K. DAVIS, ADMINISTRATIVE LAW: CASES - TEXT - PROBLEMS 5 (1965). *See also* Kirp, *supra* note 5, at 840 n.113; Nader, *Disputing Without the Force of Law,* 88 YALE L.J. 998, 1007 (1980).
61. H. ROSS, *supra* note 60; R. WEATHERLEY, *supra* note 47; Galanter, *Justice in Many Rooms, supra* note 8; Mnookin & Kornhauser, *Bargaining in the Shadow of the Law: The Case of Divorce,* 88 YALE L.J. 950 (1979).
62. The phrase is borrowed from Mnookin & Kornhauser, *supra* note 61.

b. *Who uses the hearings and for what end?*   Parents of upper and middle socio-economic status groups bring the majority of hearings.[63] They are overrepresented while parents from lower income and minority backgrounds are underrepresented.[64] This has prompted one commentator to observe that "[d]ue process and appeal procedures are used to advantage by the well-to-do and almost not at all by the poor."[65]

The middle class are usually best able to press their claims. Factors similar to those identified in other contexts seem to be at work in relation to relevance of hearings in the special education context. People in ongoing relationships are unlikely to resort to legal sanctions.[66] Parents who know that their children will have to deal with the local school district personnel for twelve years are understandably reluctant to resort to legal action, with all the anxieties that such undertakings generate, except in the most serious cases. The opportunities for reprisal even after an outcome favorable to the parents, and the difficulties of enforcing such a decision in the face of an intransigent school district,[67] pose too great a risk.

Middle and upper class parents do not face such high odds, for they have an exit strategy.[68] Their complaints typically assert the inability of the local school district to provide "appropriate" education and claim reimbursement for tuition in private schools. If this proves unsuccessful, these parents can pay for the private schooling themselves. Lower class parents do not have this option. When they are involved in hearings at all, it is most often to resist changes proposed by the school rather than to initiate change.[69] The ongoing nature of their relationship with the school system means that circumspection is probably in the best interests of these parents. This pattern points up an important limitation on the capacity of due process to bring about change in professionally run bureaucracies. It also raises questions about the wisdom of placing primary reliance on due process to effect policy change.

c. *Style of hearings.*   Adversariness and legalism seem to characterize the conduct of hearings.[70] Rather than adopting an informal negotiating format, the due process hearings tend to provide a forum for culmination of long-

---

63. M. BUDOFF & A. ORENSTEIN, *supra* note 48, at 6-11 to -12; Kirst & Bertken, *supra* note 48, at 153; Stearns, Green & David, *supra* note 48, at 104. On private school placement see M. BUDOFF & A. ORENSTEIN, *supra* note 48, at 6-11; Kirst & Bertken, *supra* note 48, at 154-55; Stearns, Green & David, *supra* note 48, at 104.

64. Kirst & Bertken, *supra* note 48, at 151-54.

65. R. WEATHERLEY, *supra* note 47, at 10. Kirst and Bertken report that where poor people do go to hearings they have a higher success rate. They suggest, however, that this may be due to the more limited nature of their claims and to the fact that they more frequently resist rather than propose changes. Kirst & Bertken, *supra* note 48, at 154.

66. *See* Galanter, *Why the "Haves" Come Out Ahead, supra* note 8; Handler, *supra* note 14; Macaulay, *Non-Contractual Relations in Business: A Preliminary Study,* 28 AM. SOC. REV. 55 (1963).

67. Budoff reports a high degree of non-compliance by school districts with decisions unfavorable to them, and continuation of the conflict. M. BUDOFF & A. ORENSTEIN, *supra* note 48, at ch. 10.

68. A. HIRSCHMAN, EXIT, VOICE AND LOYALTY (1970).

69. *See supra* note 65.

70. M. BUDOFF & A. ORENSTEIN, *supra* note 48, at 9-1; Stearns, Green & David, *supra* note 48, at 104.

term bad relations between the school and the parents.[71] Lawyers aggravate the situation, rendering proceedings more legalistic.[72] Emphasis on compliance with procedural matters, such as notices, signatures, and time deadlines, offers an easy substitute for harder substantive questions, such as the meaning to be given to the word "appropriate" in the phrase "free appropriate public education." This legalistic pattern seemed particularly evident in the earlier stages of implementation. As schools learned to comply with the forms of the law, opportunities for evasion diminished, and there was some evidence of reduced formalism. This evidence included reliance on "pre-hearing hearings" and negotiations among the participants.[73]

Parents generally reported considerable financial and psychological costs to the hearing process. They often felt themselves blamed either for being bad parents or for being troublemakers. Many perceived the school district officials to be lying:

> I've been through seizures and everything else with her, and this has been the worst affair of my life.
>
> It's been hell. Absolute hell. I seldom speak about it, even to my husband because I find that it gets me extremely upset. . . .
>
> My hands right now are shaking as I am talking to you about it. I'm cold and I get that same horrible feeling all over . . . . [b]ut I feel that it is very difficult to go in and sit across from someone 2 or 3 feet away and have them lie blatantly and not be able to say anything about it.[74]

School districts regarded the hearings as expensive, time consuming, and a threat to their professional judgment and skill. The private school placements which parents often sought are enormously costly and also carry an implied criticism of the public school program. Directors of special education programs often regarded parents seeking these placements as "ripping off" the school system, depriving other children of the benefits that would otherwise accrue to the public school program.[75] They complained about inconsistency in interpreting the appropriateness criterion from one hearing to the next and difficulties in accounting to the school board for expensive new services endorsed in hearings.[76] Special education administrators see themselves as caught in a cross-fire between parents and school boards who blame them for failing to hold the line on expensive new services.

Some school districts which have experienced a number of hearings have developed an array of defensive strategies. There are reports of districts that stick to the letter of the law but protect themselves by tape-recording IEP meetings, retaining lawyers, tightening procedures,[77] and interpreting educa-

---

71. M. BUDOFF & A. ORENSTEIN, *supra* note 48, at 9-1 to -2, 13-15, 14-27; Stearns, Green & David, *supra* note 48, at 101.

72. M. BUDOFF & A. ORENSTEIN, *supra* note 48, at 9-9.

73. *Id.* at 13-25; Stearns, Green & David, *supra* note 48, at 104.

74. M. BUDOFF & A. ORENSTEIN, *supra* note 48, at 9-29.

75. *Id.* at 13-43; Stearns, Green & David, *supra* note 48, at 108. Kirst & Bertken, *supra* note 48, at 163, warn of distortions in the allocation of public funds.

76. M. BUDOFF & A. ORENSTEIN, *supra* note 48, at 13-24 to -25.

77. Kirst & Bertken, *supra* note 48, at 159.

tion and related services narrowly.[78] Other districts negotiated extra services with parents who promised not to pursue a hearing, or threatened to demand a hearing in order to coerce parents into accepting an IEP.[79]

While a few participants in due process hearings regarded them as positive experiences, allowing some sort of catharsis and a forum in which an independent party could suggest a solution,[80] most held a negative view. In many instances, hearings have become an additional weapon with which the disputants can bludgeon one another. Parents see themselves as pursuing the best interests of their child, while the school district is anxious to preserve limited resources.

The negative effects of the due process hearings should not be exaggerated. Even though they impose a high economic and psychological cost on all involved, their incidence is concentrated in relatively few school districts. Furthermore, these are districts where parents have a long history of dissatisfaction with the school system.[81] The hearings provide an arena in which old conflicts are played out, and sometimes escalated. In view of this, the assertion that the introduction of due process procedures has caused relations between schools and parents to deteriorate must be treated with extreme caution.

V

THE APPROPRIATENESS OF THE LEGALIZATION MODEL: THE WIDE CONTEXT

A. Introduction

The implementation studies discussed in part III assess the appropriateness of legalization in special education without either considering the wider context of the education system or proposing plausible alternative means to rectify the indisputable abuses of the past. Focusing exclusively on the due process procedures and identifying only the undesirable effects associated with them misses the broader institutional changes associated with the legislation, of which due process procedures form an integral component.

Passage of the EAHCA has had an enormous effect on special education. More than 230,000 children were identified and provided with education within the first two years after passage of the law, and the rate of increase is steady.[82] Although appropriations are now falling below authorizations, there has been an infusion of $950 million in federal funds over the first two years

---

78. *See* M. BUDOFF & A. ORENSTEIN, *supra* note 48, at 13-14 to -15.
79. Stearns, Green & David, *supra* note 48, at 103.
80. M. BUDOFF & A. ORENSTEIN, *supra* note 48, at 9-29 to -30, 14-15.
81. *See id.* at 8-1 to -4; *cf.* Hassell, *supra* note 45; who seems to attribute the pathologies of schools districts with a large number of hearings to "excessive legal intervention".
82. *Hearings on the Implementation of P.L. 94-142 Before the Subcomm. on Select Education of the House Comm. on Education and Labor*, 96th Cong., 1st Sess. 297, 299 (1979). (Evidence of Edwin W. Martin, Deputy Commissioner, Bureau of Education for the Handicapped, Office of Education, Department of Health, Education and Welfare).

of the program, increasing to over $800 million per year in 1980 and 1981.[83] While reduced substantially under the Reagan Administration, special education has proved to be less of a casualty than other social welfare programs.[84] This enormous increase in special education expenditure has not only produced cash benefits but has also augmented the prestige and attractiveness of special education as a field of endeavor. The formal procedures mandated by the EAHCA are in place, and many new programs are being developed in school districts.

Much of this change might have been achieved without reliance on a legalized policy style. Implicit in the criticisms of due process procedures is the suggestion that the policymakers were wrong in believing that the legalized model was essential to achieve their purposes, and that legalization is inappropriate in the context of education. Even if one remains skeptical about the causal links between the due process hearings and the effects attributed to them by the studies canvassed in part III, there is good reason to be concerned about the appropriateness of the due process procedures.[85] It may be that some issues, including education, are not amenable to legalized treatment.[86] To determine whether special education is amenable, one must study the effects of legalization by looking beyond the hearing process to the impact of legalization on the wider institutional setting.

B. Legalization and Delegalization

Although legalization is a relatively new phenomenon in education,[87] it is more prevalent in public life where there are alternating periods of reliance on formal, procedural justice and informal, substantive justice.[88] The civil rights movement and the War on Poverty heavily emphasized rights, lawyers, courts, and formal procedures.[89] Those who studied those movements in the late 1960's and early 1970's began to doubt the extent to which substantive goals could be achieved through the legal model, especially where the poor were the intended beneficiaries.[90] The mid-1970's, by contrast, saw a growing interest in delegalization, emphasizing informal methods of dispute resolu-

---

83. *Id.* at 96, 97-98, 107. (Evidence of Frederick J. Weintraub, Assistant Executive Director for Governmental Relations of the Council for Exceptional Children).

84. The cutbacks for fiscal years 1982 and 1983 amount to 29.6 percent. CHILDREN'S DEFENSE FUND, A CHILDREN'S DEFENSE BUDGET: AN ANALYSIS OF THE PRESIDENT'S BUDGET AND CHILDREN 4 (1982).

85. On the question of the use of due process procedures in the context of school discipline, see Kirp, *supra*, note 5, and in schools generally, see Pittenger & Kuriloff, *supra* note 45, at 89-90.

86. Lon Fuller described such issues as "polycentric issues." Fuller, *The Forms and Limits of Adjudication*, 92 HARV. L. REV. 353, 371 (1978).

87. *See* Kirp, *supra* note 5.

88. *See* Abel, *supra* note 7.

89. *See, e.g.*, three articles by Reich, *Midnight Welfare Searches and the Social Security Act*, 72 YALE L.J. 1347 (1963); *The New Property*, 73 YALE L.J. 733 (1964); *Individual Rights and Social Welfare: The Emerging Legal Issues*, 74 YALE L.J. 1245 (1965).

90. *See* Galanter, *supra* note 66; Handler, *supra* note 14.

tion, arbitration, mediation, negotiation, ombudsmen, and community dispute resolution centers.[91]

Underlying this dynamic is the Janus-faced nature of legalization. In its positive aspect, legalization makes several promises. It is a vehicle through which individual citizens may redress the imbalance between themselves and the state or other powerful opposing interests. It provides access to individuals unable to summon the political resources needed to obtain a legislative majority in modern politics. It offers principled decisionmaking in an impartial, procedurally balanced forum. It emphasizes accountability, administrative regularity, and the reduction of arbitrariness.[92] In its other face, legalization can turn into the arid formality of legalism.[93] Equality before the law is too often dependent on access to resources. Legalization can also lead to the sorts of pathologies—defensiveness, delay, hostility, expense—adverted to in part III. Emphasis on accountability and reduction of arbitrariness imply a mistrust of those administering policy, which in turn may inhibit the creative exercise of professional discretion and judgment.

This duality of the legal model plays itself out in the special education area. Previously, handicapped children were excluded from school and from their share of the education dollar; those given some instruction were often poorly treated by the education system. After years of unsuccessful political efforts, the courts were called on to restructure power relationships in the education organization which had excluded the handicapped, and to legitimize their claims by declaring that they had a right to a free and appropriate public education. The embodiment of this value in the law meant that handicapped children could no longer be excluded from school and that their claims to education were legitimized. Arguments to the contrary were nullified. Legal sanctions were available to enforce the right. The argument moved beyond the question of admission to the question of the *quality* of education to which the handicapped are entitled.

The EAHCA does not squarely address the difficult questions of quality and substance in special education: namely, the content of the appropriate education in a particular case. The Act provides one procedure for giving effect to the right to a free appropriate public education, the IEP, and another for enforcing it, the due process hearing. Beyond specifying a minimum criterion of compliance with state educational agency standards, the legislative definition relies on the IEP to give substance to the term "appropriate."[94] This provides little guidance for those seeking to determine what is appropriate for a specific child. Undoubtedly this will be answered in part by the due process and review procedures. But the danger, from the point of view of those seeking high quality special education, is that the emphasis on process in the legislation will leave little room for substantive arguments. The

---

91.   Nader, *supra* note 60; *see also* the works cited *supra* note 8.
92.   We owe a number of these points to a talk on legalization given by Philip Selznick to the Berkeley/Stanford Faculty Seminar on Law, Governance and Education, October 1980.
93.   *See supra* note 11.
94.   20 U.S.C. § 1401(18) (1982).

majority in the Supreme Court decision in *Rowley* took this view.[95] They found that the Act could "not be read as imposing any particular substantive educational standard upon the States."[96] Granted that no particular substantive outcome is mandated, the question of appropriateness in a particular case remains. The *Rowley* opinion is only slightly helpful in defining what is appropriate because, like the legislative definition, it leaves the problem to the IEP process.[97]

Leaving substantive determinations to a due process hearing has both the virtues and the vices of legalization. It contemplates principled arguments about the amount and type of services due to a given child. This may be preferable to such alternatives as centralized bureaucratic decisionmaking, with its attendant problems of distance and rigid categorizations, or professional judgments, often paternalistic and highly deferential to the needs of the professionals at the expense of the handicapped student. On the other hand, it leaves open the possibility of legalism: that is, strict compliance with procedures as a means of avoiding review of the substance.[98]

The legalized model creates other problems as well.[99] Handicapped children are accorded formal rights not made available to other children in the education system. There is, for instance, a tendency for rights to know no dollar limitations.[100] Yet the reality that school administrators face is that they have limited budgets and must make difficult decisions about the just distribution of those funds among competing sectors of the school system.

Ambiguity surrounding the word "appropriate" also produces tension between schools and parents. School officials complain about parents looting the public treasury to obtain private school placements and express frustration that they feel unable to put these sorts of arguments to the hearings officers. The officials' inability to use these arguments may be attributable to the tendency of due process hearings to individualize problems, but it is not a necessary interpretation of the legislation. Acting on this perception, school administrators are resorting to indirect means of protecting funds, adopting defensive or delaying tactics, and attempting to translate arguments based on the needs of the school system in general into arguments about a particular child. For their part, parents' expectations may have been raised to unrealistic levels by the law. Their concern is likely to reside exclusively with their own child; in their eyes the word "appropriate" may have come to mean whatever is appropriate regardless of the cost. This would explain parents' frustration with school districts and their perception of a lack of candor in the school officials with whom they deal.[101]

The effect of the EAHCA is to segment decisionmaking power, empow-

---

95. Board of Educ. v. Rowley, 458 U.S. 176 (1982).
96. *Id.* at 200.
97. *Id.* at 203.
98. The majority in *Rowley* seemed to envisage something approaching this position. *Id.* at 205.
99. *See generally* Fuller, *supra* note 86.
100. Mills v. Board of Educ., 348 F. Supp. 866 (D.D.C. 1972).
101. M. BUDOFF & A. ORENSTEIN, *supra* note 48, at 9-14 to -24, 13-10; Stearns, Green & David,

ering hearing officers from outside the school administration to make decisions about potentially large slices of the school's budget. It is not clear whether the hearing officer is supposed to take into account the budgetary realities of the school system as a whole, of the special education segment of that system, or just of the educational merits of the program proposed for a particular child.

While this dispute over the relevance of costs is partly attributable to the fact that entitlements of handicapped children, but not those of nonhandicapped children, are clearly spelled out, it is also partly a function of the adjudicative process. The hearing mechanism is, in its ideal form, a case-by-case process. It formally assumes that two parties are disputing in a contextual vacuum. That fiction alone is enough to give rise to considerable frustrations. Moreover, different hearing officers will render different decisions on similar cases. There is no consistent interpretation of "appropriate," and there does not appear to be much communication among hearing officers about their decisions.[102] While this may change as precedents develop, several factors— the variegated nature of appropriateness, the fact that hearing officers lack either the legal or educational expertise to render consistent judgments, and the variability of schools and handicapping conditions—make consistency unlikely.

Modest changes in the law would improve the situation. For one, the legislation should be amended to make it clear that arguments based on the overall needs of the school system (subject to proof and open to challenge in the hearing) are germane to the question of appropriateness.[103] Use of informal dispute resolution techniques seems to be producing good results and should be encouraged.[104] Greater information, attention to problems at an early stage, and the use of mediation prevent the escalation of conflict in a significant number of cases.[105]

The broadest concerns relate to the effects of legalization of special education on the school as a bureaucratic/professional organization.[106] Schools face serious problems of coordination, confronting acutely complex questions of distributive justice among different elements of their program, of management vis-a-vis their own professional staff, and of accountability to the community, especially to the parents of currently enrolled students. The meaning

---

supra note 48, at 108 & 113; see also Kirst & Bertken on the potential for distorting funds, *supra* note 48.

102. M. BUDOFF & A. ORENSTEIN, *supra* note 48, at 13-24; Stearns, Green & David, *supra* note 48, at 107-08.

103. A recent case maintained that, in view of P.L. 94-142, the 180-day limitation on the school year could not be maintained for seriously handicapped children. This may imply a very broad interpretation of "appropriate" which would exacerbate the potential for distortion of school finances. Armstrong v. Kline, 476 F. Supp. 583 (E.D. Pa. 1979), *remanded sub nom.* Battle v. Pennsylvania, 629 F.2d 269 (3d Cir. 1980), *cert. denied,* 452 U.S. 968 (1981). *But cf. Rowley,* 458 U.S. 176 (1982) (Supreme Court chose relatively narrow interpretation of appropriate).

104. M. BUDOFF & A. ORENSTEIN, *supra* note 48, at ch. 12; Stearns, Green & David, *supra* note 48.

105. M. BUDOFF & A. ORENSTEIN, *supra* note 104.

106. See the discussion of law in the context of discrimination in L. MAYHEW, *supra* note 6.

of a good education is controversial, and limited in any case by funding realities. Potential lines of conflict run in every direction: between school board and principal, school board and teachers, teachers and principal, teacher and student, and teacher and parents.

The effect of legalization on special education entails a radical reorientation of this complex network. It empowers what was previously an out group; the handicapped must now be included in policy decisions. No one in the school system can maintain that handicapped children should be excluded from school, at least not publicly. The force of the state and the moral authority of the law is available to the handicapped. In arguments over services and resources the claimants can point to their legal entitlement to rebut the arguments of their opponents. The IEP has the force of law, and parents and special education teachers can use this to press their claims on behalf of handicapped children. Parents of the handicapped can also look to the law rather than to the generosity of the school system to define their entitlement. In short, the EAHCA effects a shift in bargaining power and prevents the claims of the handicapped from being fobbed off. As has been said in the context of anti-discrimination laws: "We like to use reason, not force. It isn't right to talk reason out of one side of your mouth and law out of the other, but before the law was passed they weren't as willing to listen to reason."[107]

Legalization has also improved the status of the special education professional. In an era of shrinking education budgets, special education has received an infusion of new money. It has become an attractive area for new teachers and a way for existing teachers to earn additional salary and avoid retrenchment. Special education teachers are assuming places in school administration that they had not held earlier. This development too will affect the organizational goals of schools and strengthen the perceived legitimacy of the claims of the handicapped.

The pathologies of legalization must also be acknowledged. There is some evidence that the values promoted by the legislation are provoking resistance from the education community. Despite increased funding, there are too few resources to treat all handicapped children individually.[108] By distinguishing the handicapped children from the regular school network and granting them rights not enjoyed by other school children, the law potentially distorts the allocation of resources. This potential is aggravated by the legal model which treats the parties to a dispute as discrete from the system in which they are located.

Further, legalization betrays a mistrust of schools. It may inhibit the discretion of professionals[109] whose judgment should be exercised creatively on

---

107. *Id.* at 275.

108. R. WEATHERLEY, *supra* note 47, at 73, 141-50 (pointing out the tensions involved in requiring bureaucracies to treat their clientele as individuals).

109. We are not alone in saying that the situation is poised to go either way. *See* Schlechty & Turnbull, *Bureaucracy or Professionalism: Implications of P.L. 94-142*, 29 J. TCHR. EDUC., Nov.-Dec. 1978, at 34.

behalf of the child.[110] In the past that distrust may have been deserved. But legalization can be a blunt instrument, undermining healthy as well as malevolent exercise of discretion. Special education teachers now find themselves as "defendants" in due process hearings. This represents a marked change from their self-perception, prior to passage of the EAHCA, as lone advocates for the handicapped child. From the viewpoint of the handicapped it would be disastrous to alienate this group, particularly in view of their role as primary service providers and their new status in the school hierarchy. Encouraging mediation and negotiation, rather than due process hearings, should diminish this danger. Moreover, resolution of the appropriateness issue should release special educators from the somewhat false position in which they currently find themselves having covertly to argue on behalf of the needs of the school system. Once recognized as legitimate, the system's needs could be advanced openly by representatives of the wider interests, leaving special educators to put the case for their component of the system. Parents would be less likely to maintain unreal expectations. In this way, parents and teachers could be reunited in the task of providing the best education, within budget constraints, for handicapped children.

Finally, the utility of the due process hearing as a compliance device is dubious. Individualization, lack of coordination, and the settlement of strategic cases to avoid hearings suggest systemic problems which may be missed by the individualized nature of the hearings. Hearings alone are ill-suited for the task of precipitating systemic review and reform.[111] Agency-wide review, litigation, and political change remain key parts of appraising and modifying any program.

Only in the context of those wider considerations may the appropriateness of legalization be assessed. Legalization jolted the education system into according handicapped children a fair share of the education pie. As the system comes to accept the presence of handicapped children and recognizes the legitimacy of their claims, and as special education teachers acquire new status in school hierarchies, there are sound reasons to diminish reliance on some aspects of the legalized structure of special education.

---

110. On the subject of growing government intervention in the classroom, see the following:
> In such a climate the teacher might be forgiven if he or she feels whipsawed, disaffected and even resentful. Teachers, I think, have been highly desirous of responding to educational concerns featured in the mass media, and they see themselves as having tried earnestly and sometimes valiantly to meet the objectives that seem important at any given time for the schools; but they become confused and angry because of the rapid change in educational priorities their resistance to external influence stiffened. I believe that this resistance to external influence, however beneficial that influence potentially may be, has been one unanticipated result of government activity in the curriculum field.

Atkin, *supra* note 45, at 96.

111. *See* Mashaw, *The Management Side of Due Process: Some Theoretical and Litigation Notes on the Assurance of Accuracy, Fairness and Timeliness in the Adjudication of Social Welfare Claims,* 59 CORNELL L. REV. 772 (1974).

VI

CONCLUSION

Development of special education policy occurred during the heyday of legalization, but the continued prominence of legalization as a policymaking style seems less likely. The force of the civil rights era, which gave so much impetus to the development of the special education policy, is spent. The rhetoric of rights has waned as calls for smaller government, lower taxes, and budget cuts produce a climate skeptical of new claims on the public sector and doubtful about many of the old ones. These rights may themselves be trimmed back by budget cuts, legislative repeal, and judicial circumspection.

This is not to suggest, however, that legalization will disappear from public life, for the values it symbolizes are too deeply embedded in the political culture. Oscillation between legalization and delegalization, reflecting the tension between procedural and substantive justice, is the likely pattern for the future. The lessons to be learned from the special education history speak to individuals' rights to enjoy essential public services and to participate in decisions affecting delivery of those services. These values remain fundamental in American public life. Yet there are also lessons to be learned about the impact of law on complex organizations and the balancing of all interests within those organizations.

Legalization is a powerful tool which needs to be understood and used with sensitivity. In the long run, there can be no easy solution to the difficult questions of distribution in organizations with conflicting interests competing for limited funds. Outright exclusion, such as handicapped children suffered, is no answer; neither is the enfranchisement of one group with little effort to relate that group's needs to those of other claimants. Those who would undertake the legalization of a policy area must take careful account of the context into which the policy is introduced, for only in this way can the appropriateness of legalization be weighed against alternative policy courses.

3

IS JUSTICE SERVED BY DUE PROCESS?: AFFECTING THE OUTCOME OF SPECIAL EDUCATION HEARINGS IN PENNSYLVANIA

PETER J. KURILOFF*

I

INTRODUCTION: THE EAHCA, DUE PROCESS, AND THE LEGALIZATION OF EDUCATION

The Education for All Handicapped Children Act of 1975 (EAHCA)[1] has been described as the major piece of social legislation passed during the 1970's.[2] Certainly it represented a major step in what Kirp and Kirp called the legalization of education.[3] Those who shaped the reform in Congress believed such a step was necessary to bring about a much needed reordering of priorities in education.[4] Indeed, for those unaccustomed to dealing with a variety of seriously handicapping conditions, the extension of a right to a free, "appropriate" education in the "least restrictive environment" represented a radical departure from traditional practice.[5]

By now, anyone involved with elementary or secondary education is familiar with at least the gross outlines of the law. What is important to emphasize is its basically procedural nature. Essentially, the EAHCA established one set of procedures for giving substance to the right to education and another set to protect that right. Congress, through its definition of "appro-

* Associate Professor of Education, University of Pennsylvania. The research reported here was supported, in part, by a grant from the National Institute of Education (Project No. Neg. -003-0192). I wish to express my special appreciation for the steadfast support and excellent advice of the Project Officer, Mr. Ronald Anson. In addition, I would like to thank Professors Arthur Dole, William Buss, Katharine Bartlett, and Judith Wegner for their careful critiques of earlier drafts of this paper. Professor Paul McDermott was very helpful on statistical matters. My research assistant, Sara Wedeman, was also of much help. Finally, I want to thank my graduate student and colleague, Steven Goldberg, Esq., for his many substantive and editorial suggestions.

1. Pub. L. No. 94-142, 89 Stat. 773 (1975) (codified as amended at 20 U.S.C. §§ 1400-1461 (1982)).

2. Pittenger & Kuriloff, *Educating the Handicapped: Reforming a Radical Law*, 66 PUB. INTEREST 72 (1982).

3. Kirp & Kirp, *The Legalization of the School Psychologists' World*, 14 J. SCH. PSYCHOLOGY 83 (1976).

4. Neal & Kirp, *The Allure of Legalization Reconsidered: The Case of Special Education*, LAW & CONTEMP. PROBS., Winter 1985, at 63.

5. *See* Pittenger & Kuriloff, *supra* note 2; *see also* Kirp, Buss & Kuriloff, *Legal Reforms of Special Education: Empirical Studies and Procedural Proposals*, 62 CALIF. L. REV. 40-155 (1974) (analysis of the early impact of those reforms which preceded and provided a model for the EAHCA).

priate," does not guarantee any particular level of substantive education.[6] Recognizing that such tasks could only be accomplished for individual children within specific contexts by trained professionals, Congress instead required an individualized education program (IEP) for each child.[7] This requirement was reinforced by a set of elaborate bureaucratic requirements, which include not only recordkeeping and periodic review of all children placed in special education, but also detailed instructions regarding how children should be assessed, with what kinds of instruments the testing should be done, by whom, and in what language.[8] The underlying assumption was that to the extent these mechanisms were faithfully employed, "general" justice would be served, and, therefore, all children would be afforded free, appropriate education.

Since Congress also knew that it was asking the same professionals who had excluded handicapped children in the past to now ensure their right to an appropriate education, it developed a second set of procedures for protecting that right.[9] The most dramatic of these was the right to an impartial hearing, in a procedurally balanced forum, for parents dissatisfied with a school's classification or placement decision.[10] Traditionally, courts and legislatures have used such due process hearings to guarantee accuracy in factfinding, participation in decisionmaking, and the perception of fairness to persons faced with the potential loss of liberty or property through acts of government.[11] Ordinarily, they have concluded that the required degree of procedural safeguards should be determined by balancing the ability of various procedures to protect the private interest in question against the public costs of providing the procedures all in light of the importance of the interest at stake.[12]

In the case of special education hearings, Congress appears to have found that the interests of exceptional children so outweigh what Buss, Kuriloff, and

---

6. Board of Educ. v. Rowley, 458 U.S. 176, 189-90 (1982). Indeed, the language of the statute is circular:

> The term 'free appropriate public education' means special education and related services which (A) have been provided at public expense, under public supervision and direction, and without charge, (B) meet the standards of the State educational agency, (C) include an appropriate preschool, elementary, or secondary school education in the State involved, and (D) are provided in conformity with the individualized education program required under section 1414(a)(5) of this title.

20 U.S.C. § 1401(18) (1982); 34 C.F.R. § 300.4 (1984). In *Rowley,* Justice Rehnquist, writing for the majority, described this definition as tending "toward the cryptic rather than the comprehensive." 458 U.S. at 188. Justice White, dissenting, argued that while the statutory language was not particularly clear, the legislative history provided a workable definition, and one more broadly drawn than the constricted view adopted by the Court. 458 U.S. at 213-16 (White, J., dissenting).
7. *See* 20 U.S.C. §§ 1401(19), 1412(4), 1414(a)(5) (1982). For a general discussion of congressional intent, see Neal & Kirp, *supra* note 4.
8. *Compare* 20 U.S.C. §§ 1412(5) *with* 34 C.F.R. §§ 300.340-.349, .530-.543 (1984).
9. 20 U.S.C. § 1415 (1982).
10. *Id.*
11. Friendly, *"Some Kind of Hearing,"* 123 U. PA. L. REV. 1267, 1270-75 (1975).
12. W. BUSS, P. KURILOFF, & T. PAVLAK, DISCIPLINARY DUE PROCESS: AN EMPIRICAL FEASIBILITY STUDY OF PROCEDURAL DUE PROCESS, SCHOOL DISCIPLINE, AND EDUCATIONAL ENVIRONMENT 12-16 (N.I.E. Project No. 7-015, 1981). Buss, *Easy Cases Make Bad Law: Academic Expulsion and the Uncertain Law of Procedural Due Process,* 65 IOWA L. REV. 1, 39-48 (1979).

Pavlak term the out-of-pocket and disruptive costs of conducting hearings to protect those interests,[13] as well as any potentially negative, long-range consequences affecting the relationship between professional educators, students, and parents,[14] that such interests require adversary hearings closely imitating the judicial model. Parents must be notified in writing of any proposed alteration in their child's classification or placement, and the reasons for it.[15] If they are dissatisfied with any part of the proposal, a timely hearing presided over by an impartial hearing examiner, is available upon their request.[16] At the hearing they have a right to legal counsel, to subpoena records, and to examine and cross-examine witnesses.[17] The hearings may be open or closed to the public, at the parents' discretion, and a record of the proceedings must be kept.[18] Finally, at the conclusion of the hearing, the parents have the right to receive a timely written decision, detailing the reasons for a given conclusion, [19] and to appeal an adverse decision to the state department of education[20] and to state or federal court if necessary.[21]

Taken together, the safeguards mandated by Congress satisfy all the major elements of due process generally thought to be essential to a fair hearing.[22] Despite the fact that such elaborate procedures represent a major new intrusion of the judicial model into the field of education, little research exists on the consequences of introducing them,[23] and none examines the effectiveness of such procedures in resolving educational disputes justly. The purpose of this article is to describe research which attempts to do the latter. I first

---

13. W. Buss, P. Kuriloff & T. Pavlak, *supra* note 12, at 1-16, 21-23.

14. These consequences have been discussed in detail in both judicial decisions and legal periodicals. *See, e.g.,* Goss v. Lopez, 419 U.S. 565, 584-99 (1975) (Powell, J., dissenting) (expressing concern over the Court's intrusion on the functioning of state and local education systems); Mashaw, *The Supreme Court's Due Process Calculus for Administrative Adjudication in* Mathews v. Eldridge: *Three Factors in Search of a Theory of Value,* 44 U. Chi. L. Rev. 28 (1976); Michelman, *Formal and Associational Aims in Procedural Due Process,* in Due Process 126 (J. Pennock & T. Chapman eds. 1977); Kirp & Jensen, *What Does Due Process Do?,* 73 Pub. Interest 75 (1983); *cf.* Tinker v. Des Moines Indep. Community School Dist., 393 U.S. 503, 515-26 (1969) (Black, J., dissenting) (expressing concern that Court's protection of students' free speech rights might lead to disruption of learning process in public schools). Perhaps the work that addresses the issue most directly as it relates to special education is Kirp, Buss & Kuriloff, *supra* note 5.

15. 20 U.S.C. § 1415(b)(1)(C) (1982), 34 C.F.R. § 300.504-.505 (1984). For a further explanation of the requirements, see S. Goldberg, Special Education Law: A Guide for Parents, Advocates and Educators 19-46 (1982).

16. 20 U.S.C. § 1415(b)(2) (1982); 34 C.F.R. § 300.506-.507 (1984).

17. 20 U.S.C. § 1415(d) (1982); 34 C.F.R. § 300.508 (1984).

18. 20 U.S.C. § 1415(d) (1982); 34 C.F.R. § 300.508 (1984).

19. 20 U.S.C. § 1415(d) (1982); 34 C.F.R. § 300.508 (1984).

20. 20 U.S.C. § 1415(c) (1982); 34 C.F.R. § 300.510 (1984).

21. 20 U.S.C. § 1415(e) (1982); 34 C.F.R. § 300.511 (1984).

22. *See* Friendly, *supra* note 11, at 1279-95 (setting forth the elements of a fair hearing).

23. The major works are P. Hill & D. Madey, Educational Policymaking Through the Civil Justice System (Rand Institute for Civil Justice, 1982); M. Budoff & A. Orenstein, Due Process in Special Education: Legal and Human Perspectives, (HEW Bureau of Educ. for the Handicapped, Grant No. G007502322, 1979); P. Kuriloff, D. Kirp & W. Buss, When Handicapped Children Go to Court: Assessing the Impact of the Legal Reform of Special Education in Pennsylvania (N.I.E. Project No. Neg. -003-0192, 1979). Most of it suffers from serious methodological weaknesses and extreme caution should be exercised in drawing conclusions from it. For a fuller discussion of these problems, see Neal & Kirp, *supra* note 5.

examine the assumptions underlying the imposition of due process hearings, showing they are used in the customary belief that they produce factually accurate, legally faithful decisions. In that respect, such outcomes represent an important part of what is understood as fair or just. I then argue that this ideal of justice cannot be assessed in special education hearings because professionals cannot agree on standards necessary to establish the accuracy of decisions. Instead, I suggest that a party's ability to influence administrative hearings in a desired direction by effectively using due process elements may be a reasonable substitute for accuracy. It is in the sense of this value—ability to influence outcome—that the term justice is used in this article.

Therefore, research on the capacity of special education hearings to produce equitable outcomes must examine the degree to which variations in the ways participants use the procedural elements of due process predict their ability to influence the outcome of the hearings in their favor. The finding of predictive relationships alone, however, will not be meaningful unless those relationships are examined in relation to the predictive power of other independent variables (such as the size of the district and the gender of the child). Such variables, although arguably irrelevant to the issues being decided in the hearing, might nevertheless affect outcome. After operationally defining the variables examined in the research, I describe how they were measured and the results of the inquiry. I conclude by arguing that on balance, the first four years of experience in Pennsylvania suggest that due process enables parents who use its elements effectively to influence the course of decisions, and in that sense to promote justice.

II

DUE PROCESS, PARTICIPATION, ACCURACY, AND FAIRNESS

Congress protects handicapped children's right to an appropriate education with a full panoply of procedural safeguards. Traditionally, the presence of such measures indicated that a vital private interest was at stake. Underlying the belief that the more important a private interest is, the more closely procedural safeguards must approximate those available in a trial, is the assumption that such procedures, beyond securing participation in decision-making, do in fact support *accuracy* in fact-finding and *fairness*. In the complex area of social welfare claims, which provide a rough analogy to the problem of determining an "appropriate" education, accuracy has been defined as "the correspondence of the substantive outcome of an adjudication with the true facts of the claimant's situation and with an appropriate application of relevant legal rules to those facts."[24] Fairness, in this framework, becomes "the degree to which the process of making claims determinations tends to produce accurate decisions."[25]

---

24. Mashaw, *The Management Side of Due Process: Some Theoretical and Litigation Notes on the Assurance of Accuracy, Fairness, and Timeliness in the Adjudication of Social Welfare Claims,* 59 CORNELL L. REV. 772, 774 (1974).

25. *Id.* at 775.

It takes little thought to realize that the link between procedures, as inputs, and accuracy and fairness, as products, is impossible to establish empirically.[26] In real life there are simply no external criteria for confirming the "true facts" of a situation. If there is no way to establish what is "accurate," how can due process be evaluated? One answer is to assess how well decisions made in such hearings withstand appeal.[27] Unfortunately, in special education hearings, the usefulness of the ability to withstand appeal as a measure of accuracy and fairness is suspect. If no objective, external standard exists in any kind of "truth"-determining hearing, it is especially obvious when determinations involve equally acceptable inferences from one set of "facts." And, while review may be an excellent test of a lower court's application of the law in traditional adjudications, decisions in special education at the local level emerge from a different legal framework than appeals at the state level. This appears to be the case in social security appeals.[28] Kirp and Jensen seem to imply that that is also true of the special education appeals process in Pennsylvania.[29]

Mashaw argues that absent external standards and comparability between local and state hearing officers, consistency in adjudication may be the nearest possible approximation of accuracy.[30] But he goes on to cite a General Accounting Office study of social security appeals indicating little agreement among state agencies and between state agencies and federal decisionmakers.[31] Given the potential variety and complexity of special education

---

26. Although not within the scope of the present study, it would be possible to measure fairness to the extent it is defined independently of outcome, by assessing participants' perceptions of the results of their hearings. Do they think the outcome was fair, whether or not they achieved their goals? But fairness may also be defined in terms of participants' feelings about their experience in the hearings. Instead of assuming that they have been treated in a "fundamentally fair" fashion because they have participated in a trial-like hearing, the researcher could ask them if the hearing process was fair. Of course, it is hard to imagine that the perception of fairness will not be somewhat enhanced simply by allowing people to participate in decisions which affect their lives. See Yudof, *Legalization of Dispute Resolution, Distrust of Authority, and Organizational Theory: Implementing Due Process for Students in the Public Schools,* 1981 Wis. L. Rev. 891, 921 & n.119. Indeed, there is some empirical evidence to support the proposition that, independent of outcome, people who have the opportunity to argue their cases in an impartial forum feel more fairly treated than those who do not. J. Thibaut & L. Walker, Procedural Justice: A Psychological Analysis (1975). It is not difficult to imagine that they might also experience greater feelings of dignity and self-respect. This was one of the explicit premises underlying the Supreme Court's decision in Goss v. Lopez, 419 U.S. 565 (1975). Such values may be even more important in special education cases, where there is so much professional uncertainty about what constitutes an appropriate outcome. (A study of parental perceptions of the fairness of both the process and outcome of special education hearings in Pennsylvania is currently being conducted by S.S. Goldberg.).

27. Friendly, *supra* note 11, at 1294-95; Mashaw, *supra* note 24, at 785-87.

28. Mashaw, *supra* note 14, at 43-44. Mashaw points out that the Disability Insurance Manual, which is designed to promote consistency at the state level by objectifying the disability standard, is not used by administrative law judges in the hearings. Instead, they apply the statutory standard, together with regulatory medical listings—listings that Mashaw claims are usually irrelevant to cases reaching the hearing stage. He attributes these differences to the bureaucratic structure of decision-making at the state level, using relatively specific standards, as opposed to a local hearing process designed to foster individualized justice according to more general, statutory criteria. *Id.*

29. Kirp & Jensen, *supra* note 14, at 81-84.

30. Mashaw, *supra* note 14, at 43-45.

31. *Id.* at 44-45 & n.56 (citing unpublished GAO study).

claims, it is likely that a similar study in this area would produce similar results. Again, Kirp and Jensen's examination of special education appears to corroborate this hypothesis.[32] To the extent this is correct, evaluating the linkage between procedures and outcome must depend on something other than the robustness of decisions under review.

While it might be possible to test the linkage in a laboratory experiment when the decision is confined to the simple binary choice between guilt and innocence, the problem increases in difficulty when it involves a real crime, and may become hopeless when the issue is what constitutes an "appropriate" education for a particular child. In the first place, there is abundant evidence to suggest that equally well-trained professional educators, working in good faith and under the best of circumstances in a nonadversary context, cannot agree on either the assessment or placement of handicapped children.[33] These findings are consistent with those from other fields indicating, for example, that psychiatrists cannot agree on psychiatric diagnoses[34] or clinical psychologists on emotional and behavioral disorders.[35]

In the second place, while it may be possible to assign such disagreements in psychiatric and psychological cases to a lack of current knowledge, the problem in educational decisionmaking is the assumption that there is one "best" or most "appropriate" placement. In fact, a whole range of programs exist that can help a particular child, and the degree to which they do depends on a mix of variables ranging from the child's current status and personality to the personality of the particular teacher and the nature of the other children in the class. Thus, choosing an appropriate program depends on the amount of knowledge about the child, what resources are available *and* the art of matching them effectively.

If the linkage between procedural safeguards and justice is to be tested for special education hearings, then an outcome criterion other than accuracy must be found. In the context of special education, the most straightforward alternative to "fairness as accuracy" may be the capacity of parents to influence the hearing officer's decision in their favor. Although not as grand a value as "Truth," the interest in being able to influence adminstrative decisionmaking, when it involves participants' vital concerns, has been recognized

32. Kirp & Jensen, *supra* note 14.

33. *See* Flor, Service Provider Agreement and Special Education Reform, *reprinted in* 39 DISSERTATION ABSTRACTS INTERNATIONAL 6061A (1979) (doctoral dissertation, Univ. of Pennsylvania, 1978); McDermott, *Sources of Error in the Psychoeducational Diagnosis of Children,* 19 J. SCH. PSYCHOLOGY 31 (1981).

34. Freeman, *A Reliability Study of Psychiatric Diagnosis in Childhood and Adolescence,* 12 J. CHILD PSYCHOLOGY & PSYCHIATRY 43 (1971); Sandifer, Pettus & Quade, *A Study of Psychiatric Diagnosis,* 139 J. NERVOUS & MENTAL DISEASE 350 (1964); Sandifer, Hordern, Timbury & Green, *Psychiatric Diagnosis,* 114 BRIT. J. PSYCHIATRY 1 (1968); Spitzer & Fleiss, *A Reanalysis of the Reliability of Psychiatric Diagnosis,* 125 BRIT. J. PSYCHIATRY 341 (1974).

35. Achenbach, & Edelbrock, *The Classification of Child Psychopathology: A Review and Analysis of Empirical Efforts,* 85 PSYCHOLOGICAL BULL. 1275 (1978); Little & Shneidman, *Congruencies Among Interpretations of Psychological Tests and Anamnestic Data,* in 73 PSYCHOLOGICAL MONOGRAPHS: GENERAL AND APPLIED, Whole No. 476 (1959); Zubin, *Classification of the Behavior Disorders,* 18 ANN. REV. PSYCHOLOGY 373 (1967).

in the legal literature.[36] Using it, the linkage between procedures and outcome need not remain simply an irreducible article of democratic faith. While it brings us no nearer to a standard of accuracy (or truth), it does allow us to develop an important, measurable standard of justice by comparing what parents want with what hearing officers give them.[37] It is then possible to correlate the relative ability of participants to use the procedural elements of due process effectively to achieve "justice," defined as what parents want from the system.

But participants do not use the elements of due process in a vacuum. It is certainly reasonable to wonder if other variables, irrelevant to the issues under consideration at a hearing, but nonetheless socially influential, may operate to skew the results, thereby undermining any conclusions which could be drawn from the due process variables themselves. Within this framework, it is possible to ask to what extent the success of participants in special education hearings is a function of their effective use of the elements of due process, and to what extent it is a function of other, less relevant characteristics such as the child's age and gender and the district's wealth and urbanization. Answers to such questions may prove the best possible gauge of how well justice, as used here, is served by special education hearings.

III

THE RESEARCH QUESTIONS

To discover if the outcomes of the hearings—the degree to which parents are able to influence decisions in directions they desire—are related to the effective use of those procedural safeguards which traditionally have been held to support accuracy and fairness, the quality of use must be measured. How much contact did the parties have prior to going to a hearing? How well did parents prepare, independent of such efforts to work with the school? In the hearing, how well did the parties present their cases and support their arguments with witnesses and exhibits? How effectively did they cross-examine opposing witnesses? Did having a lawyer or other advocate materially improve their performance? In addition, the impartiality of hearing officers, while not under the control of either party, has been cited as the single most important element of due process.[38] How impartial were they, and did evidence of bias correlate with the decisions they made? Were

---

36. *See, e.g.,* Buss, *supra* note 12, at 17-21, 44-45, 94-95; Mashaw, *supra* note 14, at 37-39; Friendly, *supra* note 11, at 1270-75; Yudof, *supra* note 26, at 921 & n.119. *Contra* Michelman, *supra* note 14, at 148-53.

37. Legal scholars such as Buss, *see supra* note 12, and Friendly, *see supra* note 11, would probably argue for an intermediate procedure that checks the relationship between this measure of justice and the presence (or absence) of each individual procedural element, and then between it and the amount of elements available, before attempting to relate it to the quality of the participants' use of the elements. The reality of special education hearings in Pennsylvania was the lack of variation in the number of elements the hearings contained. As a result, it was impossible to examine how combinations of different elements explained outcome in a statistical sense.

38. Friendly, *supra* note 11, at 1279-80.

hearing officers who worked for districts more often favorable to schools than those who worked for intermediate units or colleges? Once all of these performance aspects in hearings are quantified, it is possible to see how they relate to outcome.

But as important as it is to know if effective use of the elements of due process could predict the outcome of hearings, it is equally important to know how two other sets of independent variables describing characteristics of the child and the school district related to it. *If* the process operated justly, some of these variables would be relevant to outcome, while others would not. Thus, except under very unusual circumstances, a child's age or sex should not influence the outcome of his or her case. Neither should the year of the hearing nor the child's prior involvement with special education. But the placement and services demanded by the parties might be relevant to a decision, not just for obvious reasons relating to the degree of their reasonableness or feasibility, but also as they became part of a knowing "bargaining strategy." Again, since Pennsylvania covers the excess cost of special education,[39] the socioeconomic status of districts should not affect outcome, except perhaps in urban districts, where the impact of a variety of cross-cutting factors (desegregation, bureaucratic rigidity, a weak local tax base, and the like) may impede local efforts to provide quality services, and therefore make it difficult to counter parental claims.[40] Only by examining the correlation of these variables to the outcomes of hearings independently, as well as in relation to the correlation of the elements of due process with those outcomes, will it be possible to gauge the efficacy of due process as a vehicle for the just resolution of disputes in special education.

IV

Method

A.   The Due Process Hearing Transcripts

To answer these questions, we did a careful content analysis of the written transcripts of the first four years of hearings in Pennsylvania. Since those hearings were conducted under the rules set forth in *Pennsylvania Association for Retarded Children v. Pennsylvania* (*PARC*),[41] they were centralized and readily obtainable, once permission was obtained from the Deputy Attorney General in charge of the *PARC* case. The *PARC* due process regulations initially applied to retarded children, then were expanded to include all handicapped children, and finally, in 1976, were modified once again to include gifted

---

39.   *See* Pa. Stat. Ann. tit. 24, §§ 13-1373 to -1376 (Purdon Supp. 1984-85) (reimbursement by state to approved schools providing special education).
40.   For a discussion of how such cross-cutting factors can affect a major school system such as Philadelphia's, see P. Kuriloff, S. Wedeman & J. Day, The Impact of Chapter 2 Block Grants in Pennsylvania, Final Report to the E.H. White Company for the National Institute of Education (1983) (available from the senior author).
41.   334 F. Supp. 1257 (E.D. Pa. 1971) (per curiam) (injunction and consent agreement), *modified*, 343 F. Supp. 279 (E.D. Pa. 1972).

children.[42]

Using the first four years of hearings involved a trade-off. It limited our ability to generalize from the findings to hearings involving retarded children or those suspected of being retarded—children usually classified as either mentally retarded, learning disabled (LD), or brain injured (BI). It eliminated, however, the potentially serious confounding effects of hearings involving very different types of exceptional characteristics—physical disability, hearing impairment, severe retardation, and giftedness, for example. The choice nevertheless included a sample reflecting at least 60 percent of the total number of Pennsylvania cases (prior to 1983) and probably as many as 75 percent (if, as is likely, cases involving learning disability and brain injury followed a pattern similar to the present).[43] Possibly this also reflects about 50 percent (and up to 70 percent) of cases nationwide, as reported by Smith,[44] given all other caveats applicable because of differences in state classification procedures.[45]

Parents requested 480 hearings during the period covered by the study. Of those, 172 actually resulted in hearings. We examined the full record of 168 such hearings. The transcripts were extremely varied. They ranged from a few pages, reflecting a hearing that lasted less than an hour, to over 200 pages, reflecting hearings lasting over two days. In certain hearings, parents appeared without representation and with little more than a feeling that their child was not retarded. In others, parents, sometimes represented by an attorney, secured several professional witnesses to support a sophisticated claim. The form of the hearings varied just as much as their substance. Some resembled court cases, with highly structured presentations followed by cross and redirect examinations. Others seemed little more than parallel monologues interrupted occasionally by the hearing officers' plaintive attempts to clarify and relate them.

B. The Due Process Coding Instrument

After the project administrator removed all identifying material from transcripts which parents elected to close to the public, all the transcripts were coded, using the *Due Process Coding Instrument*[46] and the *Due Process Coding*

---

42. 22 PA. ADMIN. CODE ch. 13 (1984) (the *PARC* due process regulations as amended); 22 PA. ADMIN. CODE §§ 13.21-.23 (1978) (expression to all gifted and/or talented children). Catherine D. Pittenger, Civil No. 74-2435 (E.D. Pa. June 27, 1975) (expansion of state due process regulations to all handicapped children).

43. *See* O'Connor, Information Concerning Special Education Hearings (Memorandum to the Pennsylvania State Attorney Panel for Special Education, Technical Assistance Group for the Right to Education, 1983).

44. Smith, *Status of Due Process Hearings*, 48 EXCEPTIONAL CHILDREN 232, 234 (1981).

45. As of 1981, there had been 555 hearings in Pennsylvania, 314 (57 percent) involving retarded children and 108 (19 percent) involving learning disabled (LD) or brain injured (BI) children. *Id.* The national figures, based on Smith's work, appear closer to 35 percent and 20 percent, respectively. *Id.*

46. Kuriloff & George, *Due Process Coding Instrument*, in P. KURILOFF, D. KIRP & W. BUSS, *supra* note 23, app. IV.

Manual. [47] The instrument contained 207 items describing the child, the pre-hearing behavior of the parents (as inferred from their hearing behavior), the behavior of parents at the hearing, behavior of the school personnel, and the behavior of the hearing officer. Of these, some covered factual variables, such as the child's age, the number of witnesses called by the parents and the school, and the hearing officer's professional affiliation. Others described such things as the central issues of the case and the central arguments used by the parents and the school. Besides explicitly describing aspects of parents' and school personnel's behavior that indicated how effectively they used the elements of due process, the items also covered a number of variables we felt might mediate the outcome of the hearings, such as the size of the district and the number of years the child spent in special education prior to the hearing. A final set of items rated various aspects of the hearing officers' behavior and whether their decisions favored the parents or the schools. This measure, the dependent variable, described the overall outcome of the case in relation to what the parents demanded on a five-point Likert scale ranging from: 1 = Complete Loss, where parents do not receive the placement they request or any desired services arguably relevant to their case, to 5 = Complete Win, where parents win desired placement and the majority of desired services. Appendix A describes the thirty variables used for the present analysis.

C.   Coding and Reliability

An initial group of three coders, blind to the purposes of the study, were trained on a typical transcript. After roughly 50 hours of work together, they independently coded three randomly selected transcripts. The few discrepancies that emerged were again discussed until consensus was reached on the coding of all items. After this, six new transcripts were drawn at random and again coded independently by each coder. At this point the coders agreed, on the average, about 98 percent of the time on factual items, such as the child's age, and 93 percent of the time on the scaled items, such as rating the quality of the parents' presentation. Two new teams of three coders each were then added and trained in a similar manner. Coding the same six transcripts, there were no significant differences when the internal agreement of each team's members, agreement among the teams, and agreement among all the individuals, were compared. The same procedures were used to train coders to rate the hearing officers' decisions. Again, agreement was quite high, averaging 97 percent for factual items and 90 percent for scaled items such as the degree of hearing officer partiality.

Having established an acceptable degree of reliability, the 168 transcripts were divided among the nine transcript coders, and the hearing officer recommendations among the three recommendation coders. Each coder's work was

---

47.   Kuriloff & George, *Due Process Coding Manual*, in P. KURILOFF, D. KIRP & W. BUSS, *supra* note 23, app. V.

checked thoroughly by a research supervisor and any discrepancies were reconciled through discussion eventually reaching a consensus.

V

RESULTS

A. Who Won?

It does not make sense to try to predict the outcome of a due process hearing using either procedural elements or potential mediating variables, unless parents (or schools) in fact "won" some substantial portion of the cases. If parents never won, or won only an insignificant percentage of them, no credible claim may be made for the effectiveness or fairness of the hearings.

When hearing officers' decisions were compared to what parents demanded, we found that parents won, in whole or in part, in 59 out of the 168 cases, losing in 104 (in the remaining 5 hearings, the hearing officer's decision was so different from what the parent or school wanted, that it could not be counted). In other words, parents achieved some form of victory in 35 percent of the hearings. This parallels roughly the winning percentage that was found in Massachusetts and in a nationwide survey of forty-two states, certainly suggesting that parents are able to achieve some satisfaction in a significant portion of the hearings.[48]

When the cases are segregated into those classifying children and those involving disputes over the content and quality of programs, the picture becomes clearer. Of 114 cases in which classification issues were central, parents won 33, or 28 percent. Of the 87 cases involving content or quality, parents won 43, or 49 percent (33 cases involved both kinds of issues so the sum does equal 168). Content or quality questions were much more likely to arise in more seriously retarded children, many of whom had a long and often rocky history with public schools prior to the *PARC* case.[49] Below, I will address the question whether this result can be explained by the fact that hearing officers tended to right past wrongs against seriously retarded chil-

---

48. For the Massachusetts analysis, see M. BUDOFF & A. ORENSTEIN, *supra* note 23; for the nationwide results, see Smith, *supra* note 44. Much worse results for parents have been reported by Kirp and Jensen , *supra* note 14. The problem seems to lie in what criteria are used to determine whether a party has won. While Smith did not indicate the criteria used in his survey, Kuriloff, Kirp, and Buss described parents as partial winners whenever a decision granted them any of their substantial demands. P. KURILOFF, D. KIRP & W. BUSS, *supra* note 23, at 158. Budoff and Orenstein, using an adaptation of the methodology developed by Kuriloff, Kirp and Buss, employed similar criteria with similar results. A careful examination of the source of, Kirp and Jensen's 4 percent win rate shows that it includes only parents whose claims were *fully* successful. O'Connor, Special Education Due Process Hearings in Pennsylvania 6 (Paper presented at the international convention of the Council for Exceptional Children) (April 16, 1981). Read more liberally, O'Connor's data suggest that parents won between 31 and 42 percent of the cases, a result which would be consistent with the other studies cited here.

49. Pennsylvania Ass'n for Retarded Children v. Pennsylvania, 334 F. Supp. 1257 (E.D. Pa. 1971) (per curiam) (injunction and consent agreement), *modified*, 343 F. Supp. 279 (E.D. Pa. 1972); *see supra* text accompanying notes 41-42.

dren and show less concern about the unproven dangers of EMR (educably mentally retarded) versus LD or BI placement (around which most classification battles raged), or by the fact that parents of more seriously handicapped children simply did a better job pleading their case in the hearings.

B.   The Relationships Among Selected Child Variables, Elements of Parental Behavior, and the Outcome of Hearings

Table I presents the correlations[50] among variables describing the child, key aspects of the parents' hearing performance, and the hearing officer's decision. Aside from their decision to open or close the hearing to the public, it reveals a consistent set of moderate to strong, significant relationships. Of the twelve variables, nine were associated with outcome.

While neither the age nor the sex of the child was related to outcome, previous special education experience ($r=.34$), current placement ($r=.31$), and the restrictiveness of placement ($r=.19$) were. Parents of children who had spent time in special education, who had more serious handicaps, and whose placements were more restrictive, tended to win their hearings more often than parents of children who had never been in special education, who were less serioiusly handicapped, and who had been placed in less restrictive environments.

But winning was not merely a matter of having a more seriously handicapped child; a finding of that alone would tend to cast doubt on the value of using the procedures well. Parents who presented their cases better also won more often than those who did not. With the exception of the decision to have a lawyer and to close hearings to the public, there were significant, moderate correlations between outcome and the number of exhibits parents presented ($r=.24$), the number of witnesses they called ($r=.42$), their preparation for the hearing—not including contact with the school—($r=.30$), the degree to which their demands taxed the school's resources($r=.32$), the effectiveness of their questioning of school witnesses ($r=.30$), and the overall quality of their presentation ($r=.39$). Furthermore, these variables correlated significantly (and moderately to strongly) with each other. The presence of a lawyer representing parents correlated .45 with the number of exhibits they used and the number of witnesses they called, .76 with the quality of their questioning, and .65 with the overall quality of their presentation. There were, in addition, equally strong interrelationships among these variables. The number of exhibits parents entered correlated .52 with the number of witnesses they called, .55 with their prior preparation, .45 with the quality of their questioning, and .59 with the overall quality of their presentation. The

---

50.   A correlation expresses mathematically the strength of the relationship between two variables. Correlations range from $+1$ to -1. A complete lack of relationship is expressed as "$r=0$," a perfect relationship as "$r=+1$" or "$r=-1$" (the negative sign indicating an inverse relationship). Multiple correlations express the strength of the relationship among several independent variables and a "criterion" variable in such a fashion that it is possible to see the "unique" contribution of each independent variable to the overall correlation ("prediction" or "explanation").

TABLE 1

CORRELATION MATRIX*

RELATIONSHIPS AMONG CHILD-RELATED VARIABLES, SELECTED MEASURES OF PARENT BEHAVIOR, AND HEARING OUTCOME

Variables	1	2	3	4	5	6	7	8	9	10	11	12	13	14	15	16
Child Variables																
1. Age	1	-.12	.21	.31	-.08	-.04	.13	-.02	-.02	.12	-.07	-.07	.03	.10	-.01	.09
2. Sex		1	-.09	-.08	-.04	.02	-.02	.02	-.01	.04	.04	-.02	-.18	-.01	-.03	-.02
3. Previously in Special Education			1	.62	.28	.06	.52	.36	.31	.23	.24	.34	.37	.33	.42	.34
4. Current Placement				1	-.02	.03	.72	.38	.33	.24	.07	.32	.44	.34	.33	.31
5. Current Restrictiveness					1	.10	.28	.48	.21	.11	.40	.37	.29	.21	.37	.19
Parent Variables																
6. Hearing Open?						1	.08	.09	-.01	-.09	-.09	-.01	.06	-.02	.02	.10
7. Placement Wanted							1	.38	.33	.23	.19	.34	.45	.33	.40	.30
8. Restrictiveness Wanted								1	.35	.22	.36	.37	.45	.27	.39	.20
9. Preparation									1	.57	.55	.70	.38	.58	.71	.30
10. Lawyer Directs										1	.45	.45	.21	.76	.65	.13
11. Number of Exhibits											1	.52	.18	.45	.59	.24
12. Number of Witnesses												1	.37	.55	.68	.42
13. Demands Tax School Resources													1	.31	.40	.32
14. Quality of Questioning														1	.73	.30
15. Quality of Presentation															1	.39
Hearing Officer Decision																
16. Outcome																1

* N = 168; p < .05 for any correlation of .15 or more.

number of witnesses correlated .70 with prior preparation, .55 with the quality of their questioning, and .68 with the overall quality of their presentation. The quality of their questioning correlated .73 with their overall effectiveness.

These dimensions of presentation were not as strongly, though still significantly, related to the degree to which parental demands taxed schools' resources. Such demands correlated .21 with representation by counsel, .18 with the number of exhibits, .37 with the number of witnesses, .31 with the quality of questioning, and .40 with the overall quality of presentation. It seems likely that making a larger number of costly demands was often part of parents' strategy for winning a hearing.

To bring the matter full circle, however, all the dimensions of performance we measured, with only one exception, were also moderately and significantly related to the child's current placement: $r = .24$ with having a lawyer direct the case; $r = .32$ with the number of witnesses; $r = .33$ with prior preparation; $r = .44$ with taxing the school's resources; $r = .34$ with effectiveness of questioning; and $r = .33$ with overall quality of presentation. Only the number of exhibits was unrelated to the current placement's restrictiveness. Similarly, with only one exception (having a lawyer direct the case), the current degree of restrictiveness was related to all the elements of performance ($r = .40$ with exhibits, $r = .37$ with witnesses, $r = .21$ with prior preparation, $r = .29$ with taxing the school, $r = .21$ with questioning, and $r = .37$ with overall quality). In other words, the more severe the child's disability, the better the parents argued the case.

These findings show that while the results of the hearings were not related to irrelevant variables such as the age and gender of the child, they were associated with other intervening variables. Rather than skewing the results, however, those variables help to explain them further. Of course, it seems logical that the degree to which parental demands taxed school resources was also related to the seriousness of the child's handicap. Yet beyond that obvious relationship, the correlation of *all* key performance variables with severity of handicap, together with the other relatively strong correlations among performance variables, *including* making demands on the school, suggest that parents of more seriously retarded children tended to be more effective in the hearings than parents of less retarded children, perhaps because they had had more experience battling the school.

C. The Relationships of Selected Elements of the School's Hearing Performance and Outcome

A different picture emerges when the relationship between outcome and key aspects of the school's performance in hearings is examined. In terms of intervening variables, parents from more urbanized districts, and districts within intermediate units (I.U.)[51] with larger populations, tended to

---

51. In Pennsylvania, the state's 501 school districts are organized into 29 intermediate units which provide ancillary services, including much special education, that districts would find difficult or prohibitively expensive to supply on their own.

TABLE 2

CORRELATION MATRIX*

RELATIONSHIPS AMONG CHILD-RELATED VARIABLES, DISTRICT SIZE, SELECTED MEASURES OF SCHOOL BEHAVIOR AND HEARING OUTCOME

Variables	1	2	3	4	5	6	7	8	9	10	11	12
Child Variables												
1. Current Placement	1	-.02	-.34	.74	.02	-.12	.16	-.15	-.14	-.21	-.27	.31
2. Current Restrictiveness		1	-.21	.08	.28	.00	.09	-.20	-.17	-.07	-.10	.19
School Variables												
3. District Urbanization			1	-.28	.16	.14	-.27	.25	.20	.27	.21	-.27
4. Placement Wanted				1	-.14	-.20	.11	-.31	-.11	-.33	-.30	.31
5. Restrictiveness Wanted					1	.02	-.07	.09	.10	.15	.07	.06
6. Prehearing Involvement with Parents						1	.00	.06	.08	.27	.21	-.12
7. Lawyer Directs Case							1	.11	.04	.03	.15	.13
8. Number of Exhibits								1	.18	.26	.31	-.13
9. Number of Witnesses									1	.14	.25	-.04
10. Compliance										1	.54	-.25
11. Quality of Presentation											1	-.39
Hearing Officer Decision												
12. Outcome												1

* N = 168; p < .05 for any correlation of .15 or more.

win their cases somewhat more frequently then those from less urbanized districts or intermediate units with smaller populations (r= −.27 and r=.20, respectively).[52] Neither the educational level nor the median family income level of a district's I.U. were associated with outcome.[53]

In terms of school performance variables, the normality of placement proposed by the school was related significantly to parental success (r=.31), while the restrictiveness of the proposed placement was not.[54] Neither was the school's prehearing involvment with the parents, the number of witnesses or exhibits the school presented, nor its having a lawyer present its case. What did matter was the degree to which the school met such requirements of the law as conducting a broad evaluation, presenting a flexible prescription, and proposing an individualized program that followed from the evaluation and prescription (r= −.25) and the overall quality of the school's presentation (r= −.39). In other words, parents tended to lose their cases when schools asked for more mildly handicapped placement categories, when schools followed the procedural aspects of the law, and when, in the judgment of the coders, schools presented their cases well. Parents tended to win when schools did not do those things. Furthermore, as the data in Table 1 reveal, for parents the logically related elements of the adversary process held together in a coherent pattern. But the data in Table 2 show that for schools, those elements were much less strongly related.

The presence of a lawyer who actively managed the case for the school did not correlate significantly with the number of witnesses the school called, the number of exhibits it presented, or with the school's compliance. Furthermore, it was only weakly related to the overall quality of the school's presentation (r=.15). The number of exhibits and witnesses the school offered were modestly related (r=.18) and both of these, in turn, correlated with the overall quality of the school's presentation (r=.31 and r=.25, respectively). Finally, a school's compliance was significantly and moderately related to its involvement with parents prior to the hearing (r=.27) and strongly related to

---

52. The direction of the sign in these two correlations is a function of the way urbanization and size were coded. The text presents the proper interpretation of the relationships.

53. Socioeconomic status (SES) data (a measure combining mean income and mean educational attainment of persons over 25 within the I.U.'s) on I.U.'s were used because district census data were not available. Since the SES of districts within I.U.'s varies greatly, these correlations must be viewed as providing, at best, approximations of the strength of any real relationships among SES variables and the outcome of hearings. For that reason, it did not seem wise to use them in larger correlational or multiple regression analyses. The only demographic variable employed for those was a measure of district urbanization.

54. The terms "normality" and "restrictiveness" are not opposites. Normality of a placement, as used here, refers to the degree to which the IQ's or social behavior of children placed in the class deviate from what is considered "normal" by state standards. (For the state's definition of exceptional children, see PA. STAT. ANN. tit. 24, § 1371 (Purdon Supp 1984-85).). Such a placement could be in any of a variety of more or less "restrictive" locations. The restrictiveness of a child's placement refers to how close it is to the usual setting in which an ordinary child of ordinary intelligence would be taught. Thus, a class in a regular school would be defined as less restrictive than a class in a special school, and a class in a special school would in turn be considered less restrictive than one in a state hospital. For the rankings of normality and restrictiveness used in the present study, see Appendix A, *infra*.

the overall quality of its presentation (r=.54). Yet, most of these elements of presentation were no more strongly related to each other than to the school district's size, the child's current placement, or the placement the district was requesting.

There were significant though modest positive correlations between the urbanization of the school district and the number of exhibits (r=.25) and witnesses (r=.20) it employed, as well as the degree of its compliance with the law (r=.27). Urbanization was also correlated with the overall quality of the school's presentation (r=.21). In fact, with the exception of their tendency to be less often represented by counsel (r=−.27), less urban school districts behaved in ways that were arguably more effective in hearings than did more urban districts.[55] They also seemed to comply more with the law (r=.27). Furthermore, urbanization was negatively related to the school's desired placement (r=−.28), but positively, if weakly, related to the restrictiveness of that placement (r=.16). More urban school districts tended to ask for lower classifications than less urban districts, and for placements in less restrictive environments. Perhaps this indicates that less urban districts tended to heed the principle of normalization, but once they classified a child as seriously handicapped, their choice of facilities was narrower. These districts simply lacked the types of differential services commanded by more urban districts. Whatever the reason, the fact that less urban districts acted more effectively and complied more fully with the principle of normalization probably explains the fact that they tended to win more often than more urban districts (r=−.27). Moreover, parents tended to win more often in more urban districts while losing more often in less urban ones.

The child's current placement correlated significantly but weakly with the school's active use of a lawyer (r=.16) and negatively with the number of exhibits it presented (r=−.15), its compliance (r=−.21), and the overall quality of its presentation (r=−.27). Taken together, these findings suggest that schools had a slight tendency not to argue their cases as well as the seriousness of the child's handicap increased. They also tended, to argue their cases less well as the seriousness of the placement they *requested* increased. The placement the school requested was moderately negatively related to its number of exhibits (r=−.31), the degree of its compliance (r=−.33), the amount of its involvement with parents prior to the hearing (r=−.20), and the overall quality of its presentation (r−.30); it was unrelated, however, to the school's having a lawyer manage its case. This suggests, at least in the early years after *PARC*, that schools did not fully understand the necessity of careful preparation when they were asking for a less normalized placement or appreciate the burden of defending decisions regarding children already in a placement for the more seriously handicapped. It is interesting to note that a school's reported contact with parents tended to decrease as the severity of

---

55. *See supra* note 52.

the placement it requested increased. Certainly, this could have been a factor contributing to the need for a hearing in the first place.

D. The Relationship Between Selected Hearing Officer Variables and Outcome

An impartial hearing officer has long been the sine qua non of procedural fairness. Yet as Judge Friendly has noted, while strong disagreement arises over how much prior participation constitutes bias, "there is wisdom in recognizing that the further a tribunal is removed from the agency and thus from any suspicion of bias, the less may be the need for other procedural safeguards . . . ."[56] Table 3 presents data which reflect the relationships, both to each other and to hearing outcome, of four measures of hearing officer characteristics and behavior, including bias.[57]

The table reveals significant, though very modest, relationships between hearing officer affiliation and parents' winning (r=.15), and between hearing officer partiality toward parents and parents' winning (r=.15). It also reveals an equally weak, though significant, relationship between the activity level of the hearing officer during the hearing and outcome (r=−.17). This means that parents fared better when the hearing officer was less directly associated with local schools, less active during the hearing, and more biased in favor of the parents. Parents did worse if the primary work affiliation of the hearing officer was with the local schools, if the hearing officer was more active during the hearing, and if he or she was more biased in favor of the school.

TABLE 3

CORRELATION MATRIX*

THE RELATIONSHIPS AMONG SELECTED HEARING OFFICER VARIABLES AND HEARING OUTCOME

	1	2	3	4	5
1. H. O. Affiliation	1	.01	.03	.18	.15
2. H. O. Does Most Questioning		1	.27	−.08	−.17
3. H. O. Complies With Law			1	.17	−.00
4. H. O. is Partial				1	.15
5. Outcome					1

* N = 168; p < .05 for any correlation of .15 or more.

---

56. Friendly, *supra* note 11, at 1279.

57. Following standard criteria specified in Kuriloff & George, *supra* note 46, bias was judged by rating the hearing officers' total verbal behavior (as it appeared in the transcripts) for partiality to either parents or school districts. In particular, judges rated whether hearing officers favored one side or the other by refusing to admit arguably relevant testimony, by calling testimony or evidence into question after admitting it, by clarifying some responses or statements as opposed to others, by discrediting some witnesses, or by showing differential anger or impatience. The rating scale, together with the actual items employed, may be found in Appendix A, *infra*.

VI

FACTOR ANALYSIS

Factor analysis[58] of the thirty independent variables helps clarify the underlying meanings suggested by the preceding analysis of individual groups of correlations. The analysis resulted in the identification of four coherent factors, each meeting the criteria of (1) accounting for at least 5 percent of the overall variation and (2) having an Eigen Value over 1.5. Only two of the factors, however, had more than two loadings over .40, and even those were

TABLE 4

OBLIQUE FACTOR STRUCTURE*

Factor	Item	Factor Loading
I. Quality of Parents' Presentation	Lawyer Present for Parents	.88
	Effectiveness of Parents' Questioning	.84
	Hearing Officer Does Most of the Questioning	−.76
	Quality of Parents' Presentation	.72
	Lawyer Presents School's Case	.66
	Parents' Preparation	.61
	Number of Parental Exhibits	.50
	Number of Parental Witnesses	.49
II. Quality of School's Presentation	Quality of School's Presentation	.75
	Degree of School's Compliance with Law	.73
III. Normalization of Current Placement	Restrictiveness of Current Placement	.63
	Restrictiveness of Placement School Wants	.60
IV. Child's Current Classification	Child's Current Placement	.96
	Placement School Wants	.80
	Placement Parents Want	.78
	Child Previously in Special Education	.47

* After rotation with Kaiser Normalizations.

---

58. A correlation expresses the relationship between two variables. When many variables are being used to understand a phenomenon, a statistical technique called factor analysis may be employed. Factor analytic techniques enable the researcher to determine whether any underlying patterns of relationships exist among a complex array of correlation coefficients. Such patterns, or factors, are then examined to see if they may be taken as "source variables" accounting for the observed interrelationships in the data. Factor analysis is principally used to explore variables in order to discover patterns and to confirm theoretically derived hypotheses about the structure of phenomena. In the present study, I used it to validate inferences drawn from the welter of intercorrelations discussed in the preceding sections of this paper. For a clear, useful description of the various types of factor analyses, see Kim, *Factor Analysis*, in STATISTICAL PACKAGE FOR THE SOCIAL SCIENCES 468 (2d ed. 1975).

quite difficult to interpret. When an oblique rotational method (which allows factors to be correlated) was used to arrive at a terminal solution, this problem was overcome, yielding four clear, theoretically meaningful factors, each of which complemented the other findings of this research.[59]

As can be seen in Table 4, Factor 1, *Quality of Parents' Presentation,* loaded heavily on the active participation of a lawyer (.88), the effectiveness of the questioning (.84), and the overall quality of the parents' presentation (.72). All of the other elements of presentation appear in the factor with decreasing loadings. The only item to load negatively on this factor, whether the hearing officer did most of the questioning (−.76), also appears to fit, as it suggests that hearing officers tend to take over when parents are not making a strong case for themselves. Factor 2, *Quality of School's Presentation,* only loaded heavily on the overall quality of the school's presentation (.75) and the school's compliance with the law (.73). Factor 3, *Normalization of the Current Placement,* loaded most heavily on the restrictiveness of the child's current placement (.63) and the restrictiveness of the placement the school wanted (.60). Factor 4, *Child's Current Classification,* loaded very heavily on the child's current placement (.96), the placement the school wanted (.80), and the placement the parents wanted (.78); it loaded less heavily on the child's having been in special education (.47).

Together, the factors strongly support the reality of the patterns inferred from the individual correlations among the variables: effective hearing behavior for parents required use of the full panoply of adversary skills, while for schools it seems to involve a combination of compliance with evaluation requirements and overall skill in presentation. Such skill depended more on organization and clarity, and less on direct combativeness. The restrictiveness of the child's current placement and agreement between school and parents over his or her classification appear to represent intervening variables that affected the hearing process.

VII

PREDICTING OUTCOME: MULTIPLE REGRESSION ANALYSIS

Discussion of the zero-order correlations of the independent variables with outcome, along with discussion of the interrelationships among the predictor variables, raises the question of how these variables might combine to account for outcome. Table 5 presents a summary of the results of a regression analysis designed to answer that question. Only the three variables that made a significant ($p < .05$) contribution to the multiple R are included. The variable most strongly correlated with outcome was the number of wit-

---

59. This result makes sense given Kim's argument that while "orthogonal factors are mathematically simpler to handle . . . oblique factors are empirically more realistic." Kim, *supra* note 55, at 474. This seems especially true given the inherent intercorrelation of factors examined in this study.

TABLE 5

MULTIPLE REGRESSION SUMMARY: PREDICTING HEARING OUTCOME*

Step	Variable	Simple r	Multiple R	Multiple R^2	R^2 Change
1.	No. of Parental Witnesses	.42	.42	.18	.18
2.	Quality School's Presentation	−.39	.55	.31	.13
3.	Child Previously in Special Education	.34	.57	.33	.02

 * N=168.

nesses employed by the parents. Alone, it accounted for 18 percent of the variation. After it was entered, two more variables reliably explained an additional 15 percent of the variation in outcome. The first of these, overall quality of the school's presentation, accounted for 13 percent. Once it was entered, the second, whether the child had previously been in special education, added another 2 percent. Together, the three variables explained a considerable 34 percent of the variation in outcome.

VIII

DISCUSSION

When viewed together, the zero-order correlations, the factor analysis, and the multiple regression all suggest that the way participants used the elements of due process was associated with the results they achieved. Parents who performed well in one aspect of the hearings tended to perform well in other aspects, and such performance was in turn related to winning their cases. The fact that being represented by a lawyer did not correlate significantly with outcome, but did relate to the other elements of effective presentation, does not detract from this conclusion. Instead, it suggests that while lawyers could help with the process, they were not essential to it.

The results of the multiple regression analysis capture this process well. The number of witnesses parents called was one of the aspects of their performance that *should* have been related to outcome if the hearings were working in a way that enabled people who used the procedures effectively to influence the decisions in their favor. Indeed, since determining the number of witnesses simply involved counting those appearing in the transcripts, it may have been our most reliable proxy for the quality of parent performance. Recall that the number of witnesses correlated very strongly with the number of exhibits parents entered, the quality of their questioning, the presence of an active lawyer, and the overall quality of their presentation.[60]

The fact that the overall quality of the school's presentation explained the most additional variation in outcome, once the number of parental witnesses was entered into the equation, increases our faith in the integrity of the hearing process. It meant that parents' success was not only related to their own relative effectiveness but also to the school's relative ineffectiveness:

---

60. *See supra* Table 1.

good performance by parents combined with poor school performance to predict a decision favorable to parents.

The third variable in the regression appears to accord with this view as well. Parents of children with previous experience in special education may have won more often because hearing officers held schools to a higher standard in such cases than in cases involving children who were for the first time being considered for special education. The data also shows, however, that parents of children already in special education developed considerable expertise in advocacy. Recall that previous assignment to special education correlated moderately with the number of parent exhibits and witnesses, the quality of questioning, and the overall quality of their presentation.[61]

Taken together, these findings suggest that, for the first four years in Pennsylvania at least, the expected and logical relationship between the elements of effective performance for parents and outcome pertains. For schools, the expected elements of effective performance were also related, but not as strongly. These findings suggest that what it took to win was somewhat different for the two parties.

Perhaps the style of the schools' presentations reflected the fact that hearing officers were holding them to the letter of the new law because of the schools' legal duty to "go forward"—to present the program they viewed as "appropriate" to meet the needs of the child, as well as their reasons for it, prior to the parents' presentation. This may have made the other, more conventional elements of the adversary process less important for schools. Apparently, schools did not have to rebut parents' arguments through cross-examination, or develop overwhelming arguments of their own through the orderly presentation of witnesses and exhibits. What they had to do, it seems, was to convince the hearing officer that they were acting in good faith and within the framework of the law. It was sufficient to demonstrate that they followed the necessary evaluation and prescription procedures, and that in classification and programming they attempted to provide the most normal setting possible.

In contrast, hearing officers' concern for parents appears to be twofold. First, they appear to pay close attention to what the parents demanded and how persuasively they argued for it. Second, they seemed to have assessed carefully how effectively the parents argued against what the school proposed. The results of these different attitudes towards parents and schools seem to reflect a certain tension within the law itself. A tension that at once invites parents to attack the school's position while simultaneously implying that schools, represented by professionals, should avoid an adversary stance in favor of serving the best interest of the child.

---

61. *Id.*

IX

MORE QUESTIONS TO ANSWER

Due process in special education has worked in practice as a quasi-judicial, equalizing forum, just as its advocates envisioned.[62] Parents who make relatively effective use of the available procedural safeguards are more likely to influence the decision than parents who make relatively less effective use of them. Care must be taken, however, to make neither too much nor too little of this central finding.

This study does not examine whether the results parents achieve are less a function of their inherent skills than an effect of their socioeconomic status. In a subsample of forty-two parents, drawn from the 168 cases reviewed here, we found no relationship between the results parents received and their occupational status.[63] And in a larger, though less systematic sample, Kirst and Bertken actually found that poor parents in California, though seriously underrepresented in the sample, won more frequently than their wealthier counterparts.[64] Further research is needed to discover what lies behind these findings. Are they simply artifacts of the pre-EAHCA era, when the handicapped children of poor parents received such poor educational services that hearing officers, during the first years of the reform, had no choice but to differentially reward them? Or are poor parents asking for different, and more easily granted programs and services than rich parents? Yet, an even more pressing question arises if Neal and Kirp are correct in suggesting that the hearings have been used largely by middle class people.[65] Then the issue becomes one of equal access, and the question whether the hearings are effective vehicles for allowing parents to influence educational decisions must be understood within the context of the question of "which parents?"

Again, the present study looks only at hearings involving children thought to be retarded by one party to the dispute. Do hearings work the same way for other kinds of handicapped children? The research of Budoff and Orenstein,[66] who, using an instrument adapted from our own work,[67] found a similar factor structure for Massachusetts hearings primarily involving children classified as learning disabled and emotionally disturbed, suggests that they may. Unfortunately, Budoff and Orenstein did not attempt to develop a predictive model from their findings. Such a model would make a considerable contribution when compared to the present findings.[68]

---

62. Gilhool, *The Uses of Litigation: The Right of Retarded Children To a Free Public Education,* 50 PEABODY J. EDUC. 120 (1973); P. KURILOFF, D. KIRP & W. BUSS, *supra* note 23, at 169-81; Neal & Kirp, *supra* note 4.
63. Kuriloff & Hoffman, Parents React to Due Process Hearings (unpublished raw data, 1976) (available from the senior author).
64. Kirst & Bertken, *Due Process Hearings in Special Education: Some Early Findings from California* in SPECIAL EDUCATION POLICIES: THEORY, HISTORY, IMPLEMENTATION, AND FINANCE 136 (1983).
65. Neal & Kirp, *supra* note 4, at 78.
66. M. BUDOFF & A. ORENSTEIN, *supra* note 23.
67. Kuriloff & George, *supra* note 46.
68. M. BUDOFF & A. ORENSTEIN, *supra* note 23.

Finally, this study does not look at the question of the satisfaction of parents who have gone through hearings. Neal and Kirp's review suggests that parents often feel blamed by school districts for being either bad parents or troublemakers, while school personnel often feel that the mere request for a hearing impugns their professional judgment and dedication to promoting the welfare of children.[69] Are the outcomes of hearings worth such emotional costs?

Perhaps they are, for those parents who feel that they have at last "had their day in court," but perhaps not, for those who, having gone through the battle, find that despite the hearing nothing substantial has changed for their children. Even here, however, we are talking about only a tiny fraction of those parents eligible for hearings. Assuming that the orders of the hearing officers have been uniformly implemented in every case, the programs of some 742 children in the forty-two states surveyed by Smith have been altered as a result of hearings.[70] Yet of course, the simple availability of due process has a subtler "ripple effect" which is difficult to measure. We simply do not know to what extent districts, eager to avoid future reversals, or wishing simply to avoid hearings altogether, have become more responsive to parental concerns—or at least, to what they believe a hearing officer might require. One study has found that school psychologists reported much change in that direction.[71] The present research indicates that due process hearings in special education may indeed serve the value of "equalization" envisioned by Professor Mashaw,[72] giving parents the tools to alter a balance that has too often been tipped against them in the past. Whether (as the authors of both *PARC* and the EAHCA had hoped) the hearings extend beyond that form of individual justice to become a major instrument for institutional reform remains perhaps the central research question for those interested in evaluating the long-term consequences of imposing due process on American education.

---

69. Neal & Kirp, *supra* note 4, at 79.
70. Smith, *supra* note 44, at 235.
71. P. KURILOFF, D. KIRP & W. BUSS, *supra* note 23, at 56-60.
72. Mashaw, *supra* 14, at 52-54.

APPENDIX A

DESCRIPTION OF VARIABLES USED IN MULTIPLE REGRESSION ANALYSIS TO
PREDICT HEARING OFFICER DECISION (OUTCOME) IN DUE PROCESS HEARINGS

Variable ID	Variable Name	Content	Range
	I. Variables Describing Selected Child Characteristics		
03	Year of Hearing	2 = 1972 3 = 1973 4 = 1974 5 = 1975	2-5
05	Age	Chronological Age Rounded to the Nearest Year	0-20
06	Sex	1 = male 2 = female	1-2
07	Child Previously in Special Education	0 = no 1 = yes	0-1
Genl 8	Normality of Child's Placement	0 = not yet school age 1 = normal classroom 2 = transition class or resource room 3 = classroom for LD, SED, BI, EMR or physically handicapped 4 = combined EMR-TMR class 5 = TMR classroom 6 = low trainable classroom 7 = SMR-PMR class 8 = temporary homebound instruction 9 = exclusion	1-9
Fac 8	Restrictiveness of Placement	0 = none 1 = classroom in regular public school 2 = public school classroom building unspecified 3 = classroom run by I.U. in regular public school 4 = classroom in special public district education building 5 = classroom run by I.U. in I.U. building 6 = private facility 7 = state instruction	1-7
	II. Variables Describing Parent Performance		
507	Parent Involvement with School Prior to Hearing	Sum of scores for items V48 to V63 after weighting for difficulty of making type of contact[a] 0 = no on V48-V63	0-19

---

[a] Items may be found *infra* app. B, p. 117.

		1 = yes on V48, V49, V54, V57, V58, V60-V63 2 = yes on V51, V52, V55, V59 3 = yes on V50, V53, V56	
508	Parent Involvement Preparing for Hearing Independent of School	Sum of scores for items V64-V81 after weighting as follows: 0 = no contact 1 = nonprofessional contact 4 = professional contact 9 = professional contact, written evaluation obtained	0-87
01	Hearing Open or Closed	0 = closed 1 = open	0-1
38	Lawyer Directs Case for Parents	0 = no 1 = yes	0-1
505	Number of Exhibits Parents Enter	Sum of scores for items V40-V42[b] 0 = none	0-18
506	Number of Witnesses Parents Employ	Sum of scores for items V43-V45, V47[c] 0 = none	0-9
Genl 9	Placement Parents Want	Same as Genl 8	0-9
Fac 9	Restrictiveness Parents Want	Same as Fac 8	0-7
509	Degree Parent Demands Tax School Resources	Sum V89-V91[d] For V89 Program Location 0 = not relevant 1 = program exists in district 2 = program exists in I.U. or state facility 3 = program exists in private facility 4 = program must be created For V90 Transportation 0 = not relevant 1 = readily available 2 = available but inconvenient 3 = not available, transportation must be purchased For V91 Support Services 0 = not needed 1 = readily available 2 = partially or infrequently available 3 = not available, must be created	0-10

---

[b]   Items may be found *infra* app. B, p. 117.
[c]   Items may be found *infra* app. B, p. 117.
[d]   Items may be found *infra* app. B, p. 117.

88	Effectiveness of Parents' Questioning	1 = no questioning 2 = questioning, but not challengingly 3 = questions, challenges, but not within coherent framework 4 = questions, challenges within narrow framework 5 = questions, challenges, within broad framework	1-5
87	Overall Quality of Parents' Presentation	1 = no presentation 2 = presentation subjectively based 3 = presentation objectively based but not adequately supported 4 = presentation objectively based, supported but not well organized 5 = presentation, objectively based, supported, well organized and argued	1-5

III. Selected Variables Describing School Districts

04	District Urbanization	1 = urban school district 2 = suburban school district 3 = rural school district	1-3
IUPOP	Intermediate unit population	Mean population of counties making up each I.U.	27,967 to 1,948,608 (people)
IUMIC	Intermediate unit income level	Weighted average of median incomes of counties making up I.U.	7,596 to 12,747 (dollars)
IUED	Intermediate unit educational level	Weighted average of median educational achievement in years, of people over 25 in counties making up I.U.	10.90 to 12.20 (years)

IV. Selected Variables Describing School District Performance

504	School's Involvement with parent prior to the hearing	Sum of scores for items V29-V31[e] 0 = no 1 = yes	0-3
14	Lawyer Directs Case for School	0 = no 1 = yes	0-1
501	Number of Exhibits Entered by School	Sum of scores for items V15-V17[f] 0 = none	0-39
502	Number of Witnesses Em-	Sum of scores for items V18-V22[g] 0 = none	0-10

---

[e] Items may be found *infra* app. B, p. 117.
[f] Items may be found *infra* app. B, p. 117.
[g] Items may be found *infra* app. B, p. 117.

	ployed by School		
Genl 10	Placement School Wants	Same as Genl 8	0-9
Fac 10	Facility School Wants	Same as Fac 8	0-7
503	Degree to which School Addresses *PARC* requirements	Sum of scores for items V23-V28[h] 0 = no 1 = yes	0-6
36	Overall Quality of School's Presentation	Same as V87	1-5

V. Selected Variables Describing Hearing Officer Affiliation and Behavior

92	Hearing Officer Affiliation	1 = employed by school district 2 = employed by I.U. 3 = employed by college or university	1-3
93	Hearing Officer Does Most of the Questioning	0 = no 1 = yes	0-1
510	Degree to which Hearing Officer Adheres to *PARC* Requirements	Sum of V94, V96-V99[i] 0 = no 1 = yes	0-5
511	Hearing Officer Partiality	Sum of V100-V105[j] after weighting as follows: 1 = totally biased toward school 2 = leaning toward school 3 = impartial 4 = leaning toward Parent 5 = totally biased toward Parent	2-10
217	Hearing Officer Decision (Outcome)	1 = complete loss for Parent 2 = partial loss 3 = compromise 4 = partial win for Parents 5 = complete win for Parents	1-5

---

[h] Items may be found *infra* app. B, p. 118.
[i] Items may be found *infra* app. B, p. 118.
[j] Items may be found *infra* app. B, p. 118.

APPENDIX B

SELECTED VARIABLES

507. Parents involvement with school prior to due process hearing (prior to the hearing, which of the following people were consulted by the parents?)
48. Principal . . . . __
49. School psychologist . . . . __
50. Other teachers . . . . __
51. Classroom teacher (child's present) . . . . __
52. Classroom teacher (child's past) . . . . __
53. Classroom teacher (child's proposed) . . . . __
54. Guidance counselor . . . . __
55. Director of special education (I.U. or district) i.e., person who is in charge of special education . . . . __
56. Attorney for school . . . . __
505. How many exhibits in each of the following groups were submitted as evidence by the parents? . . . . __
40. Diagnostic exhibits . . . . __
41. Exhibits relating to child's performance in school . . . . __
42. Exhibits pertaining to child's family background and home performance . . . . __
506. How many witnesses in each of the following groups appear for the parents? . . . . . . __
43. Medical . . . . __
44. Psychological . . . . __
45. Educational . . . . __
46. Nonprofessional . . . . __
47. Other professional (list below and give total to right) . . . . __

_____   _____

_____   _____

509. Degree to which demands of parent's tax school resources . . . . __
89. Program location (rate 0-4) . . . . __
90. Does transportation to program exist? (rate 0-3) . . . . __
91. Are support services available? (rate 0-3) . . . . __
504. School involvement with parent prior to hearing . . . . __
29. Has the school's evaluation been explained to the parents? . . . . __
30. Has procedure by which school arrived at placement decision been explained to the parents? . . . . __
31. Has content of program child will be in been explained to parents? . . . . __
501. How many exhibits in each of the following groups were submitted as evidence by the school district or intermediate unit? . . . . __
15. Diagnostic exhibits . . . . __
16. Exhibits relating to child's performance in school . . . . __
17. Exhibits pertaining to child's family background and home performance . . . . __
502. How many witnesses in each of the following groups appear for the school? . . . . . . __
18. Medical . . . . __
19. Psychological . . . . __
20. Educational . . . . __
21. Nonprofessional . . . . __
22. Other professional (list below and give total number to the right) . . . . __

_____   _____

_____   _____

503. Degree to which the school addresses the issues of the consent decree .... __
23. Did the school prepare a psychological evaluation .... __
24. Was the school's evaluation broad (versus narrow)? .... __
25. Did the school prepare a prescription which follows from their evaluation? .... __
26. Was the school's prescription flexible and individualized (versus rigid and narrow)? __
27. Did the school propose a program which followed from the prescription? .... __
28. Was the school's program created to meet individual needs? .... __
510. Degree to which the hearing officer adheres to the requirements of the consent degree .... __
94. Does the hearing officer explain appeals procedures? .... __
96. Does the hearing officer attempt to find out from the parent or school if there is a need for the proposed change? (i.e., does he/she inquire into the quality of the evaluation?) .... __
97. Does the hearing officer try to find out whether there is a fit between evaluations and prescription? Does the hearing officer examine the relationship between the evaluation and the prescription? .... __
98. Does the hearing officer try to find out if the program is adequate to meet the prescription? .... __
99. Does the hearing officer address him/herself to the concept of normalization? ..... __
511. Degree to which the hearing officer attempts to run an impartial hearing (each question should be addressed twice, once using the bias scale and once as yes/no) __
101. Does the hearing officer refuse to admit arguably relevant testimony .... __
102. Does the hearing officer admit evidence after expressing doubts about admissibility? __
103. Does the hearing officer make statements or inquiries reasonably necessary to clarify or respond to statements of parents and/or school, and/or their witnesses? .... __
104. Does the hearing officer make statements or inquiries necessary to ensure that parents' or school's stories come out completely? .... __
105. Does the hearing officer show anger, impatience, or sarcasm toward either side? ... __

4

SPECIAL EDUCATION IN ENGLAND AND WALES

WILLIAM G. BUSS*

I

INTRODUCTION

The three most controversial aspects of special education law in the United States are the integration of special and regular children into a joint "mainstream" education, the formal procedural rights of parents to challenge education decisions, and the significant involvement of courts in reviewing decisions of professional educators. The British Parliament has recently enacted legislation that goes far in the direction of making the first two of these features an integral part of the law of England and Wales.[1] The new legislation, the Education Act 1981 (referred to in this article as "EA 1981"), has become effective too recently to generate sufficient experience from which to evaluate its actual implementation.[2] Therefore, this article will analyze the statute itself together with regulations and other government publications extending, elaborating or providing background to the legislative provisions.[3] As interpretations of and questions arising under the new legislation in Britain may sometimes be more sharply brought into focus in the light of comparable provisions of American law, selective comparisons will be made to the Education for All Handicapped Children Act (EAHCA).[4]

Basic and pervasive differences between the United Kingdom and the United States and between the British and American legal systems must qualify and caution an American's understanding of the special education law

---

* Theodore C. Michels Professor of Law, University of Iowa.

The author would like to acknowledge and express appreciation for the work done on this article by Patricia Blackford, Nancy Meloy, and James Fishkin, members of Iowa College of Law classes, respectively, of 1984, 1985, and 1986.

1. Education Act, 1981, ch. 60, received Royal Assent Oct. 30, 1981. Separate, comparable legislation that has been enacted for Scotland will not be considered here.

2. For most of its provisions, the new act became effective April 1, 1983.

3. In the spring and summer of 1983, I had the opportunity to discuss the background, meaning and anticipated implementation of EA 1981 with several British educators who were concerned with special education through the University of Durham, local educational authorities, private organizations and the Department of Education and Science. These people were extremely generous with their time and provided me with invaluable assistance.

4. Pub. L. No. 94-142, 89 Stat. 774 (1975) (codified as amended at 20 U.S.C. §§ 1400-1421 (1982)). Systematic comparative treatment would require consideration of § 504 of the Rehabilitation Act of 1973, 29 U.S.C. § 794, and of state legislation as well.

Professor David Kirp has written a fascinating and provocative article which compares, generally unfavorably, the "professional" British approach with the American "legal" approach to special education decisionmaking. Kirp, *Professionalization as a Policy Choice: British Special Education in Comparative Perspective*, 34 WORLD POL. 137 (1982).

governing England and Wales.[5] There is no Bill of Rights or Equal Protection Clause in the United Kingdom. There is no concept, in the American sense, of individual "constitutional" legal rights in British law.[6] There is, accordingly, nothing in British law that can be compared to the United States Supreme Court's decisions dealing with equality and racial segregation[7] or to decisions of lower federal courts dealing with the constitutional rights of handicapped students.[8] Under the British constitutional system, individual interests are always, ultimately, subordinate to the legislative power. The paramount doctrine is Parliamentary sovereignty.[9]

There is also a fundamental difference between the unitary British system and the dual (federal) system of the United States. In the United Kingdom, *all* legislative power is vested in the "Queen in Parliament"; there is nothing comparable to the sovereignty of the several states in the United States. Therefore, if there is to be legislation dealing with special education in the United Kingdom, it will be enacted by the Parliament of the United Kingdom. In this respect, EA 1981 is not at all remarkable. By contrast, the conventional wisdom in the United States is that education is a subject for state legislation. A comprehensive piece of federal legislation, like the EAHCA, is an aberration. In the light of this apparent difference, one might conclude that there is a greater degree of comparability between the EAHCA and EA 1981 than would ordinarily be possible. In a sense, this is no doubt true. Yet the basic difference does remain. Unlike the situation in England and Wales under the new British legislation, the law of special education in the United States remains a complicated amalgam of federal and state legislation. That is true both in terms of the EAHCA itself and more generally in terms of the existence of overlapping state and federal law. There is little doubt that the Supreme Court's restrictive interpretation of the EAHCA in *Board of Education v. Rowley*[10] was substantially influenced by "federalism" values and the persistent resistance to recognition of "undue" federal power in education.[11] No such consideration will influence the interpretation of EA 1981.

In one important way, a focus on the contrast between the American federal and the British unitary legal systems masks a significant common feature of the two educational systems. In both countries, there is a strong tradition of local control of education. No doubt, this means that positive legislation provides a less complete picture of reality in both systems than it first appears

---

5. Of course these grounds for caution are pointedly relevant for an American legal scholar writing about the British legal system's treatment of a difficult educational problem.

6. Under treaty commitments, however, individual rights claims of British subjects may be taken to the European Court of Human Rights. *See* S. BAILEY, D. HARRIS & B. JONES, CIVIL LIBERTIES: CASES AND MATERIALS 17-32 (1980); R. BEDDARD, HUMAN RIGHTS AND EUROPE (2d ed. 1980).

7. *E.g.*, Brown v. Board of Educ., 347 U.S. 483 (1954).

8. *E.g.*, Mills v. Board of Educ., 348 F. Supp. 866 (D.D.C. 1972); Pennsylvania Assoc. for Retarded Children v. Commonwealth, 334 F. Supp. 1257 (E.D. Pa. 1971), 343 F. Supp. 279 (E.D. Pa 1972).

9. *See* S. DE SMITH, CONSTITUTIONAL AND ADMINISTRATIVE LAW 73-104 (4th ed. 1981).

10. 458 U.S. 176 (1982).

11. *See* Yudof, *Education for the Handicapped: Rowley in Perspective*, 92 AM. J. EDUC. 163, 173 (1984).

to do. Local authorities are the primary educational providers in both countries, and it is they who must directly put educational policy changes into
effect. The variation in educational resources and preferences from area to
area will inevitably qualify the implementation of educational policies set at
national (or state) levels.

A fundamental difference of relatively recent vintage between the
legal/educational systems of the United States and the United Kingdom concerns the role of the judiciary. The ubiquitously quoted observation of de
Tocqueville that all issues in America eventually become legal issues is not a
recent revelation. But it is widely accepted, with varying emotions, that there
has been a quantum leap in litigation and judicial activism in the last quarter
century in many areas of public policy, including education.[12] The situation
in the United Kingdom could not be more different. In the leading text on
education law in the United Kingdom,[13] there is no index entry for "judicial
review" or any comparable subject encompassing the action of the courts in
enforcing British education laws. The omission is not a flaw of scholarship
but an accurate reflection of the British system. Of course, education cases
are occasionally litigated in the United Kingdom,[14] and the British legal
system provides for legal challenges to educational decisions. But judicial
involvement has been rare indeed, and there is simply nothing in the British
experience comparable to regular and extensive litigation of educational
policy issues in the United States.[15]

The advent of comprehensive special education legislation in England and
Wales should be deeply interesting to Americans. Despite all of the cultural,
legal and political differences between the two countries, fundamental values
are shared and fundamental similarities remain. Certainly, there is a very
great similarity in the conditions and educational needs of handicapped children in the United States and the United Kingdom. The United States can
learn from the successes and failures that emerge from the new legislative
framework for providing special education in England and Wales. At this preliminary juncture one cannot say how the law will be carried out, but, by
examining the legislative framework now, one can be in a better position to
understand the actual implementation that is beginning to take place.

Consideration of EA 1981 in this article will focus on several questions:

(1) Which children are entitled to a special education under the statute?

(2) What is the nature of the procedural rights given to parents?

(3) What enforcement mechanisms does the statute establish for assuring
compliance by responsible officials?

---

12. *But see* Galanter, *Reading the Landscape of Disputes: What We Know and Don't Know (And Think We
Know) About Our Allegedly Contentious and Litigious Society,* 31 U.C.L.A. L. REV. 4 (1983).
13. G. TAYLOR & J.B. SAUNDERS, THE LAW OF EDUCATION (8th ed. 1976).
14. *See, e.g.,* Secretary of State for Educ. and Science v. Metropolitan Borough of Tameside,
[1976] 3 All E.R. 665; Cumings v. Birkenhead Corp., [1971] 2 All E.R. 881.
15. Not everyone concedes that the British judiciary has stayed so clear of policymaking. *See*
J.A.G. GRIFFITH, THE POLITICS OF THE JUDICIARY (2d ed. 1981) (includes subsection on "student"
cases).

(4) Is there any role for the courts in the implementation of EA 1981?

(5) What, if any, content can be given to the special education required to be provided?

(6) Specifically, what sort of integration (mainstreaming) is required and under what circumstances must it be provided?

Although these questions are not totally separable, an attempt will be made to deal with them discretely as well as to note the interrelationships.

II

CHILDREN WITH A STATUTORY ENTITLEMENT TO SPECIAL EDUCATION

The Education Act 1981 makes important revisions in the law of special education in England and Wales, but it does not establish legal recognition of special education for the first time. Special education has been supported at some level of government in the United Kingdom since at least 1874[16] and became an integral part of British education with the enactment of the Education Act 1944 ("EA 1944").[17] Further enactments of education law in the 1970's have resulted in an educational policy under which all children are entitled to an education[18] and which presumes, in principle, that special education should be provided on an integrated (mainstreamed) basis.[19] Thus there was a substantial precedent of special education legislation in existence before the specific policy studies leading to EA 1981 were undertaken. Those studies which were immediate sources of EA 1981 were the "Warnock Report," *Special Educational Needs, a Report of the Committee of Enquiry into the Education of Handicapped Children and Young People,*[20] and the government "White Paper," *Special Needs in Education,*[21] which followed the Warnock Report.

The Warnock Report had its beginning in 1973. At that time, Margaret Thatcher, MP, then Secretary of State for Education and Science, proposed to appoint a committee (not actually established until 1974)

> To review educational provision in England, Scotland and Wales for children and young people handicapped by disabilities of body or mind, taking account of the medical aspects of their needs, together with arrangements to prepare them for entry into

---

16. *See* SPECIAL EDUCATION NEEDS, A REPORT OF THE COMMITTEE OF ENQUIRY INTO THE EDUCATION OF HANDICAPPED CHILDREN AND YOUNG PEOPLE, CMND. 7212, at 9-12 (1978) (London School Board established class for deaf in 1874) [hereinafter cited as Warnock Report, after the committee chairman, Mary Warnock]. Prior to government-supported education, which began with the Elementary Education Act in 1870, *see* H.C. DENT, EDUCATION IN ENGLAND AND WALES 9 (2d ed. 1982), there were private schools for disabled children and custodial institutions for "mentally defective" children. *See* Warnock Report at 8-9.

17. Education Act, 1944, 7 & 8 Geo. 6, ch. 31, §§ 8, 33, 34; *see* Warnock Report, *supra* note 16, at 18-25; S. TOMLINSON, A SOCIOLOGY OF SPECIAL EDUCATION 49-52 (1982).

18. Education (Handicapped Children) Act, 1970, ch. 52 (severely mentally retarded). *See* Warnock Report, *supra* note 16, at 28-29.

19. Education Act, 1976, ch. 81, § 10. By its terms, section 10 was to become operable on a date specified by the Secretary of State for Education and Science, *id.* § 10(3). This date was never set, and section 10 was eventually replaced by the provisions of EA 1981. *See* EA 1981, sched. 4 (repealing § 10).

20. *See supra* note 16.

21. SPECIAL NEEDS IN EDUCATION, CMND. 7996 (1980) [hereinafter cited as White Paper].

employment; to consider the most effective use of resources for these purposes; and to make recommendations.[22]

The Committee received evidence from approximately 250 organizations and 120 individuals.[23] Published in May 1978, the committee's report consisted of 366 pages, excluding appendices and index, of extensive discussion on a wide variety of special education topics—history, assessment, placement (including mainstreaming), curriculum, children younger and older than compulsory attendance ages, parental involvement, voluntary organizations, transition to adult life, teacher education, staffing, role of health and social services, recordkeeping (including confidentiality), and research and development. The report's 220 recommendations, for which no cost estimates were prepared,[24] were almost entirely devoted to structural and procedural methods of delivering special education and were virtually silent about the details of the education that would be delivered.[25] Teacher training and educational provisions for children under five and for those over sixteen were listed as the "Three Areas of First Priority."[26] The report also placed considerable stress on the adoption of a noncategorical approach to educating children with special educational needs[27] and proposed substantial revision in the process of assessing and meeting these needs.[28]

According to the White Paper, the government decided to reform the law in the light of the Warnock Committee's findings.[29] The White Paper summarized the government's position and its proposals for legislation. Although some specific Warnock recommendations were rejected, the White Paper accepted the substance of the Warnock Report. It proposed to adopt the major Warnock recommendations for replacing categories of handicap by a more open approach that identified children with special educational needs and arranged to meet those needs. In tension with the Warnock Report's assumption that meeting those needs would be expensive and that the required funds would be forthcoming, the White Paper was full of admonitions about the unavailability of funds and the necessity of making do within the limitations of the "current economic situation."[30]

The statute that was enacted as an outgrowth of the work of the Warnock

22. *See* Warnock Report, *supra* note 16, at 1.
23. *See* Warnock Report, *supra* note 16, app. A.
24. *See* Warnock Report, *supra* note 16, at 325-26, 329. In part, the absence of cost estimates was claimed to be a calculated avoidance of what could have become a point of vulnerability in view of the difficulty and impeachability of most cost estimates. *See* The Times (London) Educational Supplement, May 26, 1978, at 1, col. 1.
25. *See* Kirp, *Professionalization as a Policy Choice: British Special Education in Comparative Perspective,* 34 WORLD POL. 137, 157 (1982).
26. Warnock Report, *supra* note 16, at 336-37. *See also id.* at 327-28, 329-34.
27. *See id.* at 42-49, 338.
28. *See id.* at 50-72, 339-41.
29. *See* White Paper, *supra* note 21, at 5 ¶ 1. The Warnock committee was established under one Conservative government, and the committee's work led to a White Paper and the enactment of EA 1981 under a different Conservative government. In between, the committee work and its report were completed during a Labor government.
30. *Id.* at 11 ¶ 28; *see id.* at 8-9 ¶ 20, 10-11 ¶ 25, 11-12 ¶ 31, 12 ¶ 34, 13 ¶¶ 36 & 38, 16 ¶¶ 47-48, 21 ¶ 65, 22 ¶ 70, 23 ¶ 73.

Committee and the government White Paper, EA 1981, bears a superficial resemblance to the EAHCA in its broad outline: it identifies children needing special education;[31] it provides for a method to analyze and specify those special educational needs;[32] and it then entitles the child to the education specified.[33] Both statutes impose various duties on the local educational unit[34] to determine and provide the required education. Both statutes give the child's parent (and also, under the EAHCA, the child) various rights to participate in the decisionmaking process and to challenge decisions of education officials. Both statutes subject the decisions of the local educational officials to review by other government authorities.[35] Both statutes include provisions requiring integration (or "mainstreaming") under specified conditions, and both statutes otherwise leave the substantive content of the education to be provided essentially free of any express prescription.

Under the approach of both statutes, each of which begins with a definition of which children are "special," there is an unavoidable linedrawing problem. A distinction must be drawn between children who are "regular" or "ordinary" and children who are "special." Some ordinary children, it is assumed, may have more difficulty in school than others—whether from mental, emotional, social, or physical causes—but they are not "special" until they have crossed a line separating differences in kind. In both the United Kingdom and the United States, much experience indicates that this line is often hard to draw and is often drawn erroneously.[36] This linedrawing is especially difficult and error prone when the handicapping category is one identified by symptoms without physiological or medical causes.[37] Nevertheless, very much of what is done, and what the law expects and permits to be done, assumes that these differences in kind exist. Rhetorically, the Warnock Report strongly resisted categorical distinctions between special and regular education. However, it was unable to escape from a conceptual framework based on the distinction between ordinary and special children.[38] EA 1981 follows Warnock in relying upon the distinction between children who need special education and children who do not.

---

31. "Handicapped child" under the EAHCA; child who has "special educational needs" under EA 1981.
32. In an "individualized education program," or "IEP," under the EAHCA; in a "statement" under EA 1981.
33. A "free appropriate public education" under the EAHCA; "special educational provision" under EA 1981.
34. "Agency" under the EAHCA; "authority" under EA 1981.
35. The EAHCA, but not EA 1981. expressly includes courts as one such reviewing body.
36. D. GALLOWAY & C. GOODWIN, EDUCATING SLOW LEARNING AND MALADJUSTED CHILDREN: INTEGRATION OR SEPARATION? 6-12 (1979); 1 ISSUES IN CLASSIFICATION OF CHILDREN vii, 159-317 (N. Hobbes ed. 1975); 2 *id.* at 502 *passim;* D. KIRP & M. YUDOF, EDUCATIONAL POLICY AND THE LAW 542 (2d ed. 1982); D. PRITCHARD, EDUCATION AND THE HANDICAPPED 214-16 (1963); Warnock Report, *supra* note 16, at 38 ¶ 3.7, 42-43 ¶ 3.23; Kirp, *Schools as Sorters: The Constitutional and Policy Implications of Student Classifications,* 121 U. PA. L. REV. 705, 719 (1973); Kirp, Buss & Kuriloff, *Legal Defense of Special Education: Empirical Studies and Procedural Proposals,* 62 CALIF. L. REV. 40, 43 (1974).
37. *See* S. TOMLINSON, *supra* note 17, at 65-72, 96.
38. The Warnock Commission was well aware of its dilemma. *See* Warnock Report, *supra* note 16, at 43, 69.

Despite the linedrawing difficulties, the general statutory scheme adopted by EA 1981 and the EAHCA seems to make sense. The remaining sections of this article consider some of the details of EA 1981 concerning the administrative and judicial roles in enforcing this statutory scheme and the procedural and substantive rights of parents and children. This section focuses on identifying the children who are given a right[39] to special education under EA 1981.

To identify the statutorily protected children, one must begin by looking at certain basic assumptions and recommendations of the Warnock Report. First, the Warnock Report determined that the number of children needing special education amounted to approximately 20 percent of school enrollment, rather than the 2 percent which had been reported in the past.[40] This dramatic increase in the estimated number of special children was based upon empirical studies of various school populations,[41] and it was also a product of a revised and expanded concept of which children should be regarded as special.[42]

Second, the Warnock Report recommended that the past practice within England and Wales of reporting "handicapped children" by specific categories of handicap be abandoned.[43] This approach was found to be undesirable for several reasons. First of all, the labels themselves were often stigmatizing. For example, the largest category was called "Educationally Subnormal (Moderate)" (ESN(M)).[44] Furthermore, the categorical approach was thought to be both rigid and inaccurate. It reduced an unlimited number of educationally disadvantaging conditions into a few categories. Correspondingly, it encouraged the creation of a relatively few, predetermined, educational treatments corresponding to the handicap categories. Thus, for example, if a child was diagnosed as an ESN(M), he was given the educational placement established for all children who were ESN(M)'s. Finally, a fundamental purpose of the Warnock recommendations was to wipe out "the sharp distinction between two groups of children—the handicapped and the non-handicapped."[45] A better system, according to the Warnock Report, would be to identify children who were in any manner in need of special education and then to determine what that need required without any predetermined programmatic restraints. The child's education was to be fitted to the child's needs rather than the child fitted to preexisting educational placements.

---

39. The statute does not talk about "rights" of children, and the U.S. concept of student rights or children's rights may not translate well into British thinking. However, the statute clearly does describe duties owed to certain children or their parents, and it characterizes certain parental safeguards as "rights." *See, e.g.,* EA 1981, §§ 5(7), 7(9)(b). Both the Warnock Report and the White Paper do speak of "rights." *See* Warnock Report *supra* note 16, at 48 (rights of parents), 106 (children may use as of right the general facilities available at school); White Paper, *supra* note 21, at 18-19 ¶¶ 58-59. For convenience, the children to whom a statutory duty is owed under EA 1981 will sometimes be characterized as having "rights."
40. *See* Warnock Report, *supra* note 16, at 37-41.
41. *Id.*
42. *See id.* at 43-48.
43. *See id.* at 42-43.
44. Roughly corresponding to Educable Mentally Retarded (EMR) in the United States.
45. *See* Warnock Report, *supra* note 16, at 43.

Under a third basic assumption of the Warnock Report, "only a minority of children who have been ascertained as needing special education will be recorded."[46] The system of recording was expressly designed "to safeguard the interests of the minority of children with special educational needs who have severe and complex disabilities or difficulties."[47] (This group could be called the "narrow group" of children who need special education.) This recommendation obviously assumed that there is also a distinct and larger group of *unrecorded* children having special educational needs. (This group could be called the "wider group" of children who need special education.)[48] The Warnock Report recommended that this "wider group" of children having special educational needs receive appropriate statutory protection outside the formal recording process.[49]

The general understanding is that all of these elements from the Warnock Report have found their way into EA 1981. There is room to question, however, whether any statutory status has been given to the Warnock Report's assumptions concerning the number of children needing special education or the division of those children into "narrow" and "wider" groups. It is also questionable whether the statute supports the recommendation that the "wider" group of children needing special education receive statutory protection. EA 1981 does clearly adopt the Warnock Report's recommendation to replace handicap categories by a more general yet more individualized approach to educational need. In fact, the resulting innocuous statutory definition of children with "special educational needs"[50] may be partly responsible for the confusion about what the statute does. The term, "special educational needs," has meaning, without definition, in a general, descriptive sense. But it also has a *different*—somewhat artificial—meaning as used in EA 1981. Broadly speaking, children who have "special educational needs" under the Act are children who are entitled to "special educational provision"; more narrowly, *at least some* children who have "special educational needs" are children for whom a statement specifying the special educational provision must be made and maintained.[51] This statement-making process is what the Warnock Report called "recording."

As Warnock contemplated, and as it is now widely assumed,[52] there may

---

46. *See id.* AT 48 ¶ 3.44; *see also id.* at 45 ¶ 3.31.
47. *Id.* at 45 ¶ 3.31; *see also id.* at 72 ¶ 4.79, 338 ¶ 4.
48. *See id.* at 45-48.
49. *See id,* at 48 ¶ 3.42, 338 ¶ 5.
50. EA 1981, § 1. "Special educational needs" are defined as needs of a child who has a "learning difficulty" which "calls for special educational provision." *Id.* § 1(1). "Learning difficulty" and "special educational provision" are themselves operationally defined terms: a child has a "learning difficulty" if he has "greater difficulty in learning than the majority of children his age," *id.* § 1(2)(a), *or* if he has a "disability which either prevents or hinders him from making use of educational facilities of a kind generally provided," *id.* § 1(2)(b). "Special educational provision" is educational provision "additional to" or "different from" the educational provision generally made available in regular schools. *Id.* § 1(3)(a).
51. *See id.* §§ 1, 5-7.
52. *See* Hannon, *The Education Act 1981: New Rights and Duties in Special Education,* 1982 J. Soc. WELFARE L. 275, 281; *see also* authorities cited *infra* note 66; Masters, *Cooperation—the Key to Success,* CONTACT, Winter 1982, at 56.

well be children who need special education in its general, descriptive sense but who do not go through the recording process culminating in a statement. The statute neither compels nor precludes that result. Under the statute, it is possible that all children who, descriptively, need special education could be identified as children who, definitionally, have "special educational needs" and receive a formal statement.[53] If, as seems likely, the statute is construed consistently with the Warnock Report to recognize a "wider group" of children who are not entitled to a statement, though in some sense need special education, an important interpretive question arises.

May some of these children come within the statutory definition of "special educational needs" and be entitled to special educational provision even though they are not entitled to a statement? Or do all children not entitled to a statement fall outside the definition of children who have "special educational needs"? At least in a narrow sense, the answer to this question turns on the language of sections 5(6) and 7(1) of EA 1981. According to section 7(1), where an assessment has been made,

> the local educational authority . . . shall, if they are of the opinion that they should determine the special educational provision that should be made for [the child], make a statement of his special educational needs and maintain that statement . . . .[54]

Read literally, this language seems to say that the local educational authority has discretion to decide whether they "should" determine the special educational provision or not.

Nothing in EA 1981 provides the slightest suggestion of the standard for making this decision. The Warnock Report and the White Paper indicate that the statement process ("recording") should be reserved for those cases involving the most severe and difficult forms of handicap and thus justifying the administrative costs of the statement-making and -maintaining process.[55] So far as EA 1981 itself is concerned, however, the local authority is seemingly left with arbitrary power to select, from among children defined by Parliament to have "special educational needs," those who will receive the special statutory protection related to a statement. Furthermore, nothing in EA 1981 suggests what entity other than the local educational authority is to determine the special educational provision, and nothing in EA 1981 suggests any mechanism for making this determination.[56] The White Paper suggests, however, that this determination might be made informally through some combination of parent, teacher, school, and local educational authority.[57]

---

53. The definitions of section 1, *see supra* note 50, may reveal an expectation that some difficulties in learning are not "significantly" greater than those of a majority of same-age children or that some disabilities do not "impede" or "prevent" use of educational facilities and thus do not implicate a statutory "learning difficulty"; or that a statutorily implicated "learning difficulty" need not "call for special educational provision" and thus will not bring into play the technical concept of "special educational needs." That the statute discloses such an expectation does not demonstrate that the expectation will be realized in the statute's application.

54. Section 5(6) covers the decision by an LEA that "they are not required to determine the special educational provision."

55. *See supra* text accompanying note 47; White Paper, *supra* note 21, at 10 ¶ 24.

56. *See* Hannon, *supra* note 52, at 281.

57. *See* White Paper, *supra* note 21, at 10-11 ¶¶ 25-28; 15 ¶ 45; 16 ¶ 47.

Under an alternative reading of section 7(1) (and section 5(6)), the local educational authority's responsibility is to decide whether the child has "special educational needs"; if the child has such needs, then the local authority "should determine the special educational provision that should be made" for the child, and must make and maintain a statement. Admittedly, the statutory words of section 7(1) are only awkwardly designed for such an interpretation.[58] Still, the words will bear that reading, and it seems a less problematic reading of the statute as a whole for reasons already given.

Under the literal reading of section 7(1) (and section 5(6)), the "wider group" of children would be within EA 1981, but EA 1981 would provide no mechanism for enforcing the duty owed to these children.[59] Under the alternative reading, the "wider group" of children would have no rights under EA 1981, but all children who had "special educational needs" would be entitled to a statement and the statutory protection associated with a statement. Neither reading is wholly consistent with the promise of the Warnock Report, which anticipated both that the "wider group" of children would be within the statute and that these children would have some meaningful statutory protection.[60]

The generally accepted understanding, as well as the position of the Department of Education and Science,[61] is that this "wider group" of children who need special education do have statutory protection even though they do not come within the formal protection of EA 1981 associated with the "statement." At first blush, it appears that there is support for this conclusion in section 2 of EA 1981, which seems to follow the recommendation of the Warnock Report[62] in amending section 8 of EA 1944. According to the EA 1981 amendment, section 8 of EA 1944 (the basic education law of England and Wales) requires local educational authorities to see that *special educational provision* is made for pupils who have *special educational needs*.[63] Upon reflection, however, it can be seen that this provision merely begs the interpretive question just considered. If, taking the "literal" interpretation, section 7(1) requires a local educational authority to determine the special educational provision in *only some* of the instances involving children with special educational needs, then the "wider group" is covered by EA 1981's amendment of

---

58. The statutory language is not even designed well for the "literal" reading. A duty to decide whether or not a statement is required to meet a child's special education needs would have been clearer and more to the point. *Cf.* White Paper, *supra* note 21, at 14 ¶ 39.

59. *See* Hannon, *supra* note 52, at 281.

60. *See* Warnock Report, *supra* note 16, at 48 ¶ 3.42; *see also id.* at 338 ¶ 5.

61. Correspondence from representative of Division of Special Education, Dept. of Educ. & Science (Oct. 17, 1984). *See also* text accompanying notes 65 & 66; authorities cited note 66; Masters, *supra* note 52.

62. *See supra* note 60.

63. EA 1981, § 2(1). Section 8(1) of EA 1944 imposes a duty on LEA's "to secure" sufficient primary and secondary schools for their areas, specifically requiring that the schools afford opportunities for education in view of the student's ages, abilities and aptitudes. Prior to its replacement by the new provisions of EA 1981, § 8(2)(c) of EA 1944 provided that LEA's have regard "to the need for securing that provision is made for pupils who suffer from any *disability of mind or body* by providing, either in special schools or otherwise, special educational treatment, that is to say, education by *special methods appropriate for persons suffering from that disability.*" (Emphasis supplied).

EA 1944. If the alternative interpretation is correct, however, the section 8 (EA 1944) duty applies only to children receiving the full, formal, statement-related protection of EA 1981, for only they have "special educational needs".[64]

Does choosing between these interpretations concerning the "wider group" matter? It depends. If the widely accepted view is that the statute has adopted the policy recommended by Warnock, it may not matter at all—at least until such time as some person or government entity has a strong interest in arguing for a limited interpretation of EA 1981. The position of the Department of Education and Science is evidenced by its explanatory circular,[65] which treats students in the "wider group" as if they had statutory entitlement apart from their not receiving statement protection. According to the circular, EA 1981 "places a wider obligation on LEA's [local education authorities] to secure that adequate provision is made for children with special educational needs."[66] Perhaps revealingly, the circular goes on to describe the "general principles"—matters outside the direct mandate of the statute—which should apply for the children in the "wider group."[67]

Whether the correct interpretation concerning the exclusion or inclusion of the "wider group" from EA 1981 matters also depends on exactly how large that group is. As already pointed out, the Warnock Report concluded that the school-age population of children who need special education at some time is nearer to 20 percent than the 2 percent previously recognized and treated as handicapped.[68] The Warnock Report implied that a substantial part of this additional 18 percent included children with less serious, temporary, or occasional difficulties[69] and implied that these children would make up the "wider group" who would not receive the formal ("recording") treatment.[70]

The Warnock Report also contains conflicting signals about the relationship between the old 2 percent group and the new recommended narrow group of children who should be recorded and entitled to extensive statutory

---

64. Under section 8(1) of EA 1944, the LEA's general duty to educate children according to their "ages, abilities, and aptitudes," see note 63 supra, clearly survives EA 1981. The terms "abilities" and "aptitudes" could be construed broadly enough to cover any "wider group" of children who need special education but who are shut out of EA 1981. In that sense, there may be some statutory protection for the "wider group." But such protection in no sense stems from EA 1981. As a matter of statutory right, it is the protection that has existed since 1944. That is not what Warnock was talking about nor what EA 1981 is generally understood to do. See also EA 1981, § 21(2); id. sched. 3, § 6.

65. DEPARTMENT OF EDUCATION AND SCIENCE, CIRCULAR 1/83, ASSESSMENTS AND STATEMENTS OF SPECIAL EDUCATIONAL NEEDS (January 31, 1983) [hereinafter cited as DES CIRCULAR 1/83].

66. Id. at 1 ¶ 2. To the same effect, see ADVISORY CENTRE FOR EDUCATION, SPECIAL EDUCATION HANDBOOK 4-5 (1983); cf. DEPARTMENT OF EDUCATION AND SCIENCE, CIRCULAR 8/81, EDUCATION ACT 1981, 3 ¶ 9 (December 7, 1981) (characterizing the "wider" group as "children with special educational needs") [hereinafter cited as DES CIRCULAR 8/81].

67. DES CIRCULAR 1/83, supra note 65, at 1-2.

68. See supra note 40.

69. See Warnock Report, supra note 16, at 40, 47-48, 100; see also DES CIRCULAR 8/81, supra note 66, at 3 ¶ 9.

70. See Warnock Report, supra note 16, at 47-48, 72 ¶ 4.79, 100; see also White Paper, supra note 21, at 10 ¶ 24, 14 ¶ 39; DES CIRCULAR 8/81, supra note 66, at 3 ¶ 9.

protection. Children previously classified as ESN(M) and maladjusted were the two largest components of the old 2 percent group,[71] and children previously given "remedial" instruction and children considered "disruptive" students were not "special" at all—in recognized statutory terms—prior to EA 1981.[72] Yet the Warnock Report indicates ESN(M), maladjusted, remedial, and disruptive students are prime candidates for integrated education in ordinary schools.[73] At times, the Warnock Report seems to suggest that children educated in ordinary schools are part of the "wider group," not to be recorded and formally safeguarded.[74] But the Warnock Report also leaves no doubt that, for such integrated education, additional or different educational provision would be required in the form of supplementary resources and curricular adjustment.[75]

Of course, it would be *possible* under the statute that some children receiving an integrated education would be entitled to statements, while others would be part of the "wider group" not entitled to statements.[76] Indeed, nothing in the vague statutory definitions of "special educational needs" and "special educational provision"—nor in the statutory procedures through which these labels are attached to particular children—forces the Warnock assumptions and the statutory operation to be congruent. Although the Warnock background is likely to influence the interpretation of the Act, it seems likely that the perceived consequences of interpretation will be even more influential. For example, if children without statements are found to be totally outside EA 1981, it is likely that more children will be found to be entitled to statements. Conversely, if all children who have special educational needs are entitled to statements, it is likely that "special educational needs" will be read narrowly to avoid an undue burden on the statement-making process.

It will be interesting to compare the total number of children brought within the statutory coverage with the Warnock figures or, for that matter, with the total number of children reported on the old categorical basis. It will also be interesting to learn just which children are within and without the new statutory scheme and how the identity of each group compares with the particular handicap categories covered under prior law. Following the Warnock Report and the more neutral terminology of EA 1981, the new forms used for collecting data no longer report children by the old handicap categories.[77] Instead, the new forms are divided by "curriculum types"—Mainstream Plus Support, Modified or Developmental—and call for additional information concerning children in each curriculum type on the basis of ten "aspects of disability." While these ten disability "aspects" are comparable to the old

71. *See* White Paper, *supra* note 21, at 8 ¶ 20.
72. *See* Warnock Report, *supra* note 16, at 46-47; S. TOMLINSON, *supra* note 17, at 63-64, 69.
73. *See* Warnock Report, *supra* note 16, at 219-20, 221-23.
74. *See id.* at 45 ¶ 3.31, 48 ¶ 3.44, 60 ¶ 4.35, 61 ¶¶ 4.39-.40, 70 ¶¶ 4.71-.72.
75. *See id.* at 108-14.
76. *See* White Paper, *supra* note 21, at 14 ¶ 41.
77. *See* DEPARTMENT OF EDCUCATION AND SCIENCE, FORM 7M (1984).

handicap categories, they are subdivided somewhat differently.[78] Moreover, instead of reporting each student in one "aspect" (the pattern followed under the old handicap categories), each student can be reported in as many "aspects" as descriptively apply.[79]

This new data collection approach obviously will give more complete relevant information than did the old approach. The very fact that a new approach has been adopted, however, will substantially limit any attempt to compare the particular educational provision being made available for students having a particular disadvantage under the old and new law. More generally, the lack of congruency of the old and new reporting approaches will impede any comparison of children included and excluded under the old and new statutory coverage. The system of collecting data under the new special educational law may create ambiguity in still one other aspect. In completing the new forms for this purpose, Head Teachers in ordinary schools are asked to report on students having "special educational needs." Nothing in the form itself is calculated to alert respondents to the specialized usage of that phrase under the statute. The directions to the Head Teachers, however, indicate that, after a transitional period, this term will refer only to those students "for whom a statement is maintained."[80] Consequently, if the instructions are heeded, the special students reported will not include those in the "wider group"—those who, in the common vernacular, have special educational needs (but do not qualify for a statement); there would be no systematic count of this group. Of course, if the directions are not understood or not followed for any reason, some reports may include special children in the "wider group" as well.[81]

One early indication of children who will be placed in the "wider group"

---

78. Compare the old handicap categories listed in DES FORM 7M (1983):
   (a) blind;
   (b) partially sighted;
   (c) deaf;
   (d) partially hearing;
   (e) educationally sub-normal;
   (f) epileptic;
   (g) maladjusted;
   (h) physically handicapped;
   (i) pupils suffering from speech defect;
   (j) delicate;
with new aspects of disability listed on DES FORM 7 (1984):
   (1) physical;
   (2) epilepsy;
   (3) communication: speech;
   (4) communication: language;
   (5) blind;
   (6) partially sighted;
   (7) deaf;
   (8) partially hearing;
   (9) behavioural/social;
   (10) emotional.
79. *See* Instructions accompanying DES FORM 7 (1984).
80. *Id.*
81. In one part of the form, students in "special classes" (as designated by the local authority—

has been provided by the Department of Education and Science. In its Circular 1/83, DES has advised that local educational authorities may exclude from formal protection children for whom "additional tuition and remedial provision" is provided from ordinary schools' "own resources"; children attending "a reading centre"; children attending "a unit for disruptive pupils"; children having only a need "of short duration"; children placed "for a short period" in a special school for assessment with the parent's agreement; and children placed temporarily in a hospital special school as a result of admission to the hospital on medical grounds.[82] It would be very difficult to conclude that none of these children are children who have "special educational needs." They are apparently designated as children with special educational needs who are nonetheless not entitled to statement protection.[83] Perhaps this designation is understandable as to those whose handicapping condition or status may be of short duration. It is much more difficult to understand as to disruptive children and children with remedial problems.

This difficulty points up the darker underside of the uncertainty about the "wider group" excluded from all or some of the EA 1981 protection. The preceding discussion has proceeded on the unstated assumption that parents of handicapped children would not want their children to be part of the "wider group" if the wider group receives no protection under EA 1981. It is common knowledge, however, that parents often regard it as a bane rather than a boon to have their children assigned to "special education." Professor Tomlinson has criticized Warnock and EA 1981 on the ground that a larger special education net would be cast for children, who would be mainly working class and who would be dragged down by stigmatizing labels and inferior education.[84] Parents who share this concern might welcome placement of their children in the "wider group" if that meant, in effect, that these children would be left alone—left without "special" labels and special treatment. It is possible, as Tomlinson evidently fears, that from the perspective of such parents, these children may have the worst of both worlds: a special label and different education but no meaningful statutory protection.[85] The possibility of such a result would be enhanced by a reading of the statute under which certain children can be categorized and treated differently as children with "special educational needs," yet not protected under the statutory provisions concerning statements.

---

but not the school) must be reported, and there is no warning direction here tying the reported students to the statement.

82. DES CIRCULAR 1/83, supra note 65, at 4 ¶¶ 15, 16.

83. Letter from representative of Div. of Special Educ., Dept. of Educ. & Science (Oct. 17, 1984); see also DES CIRCULAR 1/83, supra note 65, at 4 ¶ 15. But see id. at 3 ¶¶ 12, 13 (suggesting that these students are not children with [special] "needs" requiring "special educational provision").

84. See S. TOMLINSON, supra note 17, at 68-72, 177.

85. See Hannon, supra note 52, at 281.

III
PARENTAL RIGHTS AND PROCEDURAL DUE PROCESS

There may be some uncertainty about which children receive what protection under EA 1981. There can be no question that EA 1981 provides very extensive procedures through which parents may participate in determining the statutory coverage. In this respect, EA 1981 is comparable to the EAHCA. The EAHCA contains two distinct procedural features. The first conforms to the classic procedural due process model—full-blown administrative hearing before an impartial tribunal.[86] The second, more innovative, procedural feature of the EAHCA is the right of parental (and sometimes student) participation in the development and preparation of the student's "individualized education program."[87] EA 1981 contains both of these procedural features, although the statutory provisions differ considerably in detail from their American counterparts.

The right of parents to participate meaningfully in the control of their children's education reflects a long-standing principle of the British educational system. Local educational authorities are enjoined by the basic education statute in England and Wales, EA 1944, to follow the general principle that, consistent with efficiency of instruction and avoidance of unreasonable expenditures, "pupils are to be educated in accordance with the wishes of their parents."[88] That general principle is given multiple application through the several distinct rights of participation given to parents of special education children by EA 1981. The full flavor of the statute in this respect can best be seen by viewing the assessment process chronologically.

(1) At the threshold stage, when the authority is of the opinion that a child either has special educational needs or probably has such needs, the first thing the authority must do is inform the parent that the authority proposes to make an assessment of the child's special needs. In addition to announcing the proposed assessment, the notice must inform the parent of the procedure to be followed, the name of the officer of the authority from whom the parent may obtain information, and the parent's right to make representations and submit written evidence within a specified period.[89]

(2) Next, the authority must take into account any parental representations or submissions and decide whether, given that consideration, it is "appropriate" to make the assessment.[90] Whichever way it decides, the parents must be notified in writing of the decision.[91]

(3)(a) If the authority decides not to make an assessment at this juncture, it apparently has no further obligation to explain its actions to the parents con-

---

86. 20 U.S.C. § 1415 (1982).
87. *Id.* § 1401 (1982).
88. Education Act 1944, § 76; *cf.* Pierce v. Society of Sisters, 268 U.S. 510, 534-35 (1925) (constitutional right of parents to influence children's education); State *ex rel.* Kelley v. Ferguson, 95 Neb. 63, 144 N.W. 1039 (1914) (common law right of parents to control children's education).
89. EA 1981, § 5(3).
90. *Id.* § 5(4).
91. *Id.* § 5(5), (7).

cerning that decision. Quite independently of the process just described, however, the parents have a right to request an assessment at any time, and "the authority shall comply with the request unless it is in their opinion unreasonable."[92] (b) If the authority, following the described process of proposing an assessment, notifying parents, and considering parent submissions, decides to go forward with the assessment, the written notice of the decision must include the "reasons for making it."[93] The statute gives the parent no forum for challenging this affirmative decision, but presumably the reasons supplied to the parent in writing may be relevant to subsequent proceedings in which parents do have procedural rights.

(4) When, during the assessment stage, an examination of the child takes place, the parents must be notified in advance of the purpose of the examination, the name of the officer of the authority from whom the parent may obtain information, and the parent's right to be present during the examination and to submit information.[94]

(5) Following the assessment, the authority must decide, in the somewhat obscure statutory words, whether they are "required" to (or "should") determine the special educational provision that should be made for the child with special needs.[95] If the decision is *not* to determine the required "provision," the parent must be notified of a right of appeal from this (negative) decision,[96] and the parent may take an appeal to the Secretary of State.[97] As in the case of a decision to assess, an affirmative decision to proceed to determine the required special educational provision is not subject to appeal.

(6) At the penultimate stage, just short of making the statement specifying the required special educational provision, another round of procedural rights comes into play. The authority is required to serve on the parent (i) the proposed statement and (ii) an explanation of the parent's procedural rights.[98] Specifically, if the parent "disagrees" with any part of the proposed statement, the parent may (i) "make representations" about the content of the proposed statement and (ii) meet with an officer of the authority to discuss the statement.[99] If, following this meeting, the parent disagrees with any part of the assessment, the authority is required to arrange one or more meetings between the parents and the persons who have given advice in connection with the assessment and any other "appropriate" persons,[100] "as they con-

---

92. *Id.* § 9(1).
93. *Id.* § 5(5).
94. *Id.* sched. 1, pt. I, § 2(2), (3). Apparently, the parent has no right to submit information in the unlikely event the child is not examined during the assessment, since the statute only mentions the submission of information in conjunction with the examination.
95. *Id.* §§ 5(6), 7(1); *see supra* note 50.
96. EA 1981, § 5(7).
97. *Id.* § 5(6). The Secretary of State may only direct the local authority to "reconsider." *Id.* § 5(8). A reconsidered and *unreasonably* reaffirmed decision might lead to a reversal under a second appeal taken outside EA 1981, pursuant to EA 1944, §§ 68 or 99. *See* discussion of *Tameside* case, *infra* part V.
98. EA 1981, § 7(3).
99. *Id.* § 7(4).
100. *Id.* § 7(5), (6). "Appropriate person" means the person who gave the relevant advice or

sider will enable the parents to discuss relevant advice."[101] The statute does not suggest a limitation on the number of appropriate persons with whom these advisory discussions could be requested, but it does require that the request for such meetings be made within fifteen days of the preceding meeting with an officer of the authority.[102]

(7) Following the previously described consultation process, final decision is at hand. The authority must (i) make a statement "in the form originally proposed" or (ii) make it in modified form or (iii) "determine not to make a statement."[103] If choice (ii) is adopted, there would evidently be a new round at the penultimate stage, presumably with parent input limited to the modifications and their effect. If choice (iii) is adopted, it is arguable that the case would be like any other determination by the authority not to follow an assessment with a statement, and consequently, the parent would have a right of appeal to the Secretary of State.[104] This might seem an odd result at first, since the parents would seem to be given a right to appeal the very decision that they would want. The parents might object to the statement proposed, however, while desiring some different statement that the local authority did not offer.

(8) Choice (i), the making of a statement, actuates a new duty by the authority to notify the parents. This time the notice encompasses a copy of the statement (which must include the advice and other details concerning assessment and the determination of what the child's needs require);[105] the name of the person to whom the parent may apply for information and advice concerning the child's needs; and information concerning the parent's right of appeal "against the special educational provision specified in the statement."[106] Up to this point, the very considerable rights of parental participation consist of consultation and requests for review by the Secretary of State. The parental appeal against the specified special educational provision triggers a very different set of rights to a hearing before a local appeal committee.

These hearing rights cannot be easily traced to the Warnock Report. Professor Kirp reports that a delegation from the Warnock Committee was appalled by what they saw in the United States of the conversion of professional judgments about special education into adversarial combat.[107] The Warnock Report contained many recommendations concerning parental par-

---

any other person who, in the opinion of the authority, is the appropriate person to discuss it with the parent. *Id.* § 7(6).

101. *Id.* § 7(5), (6).

102. *Id.* § 7(7).

103. *Id.* § 7(8). The statute says those options are available "[w]here any such representations are made." *Id.* There is no reason to suppose that an authority would be precluded from modifying or retracting a proposed statement simply because the parents had not activated the consultation process and made no representations.

104. *See supra* text accompanying notes 96 & 97.

105. Education (Special Educational Needs) Regulations 1983, § 10, STAT. INST. 29 (1983).

106. EA 1981, § 7(9).

107. *See* Kirp, *supra* note 25, at 160. Kirp quotes Mrs. Warnock (from the Times (London) Educational Supplement) as saying, "There is something deeply unattractive about the spectacle of someone demanding his own rights." *Id.*; *see also id.* at 151.

ticipation and cooperation,[108] but only a single recommendation concerning parental legal rights to contest a child's special education.[109] That was the right to appeal to the Secretary of State for Education and Science[110] from a decision of the local educational authority *not* to require special education (in addition to the already existing right to appeal a decision requiring special education).[111] The recommendation evidently intended to authorize a broader appeal than the one that already existed on the general ground that the local authority had acted unreasonably.[112]

Between the issuance of the Warnock Report in 1978 and the enactment of EA 1981, however, Parliament enacted the Education Act 1980 ("EA 1980").[113] Under this statute, procedures were established for facilitating parent appeals from school assignment decisions of local education authorities.[114] EA 1980 expressly excluded special education decisions from this procedural framework.[115] This exclusion was, perhaps, no more than reasonable since the introduction of legislation to implement the recommendations of the Warnock Report and of the related government White Paper on special education was clearly imminent. When that legislation was introduced, however, the issue could hardly be avoided. Under EA 1981 parents were given identical hearing rights ("procedural due process") to challenge special education decisions to an appeal committee, constituted substantially like the appeal committees under EA 1980.[116]

It is not easy to imagine the nature and degree of formality of the proceedings before an appeal committee under EA 1980 and EA 1981. Appeal committees must be created by each local authority. The committees consist of three, five or seven persons with membership limited in various respects to achieve a degree of neutrality and impartiality.[117] The appeal committees of EA 1981 (and EA 1980) come under the supervision of the Council of Tribunals, which has issued a Code of Practice to provide advisory guidance for the operation of these appeal committees.[118] The statute requires that the parent have an opportunity to make "oral representations"[119] and the Code of Prac-

---

108.   *See* Warnock Report, *supra* note 16, at 150-61 ("Parents as Partners").
109.   *See id.* at 71 ¶ 4.74, 341 ¶ 31. The report also recommends parental rights of access to student records. *See id.* at 70-71 ¶¶ 4.70, 4.73.
110.   *See id.* at 71 ¶ 4.74.
111.   *See* EA 1944, § 34(6); *see also* Hannon, *supra* note 52, at 279 & n.38.
112.   EA 1944, § 68; *see infra* part V of this article.
113.   Education Act, 1980, ch. 20.
114.   EA 1980, §§ 6-7; *id.* sched. 2, pt. I, § 1.
115.   EA 1980, § 9(2).
116.   The composition is not changed by statute but the Secretary of State "expects" an appeal committee under EA 1981 to include members with "relevant knowledge of special education." DES CIRCULAR 1/83, *supra* note 65, at 11 ¶ 54.
117.   EA 1980, sched. 2, pt. I, § 1. The government representatives (members of authority or education committee) may not outnumber the nongovernment members (persons "with experience in education," persons acquainted with educational conditions in the area, or parents) by more than one, *id.* § 1(4); a teacher may not be on a committee considering admission of a child to that teacher's school, *id.* § 1(7); no person who made or discussed a decision may be on an appeal committee considering that decision, *id.* § 1(6).
118.   *See* ADVISORY CENTRE FOR EDUCATION, SPECIAL EDUCATION HANDBOOK 29-30 (1983).
119.   EA 1980, sched. 2, pt. II, § 6.

tice assumes that the parents will be permitted to present expert witnesses.[120] The statutory schedule provides that an appeal committee may allow a parent to be accompanied by a friend or to be represented.[121] The Code of Practice indicates that committees should ordinarily grant this permission but "legal representation will seldom be necessary or appropriate."[122] No doubt that bit of advice in the Code of Practice would bring a smile to the faces of American critics of "proceduralization." The appeal committee's decision is required to state the grounds on which it is made.[123] The appeal is to be held in private "except when otherwise directed by the authority."[124] Also, the Code of Practice recommends that the clerk of the committee "should keep brief notes . . . as the authority may agree is appropriate" and states that "such documents will not be public."[125]

If EA 1980/EA 1981 hearings stay fairly close to the letter of the law, the "due process" afforded will be substantially less than what is required under the EAHCA. Under the EAHCA parents have an express right to submit evidence, obtain compulsory process for the attendance of witnesses, cross-examine witnesses, be represented by counsel, obtain a verbatim transcript, and obtain judicial review.[126] None of these procedural safeguards are clearly and fully guaranteed under EA 1980 and EA 1981. The absence of a clear right to counsel in appeal committee proceedings probably reflects the general pattern in informal administrative proceedings in the United Kingdom.[127] But it also seems to reflect, as does the conclusion of the Code of Practice, that legal representation would seldom be necessary or appropriate, the commitment to a "professional" approach that Professor Kirp saw in the Warnock Report.

The American and British statutes have also adopted different approaches to impartiality. The EAHCA requires an independent and impartial hearing officer, and that requirement has been construed to insulate the hearing officer from any control by either the state or local educational officials.[128] By contrast, EA 1980 and EA 1981 leave a dominant role to the local authority in the appeal committee process. The appeal committees are appointed by the local authority and are likely to have majorities which are members of the authority or the education committee of the authority.[129] Thus, despite the

---

120. *See* SPECIAL EDUCATION HANDBOOK, *supra* note 118, at 30.

121. EA 1980, sched. 2, pt. II, § 6.

122. *See* SPECIAL EDUCATION HANDBOOK, *supra* note 118, at 30.

123. EA 1980, sched. 2, pt. II, § 9.

124. *Id.* sched. 2, pt. II, § 10. But a member of the local authority and a member of the Council on Tribunals may attend as observers. *Id.*

125. *See* SPECIAL EDUCATION HANDBOOK, *supra* note 118, at 30.

126. *See* 20 U.S.C. § 1415(d), (e) (1982).

127. *See* M. BELOFF & G. PEELE, THE GOVERNMENT OF THE UNITED KINGDOM 354 (1980); T. HARTLEY & J. GRIFFITH, GOVERNMENT AND LAW 340 (2d ed. 1981).

128. *See* 34 C.F.R. §§ 300.506, .507, .510 (1984); Grymes v. Madden, 672 F.2d 321 (3d Cir. 1982); Robert M. v. Benton, 634 F.2d 1139 (8th Cir. 1980); Vogel v. School Bd. of Montrose, 491 F. Supp. 989 (W.D. Mo. 1980).

129. EA 1980, sched. 2, pt. I, § 1.

checks designed to increase the level of impartiality,[130] it is difficult to see the committees as truly independent entities.

Approximately 9000 appeals were taken in the first year of implementation of EA 1980.[131] About 3000 of these appeals resulted in decisions by an appeal committee reversing the original assignment decision of the local educational authority.[132] A reversal rate of 1 in 3 and 3000 total reversals are surprising figures. These results may suggest that the appeal committees are far more impartial than they appear to be. These results, however, may not be accurate predictors of special education appeals under EA 1981. It is possible that the results of the EA 1980 appeals are explainable on the basis of the kind of issues involved in those cases. When it comes to deciding which ordinary school regular students should attend, the appeal committees may operate very much as a jury of peers despite the authority's potentially controlling position. For regular school placement cases, the issues are not complicated, committee members can readily identify with complainants, and there is no reason to defer to anyone's professional expertise.

Despite the substantial similarity of appeal committee procedures under EA 1980 and EA 1981, there is a fundamental difference between the two when it comes to the effect of the appeal committee's decision. Under EA 1980, the decision of the appeal committee is binding upon both the local education authority and the parent. In the incorporation of the local appeal committee process into EA 1981, an interesting compromise was struck. An appeal committee decision adverse to the local education authority is advisory only.[133] It requires the local authority to reconsider its decision, but it is not binding on the authority.[134] If the local authority rejects the committee recommendation, however, the parents may appeal to the Secretary of State.[135] The parents may also appeal to the Secretary of State from an appeal committee decision confirming the decision of the local authority.[136] The government defended the bill that became EA 1981 on the ground that special education parents received two appeals while the "ordinary" parents, under EA 1980, received only one.[137]

It seems questionable whether many parents would exchange an appeal to a local hearing panel with final authority for an appeal to an advisory hearing panel followed by a second appeal to the Secretary of State. Obviously, the advantage of that trade-off depends entirely upon the substance of the appeal that will be available from the hearing panel and from the Secretary of State. In EA 1980's first year of application, 3000 out of 9000 appeals to local appeal

---

130. *Id.* sched. 2, pt. I, § 1(3).
131. *See* DEPT. OF EDUCATION AND SCIENCE PRESS RELEASE #76/83, NEW ARRANGEMENTS FOR SCHOOL ADMISSION HAVE WORKED WELL, SAYS EDUCATION SECRETARY (March 16, 1983) [hereinafter cited as DES PRESS RELEASE #76/83].
132. *Id.*
133. *See* EA 1981, § 8(4), (5).
134. *See id.* § 8(5).
135. *See id.* § 8(6)(b).
136. *See id.* § 8(6)(a).
137. *See, e.g.,* SPECIAL EDUCATION HANDBOOK, *supra* note 118, at 15.

committees were successful. Although EA 1980 itself provided no means of further review of the appeals that were unsuccessful at the local level, an appeal to the Secretary of State was available under sections 68 and 99 of EA 1944. Of the 6000 unsuccessful local appeals under EA 1980, 313 complaints were taken to the Secretary of State under these general provisions. None were successful.[138] These results, on the surface, suggest that the special education parents did not get a great bargain in the two-level appeal.

It would be simplistic, though, to conclude from these figures that meaningful review by the Secretary of State under EA 1981 will not be available.[139] In the first place, the bare statistics of appeals under EA 1980 tell us nothing about the merits of any claim brought to the Secretary of State under that statute. Secondly, the cases that came to the Secretary of State under EA 1980 had already lost once. Even assuming a substantial variety of conditions and attitudes from area to area, one has to assume that a large part of the strongest parent claims had already succeeded at the local hearing panel and did not reach the Secretary of State. Their poor success rate is probably not relevant to cases under EA 1981 in which a parent claim has been upheld by the appeal committee but rejected again on reconsideration by the local authority. Under EA 1981, these potentially strongest cases will be the ones most likely to go to the Secretary of State. When they do, they will arrive with the support of their own merits plus a favorable committee recommendation.

Appeals under EA 1981 are likely to be viewed differently for still a third important reason. The EA 1980 complainants who failed to convince a local panel were forced to rely upon the general appeal provisions of EA 1944. Under those provisions, the local authority's decision can be reversed only if it is unreasonable. Under the *Tameside* decision, that means *objectively* unreasonable—not simply unreasonable in the Secretary of State's best judgment.[140] EA 1981 presents an entirely different situation. It not only expressly authorizes the appeal from the adverse local decision, but it also expressly gives the Secretary of State broad discretion in the review. An in-between case will be presented under EA 1981 when parents who have lost at the appeal committee level exercise their statutory right to obtain an appeal from the Secretary of State. They will be coming as two-time losers, and without the advantage of a favorable appeal committee action, but the statutory provisions expressly giving the Secretary of State broad power to consider appeals will still be applicable.

At this writing, because EA 1981 has so recently gone into effect, there is little experience under that statute to form a basis of comparison between the effect of the respective appeals under EA 1980 and EA 1981. Of the few appeals taken thus far under EA 1981, the parents have already had some success.[141]

---

138. *See* DES Press Release #76/83, *supra* note 131.
139. *See supra* note 138.
140. *See* discussion of *Tameside, infra* part V.
141. Out of 18 appeals from the Local Educational Authority's decision rejecting a hearing committee recommendation, the LEA's decision was confirmed by the Secretary of State in five cases, the

The statute specifies that the parent's appeal under EA 1981 is "against the special educational provision specified in the statement."[142] It would seem quite unreasonable to attempt to isolate the "educational provision specified" from the assessment of the student's needs and the expert advice or other basis of the determination of the special educational provision. This conclusion is strongly reinforced by the breadth of the reviewing power of the Secretary of State. The Secretary of State not only has the power to direct the local authority to cease to maintain the statement at all, but also has the power to amend the statement "as he considers appropriate."[143] Although the Secretary of State's power of review is exercisable only "after consulting" with the local authority, every aspect of the statement is open on appeal to the Secretary of State. It would take very unambiguous statutory language to suggest that the advisory appeal to the appeal committee is more restrictive. The characterization of the parent's appeal as "against the special educational provision" is not such language.

There is one surprising twist in the appeal committee framework of EA 1981. As discussed in the preceding section, children who do not have "special educational needs" within the narrow statutory terminology are not the subject of a statement, even though they may need special education. Therefore, these children are entitled to none of the procedural rights before an EA 1981 appeal committee (or, subsequently, to the Secretary of State). These children thereby fall back under the 1980 act and its appeal structure.[144] EA 1980, as amended by EA 1981, excludes from its appeal provisions "children in respect of whom statements are maintained" under EA 1981.[145] So, children not entitled to statements under EA 1981 are not within the exclusion of section 9 of EA 1980. Accordingly, children who need special education but for whom statements are not maintained under EA 1981 are entitled to appeal to EA 1980 committees. An appeal under EA 1980 is limited to the question of correct school placement in ordinary schools[146] for which the Act gives explicit parental preference and imposes certain other specified limitations.[147] EA 1980 certainly was not drafted with the intention of accommodating special education assignments that fell through the cracks of the anticipated special education legislation that became EA 1981. Nevertheless, EA 1980 does give these children a right to appeal their ordinary school assignment to a local appeal committee, and the circumstances producing special educational needs for them would seem to be relevant to the committee's school assign-

---

appeal committee's recommendation was accepted by the Secretary of State in six cases, and seven cases were unresolved as of December 18, 1984. There have also been 26 appeals to the Secretary of State from LEA decisions not to assess a student under § 5(6); 15 cases were remitted to the LEA for reconsideration. Telephone conversation with representative of the Division of Special Education, Department of Education and Science (Dec. 18, 1984).

142. EA 1981, § 8(1).
143. *Id.* § 8(7).
144. *See* White Paper, *supra* note 21, at 16 ¶ 50.
145. EA 1981, sched. 3, § 14 (amending EA 1980, § 9(2)).
146. *See* EA 1980, § 7.
147. *Id.*

ment decision. Of course, whereas the generally more extensive protection of EA 1981 yields only an *advisory* local committee decision, the children relegated to EA 1980 appeal committees for protection of their special needs will receive a committee decision *binding* on the local education authority.

Whatever limitation or weaknesses one may find in particular provisions concerning the procedural rights of parents under EA 1981, it seems indisputable that their rights of participation in various phases of the process of assessment and provision of special education are extensive. Still, the basic question remains whether this participation will have utility. Will it lead to better special education? Will it, at least, lead to special education more nearly in line with parental wishes? At the very least, will it give parents a positive feeling of meaningful participation? In the first instance the answer to those questions will turn on whether parents know and understand their rights and believe that they matter.[148] The effectiveness of the parental participation will be influenced by such variables as what they know; how articulate they are; and how comfortable they feel in their relationships with school officials, teachers, advisors and other participants.

One factor which may significantly influence the extent and effectiveness of parental involvement concerns the availability and activity of voluntary organizations concerned with children's rights or education.[149] Such organizations were involved in the legislative process that produced EA 1981.[150] EA 1981 itself requires that, when an Area or District Health Authority working with a child under five believes the child has or probably has "special educational needs," the authority has a duty to inform the parent or a particular voluntary organization "likely to be able to give the parent advice or assistance."[151] There is no other requirement to bring such voluntary organizations to the parent's attention.

Still, a number of such organizations appear to be taking an active interest in the implementation of EA 1981, particularly its integration features. For example, the Advisory Centre for Education (ACE) publishes a monthly periodical and other literature dealing with student rights.[152] ACE has published a heavily used handbook explaining EA 1981[153] which includes, among other things, a list of addresses and telephone numbers of other organizations and offices that might have relevant information; a checklist of special educational needs; tactical advice to parents in dealing with local or central education

---

148. In the United States, where parental legal rights are more prevalent, it is generally assumed that a selective group of middle class parents are the dominant users of such rights. *See generally* Clune & Van Pelt, *A Political Method of Evaluating the EAHCA and the Several Gaps of Gap Analysis*, LAW & CONTEMP. PROBS., Winter 1985, at 7. Professor Tomlinson is very skeptical that the mainly working class parents affected by special education decisions will exercise their rights under EA 1981. *See* S. TOMLINSON, *supra* note 17, at 108-18.

149. *See* Kirp, Buss & Kuriloff, *Legal Reforms of Special Education: Empirical Studies and Procedural Proposals*, 62 CALIF. L. REV. 40, 96, 114 (1974). *See generally* Warnock Report, *supra* note 16, at 309-17.

150. Rosenberg, *In On the Act*, presented on *Sunday Evening*, (BBC Radio, 1981) (tape on file with the author).

151. EA 1981, § 10(2).

152. WHERE (published ten times a year).

153. SPECIAL EDUCATION HANDBOOK, *supra* note 118.

authorities, including sample letters for parents to use in various situations; and examples of integrated education schemes actually in existence. A division of the Spastics Society, the Centre for Studies on Integration in Education, has been created for the express purpose of monitoring the process of integration. Among other activities, this organization has compiled a list of professional experts who might be available to assist parents in presenting their own point of view.[154] The value of such organizations may be found not simply in their technical assistance but also in their helping parents to feel a sense of common enterprise rather than individual isolation.

The impact of parental procedural rights will depend also on whether the Secretary of State assumes an active role. If the parent viewpoint is never advanced through appeals to the Secretary of State or through effective informal action by the Secretary of State, the procedural rights of parents will obviously be less valuable. The ultimate question is whether local authorities will listen to and be influenced by parents—or, more accurately, to what extent they will listen and be influenced. No doubt it will depend on the parent and on the authority, as well as the merit of the parents' particular views, the quality with which they are presented, the supporting contribution of voluntary organizations and the position which the Secretary of State carves out for his office under EA 1981. So, in the end, the answer to the question about the value of creating parental rights depends on circularly interacting considerations: The parents will become more active if they are having an impact, and their impact will depend upon their activity, and so on and so on.

The use and utility of parental procedural rights may be indirectly affected by their cost. It seems clear that the statutory procedures put in place for parents are expensive. Totally without parental involvement, the assessment procedures required by EA 1981 demand heavy expenditures of time by local authorities and their expert advisors. The burden is significantly increased as a result of conferring rights on parents. In the absolutely minimal situation in which the affected parent makes no submissions, asks for no meetings and takes no appeals, the local authority still has the burden of preparing and sending the proper notices and of structuring the administrative operations of the school to anticipate parental involvement.[155] At the other end of the spectrum, if the parent takes the opportunity to participate extensively at every stage of the process, the expenditure of time and other resources would be truly massive. Plainly, there would be a point at which innumerable meetings between every parent and every school official and every advisor involved in the assessment process of every child would tend to bring the system to a halt.[156] However convincing the case for procedures to achieve the best possible education of children with special educational needs and to afford par-

---

154. *See id.* at 18.

155. Notices must be sent in a language that will facilitate understanding by the parent. DES CIRCULAR 1/83, *supra* note 65, at 14 ¶ 70.

156. Even though only those students for whom the formal process ends with a statement are entitled to special education, most of the parental procedural rights take hold at various stages prior to the actual making of a statement.

ents their proper role in controlling the education of their children, it remains true that these procedures can create a substantial drain on always limited educational resources. The very generosity of the procedures could contribute to their inutility. The local education authorities could perform their duties, and the Secretary of State could exercise his powers, in a way that discouraged parents from exercising their rights. Such discouragement might result if parental "overuse" is feared. Again, an element of circularity is involved, because apprehension of excessive resort to parental procedural rights might well be influenced by what parents actually do. Only experience will disclose whether the implementation of EA 1981 achieves a golden mean in which parental rights are used effectively and prudently.

IV

ADMINISTRATIVE ENFORCEMENT

As just outlined, one striking feature of the administrative machinery created by EA 1981 is its elaborate procedural detail, an important ingredient of which is the extensive rights of parents. In this important respect, EA 1981 strongly emulates and, in places, surpasses the EAHCA. In contrast to their shared penchant for procedural profusion, EA 1981 and the EAHCA have adopted enforcement provisions that are generally quite different. Under the terms of the EAHCA, federal funds to support special education are made available to state and local education agencies on the condition that the requirements of the national law are satisfied. Compliance by state and local recipients is enforceable by withdrawal of federal funds[157] or by action culminating in judicial review and judicial decree.[158] As a practical matter, a substantial part of the enforcement effort is left to the supervisory and monitoring actions of the responsible state education agency, the direct recipient of federal funds.[159]

The administrative framework of EA 1981 differs from that of the EAHCA in at least three important respects. First, EA 1981 provides no funding incentive. Second, under the British system, there is no administrative enforcement by an intermediate government unit—between national and local authorities—comparable to the role of the fifty states in the American federal system. Consequently, the instrument of educational authority of the national government in England, the Secretary of State for Education and Science, is given a central enforcement role under EA 1981. Third, EA 1981 itself contains no provision for judicial review and enforcement. Despite the absence of statutory provisions in EA 1981, however, the courts are not clearly denied a role in enforcing the special education law. This potential role will be considered in the following section. The present section will concentrate upon the role of the central educational authority in enforcing the

---

157. 20 U.S.C. § 1416 (1982).
158. *See id.* § 1415(e)(2) (1982).
159. *See id.* §§ 1412-1413 (1982).

requirements of EA 1981, one element of which is the lack of any funding component under the new law.

EA 1981 imposes primary responsibility on local education authorities to implement its requirements. In this respect, EA 1981 is wholly like the EAHCA. In England and Wales, as in the United States, local education authorities are the primary providers of educational services by government. Under EA 1981, it is the local authorities that must, in the first instance, identify children who may have special educational needs;[160] decide whether to assess those children;[161] appoint expert advisors;[162] provide required information to these advisors;[163] consider the advisors' advice;[164] decide after assessment whether a statement should be maintained;[165] decide when to reassess children and revise statements;[166] establish appeal committees;[167] engage in the hearing process before these committees;[168] reexamine a previous determination in light of the appeal committee recommendations;[169] serve notices on parents;[170] consider parental representations and submissions;[171] and arrange for the special educational provision to which a child is entitled.[172]

The enforcement of EA 1981 will largely depend upon the competence, manner and spirit with which these responsibilities are carried out. Despite the availability of parental appeals and review by the Secretary of State, it seems reasonable to suppose that parental acquiescence will be the rule and parental challenge the exception. It seems likely that only a small portion of the actions of local authorities will be scrutinized by administrative hearings and still fewer will be reconsidered by the Secretary of State. Consequently, the most thorough compliance can be expected to take place where the local authorities have the greatest commitment to the policies reflected in the Warnock Report and EA 1981, where the local authorities have the most resources, and, perhaps, where there is the greatest involvement of voluntary child-support organizations that influence local decisionmaking.

While the statute places the primary task of implementation on the local education authority, it reserves the last word on most important questions to the Secretary of State for Education and Science. Furthermore, unlike the U.S. system under the EAHCA, there is no intermediate authority like the state governments to provide substantial opportunity for independent goals

---

160. EA 1981, §§ 2(1), 4(1).
161. *Id.* § 5(1)-(5).
162. *Id.* sched. 1, pt. I, § 1.
163. *See* Education (Special Educational Needs) Regulations 1983, § 4(4), STAT. INST. 29 (1983).
164. *See* EA 1981, § 7(5), (6); *id.* sched. 1, pt. I, § 1; Education (Special Educational Needs) Regulations 1983, §§ 4-7, 8(b), STAT. INST. 29 (1983).
165. EA 1981, § 7(1).
166. *Id.* §§ 7(10), 9(2); *id.* sched. 1, pt. II, § 5.
167. *Id.* § 8(1), (2); EA 1980, sched. 2, pt. I, § 1.
168. EA 1980, sched. 2, pt. II (implication).
169. EA 1981, § 8(5).
170. *Id.* §§ 5(3), 5(5), 5(7), 7(3), 7(9), 8(5); *id.* sched. 1, pt. I, § 2.
171. *Id.* §§ 5(4), 7(8).
172. *Id.* §§ 7(2), 2(4); *cf. id.* § 2(2).

of the state—or simply bureaucratic inefficiencies—to intervene and deflect national policies. The absence of such an administrative encumbrance in England and Wales means that the Secretary of State is in a much stronger position to see to the implementation of national educational policy.

The Secretary of State exercises his powers by issuing general regulations that elaborate and define the legislation and by reviewing individual decisions of local authorities. Under the rulemaking power, the Secretary of State prescribes or elaborates the frequency of assessments for children for whom statements are maintained;[173] identifies the advice which a local authority must seek in making assessments;[174] describes the manner of conducting such assessments and other matters relating to assessments;[175] specifies the requirements for qualification as a special school;[176] and specifies the requirements for qualification as an independent school[177] approved to educate children with special educational needs.[178]

The Secretary of State's adjudicatory authority over decisions of local authorities empowers him to review[179] all decisions concerning requests of parents to remove a child from a special school;[180] approval of independent schools;[181] placement of students in unapproved schools;[182] and closing of special schools.[183] Under these provisions, the Secretary of State would make decisions affecting the kind and quality of special education provided in the schools in which a child with special educational needs could be placed. Bearing even more directly upon a child's special education is the Secretary of State's power under EA 1981 to review local decisions affecting assessment, statements and determination of a child's special educational provision.[184]

---

173. *Id.* § 7(10).
174. *Id.* sched. 1, pt. I, § 1(1), (2).
175. *Id.* sched. 1, pt. I, § 1(3).
176. *Id.* § 12(1), (2).
177. In American terms, a "private" or fee-receiving school.
178. EA 1981, § 13(1), (2).
179. Although none of the statutory provisions cited in this paragraph use the term "appeal," it seems doubtful that that variation in wording alone alters the nature of the Secretary of State's reviewing power. For example, EA 1981, § 11(2) states that a parent, aggrieved by a local authority's refusal to consent to the withdrawal of a student from a special school, "may *refer* the question to the Secretary of State, who shall give such direction thereon as he thinks fit" (emphasis added). Section 18(1), a miscellaneous provision, authorizes the Secretary of State to examine the child concerned "[w]here any question arising under this Act is *referred* to the Secretary of State" (emphasis added). It would be unsound to construe this language to cover only those questions which involved a "reference" and not questions which involved an "appeal."

However, the Secretary of State's decisions concerning approval of independent schools and consent to placement in unapproved independent schools appear to be initial decisions rather than reviews of local authority decisions.
180. EA 1981, § 11(2).
181. *See id.* § 11(3)(a).
182. *Id.* § 11(3)(b).
183. *Id.* § 14(1).
184. The Secretary of State has plenary power to confirm, modify or reverse the ultimate decision of the local authority concerning the educational provision to be made for the student. EA 1981, § 8(7). But, on an appeal from a local decision, following assessment, *not* to determine the special educational provision, i.e., not to maintain a statement, the Secretary of State's power is to "direct" the local authority to "reconsider." *Id.* § 5(8).

The decision of the local authority *not* to assess, upon request, is left to its discretion. In the case

Although the statute gives the Secretary of State the power to adjudicate these various issues on review, the Secretary of State may defer to local decisions already made. It is even arguable that some deference is legally required. It seems unmistakable, however, that the statute confers considerable independent authority on the Secretary of State; most unmistakable is the Secretary of State's power, after consultation, to revise any part or all of the local authority's statement specifying a child's special educational provision.[185]

In their book on education law, Taylor and Saunders write, "Students of the Education Acts 1944-75 can be in no doubt as to who is the senior partner in the educational system."[186] They mean the Secretary of State for Education and Science. Arguably, the eight judges on the bench of the Court of Appeals and the House of Lords showed that they had not learned this elementary lesson when they resolved a national-local controversy in favor of the local education authority in their judgments in *Secretary of State for Education and Science v. Metropolitan Borough of Tameside*.[187] Nevertheless, whatever may have been true under other legislation, and whatever should have been true in the *Tameside* dispute, it is difficult to resist the conclusion that the Secretary of State is indeed the senior partner under EA 1981.

If the Secretary of State is the senior partner, there is a junior partner as well, one that the Secretary of State will not ignore. Rather than exercising his significant power under EA 1981 in a coercive manner, the Secretary of State for Education and Science is likely to encourage local decisionmakers to adopt particular views of educational policy under EA 1981 through persuasion. For example, although Department of Education and Science circulars have no binding legal effect, they are likely to carry substantial weight in shaping the views of local authorities about the requirements of EA 1981. DES Circular 1/83, in particular, seems destined to influence significantly the views of local authorities about their obligations under EA 1981.

The Secretary of State has a variety of ongoing contacts with educational officials at all levels and a variety of means of disseminating the department's views. One important contact between the Secretary of State and local authorities is Her Majesty's Inspectorate (the Inspectorate).[188] The Inspectorate has no power to direct local decisions and, strictly speaking, it is not

---

of a child for whom no statement is maintained, the authority is to assess unless to do so is "in their opinion unreasonable," *id.* § 9(1); in the case of a child for whom a statement is maintained, the authority is to assess unless "they are satisfied that an assessment would be inappropriate." *Id.* § 9(2). Even in this situation, the Secretary of State has regulatory power over the frequency of assessments, *see id.* § 7(10), and it is arguable that there would still be an appeal under the Secretary of State's general authority to reverse unreasonable local actions. *See* EA 1944, § 68. *See generally* discussion of *Tameside* case, *infra* part V.

There is no specific provision in the act for appeal from the local *affirmative* decisions to assess or, following assessment, to make a statement. Those actions of the local authority would merge into the determinations of what educational provision should be specified in the statement and thus would be indirectly subject to appeal as part of the appeal against the educational provision specified.

185.   EA 1981, § 8(7); *see also* the Secretary of State's power "to examine the child concerned" in connection with any question referred to the Secretary of State, *id.* § 18(1).

186.   G. TAYLOR & J.B. SAUNDERS, THE LAW OF EDUCATION 4 (8th ed. 1976).

187.   [1976] 3 All E.R. 665. *See* discussion of *Tameside* case, *infra* part V.

188.   *See generally* H.C. DENT, EDUCATION IN ENGLAND AND WALES 63-64 (2d ed. 1982).

part of the administrative machinery under the Secretary of State. Rather, it is an independent body that serves as a consultant to both central and local education authorities. The Inspectorate is likely to have a centralizing effect on the application of the act: despite its independent position, it can understand and support the central authority's position; despite its lack of directive power, it can influence opinion at the local level because of the stature and status of its personnel.

In the preceding section, it was suggested that the cost of procedural rights under EA 1981 might prove to be a built-in deterrent to their use. Obviously, that tendency would be minimized if EA 1981 included a substantial commitment of funds to pay for expensive procedures. In fact, the opposite is true. There is no funding component in EA 1981. The Warnock Report assumed that carrying out its recommendations would require the commitment of substantial resources.[189] It is not surprising that the enactment of Warnock policies in EA 1981 without the concomitant financial support has been subject to criticism.[190] In the United States, the EAHCA has been criticized for imposing duties on local education authorities that are greatly in excess of the federal subsidy provided.[191] The absence of any commitment of national funds could significantly weaken the position of the Secretary of State in enforcing EA 1981. The failure to provide the resources needed to support EA 1981 may give the appearance that the national government is really not serious about special education after all. This weakness in the national policy will be felt by local authorities on whom the economic burden will fall and by the staff of the Department of Education and Science responsible for implementation. The Department will find it more difficult to press for expensive solutions under EA 1981 when the national purse is empty for such purposes. For their part, the local authorities will be in a position to question the obligation to adopt costly special education programs for which no national revenues have been committed. In this bargaining posture, it will be easy for each side to fall back on the view that EA 1981 leaves very much to local discretion.

The general lack of resources to implement EA 1981, and the corresponding subversion of administrative enforcement, is qualified in two respects. First, the Secretary of State has allocated some of his discretionary funds to provide supplementary funding of in-service special education training of teachers.[192] Such training was one of the specific purposes for

---

189. *See* Warnock Report, *supra* note 16, at 106-14, 325-26, 329.

190. *See* The Times (London) Educational Supplement, Mar. 6, 1981, at 6, col. 1; *id.* Feb. 27, 1981, at 6, col. 1. The criticism was foreshadowed in comments on the Warnock Report, *see* The Times (London) Educational Supplement: Scotland, Oct. 6, 1978, at 2, col. 3; The Times (London) Educational Supplement, May 26, 1978, at 5, col. 1, 6, cols. 1-2.

191. *See, e.g.,* Pittenger & Kuriloff, *Educating the Handicapped: Reforming a Radical Law,* PUB. INTEREST, Winter 1982, at 86-89, 94-96.

192. *See* Education Act, 1962, 10 & 11 Eliz. 2, ch. 12, § 3(a) (authorizing the Secretary of State to make grants for teacher training). Approximately £1.2 million were provided by the Secretary of State to local authorities in the 1983-84 academic year, and £2.2 million in 1984-85—a small part of the total funds spent on in-service training by local authorities. In addition, £2.25 million has been made available for the purchase of microelectronic equipment for special education in 1985-86 under the Education (Grants and Awards) Act, 1984, ch. 11. Correspondence with representative of

which the Warnock Report anticipated the need for funds.[193] The total amount of money involved is relatively small, especially compared to the need for teacher preparation to provide special education as fully as contemplated by Warnock.

Second, resources are being made available indirectly as a result of the declining school-age population in Britain. The Warnock Report[194] and the White Paper[195] both noted this phenomenon.[196] Falling enrollments result in inefficiently used educational resources—teachers, buildings, equipment— which could be diverted to meet the additional demands on educational suppliers created under EA 1981. This transfer of resources would work well in some situations but not others. For example, to the extent that special equipment is needed, existing equipment is not likely to do the job, although any available funds for replacement of the existing equipment could be used instead for the needed special equipment. Teachers unneeded in ordinary schools may not be prepared, qualified or able to teach in special schools; unneeded special schools cannot supply the access ramps needed by the handicapped to use ordinary schools—but, in both instances, funds allocated for support of unneeded teachers or maintenance of unneeded schools may be released for teacher training or ramp construction. Excess space in separate special and ordinary schools is less costly to maintain if the children from two schools are "integrated" and one of the schools is discontinued.[197]

By subsidizing some teacher training for special education, the government has demonstrated at least a symbolic commitment to special education. Through the resources made available as a result of demographic change, the local education authority's capacity to meet burdensome obligations under EA 1981 is improved. In both respects, the power—and perhaps the likelihood—of the Secretary of State for Education and Science to enforce EA 1981 is strengthened. However much the natural mode of enforcement may be to proceed through accommodation, realization of the promise of the Warnock

---

Div. of Special Educ., Dept. of Educ. & Science (Oct. 17, 1984). *See also* DEPARTMENT OF EDUCATION & SCIENCE PRESS RELEASE #284/82, PRIORITY AREAS ANNOUNCED FOR IN-SERVICE TEACHER TRAINING GRANTS (Dec. 6, 1982).

193. *See* Warnock Report, *supra* note 16, at 108 ¶ 7.23, 112 ¶¶ 7.36-.37, 226-45, 332-34.

194. *See id.* at 326 ¶ 19.6.

195. *See* White Paper, *supra* note 21, at 9 ¶ 20.

196. *See* The Times (London) Educational Supplement, May 26, 1978, at 2, col. 3.

197. The Secretary of State's powers under EA 1981 include considerable control over the use of special schools. *See, e.g.,* EA 1981, § 14; *see also id.* § 11(2) (approval of parents' removal of student from special school); *id.* § 12(1) (approval of special schools).

The possibility of obtaining school-use efficiencies through integration is suggested by figures supplied by the Special Education Division of the Department of Education and Science. From January 1981 to January 1983, the number of special students enrolled in ordinary classes increased from 10,369 to 22,592; during the same period, the number of special students enrolled in separate units in ordinary schools decreased from 16,456 to 15,378. During the same period, the number of children in special school decreased by 2376. These figures seem to show a net increase in children in ordinary schools of 11,145 and suggest that some of the increase represents a shift from separate to integrated classes. Of course, it is impossible to determine how much of the enrollment changes were a result of demographic changes, a shift in attitude by parents and educators toward integrated education, or some combination of these and other factors.

Report and EA 1981 may well depend on the Secretary of State's determination to override local decisions when meaningful enforcement so requires.

V
THE ROLE OF THE COURTS

One cannot wholly separate the question of administrative enforcement by the Secretary of State for Education and Science from the question of judicial enforcement through judicial review of administrative action. The power of the Secretary of State under EA 1981 is ultimately dependent upon what the statute is read to mean by the courts. As a close alternative, a controlling reading could be provided by the joint perception of the Secretary of State and local education authorities of what the ultimate judicial determination would be. If the Secretary of State and the local authorities assumed there would be no judicial review of administrative action, they would have to work out their views of powers and duties under EA 1981 within a very different framework. As long as judicial review is a possibility, the anticipated judicial position is an important determinant of the national-local allocation of power.

In the last thirty years, we have become accustomed to the fact that American courts often take a very active role in deciding controversial issues of public policy in enforcing both constitutional and statutory rights. The EAHCA encourages this role by assigning courts important responsibilities in connection with a student's right to a "free appropriate public education." Under the EAHCA any party aggrieved by the decisions made through a specified administrative process is entitled to bring an action in a state or federal district court, which is given power by the statute to receive the administrative record, hear additional evidence and grant such relief as it determines is appropriate.[198]

In *Board of Education v. Rowley*,[199] the Supreme Court held that this provision does not authorize the federal courts "to substitute their own notions of sound educational policy for those of the school authorities."[200] The court's responsibility, rather, is to determine whether the education authorities have complied with required statutory procedures and whether they have developed an educational program "reasonably calculated to enable the child to receive educational benefits." [201] Although the importance of judicial review under the EAHCA has been somewhat diminished by the *Rowley* case, a significant statutory responsibility for the courts remains. One somewhat ambiguous Supreme Court decision is not likely to bring about an abrupt change in judicial behavior.[202]

---

198. 20 U.S.C. § 1415(e)(2) (1982).
199. 458 U.S. 176 (1982).
200. *Id.* at 206.
201. *Id.* at 207.
202. For examples of post-*Rowley* cases refusing to defer to educational decisionmakers, *see* Roncker v. Walter, 700 F.2d 1058 (6th Cir.), *cert. denied*, 104 S. Ct. 196 (1983); Doe v. Anrig, 692 F.2d 800 (1st Cir. 1982).

In contrast, under EA 1981, no role whatsoever is created for the courts. Perhaps the best indication of the general lack of expectation of any involvement of the British judiciary in connection with special education comes from the handbook on EA 1981 prepared by the Advisory Centre for Education (ACE). Written for the express purpose of advising parents of their rights and tactical approaches possible under the new Act, the handbook refers to possible judicial relief only once, in a passing comment that parents might consider going to the European Court of Human Rights.[203] It does not contain one word concerning any British court.

Despite these strong indications to the contrary, there is a judicial role in interpreting EA 1981, and it could turn out to be significant. While there has not been judicial activism of the magnitude of that in the United States, British courts have experienced a shift toward a more active role in many areas. Perhaps the clearest example of this change is in the judicial review of administrative action.[204] Administrative action is presumptively subject to judicial review to prevent action beyond the statutory power of the administrative body.[205] There are available procedures—such as mandamus or injunction or declaratory judgment—for invoking judicial review of the action of the Secretary of State.[206] In a number of cases the courts have interceded to reverse the exercise of administrative discretion that, until recently, would not have been thought subject to judicial review.[207] One can point specifically to relatively recent examples of significant judicial decisions in the area of education: upholding a race discrimination charge of a student;[208] reversing the exercise of discretion of the Secretary of State for Education and Science;[209] and enjoining the closing of a school by a local education authority.[210]

No doubt the most famous of these cases, and apparently the case most relevant to education, is *Secretary of State for Education and Science v. Metropolitan Borough of Tameside.*[211] Lord Denning, Master of the Rolls, succinctly stated what the case was about:

> There is a controversy on this question: should the grammar schools be turned into comprehensive schools? Most educationalists and parents know what the controversy is all about, but for others who do not know the background perhaps I may say a word. The difference lies in the way the children are selected on and after the age of 11. In order to go to a grammar school, a boy or girl of age 11 has to show some marked

203. SPECIAL EDUCATION HANDBOOK, *supra* note 118, at 20.
204. *See* S. DE SMITH, CONSTITUTIONAL AND ADMINISTRATIVE LAW 560-68, 582-93 (4th ed. 1981); H.W.R. WADE, CONSTITUTIONAL FUNDAMENTALS 41-46 (1980).
205. *See* S. DE SMITH, *supra* note 204, at 560-68.
206. *See id.* at 594-607.
207. *See* Laker Airways Ltd. v. Department of Trade, [1977] Q.B. 643; Congreve v. Home Office, [1976] Q.B. 629; Anisminic Ltd. v. Foreign Compensation Comm'n, 1969 2 A.C. 147; Padfield v. Minister of Agriculture, Fisheries & Food, 1968 A.C. 997.
208. Mandla (Sewa Singh) v. Dowell Lee, 1983 2 A.C. 548, [1983] 2 W.L.R. 620 (private school).
209. Secretary of State for Educ. & Science v. Metropolitan Borough of Tameside, [1976] 3 All E.R. 665.
210. Legg v. Inner London Educ. Auth., [1972] 3 All E.R. 177.
211. [1976] 3 All E.R. 665.

ability or aptitude. When he gets there, he or she will mingle with other bright young-sters and be taught there right through until the age of 18. But a comprehensive school takes any boy or girl of age 11 without reference to his or her ability or apti-tude. The bright and the dull start together in classes, but they are divided into dif-ferent streams as they develop in ability or aptitude. They remain at the comprehensive school until they are 16. Most of them then leave to go to work. But those who wish can go on for two more years at a sixth form college where they are given more advanced teaching. That is from 16 to 18.[212]

At the time of the *Tameside* litigation, the Labor government in power in the United Kingdom was strongly supportive of comprehensive education. The control of the local education authority of Tameside, however, had just changed from the Labor Party to the Conservative Party. While they had local control, the Labor Party had developed and begun to implement a plan for the replacement of the grammar-secondary modern system by the compre-hensive system. Under the Conservatives, who had campaigned against the elimination of grammar schools, an attempt was being made to delay imple-mentation of that part of the approved plan that called for the conversion of certain grammar schools into comprehensive schools.

The Secretary of State directed the local authority to implement the plan according to schedule. When the local authority refused, the Secretary of State applied for, and received, an order of mandamus ordering the authority to go forward with the plan. On appeal, the Court of Appeals, affirmed by the House of Lords, decided that the mandamus should not have been issued and discharged the order. Three judges on the Court of Appeals and five judges of the House of Lords all agreed with this decision, largely for the same reason. For simplicity, this article refers to their several judgments as the judgment of the "court." The legal issue in the case centered on the Secre-tary of State's power under section 68 of EA 1944, which provides:

> If the Secretary of State is satisfied, either on complaint by any person or otherwise, that any local education authority . . . have acted or are proposing to act unreason-ably with respect to the exercise of any power conferred or the performance of any duty imposed by or under this Act, he may . . . give such directions as to the exercise of the power or the performance of the duty as appear to him to be expedient.[213]

The court had little difficulty in rejecting the contention that the word "satis-fied" in the first line of section 68 meant that the Secretary of State had an essentially unbridled "subjective discretion" to decide that the local authority had acted "unreasonably" and thus, without more, the power to direct the authority to implement the pending plan for comprehensive secondary schools. On the contrary, the court decided, the Secretary of State must have an objective basis for a determination that the local authority "have acted or are proposing to act unreasonably."[214]

It was the Secretary of State's position that the delay in implementing a plan already well advanced would be disruptive to the education of children in the area affected. The local authority argued just the opposite—that going

---

212. *Id.* at 667.
213. E.A. 1944, § 68.
214. [1976] 3 All E.R. 665, 670-71.

forward on schedule would be disruptive. Much of the controversy, in the court's treatment of the problem under section 68, turned on one narrow factual issue. There were 783 pending applications for grammar school at a time when, because of the implementation of the plan to that point, there were only 240 places. The Secretary of State argued that it would not be educationally feasible to select the 240 out of 783 applicants in the time available. The local authority disagreed. The court concluded that, at most, this was a disagreement between reasonable points of view and that there was no objective basis for the Secretary of State to characterize the disagreement as evidence of unreasonableness.[215]

The court was evidently influenced by several considerations. First, it was dealing with two distinct administrative bodies, each having a legitimate claim for discretion and respect. Second, local education authorities have broad primary responsibility for educating children in their respective areas. Third, there was no general legal duty for local authorities to adopt the comprehensive system. Fourth, apart from the legal framework, there was no objective basis for choosing one of the two fundamentally different approaches to education represented by the Secretary of State's and the local authority's positions. Fifth, there was no objective basis for concluding that the local authority would not be able to select the 240 places in an orderly manner in the time available; in fact there was a basis in the record for believing that the authority would be able to do so. Sixth, upholding the Secretary of State would have entailed a judgment that the local authority had acted improperly. In the court's view, it was no small matter to charge public officials with acting unreasonably with respect to the performance of any duty imposed on them by the Education Act.[216] For those who believe there is a conservative political bias to the British judiciary,[217] two other factors would very likely be mentioned: In a case embracing fundamental differences over political and educational philosophy, the court came down on the side of the Conservative party and the elite system of education.

For purposes of construing EA 1981, there are many messages one can read in the *Tameside* judgments. One series of messages might suggest that the role of the Secretary of State for Education and Science is far more limited than it appears on the face of the statutes. Very broadly, *Tameside* may indicate that, where significant policy issues are implicated, the courts may intervene in unpredictable ways. More narrowly, *Tameside* seems to demonstrate that judicial intervention into educational policy in a nondeferential fashion is a reality, not just a remote possibility. *Tameside* certainly can be read to suggest judicial bias in favor of decentralization and local control. And, of course, in its reading of the phrase, "If the Secretary of State is satisfied," to pose an objective rather than a subjective test, the court indicated that statutory language may be construed in surprising ways. These are sobering thoughts.

---

215. *Id.* at 672, 676.
216. *Id.* at 671.
217. *See* J.A.G. GRIFFITH, THE POLITICS OF THE JUDICIARY 236-40 (2d ed. 1981).

They suggest not only that the courts might have a role under EA 1981 but that the judicial role might drastically limit the power that EA 1981 seems to confer on the Secretary of State for Education and Science.

Although *Tameside* is plainly a significant precedent, it does not support a restrictive view of the Secretary of State's power under EA 1981. In *Tameside,* the real dispute was a political dispute between groups representing two distinct philosophies of educational policy. In that case, the Secretary of State represented the Labor Party and the new comprehensive education; the managers of the local authority represented the Conservative Party and the old hierarchical approach to education. Special education has not been a partisan issue in Britain. Not only did *Tameside* involve a dispute over educational policy, it involved a dispute in which the real parties in interest were the state and local governments. Within the affected educational community, there were parents (and perhaps students) who cared about the outcome of the policy struggle. But these parents were in no sense litigants or grievants or "parties."

In sharp contrast, under EA 1981 the parents (and students) will be asserting individual claims for statutory entitlements. *Tameside* does not offer any clue to how the British judiciary might respond to an attempt to invoke judicial review involving an individual claim of right—either in the situation where the individual's and Secretary of State's positions are together or in the situation where the individual and the Secretary of State take opposing positions. Finally, under EA 1981, unlike the situation in *Tameside,* there will be a recommendation by an appeal committee, a third administrative body to which some deference might or might not be given by the courts.[218]

All of these considerations indicate that *Tameside* may be an inconclusive precedent from which to evaluate the power of the Secretary of State under EA 1981. However, the most persuasive argument that the *Tameside* decision will not limit the Secretary of State's power under EA 1981 is based on its fundamentally different statutory scheme. The statute involved in *Tameside,* section 68 of EA 1944, creates a general supervisory power in the Secretary of State over any and every action of local education authorities. The controlling standard of section 68 is whether the local authority has or will act "unreasonably." As construed by the *Tameside* court, this vague standard requires a finding that the local authority has failed to perform a duty. EA 1981 seems sharply different. The central statutory provision, section 8(7), gives the Secretary of State power, "after consulting with the local education authority," to:

> (b) amend the statement so far as it specifies the special educational provision and make such other consequential amendments to the statement as he considers appropriate; or
> (c) direct the local education authority to cease to maintain the statement.

This provision applies to only one quite specific educational matter: the local

---

218. Compare the Administrative Law Judge under the National Labor Relations Act. *See* Universal Camera Corp. v. NLRB, 340 U.S. 474 (1951).

authority's statement of the child's special education provision. It does not entail any requirement of a pejorative finding such as a suggestion that the local authority has violated its duty. On the contrary, section 8(7) of EA 1981 gives the Secretary of State plenary power to substitute his or her judgment for that of the local authority. It is the Secretary of State's own conception of the statute that is to be enforced under EA 1981.

Although the *Tameside* decision provides no basis for nullification of the apparently significant power given to the Secretary of State for Education and Science by EA 1981, *Tameside* remains important for EA 1981. As seen in the preceding discussion, *Tameside* reveals that there is a potentially significant role for the courts in the enforcement of education legislation. That role would seem to include affirmatively enforcing the Secretary of State's exercise of statutory power, and it might include requiring a reluctant Secretary of State to use that power. Specifically, it might include requiring the Secretary of State to consider an individual claim of right under EA 1981. It is even possible, though far less likely, that the court might reverse the Secretary of State's rejection of such an individual claim. That is, it would be possible for a court to conclude that the Secretary of State need not defer to local judgments and, at the same time, to conclude that the Secretary of State must recognize statutory rights. Such an exercise of judicial power would be partly dependent upon a determination that EA 1981 creates substantive rights, a question to be explored in the next two sections of this article.

EA 1981 does clearly create procedural rights. The courts might be requested to enforce either the parental consultation rights established at various stages of the EA 1981 assessment process or the hearing rights before an appeal committee at the final stage of development of a statement of special educational provision. These rights are akin to the rights recognized under the rules of "natural justice," the British counterpart of American procedural due process.[219] In the absence of any specific statutory authority, the rules of natural justice extend to any person or body deciding issues affecting the rights or interests of individuals where a reasonable citizen would have a legitimate expectation that the decisionmaking process would be subject to some rules of fair procedure. That would cover decisions affecting a student's special education. But the availability of natural justice, like procedural due process, is riddled with qualifications. It is usually thought to be unavailable where the decision in question involves expertise or professional judgment,[220] and therefore it is arguably not applicable to special education in the absence of the specific statutory authority contained in EA 1981.

Since EA 1981 has brought natural-justice-like procedures into the special education area, the courts might be influenced by the principles of natural justice in construing and enforcing those procedures. As usually stated, the rules of natural justice include the right to a fair hearing[221] and the rule

---

219. *See* P. JACKSON, NATURAL JUSTICE (2d ed. 1979); S. DE SMITH, *supra* note 204, at 569-82.
220. *See* P. JACKSON, *supra* note 219, at 126-28.
221. *See id.* at 60-83; S. DE SMITH, *supra* note 204, at 572-77.

against bias.[222] Although neither branch of natural justice would require a fixed set of predetermined procedures,[223] natural justice might influence the courts' determination as to whether parents have been given an adequate opportunity to present their position to an appeal committee under EA 1981[224] and whether the appeal committee was sufficiently impartial.[225]

EA 1981 plainly relies upon the specified procedures as an important means of protecting the right to receive the "special educational provision" appropriate for each child's "special educational needs." It would be an important contribution to the achievement of the statutory promise for the court to enforce these guaranteed procedural rights, whether or not influenced by natural justice principles. Although there is a strong British distaste for judicial activism, the prospect of judicial enforcement of specific statutory rights does not seem merely an American fantasy.[226] It does seem extremely unlikely that the British courts would act in other than a deferential manner or in other than extraordinary instances of statutory violation. But even rare judicial intervention and the existence of potential judicial enforcement could go far in strengthening parent claims for meaningful procedural involvement and in stiffening the Secretary of State's will to insist that local authorities recognize those rights.

VI

CONTENT OF THE SPECIAL EDUCATION ENTITLEMENT

Whether the rights and duties created by EA 1981 are enforced by the courts or left to be enforced entirely by the Secretary of State and local educational authorities, the ultimate question about required special educational entitlement is the same: What substance, if any, is encompassed by the right to "special educational provision"? On the surface, the answer is disarmingly circular: A child with "special educational needs" is entitled to the "special educational provision" which is specified in the "statement"; the "provision" so specified is what the local education authority decides, following assessment, the child "needs."[227] Professor Kirp has contrasted the Warnock

---

222. See P. JACKSON, supra note 219, at 26-59; S. DE SMITH, supra note 204, at 569-72.

223. See P. JACKSON, supra note 219, at 1-25; S. DE SMITH, supra note 204, at 569.

224. Compare Regina v. Deputy Indus. Injuries Comm'r, [1965] 1 Q.B. 456, 490 (per Lord Diplock, dictum, cross-examination required); Pett v. Greyhound Racing Ass'n Ltd., [1969] 1 Q.B. 125 (right to counsel) with Kavanaugh v. Chief Constable of Devon and Cornwall, [1974] Q.B. 624, 633 (no right to cross-examination); Regina v. Race Relations Bd., ex parte Selvarajan [1975] 1 W.L.R. 1686, 1694 (per Lord Denning, Master of the Rolls, dictum, no right to counsel).

225. Compare Hannam v. Bradford Corp., [1970] 1 W.L.R. 937 (contrary to natural justice for school governors to sit as members of subcommittee of local education authority in teacher dismissal case) with Ward v. Bradford Corp., 70 Knight's Local Gov't R. 27 (1971) (permissible despite language to contrary for school governors to initiate charges and make decision in student expulsion).

226. See cases cited supra notes 207-09 & 222-23; authorities cited supra notes 204, 212.

227. It is well known that the same sort of circularity characterizes the EAHCA. A handicapped child is entitled to a "free appropriate public education"; this appropriate education is what the child's "individualized education program" ("IEP") calls for; the IEP specifies an educational program for the child on the basis of a meeting, the purpose of which is to evaluate the child's needs and determine how those needs should be met.

Report's "professional" approach to the American "legal" approach.[228] Despite this difference, the Warnock Report and, in its wake, EA 1981 are like the EAHCA in substituting procedure for substance. As previously outlined, EA 1981 contains elaborate procedures relating to the process of assessment and determination of a child's special needs and special educational provision. The statute itself specifies no educational content for what should be provided.[229]

The implicit claim of EA 1981 (like the EAHCA) is that if one follows the specified procedures, the correct educational program will be found for each child having a special educational need.[230] Accepting that claim, to say the least, requires an act of faith. The Warnock Report was notably lacking in description or analysis of the educational program to be provided for the broad array of children who, according to the report, will need special education.[231] Surely, this absence must reflect the state of knowledge—or lack thereof—concerning the curriculum for special education.

It does not quite follow that EA 1981 should be construed to contain no substantive constraints whatsoever. There are glimmerings in the Warnock Report and in EA 1981 and related regulations indicating that it is not quite correct to conclude that "whatever is [procedurally correct] is right."[232]

First, regulations issued under express statutory authority indicate that special students are to receive *educational benefits*.[233] No doubt that is a bland standard, and perhaps it is also a self-evident one. But it very clearly says that, however unblemished the procedural path followed, a special student has not received his statutory entitlement if the statement calls for a provision yielding no educational benefit.[234] Merely providing custody or care would not satisfy this standard. Arguably, the question is not actual benefit but rather whether the statement is *designed* to produce an educational benefit.[235] Even if the focus is on the statement rather than the delivery of services, the

---

228. Kirp, *supra* note 25.

229. EA 1981 does require that the education be provided in ordinary schools if statutorily specified conditions are met, EA 1981, § 2(2), (3), (7), but it is arguable that the policy objectives served by integration are social rather than educational. *See infra* discussion in part VII.

230. It is at least arguable that EA 1981 makes a stronger claim that the correct ("professional") decision will result than does the EAHCA; with its greater emphasis on legality, the EAHCA may be more agnostic about a "right answer" and often more willing to settle for giving parents what they want. *See* Kuriloff, *Is Justice Served by Due Process?: Affecting the Outcome of Special Education Hearings in Pennsylvania,* LAW & CONTEMP. PROBS., Winter 1985, at 89.

231. *See* Warnock Report, *supra* note 16, at 205-25; Kirp, *supra* note 25, at 157; S. TOMLINSON, *supra* note 17, at 134-54.

232. *See* A. POPE, ESSAY ON MAN, Epistle I, line 294. Professor Kirp's charge would be that, according to Warnock, whatever the professionals say is right. *See* Kirp, *supra* note 25, at 157.

233. Education (Special Educational Needs) Regulations 1983, §§ 4(2)(c), 10(1)(c)(ii), STAT. INST. 29 (1983).

234. The claim that a special student must receive education that benefits him is consistent with the assumption, characterizing British law since at least 1971, that all special students are educable. *See* Education (Handicapped Children) Act, 1970, ch. 52, § 1(1)(a).

235. *Rowley* strongly suggests that, under the EAHCA, the emphasis should be on the IEP rather than actual benefit, *see* Board of Educ. v. Rowley, 458 U.S. 176, 203-04 (1982), but the *Rowley* opinion is ultimately ambiguous on this point. *See id.* at 200-01.

extensive provisions in the act for reassessment and statement revision[236] substantially reduce the significance of that difference. When experience demonstrates that the education specified in the statement is producing no benefit, it can no longer be thought that the statement is calculated to produce benefits.[237] Determining the *level* of benefit needed to satisfy EA 1981 is likely to be problematic.[238]

A second standard giving content to "special educational provision" under EA 1981 is the Warnock Report's view that a special student is entitled to individualized education. The essence of the Warnock Report, and of the White Paper and EA 1981 following it, is that each child having special educational needs is to have an educational program tailored to meet *that child's* particular educational needs. It does not follow that each special student's educational program must be different from that of every other student. EA 1981 plainly contemplates that special students will commonly be educated in schools, and any form of "school education" contemplates some group process under which students are treated jointly much of the time. The shift from selective to comprehensive schools in England and Wales further reflects an educational judgment favoring common rather than atomized education for children within a broad range of ability.[239] A comparable preference for mixing educationally differing children is evidenced by the mainstreaming provisions in EA 1981.[240]

However paradoxical, the clear educational policy against isolation must be reconciled with the mandate of EA 1981 to shape a child's education in accordance with the child's individual needs. The Warnock Report's condemnation of a categorical approach has been adopted as national policy by EA

---

236. EA 1981, §§ 2(4), 7(10), 9(2); *id.* sched. 1, pt. II, §§ 5-6.

237. *See* DES CIRCULAR 1/83, *supra* note 65, at 11-12; *cf.* Castenada v. Pickard, 648 F.2d 989, 1010 (5th Cir. 1981) (failure of educational program to overcome language barriers would demonstrate program to be inappropriate).

238. In this respect, the history of litigation under the EAHCA is instructive. *See* Board of Educ. v. Rowley, 458 U.S. 176 (1982). The equal protection background of the EAHCA had suggested that the EAHCA contained an equality principle under which an "appropriate" education was measured by comparison to the education of "regular" or "ordinary" children. *See* Rowley v. Board of Educ., 483 F. Supp. 528, 534 (S.D.N.Y.) (handicapped child must have opportunity to achieve his or her full potential commensurate with the opportunity provided to other children), *aff'd,* 632 F.2d 945 (2d Cir. 1980), *rev'd,* 458 U.S. 176 (1982); Buchholtz v. Iowa Dep't of Pub. Instruction, 315 N.W.2d 789, 793 (Iowa 1982) (equality requires a "parity of educational opportunity" between handicapped and nonhandicapped children); Note, *Enforcing the Right to an "Appropriate" Education: The Education for All Handicapped Children Act of 1975,* 92 HARV. L. REV. 1103, 1126-27 (1979) (concept of appropriateness requires "equal opportunity for individual development"). But, in *Rowley,* the Supreme Court rejected this approach and substituted a reading of appropriate education that required a "benefit" to the handicapped child. Although the Court concluded that the benefit need not be the maximum possible, the question whether "any" benefit or "some" benefit or, indeed, a "substantial" benefit is required was pointedly left open. Noting that the child in *Rowley* was receiving "substantial specialized instruction and related services and . . . performing above average," the Court wrote, "[w]e do not attempt today to establish any one test for determining the adequacy of educational benefits conferred upon all children covered by the Act." 458 U.S. at 202.

239. *See generally* E.S. CONWAY, GOING COMPREHENSIVE (1970); A. GRIFFITHS, SECONDARY SCHOOL REORGANIZATION IN ENGLAND AND WALES (1971); W.K. RICHMOND, EDUCATION IN BRITAIN SINCE 1944, 94-112 (1978); N. WRIGHT, PROGRESS IN EDUCATION ch. 4 (1977).

240. *See infra* part VII.

1981, and the elimination of handicap categories would seem to entail more than a difference in terminology. The Warnock recommendations should preclude a process by which a student can be assigned to a school or an educational program of a particular kind simply because the student can be characterized by the same general label as other students so assigned. The student's individual statement must, somehow, be designed to accommodate the exigencies of school and the unique needs of the individual child. Broad discretion will undoubtedly be permitted, but a clear failure to exercise the judgment required to achieve an accommodation should entail a failure to satisfy EA 1981.

A third standard for determining the content of a "special educational provision" follows from EA 1981's requirements concerning the ingredients on which a special student's statement is based. The statute requires that parents have the opportunity to submit evidence and make representations.[241] The statute also requires that the local education authority obtain advice from medical, psychological and educational experts, and it authorizes the authority to obtain advice from others designated by regulation or selected by the authority.[242] Furthermore, those giving advice must take into account other information called to their attention.[243] The statute does not say, in so many words, that the authority's decision must be based upon the advice received or on the resulting record. However, it would be hard to square unbridled local discretion with a statutory pattern that constantly interweaves specific decision and information gathering, makes education authorities consult advisors, makes advisors consult persons with specified knowledge or information, directs the authority to make its decision concerning educational provision "after considering" parental representations and subjects the local decision to a broad review by the Secretary of State. Furthermore, the Secretary of State's regulations expressly require an education authority to consider various factors contributing to the assessment,[244] and they require that the evidence, advice and information considered be made part of the statement.[245] Finally, DES Circular 1/83 seems to assume that the advice on the record imposes limitations on the authority's discretion, at least as a practical matter, when it warns consultants that they should avoid discussion of "eventual placement" so as not to preempt the LEA's decision.[246]

The DES circular also indicates that the local authority's decision is circumscribed to some degree by the record it is obligated to compile.[247] If the advisors say that the child is mildly retarded and well adjusted, it will not do to provide the child with home education and braille textbooks. There will nec-

---

241. EA 1981, §§ 5(3), 7(4).
242. *Id.* sched. 1, pt. I, § 1(2).
243. *See* Education (Special Educational Needs) Regulations 1983, § 4(3), STAT. INST. 29 (1983); *see also id.* § 7(2) (psychologist advisor must consult other psychologists thought to have information).
244. *See id.* § 8 (representations made by and evidence submitted by parents; professional advice; health and welfare information submitted by any district health or social services authority).
245. *See id.* § 10(1)(d).
246. DES CIRCULAR 1/83, *supra* note 65, at 7 ¶ 35.
247. *Id.* at 8 ¶ 39.

essarily be considerable room for judgment in determining whether statement and advice are compatible,[248] but the findings of the assessment process should impose some constraint on the range of permitted content of the resulting statement.

As stressed throughout this article, the local education authorities will have the main responsibility for implementing EA 1981. This conclusion is underscored by the tradition of local control in British education, the primary obligation placed on local authorities by EA 1981 to determine "special educational provision,"[249] and the specific suggestions in EA 1981 that local variation is contemplated.[250] DES Circular 1/83 states that "the Secretary of State for Education and Science hopes that appeals will seldom prove necessary."[251] Although that hope may suggest that local authorities will be given considerable discretion to work things out with parents, it certainly does not suggest that the Secretary of State will fail to enforce the act when appeals do "prove necessary." All local authorities in England and Wales are subject to the *same* statutory standard to provide "special educational provision," and the local determinations are subject to a broad, seemingly discretionary, national review by the Secretary of State for Education and Science.[252]

Thus, it would seem that there is a national dimension to the standard governing the required special educational provision. Requirements that a special student receive educational benefits, individualized education and educational provision based on the assessment process would permit a range of local variation but would also set limits to such variation. It is to be expected that the Secretary of State will be slow to assert that such limits have been reached, but the Secretary of State presumably has the power and duty to refuse to tolerate a breach of the statutory limits. For example, if the Secretary of State believed that research had established that autistic children should be educated in segregated settings, the Secretary of State might reverse a local decision that disregarded that research and called for integrated education of an autistic child in an ordinary school. Or, if the Secretary of State were convinced that catheterization of a special student is a simple, inexpensive, easy-to-learn procedure,[253] the Secretary of State might reverse a local decision which refused to include catheterization in the applicable statement.[254]

---

248. The Secretary of State has expressly stated that "Where it has not proved possible to reconcile differences in the advice submitted," the local authority must decide "the weight to be given to different kinds of advice." *Id.* at 8 ¶ 39.

249. *See supra* notes 160-72 and accompanying text.

250. *See* EA 1981, § 1(2)(b) (kind of facilities "generally provided in schools, within the area of the local authority"); *id.* § 1(3)(a) (educational provision made generally "in schools maintained by the local education authority"); *id.* §§ 2(3), 2(7) (conditions for integration evidently dependent on peculiar facts of each school such as available resources). Of course, separate appeal committees will be established for each authority, and each authority will obtain its own professional advice. *See supra* part III.

251. DES CIRCULAR 1/83, *supra* note 65, at 10 ¶ 54.

252. *See supra* pp. 138-40.

253. *See* Irving Indep. School Dist. v. Tatro, 104 S. Ct. 3371 (1984).

254. The Secretary of State's Regulations require the statement to specify educational "facilities

The Secretary of State might also override a local decision that appeared to be inconsistent with national norms established by the letter or spirit of a law other than EA 1981. For example, official action that results in a disproportionate racial impact can violate the Race Relations Act of 1976.[255] The Secretary of State might conclude that a violation of the Race Relations Act was implicated by a statement specifying a particular educational provision,[256] if information available to the Secretary of State indicated that a significantly higher proportion of West Indian children than of white children in the area received that particular special educational provision.[257]

As pointed out in an earlier section, EA 1981 included no funding component despite the Warnock Report's assumption that its proposals would be expensive to implement. Consequently, the central government's inclination to press for changes in special education and the inclination of local education authorities (as well as their capacity) to adopt expensive changes are probably weakened. It would seem an extreme position to argue that absence of funding should mean that the duties imposed by the act have been nullified. EA 1981 was enacted, and its duties imposed, with full awareness that the revenues needed to facilitate implementation were not to be provided.[258] Still, as a practical matter, the absence of national funding can be expected to increase local variation in the substantive content given to the act's requirements.

---

and equipment" and "staffing arrangements," Education (Special Educational Needs) Regulations 1983, § 10(1)(a), STAT. INST. 29 (1983), and noneducational provision of which "advantage should be taken if the child is properly to benefit from the special educational provision," *id.* § 10(1)(c)(ii).

255. § 1. Racial Discrimination:
(1) A person discriminates against another . . . if—
(b) he applies to that other a requirement or condition which he applies or would apply equally to persons not of the same racial group as that other but— (i) which is such that the proportion of persons of the same racial group as that other who can comply with it is considerably smaller than the proportion of persons not of that racial group who can comply with it; and (ii) which he cannot show to be justifiable irrespective of the colour, race, nationality or ethnic or national origins of the person to whom it is applied.
Race Relations Act, 1976, ch. 74, § 1.
   The act was patterned on the theory of Griggs v. Duke Power Co., 401 U.S. 424 (1971), a case involving employment discrimination under Title VII of the Civil Rights Act of 1964. This theory has been applied to special education situations. *See* Larry P. v. Riles, 495 F. Supp. 926 (N.D. Cal. 1979), *aff'd,* 1983-84 EDUC. HANDICAPPED L. REP. (CRR) 555:304 (9th Cir. 1984).
   256. The Race Relations Act applies to education, *see* Race Relations Act §§ 17-19 (Current Law Statutes Annotated, 1976 Vol. 2). It may be arguable that this application would be negated by § 35, which says that Parts II-IV (including §§ 17-19) do not render unlawful "any act done in affording persons of a particular racial group access to facilities or services to meet the special needs of persons of that group." However, this section appears to be talking about racially conscious "affirmative action"—for example, as the statutory annotation suggests, to satisfy special language needs of "groups whose first language is not English." *Id.*, Part VI, § 35, General Note.
   257. The critical inquiry in applying the Race Relations Act would probably focus on the question of whether discriminatory impact was "justifiable irrespective of . . . race," § 1(1)(b)(ii); *see supra* note 255. *See generally* B. COARD, HOW THE WEST INDIAN CHILD IS MADE EDUCATIONALLY SUBNORMAL; D. GALLOWAY & C. GOODWIN, EDUCATING SLOW-LEARNING AND MALADJUSTED CHILDREN: INTEGRATION OR SEGREGATION? 9, 23-24 (1979); S. TOMLINSON, *supra* note 17, at 155-71.
   258. Nevertheless, critics of the White Paper, which anticipated the lack of funding, did argue that implementation of the Warnock Report without national financial support would permit local authorities to do what they wanted to do. *See* The Times (London) Educational Supplement, Aug. 22, 1980, at 6, col. 6.

Furthermore, in determining what the act's standards require, the cost of providing special education will inevitably be a consideration. The expense of proposed special education could influence judgments about the required level of benefit to be provided, the extent to which individual needs should be accommodated, the extent to which the advice contained in the statement should be followed or the relevance of local resources in determining permissible departures from national norms. Conceptually, the cost might be considered a defensive factor, justifying a failure to provide the special educational provision otherwise mandated by EA 1981. Or, assuming EA 1981 to be an enactment of a pragmatic compromise to meet special needs to the extent it was feasible to do so, cost might be treated as a factor integrally involved in the determination of the special educational provision required by EA 1981. However conceptualized, cost considerations will necessarily have a bearing on what "special educational provision" EA 1981 is determined to require.[259] The difficult problem will be in finding a formula that concedes the relevance of cost but does not make cost a consideration that overwhelms all others.[260]

Plainly, EA 1981 leaves the initial determination of "special educational provision" to local decision, subject to the constraints produced by procedural safeguards, parental involvement and administrative review by the Secretary of State. As argued in this section, special educational provision mandated by the act seems to entail some minimal national substantive content concerning educational benefit, individualization and record-relatedness—presumably all somehow discounted by cost considerations. If substantive standards do exist, they govern both the initial decision of the local education authority and the reviewing decisions of the Secretary of State for Education and Science. Those standards would also apply in the instance of review by the courts, which might uphold the Secretary of State's application of the governing substantive standards as well as require such application by the Secretary of State.

VII

MAINSTREAMING

The Warnock Report advocated the education of children with special education needs in ordinary schools and ordinary classrooms whenever condi-

---

259. Although American courts applying the EAHCA have often seemed to treat cost as immaterial to the requirements of an "appropriate" education, *see, e.g.*, Board of Educ. v. Rowley, 458 U.S. 176, 203-04 (1982), cost has inevitably affected decisions, *see, e.g.*, Lora v. Board of Educ., 456 F. Supp. 1211, 1293 (E.D.N.Y. 1978), *vacated and remanded*, 623 F.2d 248 (2d Cir. 1980); Darlene L. v. Illinois State Bd. of Educ., 568 F. Supp. 1340, 1345 (N.D. Ill. 1983). The courts have commonly phrased their consideration of costs in terms of the need to allocate resources among competing *special educational* needs. *See* Age v. Bullitt County Pub. Schools, 673 F.2d 141, 145 (6th Cir. 1982); Roncker v. Walter, 700 F.2d 1058, 1063 (6th Cir.) (instructions in remanding), *cert. denied*, 104 S. Ct. 196 (1983); Stacey G. v. Pasedena Indep. School Dist., 547 F. Supp. 61, 78 (S.D. Tex. 1982).

260. *See* Bartlett, *The Role of Cost in Educational Decisionmaking for the Handicapped Child*, LAW & CONTEMP. PROBS., Spring 1985, at 7.

tions made it possible to provide quality education in that setting.[261] The Warnock Committee recognized that the integration of special education reflected a movement that reached well beyond British shores (including, of course, the EAHCA in the United States) and that it was not new in Great Britain. The principle of integration had long been accepted in aspirational terms.[262] As the Warnock Report explained it, integrated education reflected a "consensus of public feeling that handicapped people should, so far as possible, be enabled to take their place in the general community."[263] In 1976, while the Warnock Committee was conducting its enquiry, the principle was enacted into law.[264] This law, generally referred to simply as "section 10," left the implementation date to be set by the Secretary of State for Education and Science, a step that was never taken.[265] The Warnock Committee, however, assumed that section 10 was the law. As a consequence, the Warnock Committee treated the integration issue as a given rather than something to be addressed, and as a result, its treatment of the issue in its report appears to reflect a noncommital position.

The Warnock Report's approach to integration, or "mainstreaming," might best be described as cautious. The principle of integration was endorsed, but considerable emphasis was given to the difficulties and burdens of integrating special education. The Warnock Report expressly concluded that certain conditions—teacher training, financial support, suitable facilities—must all be fulfilled in order for special education in ordinary schools to be successfully achieved.[266] The White Paper also subscribed to integration in principle, but the Government's position reflected caution and perhaps skepticism about integration.[267]

Without any provision expressly addressed to integration in EA 1981, the "special educational provision" required to be made available for children with "special educational needs" might well have been construed to require education in an ordinary school or classroom for particular children, possibly for many such children. Such an application of EA 1981 would have seemed especially likely in view of the Warnock Report's general approval of integrated education.[268] In fact, EA 1981 includes an express duty to educate children with "special educational needs" in ordinary schools,[269] subject to

---

261. *See* Warnock Report, *supra* note 16, at 99-120.

262. *See id.* at 32-35.

263. *Id.* at 115 ¶ 7.46.

264. EA 1976, § 10, amending EA 1944, § 33(2).

265. EA 1981, sched. 4 (repealing § 10); *see* White Paper, *supra* note 21, at 13 ¶ 36, 14 ¶ 41.

266. Warnock Report, *supra* note 16, at 120 ¶ 7.61.

267. *See* White Paper, *supra* note 21, at 13, 14 ¶ 41.

268. At least such an application would seem reasonable in the absence of an unexplained repeal of § 10.

269. Where a local education authority arrange special educational provision for a child for whom they maintain a statement under Section 7 of this Act it shall be the duty of the authority, if the conditions mentioned in subsection (3) below are satisfied, to secure that he is educated in an ordinary school.
EA 1981, § 2(2).

several specified conditions.[270]

There is no clear statutory duty to integrate *classrooms* under EA 1981. Section 2(2) of EA 1981, like its predecessor, section 10, prescribes only education in an ordinary *school*. EA 1981 supplements this requirement by adding a duty to see that a child who has special educational needs and who is being educated in an ordinary school "engages in the *activities* of the school together with children who do not have special educational needs."[271] On one occasion the Warnock Report referred to the importance of regular and special children sharing "experience through both curricular and extra-curricular activities."[272] By their use of the word "activities" in section 2(7), it is possible that the drafters of EA 1981 meant to incorporate the Warnock Report's reference to activities both within and outside the classroom, and thus to include integration of the educational process in ordinary classrooms. That interpretation would be supported by the White Paper, which expressly criticized section 10 because it "merely place[d] a handicapped pupil in an ordinary school, which does not by itself guarantee that the child will be educated in association with children who are not handicapped."[273] A contrary view is suggested by the fact that the Warnock Report does not generally talk about classroom integration as the joint participation in "activities."[274] Furthermore, neither the Warnock Report nor the White Paper convey an unqualified enthusiasm for mainstreaming, as already pointed out. It is possible that sections 2(2) and 2(7) will be read together to require classroom integration when the statutory conditions are satisfied.[275] Even if such a reading is not adopted, classroom integration might still be required as part of the special educational provision determined through the assessment process.[276]

Section 2(3) of EA 1981 contains four conditions controlling the duty to

---

270. The conditions are that account has been taken, in accordance with Section 7, of the views of the child's parent and that educating the child in an ordinary school is compatible with —
　　(a) his receiving the special educational provision that he requires;
　　(b) the provision of efficient education for the children with whom he will be educated; and
　　(c) the efficient use of resources.
Id. § 2(3).

271. Where a child who has special educational needs is being educated in an ordinary school maintained by a local education authority it shall be the duty of those concerned with making special educational provision for that child to secure, so far as is both compatible with the objectives mentioned in paragraphs (a) to (c) of subsection (3) above and reasonably practicable, that the child engages in the *activities* of the school together with children who do not have special educational needs.
EA 1981, § 2(7) (emphasis supplied).

272. Warnock Report, *supra* note 16, at 106 ¶ 7.15.

273. White Paper, *supra* note 21, at 13 ¶ 36.

274. *See* Warnock Report, *supra* note 16, at 101 ¶ 7.9, 102-05.

275. By contrast with the ambiguity of EA 1981, the EAHCA clearly requires handicapped children to be educated with children who are not handicapped "to the maximum extent appropriate." Special classes, separate schooling or other "removal from the *regular educational environment*" may occur only when, by reason of the nature or severity of handicaps, "education in *regular classes* with use of supplementary aids and services cannot be achieved." 20 U.S.C. § 1412(5)(B) (emphasis added).

276. It is possible that the draftsmen of the statute, having in mind such a voluntary understanding, drafted the statute in a way that excluded certain students from the class of students having statutory rights with the hope that they would be so integrated but without giving them any right to demand classroom integration.

integrate: (1) account must be taken of the views of the parent; (2) education in an ordinary school must be "compatible with" the child's receiving "the special educational provision that he requires"; (3) integration must be compatible with "efficient education" for the other children; and (4) it must be compatible with the "efficient use of resources." Under section 2(2), the duty to educate children with "special educational needs" in ordinary schools exists if the conditions of section 2(3) are satisfied. Under section 2(7) the integration duty includes a subordinate duty to ensure that the special child engages in school activities with ordinary children so far as is compatible with the conditions of section 2(3) and reasonably practicable. Read literally, these subsections indicate that the basic duty to integrate students depends on the answer to either/or questions: Is each condition satisfied or not? By contrast, the subordinate duty to integrate activities depends on the answer to a question of degree: How much integration is consistent with the statutory standards?

Why distinct approaches should be adopted for EA 1981's integration provisions is not clear,[277] and it may be that a literal reading will be rejected. In any event, the seeming rigidity of the section 2(2) approach is softened by the vague conditions of section 2(3) on which it depends.

Of greatest practical importance in relieving section 2(2) of its rigidity is the fact that the same decisionmakers who decide a child's special educational provision also decide whether the conditions of section 2(3) have been satisfied. If they conclude that under no circumstances can special education in an ordinary school satisfy all of the statutory conditions, they must of course reject integration. However, in all other cases, they are in a position to write the child's statement in a way that will encompass such integration as is consistent with the statutory conditions.[278]

The four conditions of section 2(3) are variously traceable to section 10, the Warnock Report and the White Paper. Only the White Paper directly focused on the importance of giving an "opportunity for the expression of parental preference."[279] The Warnock Report emphasized parental involvement generally in the assessment/placement process. The parent's view seems a plainly relevant consideration in evaluating the desirability of pro-

---

277. The mainstreaming duty of the EAHCA clearly operates along a continuum. The "regular educational environment" is the ideal, but achievement of that ideal is a *relative* matter; integration must be achieved to the "maximum extent appropriate." These notions have been encapsulated in the nonstatutory phrase, "least restrictive environment," and in detailed regulations under the EAHCA. 34 C.F.R. §§ 300.550-.556 (1984).

278. The statutory wording of section 2(2) seems to indicate that the duty to decide whether the conditions for integrated education are satisfied arises at the point of *arranging* special educational provision—that is, after the educational provision has been determined and the student's statement prepared. This would suggest that integration is distinct from the process of assessment and determination of the special educational provision that is required. But that construction is so totally at war with the Warnock Report and common sense that it should be rejected in the absence of a clearer statutory mandate. Also, the regulations clearly contemplate that the statement will specify the kind of school and, if possible, the particular school recommended. Education (Special Educational Needs) Regulations 1983, § 10(1)(b)(i), STAT. INST. 29 (1983).

279. White Paper, *supra* note 21, at 13 ¶ 36.

viding special education in an ordinary school. In particular, mainstreaming is likely to fail without parent support under some circumstances and likely to succeed only with it in other circumstances. EA 1981 does not give the parent a veto over integration, nor does it answer the question of how much weight the parent's views should carry.[280]

Under the second condition set out in section 2(3), education in an ordinary school is not required if it would be incompatible with the special educational provision the child requires.[281] The White Paper had criticized section 10 for failing to take sufficient account of the individuality of needs and the possibility that some children would do better in segregated schools.[282] Yet section 10 had conditioned integration on practicability and compatibility with "efficient instruction,"[283] and the Warnock Report had construed these provisions to present difficult decisions for some children as to where the "balance of advantage lies" between integration and segregation.[284] EA 1981 purports to make this consideration more explicit, but the resulting provision is not free from ambiguity. The wording of sections 2(2) and 2(3)(a), requiring a child to be educated in an ordinary school if that is compatible with the child's receiving the required special educational provision, suggests that education is one thing and integration is something entirely different.[285] If integration is treated as serving values other than education (and even if integration is regarded as one aspect of special educational provision), it is arguable that EA 1981 leaves unanswered an important question about tradeoffs. Integration might be regarded as such an important value that its availability would justify some decline of quality in the education otherwise available.[286] Whether, and to what extent, section 2(3) permits or requires such a balancing of incommensurate values is unclear. Presumably, more weight would be given to integration if it were thought to be an educational component which enhanced educational quality directly.

The third condition of section 2(3) is that integrated education must be

---

280. The principle of parental control of a child's education in British law may push in the direction of giving the parents' view considerable weight. *But see* Cumings v. Birkenhead, [1971] 2 All E.R. 881, 884 (parent preference only one consideration).

281. Under the EAHCA the duty to integrate is excused "only when" integrated education "cannot be achieved satisfactorily." 20 U.S.C. § 1412(5)(B) (1982).

282. White Paper, *supra* note 21, at 13 ¶ 36.

283. Under section 10, integration was not required "[w]here the education of the pupils in such schools as aforesaid— (a) is impracticable or incompatible with the provision of efficient instruction in the schools; or (b) would involve unreasonable public expenditure." EA 1976, § 10(1).

284. Warnock Report, *supra* note 16, at 115 ¶ 7.47; *see id.* at 116-18.

285. *See, e.g.,* The Times (London) Educational Supplement, Dec. 11, 1981, at 8, col. 1. Such a connotation would include an ironic twist. The Warnock Report, and even more, Mrs. Warnock herself, attempted to deflect criticism of and concern over integration by focusing attention on "how" students were educated rather than "where." *See* Warnock Report, *supra* note 16, at 115 ¶ 7.47 ("Parliament's concern with QUALITY of special education as well as its LOCATION"); The Times (London) Educational Supplement, May 19, 1978, at 1, col. 5.

286. Some American cases have seemed to assume that a trade-off is available and that an integrated education is sometimes to be preferred to a nonintegrated—though otherwise superior—education. Roncker v. Walter, 700 F.2d 1058, 1063 (6th Cir.), *cert. denied,* 104 S. Ct. 196 (1983); Springdale School Dist. #50 v. Grace, 693 F.2d 41, 43 (8th Cir. 1982), *cert. denied,* 103 S. Ct. 2086 (1983).

compatible with efficient education for the *other* children. This condition was a significant concern of the Warnock Report;[287] it was explicitly anticipated by the White Paper;[288] and, according to Warnock, it was part of what section 10 embraced in conditioning integration on compatibility with "efficient instruction."[289] Once again, the question of how the interest of the other children is to be balanced against the interest in integration is an open question under the statute. Just what effects will be "compatible" with integration? Or, when will an effect be regarded as compromising "efficient education"? It cannot be contradicted that bringing "special" children into ordinary schools and especially ordinary classrooms is likely to change the educational milieu. That change may include adverse effects. One might say that such potential adverse effects are an inevitable concomitant of mainstreaming special students and thus a factor necessarily to be considered.[290] Yet by singling out this factor expressly, EA 1981 may be understood to give a negative thrust to integration that would not be inevitable, and to put a thumb on the side of the scales disfavoring integration. Certainly, if some isolated statements in the Warnock Report are taken to express the meaning of section 2(3),[291] it may be difficult indeed to satisfy the condition that integration be compatible with efficient education of other children.

The fourth condition on which the duty to integrate depends is cost: integration must be compatible with "the efficient use of resources."[292] There are direct antecedents of this condition in section 10,[293] the Warnock Report,[294] and the White Paper.[295] The Warnock Report spelled out the cost implications of special education, and especially of integrated special education, in

---

287. *See* Warnock Report, *supra* note 16, at 116-17.

288. *See* White Paper, *supra* note 21, at 14 ¶ 41.

289. *See* Warnock Report, *supra* note 16, at 116 ¶ 7.50.

290. The question whether the effect on "other" children may be a proper consideration in deciding "appropriate" education or mainstreaming issues under the EAHCA has not been decided by American courts but has been noted in passing by commentators. *See* Turnbull, Brotherson, Wheat & Esquith, *The Least Restrictive Education for Handicapped Children: Who Really Wants It?*, 16 FAMILY L.Q. 161, 190 (1982); Note, *supra* note 238, at 1123; *see also* 34 C.F.R. § 300.552, comment (1984); Roncker v. Walter, 700 F.2d 1058, 1063 (6th Cir.), *cert. denied*, 104 S. Ct. 196 (1983).

291. For example:

It follows that the arrangements must not work to the disadvantage of any group of pupils in the school, for example in the allocation of resources or amenities, or in the range of academic or social opportunity. Further, we read "efficient instruction" as encompassing the "wholeness" of need which individual pupils may have, their need, for example, for the companionship of children of like age, condition and background, or in some cases for the intimate community that a small school is especially able to provide.

Warnock Report, *supra* note 16, at 116-17.

292. The reported American cases reveal that the courts have been surprisingly grudging in making any concession to arguments based on the out-of-pocket cost of mainstreaming. Springdale School Dist. #50 v. Grace, 693 F.2d 41, 43 (8th Cir. 1982) (ordered mainstreaming although more expensive), *cert. denied*, 103 S. Ct. 2086 (1983); Yaris v. Special School Dist., 558 F. Supp. 545, 559 (E.D. Mo. 1983), *aff'd*, 728 F.2d 1055 (8th Cir. 1984); Espino v. Besteiro, 520 F. Supp. 905 (S.D. Tex. 1981) (ordered mainstreaming although more expensive).

293. Integration is not required if it "would involve unreasonable public expenditure." EA 1944, § 33(2)(a), added by EA 1976, § 10(1).

294. *See* Warnock Report, *supra* note 16, at 118 ¶ 7.55.

295. *See* White Paper, *supra* note 21, at 14 ¶ 41.

detail.[296] The absolute indispensability of being able to provide those things which money must buy to make integration work was stressed. Consequently, when it became clear that no new money would accompany the enactment of EA 1981, great anxiety about the emasculation of the Warnock recommendations was expressed.[297] Some feared that integration without the needed support would be carried out with disastrous educational results.[298] Others feared that the decision to integrate or not would be left to local choice, which, in many cases, would mean no integration.[299] At the very least, it was understood that the absence of funding would place the burden of integration on local education authorities and, because of the substantial variation in means, would result in considerable unevenness in the process of integration.[300]

My discussions with educators in the spring in 1983, just prior to EA 1981's implementation, and my review of the written reactions to EA 1981 left me with the impression that EA 1981 was *perceived* to contain a far more forceful integration requirement than the act or its background seems to justify. There seems to be little doubt that EA 1981 contains only a mild duty to mainstream children who need special education; when combined with the empty budget, that duty may become very attenuated indeed. Yet, integration in England and Wales does seem to have increased in recent years.[301] Perhaps, as the Warnock Report observed, movement in that direction is likely to continue.[302] Perhaps mainstreaming special education is simply an idea whose time has come.[303] Whether, and to what extent, EA 1981 contributes to the integration of special education in England and Wales will probably depend far more on its winning the support of the education community, especially teachers,[304] and on the perceived success or failure of integration in the near future than it will depend on the statutory mandate.

VIII

CONCLUSION

A discussion of a statute at the very beginning of its implementation is

---

296. *See* Warnock Report, *supra* note 16, at 118 ¶ 7.56.
297. *See* The Times (London) Educational Supplement, Oct. 16, 1981, at 12, col. 5; *id.* Mar. 6, 1981, at 6, col. 1; *id.* Feb. 27, 1981, at 6, col. 1.
298. *See* The Times (London) Educational Supplement, Feb. 29, 1980, at 1, col. 1; *id.* July 14, 1978, at 7, col. 1 (risk of an "unholy alliance" between those "doctrinaire enough to support integration for its own sake" and those "who wanted to cut public expenditure"); *id.* Oct. 9, 1980, at 5b, col. 2; *id.* Apr. 12, 1980, at 3f, col. 4.
299. *See id.*, Aug. 22, 1980, at 6, col. 6; The Times (London) Educational Supplement: Scotland, Oct. 13, 1978, at 3, col. 1.
300. *See* Warnock Report, *supra* note 16, at § 119 ¶¶ 7.59-.60. *See generally id.* at 114-20; The Times (London) Educational Supplement, Dec. 11, 1981, at 8, col. 1; *id.* Mar. 6, 1981, at 6, col. 1.
301. *See* Warnock Report, *supra* note 16, at 99 ¶ 7.2, 119 ¶ 7.59; *supra* note 197.
302. *See id.* at 99 ¶ 7.2, 120 ¶ 7.61.
303. *See id.* at 99.
304. *See* The Times (London) Educational Supplement, Oct. 16, 1981, at 12, col. 5 (survey and guidelines sent to Head Teachers by membership association); The Times (London), Oct. 9, 1980, at 5b, col. 2; *id.* Apr. 12, 1980, at 3f, col. 4; Daily Telegraph, Mar. 26, 1979, at 10, col. 4.

necessarily inconclusive. At this stage questions of meaning and interpretation depend largely on future experience. Speculation aside, and even "true meaning" aside, what will the statute be interpreted to mean *in fact*? Which children will actually be covered and afforded special education under the Act? What procedures will actually be made available to parents and followed in the appeal committees? Will the Secretary of State read the statute as affording parents meaningful appeals on the merits of individual cases or will the appeals merely rubber stamp local decisions? Will the courts be called upon to enforce provisions of the act? If so, to what extent will they do so in a deferential manner—and deferential to which administrative body? What content, if any, will be given to the "special educational provision" that these children are entitled to receive? Which children will be integrated in ordinary classrooms and/or in ordinary schools?

Beyond these questions that focus on interpretation, there are questions concerning the implementation of the policy embodied in the new statute. Will special education, along with education generally, continue to be starved for adequate resources? Will the change in labeling emphasized so strongly by the Warnock Report affect attitudes of educators, parents and children in a salutary fashion? Will voluntary organizations attain a level of vitality and durability that will make them a significant (or a more significant) political force in the administration of special education at the school level? What changes, if any, will be made in the educational programs and services provided to children with special needs? To what extent will parents use the appeal committee procedures? What effect will the process of administrative hearings have on educational provision and on the parent's sense of participation in educational decisionmaking? If the court's jurisdiction is invoked successfully, will judicial involvement enforce or undermine the best spirit of the Warnock Report?

Of course, beyond these questions, is the ultimate empirical question: will these statutory changes, however implemented, enhance the quality of the edcuation of children with special educational needs and the quality of the lives they are helped by education to lead? For all of these questions, the conclusion must be that we must wait and see.

5

VARIATIONS ON A THEME—THE CONCEPT OF EQUAL EDUCATIONAL OPPORTUNITY AND PROGRAMMING DECISIONS UNDER THE EDUCATION FOR ALL HANDICAPPED CHILDREN ACT OF 1975

JUDITH WELCH WEGNER*

I

INTRODUCTION

[I]t is in the national interest that the Federal Government assist State and local efforts to provide programs to meet the educational needs of handicapped children in order to assure equal protection of the law.[1]

Congress' desire to assure that traditionally disadvantaged children receive equal educational opportunities has been a major theme running throughout much of the federal education legislation adopted in the last twenty years.[2] The theme is an elusive and complex one. Scholars considering the scope of the Constitution's equal protection guarantee have disagreed sharply and repeatedly regarding which of several possible interpretations should be afforded the concept of "equal educational opportunity."[3] Looking beyond the constitutional arena, educators and philoso-

---

* Associate Professor of Law, University of North Carolina School of Law. Research for this article was supported by a grant from the North Carolina Law Center. The author wishes to express her appreciation to Kate Bartlett for her ever-thoughtful comments on the subject of this article and related matters, to Sally Sharp for her careful review of an earlier draft, and to Brian Caldwell for his invaluable research assistance. Insights gained by the author through discussions with staff of the Office of Special Education and Office of Civil Rights during her tenure as Special Assistant to United States Secretary of Education Shirley M. Hufstedler also contributed immeasurably to the work on this article. The views here presented are, of course, those of the author.

1. 20 U.S.C. § 1400(b)(9) (1982). Education for All Handicapped Children Act of 1975, Pub. L. No. 94-142, § 3(b)(9), 89 Stat. 773, 774.

2. *See, e.g.,* S. REP. No. 146, 89th Cong., 1st Sess., *reprinted in* 1965 U.S. CODE CONG. & AD. NEWS 1446, 1449-50 (discussing Elementary and Secondary Education Act of 1965, Pub. L. No. 89-10, 79 Stat. 27, designed to provide full opportunity for a high quality program of instruction in basic skills so as to overcome effects of poverty and to provide a "basic floor" of services for all adults and children in the United States); *see generally* Levin, *Equal Educational Opportunity for Special Pupil Populations and the Federal Role,* 85 W. VA. L. REV. 159 (1983); Tolette, *The Propriety of the Federal Role in Expanding Equal Educational Opportunity,* 52 HARV. EDUC. REV. 431 (1982).

3. Important early analyses of this question include Kurland, *Equal Educational Opportunity: The Limits of Constitutional Jurisprudence Undefined,* 35 U. CHI. L. REV. 583 (1968); Schoettle, *The Equal Protection Clause in Public Education,* 71 COLUM. L. REV. 1355 (1971); Yudof, *Equal Educational Opportunity and the Courts,* 51 TEX. L. REV. 411 (1973). More recent scholarship has continued to examine competing definitions of constitutional equal protection. *See, e.g.,* Baker, *Outcome Equality or Equality of Respect:*

phers have recognized that the concept of equal opportunity is inherently a protean one which may take different shapes depending not only upon the context in which it is applied, but also upon which of a number of possible objectives are sought to be achieved in a particular context.[4]

Lawmakers seeking to embody the concept of equal educational opportunity in statutory form may hope, through legislative specificity, to avoid some of the uncertainty of interpretation associated with the Constitution's terse equal protection guarantee. The development of a detailed statutory scheme necessitates a rather intricate statement of the equal educational opportunity theme, however, and such intricacy may well compound rather than simplify the problem of interpretation. Such a scheme may include numerous points at which imprecise or ambiguous guidance is provided concerning which of several subtly different conceptions of equal educational opportunity should control. Problems of interpretation may also arise due to internal tensions created when this highly nuanced concept is given different form in several of a statute's myriad provisions.

The Education for All Handicapped Children Act of 1975 (EAHCA or the Act)[5] illustrates the interpretive problems that have arisen when the already elusive concept of equal educational opportunity is given more complex statutory form. Congress' concern with the limited educational opportunities available to handicapped children spurred the enactment of this measure in

---

The Substantive Content of Equal Protection, 131 U. PA. L. REV. 933 (1983); Levin, *The Courts, Congress, and Educational Adequacy: The Equal Protection Predicament,* 39 MD. L. REV. 187 (1979).

4. *See, e.g.,* D. RAE, EQUALITIES (1981) (describing more than 108 distinct interpretations of equality involving numerous variables including whether the subject of equality is individual-regarding, segmental, or block-regarding; whether means-regarding or prospect-regarding equal opportunity is involved; whether the equality is lot-regarding or person-regarding; and whether equality is relative or absolute); A. WISE, RICH SCHOOLS, POOR SCHOOLS 143-59 (1967) (outlining nine definitions of equal educational opportunity, including a "negative definition" (child's opportunity does not depend on parents' economic circumstances or location within state); "full opportunity" definition (schools must give child every conceivable assistance in developing his abilities); "foundation" definition (schools provide satisfactory minimum educational offering in form of minimum outlay on each pupil); "minimum attainment" definition (schools must allocate adequate resources to allow each student to reach a specified level of achievement); "leveling" definition (schools allocate resources in inverse proportion to students' abilities); "competition" definition (schools allocate resources in direct proportion to students' abilities); "equal dollars per pupil" definition (schools allocate same level of resources to each student); "maximum variance ratio" definition (schools allocate resources to pupils at a level which falls within a set percentage of deviation from expenditures of other school districts); "classification" definition (schools provide students with certain characteristics the same program of educational services which are provided to students with corresponding characteristics elsewhere in the state)); Joseph, *Some Ways of Thinking About Equality of Opportunity,* 33 WESTERN POL. Q. 393 (1980) (distinguishing between equality of result and formal, compensatory, competitive, and developmental types of equality of opportunity); Coleman, *The Concept of Equality of Educational Opportunity,* 38 HARV. EDUC. REV. 7, 16-17 (1968), *reprinted in* EQUAL EDUCATIONAL OPPORTUNITY 9 (1969) (discussing types of inequality including inequality with respect to community's tangible and intangible inputs into schools, with respect to racial composition of school populations, with respect to consequences of schools for individuals with equal backgrounds and abilities, with respect to consequences for those with unequal backgrounds and abilities, and with respect to relative intensities of school and home influences).

5. Pub. L. No. 94-142, 89 Stat. 773 (codified as amended at 20 U.S.C. §§ 1400-01, 1405-06, 1411-20, 1453, 1232 (1982)).

1975.[6] It responded to a well-documented pattern of unequal opportunity, which has resulted in the outright exclusion of handicapped children from schools in many cases and their placement in poorly supported, ineffective special classes in many others.[7] Congressional action was triggered by a rising tide of constitutional litigation such as *Pennsylvania Association for Retarded Children (PARC) v. Pennsylvania*[8] and *Mills v. Board of Education.*[9] Both

---

6. Congress had originally authorized federal financial assistance for special education in 1966. Elementary and Secondary Education Amendments of 1966, Pub. L. No. 89-750, § 161, 80 Stat. 1191, 1204-08 (repealed by Pub. L. No. 91-230 § 622, 84 Stat. 188; current version in scattered sections in 20 U.S.C. §§ 1400-1461) (adding new Title VI to Elementary and Secondary Education Act of 1965, Pub. L. No. 89-10, 79 Stat. 27). Four years later, the Education of the Handicapped Act was enacted. Pub. L. No. 91-230, Title VI, §§ 601-622, 84 Stat. 175-88 (1970) (codified in scattered sections in 20 U.S.C. §§ 1400-1461 (1982)). Part B of that Act authorized grants to the states and outlying areas to assist them in initiating, expanding, and improving programs for the education of the handicapped. *Id.* at § 611(a); 84 Stat. 178, (amended by Pub. L. No. 94-142, § 5, 89 Stat. 773, 776, current version at 20 U.S.C. § 1411). Amendments to the 1970 legislation were adopted in 1974, as a first step in modifying the federal funding formula subsequently revised by the EAHCA. *See* Education of the Handicapped Amendments of 1974, Pub. L. No. 93-380, §§ 611-621, 88 Stat. 579-85 (codified at 20 U.S.C. §§ 1401-1461 (1982)). The 1974 amendments also contained the seeds of several important substantive provisions now found in the EAHCA. *See* Comment, *The Least Restrictive Environment Section of the Education for All Handicapped Children Act of 1975: A Legislative History and An Analysis*, 13 GONZAGA L. REV. 717, 762-67 (1978).

The 1975 legislation was adopted following extensive hearings. *See Education for All Handicapped Children, 1975 Hearings Before the Subcomm. on the Handicapped of the Senate Comm. on Labor and Public Welfare on S. 6*, 94th Cong., 1st Sess. (1975); *Education for All Handicapped Children, 1973-74, Parts 1-3; Hearings Before the Subcomm. on the Handicapped of the Senate Comm. on Labor and Public Welfare on S. 6*, 93rd Cong., 1st & 2d Sess. (1973-74); *Financial Assistance for Improved Educational Services for Handicapped Children: Hearings Before the Select Subcomm. on Education of the House Comm. on Education and Labor on H.R. 70*, 93rd Cong., 2d Sess. (1974).

7. *See generally* Lazerson, *The Origins of Special Education*, in SPECIAL EDUCATION POLICIES 15 (J. Chambers & W. Hartman eds. 1983); Burgdorf & Burgdorf, *A History of Unequal Treatment: The Qualifications of Handicapped Persons as a "Suspect Class" under the Equal Protection Clause*, 15 SANTA CLARA L. REV. 855, 868-83, 899-910 (1975).

8. 343 F. Supp. 279 (E.D. Pa. 1972); *see also* 334 F. Supp. 1257 (E.D. Pa. 1971) (earlier consent decree). In *PARC*, mentally retarded residents of the Pennsylvania state institution at Pennhurst alleged that they had been improperly denied any meaningful education. Since scientific evidence had established that all children, including developmentally disabled children, have the capacity to learn, plaintiffs asserted that no rational basis existed to justify the state's failure to provide suitable educational opportunities, and that the state's action therefore violated the equal protection clause of the federal constitution. Moreover, plaintiffs claimed that the state's exclusion of a vague category of "uneducable" children from such opportunities, without the benefit of notice or a hearing, violated the due process clause. The state agreed to end proceedings pursuant to a negotiated consent decree. In its order approving that decree, the three-judge federal court reserved its judgment on the merits, but stated that plaintiffs had stated a "colorable constitutional claim." 343 F. Supp. at 288 n.19.

The *PARC* decision has been the subject of extensive scholarly commentary. *See, e.g.,* Haggerty & Sacks, *Education of the Handicapped: Towards a Definition of an Appropriate Education*, 50 TEMP. L.Q. 961, 966-75 (1977); Kirp, Buss & Kuriloff, *Legal Reform of Special Education: Empirical Studies and Procedural Proposals*, 62 CALIF. L. REV. 40, 58-82 (1974); Neal & Kirp, *The Allure of Legalization Reconsidered: The Case of Special Education*, LAW & CONTEMP. PROBS., Winter 1985, at 63, 69-70.

9. 348 F. Supp. 866 (D.D.C. 1972). *Mills* was brought on behalf of mentally, physically, and emotionally disturbed children who had been excluded from educational opportunities in the District of Columbia schools. *Mills* squarely held that exclusion of handicapped children from public education violated the Fifth Amendment. *Id.* at 875. *Mills* added to the *PARC* reasoning in two noteworthy respects. First, the *Mills* court rejected the District's putative cost defense, holding that the problem of insufficient funds faced by the school board could not be permitted to result in an outright denial of educational opportunity to handicapped children, nor could the inadequacies of the school system bear more heavily on the exceptional or handicapped child than on his nonhandicapped counter-

cases had recognized that handicapped children were entitled to participate in the nation's schools by receiving educational services appropriate to their special needs. The resulting legislation sought, to a significant extent, to incorporate this developing constitutional doctrine into federal law applicable throughout the fifty states.[10] Congress went further, however, elaborating upon the already intricate equal educational opportunity theme by introducing novel and important statutory variations.[11]

This article explores the equal educational opportunity theme as it is embodied in the EAHCA's educational programming requirements. It will focus on three key questions. First, it will consider the level and extent of services which must be provided under the Act to address handicapped children's educational needs. Specifically, it will discuss the courts' efforts to determine whether the mix of services to be afforded must guarantee a handicapped child only minimal educational opportunity, opportunity equivalent to that provided his nonhandicapped peers, or some more optimal opportunity. Second, the article will consider which of a handicapped child's many needs must be met at public expense pursuant to the EAHCA. To this end, it will examine the problems encountered when parents seek services which simultaneously address both a child's educational needs and his emotional and custodial needs, services which have traditionally been regarded as noneducational in nature and thus beyond the range of schools' responsibilities to nonhandicapped children. Third, the article will explore the special problems which

---

parts. *Id.* at 876. Second, the court issued an extensive remedial order which foreshadowed many of the substantive provisions included in the EAHCA. Among these were the requirements that all handicapped children be served, that each child be provided an "appropriate" education suitable to his individual needs, that children be placed in the most normal setting in which they could function effectively, and that they and their parents be afforded notice and an opportunity for a hearing before potentially adverse changes in placement were made. *Id.* at 878-83.

For more extensive discussion of the *Mills* decision, see generally those secondary sources which address the *PARC* case, cited *supra* note 8.

For a further discussion by early proponents of handicapped children's constitutional right to equal educational opportunity, see also Dimond, *The Constitutional Right to Education: The Quiet Revolution,* 24 HASTINGS L.J. 1087 (1973); Handel, *The Role of the Advocate in Securing the Handicapped Child's Right to an Effective Minimal Education,* 36 OHIO ST. L.J. 349 (1975); Herr, *Retarded Children and the Law: Enforcing the Constitutional Rights of the Mentally Retarded,* 23 SYRACUSE L. REV. 995 (1972).

10.   The legislative history of the EAHCA is replete with references to *PARC* and *Mills. See, e.g.,* S. REP. No. 168, 94th Cong., 1st Sess. 6, *reprinted in* 1975 U.S. CODE CONG. & AD. NEWS 1425, 1430 (discussing *PARC* and *Mills* decisions); *id.* at 9, *reprinted in* U.S. CODE CONG. & AD. NEWS at 1433 (stating that "over the past few years, parents of handicapped children have begun to recognize that their children are being denied services which are guaranteed under the Constitution. It should not be necessary for parents throughout the country to continue utilizing the courts to assure themselves a remedy."); H.R. REP. No. 322, 94th Cong., 1st Sess. 3-4 (1975) (discussing *PARC, Mills* and various state court decisions).

11.   For commentary which provides a useful summary of the Act's principal provisions, see generally L. ROTHSTEIN, RIGHTS OF PHYSICALLY HANDICAPPED PERSONS 25-48 (1984); Blakely, *Judicial and Legislative Attitudes Toward the Right to an Equal Education for the Handicapped,* 40 OHIO ST. L.J. 603, 615-33 (1979); Colley, *The Education for All Handicapped Children Act (EHA): A Statutory and Legal Analysis,* 10 J. LAW & EDUC. 137 (1981); Krass, *The Right to Public Education for Handicapped Children: A Primer for the New Advocate,* 1976 U. ILL. L.F. 1016, 1063-77; Stark, *Tragic Choices in Special Education: The Effect of Scarce Resources on the Implementation of Pub. L. No. 94-142,* 14 CONN. L. REV. 477 (1982). For an excellent review of procedural problems raised in litigation under the Act, see Hyatt, *Litigating the Rights of Handicapped Children to an Appropriate Education: Procedures and Remedies,* 29 UCLA L. REV. 1 (1981).

have arisen in determining whether noninstructional medical services, traditionally unavailable to nonhandicapped students, must be provided by school systems as a result of this federal legislation. In particular, it will focus on the recent debate regarding the availability of clean intermittent catheterization and psychotherapy services, which some have urged should be regarded as nondiagnostic, nonevaluative medical services that need not be provided under the EAHCA.

The article will argue that these controversies can be more fully understood by examining the equal educational opportunity theme that unites them. It will demonstrate that the courts which have been asked to address each of the three questions just described have done so in ways that reflect underlying uncertainty as to whether and how the concept of equal educational opportunity bears upon their resolution of various programming disputes. It will urge that recognizing the important role of equal educational opportunity as a source of uncertainty, and identifying and evaluating the competing interpretations of that concept that have emerged to date in the three contexts of interest here, provides helpful insight into the substantive requirements of the EAHCA.

Parts II and III will consider the level and extent of services required to be provided under the EAHCA. Reserving the more specific questions discussed in subsequent portions of this paper, part II will focus on pertinent legislative history and upon early cases interpreting the Act's requirement that all handicapped children be afforded a "free appropriate public education" (FAPE). Part III will examine the United States Supreme Court's landmark decision in *Board of Education v. Rowley*[12] and conclude that the Court's interpretation of the Act's FAPE requirement as guaranteeing a minimally equal level of educational opportunity to handicapped children is a legitimate and necessary reading of the Act.

Part IV will discuss judicial efforts to delineate the scope or range of handicapped children's needs which must be addressed by the schools pursuant to the EAHCA. It will suggest that novel questions are posed by the juxtaposition of this statutory scheme with the traditional approach to meeting the educational, but not noneducational, needs of nonhandicapped children in the nation's schools. It will argue that the EAHCA supplants this traditional scheme by embodying an inclusionary, rather than exclusionary, approach to defining educational needs, that is, one that requires that services be provided where needed for educational purposes, even if noneducational needs are at the same time addressed. It will also suggest that courts should go farther and abandon the classic dichotomy between educational and noneducational needs, instead recognizing that all needs that directly or indirectly affect a child's educational performance must be addressed pursuant to the EAHCA, subject, of course, to the substantial limitations on the level and extent of services, and the types of services required, described in parts II, III and V.

---

12.   458 U.S. 176 (1982).

Part V will consider whether certain services, reasonably described as medical in nature, must be provided by school districts under the Act. It will argue that textual references to medical services clearly limit districts' obligations in this regard, but that it is less certain whether the EAHCA's nonevaluative, nondiagnostic medical services exception is partial or complete. It will urge that this provision can reasonably be interpreted as a partial exception designed to limit schools' responsibilities in view of the particularly expansive definitions of equal educational opportunity possibly or actually embodied elsewhere in the Act. It will argue that this approach is consistent both with the Supreme Court's determination, in *Irving Independent School District v. Tatro*,[13] that clean intermittent catheterization is a related service, and with the judgment of a number of lower courts that intensive psychological services, in the form of psychotherapy, may be required in certain cases.

II

LEVEL AND EXTENT OF SERVICES PRIOR TO *ROWLEY*

Disputes often arise between parents and school officials regarding the level and extent of educational services to be provided a particular child.[14] Disagreement concerning the level and extent of educational programming is most commonly voiced in practical terms: what pupil-teacher ratio must be employed in a class for emotionally disturbed students;[15] how many months of instruction need be provided;[16] must a teacher's aide be retained to accompany a handicapped child to mainstream classes;[17] and what method of instruction should be adopted for mentally retarded students' basic life-skills instruction.[18]

---

13.   104 S. Ct. 3371 (1984).

14.   *See generally* Kirst & Bertken, *Due Process Hearings in Special Education: Some Early Findings From California*, in SPECIAL EDUCATION POLICIES 136 (J. Chambers & W. Hartman eds. 1983) (reporting that in California administrative hearings studied, more than 22 percent of cases involved requests for related services or an extended school year, while more than 70 percent of cases involved demands for services allegedly available only through private day programs which traditionally have provided more intensive services than those available through many public schools. *Id.* at 142-43.); Kuriloff, *Is Justice Served by Due Process?: Affecting the Outcome of Special Education Hearings in Pennsylvania,* LAW & CONTEMP. PROBS., Winter 1985, at 89.

15.   *See* Colin K. v. Schmidt, 536 F. Supp. 1375, 1386-87 (D.R.I. 1982), *aff'd,* 715 F.2d 1 (1st Cir. 1983).

16.   *E.g.,* Crawford v. Pittman, 708 F.2d 1028 (5th Cir. 1983); Armstrong v. Kline, 476 F. Supp. 583 (E.D. Pa. 1979), *remanded sub nom.* Battle v. Pennsylvania, 629 F.2d 269 (3d Cir. 1980), *cert. denied,* 452 U.S. 968 (1981); Yaris v. Special School Dist., 558 F. Supp. 545 (E.D. Mo. 1983), *aff'd,* 728 F.2d 1055 (8th Cir. 1984); Stacy G. v. Pasadena Indep. School Dist., 547 F. Supp. 61, 79-80 (S.D. Tex. 1982); Georgia Ass'n of Retarded Citizens v. McDaniel, 511 F. Supp. 1263 (N.D. Ga. 1981), *aff'd,* 716 F.2d 1565 (11th Cir. 1983), *vacated,* 104 S. Ct. 3581 (1984), *aff'd as modified,* 1984-85 Educ. Handicapped L. Rep. (CRR) (11th Cir. 1984) (on EAHCA grounds only); Bales v. Clarke, 523 F. Supp. 1366 (E.D. Va. 1981); Anderson v. Thompson, 495 F. Supp. 1256, 1265-67 (E.D. Wis. 1980), *aff'd,* 658 F.2d 1205 (7th Cir. 1981); Birmingham & Lamphere School Dists. v. Superintendent of Pub. Instruction, 120 Mich. App. 465, 328 N.W.2d 59 (1982).

17.   *See In re* Brookfield Pub. Schools, 1982-83 EDUC. HANDICAPPED L. REP. (CRR) 504:166 (Mass. SEA 1982).

18.   *See In re* Marin County Office of Educ., 1982-83 EDUC. HANDICAPPED L. REP. (CRR) 504:162 (Cal. SEA 1982).

These concrete problems mask a more deep-seated theoretical conflict, however. Many school districts believe that their obligation to handicapped children is a relatively limited one which requires them to provide such children with sufficient educational programming to allow the children to derive "some benefit" from their educational experience. In those districts' view, this is all they are obliged to provide to any student, all they can measure, and all they can afford. In more theoretical terms, this "some benefit" standard might well be characterized as a first derivative of the "minimum attainment" definition of equal educational opportunity recognized by school finance theorists.[19] Under that definition, resources are to be allocated so that every student reaches a specified level of achievement.[20] In contrast, the "some benefit" approach, of interest here, would assure students of receiving resources needed to make some incremental progress toward their educational goals, without guaranteeing the means necessary to the actual achievement of those goals.

Parents have often espoused competing views. They tend to reject the "some benefit" standard, which assures handicapped children a minimal opportunity, in instances in which other children receive services designed to facilitate their attaining a more than minimal level of achievement. Parents have generally preferred either of two alternative approaches that reflect a more broadly conceived interpretation of equal educational opportunity.

On the one hand, parents may urge that an "equivalent opportunity" be provided their handicapped child. Thus, if a nonhandicapped child receives programming that gives him a good chance to achieve appropriate educational goals, a handicapped child should likewise be entitled to a good education, taking his handicapping condition into account. In theoretical terms, this "equivalent opportunity" standard perhaps most closely resembles another vintage definition of equal educational opportunity proposed in the aftermath of *Brown v. Board of Education*:[21] the provision of equal tangible and intangible educational inputs for all school children.[22] The "equivalent opportunity" standard described here differs from this vintage definition in certain respects, however. The "equivalent opportunity" standard entails comparison of tangible services and facilities, such as pupil-teacher ratios, rather than intangible factors, such as teacher morale. Such tangible factors may, however, defy comparison in much the same way that intangibles do, in view of the inherent differences in expenditures, facilities, design, and other program characteristics that are associated with regular and special education programs of equivalent quality. Moreover, a determination of "equivalent opportunity" for present purposes seems to envision comparison not just between programs for handicapped and nonhandicapped children generally, but also between individual handicapped children and their handicapped or

---

19. The minimum attainment definition is discussed in A. WISE, *supra* note 4, at 151.
20. *Id.*
21. 347 U.S. 483-(1954).
22. Coleman, *supra* note 4, at 17.

nonhandicapped peers. The "equivalent opportunity" standard therefore requires even more complex comparative analysis than would be contemplated under an application of the vintage standard to ensure equality of opportunity between and among schools or school districts.

Alternatively, parents may argue that schools should provide a handicapped child with an "equalized" educational opportunity, by affording him whatever services are needed to minimize the effects of his handicapping condition, thereby allowing him to benefit as nearly as possible from the same educational opportunities that are available to his nonhandicapped peers. This argument may be particularly appealing to parents of physically impaired students who could be fully integrated into mainstream classes if adequate means of translation were provided or physical barriers overcome. Viewed from a more theoretical perspective, the "equalized educational opportunity" standard represents a blend of two traditional definitions of equal educational opportunity. It resembles the "leveling" definition of that concept, which asserts that resources should be allocated in inverse proportion to students' abilities,[23] for it contemplates that handicapped children would be provided with whatever services are necessary to allow them to compete as nearly as possible on an equal footing with their nonhandicapped peers. It also resembles the "full opportunity" definition of "equal educational opportunity," which assumes that all students will be given adequate resources to allow them to develop their individual abilities to the limit.[24] Under the "equalized educational opportunity" standard, however, full opportunity would be provided only to handicapped children, and only where, in the absence of full opportunity, those children would be unable to profit from generally available educational opportunities to the same extent as their nonhandicapped peers.

Congress and the courts, no less than schools and parents, have been troubled by such deep-seated conflicts, reflecting a fundamental uncertainty regarding the interpretation of the concept of equal educational opportunity as it applies to the level and extent of educational programming under the Act. Section A of this part discusses pertinent portions of the EAHCA's statutory text and legislative history. Section B reviews early judicial decisions regarding the level and extent of services required. The Supreme Court's efforts to resolve this uncertainty are the subject of part III.

A. Congressional Guidance

The EAHCA's substantive mandate is a deceptively simple one. In order to qualify for categorical federal assistance, states and subsidiary local educational agencies must agree to ensure that handicapped children[25] within their

---

23. A. WISE, *supra* note 4, at 152-53.
24. *Id.* at 148-49.
25. "Handicapped children" protected by the Act include "mentally retarded, hard of hearing, deaf, speech impaired, visually handicapped, seriously emotionally disturbed, orthopedically impaired, or other health impaired children, or children with specific learning disabilities, who by reason thereof require special education and related services." 20 U.S.C. §1401(1) (1982). Regulations defining each of the listed handicaps appear at 34 C.F.R. § 300.5 (1984).

jurisdictions receive a "free appropriate public education."[26] A "free appropriate public education" is, in turn, composed of two programmatic components: "special education" and "related services."[27] The free appropriate public education required to be provided any individual child is determined through an innovative consultation process. After a child has been identified as handicapped, he is evaluated and a meeting of parents, teachers, other professionals, and perhaps the child himself is convened to develop the child's own "individualized education program" (IEP).[28] The IEP includes a statement of the child's present levels of educational performance, his annual goals and short-term instructional objectives, the educational services he is to receive and the setting in which they are to be provided, the initiation date and duration of those services, and the criteria and evaluation procedures to be used in determining whether those instructional services are being achieved.[29] Parents who object to a proposed IEP may invoke their due process rights to an administrative appeal.[30] Either parents or school officials may then pursue an additional appeal in state or federal court.[31]

For present purposes, the critical textual provisions are those which define "special education" and "related services," for it is in these provisions that Congress endeavored to establish the broad contours of the educational programming available under the Act. "Special education" is defined as "specially designed instruction, at no cost to parents or guardians, to meet the unique needs of a handicapped child, including classroom instruction, instruction in physical education, home instruction, and instruction in hospi-

---

26. *See* 20 U.S.C. § 1412(2)(B) (1982) ("In order to qualify for assistance under this part . . . a State shall demonstrate . . . that . . . (1) [it] has in effect a policy that assures all handicapped children the right to free appropriate public education, (2) [it has developed a plan to assure that] (B) a free appropriate public education will be available for all handicapped children between the ages of 3 and 18 within the State. . . ."); *id.* § 1414(a) ("A local educational agency . . . which desires to receive payments . . . for any fiscal year shall submit an application . . . [which] shall . . . (1)(C) establish a goal of providing full educational opportunities to all handicapped children, including . . . (ii) the provision of, and the establishment of priorities for providing, a free appropriate public education . . . .").

27. *See id.* § 1401(18) (defining "free appropriate public education" as "special education and related services which (A) have been provided at public expense under public supervision and direction, and without charge, (B) meet the standards of the State educational agency, (C) include an appropriate preschool, elementary, or secondary education in the State involved, and (D) are provided in conformity with the individualized education program required under section 1414(a)(5) of this title").

28. *See id.* § 1401(19).

29. For a detailed discussion of specific problems likely to arise in the development of a child's IEP, see 34 C.F.R. § 300 App. C (1984) (notice of interpretation of federal regulations governing development of IEP's); *Id.* §§ 300.341-.349.

30. *See* 20 U.S.C. § 1415(b) (1982) (describing procedural safeguards, including right of parents or a guardian to examine relevant records, to obtain independent educational evaluation, to receive written prior notice of proposed changes in evaluation, programming, or placement, and to file complaint triggering impartial administrative hearing by state educational agency); 34 C.F.R. § 300.500-.514 (1984) (governing due process rights).

31. *See id.* § 1415(e)(2) (describing right of party aggrieved by findings and decision of impartial hearing officer to bring civil action in state court of competent jurisdiction or in federal district court, and requiring court to "receive the records of the administrative proceedings, [to] hear additional evidence at the request of a party and, basing its decision on the preponderance of the evidence, [to] grant such relief as [it] determines is appropriate").

tals and institutions."[32] "Related services," in turn, include "such developmental, corrective, and other supportive services . . . as may be required to assist a handicapped child to benefit from special education . . . ."[33]

This statutory language is, unfortunately, ambiguous. Although the definition of "special education" indicates that instruction is required "to meet the unique needs" of each handicapped child, it does not clearly specify whether "meeting" such needs entails merely addressing those needs, fully satisfying those needs, or something in between. Similarly, the key term "benefit," included in the "related services" definition, is susceptible to several interpretations. The benefit provided might take the form of minimal, incremental progress toward the child's educational objectives, progress toward those objectives to the same extent as the child's nonhandicapped peers, or enjoyment of the maximum benefits conceivable. Thus, the statutory language is arguably amenable to any of the three interpretations of equal educational opportunity—some benefit, equivalent benefit, or equalized benefit—introduced above.[34] Other statutory provisions provide little additional insight on this point.[35]

The statute's legislative history is no more enlightening. Committee reports discussing the FAPE requirement and pertinent definitions do little more than restate the statutory text.[36] General statements of a desire to ensure that handicapped children receive "equal educational opportunities"

---

32. *Id.* § 1401(16).

33. *Id.* § 1401(17).

34. See *supra* text accompanying notes 19-24.

35. The EAHCA also contains several references to Congress' desire that handicapped children be provided with "full equality of educational opportunity" or "full educational opportunity." See 20 U.S.C. § 1400(b)(3) (1982) ("Congress finds that . . . more than half of the handicapped children in the United States do not receive appropriate educational services which would enable them to have full equality of opportunity"); *id.* § 1412(2)(A)(i) (State eligibility conditioned upon development of plan with policies and procedures which the State will undertake to assure that there is established "a goal of providing full educational opportunity to all handicapped children"); *id.* § 1414(a)(1)(C) (local educational agency desiring to receive funds under EAHCA must submit application to state educational agency which "establish[es] a goal of providing full educational opportunites to all handicapped children").

Arguably, this language suggests that Congress intended to require that the needs of handicapped children must be met as fully as possible, that is, that they be afforded an "equalized" educational opportunity. As this article demonstrates, however, the concept of equal educational opportunity bears on a number of aspects of the statutory scheme, and a similar interpretation of this concept need not have been intended in each of these differing contexts. Federal regulators appear to have recognized as much, for they carefully distinguished the terms "free appropriate public education" and "full educational opportunity goal" in commentary to 1977 EAHCA regulations. In their view the phrase "full educational opportunity goal" is broader in scope than "FAPE" because it covers children aged birth through 21, includes a planning as well as programming function, allows local educational agencies to set their own timetables for meeting that goal, and calls for the provision of additional facilities, personnel, and services to further enrich a handicapped child's educational opportunity beyond that mandated under the FAPE requirement. 42 Fed. Reg. 42,506 (1977). The inclusion of references to "full educational opportunity" elsewhere in the statute is thus of limited assistance in interpreting the critical FAPE standard and related definitions.

36. See, e.g., S. REP. No. 168, 94th Cong., 1st Sess. 10, *reprinted in* 1975 U.S. CODE CONG. & AD. NEWS 1425, 1434; H.R. REP. No. 332, 94th Cong., 1st Sess. 18 (1975); S. REP. No. 455, 94th Cong., 1st Sess. 29-30 (1975).

are scattered throughout reports, hearings, and floor debates.[37] More specific comments hint at a wide range of underlying views. For example, some proponents suggested that the legislation was designed to require school systems to provide equal educational opportunities which conformed to constitutional mandates.[38] Others desired that "equivalent"[39] or "full"[40] educational opportunities be afforded. In sum, Congress provided only limited guidance concerning the level and extent of services to be required, merely suggesting, in a general way, that some sort of equality-based standard might reasonably be employed.

B. Early Judicial Response

Faced with limited legislative and administrative[41] guidance, the courts were initially left to their own devices to clarify the substantive standard to be used in assessing the sufficiency of educational programming under the EAHCA. Perhaps not surprisingly, early court decisions in many instances gave lip service to some sort of equality-based standard, but split sharply over the precise type of equality they believed the statute guaranteed.

The greatest number of cases spoke generally of Congress' desire to ensure "equal educational opportunity," but adopted a restrictive "some benefit" test in order to determine whether an "appropriate" education had been provided.[42] The test was variously stated and variously applied. At times, the courts spoke of the existence or absence of regression or other harm.[43] In some instances, this standard seems to have been applied because evidence of

---

37. *See, e.g.,* S. Rep. No. 168, 94th Cong., 1st Sess. 9, *reprinted in* 1975 U.S. Code Cong. & Ad. News 1425, 1433; 121 Cong. Rec. 19,483 (1975) (remarks of Sen. Randolph); *id.* at 19,504 (Sen. Humphrey); *id.* at 19,505 (Sen. Beall); *id.* at 23,704 (Rep. Brademas); *id.* at 25,540 (Rep. Grassley); *id.* at 37,030-31 (Rep. Mink); *id.* at 37,412 (Sen. Taft); *id.* at 37,413 (Sen. Williams); *id.* at 37,418-19 (Sen. Cranston); *id.* at 37,419-20 (Sen. Beall); *Education for All Handicapped Children 1973-74 Hearings Before the Subcomm. on the Handicapped of the Senate Comm. on Labor and Public Welfare on S. 6,* 93d Cong., 1st Sess. (1973), part 1, at 31 (Sen. Williams).

38. 121 Cong. Rec. 37,413 (1975) (remarks of Sen. Williams); *see also supra* note 10 (discussing portions of the legislative history that reflect a desire to embody constitutional principles of early cases into statutory form).

39. 121 Cong. Rec. 19,483 (1975) (remarks of Sen. Stafford).

40. *See, e.g.,* 121 Cong. Rec. 19,482-83 (1975) (remarks of Sen. Randolph); *id.* at 23,703-05 (Rep. Brademas); *id.* at 25,538 (Rep. Cornell); *id.* at 37,025 (Rep. Perkins); H.R. Rep. No. 332, 94th Cong., 1st Sess. 11 (1975); *see also id.* at 13 (handicapped child requires tailored educational plan to achieve his "maximum potential").

41. Applicable EAHCA regulations focus significantly on the types of services to be provided pursuant to the Act. *See, e.g.,* 34 C.F.R. § 300.13 (1984) ("related services" definition); *id.* at § 300.14 ("special education" definition); *id.* at §§ 300.305-.307 (availability of programs and services such as art, music, vocational education, athletics, health services, and physical education). The regulations do not elaborate upon the level and extent of services to be provided, however.

42. *See* Age v. Bullitt County Pub. Schools, 673 F.2d 141, 144 (6th Cir. 1982); Colin K. v. Schmidt, 536 F. Supp. 1375, 1387 (D.R.I. 1982), *aff'd,* 715 F.2d 1 (1st Cir. 1983); Bales v. Clarke, 523 F. Supp. 1366, 1370 (E.D. Va. 1981); Anderson v. Thompson, 495 F. Supp. 1256, 1266 (E.D. Wis. 1980), *aff'd,* 658 F.2d 1205 (7th Cir. 1981).

43. *See, e.g.,* Age v. Bullitt County Pub. Schools, 673 F.2d 141, 144 (6th Cir. 1982) (undue interference with development of skills); Colin K. v. Schmidt, 536 F. Supp. 1375, 1387 (D.R.I. 1982) (stagnation or regression), *aff'd,* 715 F.2d 1 (1st Cir. 1983); Bales v. Clarke, 523 F. Supp. 1366, 1370 (E.D. Va. 1981) (extraordinary or irretrievable regression); Anderson v. Thompson, 495 F. Supp. 1256, 1266 (E.D. Wis. 1980) (irreparable loss of progress), *aff'd,* 658 F.2d 1205 (7th Cir. 1981).

harmful programming presented such strong proof of a statutory violation that it was unnecessary to consider whether some more stringent standard might otherwise apply.[44] In other cases, however, it was apparent that the courts regarded the absence of harm, coupled with programming which allowed the child to make some educational gain, as sufficient to satisfy the Act's requirements.[45] At times, the courts articulated the test in slightly different terms, asking whether the programming had afforded the child an opportunity to make "some progress" toward his educational objectives.[46] Surprisingly, in view of the apparent laxity of the "some benefit" standard, a significant number of cases determined that the challenged programming failed to comply with the statutory requirement.[47]

In a second class of cases, courts at least gave lipservice to a modified "equivalence of opportunity" standard.[48] However, no reported decision appears to have attempted to apply such a test in a literal fashion by comparing the objectives of nonhandicapped students against the services provided, and contrasting that shortfall with the corresponding shortfall in opportunity afforded handicapped students in order to determine the relative quality of the respective educational programs.[49] However, two alternative approaches to determining "equivalence" were used, in each case without explicitly acknowledging the logic underlying the courts' analysis. First, some courts relied upon evidence in the Act's legislative history to conclude that handicapped students should generally be guaranteed an opportunity to gain

---

44. *See, e.g.*, Colin K. v. Schmidt, 536 F. Supp. 1375, 1387 (D.R.I. 1982), *aff'd*, 715 F.2d 1 (1st Cir. 1983).

45. *See, e.g.*, Age v. Bullitt County Pub. Schools, 673 F.2d 141 (6th Cir. 1982).

46. *See, e.g.*, Norris v. Massachusetts Dep't of Educ., 529 F. Supp. 759, 767 (D. Mass. 1981) (failure to achieve significant growth, lower than expected skill development); Gladys J. v. Pearland Indep. School Dist., 520 F. Supp. 869, 877-78 (S.D. Tex. 1981); Anderson v. Thompson, 495 F. Supp. 1256, 1266 (E.D. Wis. 1980), *aff'd*, 658 F.2d 1205 (7th Cir. 1984).

47. Parents succeeded in demanding more extensive programming in several cases. *See* Colin K. v. Schmidt, 536 F. Supp. 1375 (D.R.I. 1982), *aff'd*, 715 F.2d 1 (1st Cir. 1983); Norris v. Massachusetts Dep't of Educ., 529 F. Supp. 759 (D. Mass. 1981); Gladys J. v. Pearland Indep. School Dist., 520 F. Supp. 869 (S.D. Tex. 1981); Anderson v. Thompson, 495 F. Supp. 1256 (E.D. Wis. 1980), *aff'd*, 658 F.2d 1205 (7th Cir. 1981). However, the school systems in large part prevailed in others. *See* Age v. Bullitt County Pub. Schools, 673 F.2d 141 (6th Cir. 1982); Rettig v. Kent City School Dist., 539 F. Supp. 768 (N.D. Ohio 1981), *aff'd in part, vacated and remanded in part*, 720 F.2d 463 (6th Cir. 1983), *cert. denied*, 104 S. Ct. 2379 (1984); Bales v. Clarke, 523 F. Supp. 1366 (E.D. Va. 1981).

48. *See, e.g.*, Springdale School Dist. v. Grace, 656 F.2d 300, 305 (8th Cir. 1981), *vacated*, 458 U.S. 1118 (1982), *aff'd on rehearing*, 693 F.2d 41, *cert. denied*, 103 S. Ct. 2086 (1983); Gladys J. v. Pearland Indep. School Dist., 520 F. Supp. 869, 875 (S.D. Tex. 1981); Hines v. Pitt County Bd. of Educ., 497 F. Supp. 403, 406 (E.D.N.C. 1980) (quoting Rowley); Rowley v. Board of Educ., 483 F. Supp. 528, 533-34 (S.D.N.Y.), *aff'd*, 632 F.2d 945 (2d Cir. 1980), *rev'd*, 458 U.S. 176 (1982). This position was also espoused by an influential student law review note which had taken the position that the EAHCA guaranteed handicapped children equal opportunity for individual development that is defined in relationship to the level of opportunity accorded nonhandicapped children in light of services provided to the general student population within a given district. *See* Note, *Enforcing the Right to an "Appropriate" Education: The Education for All Handicapped Children Act of 1975*, 92 HARV. L. REV. 1103, 1125-27 (1979).

49. The district court in *Rowley* purported to do so, but as explained more fully in section C, instead adopted a more comprehensive equalized opportunity standard. *See infra* notes 59-62 and accompanying text.

skills needed to assure self-sufficiency.[50] At least arguably this approach rests upon the premise that self-sufficiency is the underlying goal of both handicapped and nonhandicapped students; since the system of regular education allows nonhandicapped children to make substantial progress toward that objective, so should the system of special education. Second, at least one court assumed that the opportunities available to handicapped students must be determined by a balancing of their needs against the available resources.[51] By implication, this balancing process must likewise be used to determine what programming would be provided nonhandicapped students.[52] The use of an independent balancing calculus for each group might, in at least some circumstances, result in comparable levels of service without the need to engage in literal comparisons between the services afforded handicapped and nonhandicapped students.

Finally, at least one case appears to have adopted an "equalized opportunity standard."[53] It is to that case—the *Rowley* case—that we now turn.

III

LEVEL AND EXTENT OF SERVICES: *ROWLEY* AND BEYOND

A. The *Rowley* Decision

The facts of the *Rowley*[54] case are, by now, well known.[55] Amy Rowley, an intelligent, highly motivated youngster, suffered, since birth, from a significant hearing impairment. Her parents, also deaf, raised Amy using the "total communication" system of instruction, teaching her to use sign language but also to rely on her limited residual hearing to develop excellent lipreading skills.[56] When Amy entered first grade in the Hendrick Hudson School Dis-

---

50. *See, e.g.,* Stacey G. v. Pasadena Indep. School Dist., 547 F. Supp. 61, 77 (S.D. Tex. 1982); Rettig v. Kent City School Dist., 539 F. Supp. 768, 777 (N.D. Ohio 1981), *aff'd in part, vacated and remanded in part,* 720 F.2d 463 (6th Cir. 1983), *cert. denied,* 104 S. Ct. 2379 (1984); Gladys J. v. Pearland Indep. School Dist., 520 F. Supp. 869, 875 (S.D. Tex. 1981); Campbell v. Talladega County Bd. of Educ., 518 F. Supp. 47, 54 (N.D. Ala. 1981); Armstrong v. Kline, 476 F. Supp. 583, 604 (E.D. Pa. 1979), *remanded sub nom.* Battle v. Pennsylvania, 629 F.2d 269 (3d Cir. 1980).

51. *See* Pinkerton v. Moye, 509 F. Supp. 107, 112 (W.D. Va. 1981).

52. *See* Bales v. Clarke, 523 F. Supp. 1366, 1371 (E.D. Va. 1981). ("No language in federal law can properly be read as mandating that costs may not be considered in determining what is appropriate for a child—handicapped or nonhandicapped.").

53. Rowley v. Board of Educ., 483 F. Supp. 528, 534 (S.D.N.Y.), *aff'd,* 632 F.2d 945 (2d Cir. 1980), *rev'd,* 458 U.S. 176 (1981) (discussed *infra* at notes 58-61 and accompanying text). Other courts rejected a similar but more expansive test which would have required school districts to provide handicapped children with an education designed to allow them to achieve their maximum potential. *See, e.g.,* Stacey G. v. Pasadena Indep. School Dist., 547 F. Supp. 61, 78 (S.D. Tex 1982).

54. 483 F. Supp. 528 (S.D.N.Y.) *aff'd,* 632 F.2d 945 (2d Cir. 1980), *rev'd,* 458 U.S. 176 (1982).

55. The Supreme Court's decision in *Rowley* has already received substantial scholarly attention. *See, e.g.,* Beyer, *A Free Appropriate Public Education,* 5 W. NEW ENG. L. REV. 363 (1983); Zirkel, *Building an Appropriate Public Education from* Board of Education v. Rowley: *Razing the Door and Raising the Floor,* 42 MD. L. REV. 466 (1983); Note, Board of Education v. Rowley: *The Supreme Court Takes a Conservative Approach to the Education of Handicapped Children,* 61 N.C.L. REV. 881 (1983); DuBow, *EHLR Analysis: Application of* Rowley *by Courts and SEAs,* 1982-83 EDUC. HANDICAPPED L. REP. (CRR) SA-107 (Supp. 93, April 1, 1983); *EHLR Analysis: What* Rowley *Means,* 1982-83 EDUC. HANDICAPPED L. REP. (CRR) SA-29 (Supp. 84, Nov. 12, 1982).

56. For a detailed discussion of the total communication method, and other systems of deaf

trict, in Peekskill, New York, school administrators agreed that she should be placed in a regular classroom and provided with a special hearing aid, a tutor for the deaf who would meet with Amy on a daily basis, and three hours per week of speech therapy. Amy's parents requested that she also be provided a sign language interpreter to accompany her to class, so as to ensure that Amy would continue to rely upon the total communication method. The school district refused to incorporate this additional element into Amy's IEP, citing an earlier determination that a sign language interpreter had been unnecessary to Amy during her participation in the district's kindergarten program, and Amy's good social adjustment and better than average academic performance in the absence of such additional assistance.[57] The Rowleys unsuccessfully pursued state administrative remedies, and ultimately commenced proceedings in federal district court.

The trial court held in favor of the Rowleys, concluding that the school district's refusal to provide Amy with a sign language interpreter had, indeed, resulted in denial of a "free appropriate public education."[58] The court concluded that the EAHCA's requirement that handicapped children be provided an "appropriate" education meant that Amy should receive something more than an "adequate" education, yet something less than an education which would enable her to achieve her "full potential."[59] Instead, the court stated, the Act required that Amy "be given an oportunity to achieve [her] full potential commensurate with the opportunity provided to other children."[60]

In the court's view, in order to implement this standard, a reviewing court must necessarily examine three subsidiary questions. First, the potential of the handicapped child in question must be calculated. Second, the child's performance must be assessed and compared to his or her potential. Third, the corresponding "shortfall" between potential and performance of the handicapped child must be compared to that experienced by nonhandicapped children.[61] In the case at hand, the court reasoned, Amy's potential—measured by her IQ and exceptional level of energy and motivation—was great. The shortfall in educational opportunity she suffered significantly exceeded that of her peers, because she was burdened by a substantial hearing impairment and they were not.[62] Since provision of a sign language interpreter would eliminate this incremental shortfall in educational opportunity, the school district must supply that service. Thus, although the district purported to apply an "equivalent opportunity" standard, what it adopted instead was an "equalized opportunity" standard—one that required the school district to supply whatever services were needed to minimize the effect of Amy's impairment so

---

education, see Large, *Special Problems of the Deaf Under the Education for All Handicapped Children Act of 1975*, 58 WASH. U.L.Q. 213, 223-40 (1980).

57.   458 U.S. 176, 184-85 (1982).
58.   *Id.* at 176.
59.   483 F. Supp. at 534.
60.   *Id.*
61.   *Id.*
62.   *Id.* at 535.

that she might benefit, to the fullest extent possible, from the educational opportunities available to nonhandicapped students.

A divided panel of the Second Circuit affirmed on appeal.[63] In a *per curiam* ruling, expressly limiting the holding to the facts at hand without any precedential value,[64] the appellate majority adopted the district court's reasoning by reference. Judge Mansfield dissented. He urged that an equivalent opportunity standard should be applied in order to ensure that each handicapped child receive an education that would enable him to be as free as reasonably possible from dependence on others.[65] In his opinion, this standard had been satisfied under the facts at bar.

The United States Supreme Court reversed.[66] Not surprisingly, however, the Justices were sharply divided, their three opinions reflecting a full range of equality-based approaches to resolving the ambiguity in the EAHCA's free appropriate public education requirement.

Writing for himself and four others, Justice Rehnquist concluded that the laxest of the available standards—the "some benefit" standard—should apply. Resting his analysis upon the statutory text and the legislative history,[67] he first stated that the EAHCA's requirements could be satisfied "by providing [a handicapped child with] personalized instruction with sufficient support services to permit the child to benefit educationally from that instruction."[68] In discussing the application of that standard, he noted that Congress had intended "that the services provided handicapped children be educationally beneficial, whatever the nature or severity of their handicap,"[69] and that "the benefits obtainable by children at one end of the spectrum will differ dramatically from those obtainable by children at the other end, with infinite variations in between."[70]

Justice Rehnquist was careful to observe that the Court did not attempt "to establish any one test for determining the adequacy of educational benefits conferred upon all children covered by the Act."[71] On the facts at hand, however, the majority determined that the test had been satisfied. The Court cited several factors which it believed supported this conclusion: (1) Amy's needs had been specially considered by school administrators; (2) she was receiving special services responsive to her needs; (3) she was enrolled in a regular classroom in which her educational progress was monitored and evaluated as examinations were given, grades awarded, and retention and promotion decisions reached; and (4) she was performing adequately in this

---

63. 632 F.2d 945 (1980), *rev'd,* 458 U.S. 176 (1982).
64. *Id.* at 948 & n.7.
65. *Id.* at 953.
66. 458 U.S. 176 (1982).
67. *See supra* notes 25-40 and accompanying text. The majority also emphasized Congress' desire to ensure that previously unserved children would no longer be excluded from the schools or from specialized educational services. 458 U.S. at 195-97.
68. 458 U.S. at 203.
69. *Id.* at 202 n.23.
70. *Id.* at 202.
71. *Id.*

placement, attaining passing marks and advancing from grade to grade.[72] While no one of these factors alone would necessarily have been enough to compel the Court's conclusion,[73] taken together they demonstrated that Amy was receiving an "appropriate" education.

The majority then went on to address a second question, the scope of judicial review, perhaps in order to provide an alternative holding, or perhaps simply to assure that the role of the reviewing court would not, henceforth, be misunderstood. In their view, a two-pronged inquiry is required in actions brought under section 1415(e)(2) of the Act: "First, has the State complied with the procedures set forth in the Act? And second, is the individualized educational program developed through the Act's procedures reasonably calculated to enable the child to receive educational benefits?"[74] Since the EAHCA contains detailed procedural requirements designed by Congress to afford important substantive protection, the courts should rigorously enforce such obligations.[75] On the other hand, according to the majority, reviewing courts must tread more carefully when engaging in direct substantive review. They should accord "due weight" to administrative proceedings, and should refrain from "substitut[ing] their own notions of sound educational policy for those of the school authorities which they review."[76]

In the majority's view, the Rowley dispute largely focused upon the legitimacy of the school district's decision to adopt a method of instruction other than the total communication method (which would have relied heavily upon the presence of a sign language interpreter).[77] Since the district court had sought to resolve a difference in opinion concerning the best educational methodology, rather than simply determining whether Amy had received some educational benefit from her program of instruction, it had erred in going beyond the proper scope of judicial review.[78]

Justice Blackmun concurred in the result reached by the majority, but rejected the analytical approach of the Rehnquist opinion in favor of an intermediate "equivalent opportunity" interpretation of the FAPE requirement. In Justice Blackmun's view, the critical issue was whether Amy Rowley's educational program, "viewed as a whole, offered her an opportunity to understand and participate in the classroom that was substantially equal to that given her nonhandicapped classmates."[79] In his opinion, the equivalent

---

72. *Id.* at 203 & n.25.
73. *Id.*
74. *Id.* at 206-07. The Court has recently reiterated its view that the EAHCA both creates "an elaborate procedural mechanism to protect the rights of handicapped children" and "establishes an enforceable substantive right to a free appropriate education," Smith v. Robinson, 104 S. Ct. 3457, 3468-69 (1984), and has stated that a reviewing court must satisfy itself that a child's IEP "conforms with the requirements of § 1401(19) [defining such plans]," Irving Indep. School Dist. v. Tatro, 104 S. Ct. 3371, 3377 n.6 (1984).
75. 458 U.S. at 205-06.
76. *Id.* at 206.
77. *Id.* at 184-86.
78. *Id.* at 207-08 & n.29, 209-10.
79. *Id.* at 211 (emphasis omitted).

opportunity standard was preferable both to the Rehnquist standard, which focused too narrowly on a handicapped child's achievement of a particular educational outcome (passing from grade to grade), and to the lower court's standard, which focused too narrowly on the presence or absence of a particular service rather than on the handicapped child's overall program.[80] Since Amy's program, taken as a whole, did offer her an educational opportunity substantially equivalent to that afforded her classmates, it satisfied the requirements of the Act.

Justice White, writing for himself and Justices Brennan and Marshall, dissented, preferring an "equalized opportunity" interpretation of the FAPE obligation. In the view of these three Justices, the Act's guarantee of a free appropriate public education was "intended to eliminate the effects of the handicap, at least to the extent that the child will be given an equal opportunity to learn if that is reasonably possible."[81] Since the aid of a sign language interpreter would effectively equalize Amy's opportunity to learn, one should have been provided.[82] Moreover, the dissenters concluded, the lower courts had been correct in undertaking a "full and searching"[83] judicial inquiry; Congress's explicit provision for independent judicial review contemplated just that.

B. Critique and Afterword

The Supreme Court's decision in *Rowley* may be criticized on at least one score: none of the three competing opinions withstands close analytical scrutiny. Each places a different slant on the ambiguous text and nonspecific legislative history described above.[84] Yet, because of that ambiguity and lack of specificity, none is able to refute the opposing views in an effective or convincing manner.[85]

Rather than engaging in a protracted discussion of the justifications offered in support of the majority, concurrence, and dissent, it is therefore more profitable to proceed directly to the heart of the matter by assessing the substantive merits of these three views. This section will accordingly examine the implications of the majority's standard to determine whether it assures handicapped children sufficient educational programming to provide them with meaningful educational opportunities. It will then discuss the viability of alternative standards, such as those favored by the concurrence and dissent, in order to ascertain whether a more generous standard was in fact available and might instead have been adopted. It will conclude that, when judged from

---

80. *Id.*
81. *Id.* at 215.
82. *Id.*
83. *Id.* at 218.
84. *See supra* notes 25-41 and accompanying text.
85. Both the majority and the dissent relied upon harsh words and competing portions of the legislative history to support their diverse views. *Compare* 458 U.S. at 190 n.11 (majority's criticism of dissent) *and id.* at 191-200 (majority's review of legislative history) *with id.* at 212 (dissent's criticism of majority) *and id.* at 213-14, 217-18 (dissent's review of legislative history).

this perspective, the majority's standard represents a sound and perhaps inevitable interpretation of the Act's FAPE requirement.

1. *Assurance of meaningful educational opportunity.* Whether meaningful educational opportunity will be afforded handicapped students as a result of the *Rowley* decision will depend upon the interplay of the two critical issues discussed in that decision—first, the substantive standard governing programming decisions, and second, the scope of judicial review.

A threshold question is whether *Rowley's* "some benefit" standard requires a single-pronged or double-pronged substantive inquiry. It might be contended that *Rowley* merely contemplates that each handicapped child receive some net educational benefit, without attempting to measure that benefit against the child's individual goals and objectives.[86] A much stronger case can be made for a two-pronged approach, however, since the EAHCA specifically provides that each child's educational program is to be designed with his individual needs in mind.[87] If the sufficiency of the programming to be provided is not similarly assessed with the child's unique abilities, needs, and objectives in mind, that requirement would be largely nugatory. The *Rowley* decision itself specifically recognized that the "some benefit" standard could only be applied after careful consideration of each individual child's abilities, needs, and objectives.[88] Accordingly, a two-pronged analysis of the substantive sufficiency of educational programming should be employed: This analysis requires both careful examination of the child's abilities, needs, and objectives, and an assessment of whether he is receiving some educational benefit as measured against those objectives.

The first prong of this test—examination of the child's abilities, needs, and objectives—is particularly critical. In the absence of careful and accurate judgments on these issues, the second-stage inquiry into benefit derived will be based upon an incorrect benchmark, virtually assuring that the child will not receive an "appropriate" education. Thus, if a child's goals and objectives are set at a very modest level as a result of an incorrect diagnosis of mental retardation or an erroneous assessment of the extent to which his mental capacity is impaired, an inquiry into his attainment of the established goals would fail to ensure that he has, in fact, received educational programming which "meets his unique needs."[89] Following *Rowley*, it is therefore quite likely that more attention will be focused upon the nature of individual

---

86. The *Rowley* majority at times uses broad language which could provide support for such a view. *See, e.g.,* 458 U.S. at 195 ("the Act imposes no clear obligation upon recipient States beyond the requirement that handicapped children receive some form of specialized education"); *id.* at 196 (Congress sought to ensure that handicapped children were "served" and " 'served' referred to children who were receiving some form of specialized educational services").

87. *See* 20 U.S.C. § 1401(16) quoted in text accompanying note 32 *supra.*

88. *See* 458 U.S. at 202, 203 n.25 (observing that the Court did not intend to hold that "every child who is advancing from grade to grade in a regular public school system is automatically receiving a 'free appropriate public education,' " but that Amy Rowley had received such an education in view of her actual progress, the services she had received, and the "professional consideration" she had been afforded).

89. *See, e.g.,* Campbell v. Talladega County Bd. of Educ., 518 F. Supp. 47, 55 (N.D. Ala. 1981)

handicapped children's disabilities. The precise nature of such children's educational needs—including needs for emotional as well as intellectual development—is also likely to become an even more prominent factor in educational programming decisions.[90] Finally, an increased number of challenges may well be directed to the adequacy of the objectives and goals stated in the child's IEP,[91] for unless those objectives are detailed and comprehensive in character, review of the sufficiency of educational benefits received must, at best, be cursory.

Under this first prong of the substantive inquiry into the adequacy of educational programming, judicial review may be limited when the school and the parents agree on a particular child's abilities, needs, and objectives.[92] In the event of disagreement, however, that review should be more probing. Such review necessitates careful review of professional diagnoses of the child's handicapping condition and evaluations of the impairment to his learning abilities that exists as a result. These issues are, by and large, factual in character.[93] In discussing the standard of review for such factual issues, some lower courts have tended to limit the Supreme Court's caution in *Rowley*, regarding factual review of school districts' judgments, to disagreements about educational methodology.[94] Courts have also concluded that "due weight" is afforded determinations by state and local hearing officers on other, nonmethodological issues so long as evidence adduced and findings reached in administrative proceedings are not wholly ignored by the trial court.[95] The trial court thus retains the ultimate responsibility of making factual findings on such issues as the handicapped child's abilities, needs, and

---

(FAPE not provided where program for severely mentally retarded boy did not take into account his individual needs and abilities.).

90. *See, e.g.,* Crawford v. Pittman, 708 F.2d 1028, 1033-35 (5th Cir. 1983) (must assess needs); Lee v. Thompson, 1982-83 EDUC. HANDICAPPED L. REP. (CRR) 554:429 (D. Hawaii 1983) (must consider nature and severity of handicap and areas of learning crucial to attaining self-sufficiency); *In re* J.B., 1982-83 EDUC. HANDICAPPED L. REP. (CRR) 504:319 (Vt. SEA 1983) (must first consider child's needs to determine whether vocational educational programming is appropriate; *see also infra* part IV for discussion of scope of educational needs for purposes of the EAHCA.

91. *See, e.g.,* Case No. SE-99-80, 1982-83 EDUC. HANDICAPPED L. REP. 504:267 (Ill. SEA 1983) (dispute regarding suitability of academic versus vocational objectives); *In re* Hershey Pub. School Dist. No. 37, 1982-83 EDUC. HANDICAPPED L. REP. (CRR) 504:225 (Neb. SEA 1982) (same).

92. This was apparently the case in *Rowley. See* 483 F. Supp. 528, 529 (S.D.N.Y.), *aff'd,* 632 F.2d 945 (2d Cir. 1980), *rev'd,* 458 U.S. 176 (1981).

93. *See, e.g.,* Colin K. v. Schmidt, 715 F.2d 1, 6 (1st Cir. 1983); Case No. SE-99-80, 1982-83 EDUC. HANDICAPPED L. REP. (CRR) 504:267 (Ill. SEA 1983).

94. *See, e.g.,* Roncker v. Walter, 700 F.2d 1058, 1062 (6th Cir. 1983), *cert. denied,* 104 S. Ct. 196 (1983).

95. *See, e.g.,* Abrahamson v. Hershman, 701 F.2d 223, 230 (1st Cir. 1983). *But see* Roncker v. Walker, 700 F.2d at 1062 (trial court failed to accord due weight when reversing decision of local and state hearing officers that proposed programming was inappropriate). *Roncker* may suggest that a differential standard of review is being applied depending on whether state and local hearing officers uphold or reject a local school district's decision. A federal court may fear that a hearing officer's decision in favor of a local school district may reflect favoritism toward the district's point of view, and may, therefore, step in to protect the interest of the handicapped children whom the EAHCA is designed to protect. Such a court may be inclined to give greater deference to determinations by hearing officers which necessarily reflect an independent judgment which differs from that of the school district, triggering no similar fear of favoritism.

objectives.[96] In reaching such decisions, trial courts and hearing officers are nevertheless likely to treat professional judgments as particularly persuasive, especially where such judgments are those of teachers or other personnel who have worked with the handicapped child over an extended period.[97] They may also give serious consideration to the insights of parents, who in many cases have considerable knowledge of their child's abilities and needs, regardless of their backgrounds in educational methodology.[98]

Assessment of the benefit afforded by the educational programming in question, under the second prong of the substantive standard, is likewise of great importance. The Supreme Court's decision in *Rowley* has shaped this inquiry in two key respects. First, while the benefit afforded must ultimately be evaluated in light of an individual child's narrow educational objectives, benefit itself is not a narrow concept. Instead, it includes the net advantages gained, not simply from one facet, but from the whole of the child's educational environment—the educational methods used, the personnel employed, the intensity of services afforded. Accordingly, following *Rowley*, attention has turned to the general benefit derived from the total mix of services offered a handicapped child—his overall educational opportunity—rather than the adequacy or inadequacy of a single aspect of his educational program.[99] Second, the Court clearly stated that the benefit afforded need not be sufficient to allow the child in question to actually attain his full educational potential.[100] The Court indicated that the sufficiency of the child's educational programming is to be judged by his performance in making incremental progress toward his individual educational goals. It thus established an objective threshold standard of sufficiency that appears to guarantee each handicapped child at least minimal eductional opportunity.

---

96. Abrahamson v. Hershman, 701 F.2d at 230; School Comm. v. Massachusetts Dep't of Educ. (Burlington), 736 F.2d 773, 790 (1st Cir. 1984), *cert. granted*, 53 U.S.L.W. 3414 (Dec. 4, 1984). A more limited federal interest thus exists to justify intervention by the federal courts under these circumstances. School Comm. v Massachusetts Dep't of Educ. (Burlington), 736 F.2d 773, 792 (1st Cir. 1984) (adopting "a symmetrical" approach envisioning greater judicial deference to decision of state hearing officers determining that IEP did not comply with requirements of state law), *cert. granted*, 53 U.S.L.W. 3414 (Dec. 4, 1984).

97. *See, e.g., In re* West Brookfield Pub. Schools, 1982-83 EDUC. HANDICAPPED L. REP. (CRR) 504:166 (Mass. SEA 1982) (home teacher); *In re* Brockton Pub. Schools, 1982-83 EDUC. HANDICAPPED L. REP. (CRR) 504:128 (Mass. SEA 1982) (primary teacher, therapists, evaluators); *In re* Dixie School Dist. and Marin County Special Educ. Consortium, 1982-83 EDUC. HANDICAPPED L. REP. (CRR) 504:274 (Cal. SEA 1983) (current teachers and interpreter).

98. *See* Davis v. District of Columbia Bd. of Educ., 522 F. Supp. 1102, 1109 (D.D.C. 1981) (parents' views are to be thoroughly considered; may be biased or highly probative); *In re* Madison Metropolitan School Dist., 1981-82 EDUC. HANDICAPPED L. REP. (CRR) 503:125 (Wis. SEA 1981) (parents' wishes are to be considered, but do not control). *But see* Johnston v. Ann Arbor Pub. Schools, 569 F. Supp. 1502, 1509 (E.D. Mich. 1983) (refusing to substitute mother's judgment for judgment of professionals).

99. *See, e.g.,* Rettig v. Kent City School Dist., 720 F.2d 463, 466 (6th Cir. 1983) (mix of services adequate without provision of summer classes and occupational therapy), *cert. denied*, 104 S. Ct. 2379 (1984). Cothern v. Mallory, 565 F. Supp. 701, 707-08 (W.D. Mo. 1983) (considering teacher training, integration with nonhandicapped children, and other factors).

100. *See* 458 U.S. at 192 (quoting Senate report which expressly recognized that "in many instances the process of providing special education and related services to handicapped children is not guaranteed to produce any particular outcome").

Whether even this minimal opportunity will in fact be afforded depends, however, upon the judicial review applied to this second, assessment-of-benefit facet of the test for substantive sufficiency of educational programming. Most of *Rowley's* strong cautionary language regarding the scope of judicial review seemed to be addressed to this prong of the analysis, since there was little question regarding Amy's abilities, needs, or objectives. Not surprisingly, several competing interpretations of the Court's statements regarding the scope of judicial review are possible. One view is based on the Court's repeated references to the broad authority of state and local school officials over questions of educational policy. Under this view, since all programming determinations involve decisions about educational methodology to some degree, school officials, not the courts, should be allowed to determine what constitutes adequate educational benefits, either during the local IEP development or the state administrative review process. For example, the courts would largely defer to school officials' determination of whether a seriously learning disabled child, who also suffered from associated emotional problems, would derive "some" educational "benefit" from instruction in a self-contained classroom with a 10 to 1 pupil-teacher ratio, or whether a more individualized, highly structured, and closely supervised program would instead be required.[101]

Alternatively, the Court's remarks could be seen to limit the scope of judicial review only in relatively few cases, where parents disagree with school officials regarding which of several professionally acceptable techniques or modes of instruction should be employed.[102] Under this view, trial courts would remain relatively free to reach independent, de novo judgments regarding the sufficiency of educational programming in other respects.

The appropriate scope of judicial review under the second prong of *Rowley's* substantive standard probably lies somewhere between these two extremes. The Court's rather indiscriminate references to educational method and policy probably were not limited to theories of instruction.[103] At the same time, the Court did not suggest that school officials' judgments on these questions should go altogether unchecked. Instead, the Court specifically directed that reviewing courts were to determine whether the mix of methods, personnel, and other facets of a child's educational program carried

---

101. This view was rejected in Colin K. v. Schmidt, 715 F.2d 1, 6 (1st Cir. 1983). However, other courts have adopted such a view on comparable facts. *See* Johnston v. Ann Arbor Pub. Schools, 569 F. Supp. at 1507-09 (court hesitated to substitute its judgment for that of school official in case involving 11-year-old girl with cerebral palsy who requested placement in specialized school for physically impaired after experiencing significant learning difficulties in local placement); *see also* Rettig v. Kent City School Dist., 720 F.2d 463, 466 (6th Cir. 1983) (stating that programming decisions are within state's discretion, but holding, in the alternative, that requested services were unnecessary), *cert. denied,* 104 S. Ct. 2379 (1984).

102. *See* Roncker v. Walter, 700 F.2d 1058, 1062 (6th Cir. 1983) (distinguishing decisions regarding methodology from those regarding mainstreaming), *cert. denied,* 104 S. Ct. 196 (1983).

103. The Court undertook an extended discussion of the scope of review, warning reviewing courts against using a free hand to impose substantive standards of review which are not derived from the Act itself and emphasizing that Congress had intended the Act's procedural requirements to assure compliance with its substantive requirements. 458 U.S. at 206.

him across the statutory threshold, immunizing him from harm, and assuring him of some incremental progress toward his objectives.[104] Because these latter questions are questions of fact,[105] they may be addressed by the courts without fear of violating state and local prerogatives to determine the means used to reach a statutorily mandated end.

Again under this factual review, the courts will undoubtedly accord considerable weight to the professional judgments of school personnel.[106] At the same time, the child's track record is likely to be more compelling evidence than educators' projections.[107] In doubtful cases, a court may order especially close monitoring of a child's progress to assure that his educational program will be modified if the minimum opportunity is not provided.[108] In other cases, especially where the child is so seriously impaired that a marginally effective educational program creates substantial risks (risk of harm through regression, or the risk of inability to make even some progress toward identified educational objectives), the court may well find that the program is inadequate.[109] In such instances, it is likely that the court or other reviewing body will order some specific remedy—a change in instructional personnel, a change in the type or level of sevices provided, or some other program modification—rather than leaving completely to school officials the decision regarding the proper scope of the child's program.[110]

Thus, the decision in *Rowley* appears to guarantee that, under the EAHCA, handicapped children will receive at least a minimally adequate education, one that is designed to meet their individual abilities, needs, and objectives and that will assist them in achieving at least some progress toward their goals. Although the authority of reviewing courts has been limited in at least some respects, they may be expected to continue to play a key role in ensuring that this threshold statutory standard is met. The standard adopted by the *Rowley* majority is, on its face, a sound one. This judgment is further confirmed by a comparative analysis of the more generous alternative standards proposed by the *Rowley* concurrence and dissent.

2. *Availability of Alternative Standards.* Examination of possible alternative standards suggests that the Supreme Court in *Rowley* bowed to the inevitable

---

104. *Id.* at 203 n.25 (determining that Amy Rowley received appropriate education in view of professional consideration received, special services provided, and academic progress achieved).
105. *See* Abrahamson v. Hershman, 701 F.2d 223, 230 (1st Cir. 1983); Doe v. Anrig, 692 F.2d 800, 806 & n.12 (1st Cir. 1982), *on remand*, 561 F. Supp. 121 (D. Mass. 1983), *aff'd*, 728 F.2d 30 (1st Cir. 1984).
106. *See, e.g.,* Lang v. Braintree School Comm., 545 F. Supp. 1221, 1225-26 (D. Mass. 1982).
107. *See* Doe v. Anrig, 692 F.2d at 807-08.
108. *See In re* Burton School Dist., 1982-83 EDUC. HANDICAPPED L. REP. (CRR) 504:133 (Cal. SEA 1982); *see also* Laura M. v. Special School Dist. #1, 1980-81 EDUC. HANDICAPPED L. REP. (CRR) 552:152 (D. Minn. 1980).
109. *See, e.g., In re* Burton School Dist., 1982-83 EDUC. HANDICAPPED L. REP. (CRR) 504:133 (Cal. SEA 1982); *In re* Putnam City School Dist., 1982-83 EDUC. HANDICAPPED L. REP. (CRR) 504:207 (Okla. SEA 1982).
110. *See, e.g.,* Abrahamson v. Hershman, 701 F.2d 223 (1st Cir. 1983) (custodial services for severely retarded child); *In re* Scottsbluff Pub. School, 1982-83 EDUC. HANDICAPPED L. REP. (CRR) 504:238 (Neb. SEA 1982) (preschool service for profoundly deaf child).

in adopting a "some benefit" standard for determining the sufficiency of educational programming under the EAHCA. The Court selected the only one of the three possible standards which avoided problems of justiciability that have long influenced the development of equal educational opportunity jurisprudence. Academic and judicial discussion of justiciability during the last twenty years has focused on two principal concerns. First, federal courts have hesitated to assume the task of allocating public resources in an equitable fashion to assure equality of opportunity.[111] The courts have long understood that the process of resource allocation is, by its nature, largely a political one. Except where a disadvantaged group is denied all opportunity (a strong indication that the political process has gone awry and that judicial intervention is warranted), or inhumane conditions exist,[112] the courts have generally concluded that resolution of political disputes should be left to the legislative arena.[113] This general hesitancy to assume responsibilities for resource allocation has applied equally in the educational context.[114]

Second, the courts have recognized that, even apart from resource allocation problems, it is particularly difficult to develop judicially manageable standards for determining whether educational opportunities have been allocated in an "equal" fashion.[115] Many scholars agree that "educational opportunity" does not refer to educational "output," that is, an individual's achievement of noneducational goals by using the intellectual and practical skills he acquired through education, as well as his own talent, energy, and other available resources.[116] Assuming that educational opportunity is defined in terms of "input," rather than "output," a question arises as to the precise "input" to be measured, for example, monetary contributions versus other more intangible resources.[117] In addition, scholars differ on the proper measurement of the sufficiency of that "input" to meet affected children's needs.[118] Courts have hesitated to undertake a comparison of the opportunities afforded on a school district by school district basis.[119] Comparison on a child-by-child basis could only prove significantly more cumbersome.

The "some benefit" standard surmounts both these justiciability concerns. First, it allows the courts to confine their involvement in resource allocation decisions within traditionally acceptable bounds. Rather than having to balance myriad competing claims to limited available resources, courts only must

---

111. *See, e.g.,* Dandridge v. Williams, 397 U.S. 471 (1970).
112. *See, e.g.,* Wyatt v. Stickney, 344 F. Supp. 373, (M.D. Ala. 1972) (inhumane conditions in institution for mentally retarded), *aff'd in part, remanded in part, sub nom.* Wyatt v. Aderholt, 503 F.2d 1305 (5th Cir. 1974); Gates v. Collier, 349 F. Supp. 881 (N.D. Miss. 1972) (inhumane prison conditions), *aff'd,* 501 F.2d 1291 (5th Cir. 1974).
113. Dandridge v. Williams, 397 U.S. 471 (1970).
114. *See, e.g.,* San Antonio Indep. School Dist. v. Rodriguez, 411 U.S. 1, 35 (1973).
115. *See id.* at 42; Battle v. Pennsylvania, 629 F.2d 269, 277 (3d Cir. 1980), *cert. denied,* 452 U.S. 968 (1981); McInnis v. Shapiro, 293 F. Supp. 327, 335-36 (N.D. Ill. 1968) (three judge panel), *aff'd sub nom.* McInnis v. Ogilvie, 394 U.S. 322 (1969).
116. *See, e.g.,* Haggerty & Sacks, *supra* note 8, at 972-73; Schoettle, *supra* note 3, at 1373.
117. Schoettle, *supra* note 3, at 1369-70.
118. *Id.* at 1371-72.
119. *See* San Antonio Indep. School Dist. v. Rodriguez, 411 U.S. 1 (1973).

assure that no individual is denied resources needed to allow him to receive effective, personalized instruction, and thus at least minimal access to an important, publicly funded opportunity. The "some benefit" standard thus allows the courts to adopt the least intrusive possible posture in dealing with resource allocation questions. They can require schools, without exception, to provide all students with a minimum level of opportunity, while leaving to school officials the task of allocating available resources that exceed this amount as they see fit.[120]

Second, the "some benefit" standard provides judicially manageable criteria for determining whether equal educational opportunity has been afforded. On the one hand, it assumes that opportunity comprises the sum total of all facets of a handicapped child's educational environment, thereby shielding a reviewing court from demands that it evaluate the adequacy of independent components of that environment—for example, teaching skill, or method and intensity of instruction—which are peculiarly insusceptible to judicial review. On the other hand, it requires the reviewing court to assess the adequacy of the child's educational program in practical and measureable terms, by focusing on the individual handicapped child alone, without the need for assessing and comparing the opportunity afforded any other children enrolled in the public school system. As in *Rowley*, a court need only inquire whether the child's needs and objectives have been properly determined (e.g., was the extent of Amy's hearing impairment accurately diagnosed and her instructional objectives reasonably defined to include at least normal academic progress for a child of her age?), and whether the child can reasonably be expected to make some discernible progress toward those objectives (Can Amy continue to achieve at or above normal grade level?).

Neither of the competing alternative standards could similarly surmount these two longstanding justiciability concerns. Each of the possible formulations of the "equivalent opportunity" test runs afoul of one or another justiciability problem. Under the more viable of the two pre-*Rowley* "equivalent opportunity" approaches, for example, a reviewing court would be required to balance the opportunity afforded the handicapped child against the resources available. Therefore, a court would be required to engage directly in the allocation of public resources, without the assistance of any judicially manageable guidelines.[121] Under Justice Blackmun's approach in *Rowley*, direct comparison of opportunities afforded handicapped and nonhandicapped children would be required, again with no hint of how the possibly very different components of these educational programs would be assessed, averaged, and translated into units appropriate for comparison.

Similarly, the "equalized opportunity" standard is seriously flawed. In theory, this standard would not require direct consideration of allocation issues. Instead, school districts would have to afford those services needed to

---

120. *See* Bartlett, *The Role of Cost in Educational Decisionmaking for the Handicapped Child*, LAW & CONTEMP. PROBS., Spring 1985, at 7.

121. *See supra* note 51 and accompanying text.

minimize the effects of a child's handicapping condition, regardless of cost, unless they could offer a statutory cost defense.[122] In practice, however, there would undoubtedly be insufficient resources to provide the optimal services necessary to overcome the effects of a child's handicap to the maximum extent possible. The courts would thus be inexorably drawn into allocating the resulting shortfall in overall resources between handicapped and nonhandicapped students. Since no judicially manageable standards for that process of allocation are provided, this option is an unpalatable one.

Even if the sufficiency of public resources posed no problem, an additional difficulty would remain. Under the equalized opportunity test, the court would be expected to determine whether the educational services provided were those which most nearly minimized the effects of a particular child's handicap, thereby allowing him to benefit as fully as possible from the opportunities afforded nonhandicapped students. This task is a troublesome one. As was the case in *Rowley*, the standard would draw the courts into deciding, on a recurring basis, which of several possible techniques should be used to minimize the effects of a child's handicap as fully as possible. Since there is often considerable professional disagreement concerning which is the "best" instructional technique currently available, use of the "equalized opportunity" standard would force the courts to resolve issues that are peculiarly beyond the judicial province. Thus, for this reason as well, the "equalized opportunity" standard presents serious justiciability problems.

Recent developments under state special education statutes confirm these observations. Following the Supreme Court's decision in *Rowley*, it was predicted that state courts might choose to impose a more stringent standard under state law than that adopted by the Court for purposes of the EAHCA.[123] Although litigants have attempted to invoke a more stringent state standard in a number of administrative appeals and cases, the approach has generally been unsuccessful.[124] In several instances, it has been determined that state law requires the adoption of educational objectives that reflect a handicapped child's maximum potential.[125] However, no more than measurable progress toward those objectives has generally been required,

---

122. *See* Bartlett, *supra* note 120, at 38.
123. *See* Zirkel, *supra* note 55, at 487-91.
124. *See, e.g.*, Max M. v. Thompson, 566 F. Supp. 1330 (N.D. Ill. 1983) (interpreting Illinois law); Cothern v. Mallory, 565 F. Supp. 701 (W.D. Mo. 1983) (interpreting Missouri law); Harrell v. Wilson County Schools, 58 N.C. App. 260, 293 S.E.2d 687 (1982), *appeal dismissed*, 306 N.C. 740, 295 S.E.2d 759, *cert. denied*, 460 U.S. 1012 (1983); *In re* Traverse Bay Area Intermediate School Dist., 1982-83 EDUC. HANDICAPPED L. REP. (CRR) 504:140 (Mich. SEA 1982); *cf.* Buchholtz v. Iowa Dep't of Pub. Instruction, 315 N.W.2d 789, 793 (Iowa 1982) (pre-*Rowley* decision).
125. *See* Cothern v. Mallory, 565 F. Supp. 701 (W.D. Mo. 1983) (Missouri statute requires schools to meet the needs and maximize the capabilities of handicapped children); Harrell v. Wilson County Schools, 58 N.C. App. 260, 265, 293 S.E.2d 687, 690 (1982) (interpreting North Carolina State statute guaranteeing an "appropriate" education in light of legislative purpose to ensure every child an opportunity to achieve his full potential and concluding that statute embodied standard proposed by *Rowley* dissenters); *In re* Traverse Bay Area Intermediate School Dist., 1982-83 EDUC. HANDICAPPED L. REP. (CRR) 504:140 (Mich. SEA 1982) (interpreting Michigan state statute as requiring provision of education designed to achieve child's maximum potential); Buchholtz v. Iowa Dep't of Pub. Instruction, 315 N.W.2d 789, 793 (Iowa 1982) (interpreting Iowa statute to require

consistent with the federal "some benefit" test.[126]

In sum, the Supreme Court in *Rowley* very likely had little choice but to adopt a "some benefit" standard for determining the sufficiency of educational programming under the EAHCA. While that standard does not afford the degree of protection that some advocates would prefer, it continues to afford courts adequate leeway to ensure that some meaningful educational opportunity is afforded each handicapped child.

IV
SCOPE OF EDUCATIONAL NEEDS

As has just been described, a handicapped child's abilities and attendant needs, goals and objectives, play a critical role in determining the level and extent of services provided pursuant to the EAHCA. A second, related question accordingly comes readily to mind: What range of needs must school districts address in developing a child's educational program?

Careful analysis of this question is required, for the stakes are high. If the range of needs to be addressed under the EAHCA ("educational needs") is a narrow one, and schools are relieved of any obligation to provide services which respond to noneducational needs, the extent of services available under the Act may be significantly curtailed. If, on the other hand, educational needs are defined as very broad in scope, school districts may regularly face demands for a wide array of very expensive noninstructional services. Not surprisingly, for example, the scope of educational needs to be addressed under the Act has become a recurrent question in cases in which parents have requested placement of severely impaired children in intensive, comprehensive residential programs. School districts have agreed, in many instances, to cover costs of instructional services attendant to such placements. However, they have declined to pay for expensive[127] counseling, custodial and medical services which often form an integral part of such residential programs, arguing that such noninstructional services address noneducational needs

---

provision of a level of education commensurate with the level provided each child who does not receive special education).

126. *See* Cothern v. Mallory, 565 F. Supp. 701 (W.D. Mo. 1983) (programming provided child with Down's syndrome sufficient under both state and federal standards despite parents requests for additional services and more fully trained personnel); Harrell v. Wilson County Schools, 58 N.C. App. 260, 293 S.E.2d 687 (1982) (hearing impaired child received sufficient education under both federal and state standards where she was placed in mainstream setting with unspecified amount of assistance from resource personnel and was "progressing with her studies"); *In re* Traverse Bay Area Intermediate School Dist. 1982-83 EDUC. HANDICAPPED L. REP. (CRR) 504:140 (Mich. SEA 1982) (profoundly hearing impaired child need not be provided cued speech interpreter while enrolled in mainstream classes for substantial part of day, notwithstanding state statute incorporating maximum potential standards); Buchholtz v. Iowa Dep't of Pub. Instruction, 315 N.W.2d 789 (Iowa 1982) (child with learning disability not guaranteed "best" education available in neighboring school district under Iowa "commensurate education" standard). *But see* David D. v. Dartmouth School Comm., 1984-85 EDUC. HANDICAPPED L. REP. (CRR) 556:215 (D. Mass. 1984) (awarding relief based on more protective Massachusetts state law); Geis v. Board of Educ., 1984-85 EDUC. HANDICAPPED L. REP. (CRR) 556:208 (D.N.J. 1984) (awarding relief based on more protective New Jersey state law).

127. *See* Stanger v. Ambach, 501 F. Supp. 1237, 1241-42 (S.D.N.Y. 1980) (discussing residential placement that would cost $53,832 for the 1980-81 year); Stark, *supra* note 11.

outside the realm of their statutory obligations.[128] Parents, on the other hand, have urged that the full range of instructional and noninstructional services are needed to allow their child to make even minimal educational progress, and that such programming should accordingly be deemed to address educational needs.

Debate over the scope of educational needs may be motivated by practical concerns to avoid substantial drains on limited school budgets and to protect the welfare of severely impaired children, but it is often waged in more theoretical terms which once again can fruitfully be examined by reference to the concept of equal educational opportunity. The position of many school districts that the scope of educational needs under the Act should be narrowly defined rests on the unstated premises that the EAHCA is designed to assure equal educational opportunity, and that such opportunity can best be defined by reference to the traditional school system. In that context, educational needs are commonly understood to be synonymous with needs uniquely and historically addressed by educational institutions, through provision of instructional services by trained personnel. Noneducational needs are those historically addressed by other institutions, through the provision of other types of services by personnel with different sorts of training. Under this approach, a dichotomy is assumed to exist between mutually exclusive classes of educational and noneducational needs. If this *exclusionary* approach were incorporated as an aid in determining the scope of needs to be addressed under the EAHCA, it would therefore follow that programming which meets noneducational needs falls outside the range of schools' statutory obligations.

A different view of equal educational opportunity has underlain arguments of parents and advocates in support of a broader interpretation of the scope of educational needs under the EAHCA. They have claimed that the Act contemplates a more substantial modification of the traditional approach to defining schools' responsibilities to address children's educational needs, and have urged that the traditional dichotomy between educational and noneducational needs be recast or replaced by an *inclusionary* approach to the definition of educational needs. Under this view, the assumption that educational and noneducational needs are mutually exclusive would be rejected, and programming required to address a child's educational needs would be provided, even though it simultaneously responds to noneducational needs.

Section A explores the guidance provided by the text of the Act and agency regulations regarding which of these alternative interpretations should be employed. Section B demonstrates that the weight of case law has correctly adopted a broad inclusionary approach to delineating those needs that are to be regarded as educational in character, for purposes of the EAHCA.

---

128. School districts have also urged that placement in residential programs would violate the statutory requirement that handicapped children be educated in the least restrictive environment.

A. Statutory and Regulatory Text

While neither statutory text nor pertinent regulatory provisions are free of ambiguity, both suggest that a broad inclusionary interpretation of educational needs is preferable. Educational need, for purposes of the EAHCA, cannot be understood by referring to a single section of the statute. Instead, one must discern the significance of several interlocking provisions. The definitions of "special education" and "related services" provide a critical starting point. The special education component of a child's free appropriate public education is to include "instruction . . . to meet [his] unique needs."[129] This unqualified reference to the child's needs suggests that the instruction in question may have to address the full spectrum of needs experienced by the child. In addition, the related services to be provided are defined in broad terms. For example, "supportive" and "psychological services" may be required, services which necessarily both foster a child's academic performance and respond to his emotional needs.[130]

A limit upon school systems' obligations to meet handicapped children's needs appears elsewhere in the Act, however. Special education and related services must be supplied only as required to ensure that a child receive a free appropriate public education.[131] EAHCA defines that education, in turn, as the composite of services identified through the IEP development process.[132] The IEP is to include a "statement of present levels of educational performance," a statement of "annual goals, including short-term instructional objectives," and criteria for determining whether these objectives are being achieved.[133]

This language could be interpreted narrowly as focusing upon the process of instruction, confirming some schools' exclusionary view that emotional and custodial needs remain beyond the scope of their responsibilities. However, a broader interpretation seems more supportable. The educational performance and instructional goals in question are those of the full range of handicapped children identified elsewhere in the Act.[134] Thus, because of their seriously impaired abilities, some children require instruction in coping and self-care skills in addition to, or instead of, traditional academic instruction. Congress was fully advised of this fact during extensive hearings which preceded the EAHCA's enactment.[135] Moreover, Congress was also aware that it might be impossible to provide instruction that allows such children to make even limited progress toward the attainment of these skills except through

---

129. 20 U.S.C. § 1401(16) (1982).

130. *See infra* text accompanying note 175 for quotation of this portion of the "related services" definition.

131. 20 U.S.C. § 1401(18) (1982) (a definition of "free appropriate public education" is quoted *supra* at note 27).

132. *Id.*

133. 20 U.S.C. § 1401(19) (1982).

134. *See supra* note 25 for the definition of "handicapped children" which includes mentally retarded and seriously emotionally disturbed children.

135. *See* 1973 Senate Hearings, *supra* note 6, at 99, 391-92, 798, 808.

means that simultaneously address their emotional and custodial care needs.[136] The better reading of these provisions is, therefore, that they justify a broad inclusionary interpretation.

Agency regulations, while also ambiguous, appear likewise to support this broad view. EAHCA regulations regarding the availability of residential programming state: "If placement in a public or private residential program is necessary to provide special education and related services to a handicapped child, the program, including nonmedical care and room and board, must be at no cost to the parents of the child."[137] A cryptic comment accompanying the rule has proved more important than the statutory text: "This requirement applies to placements which are made by public agencies for educational purposes . . . ."[138] This regulation, and the accompanying comment, clearly indicate that schools may have to address custodial care needs. Moreover, the regulators' reference to "educational purposes," rather than "educational needs," may suggest a desire to abandon the traditional dichotomy between educational and noneducational needs. The word "purposes" can reasonably be seen to embrace a wider range of needs, in effect redefining the notion of educational needs in a more comprehensive fashion such as that required by the inclusionary interpretation under consideration here. The regulation is not, however, altogether free from ambiguity in this regard. One construction of the reference to "educational purposes" is that it is an express recognition that some residential placements may be made because of children's emotional needs, and that those placements need not be funded publicly. The regulation, though, makes no reference to schools' responsibilities to address custodial care needs which exist in nonresidential settings and which may likewise give rise to educational needs or affect schools' abilities to address instructional needs in an effective fashion. Although the statutory and regulatory text provides some guidance concerning the definition of educational needs to be adopted for purposes of the EAHCA, it is not surprising that the issue has continued to spur debate and has accordingly required resolution by administrative hearing officers and by the courts.

B.   Judicial and Quasi-Judicial Interpretations

As suggested above, there is a pronounced split in quasi-judicial and judicial interpretations of the scope of educational needs which must be addressed under the EAHCA. The following discussion examines and evaluates a typical administrative hearing officer decision adopting a narrow exclusionary approach, and then traces the courts' development of a better reasoned inclusionary interpretation.

---

136.   *Id.*
137.   34 C.F.R. § 300.302 (1984).
138.   *Id.*

1. *Exclusionary Approach. In re M.J.S.* is a recent New Jersey hearing officer decision which exemplifies the exclusionary approach.[139] In that case, the father of a 17-year-old emotionally disturbed girl requested that she be provided with residential programming. The girl had become a routine truant and an alcohol and drug abuser following her parents' divorce. She was placed by her parents in a residential program, where she performed above average academically until removed for treatment and evaluation in a specialized hospital facility. The hospital staff recommended that upon release she be placed again in a residential setting in order to receive both an appropriate academic program and training in behavior modification accompanied by therapy, the latter designed to deal with her emotional needs. After an unsuccessful attempt to place the girl in local programming, including some mainstream classes, the school system agreed that her educational program should be revised. While expressing a willingness to fund the educational component of the proposed residential program, the school refused to cover other expenses such as those associated with room and board. The board supported this position by contending that it could provide an adequate local private day program for the girl in order to meet her educational needs. It further contended that residential programming was being requested for noneducational purposes—specifically to meet her emotional needs and to relieve her father of undesired supervisory responsibilities which interfered with his business career.

The state hearing officer generally upheld the position taken by the school system. She stated that, although she accepted the unanimous testimony of professional witnesses that residential programming was indicated in the case at hand, she was convinced that such programming was required because of separate noneducational needs:[140] the girl's behavior and emotional problems, and her home situation. In support of this position, the hearing officer cited the evaluating hospital's bifurcated description of the residential program it recommended, one which included both an academic component and a behavior modification-therapy component.[141] The fact that these two components could be separately described served, for the hearing officer, as ample evidence that the modification-therapy component, and thus the overall program, was sought to address the girl's emotional needs.

---

139. 1982-83 EDUC. HANDICAPPED L. REP. (CRR) 504:302 (N.J. SEA 1983). Other administrative hearing officer decisions involving a similar dichotomy between educational and emotional or psychiatric needs include: *In re* P., 1982-83 EDUC. HANDICAPPED L. REP. (CRR) 504:148 (Conn. SEA 1983); Case No. 81-22, 1982-83 EDUC. HANDICAPPED L. REP. (CRR) 502:331 (Conn. SEA 1981); Case No. 80-24 (Jimmy F.), 1980-81 EDUC. HANDICAPPED L. REP. (CRR) 502:109 (Conn. SEA 1980). At least one court has adopted an exclusionary approach in distinguishing between educational and medical needs. *See* McKenzie v. Jefferson, 566 F. Supp. 404 (D.D.C. 1983) (school district not required to pay for placement of emotionally handicapped child in private psychiatric hospital where primary purpose of placement was medical, placement was not made in support of special education program, and services received fell within medical services exception to definition of "related services"). For further discussion of the application of the medical services exception as it relates to the availability of psychotherapy, see part V B 2, *infra. See also* Stark, *supra* note 11, at 513-14.

140. 1982-83 EDUC. HANDICAPPED L. REP. (CRR) 504:308, :309 (N.J. SEA 1983).

141. *Id.* at 504:308.

The *M.J.S.* decision is marked by flawed logic and by insufficient factual analysis. To begin with, the scope of the holding is unclear. The hearing officer may have narrowly determined that the school system had no obligation to supply residential programming needed to meet a child's emotional needs where that programming was not simultaneously required to satisfy her educational needs to the extent required under the EAHCA's FAPE requirements. This holding would have been consistent with the facts at hand. The hearing officer did declare the school system's proposed locally available programming "appropriate," perhaps convinced that the girl would continue to perform at an average level academically, and that this was all that was needed to satisfy the FAPE standard. If this is indeed the case's narrow holding, however, it is unclear why characterization of the requested programming as meeting the girl's emotional needs was even necessary. A reviewing authority could not require of the school district additional services which provided more than the level of opportunity guaranteed pursuant to the FAPE standard, whether designed to meet the girl's educational or emotional needs.

Accordingly, a fair interpretation of the decision is that the hearing officer intended a broader holding declaring that school systems have no obligation to provide residential programming which addresses a child's educational needs if, at the same time, that programming responds to emotional or other noneducational needs—in essence, an adoption of the exclusionary approach. Unfortunately, the rationale behind this intended holding is obscure. The hearing officer may have defined educational need narrowly to exclude the need to acquire basic nonacademic skills, so that even though a child's emotional handicap gives rise to deficiencies in coping skills, a remedy for those deficiencies must be found outside the Act.[142] This conclusion is question-

---

142. Many disputes regarding the definition of educational needs for purposes of the EAHCA involve disagreements between state agencies regarding overlapping responsibility for funding a particular child's placement in a residential setting. *See, e.g.,* North v. District of Columbia Bd. of Educ., 471 F. Supp. 136 (D.D.C. 1979) (dispute regarding responsibilities of school board and social service agency); Parks v. Illinois Dep't of Mental Health & Development Disabilities, 110 Ill. App. 3d 184, 441 N.E.2d 1209 (1982) (dispute regarding responsibility of state board of education and state mental health agency); D.S. v. Board of Educ., 88 N.J. Super. 592, 458 A.2d 129, *cert. denied,* 94 N.J. 529, 468 A.2d 184 (1983) (dispute regarding responsibility of state and local boards of education).

For an extensive discussion of this problem, see Mooney & Aronson, *Solomon Revisited: Separating Educational and Other than Educational Needs in Special Education Placements,* 14 CONN. L. REV. 531 (1982). Mooney and Aronson urge that a "but for" test be adopted in order to limit schools' responsibilities for residential placements which would be required because of emotional needs unrelated to the educational process. *Id.* at 552. There are two problems with this approach which closely parallel the problems with the *M.J.S.* decision itself. First, it is unclear under what circumstances emotional needs would be found to be "unrelated" to the educational process. If that term is used to suggest that schools need not fund residential placements where the school is required to provide a free appropriate public education, then the term complicates the inquiry, for a simpler determination of whether alternative programming would satisfy the *Rowley* standard should suffice. Alternatively, the proposal may suggest that, where compelling emotional needs can be demonstrated, a school would be relieved of any obligation to satisfy concomitant educational needs. While Congress specifically contemplated that local educational agencies could seek financial assistance from other state agencies in order to satisfy the obligations under EAHCA, Congress nevertheless envisioned that local educational agencies would remain ultimately responsible for provision of needed services. *See* S. REP. No. 168, 94th Cong., 1st Sess. 22, 24, *reprinted in* 1975 U.S. CODE CONG. & AD. NEWS 1446, 1448. While the Mooney and Aronson test might serve as a mechanism for allocating financial responsibility

able in light of the previously cited evidence of Congress' intent that the schools assist handicapped children to acquire fundamental nonacademic skills in cases in which a particular disability prevents children from acquiring such skills through more informal contact with parents and other members of the community.[143]

Alternatively, the hearing officer may have defined educational needs narrowly to exclude those that only indirectly influence educational performance. Thus she may have believed that the child in question possessed adequate coping skills which rendered attention to her emotional needs unnecessary, even though those needs indirectly affected her ability to make meaningful progress toward instructional goals and objectives as required under the definition of a free appropriate public education. This view is similarly flawed. Congress' insistence that each handicapped child receive a free appropriate public education dominates the statute and its legislative history.[144] The Congress authorized schools to employ a wide range of related services as tools to achieve this result, at least some of which work only indirectly to facilitate a handicapped child's attainment of his individual educational goals.[145] Requiring schools to address underlying emotional needs which affect a child's educational achievement would be consistent with this strategy and would work in favor of Congress' paramount remedial objective. A narrower interpretation, which instead undercuts the attainment of that objective, should accordingly be rejected.

2. *Inclusionary Approach.*   In light of the flaws evident in the exclusionary approach, it is not surprising that the alternative inclusionary approach now commands substantial judicial support. The courts' acceptance of this approach did not come easily, though, but can be traced over a period of several years.

The first step in the development of this approach occurred in *North v. District of Columbia Board of Education.*[146] *North* involved efforts to procure residential programming for a seriously emotionally disturbed 16-year-old boy who also suffered from learning disabilities and epilepsy. An initial residential placement proved unsuccessful when the provider was unable to deal with his emotional and other problems. The school system refused to arrange another similar placement, arguing that it could provide an adequate day program to meet his educational needs, that residential programming was required only

---

between local educational agencies and other state and local agencies, at least for purposes of state budgetary or accounting practice, other more viable alternatives are probably available. *See* Stoppleworth, *Mooney & Aronson Revisited: A Less than Solomon-Like Solution to the Problem of Residential Placement of Handicapped Children,* 15 CONN. L. REV. 757 (1983). In any event, their proposed approach cannot limit the ultimate responsibility of local agencies as a matter of federal law.

143. *See supra* notes 135-36.

144. *See supra* note 26; *see also* 20 U.S.C. § 1401(C) (1976) (statement of purpose); S. REP. No. 168, 94th Cong., 1st Sess. 9, *reprinted in* 1975 U.S. CODE CONG. & AD. NEWS 1433; H.R. REP. No. 332, 94th Cong., 1st Sess. 7.

145. *See infra* note 176 and accompanying text (related services include psychological and counseling services).

146. 471 F. Supp. 136 (D.D.C. 1979).

to satisfy his emotional needs, and that the appropriate social service agency, not the school system, should bear the attendant costs of such programming. The court rejected the school system's plea. The court stated that in some instances dilemmas of the sort presented would be better resolved through the instigation of neglect proceedings which would place the ultimate responsibility for a seriously impaired child's welfare with a social service agency.[147] Where, however, as in the case at hand, such an approach would cause serious injury to the child,[148] the federal education laws could be invoked. While observing that even if such laws were properly invoked, situations could arise in which emotional needs were dominant (cases in which, the court implied, the schools' responsibilities might differ), the court stated that no such determination was possible under the facts at hand since the child's emotional and educational needs were significantly intertwined.[149] In such cases, the school system could be held accountable for supplying a child with needed residential programming consistent with the EAHCA's free appropriate public education guarantee.[150]

North thus represents an important first step toward the adoption of an inclusionary approach to defining the scope of educational needs. The court recognized that educational needs may overlap emotional needs in at least some instances and that, notwithstanding this fact, such educational needs must be addressed. The court's opinion, however, is flawed in certain respects. As in other cases, the scope of the court's rationale and holding is unclear. The court does not squarely state whether the child's emotional needs themselves give rise to educational needs which must carefully be attended, or whether emotional needs which indirectly affect a child's educational progress, as a result, attain derivative status as educational needs. The court also preserved the dichotomy between educational and emotional needs, and hinted that some sort of balancing process might be required to determine whether a child's educational or noneducational need for a particular service predominates.[151] This statement accordingly suggests that an exclusionary approach might continue to be preferred, in future cases, at least in instances in which strong noneducational needs are found to exist.

The second step in the development of the inclusionary approach came two years later in *Kruelle v. New Castle County School District*.[152] In *Kruelle*, the Third Circuit addressed the obligation of the affected school system to provide a residential program for a 13-year-old profoundly mentally retarded boy who also suffered from emotional problems. The school system had resisted

---

147. *Id.* at 140.
148. The court noted that a neglect proceeding would itself have had a significant adverse effect on the child's course of treatment since his emotional problems would have been exacerbated by his perception that he had been abandoned by his parents. *Id.*
149. *Id.* at 141.
150. *Id.* at 142.
151. *Id.* at 141.
152. 642 F.2d 687 (3d Cir. 1981). *See also* Christopher T. v. San Francisco Unified School Dist., 553 F. Supp. 1107, 1119 (N.D. Cal. 1982) (following *Kruelle* approach).

the parents' efforts to procure such programming, despite evidence of a successful prior residential placement and unsatisfactory local programming. The Third Circuit affirmed a district court decision which held for the parents after rejecting the view of a state hearing officer that the requested programming was more in the nature of parenting than education.[153] While citing and purporting to rely upon *North,* the court framed the issue in a somewhat more helpful fashion by focusing directly upon whether residential placement "is part and parcel of 'specially designed instruction . . . to meet the unique needs of a handicapped child' "—that is, whether that placement is "a necessary predicate for learning" rather than unrelated to learning skills.[154] The Third Circuit went on to justify its ultimate affirmance of the district court's decision by noting that residential programming was needed in order to provide the child in question with a greater degree of consistency in programming available as a result of full time care.[155]

Kruelle demonstrates important progress in the development of the inclusionary approach to defining educational needs for at least two reasons. First, the court squarely formulated the issue at bar in terms of the child's ability to learn, recognizing that the fact that requested services might simultaneously address emotional or custodial needs was largely irrelevant or at least of secondary importance. The decision therefore opened the way for abandonment of the educational/emotional needs dichotomy preserved in *North.* Second, the court articulated a more distinct rationale for its holding than had the *North* decision. The court appeared to recognize that custodial and residential support services could address a child's need for custodial care while simultaneously performing the critical educational function of reinforcing instruction of basic life skills.

The streamlined analysis foreshadowed in *Kruelle* emerged at last in full-blown form in *Abrahamson v. Hershman.*[156] *Abrahamson* involved another seriously impaired child—a 16-year-old boy diagnosed as severely mentally retarded with behavior which was also described as autistic in character. Like the child in *North,* the child in *Abrahamson* had been previously placed unsuccessfully in a residential program. When residential placement subsequently became unavailable, the school system proposed that the child be placed in a day program operated through a consortium of several local public school systems; the school system did not include a residential component as part of his IEP. The district court held that such residential programming was necessary since the child required an extremely structured environment if he was not to regress from day to day, let alone have a chance to make any educational progress.[157] The appellate court cited the district court as stating, however, that needed residential services might be provided through placement in

153. 642 F.2d 687.
154. *Id.* at 693-94.
155. *Id.* at 694.
156. 701 F.2d 223 (1st Cir. 1983).
157. *Id.* at 226.

a group home in conjunction with the local day program.[158]

The First Circuit affirmed. It reasoned that school systems have a paramount obligation to provide each handicapped child with a free appropriate public education, one which must be afforded, in certain instances, in institutional settings which necessarily provide ancillary custodial care.[159] The First Circuit then observed that while foster care was not required to be provided, services which appeared to be custodial might, in appropriate cases, constitute a critical portion of a severely impaired child's educational program where that program was intended to help him master basic life skills.[160] The appellate court also upheld the district court's conclusion that such services may, at the school district's option, be provided through placement in a group home facility adequately equipped to meet the child's needs.[161]

Abrahamson thus confirmed that the critical issue in determining whether a child's needs are educational in character is whether they relate to his ability to master pertinent skills. The court dismissed the defendant school district's proposed dichotomy between educational and custodial needs as unwarranted, suggesting that such dichotomies will no longer be relevant to analysis under the EAHCA.[162] The court also provided an explicit rationale for its determination that the custodial care in question was educational in nature, emphasizing the fact that such custodial care and residential services themselves perform an educational function for a child who is endeavoring to master basic self-care skills. Significantly, however, the court appeared to question an alternative suggestion, noted above, that custodial needs deserve derivative status as educational needs where, if left unattended, the child in question would be denied a free appropriate public education.[163] Other deci-

---

158. *Id.*
159. *Id.* at 227.
160. *Id.* at 228.
161. *Id.* at 229.
162. *Id.* at 228-29.
163. This inference may be drawn from a brief comment on the availability of residential programming for children who suffer from poor home situations.

> This is not to say that the Act requires a local school committee to support a handicapped child in a residential program simply to remedy a poor home setting or to make up for some other deficit not covered by the Act. It is not the responsiblity of local officials under the Act to finance foster care as such: other resources must be looked to. . . . Congress did not intend to burden local school committees with providing all social services to all handicapped children.

Id. at 227-28. The court's statement might be seen to relieve schools of responsibility for providing custodial services to children who are in fact receiving an appropriate education in the local setting but who would also benefit from residential placement in order to escape difficulties at home. *See, e.g., In re* Wellesley Pub. Schools, 1982-83 EDUC. HANDICAPPED L. REP. (CRR) 504:268 (Mass. SEA 1983); *In re* Joseph K., 1982-83 EDUC. HANDICAPPED L. REP. (CRR) 502:133 (Ga. SEA 1980). The statement could also be interpreted in a broader fashion as limiting the responsibility of schools to provide some type of residential programming even where the combined force of a child's handicap and poor home setting precludes his receiving an appropriate education in the absence of such services. Federal regulations under section 504 of the Rehabilitation Act of 1973, referred to in the commentary to the EAHCA regulations described *supra* note 134, are similarly ambiguous on this point. *See* 34 C.F.R. § 104.33 app. A (1983) (regulation requiring that residential placements be provided at no cost where necessary to provide a free appropriate education to a handicapped individual, interpreted in commentary as inapplicable "[w]hen residential care is necessitated not by the student's handicap, but by factors such as the student's home conditions").

sionmakers have nevertheless adopted a contrary view, determining that residential placement should be afforded where necessary to address children's educational needs, even in several cases in which those needs were exacerbated by poor home situations.[164]

Finally, the court resolved a question left unclear under the EAHCA regulations previously discussed,[165] by determining that custodial services provided in a group home, rather than an institution, were as necessary and appropriate in addressing a child's educational needs as similar services available in a more restrictive institutional setting.[166] This result is likely to spur increased reliance on community-based residential placement as an adjunct to private day care programs, a result which may foster cost-effective delivery of services in a beneficial, more fully integrated environment.

Abrahamson should not be interpreted as requiring school districts to routinely assume responsibilities for the complete range of handicapped children's instructional, custodial, emotional, and medical needs, however. The scope of educational needs is only one of several questions which must be answered in determining the mix of programming to be afforded a given child. While an expansive, inclusionary view of educational needs lies at the core of the Act's programming requirements, other aspects of the EAHCA effectively limit the impact that might otherwise result from that interpretation. Thus, however broadly a child's needs may be defined, school districts are only obliged to respond to those needs at the level and to the extent earlier described in parts II and III. Moreover, Congress has carved out a categorical medical services exception as part of its definition of "related services,"[167] thus intervening to relieve school districts of possible obligations to address medical needs which indirectly affect a child's educational performance by restricting the types of services that might be used to do so.

The cases discussed above demonstrate, once again, that courts and quasi-judicial decisionmakers faced with problems of construction under the

---

164. *See* Doe v. Anrig, 692 F.2d 800, 808 (1st Cir. 1982) (while governing consideration is not the needs of the parents but of the child, child should not be placed in possibly hostile home environment which would adversely affect his educational development); *In re* Los Angeles Unified School Dist., 1981-82 Educ. Handicapped L. Rep. (CRR) 502:364 (Cal. SEA 1981) (where emotional problems, home problems, and educational problems intertwined, residential placement would be required); *In re* East Side Union High School Dist., 1981-82 Educ. Handicapped L. Rep. (CRR) 502:374 (Cal. SEA 1981) (although child's nonschool social environment is a major cause of her school problems, residential placement required because all that matters is that her condition makes her unable to learn); Case No. 81-14, 1982-83 Educ. Handicapped L. Rep. (CRR) 502:292 (Conn. SEA 1981) (residential placement required where student's academic progress had been minimal and parent was unwilling or unable to cope with student's presence at home). This position seems well founded for at least two reasons. First, the presence of a severely handicapped child can itself add significant stress to the home environment. Efforts to distinguish between the effects of a child's handicapping condition and the existence of independent problems in the home environment are, therefore, often neither theoretically nor practically justified. Second, the whole thrust of EAHCA appears to be to ensure that handicapped children receive an adequate education whatever the nature or source of their handicap. Only an approach which takes the child as he is and addresses his needs as they stand can accomplish this objective.

165. *See supra* text accompanying notes 137-38.

166. *Abrahamson*, 701 F.2d at 229.

167. 20 U.S.C. § 1401(17) (1982).

EAHCA have turned to the concept of equal educational opportunity for guidance. Because this concept is an ambiguous one, competing lines of interpretation have developed. Nevertheless, it is possible to evaluate such competing views to determine which comports more closely with the policies of the Act—in this case, an inclusionary approach to defining the scope of educational needs which fall within its purview. At the same time, the question of scope cannot be viewed in isolation. Instead, the use of a broadly defined notion of equal educational opportunity in this context is coupled with distinct, more narrow applications of that concept in related contexts, to describe the obligations of school districts to provide educational programming under the Act.

V

AVAILABILITY OF MEDICAL SERVICES

Even assuming the adoption of a broad definition of educational needs for purposes of the Act, an additional question frequently arises concerning the availability of certain types of nontraditional services of a medical nature needed to permit particular handicapped children to make even minimal progress toward appropriate goals and objectives. Parents have requested such services in a variety of situations. For example, they have urged schools to provide clean intermittent catheterization (CIC) to students paralyzed from the waist down who need assistance in emptying their bladders during school hours in order to avoid the risk of increased internal infections while enrolled in regular classes appropriate to their intellectual needs.[168] Parents have also sought intensive psychotherapeutic services which can only be provided through the supervision of a medically licensed psychiatrist.[169] Schools hesitate to provide such services for a variety of reasons including concern

---

168. Clean intermittent catheterization (CIC) may be defined as follows:
CIC is a very simple procedure which can be performed within five minutes. The catheter is washed with soap and water; the urethral area is wiped clean; the catheter is introduced approximately one and one-half inches into the urethra and the bladder contents drained; the catheter is withdrawn; and the amount of urine collected is measured and noted. The procedure can be taught to anyone after a training session of approximately thirty minutes, and it need not be performed by a doctor or nurse. Currently, [plaintiff's child] is catheterized at home by her parents, teenage sibling, and babysitter. However when [the child] is 8 or 9 years old, she will be able to perform CIC upon herself.
Tatro v. Texas, 625 F.2d 557, 559 n.3 (5th Cir. 1980) on remand, 516 F. Supp. 968 (N.D. Tex. 1981), aff'd, 703 F.2d 828 (5th Cir. 1983), aff'd in part, rev'd in part sub nom Irving Indep. School Dist. v. Tatro, 104 S. Ct. 3371 (1984).

169. The term "psychotherapy" has generally been used to describe diverse forms of intensive psychological intervention. See, e.g., THE ENCYCLOPEDIA DICTIONARY OF PSYCHOLOGY 551 (Harre & Lamb eds. 1983) (defining psychotherapy as "treatment of emotional and personality difficulties by psychological means"). Alternatively, the term has been seen to refer to treatment of "[a]ny form of treatment for mental illnesses, behavioral maladaptations, and/or other problems that are assumed to be of an emotional nature, in which a trained person deliberately establishes a professional relationship with a patient for the purpose of removing, modifying, or retarding existing symptoms or attenuating or reversing disturbed patterns of behavior, and of promoting positive personality growth and development." PSYCHIATRIC DICTIONARY 519 (R. Campbell, 5th ed. 1981). Professionals disagree concerning a more precise definition. See. Psychotherapy as a "Related Service," 1981-82 EDUC. HANDICAPPED L. REP. (CRR) AC15, 16, 19, 23 (Supp. 60, Nov. 13, 1981).

regarding anticipated high costs[170] and doubts concerning how provision of medical services fit within their ever-expanding institutional mission. Many schools have accordingly interpreted language in the Act as largely exempting them from any obligation to provide such "medical" services.[171]

Disputes regarding the availability of medical services have not generally been understood to involve uncertainty concerning the application of the concept of equal education opportunity. However, careful examination suggests that, as in the two contexts previously considered, disagreements concerning the interpretation to be accorded the EAHCA's medical services exception rest, in part, on differing views concerning precisely that point.

Resolution of such disputes requires a determination of whether Congress intended to remove all forms of nonevaluative, nondiagnostic medical services from its definition of related services available under the Act,[172] or whether it desired to craft a medical services exception subject to two partial limitations. Schools have urged that the medical services exception is a *comprehensive* one, designed to codify traditional practices. As noted above, nonhandicapped children have historically received an educational opportunity embodied in a common or diversified curriculum of instructional services. Through the Act, Congress required certain additional, related services to be made available.[173] With respect to medical services, however, Congress expressly declined to vary from the norm. Accordingly, it is contended, the EAHCA imposes no obligation to provide such services.

A competing argument might well be formulated in equal educational opportunity terms. While the medical services exception may be broad, it is limited in at least two respects, and it thus is better characterized as a *partial* exception. First, nonhandicapped children should not be denied de minimus medical services comparable to those provided to their nonhandicapped peers. Second, where Congress has explicitly indicated that certain other types of services (including psychological and counseling services) must be made available in order to ensure that handicapped children receive an equal opportunity to be educated in accordance with their unique needs,[174] the medical services exception should be interpreted consistent with, rather than in derogation of, that explicit requirement.

Section A reviews statutory and regulatory provisions bearing on the availability of medical services. Section B discusses the courts' interpretation of the medical services proviso in two problematic factual contexts—when parents request that their child be provided with CIC, and when parents demand that psychotherapy be provided at public expense. The analysis will conclude that the Supreme Court's recent *Tatro* decision regarding the availability of

---

170. *See* McKenzie v. Jefferson, 566 F. Supp. 404, 407 (D.D.C. 1983) (costs of outpatient psychiatric treatment approximately $23,000 per year, cost of inpatient treatment approximately $60,000 per year); *see also* Stark, *supra* note 11, at 516-18.
171. *See infra* text at note 175 for pertinent statutory text.
172. 20 U.S.C. § 1401(17) (1982).
173. *Id.*
174. *Id.*

CIC and the decisions of the majority of lower courts concerning the provision of psychotherapy are consistent with the second of the two interpretations proposed above, that which recognizes two limitations on the EAHCA's medical services exception in the interest of assuring a more broadly defined equal educational opportunity.

A. Statutory and Regulatory Text

The statutory text provides important, but cryptic, guidance. The definition of "related services" states that in "appropriate" cases the following services must be provided as part of a free appropriate public education:

> [S]uch developmental, corrective, and other supportive services (including speech pathology and audiology, psychological services, physical and occupational therapy, recreation, and medical and counseling services, *except that such medical services shall be for diagnostic and evaluation purposes only) as may be required to assist a handicapped child to benefit from special education.*[175]

This language is important both for what it gives and for what it takes away. It expressly endorses the use of corrective and supportive services which are not themselves educational in nature where required to ensure that a handicapped child's educational needs are met. At the same time the statute expressly restricts the types of medical services to be provided.

This critical exception is framed in functional terms. By specifying that medical services must be provided for diagnostic and evaluative purposes, the statute implicitly suggests provision of such services for certain other purposes is not required. Obviously excluded are provision of services designed to provide medical treatment to handicapped children, in an effort to reduce the effect of their disabling conditions, and services to afford requisite life support. Congress therefore appears to accomplish its probable objective of ensuring that general responsibility for handicapped children's medical requirements not be transferred from parents and other providers to the schools. This interpretation simultaneously assumes that the reference to diagnostic and evaluative purposes is not designed as Congress' own embodiment of a de minimis exception to a more comprehensive limitation on the availability of medical services. Consequently, the possibility remains of interpreting this provision to require the provision of de minimis medical services consistent with a narrow application of the concept of equal educational opportunity such as described above.

The EAHCA's legislative history provides limited additional guidance concerning the appropriate interpretation of the medical services proviso. The Senate bill, which served as the principal vehicle for discussion during the early stages of the EAHCA's development, included a limited list of related services and made no reference to the availability of medical services.[176] The

---

175. 20 U.S.C. § 1401(17) (1982) (emphasis added).

176. *See* S. REP. No. 168, 94th Cong., 1st Sess. 62 (1975) (" 'related services' means transportation and developmental, corrective, and other supportive services (including, but not limited to, speech pathology and audiology, psychological services, counseling services, physical and occupational therapy, and recreation) as required to assist a handicapped child to benefit from special edu-

bill reported by the House Education and Labor Committee contained the statute's current language, accompanied by a noncommital textual summary of the revised definition.[177] The Conference Committee merely noted the discrepancy between the House and Senate versions of the legislation while acceding to the inclusion of the medical services proviso that was in the House version.[178]

The EAHCA regulations issued in the wake of enactment carefully defined certain of the terms included in the statutory text. These rules included certain narrowly circumscribed "medical services" within the scope of available "related services"—"services provided by a licensed physician to determine a child's medically related handicapping condition which results in the child's need for special education and related services."[179] The regulations also stated that "related services" include "school health services," defined as "services provided by a qualified school nurse or other qualified person."[180] No commentary was provided to justify the latter provision, only a brief observation that the related services definition included in the final regulations went beyond the formulation originally published in the proposed text.[181]

EAHCA regulations currently in force thus specify that two classes of medical services are to be provided, where necessary, pursuant to the EAHCA: diagnostic and evaluative services, expressly addressed by the statute, and school health services, an invention of the regulators. Unfortunately, no justification is included in support of the later school health services requirement. One may infer from the first of the subsidiary definitions just quoted that the regulators interpreted the term "medical services" to refer to services provided by a licensed doctor, but not services afforded by other licensed professionals or by laypersons. Accordingly, the services of nurses or other persons referred to in the "school health services" definition would not be regarded as "medical services" but instead required as another type of service authorized by the more general catchall portion of the related services provision. This conclusion is confirmed both by a subsequent interpretative ruling regarding the availability of clean intermittent catherization[182] and by the approach adopted in the ill-fated 1982 regulatory revisions addressing the general avail-

---

cation, and includes the early identification and assessment of handicapping conditions in children and provision of services to such children").

177. *See* H.R. REP. No. 332, 94th Cong., 1st Sess. 42-43 (1975) (language of bill); *id.* at 27 ("related services" include "recreation, and medical and counseling services").

178. *See* S. REP. No. 455, 94th Cong., 1st Sess. 30 (1975).

179. 34 C.F.R. § 300.13(b)(4) (1984).

180. *Id.* § 300.13(b)(10).

181. 42 Fed. Reg. 42,505 (1977).

182. *See* 46 Fed. Reg. 4912 (1981) (interpretive ruling regarding the availability of CIC); *id.* at 25,614 (indefinitely postponing implementation of interpretive ruling). The interpretive ruling concluded that CIC should be provided, consistent with prevailing judicial precedent, because: CIC could be performed by unlicensed persons with minimal training; such services could be covered by the reference to "supportive services" which appeared elsewhere in the related services definition; and such services permitted children to be placed in the least restrictive environment rather than consigned to home study.

ability of medical services under the Act.[183] The merits of this approach are explored more readily after a brief exposition of relevant case law.

B. Judicial Response

A substantial body of case law is beginning to develop concerning the scope of the EAHCA's related services provision and the medical services proviso.[184] Discussion of the evolving doctrine is advanced best by concentrating upon the two fact patterns receiving the most sustained judicial attention— challenges involving the availability of clean intermittent catheterization needed by children with spina bifida and disputes concerning the provision of psychotherapy.

1. *Clean Intermittent Catheterization.* The ongoing litigation in the *Tatro* case provides an obvious focal point for examination of the availability of CIC, for it is this case which the Supreme Court recently chose as its own vehicle for exploring the scope of the EAHCA's medical services proviso.[185] Amber Tatro's story, like Amy Rowley's, is now well known. Amber was born with spina bifida and, as a result of that birth defect, suffered from orthopedic and speech impediments and a neurogenic bladder.[186] When Amber was 3 years

---

183. *See* 47 Fed. Reg. 33,836 (1982) (proposed amendments to EAHCA regulations). The proposed regulations would have deleted the school health services portion of the earlier related services definition because no reference to such services was included in the statutory definition. *Id.* at 33,838. Any other obligation any agency might have to handicapped children in making available the same services provided to nonhandicapped children would have been unaffected by this change, however. *Id.* at 33,854 (proposed 34 C.F.R. § 300.13). *See also id.* at 33,839. Moreover, the regulatory preamble specifically stated that these changes were not designed to "categorically preclude the provision of [CIC]"; instead decisions on whether that service was required would be made by public agencies on an individualized basis. *Id.* at 33,838.

The proposed regulations would also have modified the existing medical services definition in several other pertinent ways. First, the reference to licensed physicians previously included in the regulatory "medical services" definition was replaced with a broader reference to "services relating to the practice of medicine." *Id.* at 38,846 (proposed 34 C.F.R. § 300.4(10)(i)). Second, the regulations stated that public agencies were not required to provide life sustaining procedures that: (1) could be provided outside the normal school day, (2) must be performed under sterile conditions, (3) must be administered by specially trained, licensed health care professionals, or (4) entailed a significant risk of illness or more than minimal injury to the child. *Id.* Neither were schools required to provide surgical procedures, medication or the administration of medication, or individually prescribed devices such as eyeglasses. *Id.*

The proposed regulations were later withdrawn in large part. *See EHLR Round-Up: House Hearings on Proposed Regulations,* 1982-83 Educ. Handicapped L. Rep. (CRR) SA-11 (Supp. 81, Oct. 1, 1982).

184. *See, e.g.,* Department of Educ. v. Katherine D., 727 F.2d 809, 813 (9th Cir. 1983) (maintenance of tracheotomy tube is related service); Espino v. Besteiro, 520 F. Supp. 905, 911 (S.D. Tex. 1981), *rev'd on other grounds,* 708 F.2d 1002 (5th Cir. 1983) (air conditioning is related service).

185. The *Tatro* litigation endured for more than four years. *See* 481 F. Supp. 1224 (N.D. Tex. 1979), *vacated and remanded,* 625 F.2d 557 (5th Cir. 1980), *on remand,* 516 F. Supp. 968 (N.D. Tex. 1981), *aff'd,* 703 F.2d 823 (5th Cir. 1983), *aff'd in part, rev'd in part sub nom.* Irving Indep. School Dist. v. Tatro, 104 S. Ct. 3371 (1984). The *Tatro* litigation is discussed in Note, *A Confusion of Rights and Remedies:* Tatro v. Texas, 14 Conn. L. Rev. 585 (1982). For other cases involving CIC, see Tokarcik v. Forest Hills School Dist., 665 F.2d 443 (3d Cir. 1981); Hairston v. Drosick, 423 F. Supp. 180 (S.D. W. Va. 1976) (decided under section 504 of the Rehabilitation Act of 1973); *cf.* Department of Educ. v. Katherine D., 727 F.2d 809 (9th Cir. 1983) (availability of emergency services required by child with cerebral palsy whose tracheotomy tube might be dislodged).

186. Irving Indep. School Dist. v. Tatro, 104 S. Ct. 3371, 3374 (1984).

old, her parents requested that she be permitted to attend the Irving Independent School District's early childhood development program. The school district did not refuse her admission but declined to provide CIC needed by Amber if she was to be present throughout the half-day program. The Tatros brought an action for injunctive relief in federal district court under the EAHCA and section 504 of the Rehabilitation Act of 1973.[187]

The court rebuffed the Tatros when it granted defendants' motion to dismiss the EAHCA claim.[188] The district court reasoned that the related services required under the Act were of two types: (1) transportation and (2) supportive services required to assist the child to benefit from special education.[189] Because the latter category "might, if read literally, require schools to furnish every necessary life support system," the court adopted a narrowing gloss by stating that "to be related in the statutory sense, the service requirement must arise from the effort to educate."[190] The court also concluded that only those "school health services" which satisfied this restrictive interpretation of "related services" could be required.[191] The court did not, however, attempt to probe, in any detail, the significance of the medical services exclusion itself.[192]

The Fifth Circuit rejected this restrictive reading.[193] The appellate court concluded that CIC was a supportive service for purposes of the related services definition.[194] However, the panel believed that the Act contained its own limitations which would ensure that school systems could not be required to supply every extensive life support procedure a child might need.[195] The court also stressed the importance of the Act's least restrictive environment mandate,[196] stating that a determination concerning the availability of CIC should take into account the fact that a child denied such services would likely be consigned to educationally inappropriate programs of homebound instruc-

---

187.　*Id.* at 3374-75.

188.　A claim was also asserted under section 504 of the Rehabilitation Act of 1973. The lower court rejected that claim using reasoning similar to that with which it disposed of the EAHCA cause of action. 481 F. Supp. 1224, 1229 (N.D. Tex. 1981). The Court of Appeals reversed on this point as well, concluding that CIC was the sort of minimal reasonable accomodation required by that statute. 625 F.2d 557, 564-65 (5th Cir. 1980). Six members of the Supreme Court ultimately concluded that the Tatros were not entitled to relief under section 504, and attendant attorneys' fees, since "relief [was] available under the Education of the Handicapped Act to remedy a denial of educational services." 104 S. Ct. at 3379. *See also* Smith v. Robinson, 104 S. Ct. 3457 (1984) (holding that parents are not entitled to receive attorneys' fees under § 505 of the Rehabilitation Act where a remedy is available under the EAHCA but no provision is made under that statute for award of attorneys' fees).

189.　481 F. Supp. at 1227.

190.　*Id.*

191.　*Id.* at 1228.

192.　*Id.*

193.　625 F.2d 557 (5th Cir. 1980).

194.　*Id.* at 562.

195.　*Id.* at 562-63. The court cited three such limitations: (1) the requirement that the affected child be handicapped and require special education; (2) the necessity that the life support system aid the child in benefiting from special education, which the court believed limited the required services to those needed during school hours; and (3) the rule that the life support system be one which a nurse or other qualified person could provide.

196.　*Id.* at 563.

tion.[197] The case was then vacated and remanded for necessary additional proceedings.

In *Tatro II*, the district court proceeded to inquire whether, under Texas law, CIC was a medical service which could only be provided by a physician or whether it fell within the scope of the regulatory provision relating to "school health services" capable of provision by a qualified school nurse or other qualified person.[198] With the aid of briefs from state and local medical associations, the court concluded that a qualified individual acting pursuant to a physician's prescription and under a physician's supervision could provide CIC.[199] The school district appealed and a different panel of the Fifth Circuit affirmed.[200] While expressing reservations about the merits of the earlier panel's decision, the court nevertheless concluded that the analysis included in *Tatro I* represented a reasonable reading of a "delphic statute."[201] The second panel also upheld the trial court's reading of Texas law concerning the proper practice of medicine, as well as the application of that law to the facts at hand.[202]

A unanimous Supreme Court affirmed on EAHCA grounds.[203] The Court held that CIC is a supportive service which was needed by Amber Tatro to allow her to benefit from special education.[204] It further determined that the medical services exception did not apply.[205] In reaching this conclusion, the Court relied heavily upon an earlier interpretative ruling of CIC which had been issued by the United States Department of Education,[206] a ruling which the Court believed was entitled to deference as a reasonable interpretation of congressional intent.[207] The Court stated that the Secretary of Education "could reasonably have concluded that [the medical services exception] was designed to spare schools from an obligation to provide a service that might well prove unduly expensive and beyond the range of their competence."[208] The Court then explained that the provision of CIC imposed no such cost burden, and that the obligation of schools to make CIC and other school health services available merely required districts to continue to provide limited school nursing services simlar to those traditionally afforded all chil-

---

197. *Id.*
198. 516 F. Supp. 968 (N.D. Tex. 1981).
199. *Id.* at 975-77.
200. 703 F.2d 823 (5th Cir. 1983).
201. *Id.* at 826.
202. *Id.* at 827-29. The court also rejected arguments that Amber did not, in fact, require CIC in order to attend the district's half-day early childhood program, and that intervening interpretations required a reversal of its earlier determination concerning the merits of plaintiff's claim under section 504 thereby relieving the school district of liability for attorneys' fees under that provision. *Id.* at 831-32.
203. 104 S. Ct. 3371 (1984). Justices Brennan, Marshall, and Stevens dissented from the majority's determination that the Tatros could not be awarded attorneys' fees. *Id.* at 3379-80.
204. *Id.* at 3377.
205. *Id.*
206. *See supra* note 182.
207. 104 S. Ct. 3371, 3377 (1984).
208. *Id.* at 3378.

dren.[209] The Court rejected the school district's argument that CIC should be regarded as a medical service since it could only be provided pursuant to a physician's prescription under Texas law. Instead, the Court noted that minor medical services, such as the administration of medicine, were routinely provided to nonhandicapped children, concluding that "[i]t would be strange indeed if Congress, in attempting to extend special services to handicapped children, were unwilling to guarantee them services of a kind that are routinely provided to the nonhandicapped."[210] Finally, the Court cited four restrictions which it believed moderated the burdens upon school districts that might flow from the application of its de minimus limitation on the medical services exception: (1) related services such as CIC need only be provided to handicapped children in need of special education; (2) only services necessary to aid a child to benefit from such education need be supplied, not services that might be provided outside the school day; (3) only services that may be performed by a nurse or a layperson must be provided, not those which require the assistance of a physician; and (4) only de minimis medical services, not equipment, must be made available.[211]

The Court's decision in *Tatro* is a sound, well-reasoned one. The case's outcome reflected the balance of equities involved. Amber Tatro's situation was much more emotionally compelling than Amy Rowley's. A determination that CIC is a related service was required if Amber was to receive an education at all appropriate to her social and intellectual abilities, rather than being consigned to the plainly inadequate alternatives of home study or placement in a private setting catering to children with much more severe multiple impairments. Few countervailing considerations favored the school district. Provision of CIC was neither disruptive nor costly, especially when compared to the expensive placement alternatives just described. It is hardly surprising, therefore, that the Court would conclude that the Tatros should prevail.

The decision is also carefully grounded and explained. The Court made no bones about its reliance upon equal educational opportunity principles as a central basis for its decision. It disposed of the school district's proposed interpretation of the medical services exception in a single paragraph, stressing repeatedly that only a "strange" or "anomolous" reading would attribute to Congress a desire to deny handicapped children access to services available to their nonhandicapped peers.[212] The Court might have gone even further in bolstering its justification, for the EAHCA's legislative history plainly supports this position.[213]

---

209. *Id.*
210. *Id.*
211. *Id.* at 3379.
212. *Id.* at 3377-78.
213. *See, e.g.,* S. REP. No. 168, 94th Cong., 1st Sess. 12 (1975) ("The Committee points out in addition that a handicapped child has a right to receive all services normally provided a nonhandicapped child enrolled in a public elementary . . . school. Thus, he or she has a right to physical education services, *health screening,* transportation services and all other services which are provided to all children within the school system, and a right to as many options in curricula as are available to all children.") (emphasis added).

This approach provides an important theoretical underpinning absent from existing regulations and prior case law. The Education Department's "school health services" regulations[214] no longer appear rooted in an arbitrary distinction between two classes of medically trained and licensed personnel (doctors and nurses), each of whom would appear to provide medical services, that is, services designed to maintain health and prevent, alleviate, or cure disease. Instead, the requirement that certain services be provided through school nurses is explained in terms of historical tradition and the probable intention of Congress to preserve that tradition for all children. The Fifth Circuit's earlier determination that "school health services" include only those medical services that must unavoidably be provided during the school day[215] is similarly illuminated. No comparable restriction has been applied to other types of related services, such as counseling, which might well be provided outside of traditional school hours; it is therefore evident that this limiting gloss does not stem from the terms of the "related service" definition which specify that such services must be "required to assist" a handicapped child to benefit from special education. The Court's approach makes plain that the limitation flows inevitably from the fundamental premise that handicapped children should receive school health services comparable to those enjoyed by others. Since nonhandicapped children only receive school medical services that cannot be provided in off hours, that same restriction should apply to their handicapped peers.

In addition to providing a useful theoretical perspective, the Court offered needed practical guidance. Two questions are likely to emerge in the wake of the *Tatro* decision: (1) what are the obligations of school districts which do not now employ school nurses? and (2) what range of school health services other than CIC need be supplied? *Tatro* touches on each of these questions in at least a preliminary fashion.

It is plain that school districts which provide school health services must open those services to both handicapped and nonhandicapped children. Irving Independent School District apparently authorized school nurses to dispense oral medications and administer emergency injections in accordance with a physician's prescription.[216] It is therefore obliged to accommodate the needs of handicapped students for simlar, minimal medical assistance. Given these facts, the Court's holding might be viewed as a narrow one, applicable only to schools currently providing school health services through school nurses. The Court's logic would seem, however, to dictate a broader result. The Court did not rest its decision solely on Irving Independent School District's past practices. Instead, it relied upon federal regulations which had reasonably concluded that Congress had designed the medical services exception to limit school district obligations to provide costly hospital and physician services, not to supplant the traditional system of retaining school nurses on

---

214. *See supra* note 182.
215. *See supra* note 195.
216. 104 S. Ct. 3371, 3378 (1984).

school district staffs. Read in this restrictive fashion, the medical services proviso does not limit the authority of federal regulators to require all school districts to supply CIC and other supportive school health services, whether those districts have done so in the past or not. The Court thus ensured that a nationwide standard would continue to govern the minimum range of services available under the EAHCA, rather than limiting its equal educational opportunity equation to analysis of the historical practices of individual school districts. Whether districts will meet their obligations by hiring school nurses, contracting for visiting nurse assistance, or training other personnel to meet necessary requirements will be up to them.

The range of de minimis school health services that must be provided in the wake of *Tatro* is less clear. *Tatro* recognizes that at least those services that may only be provided by licensed physicians generally fall within the medical services exception and need not be supplied under the EAHCA. Thus, it is clear that schools need not pay the cost of corrective surgery or other similar procedures. At the same time, *Tatro* indicates that certain de minimis medical services that can be performed by registered nurses or other qualified personnel must be provided. Schools will be obliged to expand their current medical service offerings, increasing both the types of medical services available (providing CIC as well as dispensing medication), and the terms on which those services are offered (supplying routine as well as emergency assistance). It is obvious that state licensing laws and attendant restrictions on nurses' authority and duties will serve as an outer limit on schools' obligations under the Court's ruling,[217] and that, in any event, federal regulators are likely to defer to such authority.[218] School districts' responsibilities may well fall somewhat short of offering a full range of services that a nurse is capable of providing, however. As previously discussed,[219] the rationale of the *Tatro* decision was not simply that licensed doctors, and not nurses, are providers of medical services. Instead, the decision recognized that a certain class of nursing services traditionally had been offered nonhandicapped children, and that a comparable set of de minimis services should thus be available to handicapped children under the EAHCA. It therefore follows that only certain nursing services need be provided by local educational agencies. Which services fall within this de minimis class will likely stir continuing debate. The Court's analysis in *Tatro* suggests, however, that only those medical services which can safely be performed in the school environment, with minimal time, staff, expense, and equipment, should be seen to fall within the *Tatro* rule. Other services, such as the performance of kidney dialysis, cannot fairly be characterized as de minimis in character. Accordingly, they should be

---

217. *Id.* at 3379. ("school nursing services must be provided only if they can be performed by a nurse or other qualified person").

218. *See, e.g.,* 47 Fed. Reg. 33,839 (1982) (guideline accompanying proposed regulatory amendment specified that public agencies may look to standards, opinions, and other determinations of State medical licensing authorities in determining if certain services are medical services within the meaning of the EAHCA).

219. *See supra* text accompanying note 214.

regarded as falling within the statutory medical services exception, even if they might be provided by a nurse or other trained person acting under a physician's direction.

In sum, the Supreme Court's approach in *Tatro* both parallels and differs from its approach in *Rowley*. The equal educational opportunity theme underlies both decisions. Although *Rowley* had defined the level and extent of services under the Act in terms of a restrained "some benefit" version of that theme, *Tatro* reflects a more expansive interpretation, appropriate to its subtly different subject matter. While considerations of justiciability and cost limited the Court's choice of standard in the earlier case, similar constraints did not prevent its adoption in *Tatro* of a construction which required minimal expenditure of school district funds and which necessitated only limited, nationwide comparison of the types of services afforded handicapped and nonhandicapped children.

2. *Psychotherapy.* While many schools have agreed to provide CIC in response to pressure from federal administrative agencies and unanimous court decisions, schools have more slowly and reluctantly conceded a possible obligation to provide intensive psychotherapy when needed by children who are seriously emotionally or mentally impaired. Although psychotherapeutic services at times are offered by trained social workers and psychologists, they may also be offered by psychiatrists who are licensed physicians, or by social workers and psychologists operating under a physician's direction. At least arguably, those intensive services offered by or under the supervision of a psychiatrist may be characterized as medical in character. In the wake of *Tatro,* a dearth of definitive regulatory guidance concerning the availability of such services and an emerging split in judicial opinions on this issue is likely to result in growing uncertainty regarding the schools' obligations to provide such services at no cost.

Consistent with the EAHCA's statutory text,[220] United States Department of Education regulations specify that certain counseling and psychological services must be provided. The regulations define counseling services by reference to possible service providers, stating that such services are those "provided by qualified social workers, psychologists, guidance counselors, or other qualified personnel."[221] "Psychological services," in turn, refers to the performance of several specific diagnostic, interpretive, and counseling functions.[222] Because the regulations do not expressly include psychiatrists among the listed providers of counseling services, they may imply that schools are not obliged to supply psychotherapeutic services only available from such persons or services provided under their direction. The Department of Edu-

---

220. 20 U.S.C. § 1401(17) (1982).
221. *See* 34 C.F.R. § 300.13(b)(2) (1984).
222. *Id.* at § 300.13(b)(8):

cation's more recent pronouncements have been equivocal on this point.[223] The weight of judicial authority interprets the EAHCA to require the provision of psychotherapy in appropriate cases. *In re "A" Family* is an early representative case which adopts this view.[224] The case involved a family of a seriously emotionally disturbed, schizophrenic boy which requested the provision of intensive psychiatric services for the boy as part of a private residential program. The plaintiffs asked the Montana Supreme Court to determine whether such services were medical services, which fell beyond the scope of the definition of related services just discussed, or psychological services, which are listed without qualification as an available service within the terms of the EAHCA. After consulting a standard dictionary, the court concluded that "psychotherapy" referred to "treatment of [a] mental or emotional disorder or of related bodily ills by psychological means."[225] Since the court believed such psychotherapeutic services were expressly included within the phrase "psychological services," the court gave no further consideration to the application of the medical services proviso.[226]

A recent decision of the federal district court for the Northern District of Illinois took an opposing position. *Darlene L. v. Illinois State Board of Education*[227] involved a child diagnosed as having a severe behavioral disorder. Local school officials and the child's parents argued that she needed placement in a residential program. However, the state administrative agency charged with review of private placements refused to authorize payment for

---

"Psychological services" include:
  (i) Administering psychological and educational tests, and other assessment procedures;
  (ii) Interpréting assessment results;
  (iii) Obtaining, integrating, and interpreting information about child behavior and conditions relating to learning;
  (iv) Consulting with other staff members in planning school programs to meet the special needs of children as indicated by psychological tests, interviews, and behavioral evaluation; and
  (v) Planning and managing a program of psychological services, including psychological counseling for children and parents.
  223.   The Office of Special Education has taken a somewhat equivocal position on the issue. *See* 2 [EHA Rulings] EDUC. HANDICAPPED L. REP. (CRR) 211:19 (1978) (if state interprets psychotherapy as "medical service," local education agency is not obligated to provide such service since 34 C.F.R. § 300.13 requires medical services for diagnostic and evaluative purposes only; if state interprets psychotherapy as "counseling services," services must be provided at no cost to parents if they are listed in IEP as related services); *id.* at 211:104-:105 (1979) (where state law permits "psychotherapy" to be provided by someone other than a psychiatrist and psychotherapy is needed to assist a handicapped child to benefit from special education, psychotherapy might be considered a "related service" under Department "related service" regulations). The Office of Civil Rights, during the same period, opined that psychiatric services must be provided, where appropriate, pursuant to section 504 of the Rehabilitation Act. *See* 3 [§ 504 Rulings] EDUC. HANDICAPPED L. REP. (CRR) 257:82 (1980); *id.* at 257:57, :191, :248 (1980).
  224.   602 P.2d 157 (Mont. 1979). *See also* Papacoda v. Connecticut, 528 F. Supp. 68 (D. Conn. 1981); T.G. v. Board of Educ., 576 F. Supp. 420 (D.N.J. 1983), *aff'd*, 738 F.2d 425 (3d Cir. 1984); Max M. v. Thompson, 1984-85 EDUC. HANDICAPPED L. REP. (CRR) 556:227 (N.D. Ill. 1984) (psychotherapy provided by psychiatrist is related service, but services provided by social worker or other qualified non-physician provider are generally reimbursable costs).
  225.   602 P.2d at 165.
  226.   *Id.*
  227.   568 F. Supp. 1340 (N.D. Ill. 1983). *See also* McKenzie v. Jefferson, 566 F. Supp. 404, 412 (D.D.C. 1983).

psychiatric services provided in conjunction with the proposed placement because he concluded that such services were medical in character. The district court agreed with this interpretation. The court rejected the view that the services in question were psychological services for purposes of the EAHCA.[228] In support of its position, the court cited the EAHCA regulations' definition of psychological services which does not list psychiatrists among the possible providers of such services.[229] The court contended that psychiatrists are, by definition, licensed physicians.[230] Therefore, intensive psychotherapy afforded by such providers should be deemed medical services. Since the psychotherapeutic services sought for Darlene L. were other than diagnostic or evaluative in purpose, the school system had no obligation to provide those services at public expense pursuant to the EAHCA.[231]

Resolution of this conflict in authority requires a three-part analysis. First, are psychotherapeutic services provided by or under the supervision of a psychiatrist "psychological services" for purposes of the Act? The statute provides no direct guidance on this question, but seems indirectly to suggest that the answer should be "yes." The "related services" definition refers to both "counseling" and "psychological services,"[232] evidencing what appears to be an intent to encompass a broad spectrum of mental health services. Had Congress wished to exclude the most intensive types of mental health services from this range, it could have done so explicitly, as it did in excluding certain forms of medical services from the spectrum of related services available. Moreover, coverage of such intensive mental health services arises by implication as a result of the express coverage and protection of seriously emotionally disturbed children under the Act.[233] It is questionable whether Congress would have included such children as beneficiaries of the legislation while at the same time limiting their access to the intensive services possibly needed for attaining any meaningful educational progress.

Second, are psychotherapeutic services provided by or under the supervision of a psychiatrist "medical services" within the terms of the statute? To the extent that intensive psychotherapeutic services can only be provided by a licensed psychiatrist or under a psychiatrist's supervision, the answer would seen to be "yes," in light of the *Tatro* decision discussed above. This class of services might include the prescription of drugs. In other cases, the answer should be "no." Counseling services available from social workers or psychologists who need not possess or be supervised by a person possessing a medical license are not generally regarded as medical in nature. Indeed, Congress specifically contemplated that the services of such persons would be

228. 568 F. Supp. 1340, 1344 (N.D. Ill. 1983).
229. *Id.*
230. *Id.*
231. *Id.* at 1345.
232. 20 U.S.C. § 1401(17) (1982).
233. *See supra* note 25.

available under the EAHCA.[234] The fact that a medically trained and licensed psychiatrist can also provide similar counseling services should not transform those services so as to render them "medical" in character when performed by nonmedical personnel.[235] Instead, it suggests that psychiatrists performing certain counseling functions may themselves be providing services reasonably regarded as nonmedical in character, at least for purposes of the Act. It follows, in turn, that social workers or psychologists who work under the supervision of a psychiatrist are not necessarily supplying medical services, but may instead be functioning as adjunct providers of counseling services solely for purposes of convenience and cost control, rather than because oversight by a medically licensed psychiatrist is legally required with respect to all their activities. In a substantial number of cases, therefore, the provision of psychotherapeutic counseling services should not be regarded as medical in character and should therefore fall outside the medical services exception.

The final question, in any event, is whether the medical services proviso should be interpreted in isolation. If intensive psychotherapeutic services (including those services uniquely available from or under the supervision of a licensed psychiatrist) fall within the phrase "psychological services" but are excluded under the medical services proviso, it is necessary to determine how these two provisions are to be reconciled. Standard canons of statutory construction suggest that the more general reference to medical services should not lightly be adjudged to override the more specific treatment of psychological services.[236] Moreover, a basic rule of construction assumes that each of several listed items should be afforded independent significance.[237] This would only be the case if the "psychological services" provision is seen to stand on its own rather than narrowed consistent with the medical services proviso. Although the matter is plainly not free from doubt,[238] the better reading of the EAHCA is that the full range of intensive psychotherapeutic services should not be regarded as medical services but should instead be treated, in appropriate cases, as psychological services requiring no special analysis beyond that discussed in Parts II through IV above.[239] In effect, the

---

234. *See* S. REP. No. 168, 94th Cong., 1st Sess. 33 (1975); Irving Indep. School Dist. v. Tatro, 104 S. Ct. 3371, 3378 (1984).

235. *See* T.G. v. Board of Educ., 576 F. Supp. 420, 424 (D.N.J. 1983).

236. Fourco Glass Co. v. Transmirra Products Corp., 353 U.S. 222 (1957).

237. *See* Reiter v. Sonotone Corp., 442 U.S. 330 (1979) (canons of construction suggest that terms connected by a disjunctive be given separate meaning unless context dictates otherwise); De Sylva v. Ballentine, 351 U.S. 570, 573 (1956) (word "or" is often used as a careless substitute for the word "and").

238. *See Psychotherapy as a "Related Service,"* supra note 169.

239. To say that psychiatric services can in some instances be a related service for purposes of the Act is not, however, to conclude that psychiatric services are required by every handicapped child in every case. Under the *Rowley* decision discussed in part III *supra*, school districts would be obligated to provide such services only in those cases in which less intensive psychological services were insufficient to permit a child to benefit and make some progress toward appropriate educational goals. Thus, psychiatric services which go well beyond what is required for educational purposes do not fall within the scope of a school district's responsibilities under the EAHCA.

medical services proviso should be seen as a partial, rather than comprehensive, exception to the EAHCA's related services definition, in order to honor Congress intent that children with severe emotional impairments have access to a full range of services needed to provide an equal educational opportunity.

In sum, the concept of equal educational opportunity can once again be employed as an aid to construing ambiguous provisions of the EAHCA. As demonstrated, notwithstanding Congress' explicit limitation on the availability of medical services, a de minimis limitation on that exception has been described by reference to the concept of equal educational opportunity. The concept also serves as a useful reminder that the medical services exception should be interpreted in the context of Congress' overall plan to ensure that all children, including seriously emotionally disturbed children in need of the full range of psychotherapeutic services, should receive those services needed to allow them to make at least minimal educational progress.

VI

CONCLUSION

This article has traced the major theme of equal educational opportunity as it bears upon educational programming decisions under the EAHCA. It has been argued that this complex theme is subject to numerous competing interpretations which must be carefully explored in each of the several settings in which the theme recurs. It has been suggested that the courts have relied upon the concept as an interpretive aid in addressing three important questions under the Act: in describing the level and extent of services to be provided handicapped children, in defining the scope of their educational needs, and in delineating the types of medical services available. Finally, the article has evaluated competing interpretations adopted in the judicial decisions which address these questions and has proposed alternative interpretations, where necessary, to give fuller effect to Congress' paramount objective—assisting state and local governments to meet the educational needs of handicapped children in order to assure equal protection of the law.

PART II

6

THE ROLE OF COST IN EDUCATIONAL DECISIONMAKING FOR THE HANDICAPPED CHILD

Katharine T. Bartlett*

Do the 30 million Americans afflicted with physical or mental handicaps have a right of access, no matter what the cost, to all publically sponsored activities? That is now a central question because the price of such access promises to become very great.[1]

I

INTRODUCTION

A. The Issue of Cost in Special Education

Special education for the handicapped is expensive.[2] Estimates of the average cost of educating a handicapped child are about twice as high as the cost of educating a nonhandicapped child, with some educational placements costing six times as much or more.[3] Neither the guarantee of a free and appropriate education to handicapped children set forth in the Education for

* Associate Clinical Professor of Law, Duke University. I am indebted to Chris Schroeder and Judith Wegner for their insights during numerous conversations I had with them while I was writing this article, and to Richard Boulden, Matt Lavine, and Howard Vingan for their research assistance.

1. Hicks, *Should Every Bus Kneel?* in DISABLED PEOPLE AS SECOND CLASS CITIZENS 13-14 (1982) (quoting *Must Every Bus Kneel to the Disabled?*, N.Y. Times, Nov. 18, 1979, at 18E).

2. *See Oversight of P.L. 94-142 — The Education for All Handicapped Children Act, Part 1: Hearings before the Subcommittee on Select Education of the Committee on Education and Labor — House of Representatives,* 96th Cong., 1st Sess. 82 (1979) (statement of Walter Tice, American Federation of Teachers); J. KAKALIK, W. FURRY, M. THOMAS & M. CARNEY, THE COST OF SPECIAL EDUCATION 5 (1981) [hereinafter cited as KAKALIK] ($3577 average cost per student for handicapped child in 1977-78; $4898 average cost in the following 3-year period). Residential placements, not included in the Kakalik study, are even more expensive. *See Stark, Tragic Choices in Special Education: The Effect of Scarce Resources on the Implementation of Pub. L. No. 94-142,* 14 CONN. L. REV. 477, 491, 493 (1982). A residential placement may cost well over $50,000 per year. *See* Clevenger v. Oak Ridge School Dist., 744 F.2d 514, 517 (6th Cir. 1984) (ordering residential placement costing $88,000 per year); Stanger v. Ambach, 501 F. Supp. 1237, 1241-42 (S.D.N.Y. 1980) (discussing residential placement that would cost at least $52,410 for the 1980-81 school year).

3. KAKALIK, *supra* note 2, at 339, 343. (This study noted that, depending on the type of handicap and educational placement (excluding residential placements), the cost of educating a handicapped child is between .49 (full-time work placement for learning disabled students) and 6.78 (regular class plus part-time special teacher) times the cost of educating a nonhandicapped child. *See also* M. MOORE, L. WALKER, & R. HOLLAND, FINETUNING SPECIAL EDUCATION FINANCE 50-51 (1982) [hereinafter cited as MOORE, WALKER & HOLLAND] (depending upon the type of handicap and method of computation, the cost of special education ranges from 1.37 to 5.86 times the cost of a regular education); Marriner, *The Cost of Educating Handicapped Pupils in New York City,* 3 J. EDUC. FIN. 82, 86-88 (1977) (average cost of special education was $5897 per student, compared to $2294 per student for a regular education; average per student cost of special education ranged from $4022 to $14,072, depending on the program). The factors considered in measuring the cost of special education are discussed in MOORE, WALKER & HOLLAND, *supra,* at 45-58.

All Handicapped Children Act of 1975 (EAHCA)[4] nor the prohibition of exclusion of the handicapped from a program or activity receiving federal assistance, contained in section 504 of the Rehabilitation Act of 1973,[5] is expressly qualified by considerations of cost. Nevertheless, as the cost of special education has risen dramatically,[6] and as public concern for the quality of public education generally has sharpened,[7] cost is often a major factor in educational decisionmaking affecting handicapped children. A school district may understand that certain services sought by parents on behalf of a handicapped child would be extremely beneficial to the child, but nevertheless be concerned about the resource implications of those services. If it determines that it is "unable" to provide those services, it may reject the parents' request. If this rejection is challenged by the parents under the hearing procedures of the EAHCA, the hearing officer's understanding of the relevance of cost may determine whether a program is deemed required by the EAHCA.[8]

Despite its importance, the cost issue is unsettled. Judicial responses range from the position that cost should not be considered in decisionmaking under the EAHCA to the position that cost is an important factor to be taken into account so that a requested program that is "too" expensive need not be offered. Rather than facing the cost issue head on, some courts take cost into account indirectly in making such substantive statutory interpretations as whether a particular requested program is "educational," or whether an educational program is "appropriate," the "least restrictive alternative," or a "related service."

The absence of a clear answer to the cost issue is not surprising. The rights of handicapped children to public education, like other rights established in the 1960's and 1970's, were created without serious attention to

---

4.   Pub. L. No. 94-142, 89 Stat. 773 (1975) (codified as amended at 20 U.S.C. §§ 1400, 1401, 1405, 1406, 1411-20, 1453 (1982)). The Act applies only to those states that accept federal funds pursuant to its provisions. *Id.* § 1412. All states now accept federal funds under the Act and are covered by it. *See* Levinson, *The Right to a Minimally Adequate Education for Learning Disabled Children,* 12 VAL. U.L. REV. 253, 277 n.135 (1978) (all states except New Mexico submitted state plans under the EAHCA); 1983-84 EDUC. HANDICAPPED L. REP. (CRR) SA:104 (New Mexico legislature passed legislation requiring state board to submit a plan for EAHCA funds).

5.   29 U.S.C. § 794 (l982).

6.   *See* Stark, *supra* note 2, at 487 (In the 3-year period after passage of the EAHCA, "local school budgets for special education rose at the rate of 14 percent per year, twice as rapidly as overall operating budgets for public schools nationwide.")

7.   In 1983 there were three major studies on how to improve the quality of public education in the United States: NAT'L COMMISSION ON EXCELLENCE, A NATION AT RISK: THE IMPERATIVE FOR EDUCATIONAL REFORM (1983); Report of the Twentieth Century Fund Task Force on Federal Elementary and Secondary Education Policy, *reprinted in* MAKING THE GRADE (1983); TASK FORCE ON EDUCATION FOR ECONOMIC GROWTH, EDUCATION COMMISSION OF THE STATES, ACTION FOR EXCELLENCE: A COMPREHENSIVE PLAN TO IMPROVE OUR NATION'S SCHOOLS (1983).

8.   *See* Note, Board of Education v. Rowley: *Handicapped Children Are Entitled to a Beneficial Education,* 69 IOWA L. REV. 279, 287-88 (1983) [hereinafter cited as Note, *Board of Education v. Rowley*]; Stark, *supra* note 2, at 519-20; Note, *Enforcing the Right to an "Appropriate" Education: The Education for All Handicapped Children Act of 1975,* 92 HARV. L. REV. 1103, 1109, 1125 (1979) [hereinafter cited as Note, *Enforcing the Right*]; Note, *Defining an "Appropriate Education" Under the Education for All Handicapped Children Act,* 34 ME. L. REV. 79, 91, 96-97 (1982) [hereinafter cited as Note, *Defining an "Appropriate Education"*].

their redistributive consequences.[9] Declining to face these consequences when the rights were initially defined might have been appropriate, or at least sound advocacy, for some solutions to issues of implementation and resource allocation which now deserve serious consideration would have been rejected as "unrealistic" when the needs and potential of handicapped were so little understood. A decade later, however, the failure to confront these issues suggests naivete rather than political astuteness and risks the dilution of those rights which the EAHCA was designed to secure.[10] Consolidation of rights during this "second generation" period depends in large part upon how well their implications, including those of cost, are understood and addressed.

B. The Concept of Program Parity

I conclude in this article that cost is a legitimate factor to consider in determining the level of educational services to make available to handicapped children, as it is in determining the level of other public services. Moreover, the issue of cost should be confronted directly in educational decisionmaking, not hidden behind an analysis that purports to focus entirely on educational factors. The article focuses on the limits that should be put on considering cost in educational decisionmaking for the handicapped. I argue that although it is appropriate to take cost into account, cost considerations should not prevail to deny a handicapped child an education program that is *comparable in quality* to that provided to nonhandicapped children. This standard, which I refer to as "program parity," is similar to suggestions that educational programs for

---

9. *Compare* Goldberg v. Kelly, 397 U.S. 254, 261, 265-66 (1970) (establishing right to hearing before termination of welfare assistance benefits despite costs to government) *with* Matthews v. Eldridge, 424 U.S. 319, 334-35, 347-48 (1976) (decided six years after Goldberg v. Kelly and instituting, in cases involving termination of Social Security disability payments, a test balancing private and governmental interests, including administrative inconvenience and cost, to determine extent of due process required).

Legislation on behalf of the handicapped, such as the Urban Mass Transportation Act, 49 U.S.C. § 1612 (1982), and section 504 of the Rehabilitation Act of 1973, 29 U.S.C. § 794 (1982), has had particularly acute financial consequences, because of the increased costs of providing to the handicapped services that are generally available to others. *See, e.g.*, Dopico v. Goldschmid, 687 F.2d 644, 650 (2d Cir. 1980) (New York City should have spent six million dollars in Urban Mass Transportation Act Funds in 1980 to make public transportation accessible to the handicapped); Barnes v. Converse College, 436 F. Supp. 635, 638, 639 (D.S.C. 1977) (sign-language interpreter ordered for deaf student to cost about $1000 for one summer school session).

The financial consequences of the EAHCA did not go unnoticed in Congress. *See, e.g.*, 121 CONG. REC. 9498-99 (1975) (remarks of Senator Dole) ("Someone will have to pay for [individualized conferences], of course, and that someone will be you and me, the taxpayers."); *id.* at 9506 (remarks of Senator Baker) ("It is my feeling. . .that [the EAHCA], which contains authorizations in excess of $6 billion over a 4-year period, holds out the hope of a level of Federal support which is much greater than we are able to provide during this time of fiscal constraints."). The role of cost in defining the extent of the states' obligation to educate the handicapped, however, was not specifically addressed.

10. The Reagan Administration, partly in response to the financial stress claimed to have been caused by the EAHCA, has proposed several changes in the legislation. *See* Stark, *supra* note 2, at 524-28; *see also* Note, *Education* — Board of Education v. Rowley: *The Supreme Court Takes a Conservative Approach to the Education of Handicapped Children*, 61 N.C.L. REV. 881, 897 n.156 (1983) (drawing a connection between the financial crisis created by the EAHCA and a predicted backlash against special education); Comment, *Statutory Mandate for "Free and Appropriate Public Education" Satisfied When Handicapped Benefit from Specialized Instruction and Support Services*, 14 RUTGERS L. REV. 989, 1004-06 & n.90 (1983) (*Rowley* decision and efforts to erode EAHCA have a financial basis).

the handicapped be comparable to those of the nonhandicapped;[11] a closer examination of this standard and an analysis of its implications should enhance its appeal to policymakers and courts. It is the standard that best interprets the Act, and although it will require some redirection of the approach adopted by the United States Supreme Court in its first attempt at interpreting the Act,[12] this redirection is consistent with the institutional concerns to which the Court has been sensitive.

Program parity describes a model in which the educational needs of the handicapped child are met in the same proportion as the needs of the nonhandicapped child. It requires that sacrifices, if necessary, be equal.[13] It does not require dollar-for-dollar cutbacks in every educational program to adjust to resource shortages, but rather a downscaling that keeps programming for handicapped children at a level of quality comparable to that for the nonhandicapped. The standard of program parity thus demands that before cost is used to deny a service that would be beneficial to the handicapped child, school districts must ensure that the handicapped child's needs are met by a program that is at least comparable in overall quality to that offered to nonhandicapped children.

The program parity standard fills a gap between the nondiscrimination mandate of section 504 of the Rehabilitation Act and the affirmative requirements imposed by the EAHCA. These statutes are often read restrictively. The EAHCA has been held to ensure only a minimal level of educational benefit for handicapped children, without relation to the level of educational services afforded to others.[14] Section 504 has been held to require "equal"

---

11. See, e.g., Note, Enforcing the Right, supra note 8, at 1125 (proposing that appropriateness under the Act be defined "in relation to the actual level of educational services provided for most children within a given school system" (footnote omitted)); Colley, The Education for All Handicapped Children Act (EHA) A Statutory and Legal Analysis, 10 J.L. & EDUC. 137, 147 (1981) ("If the optimum level of services can not [sic] be provided within the resources available to a district, then every child (handicapped and non-handicapped alike) within the district must suffer a derogation of his program in relation to his educational potential."); Note, Defining Appropriate Education for the Handicapped: The Rowley Decision, 27 ST. LOUIS U.L.J. 685, 705 (1983) ("For the present, the best approach for school districts may be a good faith attempt to educate the handicapped and the nonhandicapped on the same plane.") [hereinafter cited as Note, The Rowley Decision]; Note, Defining an "Appropriate Education," supra note 8, at 109 ("provision of . . . equal educational opportunity necessary requires a comparison between that quantum of opportunity afforded to handicapped and nonhandicapped children.").

12. Board of Educ. v. Rowley, 458 U.S. 176 (1982).

13. See B. ACKERMAN, SOCIAL JUSTICE IN THE LIBERAL STATE 237-38, 261, 270 (1980). Ackerman's discussion of the concept of negative compensation is particularly applicable to rules relating to the handicapped.

"The principle of negative compensation requires X to receive an education and transactional system that permit him to explore those (perhaps very limited) options that his genetic equipment leaves open for him. These compensatory systems, moreover, need not be perfect, for the resources provided even 'normal' children hardly provide them with an ideally liberal education or perfectly flexible system of transactions. Instead, negative compensation insists that X be provided with a chance of realizing his genetic possibilities that is no less imperfect than that provided others."

Id. at 270 (italics in original).

14. Board of Educ. v. Rowley, 458 U.S. 176, 201, 203 (1982) (EAHCA requires only specialized instruction and related services which are individually designed to provide educational benefit to the handicapped child). See infra notes 125-28 and accompanying text.

access, but not affirmative efforts to assure that access is meaningful.[15] The concept of program parity reads into the affirmative mandate of the EAHCA a comparative standard, akin to the nondiscrimination prohibition explicit in section 504, directing that meaningful educational services be provided to handicapped children at a level determined in accordance with the level of services given to the nonhandicapped.

Because the EAHCA is the detailed statute, drafted specifically to handle educational decisionmaking for the handicapped, and under which most cases challenging the denial of educational services to the handicapped are brought, analysis will be focused primarily on this statute. The EAHCA requires that handicapped children be given a "free appropriate public education."[16] I contend in this article that this requirement must be interpreted by reference to a standard of fairness that relates to the educational services made available to the nonhandicapped. This contention does not depend upon a fusion of the EAHCA with section 504, nor upon an interpretation of the rather murky legislative history of the EAHCA.[17] It is derived, rather, from a recognition of the inherently flexible and necessarily interactive quality of the concept of "appropriate education." It is often said that the concept of equality has little or no meaning without reference to standards defining substantive rights.[18] Whether or not this proposition is fully correct, or helpful, it is my view that there are certain substantive rights, among them "appropriate education," that can be given sensible meaning only by reference to a comparative norm or a concept of equality.

In developing the concept of program parity, the term "parity" is used instead of "equality" to avoid the confusion that may arise from common usage of the latter term. Equality is sometimes understood to require not only that alikes be treated alike but also that unalikes be treated unalike.[19] Insofar as handicapping conditions may involve characteristics that make individuals unalike with respect to a particular service or activity, the term equality might be misunderstood to be intolerant of differences in treatment (inequality) on one level, required to achieve equality on another level. Parity in this article refers to a form of equality respecting claims to educational

---

15. Southeastern Community College v. Davis, 442 U.S. 397, 413 (1979); Timms v. Metropolitan School Dist., 722 F.2d 1310, 1317 (7th Cir. 1983); Monahan v. Nebraska, 687 F.2d 1164, 1170 (8th Cir. 1982), *cert. denied*, 460 U.S. 1012 (1983); *see* Sanders v. Marquette Pub. Schools, 561 F. Supp. 1361, 1371 (W.D. Mich. 1983) (a plaintiff is not "otherwise qualified" under section 504 "if accommodating the plaintiff would impose an undue burden on the defendant"); *see also infra* at 30-31. Numerous cases brought under both section 504 and the EAHCA have reserved judgment on section 504, applying instead the more specific provisions of the EAHCA. *See infra* note 128. Where relief is granted under EAHCA, the U.S. Supreme Court has held that section 504 is inapplicable. Smith v. Robinson, 104 S. Ct. 3457 (1984).

16. 20 U.S.C. § 1412(1) (1982).

17. *See infra* note 187.

18. *See, e.g.*, Westen, *The Empty Idea of Equality*, 95 HARV. L. REV. 537 (1982); Joseph, *Some Ways of Thinking About Equality of Opportunity*, 33 WESTERN POL. Q. 393, 399-400 (1980).

19. *See* Westen, *supra* note 18, at 539-40, 572; H.L.A. HART, THE CONCEPT OF LAW 155 (1961); *cf.* Tigner v. Texas, 310 U.S. 141, 147 (1940) ("[t]he Constitution does not require things which are different in fact or opinion to be treated as though they were the same.").

resources for handicapped children that will often need to reflect important differences between handicapped and nonhandicapped children.

The differences between handicapped and nonhandicapped children are important in defining a relationship between them — a relationship in some senses more difficult to define than that between the majority and other minority groups. Many problems exist in implementing the goal of equal educational opportunity for racial and ethnic minorities and for women. In the abstract, however, there is general agreement that members of these groups should be allowed to advance on the basis of their own merits, unhindered by inherently unequal separate schools, tracks, or programs, which are often motivated by prejudice or discriminatory purpose. This consensus cannot always exist with respect to handicapped persons, for while much of the discrimination faced by them is based upon irrational prejudice, handicaps are also often related to ability, and thus to a criterion that is otherwise considered rational for the services they seek.[20] Consequently, equal educational opportunity for handicapped children in public education may have to rest on a basis different from the commitment to other disadvantaged groups. The concept of parity accommodates the significant differences between the handicapped and nonhandicapped and describes what is possible and what is just in securing for the handicapped services for which they may not be eligible under what might otherwise seem to be fair and rational criteria.

I begin this article by describing the different ways courts have handled issues of cost arising under the EAHCA. I then examine the tensions between the structure and design of the EAHCA and the institutional context in which education is provided. These tensions arise from the EAHCA's creation of individualized rights, which must operate within an institution characterized by collective decisionmaking; from the focus in the EAHCA on the needs of an individual student without regard to his inability to compete in the merit-based system which the educational system is otherwise designed to promote; and from the imposition of national standards relating to the content of education which departs from a tradition of local and state decisionmaking in public education. I then describe the concept of program parity as a standard to mediate the tensions and resolve cost issues that arise under the EAHCA. This standard uses the existing framework for local educational decision-making to define state and local responsibility for educating the handicapped, and within that framework allows consideration of both the needs of the handicapped and the limitations of cost to which educational agencies are sensitive. It rejects a strict cost-benefit or efficiency analysis in allocating educational resources, emphasizing instead the premium that is appropriately put on the individual respect and integrity of handicapped children. It permits considerations of resource utility, however, as well as political judgments to influence decisions about the level of educational quality generally.

---

20. *See* Wegner, *The Antidiscrimination Model Reconsidered: Ensuring Equal Opportunity Without Respect to Handicap Under Section 504 of the Rehabilitation Act of 1973,* 69 CORNELL L. REV. 401, 429 (1984) [hereinafter cited as *Antidiscrimination Model*]. This point is explored further in section IV A, *infra.*

II

Judicial Responses to the Cost Issue

Before examining further the concept of program parity, I will review the responses courts have made when cost is an issue in EAHCA litigation. These responses are inconsistent, reflecting the tensions which will be explored further in part III.

A. Resolution One: Cost Not Relevant

Some courts have insisted that the cost of a program sought by the parent of a handicapped child is not relevant to whether the child has a right to that program, and thus that cost is no defense to a failure to comply with the requirements of the EAHCA.[21] This approach parallels the rejection of a broad cost defense in cases in which important constitutional rights are at stake,[22] and in cases brought under antidiscrimination statutes designed to protect members of traditionally disadvantaged classes.[23] As to claims based on specific legislation, this approach is particularly appealing when cost or administrative convenience was one of the underlying bases for the discrimination which the legislation sought to address.[24]

No constitutional basis has yet been established for the extension of special constitutional protection to handicapped children in public education. Handicap is not generally recognized as a suspect classification[25] and the

---

21. *E.g.*, Kruelle v. New Castle County School Dist., 642 F.2d 687, 695-96 (3d Cir. 1981); William S. v. Gill, 572 F. Supp. 509, 516 (N.D. Ill. 1983); Hines v. Pitt County Bd. of Educ., 497 F. Supp. 403, 408 (E.D.N.C. 1980); D.S. v. Board of Educ., 188 N.J. Super. 592, 609-10, 458 A.2d 129, 139-40 (App. Div. 1983).

22. *E.g.*, Memorial Hosp. v. Maricopa County, 415 U.S. 250, 263 (1974) ("[A] State may not protect the public fisc by drawing an invidious distinction between classes . . . so [the state] must do more than show that denying free medical care to new residents saves money."); *e.g.* Finney v. Arkansas Bd. of Correction, 505 F.2d 194, 201 (8th Cir. 1974) ("Lack of funds is not an acceptable excuse for unconstitutional conditions of incarceration"); Wyatt v. Aderholt, 503 F.2d 1305 (5th Cir. 1974) In *Wyatt*, a case involving involuntary commitment of the mentally ill, the court stated:

It goes without saying that state legislatures are ordinarily free to choose among various social services competing for . . . state funds. But that does not mean that a state legislature is free, for budgetary or any other reasons, to provide a social service in a manner which will result in the denial of individuals' constitutional rights.

Id. at 1314-15. *see also* Plyler v. Doe, 457 U.S. 202, 229 n.25 (1983) (incapacity to bear the costs of educating children of illegal aliens inadequate defense). *See generally* Wegner, *supra* note 20, at 447-48.

23. *E.g.*, City of Los Angeles Dep't of Water & Power v. Manhart, 435 U.S. 702, 716-17 (1978) (sex-biased rates of contribution to city pension plan held a violation of Title VII despite showing of difference in projected costs of plan to different sexes); Smallwood v. United Air Lines, 661 F.2d 303, 307 (4th Cir. 1981), *cert. denied*, 456 U.S. 1007 (1982) (economic considerations are not a BFOQ under the Age Discrimination in Employment Act); *see also* Lora v. Board of Educ., 456 F. Supp. 1211, 1292-93 (1978), *vacated on other grounds and remanded*, 623 F.2d 248 (1980) (city's budgetary problems no excuse for unconstitutional discrimination in classification of minority students).

24. *See, e.g.*, Orzel v. City of Wauwatosa Fire Dep't, 697 F.2d 743, 755 (7th Cir. 1983), *cert. denied*, 104 S. Ct. 484 (1983) ("It is well established that economic factors cannot be the basis for a BFOQ, since precisely those considerations were among the targets of the ADEA."); Smallwood v. United Airlines, 661 F.2d 303, 307 (4th Cir. 1981), *cert. denied*, 456 U.S. 1007 (1982).

25. Sherer v. Waier, 457 F. Supp. 1039, 1047-48 (W.D. Mo. 1978); Levy v. City of New York, 38 N.Y.2d 653, 655, 345 N.E.2d 556, 558, 382 N.Y.S.2d 13, 15 (1976), *appeal dismissed*, 429 U.S. 805

United States Supreme Court has not deemed education a fundamental right.[26] Education for the handicapped, however, is the subject of remedial legislation intended to provide protection for a minority group which previously was significantly disadvantaged in public service.[27] Moreover, one reason for traditional discrimination against the handicapped was (and remains) that the cost of serving them is too high.[28]

In some cases interpreting the EAHCA, the view that cost is not a relevant factor is expressed alongside an expansive definition of the underlying duties of school districts.[29] Many courts take this approach without express discussion of the cost issue.[30] Others reach this conclusion by reasoning that, unlike other types of legislation, the EAHCA does not mention cost as a limit on the

---

(1976); *see also* Doe v. Koger, 480 F. Supp. 225, 230 (N.D. Ind. 1979) (expressing serious doubts that handicapped students are a suspect class). *But see* Frederick L. v. Thomas, 408 F. Supp. 832, 836 (E.D. Pa. 1976) (handicapped persons are not a suspect class, but the middle-level equal protection standard applies); Fialkowski v. Shapp, 405 F. Supp. 946, 959 (E.D. Pa. 1975) (discrimination against handicapped persons should receive more than minimal judicial scrutiny); *In re* G.H., 218 N.W.2d 441, 447 (N.D. 1974) ("G.H.'s terrible handicaps were . . . 'immutable characteristic[s]' . . . to which the 'inherently suspect' classification would be applied.").

Several commentators have suggested that handicapped persons be afforded constitutional protection. *See* Burgdorf & Burgdorf, *A History of Unequal Treatment: The Qualifications of Handicapped Persons as a "Suspect Class" under the Equal Protection Clause*, 15 SANTA CLARA L. REV. 855, 905-08 (1975) (arguing that handicapped *should* be a suspect classification); Krass, *The Right to a Public Education for Handicapped Children: A Primer for the New Advocate*, 1976 U. ILL. L.F. 1016, 1036-42 (also arguing for strict scrutiny for handicapped classification); Contemporary Studies Project, *Special Education: The Struggle for Equal Educational Opportunity in Iowa*, 62 IOWA L. REV. 1283, 1354-59 (1977) (arguing for at least a "strict rationality" standard of review in handicapped cases).

26.   San Antonio Indep. School Dist. v. Rodriguez, 411 U.S. 1, 37 (1973). *But see* Plyler v. Doe, 457 U.S. 202, 221-24 (1983) (discrimination in the education provided children of illegal immigrants must serve a substantial, rather than legitimate, state goal). State courts have by and large followed the lead of federal courts in holding that education is not a fundamental right. *See* Horton v. Meskill, 172 Conn. 615, 648-49, 376 A.2d 359, 373 (1977); Thompson v. Engelking, 96 Idaho 793, 805, 537 P.2d 635, 647 (1975). *But see* Serrano v. Priest, 487 P.2d 1241, 1244, 5 Cal. 3d 584, 589; 96 Cal. Rptr. 601, 604 (1971) (education is a fundamental right.)

27.   *See* 20 U.S.C. § 1400(b)(1)-(6), (c) (1982); S. REP. No. 168, 94th Cong., 1st Sess. 9, *reprinted in* 1975 U.S. CODE CONG. & AD. NEWS 1425, 1433; H. REP. No. 332, 94th Cong. 1st Sess. 11 (1975).

28.   *See* 20 U.S.C. § 1400(b)(7)-(9) (1982); S. REP. No. 168, 94th Cong., 1st Sess. 7, *reprinted in* 1975 U.S. CODE CONG. & AD. NEWS 1425, 1431. ("In recent years [court] decisions . . . have recognized the rights of handicapped children to an appropriate education. States have made an effort to comply; however, lack of financial resources have [sic] prevented the implementation of the various decisions . . ."); H. REP. No. 332, 94th Cong., 1st Sess. 26 (1975).

29.   *See, e.g.,* Kruelle v. New Castle County School Dist., 642 F.2d 687, 693 (3d Cir. 1981) (mentally retarded child with cerebral palsy who required continuous supervision entitled to more than 6-hour day program under EAHCA); T.G. v. Board of Educ., 576 F. Supp. 420, 423 (D.N.J. 1983) (same), *aff'd,* 738 F.2d 420, 425 (3d Cir. 1984); Hines v. Pitt County Bd. of Educ., 497 F. Supp. 403, 408 (E.D.N.C. 1980) (residential hospital placement for severely emotionally disturbed child held inappropriate because of the absence of an appropriate peer group, despite high cost of private school alternatives and confusion about availability of public placement); School Comm. v. Massachusetts, 1980-81 EDUC. HANDICAPPED L. REP. 552:186 (Mass. Super. Ct. 1980) (benefits of continuity of psychiatric services justified placement with same psychiatrist despite existence of less expensive alterantive); *In re* "A" Family, 184 Mont. 145, 159-60, 602 P.2d 157, 166 (1979) (psychotherapy service in out-of-state residential placement a related service under the EAHCA); Adams Cent. School Dist. v. Deist, 214 Neb. 307, 314-18, 334 N.W.2d 775, 781-82 (retarded child entitled to residential placement even though it was not purely "educational"), *modified,* 215 Neb. 284, 338 N.W.2d 591, *cert. denied,* 104 S. Ct. 239 (1983).

30.   *E.g.,* T.G. v. Board of Educ., 576 F. Supp. 420 (D.N.J. 1983), (psychotherapy services), *aff'd,* 738 F.2d 420, 425 (3d Cir. 1984); Pires v. Pennsylvania Dep't of Educ., 78 Pa. Commw. 127, 467 A.2d 79 (1983) (residential placement outside of school district); Adams Cent. School Dist. v. Deist,

duties it creates.[31] One court, answering the argument that a placement could not be appropriate if its costs were inordinate, implied that while cost considerations motivated the drafters of the EAHCA to mandate an "appropriate" rather than the "most ideal" education, cost could not then be taken into consideration again in deciding what was appropriate.[32] The point is also made that only states that have volunteered to participate in the EAHCA are bound by it.[33] If economic hardship arises as a result, this must be addressed "through the normal political process, not through judicial emasculation of regulatory power."[34]

The conclusion that cost is not a factor to consider may also be reached alongside a very narrow definition of the duties of school districts under the EAHCA. The decision of the United States Supreme Court in *Board of Education v. Rowley*[35] may be viewed in this light. In holding that the defendant school district was required to provide only three hours of speech therapy weekly and an FM hearing aid to Amy Rowley to supplement the traditional educational program, the Court limited the scope of the EAHCA to the requirement that school districts provide each handicapped child "personalized instruction with sufficient support services to permit the child to benefit educationally from that instruction."[36] This requirement sets a low level of duty on the part of the school system, but seems to make the duty absolute, unqualified by any defense based on cost.[37]

---

214 Neb. 307, 334 N.W.2d 775 (residential placement), *modified on other grounds*, 215 Neb. 284, 338 N.W.2d 591, *cert. denied*, 104 S. Ct. 239 (1983).

31.   *E.g.*, Kruelle v. New Castle County School Dist., 642 F.2d 687, 695 (3d Cir. 1981) ("Under the Education Act, in contradistinction [to section 504 of the Rehabilitation Act], schools are required to provide a comprehensive range of services to accommodate a handicapped child's educational needs, *regardless of financial and administrative burdens. . . .*" (emphasis added); *see also* William S. v. Gill, 572 F. Supp. 509, 516 (N.D. Ill. 1983) ("[T]he appropriateness of an education is a function not of cost but of the actual or potential educational benefits conferred.").

32.   William S. v. Gill, 572 F. Supp. 509, 516 (N.D. Ill. 1983); *see also* Clevenger v. Oak Ridge School Bd., 744 F.2d 514, 517 (6th Cir. 1984).

33.   Hines v. Pitt County Bd. of Educ., 497 F. Supp. 403, 408 (E.D.N.C. 1980). All states are now covered by the EAHCA. *See supra* note 4.

34.   D.S. v. Board of Educ., 188 N.J. Super. 592, 609, 458 A.2d 129, 140 (App. Div. 1983). Through the political process it is not determined *whether*, but rather *how* the necessary funds will be appropriated. *See* Kerr Center Parents Ass'n v. Charles, 572 F. Supp. 448, 459 (D. Or. 1983) (state legislature responsible for ensuring that special education is funded in state, either by providing funds itself, or by placing burdens on local school districts); School Comm. v. Bureau of Special Educ. Appeals, 389 Mass. 705, —, 452 N.E.2d 476, 481 (1983) (state proposition "does not relieve a city or town from its educational responsibilities" to the handicapped) (unavailable in Massachusetts reporter at publication); *see also* Fallis v. Ambach, 710 F.2d 49, 50-53 (2d Cir. 1983) (absent showing of deprivation of free and appropriate education to handicapped children, EAHCA does not prevent state from reducing tuition rate at which public schools are required to reimburse private schools for education of handicapped children).

35.   458 U.S. 176 (1982).

36.   *Id.* at 203.

37.   This approach is admittedly difficult to distinguish from the approach of interpreting the substantive provisions of the EAHCA in a cost-sensitive manner. The latter approach is considered *infra* notes 44-49 and accompanying text. The *Rowley* decision is discussed further *infra* text accompanying notes 174-76.

B. Resolution Two: Cost a Defense

Courts have found a number of different ways to take cost into account under the EAHCA. These courts can be divided into those that consider the issue of cost as a potential defense to the failure to provide certain "appropriate" educational programs and those that make cost one factor to consider in interpreting the meaning of substantive provisions of the EAHCA.

There are only a handful of cases in which courts have rejected educational programs sought by parents of handicapped children expressly on grounds of cost.[38] The rationale commonly given for this approach is that if a district were required to fund extremely expensive programs for some handicapped children it would not have enough money to educate other handicapped children properly.[39] Courts have also been sensitive to the hardship placed on nonhandicapped children by diverting excessive expenditures from regular programs to programs for the handicapped.[40]

More often, courts taking cost into account have engaged in an explicit balancing process. In Pinkerton v. Moye,[41] for example, the District Court balanced the individual needs of a learning-disabled child, whose mother sought the creation of a self-contained class in the school nearest the child's home (which was 19 miles away), against the realities of limited funding faced by the school district, for which it was less costly to send the child to a school

---

38. *See, e.g.,* Rettig v. Kent City School Dist., 539 F. Supp. 768, 777 (N.D. Ohio 1981) (rejects cost-blind approach to EAHCA), *aff'd in part, rev'd in part on other grounds, and remanded,* 720 F.2d 463 (6th Cir. 1983); Bales v. Clarke, 523 F. Supp. 1366, 1371 (E.D. Va. 1981) (cost is always a factor in school placement decisions, even placement of nonhandicapped children); Pinkerton v. Moye, 509 F. Supp. 107, 112-13 (W.D. Va. 1981) (competing interests of parents and schools must be balanced). California state regulations specifically provide that cost be considered in determining a handicapped child's education placement. CAL. EDUC. CODE § 56505(i) (West Supp. 1984).

39. *E.g.,* Rettig v. Kent City School Dist., 539 F. Supp. 768, 777 (N.D. Ohio 1981) ("a school cannot spend an exorbitant amount on one child at the expense of all its other handicapped children."), *aff'd in part, rev'd in part on other grounds, and remanded,* 720 F.2d 463 (6th Cir. 1983); Pinkerton v. Moye, 509 F. Supp. 107, 113 (W.D. Va. 1981) ("Excessive expenditures made to meet the needs of one handicapped child ultimately reduce the amount that can be spent to meet the needs of the other handicapped children." (footnote omitted)); Stacey G. v. Pasadena Indep. School Dist., 547 F. Supp. 61, 78 (S.D. Tex. 1982) ("Indeed, failure to consider these sometimes conflicting interests would ultimately work to circumvent Congress' intent to educate all handicapped children as best as practicable. Excessive expenditures made to meet the needs of one handicapped child may reduce the resources that can be spent to meet the needs of the other handicapped children."); Clevenger v. Oak Ridge School Bd., 573 F. Supp. 349, 350 (E.D. Tenn. 1983) ("[T]he Court should balance the needs of the handicapped child for a free and appropriate education with the need of the State to allocate scarce funds among as many handicapped children as possible."), *rev'd and remanded,* 744 F.2d 714 (6th Cir. 1984); Roncker v. Walter, 700 F.2d 1058, 1063 (6th Cir.), *cert. denied,* 104 S. Ct. 196 (1983). ("Cost is a proper factor to consider since excessive spending on one handicapped child deprives other handicapped children."). Age v. Bullitt County Pub. Schools, 673 F.2d 141, 145 (6th Cir. 1982) ("[W]e cannot say that the State has failed to reconcile satisfactorily [the boy's] need for a free, appropriate public education with the need for the State to allocate scarce funds among as many handicapped children as possible.").

40. *See* Bales v. Clarke, 523 F. Supp. at 1366, 1371 (E.D. Va. 1981); *cf.* Note, *Enforcing the Right, supra* note 8, at 1123 (mainstreaming of handicapped children may diminish quality of education offered to other students in the class); Espino v. Besteiro, 520 F. Supp. 905, 912 (S.D. Tex. 1981) (air-conditioned classroom for benefit of handicapped child may raise complaints by nonhandicapped children who are not assigned to that classroom). *But see infra* note 73.

41. 509 F. Supp. 107 (W.D. Va. 1981).

six miles farther away. In concluding that the school district's placement of the child met the requirements of the EAHCA, the Court noted that this legislation "was not intended to totally supplant the state's prerogative in allocating its financial resources," and that "competing interests must be balanced to reach a reasonable accommodation."[42]

Courts that have engaged in this balancing process have concluded in some cases that the concern of the school district for cost did *not* justify the denial of requested services. In one such case, the court balanced the needs of a multihandicapped child who could not regulate his body temperature against the fiscal considerations of the school district and held that the cost of a fully air-conditioned classroom, as compared with the single air-conditioned cubicle proposed by the district, was a reasonable burden in light of the amount of federal funds received by the district.[43]

C. Resolution Three: Cost a Factor in Interpreting Substantive Provisions of Act

Many courts that have considered cost have done so not by a separate balancing of the interests of the child and the school district but through a cost-sensitive interpretation of the substantive provisions of the EAHCA. A number of courts, for example, have considered the cost of various alternative educational programs and the financial well-being of the school district in deciding what educational program was "appropriate." In some cases courts justify this approach by distinguishing "appropriate" from "best," and iterating that the EAHCA does not guarantee the best possible education.[44] Other courts more explicitly balance the needs of the child against the resources of the school system in determining what program is "appropriate." The First Circuit has taken this approach: "There can be little doubt . . . that in determining the 'appropriate' placement of the individual handicapped

---

42. *Id.* at 112.

43. Espino v. Besteiro, 520 F. Supp. 905 (S.D. Tex. 1981); *see also In re* El Paso Indep. School Dist., 1981-82 EDUC. HANDICAPPED L. REP. (CRR) 503:260, :263 (Tex. SEA 1982) ("The administrative and financial burden on the district of providing [a crib for a severely handicapped child attending a full day program] is not undue."); Department of Educ. v. Katherine D., 727 F.2d 809, 813-14 (9th Cir. 1983) (although, because of budgetary constraints, school system required only to make efforts that are "within reason," in-school medical services were required to be furnished to child so that the child could attend regular public school); Tokarcik v. Forest Hills School Dist., 665 F.2d 443, 458 (3d Cir. 1981), *cert. denied*, 458 U.S. 1121 (1982); *cf.* Hurry v. Jones, 560 F. Supp. 500, 511 (D.R.I. 1983) (transportation services for physically handicapped child required under section 504 of the Rehabilitation Act since the services were "financially and administratively feasible" and would not impose an undue burden on the school district), *aff'd in part, rev'd in part*, 734 F.2d 879 (1st Cir. 1984).

44. *See, e.g.,* Hessler v. State Bd. of Educ., 700 F.2d 134, 139 (4th Cir. 1983) (a state is not obligated to provide "the best education . . . that money can buy."); Age v. Bullitt County Pub. Schools, 673 F. 2d 141, 143-44 (6th Cir. 1982) (mere existence of a better program did not make the proposed program inappropriate under the Act); Bales v. Clarke, 523 F. Supp. 1366, 1371 (E.D. Va. 1981) (rejects the argument that the proper goal of an educational plan is "to achieve 'maximum educational progress' through the 'best' education available" (quoting a witness in the case)); Darlene L. v. Illinois State Bd. of Educ., 568 F. Supp. 1340, 1345 (N.D. Ill. 1983); *see also* Board of Educ. v. Rowley, 458 U.S. 176, 198-204 (1982) (students need only be able to benefit from special instruction), and *supra* note 37.

child, one must balance the important personal needs of the individual handicapped child, and the realities of limited public monies."[45] One court justified this same balancing test on the ground that cost is also a factor in determining what is appropriate for nonhandicapped children.[46]

Still other courts have linked the question of what "related services" are required under the EAHCA to the question of their cost. Thus, children with spina bifida seeking clean intermittent catheterization (CIC) have been successful in persuading courts that this rather inexpensive service is a related service to which they are entitled,[47] while many children seeking more expensive medical services, such as residential psychiatric services, have not.[48] Finally, a few courts have limited the liability of school districts for costly residential placement in psychiatric facilities by excluding those expenses not attributable to traditional "educational" services.[49]

The range of responses courts interpreting the EAHCA have given to an issue as potentially critical as cost reflects a fundamental disagreement about the basic purpose and thrust of this legislation and its place within the broader goals and institutional framework of public education. The ad hoc manner in which the issue of cost has been approached to date has created confusion and inconsistency, encouraging on the one hand superficial compliance with the law, and on the other, overstated claims on behalf of some handicapped children.

One reason for the difficulty in resolving the issue of cost in decision-making under the EAHCA is that this legislation runs counter to a number of assumptions and traditions of public education in this country. How the EAHCA takes into account those aspects of public education has an important

---

45. Doe v. Anrig, 692 F.2d 800, 806 (1st Cir. 1982) (quoting from the opinion of the district court).

46. Bales v. Clarke, 523 F. Supp. 1366, 1371 (E.D. Va. 1981).

47. Irving Indep. School Dist. v. Tatro, 104 S. Ct. 3371, 3377-78 (1984) (approving the conclusion of the Secretary of the Department of Education, that the "medical services" exclusion to the "related services" provision "was designed to spare schools from an obligation to provide a service that might well prove unduly expensive and beyond the range of their competence" (footnote omitted)); Tokarcik v. Forest Hills School Dist., 665 F.2d 443 (3d Cir. 1981), *cert. denied*, 458 U.S. 1121 (1982).

48. *See, e.g.,* McKenzie v. Jefferson, 566 F. Supp. 404, 411-12 (D.D.C. 1983) (distinguishing Irving Indep. School Dist. v. Tatro, 104 S. Ct. 3371 (1984), and Tokarcik v. Forest Hills School Dist., 665 F.2d 443 (3d Cir. 1981), *cert. denied*, 458 U.S. 1121 (1982), on grounds of cost, among other things); *see also* Stark, *supra* note 2, at 516-20 (describing practice in Connecticut of not treating psychotherapy as a "related service" for economic reasons, although most states treat psychological counseling as a related service). *But see In re* "A" Family, 184 Mont. 145, 160-61, 602 P.2d 157, 166 (1979) (psychotherapy at out-of-state residential placement is a related service); T.G. v. Board of Educ. 576 F. Supp. 420 (D.N.J. 1983) (out-patient psychotherapy is related service), *aff'd*, 738 F.2d 420, 425 (3d Cir. 1984).

49. *E.g.,* Bill D., 1980-81 EDUC. HANDICAPPED L. REP. (CRR) 502:259 (Conn. SEA 1981) (applying a state regulation); *see* Stark, *supra* note 2, at 506. *See generally* Rothstein, *Educational Rights of Severely and Profoundly Handicapped Children*, 61 NEB. L. REV. 586 (1982); Mooney & Aronson, *Solomon Revisited: Separating Educational and Other Than Educational Needs in Special Education Residential Placements*, 14 CONN. L. REV. 531 (1982).

Cost could also be taken into account in the definition of the Act's "least restrictive alternative" provision. *See* Roncker v. Walter, 700 F.2d 1058, 1066 (6th Cir.) (Kennedy, J., dissenting), *cert. denied*, 104 S. Ct. 196 (1983).

bearing on the success of its implementation. Three areas of tension between the EAHCA and the institutional context within which it must be implemented are explored in the next section.

III
The EAHCA in the Context of the Institution of Public Education: Three Tensions

The EAHCA requires that the handicapped child be provided an education that is based strictly on the needs of each individual child, and determined on a case-by-case basis, according to a federal standard of what is appropriate education. The law requires the EAHCA to be implemented in an institutional context in which decisions (both educational decisions and resource allocation decisions) are made collectively rather than on an individual basis; in which merit rather than needs per se are the organizing principle; and in which state and local government rather than the federal government control the context and quality of public education. These tensions are at the heart of the dilemma concerning the role of cost in educational decisionmaking under the EAHCA and must be explored further before any solution to this dilemma can be attempted.

A. Individualized vs. Collective Decisionmaking

1. *Educational Programing Decisions.* Perhaps the most remarkable feature of the EAHCA is its emphasis on the individual child. The EAHCA assumes that each handicapped child is unique. It requires that the level of performance of each handicapped child be individually identified;[50] that his or her needs be individually assessed[51] "in all areas related to the suspected disability";[52] that educational goals and plans for handicapped children be individually developed with "[a] statement of the specific special education and related services to be provided to the child"[53] and "[a]ppropriate objective criteria and evaluation procedures . . . for determining . . . whether the short term instructional objectives are being achieved";[54] and that an "individualized education program" be developed for each child.[55] The procedural mechanism for enforcing rights under the EAHCA maintains attention on the individual, affording parents the opportunity to have the child's educational program reviewed on a case-by-case basis, many times and at many different levels.[56]

---

50. 20 U.S.C. § 1412(2)(c) (1982); 34 C.F.R. § 300.128 (1984).
51. 20 U.S.C. § 1401(19) (1982); 34 C.F.R. § 300.346 (1984); *see* 20 U.S.C. § 1413(a)(11) (1982); 34 C.F.R. §§ 300.128, .146 (1984) (requiring evaluations of handicapped children).
52. 34 C.F.R. § 300.532(f) (1984)
53. *Id.* § 300.346(c).
54. *Id.* § 300.346(e); *accord* 20 U.S.C. § 1401(19) (1982). *See generally* 34 C.F.R. §§ 300.341, .343 (1984).
55. 20 U.S.C. § 1401(19) (1982); 34 C.F.R. §§ 300.4, .341 (1984).
56. *See* 20 U.S.C. § 1415(b)(2) (1982) (hearing before impartial hearing officer); *id.* § 1415(c) (appeal to state agency); *id.* § 1415(e) (appeal in state or federal court). These hearing and appeal rights can apparently be exercised annually. Colley, *supra* note 11, at 150.

At the hearing, the issue is limited to the needs and program of the individual child; concerns of the school system at large are not ordinarily relevant.[57]

This process of individual identification, needs assessment and programming contrasts sharply with the process of educational programming for other children.[58] Establishment of public school programs precedes the identification of the needs of the individual students who will eventually be placed in those programs. Schools are organized into grades, perhaps into tracks within grades, and/or by courses that students are expected to take. These classifications conform to what is generally expected of students of that age, level of ability, and motivation. Grades and courses have standard curricula, determined in advance by state Boards of Education, local educational agencies, or in some cases teachers, according to what is perceived by members of the profession and policymakers to be appropriate for particular collective groups of children.[59] The offering of common curriculum, indeed, has long been considered an important aspect of educational opportunity in American education. Standardization is to ensure that children are given educations that will enable them to achieve regardless of background.[60] Even the development of tracks appropriate to different types of occupational paths and electives to accommodate different interests and career goals[61] manifest planning by group rather than by individual.

Nonhandicapped students are often assessed individually according to some scale of individual performance, such as grades or scores on standardized tests. These evaluations are only gross placement devices, however, determining such questions as whether the student should progress to the next grade, what level of courses the student should take, or what sort of recommendation the student will receive for college admission or employment. Schools do not use them to tailor an individual program for a child. Students in their respective classrooms are expected to master the curriculum and are evaluated according to their success in doing so. In teaching the curriculum, the teacher will sometimes tailor the teaching technique or pace according to individuals within that class; nevertheless, the goals for the class and the individuals within that class are standard ones, and do not vary significantly

---

57. See 34 C.F.R. §§ 300.504, .506 (1984) (Parent or agency may initiate hearing on any matters discussed in § 300.504, which deals with *individual* placements.) See also discussion of Poe v. Durham County Schools, No. 82-2566 (N.C. Super. Ct. 1982), in Comment, *Age Appropriateness as a Factor in Educational Placement Decisions*, LAW & CONTEMP. PROBS., Winter 1985, at 94-98 (hearing officer refused to hear evidence relating to other similarly situated children). For a brief discussion of whether the class action vehicle is available under the EAHCA, see Note, *Enforcing the Right, supra* note 8, at 1113 n.62, 1115-18.

58. See generally P. HILL & D. MADEY, EDUCATIONAL POLICYMAKING THROUGH THE CIVIL JUSTICE SYSTEM (1982); MOORE, WALKER & HOLLAND, *supra* note 3.

59. D. TYACK, THE ONE BEST SYSTEM 45-47 (1974); P. HILL & D. MADEY, *supra* note 58, at 1.

60. Coleman, *The Concept of Equal Educational Opportunity*, 38 HARV. EDUC. REV. 7 (1968), *reprinted in* EQUAL EDUCATIONAL OPPORTUNITY 13 (1969); Resnick & Resnick, *Improving Educational Standards in American Schools*, 65 PHI DELTA KAPPAN 178, 178 (1983).

61. Resnick & Resnick, *supra* note 60, at 178.

according to the needs and abilities of each child.[62] Moreover, children (or their parents) who disagree with curricular, methodological or structural features of the system have no recourse outside whatever informal pressure they can exert; they have no legally enforceable rights to any particular type of education nor even to a right to equality in education. If dissatisfied, their only recourse is through the political, not the legal, process.[63]

2. *Resource Allocation Decisions.* The contrast between the individualized and nonindividualized approaches apparent in educational decisionmaking for handicapped and nonhandicapped children persists with respect to resource allocation decisions. Under the EAHCA, individual needs are to be identified and educational programs provided that will address those needs appropriately. This legislation attends only to the individual needs, and does not acknowledge any clash between the needs and programs of the individual and those of others. By taking no direct account of resource limitations or qualifications on the duty to provide what is appropriate, the EAHCA implies that resources *must* be made available to meet the individual needs of the handicapped child.[64]

In contrast, the framework within which competing claims for limited public school resources are usually made is one of collective decisionmaking.[65] Both the allocation of resources to public schools and the division of resources between different school programs take place in a process that is political rather than compulsory.[66] The availability of funds determines the level of a school budget,[67] and negotiations determine amounts allocated for certain needs within that budget. Through this process, the perceived needs and interests of constituent groups are evaluated, asserted, and debated. Decisions are made, usually after consideration of many alternatives. Claims or programs thought to be more worthy are honored over others less valued.

---

62. Glaser, *Adapting to Individual Differences,* in ANNUAL EDITIONS EDUCATION 80/81, at 181, 182-83 (1980).

63. *See* San Antonio Indep. School Dist. v. Rodriguez, 411 U.S. 1, 37 (1973); Lujan v. Colorado State Bd. of Educ. 649 P.2d 1005, 1018 (Colo. 1982); *cf.* Dandridge v. Williams, 397 U.S. 471, 487 (1970) (courts should not second-guess state officials allocating welfare funds). *But see, e.g.,* Pauley v. Kelly, 255 S.E.2d 859, 878 (W.Va. 1979) (individual students stated claim of action against state for discriminating school finance system); Horton v. Meskill, 172 Conn. 615, 648-49, 376 A.2d 359, 374 (1977) ("[E]lementary and secondary education is a fundamental right . . . [and] pupils in the public schools are entitled to equal enjoyment of that right . . . .").

64. *See supra* notes 31-32 and accompanying text.

65. The EAHCA contrasts even with the process through which other special groups, such as the educationally disadvantaged, compete for limited federal funds which are distributed by local administrators to only a fraction of eligible beneficiaries. In these kinds of programs, program eligibility is not equivalent to entitlement; it is only a threshold factor, allowing one to compete against others for limited resources. *See* P. HILL & D. MADEY, *supra* note 58, at 2; *see, e.g.,* 20 U.S.C. § 2732 (1982); *see also infra* note 70.

66. *See* Lujan v. Colorado State Bd. of Educ., 649 P.2d 1005, 1022-23 (Colo. l982) (members of school board, controlled by voters, determine how much money to raise for schools and how that money will be spent); Board of Educ. v. Nyquist, 57 N.Y.2d 27, 44-46, 439 N.E.2d 359, 366-67, 453 N.Y.S.2d 643, 651-52 (1982) (identifying the different levels of government involved in funding schools), *appeal dismissed,* 459 U.S. 1139 (1983).

67. Wise, *Educational Adequacy: A Concept in Search of Meaning,* 8 J. EDUC. FIN. 300, 314 (1983).

In responding to the selective creation of enforceable rights for the handicapped, school districts initially obtained extra appropriations for special education and additional services for handicapped children.[68] By the late 1970's, however, extra appropriations were more problematic and "school systems maintained the quality of special education services by diverting funds from other categorical grant programs."[69] Because other special interest groups, especially the poor, did not have individual rights enforceable in the judicial system,[70] these other groups were significantly disadvantaged with respect to the handicapped.[71] Upper and middle class parents were most able to assert their claims.[72] And it was charged that funds were pulled from programs otherwise intended for nonhandicapped children in order to serve the handicapped.[73]

The tension between the individualized decisionmaking required under the EAHCA and the institutional context within which decisions are usually made on the basis of collective considerations is destabilizing. On the one hand, some children are selected for a track that entitles them to special treatment and immunizes them from restraints, including resource restraints, to which others are subject. This seems grossly unfair to other children, who may have complaints about the quality of their own education. In response to this perceived unfairness and to genuine resource limitations, school officials (either intentionally or unintentionally) may subvert educational programming for handicapped children; they may, for example, limit their consideration in placement decisions to programs that are *already available* in a school district rather than to those programs and others that *might be made* available.[74]

---

68. P. HILL & D. MADEY, *supra* note 58, at 24.
69. *Id.* at 25.
70. Many disadvantaged groups are protected, of course, by nondiscrimination statutes. *See, e.g.,* section 601 of the Civil Rights Act of 1964, 42 U.S.C. § 2000(d) (1982) (Title VI); Section 504 of the Rehabilitation Act of 1973, 29 U.S.C. § 794 (1982); Sections 901-05, 907 of the 1972 Education Amendments, 20 U.S.C. §§ 1681-86 (1982) (Title IX). With the possible exception of Title VI, however, these statutes generally have not been interpreted to require broad affirmative steps requiring the expenditure of significant funds. *See, e.g.,* Southeastern Community College v. Davis, 442 U.S. 397 (1979) (interpreting section 504 of the Rehabilitation Act of 1973). Often any relief at all is dependent upon a showing of discriminatory intent. *See, e.g.,* Guardians Ass'n v. Civil Serv. Comm'n, 103 S. Ct. 3221 (1983) (compensating relief in a Title VI action requires proof of a discriminatory intent). Even Lau v. Nichols, 414 U.S. 563 (1974), did not clearly give a cause of action to an individual child for some educational benefit. *See* Levin, *Equal Educational Opportunity for Special Pupil Populations and the Federal Role,* 85 W. VA. L. REV. 159, 178 (1983). *See infra* notes 123-28 and accompanying text.
71. P. HILL & D. MADEY, *supra* note 58, at 25.
72. Neal & Kirp, *The Allure of Legalization Reconsidered: The Case of Special Education,* LAW & CONTEMP. PROBS., Winter 1985, at 63, 78.
73. *Id.* at 79. *See* Note, *Enforcing the Right, supra* note 8, at 1123; Stark, *supra* note 2, at 493. *See also supra* note 40. One research team has concluded that this diversion has not actually occurred. *See* P. HILL & D. MADEY, *supra* note 58, at 25; *see also* cases cited *supra* note 40; M. KNAPP, M. STEARNS, TURNBULL, J. DAVID & S. PETERSON, CUMULATIVE EFFECTS OF FEDERAL EDUCATION POLICIES ON SCHOOLS AND DISTRICTS, SUMMARY REPORT OF A CONGRESSIONALLY MANDATED STUDY 6 (1983) (no substantial effects of federal programs on nontarget students).
74. *See* Note, *Board of Education v. Rowley, supra* note 8, at 279, 286-87 (1983); Large, *Special Problems of the Deaf Under the Education for All Handicapped Children Act of 1975,* 58 WASH. U.L.Q. 213, 256 (1980); Miller & Miller, *The Handicapped Child's Civil Right as it Relates to the "Least Restrictive Environment" and Appropriate Mainstreaming,* 54 IND. L.J. 1, 5 (1978); Note, *Enforcing the Right, supra* note 8,

The law might respond to this tension either by making the process for educational programming decisions for handicapped children conform to the collective, largely political process used for nonhandicapped children, or by requiring individual assessments and programming for *every* child. Neither of these alternatives, however, is satisfactory. Folding the handicapped into the collective process of decisionmaking that works for the nonhandicapped led to the disregard of handicapped children and to their segregation in public education prior to passage of the EAHCA. The political weakness of the handicapped minority at the local district level,[75] prejudice and discomfort toward the handicapped,[76] ignorance about the capacity and value of the handicapped,[77] disagreements among professionals,[78] overburdened teachers and administrators,[79] and funding shortages[80] together continue to make fair treatment of the handicapped unlikely absent a requirement of individualized

---

at 1109-10. This charge was confirmed in one study. *See* David & Greene, *Organizational Barriers to Full Implementation of PL 94-142*, in Special Education Policies, Their History, Implementation, and Finance 115, 125-26, 132 (1983); *see also* Weatherly & Lipsky, *Street-Level Bureaucrats and Institutional Innovation: Implementing Special Education Reform*, 47 Harv. Educ. Rev. 171, 187 (1977) (similar findings in study of implementation of Massachusetts special education law requiring individual assessments).

Courts that have addressed this practice have generally rejected it. *See, e.g.*, Georgia Ass'n of Retarded Citizens v. McDaniel, 716 F.2d 1565, 1576-77 (11th Cir. 1983) (state cannot ignore needs of handicapped individuals with a policy limiting educational programs to 180 days per year), *vacated on other grounds*, 104 S. Ct. 3581 (1984); Crawford v. Pittman, 708 F.2d 1028, 1033-35 (5th Cir. 1983) (same). *See also* Note, *Defining an "Appropriate Education,"* *supra* note 8, at 110. *But cf.* Grkman v. Scanlon, 563 F. Supp. 793, 797 (W.D. Pa. 1983) (case remanded to determine most appropriate *available* alternative); Tilton v. Jefferson County Bd. of Educ., 705 F.2d 800 (6th Cir. 1983) (closing of facility for budgetary reasons not a change of placement triggering due process procedures of the Act), *cert. denied*, 104 S. Ct. 998 (1984).

75.   *See, e.g.*, Garrity v. Gallen, 522 F. Supp. 171, 224 (D.N.H. 1981) ("[w]hether out of timidity in the face of this powerful local voice, out of deference to the local taxpayers who are primarily footing the bill for education in the state, or out of sheer abdication of responsibility, the State Board of Education has failed to fulfill its responsibility" under the Act.) This is not to say, however, that the handicapped, particularly in recent years and at the national level, have been powerless. *See* Neal & Kirp, *supra* note 72, at 68-70; Finn, *Advocating for the Most Misunderstood Minority: Securing Compliance with Special Education Laws*, 14 Suffolk U.L. Rev. 505, 513 (1980). For a chronicle of the move from political powerlessness to effective advocacy, see Tweedie, *The Politics of Legalization in Special Education Reform*, in Special Education Policies 48 (1983).

76.   *See* Note, *Enforcing the Right*, *supra* note 8, at 1123, n.131; Eisenberg, *Disability as Stigma* in Disabled People as Second-Class Citizens 3 (1982); Griggins, *The Disabled Face a Schizophrenic Society*, in Disabled People as Second-Class Citizens 30 (1982); *see also infra* note 138.

77.   *See* tenBroek & Matson, *The Disabled and the Law of Welfare*, 54 Calif. L. Rev. 809, 809-10 (1966); Blakely, *Judicial and Legislative Attitudes Toward the Right to an Equal Education for the Handicapped*, 40 Ohio St. L.J. 603, 603-05 (1979); Note, *A Modern Wilderness—The Law of Education for the Handicapped*, 34 Mercer L. Rev. 1045, 1045-1048 (1983).

78.   *See, e.g.*, Age v. Bullitt County Pub. Schools, 673 F.2d 141 (6th Cir. 1982) (dispute over what method of educating the deaf is superior); Doe v. Lawson, 579 F. Supp. 1314, 1316-19 (D. Mass. 1984) (dispute over techniques of educating a severely retarded child); *In re* Marin County Office of Educ., 1982-83 Educ. Handicapped L. Rep. (CRR) 504:162 (Cal. SEA 1982) (dispute over method of vocational instruction for handicapped student); Johnston v. Ann Arbor Pub. Schools, 569 F. Supp. 1502 (E.D. Mich. 1983) (dispute over feasibility of mainstreaming). *See also* Note, *Enforcing the Right*, *supra* note 8, at 1109; Kirp, Buss & Kuriloff, *Legal Reform of Special Education: Empirical Studies and Procedural Proposals*, 62 Calif. L. Rev. 40, 47 (1974); Halligan, *The Function of Schools, the Status of Teachers, and the Claims of the Handicapped: An Inquiry Into Special Education Malpractice*, 45 Mo. L. Rev. 667, 681 (1980); Large, *supra* note 74, at 229-38.

79.   *See* Note, *Enforcing the Right*, *supra* note 8, at 1110.

80.   *See generally* Stark, *supra* note 2; *see also infra* note 118.

attention. When children are assessed according to standardized measurements used to put the handicapped into categories with pre-formulated programs, the exceptional needs of the handicapped are not likely to be understood, and responsibility for meeting those needs is not likely to be taken as seriously as for those of the nonhandicapped.

Individualized needs assessment and programming for every nonhandicapped child is also unrealistic. Although the EAHCA has led to a practice of individualizing educational programs that may spill over into procedures for nonhandicapped children, it is difficult to imagine public education operating under its current resource restraints while engaging in the kind of individualized procedures for all children that are now required only for the 10 to 12 percent of children who are handicapped.[81]

I will return to this tension between the mandate for individualized programming under the EAHCA and the practice of collective decisionmaking in public education after I have examined two other tensions also underlying the EAHCA.

B. Need vs. Merit

The focus of the EAHCA is on the needs of the handicapped child. This focus creates a certain dissonance with the merit principle upon which the public education system is largely based. Under the merit principle, individuals "should be enabled to attain some particular social good on the basis of their natural abilities and/or actual achievement and not on the basis of arbitrary or ascriptive factors."[82] This principle is a basic component of liberal political philosophy and draws support from instrumental judgments about what makes for an efficient society. A competing, but equally basic, liberal tenet stresses needs rather than merit: individuals should be afforded roughly equal chances to achieve their desired goals.[83] These two concepts are pursued simultaneously through public education: schools meet the needs of children by developing their talent so that they may achieve. Education eliminates *artificial* impediments unrelated to merit or true natural abilities[84] so that children may have the opportunity to display and develop their talents

81. MOORE, WALKER & HOLLAND, *supra* note 3, at 11.

82. Joseph, *supra* note 18, at 394; *see* Frankel, *Equality of Opportunity*, 81 ETHICS 191, 192 (1971) ("democrats and antidemocrats, socialists and adherents of free enterprise, have all apparently been able to say that they believe in at least this much—that individuals ought to have a chance to go as far as their talents permit, and that it is the mark of a good society that its best people rise to the top").

83. This concept is usually referred to as equal opportunity; one writer expresses it perhaps more precisely as that of "equality of life chances." J. FISHKIN, JUSTICE, EQUAL OPPORTUNITY, AND THE FAMILY 20, 32 (1983). Equal opportunity to participate fully in the meritocracy is often viewed as a primary goal of nondiscrimination legislation. *See, e.g.,* Blumstein, *Defining and Proving Race Discrimination: Perspectives on the Purpose vs. Results Approach from the Voting Rights Act*, 69 VA. L. REV. 633, 638-39 (1983) ("race-based discrimination violates the societal goal of a fair, individualized, and meritocratic procedural framework for decisionmaking").

84. *See* J. FISHKIN, *supra* note 83, at 32 (1983) (defining as arbitrary any factor which does not "[predict] the development of qualifications to a high degree among children who have been subjected to equal developmental conditions.").

and reach their rightful level in society based on merit.[85] The education system uses merit as the measurement of success and the basis for classification and advancement. In addition, the system seeks to make up for deficiencies of talent by affording extra help to those who need it most.[86]

Factors relating to many handicaps—physical ability, physical self-sufficiency, the ability to process letter combinations accurately, personality, discipline — may be seen either as components of talent to be used to select the child's rightful place in the meritocracy, or as impediments which should be overcome by education so that the child's achievements will match the achievements of children who are alike in ability except for the handicapping condition. When talent is defined broadly, the realm within which education seeks to modify or correct the barriers to achievement that the child brings with him to school is narrow. A restrictive interpretation of talent, on the other hand, leaves a broad realm within which education seeks to affect factors that influence educational success *including*, ultimately, academic talent itself.[87]

Under a merit system, talent may provide a valid criterion for distributing educational resources. The most talented may require the most extensive and advanced educational services as the meritocracy prepares them to make the maximum contribution to society. This will justify in some cases the distribution of resources in proportion to merit.[88] Moreover, a focus on merit nar-

---

85. *See* Bell, *On Meritocracy and Equality*, 29 Pub. Interest 29, 41-42 (1972); Wilson, *Social Class and Equal Educational Opportunity*, 38 Harv. Ed. Rev. 77, 79-80 (1968), *reprinted in* Equal Educational Opportunity 80, 82-83 (1969); Yudof, *Equal Educational Opportunity and the Courts*, 51 Tex. L. Rev. 411, 418 (1973); *see also* Plyler v. Doe, 457 U.S. 202, 221-22, (1982) ("In addition to the pivotal role of education in sustaining our . . . heritage, denial of education to some isolated group of children poses an affront to one of the goals of the Equal Protection Clause: the abolition of governmental barriers presenting unreasonable obstacles to advancement on the basis of individual merit."); Brown v. Board of Educ., 347 U.S. 483, 493 (1954) (importance of education offered on equal terms to all to enable children to succeed).

86. *See, e.g.*, Education Consolidation and Improvement Act of 1981, 20 U.S.C. §§ 3801-3876 (1982) (establishing federal program of financial assistance for education of disadvantaged children).

87. *See* Wilson, *supra* note 85, at 79, *reprinted in* Equal Educational Opportunity at 82. Wilson elaborates as follows:

The traditional liberal view of equality of opportunity which motivated the extension of public elementary and secondary education in this country would, as far as possible, remove legal and economic handicaps to the acquisition of education by intelligent and industrious youths whose parents sought their social advancement. The more radical conception calls for the provision of experiences which generate intelligence and arouse interest even where the influence of home and neighborhood may be impoverished or hostile.

Id. (footnote omitted). Charles Frankel describes as dichotomous the "educational" and "meritocratic" approaches to equal opportunity. Frankel, *supra* note 82, at 203-04; *see also* D. Rae, Equalities 65-66 (1981) (comparing "prospect-regarding" equal opportunity, defined as an equalized probability that persons will attain the same goal, to "means-regarding" equal opportunity, which equalizes external circumstances relevant to particular goals, but not those qualities about people—wit, speed, strength—that may result in "legitimately" unequal prospects of success); Fishkin, *supra* note 83, at 34-35.

The attention given to ensuring that educational assessments do not result in a disproportionate number of minority children in special education programs illustrates the perception that factors of handicap should be kept separate from sociocultural factors. *See generally* Placing Children in Special Education: A Strategy for Equity (1982) [hereinafter cited as Placing Children in Special Education].

88. Arthur Wise's "competition" definition of equality of educational opportunity would pro-

rows the range of goals that are appropriate for an educational system to pursue. If such factors as the level of ambition, attitude toward learning, extent of curiosity, and quality of personal tastes are all factored into the definition of talent, a school may remain faithful to a merit-based vision by setting goals for the child based in part on these factors, rather than by trying to modify them.

In requiring that educational services be made available to handicapped children entirely on the basis of need, the EAHCA upsets the rough balance between need and merit in public education. Under the EAHCA, the role of merit and need is reversed. Instead of identifying and meeting needs that must be met for a child to be able to find his rightful place in the educational system (and in society) based on merit, ability is assessed in order to determine the child's due in the educational system based upon need. Indeed, insofar as the EAHCA places a priority upon meeting the needs of severely handicapped children,[89] for whom the cost of education is extremely high,[90] it requires that resources be set apart for the handicapped roughly in *inverse* proportion to their "merit."

The need-based focus of the EAHCA is essential, for without it, the position of the handicapped with respect to claims for scarce resources would be extremely weak. The compensatory assistance to which a person disadvantaged by race or social class is entitled under the merit system in order that he have an opportunity to reach his true place in the hierarchy or obtain his "fair" share of society's rewards based on merit, would elude the handicapped person whose disadvantage relates directly to his innate abilities. Without coming to terms with the contrary inclinations of the merit-based system of public education, however, this focus will be difficult to maintain.

C. Federal vs. Local and State Decisionmaking: The Federalism Tension

The EAHCA establishes uniform federal procedures and standards for education of the handicapped. This uniformity is in tension with a long-standing tradition in this country of state and local control over public education.

Many important procedural and substantive issues are preempted by the EAHCA. A local school district may not, for example, decide to serve children with learning disabilities before tackling the more difficult job of providing educational services to severely retarded children,[91] or to eliminate the role of parents in the planning process,[92] or to educate all handicapped

---

mote this pattern. A. WISE, RICH SCHOOLS, POOR SCHOOLS 153-54 (1968). Because the removal of artificial barriers can be costly, however, and because in some respects the talented will not need substantial resources to find their rightful place in society, this merit-based allocation method will not always best promote a meritocratic system.

89. See 20 U.S.C. § 1412(3) (1982); 34 C.F.R. §§ 300.320-.321 (1984).

90. See KAKALIK, *supra* note 2, at 332-36 (comparing $5926 cost of educating severely retarded child with $3795 for educable retarded child and $2253 for speech-impaired child).

91. See 20 U.S.C. § 1412(3) (1982); 34 C.F.R. §§ 300.320-.321 (1984).

92. See 20 U.S.C. § 1415(b)(1) (1982); 34 C.F.R. §§ 300.343-.345 (1984).

children in segregated classrooms.[93]

The EAHCA has been described "as a model of 'cooperative federalism,' "[94] but if it is, it is a different model than that which has characterized the respective roles of local, state, and federal governments in public education in recent decades.[95] In the earliest days of public education in this country, operation and control over schools was left entirely up to local government and parents. In the nineteenth century, small, local school districts were consolidated, usually by towns, and states gradually assumed some of the control over education.[96] Today, the states rather than the federal or local governments are considered ultimately responsible for public education,[97] but consistent with the strong tradition of local control over education,[98] many responsibilities are delegated to local educational agencies.[99] Thus, states commonly issue rules and regulations pertaining to teacher cert-

---

93. See 20 U.S.C. §§ 1412(5)(B), 1414(a)(1)(C)(iv) (1982); 34 C.F.R. §§ 300.550-.556 (1984). These requirements of the EAHCA also coopt decisionmaking relating to the allocation of resources needed to satisfy them. See supra notes 64-73 and accompanying text.

94. Georgia Ass'n of Retarded Citizens v. McDaniel, 716 F.2d 1565, 1569 (11th Cir. 1983), vacated on other grounds, 104 S. Ct. 3581 (1984).

95. This shift to a certain extent was anticipated in the Senate debates over the EAHCA. See 121 CONG. REC. 19,498 (1975) ("this measure will greatly change the Federal role in the education of handicapped children in this Nation.") (remarks of Sen. Dole). Senator Dole's remarks, however, were directed at the financial burdens the legislation would create for the federal (and state) governments, not the impact on state sovereignty over the educational system. Id.

96. See Kaestle & Smith, The Federal Role in Elementary and Secondary Education, 1940-1980, 52 HARV. EDUC. REV. 384, 384 (1982); M. MILSTEIN, IMPACT AND RESPONSE: FEDERAL AID AND STATE EDUCATIONAL AGENCIES 3-4 (1976); see also Andrus v. Hill, 73 Idaho 196, 200, 249 P.2d 205, 207 (1952) ("Traditionally, not only in Idaho but throughout most of the states of the Union, the legislature has left the establishment, control and management of the school to the local community which it serves."); Board of Educ. v. Nyquist, 57 N.Y.2d 27, 46, 439 N.E.2d 359, 367, 453 N.Y.S.2d 643, 652 (1982) ("For all of the nearly two centuries that New York has had public schools, it has utilized a statutory system whereby citizens at the local level . . . have made the basic decisions on . . . operating their own schools." (quoting the amici curiae brief of 85 public school districts)), appeal dismissed, 459 U.S. 1138 (1983).

97. See 121 CONG. REC. 19,498 (1975) (statement of Sen. Dole) ("Historically, the States have had the primary responsibility for the education of children at the elementary and secondary level.").

98. See Milliken v. Bradley, 418 U.S. 717, 741 (1975) ("No single tradition in public education is more deeply rooted than local control over the operation of public schools. . . ."); Washington v. Seattle School Dist., 458 U.S. 457, 477-49 (1982) (describing the duties of local school boards); San Antonio Indep. School Dist. v. Rodriguez, 411 U.S. 1, 47-49 (1973) (tracing the history of local control over education in Texas); Martinez v. Bynum, 461 U.S. 321, 329 (1983) (education "is one of the most important functions of local government"); Brown v. Board of Educ., 347 U.S. 483, 493 (1954) ("Today, education is perhaps the most important function of state and local governments."). See also Coleman, Rawls, Nozick, and Educational Equality, 43 PUB. INTEREST 121, 123 (1976).

99. See Robinson v. Cahill, 69 N.J. 449, 458, 355 A.2d 129, 133 (1976) (running the schools has been largely delegated to local governments); Thompson v. Engelking, 96 Idaho 793, 803, 537 P.2d 635, 645 (1975) (local governments control these schools (quoting Andrus v. Hill, 73 Idaho 196, 200, 249 P.2d 205, 207 (1952)); Campbell v. Board of Educ., 193 Conn. 93, 96-97, 475 A.2d 289, 291 (1984) (state constitution requires the state to provide public education, but this obligation has been delegated to local governments); Levin, Federal Grants and Educational Equity, 52 HARV. EDUC. REV. 444, 445 (1982).

Only the State of Hawaii has not delegated power over education to local school districts. HAWAII REV. STAT. § 27-1(1) (1976); Kaden, supra note 18, at 1210.

For a brief history of the relationship between state and local government in the control of education, see M. MILSTEIN, supra note 96, at 3-6; Kaestle & Smith, supra note 96, at 384-87; see also McLaughlin, States and the New Federalism, 52 HARV. EDUC. REV. 564 (1982) (describing variations in state relationships with both local and federal educational agencies).

ification,[100] textbooks[101] and curriculum matters,[102] testing,[103] length of school year[104] and attendance guidelines,[105] but local educational agencies typically exercise considerable discretion in these areas, as well as primary control over such matters as local school finance,[106] discipline,[107] educational methodology,[108] extracurricular programs,[109] health and safety standards,[110] and other internal school matters.[111]

Earlier federal limits imposed on state and local control over education related largely to access, rather than to the substance of educational programs. The federal Constitution has been interpreted to forbid states from interfering with certain prerogatives of parents with respect to their children, but not to preclude states from structuring an educational system as they wish. Thus, parents may be able to insist upon private alternatives to public education[112] or upon the elimination of unconstitutional limitations on what is available in public schools.[113] Ordinarily, however, parents may not hinder the school in fulfilling what the school sees as its educational mission.[114]

---

100. *See, e.g.,* CAL. EDUC. CODE § 44330 (West 1978); MD. EDUC. CODE ANN. § 2-303(g) (1978); MICH. COMP. LAWS ANN. §§ 380.1531-.1535 (West Supp. 1984-85); N.J. STAT. ANN. §§ 18A:6-38, :26-1-2 (West 1968 & Supp. 1984-85).

101. *See, e.g.,* CAL. EDUC. CODE §§ 60200, 60401 (West 1978 & Supp. 1984); N.J. STAT. ANN. § 18A:34-1 (West 1968); N.C. GEN. STAT. §§ 115C-85 to -102 (1983); *cf.* MD. EDUC. CODE ANN. § 7-106 (1978); MICH. COMP. LAWS ANN. §§ 380.1421-.1437 (West Supp. 1984-85).

102. *See, e.g.,* CAL. EDUC. CODE §§ 51202-51260 (West 1978 & Supp. 1984); ILL. ANN. STAT. ch. 122, §§ 27-1 to -22 (Smith-Hurd 1962 & Supp. 1984-85); MICH. COMP. LAWS ANN. §§ 380.1151-.1174 (West Supp. 1984-85); N.J. STAT. ANN. §§ 18A:35-1 to -4.8 (West 1968 & Supp. 1984-85); *cf.* MD. EDUC. CODE ANN. § 4-110 (1978 & Supp. 1983).

103. *See, e.g.,* FLA. STAT. ANN. § 229.57 (West 1977 & Supp. 1984); N.C. GEN. STAT. §§ 115C-175 to -184 (1983).

104. *See, e.g.,* CAL. EDUC. CODE §§ 37200-37707 (West 1978 & Supp. 1984); MD. EDUC. CODE ANN. § 7-103 (1978 & Supp. 1983); MICH. COMP. LAWS ANN. § 380.1284 (West Supp. 1984-85); N.J. STAT. ANN. §§ 18A:36-1, :36-2 (West 1968 & Supp. 1984-85).

105. *See, e.g.,* ILL. ANN. STAT. ch.122, §§ 26-1, -2 (Smith-Hurd 1962 & Supp. 1984-85); MD. EDUC. CODE ANN. § 7-301 (1978 & Supp. 1983); MICH. COMP. LAWS ANN. §§ 380.1541, .1561 (West Supp. 1984-85).

106. *See, e.g.,* FLA. STAT. ANN. § 230.23(10) (West 1977 & Supp. 1984); ILL. ANN. STAT. ch. 122, §§ 17-1, -2 (Smith-Hurd 1962 & Supp. 1984-85); MICH. COMP. LAWS ANN. §§ 380.1211-.1212 (West Supp. 1984-85).

107. *See, e.g.,* FLA. STAT. ANN. § 230.23(6)(c)-(d) (West 1977 & Supp. 1984); MD. EDUC. CODE ANN. § 7-304 (1978 & Supp. 1983); MICH. COMP. LAWS ANN. §§ 380.1311-.1312 (West Supp. 1984-85).

108. *See, e.g.,* FLA. STAT. ANN. § 230.23(7) (West 1977 & Supp. 1984); MICH. COMP. LAWS ANN. § 380.1282 (West Supp. 1984-85); N.C. GEN. STAT. § 115C-47(12) (1983).

109. *See, e.g.,* MICH. COMP. LAWS ANN. § 380.1289 (West Supp. 1984-85); N.C. GEN. STAT. § 115C-47(4) (1983).

110. *See, e.g.,* FLA. STAT. ANN. § 230.23(2) (West 1977); MICH. COMP. LAWS ANN. § 380.1300 (West Supp. 1984-85).

111. *See, e.g.,* FLA. STAT. ANN. § 230.23(8) (West 1977) (transportation of students); ILL. ANN. STAT. ch. 122, § 10-22.4 (Smith-Hurd 1962 & Supp. 1984-85) (dismissal of teachers); MICH. COMP. LAWS ANN. § 380.1272 (West Supp. 1984-85) (supplying food to students and employees).

112. Pierce v. Society of Sisters, 268 U.S. 510 (1925).

113. *See* Board of Educ., v. Pico, 457 U.S. 853 (1982) (ban on books school board disliked may violate first amendment); Meyer v. Nebraska, 262 U.S. 390 (1923) (ban on teaching foreign language was unconstitutional).

114. *See* Medeiros v. Kiyosaki, 52 Hawaii 436, 478 P.2d 314 (1970) (parents may not prevent state from showing sex education films when parents have option to withdraw their children from showings). *But see* Engel v. Vitale, 370 U.S. 421 (1962) (state may not require recitation of state-

Similarly, the federal government may impose its will upon state and local governments as to who will be allowed access to public education and on what terms,[115] but it may not control the substance of what is taught in the schools. Federal aid programs, which have inserted a more tangible federal presence in education than have judicial decisions, have also been concerned primarily with enlarging access to education. These programs have tied funds for serving target populations to regulations with which local and state educational agencies must comply. These aid programs, however, are quite different in structure and intent from the EAHCA which, by comparison, is both "unusually specific"[116] and more far-reaching. First, the conditions attached to aid programs generally affect only the aid made available under the programs and do not restrict the use of other school monies.[117] The EAHCA, in contrast, only covers about 25 percent of the extra cost of educating the handicapped child or about 9 to 14 percent of the total cost of the handicapped child's education.[118] Conditions attached to other aid programs generally focus on the eligibility for new or enhanced services and programs, not the content and priorities of programs that already exist.[119] Finally, other aid

---

composed prayers in school, even if children may be excused); Abington School Dist. v. Schemp, 374 U.S. 203 (1963) (state may not require Bible readings or recitation of Lord's Prayer in schools).

115. *See* Brown v. Board of Educ., 347 U.S. 483 (1954) (racially segregated school are unconstitutional); Plyler v. Doe, 457 U.S. 202 (1982) (public schools may not exclude students who are illegal aliens). *But see* San Antonio Indep. School Dist. v. Rodriguez, 411 U.S. 1 (1973) (states not required to equalize funding to different school districts).

116. Cohen, *Policy and Organization: The Impact of State and Federal Educational Policy on School Governance*, 52 HARV. EDUC. REV. 474, 489 (1982).

117. *See, e.g.*, Education Consolidation and Improvement Act of 1981, 20 U.S.C. §§ 3801-3807 (Supp. 1984); Silverstein, Federal Approaches for Ensuring Equal Opportunity: Past, Present, and Future 15 (Nov. 1981) (unpublished paper); *see also* Bilingual Education Act, 20 U.S.C. §§ 3221-3223, 3231-3233, 3241-3242, 3251-3252, 3261 (1982); Levin, *supra* note 70, at 171-72.

118. *See* Note, *Board of Education v. Rowley, supra* note 8, at 292 n.93; Miller & Miller, *supra* note 74, at 17; Hartman, *Policy Effects of Special Education Funding Formulas*, 6 J. EDUC. FIN. 135, 151 (1981); Colley, *supra* note 11, at 137, 144.

Federal funds under the EAHCA are made available to states and distributed to local districts on the basis of the number of handicapped children served, up to a limit of 12 percent of the total school population, without regard to the nature of the services actually provided. 20 U.S.C. § 1411(a)(5)(A)(i)(d) (1982). States must distribute 75 percent of the federal funds they receive directly to local districts, *id.* § 1411(c)(l)(B), and must pay a portion of the 25 percent they retain for direct services, *id.* § 1411(c)(2)(A). States must also match the funds distributed to local districts with nonfederal funds, *id.* § 1411(c)(2)(B). This money and the portion of the 25 percent they distribute for direct services can be distributed in accordance with various reimbursement formulas which carry different sets of incentives. MOORE, WALKER & HOLLAND, *supra* note 3, at 24-26, 77-78. *See generally* Barro, FEDERALISM, EQUITY, AND THE DISTRIBUTION OF FEDERAL EDUCATION GRANTS 2 (February, 1983) (unpublished paper); Hartman, *supra*.

Appropriation levels were expected to increase from 5 percent of the extra cost of educating a handicapped child in 1977 to 40 percent in 1982. 20 U.S.C. § 1411(a)(1)(B) (1982). Actual federal appropriations have been considerably less, with only 29 percent of the possible amount (of $3.16 billion) allocated in fiscal year 1982. One estimate is that in fiscal year 1978, states received approximately $74 per handicapped child, while in 1980 and 1981, the figure was in the $200 to $250 range. Hartman, *supra*, at 153. A useful table illustrating the gap between federal funds authorized and funds appropriated under the EAHCA from 1978 to 1982 is found in Pittenger & Kuriloff, *Educating the Handicapped: Reforming a Radical Law*, 66 PUB. INTEREST 72, 87 (1982).

119. *Compare, e.g.*, School Lunch Program, 42 U.S.C. §§ 1751-1761c (1982); School Milk Program Extension Act, P.L. 85-478, 72 Stat. 276 (1958) (expired 1961); Bilingual Education Act, 20 U.S.C. §§ 3221-3223, 3231-3233, 3241-3242, 3251-3252, 3261 (1982); Career Education and De-

programs do not create enforceable individual rights for particular services, but rather only eligibility to compete for additional limited monies distributed by decisionmakers who have considerable discretion.[120]

Federal nondiscrimination statutes also differ in many respects from the EAHCA. Section 601 of the Civil Rights Act of 1964[121] prohibits discrimination in public education by the recipient of any federal funds on the basis of race, sex, or national origin. Section 504 of the Rehabilitation Act of 1973 prohibits discrimination against the handicapped by any recipient of federal funds.[122] Like federal grant-in-aid statutes, however, these statutes affect access to, but not the content of, educational programming. Thus, while Title VI may prohibit a school district from using practices which deny national origin minority children effective participation in the educational program,[123] it does not impose specific educational priorities, methods, or procedures upon school districts in implementing this nondiscrimination mandate.[124] Section 504 of the Rehabilitation Act of 1973 is likewise a nondiscrimination statute,[125] and even though it has been interpreted in the education setting according to guidelines very similar to those issued under the EAHCA[126] and has been held to require school districts to provide an appropriate education to handicapped children,[127] cases interpreting section 504 to require affirmative relief generally reach this conclusion through an analysis that piggybacks section 504 onto the more detailed and demanding provisions of the

---

velopment Program, 20 U.S.C. §§ 2501-2569 (1982), *with* 20 U.S.C. §§ 1412(5)(B), 1414(a)(1)(C)(1982); 34 C.F.R. §§ 300.500-.556(1983) (least restrictive alternative preference). *See* Levin, *supra* note 74, at 171-72.

120. *See* P. Hill & D. Madey, *supra* note 58, at 2.

121. 42 U.S.C. § 2000d (1982).

122. 29 U.S.C. § 794 (1982).

123. *See* Lau v. Nichols, 414 U.S. 563 (1974) (local schools may not refuse to teach a large number of non-English speaking children in their native languages).

124. Courts have disagreed over the nature of the affirmative duties required by schools under Title VI on behalf of non-English speaking children. *Compare* Cintron v. Brentwood Union Free School Dist., 455 F. Supp. 57, 64 (E.D.N.Y. 1978) (must comply with "Lau guidelines" drafted by the Office of Civil Rights, requiring bilingual-bicultural program) *with* Guadalupe Org., Inc. v. Tempe Elementary School Dist., 587 F.2d 1022, 1029 (9th Cir. 1978) (remedial English satisfies Title VI). *See* Levin, *supra* note 70, at 174-75. Levin also points out that it is not clear that Title VI requires any affirmative action for non-English speaking children where the number of such students is small. *Id.* at 178.

125. *See* Southeastern Community College v. Davis, 442 U.S. 397, 410-11 (1979). Title IX of the Education Amendments of 1972, 20 U.S.C. §§ 1681-1686 (1982), similarly prohibits discrimination in all aspects of public education but does not require affirmative remedies on behalf of women, except as may be necessary to remove the effects of past discrimination. 34 C.F.R. § 106.3(a) (1984).

126. *See, e.g.,* 34 C.F.R. § 104.33(a) (1984) (requirement of free and appropriate education); *id.* § 104.35 (placement and evaluation requirements); *id.* § 104.36 (procedural due process safeguards). The section 504 regulations, in fact, make explicit reference to the standards of the EAHCA. *See, e.g.,* 34 C.F.R. § 104.33(b)(2) (1984) (compliance with IEP requirement of EAHCA meets burden of free and appropriate education under section 504).

127. *See, e.g.,* Georgia Ass'n of Retarded Citizens v. McDaniel, 716 F.2d 1565 (11th Cir. 1983), *vacated on other grounds,* 104 S. Ct. 3581 (1984); New Mexico Ass'n for Retarded Citizens v. New Mexico, 378 F.2d 847 (10th Cir. 1982); David H. v. Spring Branch Indep. School Dist., 569 F. Supp. 1324 (S.D. Tex. 1983); Association of Retarded Citizens v. Frazier, 517 F. Supp. 105 (D. Colo. 1981). North v. District of Columbia Bd. of Educ., 471 F. Supp. 136 (D.D.C. 1979).

EAHCA.[128]

Federalism raises a difficult problem under the EAHCA. On the one hand, it would seem that the handicapped need the coercive power of federal government applying uniform and enlightened standards of conduct in order to reverse local prejudice and ignorance and to protect their basic interests.[129] On the other hand, state and local control of education is likely to enhance the effectiveness of education, from which all students benefit. The freedom to participate in public life, to influence political decisions, to obtain relevant information, and to hold those who act on one's behalf directly accountable, are all considered particularly valuable with respect to a governmental service such as education which, regardless of the ultimate basis of power, must be *delivered* on a local and decentralized basis. Decentralization is thought to keep local communities concerned, active, and vigilant in public school systems,[130] which then encourages accountability by those who can make the biggest difference in the quality of education—teachers and school

---

128. *See, e.g.,* Rettig v. Kent City School Dist., 539 F. Supp. 768, 776 (N.D. Ohio 1981) (collapsing discussion of EAHCA and section 504), *aff'd in part, rev'd in part on other grounds,* 720 F.2d 463 (6th Cir. 1983); Campbell v. Talladega County Bd. of Educ., 518 F. Supp. 47, 51 (N.D. Ala. 1981) (focusing on provisions of the EAHCA because they provided "a far more detailed statutory framework" than section 504); Gladys J. v. Pearland Indep. School Dist., 520 F. Supp. 869, 874-75 (S.D. Tex. 1981) (mentioning the section 504 claim and then ignoring it); *see also* North v. District of Columbia Bd. of Educ., 471 F. Supp. 136, 139 (D.D.C. 1979) (deciding for the child under both section 504 and the EAHCA without analyzing separately the applicability of each statute).

Despite the more specific provisions of the EAHCA, section 504 claims are often brought in addition to the EAHCA claims because of the different procedural requirements and remedies available under section 504. *See, e.g.,* Georgia Ass'n of Retarded Citizens v. McDaniel, 716 F.2d 1565 (11th Cir. 1983) (injunctive relief sought under section 504), *vacated on other grounds,* 104 S. Ct. 3581 (1984); Phipps v. New Hanover County Bd. of Educ., 551 F. Supp. 732 (E.D.N.C. 1982); Patsel v. District of Columbia Bd. of Educ., 530 F. Supp. 660 (D.D.C. 1982) (attorney fees available under section 504); Association for Retarded Citizens v. Frazier, 517 F. Supp. 105 (D. Colo. 1981) (plaintiffs not required to exhaust administrative remedies under section 504). The Supreme Court has put into question these strategies, holding last term that section 504 was inapplicable in a case in which relief had been granted under the EAHCA. Smith v. Robinson, 104 S. Ct. 3457 (1984) (plaintiff sought attorney fees under section 504).

The major case which responded to section 504 without also deciding the EAHCA claim held that a failure to diagnose, identify, and assimilate handicapped children into public school classes would violate the Rehabilitation Act. *See* New Mexico Ass'n for Retarded Citizens v. New Mexico, 678 F.2d 847 (10th Cir. 1982). At the time of this decision, New Mexico did not accept federal funds under the EAHCA, and thus was not subject to its provisions. *Id.* at 853.

129. *See supra* note 75; *infra* note 138 and accompanying text.

130. *See* Milliken v. Bradley, 418 U.S. at 717, 741-42 (1974) ("[L]ocal autonomy has long been thought essential both to the maintenance of community concern and support for public schools and to the quality of the educational process."); Wright v. Council of Emporia, 407 U.S. 451, 469 (1972) ("[d]irect control over decisions vitally affecting education of one's children is a need that is strongly felt in our society. . . ."); Thompson v. Engelking, 96 Idaho 793, 803, 537 P.2d 635, 645 (1975). The *Thompson* court stated:

> The American people made a wise choice early in their history by not only creating forty-eight state systems of education, but also by retaining within the community, close to parental observation, the actual direction and control of the educational program. This tradition of community administration is a firmly accepted and deeply rooted policy.

Id. at 803, 537 P.2d at 645 (quoting Andrus v. Hill, 73 Idaho 196, 200, 249 P.2d 205, 207 (1952)).

This view is often attributed to the Reagan Administration as the impetus behind efforts at greater decentralization in education. *See* Clark & Amiot, *The Impact of the Reagan Administration on Federal Education Policy,* 63 PHI DELTA KAPPAN 258, 258 (1981). *See also* Levin, *supra* note 99, at 444-45. (decentralized decisionmaking promotes accountability to those most affected by the decisions);

administrators.[131] The enhanced authority of service providers on the local level increases their effectiveness in another way as well, for when such individuals are given more responsibility they tend to act more diligently and effectively than when they are not.[132]

Decentralization also capitalizes on the positive potential of experimentation and diversity.[133] Where various solutions are possible, decentralization encourages choices that enrich liberty and freedom of choice and permits the observation and testing of hypotheses which will yield better answers for adoption by others with common problems.[134] This experimentation is thought to be especially beneficial in public education.[135]

The federalism tension in public education, like the tension between need and merit and the tension between individualized and collective decision-making, did not originate with the EAHCA but has been highlighted and aggravated by it. In the next section, I attempt to define a theoretical framework that will assist in mediating (though not eliminating) these tensions.

IV

DEFINING THE IDEAL

The tensions defined in part III arise from the attempt to assist certain individuals who, because of their special characteristics, are at a disadvantage in relation to the majority in obtaining the benefit of a public service. Such stress has been demonstrated in other areas of civil rights and is perhaps inevitable in efforts to eliminate hardship that befalls a special group from the operation of otherwise neutral rules. When these tensions have important

---

Steiner, *A Progressive Creed: The Experimental Federalism of Justice Brandeis*, 2 YALE LAW & POL'Y REV. 1, 38 (decentralization promotes civic virtue).

131. *See* David & Greene, *supra* note 74, at 122, 124.

132. *See* R. ELMORE, *Complexity and Control: What Legislators and Administrators Can Do About Implementation* (Institute of Governmental Research, Public Policy Paper No. 11, 1979), *excerpted in* M. YUDOF, D. KIRP, T. VAN GEEL & B. LEVIN, EDUCATIONAL POLICY AND THE LAW 658-75 (2d ed. 1983). *See also* Wieman v. Updegraff, 344 U.S. 183, 196 (1952) (Frankfurter, J., concurring) ("'[teachers] cannot carry out their noble task if the conditions for the practice of a responsible and critical mind are denied to them"); Odden, *Financing Educational Excellence*, 66 PHI DELTA KAPPAN 311, 312 (1984) ("The research on effective schools has made it clear that the individual school is the proper unit for educational renewal. Centralized standards and requirements may be necessary, but so is decentralized implementation. . . . Each effective school is bound together by a belief structure, a value system, and a consensual—not a hierarchical—governance system.").

133. "It is one of the happy incidents of the federal system that a single courageous state may, if its citizens choose, serve as a laboratory; and try novel social and economic experiments without risk to the rest of the country." New State Ice Co. v. Liebmann, 285 U.S. 262, 311 (1932) (Brandeis, J., dissenting); *see also* Addington v. Texas, 441 U.S. 418, 431 (1979) ("The essence of federalism is that states must be free to develop a variety of solutions to problems and not be forced into a common, uniform mold.").

134. *See* B. ACKERMAN, *supra* note 13, at 306 ("Federalist structures . . . permit the polity to make creative use of the fact that many second-best problems admit of a wide variety of legitimate solutions."). Ackerman notes as limits of federalism and other "process strategies," however, that "[w]hile they may well reduce the risk of governmental tyranny, they often increase the risk of private exploitation." *Id.*

135. *See* San Antonio Indep. School Dist. v. Rodriguez, 411 U.S. 1, 50 (1973) (local control over the educational process encourages "experimentation, innovation, and a healthy competition for educational excellence").

cost implications, they pose risks of unfairness to society at large. The creation of unique, individualized, and costly rights for the handicapped in public education burdens a system which has legitimate, worthy goals and upon which a large proportion of children depend for an essential service. There must be limits to the weight of this burden. As Bruce Ackerman states in a more general context, "[h]owever valid X's claims against his fellow citizens, it hardly follows that his treatment can serve as the *exclusive* touchstone of economic and social policy in a just society."[136]

This dilemma creates the need for a principle which will mediate the interests of particular individuals and the interests of society at large and will define a fair relationship between the entitlements of the protected class and the interests of the remainder of society. This section first outlines the characteristics of handicap relevant to the formulation of this relationship. It then reviews and evaluates various conceptions of equality that might be used as a basis for this relationship.

A. The Nature of Handicap

Handicap is not defined by a single characteristic, such as skin color, national origin, sex, or religious preference. Handicaps vary in type and degree, with differing effects upon an individual's ability and hence upon the likelihood of achieving certain educational goals.[137] Some conditions perceived to be handicaps are not in fact handicapping conditions; they are differences without significance except that which may be artificially given to them by others. Children with disfigurements or features which make them unusual or unsightly might be unwelcome in public schools, but the lack of hospitality is due not to a rational relationship between the handicapping condition and the activities that take place in the school, but rather to irrational or unreasonable discriminations attached to those handicaps by others.[138] The effects of these handicaps can be neutralized without special compensation or treatment, other than that which might make the child more welcome or understood in the educational institution.

Most handicaps, on the other hand, are true handicaps affecting the value or utility of educational services that might be offered to children who have them. The handicaps are thus *relevant* to the education which is made avail-

---

136. B. Ackerman, *supra* note 13, at 271 (emphasis added).
137. *See* Moore, Walker & Holland *supra* note 3, at 7-9; Sorgen, *The Classification Process and Its Consequences*, in The Mentally Retarded Citizen and the Law 215 (1976); Large, *supra* note 74 at 214, 238-40.
138. *See, e.g.*, State *ex rel.* Beattie v. Board of Educ., 169 Wis. 231, 232, 172 N.W. 153, 154 (1919) (paralytic boy with "slow and hesitating speech" and a "peculiarly high, rasping, and disturbing tone of voice, accompanied with uncontrollable facial contortions" and "an uncontrollable flow of saliva, which drools from his mouth onto his clothing and books, causing him to present an unclean appearance" excluded from school because "his physical condition and ailment produces a depressing and nauseating effect upon the teachers and school children; . . . he takes up an undue portion of the teacher's time and attention, distracts from the attention of other pupils, and interferes generally with the discipline and progress of the school"). For a follow-up on the child involved in this case, *see* Blakely, *supra* note 77, at 603-05.

able to handicapped children or to which they may be entitled. True handi-caps cover a wide universe, and problems of definition, identification, and professional disagreement about teaching methods and theories make predic-tions and generalizations about many of them difficult and/or controver-sial.[139] Some handicaps are mild, at least as to their impact on the objectives of public education. These can be eliminated with only modest adjustments in a child's educational program. A mobility impairment, for example, may be corrected as to nearly all activities offered to students through the availability of a wheelchair and ramps or other devices that allow free access to the educa-tional facilities. A mild speech impediment may, after a brief time, be elimi-nated by speech therapy.

Other handicaps pose greater difficulties with respect to the objects and design of public education. The educational effects of these handicaps can be virtually eliminated in some cases, but may require more than modest adjust-ments to the standard educational program in order to do so. A deaf child, for example, may need a sign-language interpreter in order to understand all of what is said in school during the day. Still other handicaps, such as severe retardation, render a child incapable at *any* cost, through existing technology, of achieving the same goals that are set for nonhandicapped children.

In addition to the variety of types and degrees of handicap, children with handicaps may differ with respect to individual tastes, interests and goals, ren-dering the effects of their handicap more or less disabling to them. These differences affect the type and degree of remediation that might be desired by a handicapped person. The blind child who wishes to become a nurse, for example, will be considerably more burdened by the legitimate requirements of the profession[140] than the blind child who wishes to be a writer or a musi-cian. Likewise, the individual's other talents, weaknesses, or life circum-stances may temper or magnify the effects of a handicap. For instance, low intelligence may aggravate the handicapping condition of deafness while a high intelligence may ameliorate it. An unstable family life may distract the handicapped child from an already difficult learning activity; a child with handicaps who enjoys a warm, stable home life, may respond extremely well to remedial assistance.[141]

The fact that handicap encompasses some of the very qualities which would otherwise render discriminations valid—ability, wit, speed, sense of humor, size, ambition, and so on—creates a dilemma which partially explains the tenacity and insidious nature of disparate treatment based upon handicap.

---

139. *See* MOORE, WALKER & HOLLAND, *supra* note 3, at 7-9, 11-12; Stark, *supra* note 2, at 488-91, 497, 504-05. *See also supra* note 78.

140. *See, e.g.*, Southeastern Community College v. Davis, 442 U.S. 397, 407 (1979) (hearing-impaired applicant for nursing program).

141. *See, e.g.*, Springdale School Dist. v. Grace, 494 F. Supp. 266, 272 (W.D. Ark. 1980) ("The home life of the child, his parents' interests and the child's cultural and sociological environment often determine the child's academic success and attainment or lack of such."), *aff'd*, 656 F.2d 300 (8th Cir. 1981), *vacated*, 458 U.S. 1118 (1982), *aff'd on rehearing*, 693 F.2d 41 (8th Cir. 1982), *cert. denied*, 461 U.S. 927 (1983); PLACING CHILDREN IN SPECIAL EDUCATION, *supra* note 87, at 16, 167-69 (home environment may affect outcome on tests and hence educational placements).

These qualities of handicap appear to provide a factual explanation for different outcomes in learning, thus confusing us as to what constitutes fair treatment. The issue of fair treatment is complicated when cost is raised as a factor to limit educational services for a handicapped child. Costs are a limiting factor, and society resists diverting resources from other purposes, especially where others assert competing claims to the resources demanded by the handicapped. The issue of cost in special education must be answered by reference to a concept of fairness relating the entitlements of the handicapped child to the claims of others. In the next section I explore and evaluate some alternatives.

B.   Alternative Forms of Equality

Because genuine, relevant differences exist between the handicapped and the nonhandicapped, certain formulations of equality that are appropriate between members of other groups seem unsatisfactory when applied to the handicapped. Formal equality, for example, providing identical legal right of access to a service, would give handicapped children permission to enter public schools, but would go no further. Because formal equality does not treat differences between individuals affecting their ability to obtain value from such service as relevant, that service will not enable the handicapped to benefit from it.[142] Formal equality requires no special accommodations or remediation to eliminate differences affecting a child's ability to use or benefit from formal access, and thus would at most only legitimate continued lack of effective access by handicapped children who cannot benefit from regular educational programs. This approach is not argued seriously in cases arising under the EAHCA,[143] and contentions that a particular type of service is not required because it has no parallel in regular education programs are generally rejected.[144]

Value equalization might seem a more attractive form of equality between the handicapped and the nonhandicapped in public education.[145] Value equalization, which equalizes the objective value of resources made available to children, makes allowances for individual abilities, tastes, and needs, requiring the distribution of resources equally to individuals who can then use the resources with some degree of (perhaps total) discretion. In education, value equalization would allow individuals to have different educational pro-

---

142.   This shortcoming follows in large part from a superficial view of what characteristics are relevant in determining equality of treatment. *See* J. FEINBERG, SOCIAL PHILOSOPHY 100 (1973).

143.   The EAHCA, in fact, specifies that funds disbursed under it are to be used only for "excess costs," that is, costs over and above the school's average annual expenditures. 20 U.S.C. §§ 1401(20), 1414(a)(1) (1982).

144.   *See, e.g.,* Kruelle v. New Castle County School Dist., 642 F.2d 687, 693 (3d Cir. 1981) (rejecting argument that 6-hour day program would be appropriate for a profoundly retarded child since nonhandicapped children had only 6-hour day program); Battle v. Pennsylvania, 629 F.2d 269 (3d Cir. 1980) (180-day rule), *cert. denied,* 452 U.S. 968 (1981).

145.   Arthur Wise calls this form of equality the "equal-dollars-per-child" definition. A. WISE, *supra* note 88, at 155-56.

grams and services so long as the programs and services required equivalent resource expenditures. Value equalization would be helpful to children whose needs are different from other children but who do not require a greater total amount of resources. Most handicapped children, however, do not fall into this category.[146] The vast majority of the needs of the handicapped are not only different from, but also greater, in terms of resources, than those of the nonhandicapped; for them, value equality will address only a portion of their needs in comparison to other children.[147] Like formal equality, value equalization has not, since the enactment of the EAHCA, been seriously advanced as the appropriate relationship between handicapped and nonhandicapped children in public education.

Equalization of results or outcomes has received more serious attention. Outcome equality "permits wide disparities in the allocation of education resources so long as the different needs of children are being met in a way that results in equality in the effects of the schooling process."[148] Because results or outcome in education depend heavily upon highly individualized factors such as personal effort, this form of equality is usually expressed in terms of equalized *opportunity*.[149] In its more extreme form, this approach would require elimination of the effects of the handicap that bear on the child's ability to benefit from the education offered to him.[150] Thus, if a nonhandicapped child receives a certain amount of resources in order to reach certain educational goals, the handicapped child would have a right to whatever resources are necessary to reach the same goal.

Differences in goals among children, both handicapped and nonhandicapped, make outcome equality problematic.[151] On the basis of these goals, the resources to which children lay claim may vary considerably.[152] A child who wishes to become an unskilled laborer may ask much less in the way of educational resources than one who decides to pursue a medical career. Factors other than handicap which may impede or facilitate the accomplishment of certain goals such as a bad diet or unstable homelife, may also affect the ability of children to benefit from education resources. If, however, the effects of handicap could be isolated (or the definition of handicap sufficiently broadened to take into account all disadvantaging factors in one's life),[153] particular goals could be set—such as reading at a "tenth grade" level or self-suffi-

---

146. *See* KAKALIK *supra* note 2, at 339-43 (10-12 percent).

147. *See supra* note 3.

148. Yudof, *supra* note 85, at 419.

149. Equality of opportunity and equality of results are often viewed as contrasting forms of equality. *See* Bell, *supra* note 85; Coleman, *supra* note 60. Both equality of opportunity and equality of results, however, focus on the end product rather than on the resources that may be required to reach that end. Ronald Dworkin refers to that end product as "welfare." Dworkin, *What Is Equality? Part 1: Equality of Welfare*, 10 PHIL. & PUB. AFFAIRS 185 (1981).

150. This approach is essentially the approach taken by the trial court in Rowley v. Board of Educ., 483 F. Supp. 528 (S.D.N.Y.), *aff'd*, 632 F.2d 945 (2d Cir. 1980), *rev'd*, 458 U.S. 176 (1982).

151. *See supra* notes 140-41 and accompanying text.

152. *See* Dworkin, *What Is Equality? Part 2: Equality of Resources*, 10 PHIL. & PUB. AFFAIRS 283, 285-86 (1981).

153. *See supra* note 87 and accompanying text.

ciency[154]—and resources distributed in a manner that would neutralize the effects of any handicap and equalize the handicapped child's chances of achieving those goals.

The more basic difficulty with outcome equality is that it puts unrealistic demands on both resources and educational goals. There is first the question of feasibility. For many children, handicaps render them incapable under the present state of the art to achieve average, or even minimal, educational goals regardless of the manner of resource allocation. Even if goals are limited to those an individual child is capable of achieving, difficulties remain. For many handicapped children, the cost of educational achievement will be extraordinarily high. The only way to address a shortfall of resources under outcome equality is to adjust the goals that *all* children are given the opportunity to achieve. This approach, however, ignores the merit-based orientation of public education, and trades off the education of "normal" and higher functioning children to the education of children of the lower ability levels.[155]

This outcome equality approach to distributing educational resources will result in a quality of education to children generally that does not serve society, or even the handicapped, well.[156] This method would be grossly inefficient in other respects as well. The gains to the handicapped child from such a distribution may be slight and the disutility of shifting resources from the nonhandicapped to the handicapped enormous. Equality may be furthered, but entirely at the expense of efficiency and common sense. For even the more thoroughgoing redistributionists, a point is reached at which the resources needed to accomplish the next increment of equality of results are considered too great in light of the sacrifices that would be required.[157]

To reduce the inefficiency and, in many cases, the infeasibility of achieving

---

154. Some courts have identified the goal of self-sufficiency as the goal of the EAHCA and the end toward which educational services should be aimed. *See* Campbell v. Talladega County Bd. of Educ., 518 F. Supp. 47, 53-54 (N.D. Ala. 1981); Armstrong v. Kline, 476 F. Supp. 583, 603-04 (E.D. Pa. 1979), *aff'd on other grounds sub nom.* Battle v. Pennsylvania, 629 F.2d 269 (3d Cir. 1980), *cert. denied,* 452 U.S. 968 (1981). *See also* Comment, *Self-Sufficiency Under the Education for All Handicapped Children Act: A Suggested Judicial Approach,* 1981 DUKE L.J. 516; Note, *Defining an "Appropriate Education,"* supra note 8, at 106-09; Note, *The Education for All Handicapped Children Act: What Is a "Free Appropriate Public Education"?*, 29 WAYNE L. REV. 1285, 1291 (1983). This approach was also suggested by Judge Mansfield, dissenting from the court of appeals' decision to affirm in Rowley v. Board of Educ., 632 F.2d 945, 952-53 (2d Cir. 1980), but was rejected by the U.S. Supreme Court. 458 U.S. 176, 201 n.23 (1981).

155. *Cf.* B. ACKERMAN, *supra* note 13, at 18 (describing the "nightmare world where all human diversity has been destroyed in the name of an equality that levels everyone to the lowest common denominator").

156. *Cf.* J. RAWLS, A THEORY OF JUSTICE 78 (1971) (describing the "difference principle," which justifies inequalities in resource allocation only if necessary to improve the position of the worse-off in society).

157. *See, e.g.,* B. Ackerman, *supra* note 13, at 270 ("[W]hatever the strain placed on statesmanly judgment the standard of negative compensation does *not* impose the insatiable demand implied by a maximizing principle."); Frankel, *supra* note 82, at 201 ("Some general system of social cost accounting, which assigns different values to the satisfaction of different wants, . . . has to be employed."); J. FISHKIN, *supra* note 83, at 46. *See also* Dworkin, *supra* note 152, at 297-300 (developing insurance model to set upward limit on extraordinary expenses for individuals with extraordinary needs); Baker, *Outcome Equality or Equality of Respect: The Substantive Content of Equal Protection,* 131 U. PA. L. REV. 933, 941 (1983); *infra* note 186.

outcome equality, one might seek instead to allocate resources so that all children have the opportunity to reach certain minimal goals, distributing any remaining resources to children with higher potential so that they may attain further goals. This reallocation principle would permit equality in the opportunity to achieve at certain minimum levels (at least insofar as a child is capable of reaching such a level),[158] higher levels being available according to criteria that *may discriminate on the basis of handicap*. This approach requires the definition of the minimum educational levels to be afforded to students regardless of handicap. The factors which make this task especially problematic are outlined below in the discussion of *Board of Education v. Rowley*.[159]

Instead of equalizing the opportunity to attain certain standardized results, one might attempt to equalize the opportunity to attain reasonable educational goals set in accordance with each child's own particular needs. This variation of equality aims at equalizing the likelihood of reaching goals that are equivalently suitable for each person,[160] and responds to limitations in resources by scaling down the programs proportionately for *all children* so that they are subjected equally to the effects of resource shortfall. This approach pursues parity, acknowledging that needs vary but that the strength of an individual's claim for limited resources should not. I develop this approach further in the following section.

C. Program Parity

Program parity requires that educational needs be identified for every child and programs hypothesized to satisfy those needs. Resource availability would then determine what portion of a child's needs could be met, and schools would adjust programs so that each child would be afforded the same portion (or relative deprivation) as others.[161] The purpose of this standard is to ensure that in allocating scarce resources, some students are not favored

---

158. See Stark, *supra* note 2, at 499; Haggerty & Sacks, *Education of the Handicapped: Towards a Definition of an Appropriate Education*, 50 TEMP. L.Q. 961, 974-75 (1977). This is essentially the approach taken by the Supreme Court in interpreting the EAHCA in Board of Educ. v. Rowley, 458 U.S. 176 (1981).

159. 458 U.S. 176 (1982); *see infra* text accompanying notes 174-76.

160. This principle might be confined to handicapped children who are incapable, regardless of program, of reaching the same goals that would otherwise be set for nonhandicapped children. It might also be appropriate, however, where there is an intolerably large disparity between the incremental advances in achievement (made possible by additional resources) attainable by handicapped and nonhandicapped children.

161. Judith Wegner has described this approach as an "equivalent opportunity" test, and criticized it for its lack of judicially manageable criteria. Wegner, *Variations on a Theme—The Concept of Equal Educational Opportunity and Programming Decisions Under the Education for All Handicapped Children Act of 1975*, LAW & CONTEMP. PROBS., Winter 1985, at 169, 184-85, 192-93. The district court in Rowley v. Board of Educ., 483 F. Supp. 528, 534 (S.D.N.Y. 1980), set forth a similar standard, but with quite different implications. This standard required that the shortfall between a handicapped child's *potential* and his or her performance be measured and then compared to the shortfall experienced by nonhandicapped children. *Id.* Because potential was determined in *Rowley* without regard to the child's physical handicap, the standard, as applied *in that case* required that the effects of the child's handicap be eliminated as far as possible. A number of commentators have made a similar move, describing first a comparability-of-opportunity standard and then applying a standard in which the effects of handicap are to be eliminated. *See* Note, *Enforcing the Right, supra* note 8, at 1125-27;

over others. More precisely, the standard ensures that decisionmakers do not disfavor members of certain targeted groups and make them absorb more than their fair share of the effects of resource scarcity.

The concept of program parity begins with the identification of "first-rate" educational programs. A first-rate educational program is not one for which improvements cannot be imagined, but rather one that is reasonably comprehensive and which adopts the highest standards of practice among professionals in the field. There is reason to believe that such programs can be identified, at least in general categories.[162] Theoretically, one could begin this process by defining an *optimal* program, and work down from there in parallel fashion for all educational programs.

There are many practical problems even at this first stage. Just as educational minimums are extremely problematic,[163] so educational maximums are elusive as well. One can nearly always imagine additional incremental services of higher quality programs that could be offered to a student to improve his opportunity for learning—additional tutoring, for example, or teacher pay raises. Moreover, developing hypothetical programs that are not ultimately affordable will be considered a wasteful effort, effort that would be better spent in providing direct educational services. Still further, comparisons of quality will be difficult, and the threshold questions to sort out nearly endless: With what children and with what programs should determination of needs and quality of program be made for purposes of comparison with the programs offered to handicapped children? By what measures will needs be determined? By what standards will the quality of programs be judged? How can shortfall be measured? On what basis could one conclude that the programs for numerous different groups of children be rated as "comparable" to a first-rate program for a handicapped child? Is it possible to compare, for example, the quality of a resource center for the learning disabled or the self-contained classroom for a moderately retarded child with the regular fifth grade program of a nonhandicapped child or the special library period for the gifted?

These difficult questions have influenced courts to avoid application of comparative standards.[164] The high degree of skepticism shown over such comparisons, however, is unwarranted. Comparative judgments about the

Note, *Attack on the EHA: The Education for All Handicapped Children Act After Board of Education v. Rowley*, 7 U. PUGET SOUND L. REV. 183, 189 n.46 (1983) [hereinafter cited as Note, *Attack on the EHA*].

162. *See* Jordan & Stultz, *Projecting the Educational Needs and Costs of Elementary and Secondary Education*, in EDUCATIONAL NEED IN THE PUBLIC ECONOMY 163, 177 (1976) (establishing weights for making cost estimates of special education based upon practices by reputedly good or high quality programs). Haggerty & Sacks, *supra* note 158, at 989 n.170.

163. *See infra* section IV D.

164. *See, e.g.*, Board of Educ. v. Rowley, 458 U.S. 176, 198 (1981) (requirement of equal educational opportunities an "unworkable standard requiring impossible measurements and comparisons"); *cf.* San Antonio Indep. School Dist. v. Rodriguez, 411 U.S. 1, 25 (1972) (no system can assure equal quality of education, except in the most relative sense); McInnis v. Shapiro, 293 F. Supp. 327, 335-36 (N.D. Ill. 1968) (three-judge panel) (no manageable standards by which court can require expenditures by schools in relation to a child's need, or in equal amounts), *aff'd sub nom.* McInnis v. Ogilvie, 394 U.S. 322 (1969).

quality of education are commonly made[165]—most persons would acknowledge the superiority of the education available in Scarsdale over Harlem—and many more refined comparisons are routinely made by educators. These judgments are at least as precise as those required under *Board of Education v. Rowley* to determine what educational services are required to permit a child to receive "some educational benefit."[166]

Even where precise comparisons are difficult, program parity is a useful general guide to decisionmaking. It is the principle — the legal, political, and moral goal — that most accurately describes the nature of the task that policymakers should adopt in ensuring and implementing education for the handicapped. It is a principle that helps to apply more specific, though still elusive, standards such as an "appropriate education," and which suggests a vision of justice for the handicapped that can guide not only judges, but also legislators, regulators, service providers, and others upon whom the fate of handicapped children in the schools ultimately rests.

Under the program parity approach, the handicapped child will not be entitled to any *particular* level of services, so long as what the child is offered is comparable to the services offered to others in the school district. This approach is vulnerable to the criticism that the handicapped child in a poorer school district will be entitled to less than his counterpart in a wealthier district. This criticism highlights a deficiency in public education generally, however, rather than a weakness in the concept of program parity. Program parity does not require that the level of education generally available to children in all districts, including poor districts, be sacrificed so that handicapped children can enjoy services that are measurably *superior* to those offered to nonhandicapped children. By the same token, handicapped children in wealthy districts will not be limited by a level of average or minimal educational entitlements; their entitlements will be equal to the level of educational services available to nonhandicapped children. Program parity reflects, but does not aggravate, the wealth disparities among school districts in this country today.

The concept of program parity directly addresses the issue of cost in special education. It affirms that cost is a legitimate factor to take into account in determining what educational program should be offered to a handicapped child, as it is already in determining the level of educational programs available to nonhandicapped children. The program parity standard requires that consideration of cost be overt, open to scrutiny by reviewing courts, parents, and the public. It requires explicit analysis of the resource allocation issue and puts that analysis into view for possible response by parents, school offi-

---

165. *See, e.g.*, EDUCATIONAL EVALUATION METHODOLOGY: THE STATE OF THE ART (R. Berk ed. 1981); Doud, *NSSE Elementary School Evaluative Criteria: A Guide to School Improvement Through Evaluation*, 56 NORTH CENT. A.Q. 402 (1983). *See also* Kaden, *Courts and Legislatures in a Federal System: The Case of School Finance*, 11 HOFSTRA L. REV. 1205, 1212 (1983) (discussing measurements of school quality by educational outputs, educational inputs, and evaluations of school programs); *cf.* A. WISE, LEGISLATED LEARNING 12-27 (1979) (educational evaluations focus on student achievement levels rather than quality of opportunities offered to students).

166. *See* 458 U.S. 176, 200-04 (1982). For a discussion of this standard, *see infra* section IV D.

cials, and elected representatives.[167]

Program parity sets substantive limits on the extent to which cost may bear on program choice, refining the assertion often made that scarcity of funding should not be permitted to bear more heavily on handicapped than on nonhandicapped children.[168] Where types of services exist that can be comparable between handicapped and nonhandicapped children, the concept of program parity suggests that the kinds of services that are offered to nonhandicapped children should ordinarily be offered to handicapped children as well. Cases holding that summer programs should be offered to handicapped children whenever they are offered to the nonhandicapped exemplify this analysis.[169] Such parallelism, however, will in most cases be absent, and even where present it may suggest services that either fall short or go beyond the duty required under the program parity standard.

Program parity would encourage further scrutiny of comparisons between educational programs offered handicapped children and nonhandicapped children, to assess whether significant disparities in quality exist. Factors such as overcrowding, high student/teacher ratios, low teacher salaries, outdated

---

167. In fact, in establishing a substantive standard under which the issue of cost is apparently, but unrealistically, irrelevant, see supra notes 35-37 and accompanying text, the Court in Board of Educ. v. Rowley, 458 U.S. 176 (1982), drives the issue of cost underground, rendering it a more dangerous, less controllable factor in educational decisions that are made for handicapped children than the standard of program parity would allow. See infra note 186.

168. See, e.g., Crawford v. Pittman, 708 F.2d 1028, 1035 (5th Cir. 1983); Yaris v. Special School Dist., 558 F. Supp. 545, 559 (E.D. Mo. 1983), aff'd, 728 F.2d 1055 (8th Cir. 1984). This analysis is supported in legislative history of the EAHCA that cites language from Mills v. Board. of Educ., 348 F. Supp. 866, 876 (D.D.C. 1972):

> If sufficient funds are not available to finance all of the services and programs that are needed and desirable in the system then the available funds must be expended equitably in such a manner that no child is entirely excluded from a publicly supported education consistent with his needs and ability to benefit therefrom. The inadequacies of the . . . Public School System whether occasioned by insufficient funding or administrative inefficiency, certainly cannot be permitted to bear more heavily on the 'exceptional' or handicapped child than on the normal child.

S. REP. No. 168, 94th Cong., 1st Sess. 23, reprinted in 1975 U.S. CODE CONG. & AD. NEWS 1425, 1447. This authority is somewhat ambiguous, for its meaning depends upon the weight given to the Mills language that no child should be entirely excluded from public education. The Supreme Court in Board of Educ. v. Rowley, 458 U.S. 176 (1982), clearly means to restrict the language in Mills to the exclusion of handicapped children from a meaningful education, not to define a right dependent upon "impossible measurements and comparisons." Id. at 198. "Mills . . . speaks in terms of 'adequate' educational services, 348 F. Supp. at 878, and sets a realistic standard of providing some educational services to each child when every need cannot be met." 458 U.S. at 193 n.15.

169. See, e.g., Yaris v. Special School Dist., 558 F. Supp. 545 (E.D. Mo. 1983), aff'd, 728 F.2d 1055 (8th Cir. 1984). If a school offers summer programs to nonhandicapped children, it would seem unfair to require handicapped children to make a showing that a summer program was necessary to prevent them from regressing in the gains experienced during the regular 180-day school year, as was at issue in Yaris. This requirement is typical in cases challenging the 180-day school year where summer programs are generally not available to any children. See Georgia Ass'n of Retarded Citizens v. McDaniel, 716 F.2d 1565, 1573-76 (11th Cir. 1983), vacated, 104 S. Ct. 3581 (1984); Battle v. Pennsylvania, 629 F.2d 269 (3d Cir. 1980), cert. denied, 452 U.S. 968 (1981); Bales v. Clarke, 523 F. Supp. 1366 (E.D. Va. 1981); see also Irving Indep. School Dist. v. Tatro, 104 S. Ct. 3371 (1984) (catheterization for handicapped child comparable to school nurse services available to nonhandicapped); Helms v. Indep. School Dist. No. 3, 750 F.2d 820 (10th Cir. 1984) (handicapped children entitled to more than twelve years of public education where handicapped children permitted to repeat grades until they graduate).

facilities, and limited materials in the school system might justify a lower level of services to handicapped children than if the school system enjoyed modern and ample facilities, the most advanced laboratory resources, the best-trained and most highly paid teachers, and the latest, innovative educational programs.[170] Comparisons with spending patterns in other school districts or states,[171] perhaps assisted by data and guidelines generated by a centralized administrative agency, would be helpful in evaluating spending patterns in a particular school district.[172]

Program parity identifies what is fair and just in terms of the district's ability to bear the cost of expensive programs. This ability to bear the cost is a factor used in resolving questions of cost under section 504 of the Rehabilitation Act of 1973[173] and other nondiscrimination statutes. Under the program parity standard, however, the ability to bear the cost explicitly goes beyond what resources the district may have reserved for the handicapped, using the broader reference point of the level of quality the district is willing to fund for programs for nonhandicapped children.

The concept of program parity mediates the tensions between the EAHCA and the institutional context of public education described in part III of this article. It integrates individualized assessments into the institutional setting of collective decisionmaking by more precisely and accurately defining the problem in both individual and collective terms: how to marshal some fair share of public resources for the individual handicapped child for a service generally available to others. It resolves this problem by coordinating individualized and collective decisionmaking. Although need must be identified individually, the required level of educational services for the handicapped

---

170. See Note, *Enforcing the Right, supra* note 8, at 1126-27; Note, *The Rowley Decision, supra* note 11, at 705.

171. See, e.g., Crawford v. Pittman, 708 F.2d 1028, 1035 n.31 (5th Cir. 1983) ("Mississippi is not now parsimonious in its aid to the handicapped. In the 1979-80 school year, the state expended almost five dollars for the handicapped for every one dollar in federal funding it received for that purpose. For the 1978-79 school year, the ratio was $7.30 to $1.00 . . ."); Garrity v. Gallen, 522 F. Supp. 171, 224 (D.N.H. 1981) (Whereas the national average of state money going to special education is 3.63 percent of every dollar spent on education, New Hampshire spends only .9 percent of every dollar on special education.); Espino v. Besteiro, 520 F. Supp. 905, 912 (S.D. Tex. 1981) (Cost of air-conditioned classroom for handicapped child minimal in relation to the amount of federal funds received by the school district and in relation to the district's total budget.); *see also* Yaris v. Special School Dist., 558 F. Supp. 545, 559 n.7 (E.D. Mo. 1983) ("[T]this court can not help but note that only one state in the country appropriates less funds than the State of Missouri for its educational system"), *aff'd*, 728 F.2d 1055, (8th Cir. 1984); Springdale School Dist. v. Grace, 494 F. Supp. 266, 272 (W.D. Ark. 1980) ("The school provides the nonhandicapped child an opportunity to learn the basics and to learn them well enough so that he might excel in his secondary school courses. But the . . . school does not turn every one of its students into academicians or professionals, or even successful secondary school students."), *aff'd*, 656 F.2d 300 (8th Cir. 1981), *vacated*, 458 U.S. 1118 (1982), *aff'd on rehearing*, 693 F.2d 41 (8th Cir. 1982), *cert. denied*, 461 U.S. 927 (1983).

172. Much of the data collection and analysis for such guidelines has already taken place. *See, e.g.*, KAKALIK, *supra* note 2; MOORE, WALKER & HOLLAND, *supra* note 3.

173. 29 U.S.C. § 794 (1982); *see* 34 C.F.R. § 104.12(c) (1984); 29 C.F.R. § 1613.704 (1984); Treadwell v. Alexander, 707 F.2d 473, 478 (11th Cir. 1983); Colin K. v. Schmidt, 536 F. Supp. 1375, 1388 (D.R.I. 1982), *aff'd*, 715 F.2d 1 (1st Cir. 1983); *see also* 29 U.S.C. § 794a(a)(1) (1982) (remedy for violation of section 504 should take into account reasonableness of cost of any necessary accommodations).

child is determined by reference to what has been determined to be available for the nonhandicapped. Data for decisionmaking is highly individualized as it is not for other children, but entitlements for the handicapped are determined, in the final analysis, as part of an integrated process in which the needs and interests of the handicapped are coordinated with the needs and interests of others.

The program parity model, similarly, mediates the tension between the need-based framework for determining educational services for the handicapped and the merit-based framework of public education. Program parity recognizes that there are differences in need and ability that will justify different treatment, but compels evenhanded consideration of the interests of both. Differences in ability between the handicapped and nonhandicapped justify neither a lower level of attention, because of the inability of the handicapped to demonstrate the same levels of "innate" ability, nor compensation for the handicapped so extensive as to eliminate as far as educationally possible the effects of that handicap without regard to resource limitations. Instead, it requires school districts to offer services based on need to the handicapped on a par with services to others whose positions in the system will still be based on merit. Merit thus retains its established place in the public education system without compromising the need-based rationale for allocating resources to the handicapped.

The program parity model also addresses the tension between the centralized standards of the EAHCA and the tradition of local control of education by focusing federal intervention on the appropriate federal interest — ending unfair treatment of the handicapped in public education — while preserving the traditional role of state and local government for determining the appropriate content and quality of educational services. As I will explain in the next section of this article, recent constructions of the EAHCA have been insensitive to the real issue of federalism. Although the legal analysis in *Board of Education v. Rowley* is replete with invocations of the demands of federalism — that matters of educational methodology should be left up to the individual states[174] and that "due weight" should be given to state administrative proceedings[175] — the educational benefit test set forth in that opinion is more offensive to basic federalism policies than the test I suggest.

D. Program Parity and Educational Minimums

Under *Rowley*, the EAHCA is satisfied só long as its procedural requirements are followed and the handicapped child is receiving "access to specialized instruction and related services which are individually designed to provide educational benefit to the handicapped child."[176] This standard, in interpreting the EAHCA to require a minimum level of education for the handicapped to be determined without respect to the benefits received by

---

174.   458 U.S. 176, 207 (1982).
175.   *Id.* at 206.
176.   *Id.* at 201.

other children, forces judgments that (1) cannot meaningfully be made, and (2) should not be directed by the federal government.

Education is a purposive enterprise. Hence, any definition of a minimum can be formulated only by reference to the function education fulfills in achieving particular goals. Although there is agreement on certain general social, political, economic, and cultural goals in public education,[177] consensus at the implementation level is impossible and probably undesirable. Communities have different needs and different priorities for their educational systems. Indeed, this diversity, which may reflect political differences of opinion and local variations in employment opportunities, is a primary reason for allocating control over education to state and local governments.[178] Disagreement may exist about the desired level of educational services. Is the minimal goal of education respecting competence economic survival, getting a job, or getting a *good* job? Disagreement may also exist about the importance of certain types of learning: Should the goal of education be intellectual development or socialization skills? basic communication and computational skills or the ability to pursue and analyze abstract ideas? vocational training or preparation for higher education, science, or the liberal arts? excellence in one field or basic coverage of many? Teaching techniques and methods also vary, some schools preferring rote learning, others the process of free inquiry. Differences of opinion are particularly numerous in the relatively new field of special education. Unitary standards suggest that the subject of regulation is susceptible to having a uniform, best answer. Because of the diversity of educational priorities, theories, methodologies and needs, however, "certainty bespeaks ignorance."[179]

Even if the goals of education could be determined, the role of education in achieving them is incremental. While minimums may have some significance with respect to certain basic goods and services such as housing and food,[180] the nature of the education process makes the notion of minimums

---

177. These include the socialization of students within our political and cultural system, the acquisition of skills to enable them to be productive members of the economic system, and the development of social skills. *See, e.g.,* Plyler v. Doe, 457 U.S. 202, 221-22 (1982) (education "provides the basic tools by which individuals might lead economically productive lives to the benefit of us all . . . . [it] has a fundamental role in maintaining the fabric of our society . . . . [and has a] pivotal role . . . in sustaining our political and cultural heritage"); Wisconsin v. Yoder, 406 U.S. 205, 221 (1972) ("some degree of education is necessary to prepare citizens to participate effectively and intelligently in our open political system"); Brown v. Board of Educ., 347 U.S. 483, 493 (1954) (education is a "principal instrument in awakening the child to cultural values, in preparing him for later professional training, and in helping him to adjust normally to his environment."); Serrano v. Priest, 5 Cal. 3d 584, 604-06, 487 P.2d 1241, 1255-56, 96 Cal. Rptr. 601, 615-16 (1947) ("[F]irst, education is a major determinant of an individual's chances for economic and social success in our competitive society; second, education is a unique influence on a child's development as a citizen and his participation in political and community life.").

178. *See supra* notes 133-35 and accompanying text.

179. Kaden, *supra* note 165, at 1242. *See* San Antonio Indep. School Dist. v. Rodriguez, 411 U.S. 1, 42 (1972) ("Education, perhaps even more than welfare assistance, presents a myriad of intractable economic, social and even philosophical problems.") (citing Dandridge v. Williams, 397 U.S. 471, 487 (1970)).

180. Michelman, *Foreword: On Protecting the Poor Through the Fourteenth Amendment,* 83 HARV. L. REV. 7 (1969). *Cf.* Karst, Serrano v. Priest's *Inputs and Outputs,* 38 LAW & CONTEMP. PROBS. 333, 344-

hopelessly elusive. One can speak of more or less education, but once beyond zero education, not of minimums. A fifth grade education generally will be more beneficial than a fourth grade education and less beneficial than a sixth grade education, but it cannot be meaningfully said that one level or another is a *minimum* level of education. Thus it is that in making educational program decisions, school officials and school boards do not in any realistic sense engage in establishing minimums, but rather in evaluating better and worse alternatives.[181] Although school finance theory presumes that states assume responsibility for a minimum level of education to be supplemented by higher service levels chosen and financed by the local system,[182] school budgets are actually set "incrementally and with reference to the availability of funds for education."[183]

Education is ordinarily valued also in relative terms. An important purpose of education is to prepare students for a competitive economy based on merit and achievement. Thus, the need for a student to learn advanced calculus, computer science, or fluent Spanish is determined in part by whether others whom a student will later face in the educational system or the job market have been trained in those subjects. For this reason, educational mini-

---

45 (1974). Even with respect to these basic human needs, the value attached to particular service levels is relative to what others receive. *See* Winter, *Poverty, Economic Equality, and the Equal Protection Clause,* 1972 Sup. Ct. Rev. 41, 71 ("no finite list of goods and services" that will remove poverty).

181. *Cf.* Miner, *Estimates of Adequate School Spending by State Based on National Average Service Levels,* 8 J. Educ. Fin. 316 (1983) (conceptualizing "adequate" level of education according to average national expenditures).

182. *See* Lujan v. Colorado State Bd. of Educ., 649 P.2d 1005, 1025 (Colo. 1982); Buse v. Smith, 74 Wis.2d 550, 570-74, 247 N.W.2d 141, 151-52 (1976); Wise, *supra* note 67, at 308-09. School finance cases often involve the interpretation of state constitutional provisions designed to define the minimum level of acceptable education in that state. *See* Lujan, 649 P.2d at 1018 ("thorough and efficient" no mandate for equal expenditure); McDaniel v. Thomas, 248 Ga. 632, 285 S.E.2d 156, 165 (1981) (state constitution requires provision of "adequate education," which means basic education and *not* equality of opportunity); Hornbeck v. Somerset County Bd. of Educ., 295 Md. 597, 619-39, 458 A.2d 758, 770-80, (1983) ("thorough and efficient education" clause does not mandate equality of expenditure); Board of Educ. v. Nyquist, 57 N.Y.2d 27, 47, 439 N.E.2d 359, 453 N.Y.S.2d 643, 653 (1982) (state constitution assures only "minimal [sic] acceptable facilities and services" in education and not equal facilities and services), *appeal dismissed,* 459 U.S. 1139 (1983); Seattle v. Washington, 90 Wash. 2d 476, 514-20, 585 P.2d 71, 93-96 (1978) (applying Wash. Const. art. 9, §§ 1, 2, to mandate state funding of a basic program of education for all children); Pauley v. Kelly, 255 S.E.2d 859, 878-79 (W. Va. 1979) ("thorough and efficient" education clause requires development of high quality statewide standards, something more than mere equality of funding to counties). *But see* Robinson v. Cahill, 62 N.J. 473, 513-14, 303 A.2d 273, 294 (1973) (applying the "thorough and efficient" education standard of the New Jersey Constitution to require equal educational opportunity).

183. Wise, *supra* note 67, at 314; *see also* A. Wise, *supra* note 88, at 145 ("In effect, educators are viewed as setting norms for all students at a level which will just exhaust available educational resources."); Karst, *supra* note 180, at 344.

In expressing the complexity of the notion of educational adequacy, Wise concludes that "adequacy is in the eye of several beholders and may be appraised formally or informally and against a uniform or flexible standard." Wise, *supra* note 67, at 310. He concludes that the concept of educational adequacy is in fact a redefinition of the problem of equal educational opportunity. *Id.* at 315. For a critique of the similar concept of "functional literacy" as a description of minimum norms, *see* Levine, *Functional Literacy: Fond Illusions and False Economics,* 52 Harv. Educ. Rev. 249 (1982); *see also* Robinson v. Cahill, 62 N.J. 515, 303 A.2d 273, 295 (1973) (describing the constitutional mandate of a "thorough and efficient education" as a relative concept).

mums are "significantly a function of the maximum."[184] Moreover, on an individual level, it is clear that the value of education is derived from what the individual child himself is able to make of what education is provided. The emphasis on the equality of *opportunity* rather than educational achievement or results recognizes that children cannot be forced to learn, that they vary in motivation and receptivity to education, and that their academic rewards will depend in large part on the nature of their voluntary engagement with what is offered to them.[185]

Not only does the minimum educational benefit standard require judgments that cannot meaningfully be made, but it requires judgments that should not be directed by the federal government. Enforcing educational standards at a particular level, even if only a "minimum" level and even if only for the handicapped, removes from local and state government a function that is particularly critical to its authority over education. Moreover, it ignores the issue of fairness of treatment for a discrete, disadvantaged group — the handicapped — which is the more appropriate domain of federal intervention.[186]

The legislative history of the EAHCA is consistent with the view that the federal interest in education is comparative rather than absolute. Concern with fairness between the handicapped and the nonhandicapped pervades this history.[187] Although there was a wide range of opinions expressed in Con-

---

184. Michelman, *supra* note 180, at 58. Michelman, who urges the minimum protection view with respect to other human needs, recognizes that this view is especially problematic with respect to education. *See id.* at 19, 47-59. *See also* Winter, *supra* note 180, at 71.

185. The school environment may, in turn, have an effect in influencing the educational aspirations and motivations of its students. *See* Katz, *Academic Motivation and Equal Educational Opportunity,* 38 Harv. Educ. Rev. 57 (1968), *reprinted in* Equal Educational Opportunity at 60 (1969); Wilson, *supra* note 85, at 80-81, *reprinted in* Equal Educational Opportunity at 83-84; *see also supra* note 141 and accompanying text (importance of home life to success in school).

186. Ironically, because of the relativity of educational norms and the subjectivity of educational minimums, the *Rowley* "some benefit" approach used in Board of Educ. v. Rowley, 458 U.S. 176 (1982), may in some cases be used to compel school districts to provide to the handicapped educational services that are excessive and unfair to the nonhandicapped. This is all the more likely if Professor Wegner is correct in her analysis that a rigorous standard must be applied to the process of identifying a child's needs and appropriate educational program. *See* Wegner, *supra* note 161, at 186-94; *see also* Zirkel, *Building an Appropriate Education from* Board of Education v. Rowley, 42 Md. L. Rev. 466, 481-84, 487 (1983) (*Rowley* may be interpreted in some circumstances to set high substantive demands on school districts); Note, *The Rowley Decision, supra* note 11, at 703-04 (courts will interpret the *Rowley* standard in light of their own theories); Colley, *supra* note 11, at 152 (suggesting there might be a reverse discrimination problem under the EAHCA).

The some benefit test, as explained above, takes no explicit account of the cost of a program. If the standard is given real teeth, and cost factors are ignored, the nonhandicapped may be forced to bear a disproportionate share of the effects of resource scarcity. Placing a duty upon a school district to provide a full-time residential placement with a full range of round-the-clock educational stimulation may have a ruinous effect on its budget and on other educational programs while achieving only a *de minimis* benefit for the handicapped. *See* Stark, *supra* note 2, at 493; Adams Cent. School Dist. v. Deist, 215 Neb. 284, 285-87; 338 N.W.2d 591, 591-92 (1983), *aff'g as modified,* 214 Neb. 307, 334 N.W. 2d 775 (1983), *cert. denied,* 104 S. Ct. 239 (1984). Thus, at the same time that the duty to provide "some benefit" may leave handicapped children at a marked disadvantage in asserting a claim for resources, it may impose a backbreaking obligation upon school districts attempting to serve a severely handicapped child for whom benefit is extraordinarily elusive.

187. *See* S. Rep. No. 168, 94th Cong., 1st Sess. 9, *reprinted in* 1975 U.S. Code Cong. & Ad. News 1425, 1433 ("This Nation has long embraced a philosophy that the right to a free appropriate public education is basic to equal opportunity. . . . It is contradictory to that philosophy when that right is

gress at the time the EAHCA was passed, the focus on equal educational opportunity is impressive. Evidence in the legislative history that many handicapped children in the United States were being entirely excluded from education was emphasized by the Supreme Court in *Board of Education v. Rowley* to justify the minimum benefit standard.[188] This concern for the total exclusion of handicapped children must be analyzed, however, in light of the fact that at the time, nonhandicapped children did have access to public education. It was *this* disparity that Congress sought to correct. This is not to say that Congress could not legitimately be concerned if it determined that no child was receiving a proper education, and undertake drastic measures to correct the situation, even assuming direct control over the nation's education system under its common power. Congress also may set out to improve the level or quality of public education in some particular way, as it has done through various federal aid-to-education programs.[189] Indeed, Congress surely intended to improve the quality of education for the handicapped in passing the EAHCA.[190] When Congress undertakes to identify a group that has been previously disadvantaged in receiving public education that is available to others, however, and requires that an "appropriate" education be provided to members of that group, the meaning of the requirement should be ascertained in light of the generally accepted federal interest in equal treatment for

---

not assured equally to all groups of people within the Nation. . . . It is this Committee's belief that Congress must take a more active role under its responsibility for equal protection of the laws to guarantee that handicapped children are provided equal educational opportunity.").

The Congressional Record also overflows with references to the goal of equal educational opportunity for the handicapped. *See* 121 CONG. REC. 19,503 (1975) (remarks of Sen. Cranston) ("[The Act's] enactment will signify a new beginning and the broadening of equal opportunity for all our children."); *id.* at 37,410 (remarks of Sen. Randolph) ("The [EAHCA] promises handicapped children the educational opportunity that has long been considered the right of every other American child."); *id.* at 25,540 (remarks of Rep. Grassley) ("[h]andicapped children have always been slighted on equal educational opportunity.").

The House and Senate reports both contained language which linked services that were to be provided to the handicapped to services that were being provided to the nonhandicapped. *See, e.g.,* S. REP. No. 168, 94th Cong., 1st Sess. 12, *reprinted in* 1975 U.S. CODE CONG. & AD. NEWS 1425, 1436. The report stated:

The Committee points out in addition that a handicapped child has a right to receive all services normally provided a nonhandicapped child. . . . Thus, he or she has a right to physical education services, . . . transportation services and all other services . . . provided to all children within the school system, and a right to as many options in curricula as are available to all children.

Id.; H. R. REP. No. 332, 94th Cong., 1st Sess. 10 (1975) ("The committee would like to see that each handicapped child to the best of his or her ability be able to participate in extracurricular activities to the same extent as nonhandicapped children."); *see also* 34 C.F.R. §§ 300.305-.306 (1984). For a more complete collection of statements relating to the Act's objectives of equal opportunity for handicapped children, see Note, *Attack on the EHA supra* note 161, at 194-96. *Cf.* Commonwealth v. School Comm. of Springfield, 382 Mass. 675-79, 417 N.E.2d 408, 414-15 (1981) (purpose of state law regarding education of the handicapped is to prevent denials of equal educational opportunity).

188. 458 U.S. 176, 191-97 (1982).

189. *See, e.g.,* National Defense Education Act of 1958, 20 U.S.C. § 401 (omitted 1982 because programs have not been funded for a number of years); Education Consolidation and Improvement Act of 1981, 20 U.S.C. §§ 3801-3876 (1982).

190. *See, e.g.,* H.R. REP. No. 332, 94th Cong., 1st Sess. 10, 11 (1975) (describing unserved population of handicapped children); 121 Cong. Rec. H7148 (remarks of Rep. Brandemas) (need for federal government to act if substantial progress to be made in education for the handicapped).

the disadvantaged, and in recognition of the relative nature of education. The alternative—a federal definition of the required level of services—embarks the federal government on an expedition outside the customary boundaries of federal intervention in education for which it is unsuited.

The minimum educational benefit standard has received some support in academic literature.[191] In addition, the United States Supreme Court has appeared to rely upon a concept of educational minimums in two recent equal protection cases. These cases require further attention.

In *San Antonio Independent School District v. Rodriguez,*[192] the Court implied that so long as every student had the opportunity for a "basic education," the state had no constitutional obligation to equalize that opportunity between school districts with varying taxing capacities.[193] Despite this opinion's apparent support of the notion of educational minimums,[194] *Rodriguez* did not actually decide whether a state is obligated to provide at least some minimal level of educational service.[195] To the extent that the Court may have implied that some minimal level of education was required, this level seemed to refer to anything higher than "an absolute denial of educational opportunities."[196] This rock bottom definition, which may be all that could be compelled by the United States Constitution, could hardly be adopted as a standard consistent with the ambitious goals of the EAHCA.

By speaking of the right of illegal alien children to a "basic education," the Court in *Plyler v. Doe*[197] may also be viewed as having endorsed the concept of educational minimums. *Plyler,* however, is an equal protection case holding that illegal alien children should have access to the public education system. Insofar as the Court speaks at all of the level of services for illegal alien children in relation to those offered to other children, the suggestion is that these services should be equivalent.[198]

It is clear that much of the concern with judicial interference in education, expressed in *Rodriguez* and *Plyler,* is a concern about the courts assuming a legislative role.[199] This concern is considerably less pertinent to an analysis of

---

191.   *See, e.g.,* Levinson, *The Right to a Minimally Adequate Education for Learning Disabled Children,* 12 VAL. U.L. REV. 253 (1978) (arguing for minimally adequate education for learning disabled children); McClung, *Do Handicapped Children Have a Legal Right to Minimum Adequate Education?,* 3 J. LEGAL EDUC. 153, 160 (1974). The minimum competency testing movement demonstrates the related belief that educational minimums can be defined. *See* McClung, *Competency Testing Programs: Legal and Educational Issues,* 47 FORDHAM L. REV. 651, 698-701 (1979); Young, *Legal Aspects of Minimum Competency Testing in the Schools,* 16 LAND & WATER L. REV. 561, 615-20 (1981); Logar, *Minimum Competency Testing in Schools: Legislative Action and Judicial Review,* 13 J.L. & EDUC. 35 (1984).
192.   411 U.S. 1 (1972).
193.   *Id.* at 36-37, 49.
194.   *See* Richards, *Equal Opportunity and School Financing: Towards a Moral Theory of Constitutional Adjudication,* 41 U. CHI. L. REV. 32, 63 (1973).
195.   411 U.S. at 36-37.
196.   *Id.* at 37.
197.   457 U.S. 202, 223, 226 (1982).
198.   "If the State is to deny a discrete group of innocent children the free public education that it offers to other children residing within its borders, that denial must be justified by a showing that it furthers some substantial state interest." Plyler v. Doe, 457 U.S. 202, 230 (1982) (emphasis added).
199.   *See Rodriguez,* 411 U.S. at 31; *cf.* A. BICKEL, THE LEAST DANGEROUS BRANCH 16-17 (1962).

what meaning should be given to federal legislation creating enforceable rights for certain individuals than it was in those cases responding to constitutional challenges to state education practices. It still raises an issue of federalism, however, insofar as the opportunity for judicial rulemaking under authority of federal legislation may enhance the risk of encroachment upon the prerogative of state and local government. A standard that requires setting a particular level of service, even a "minimum" or "adequate" level, engages a decisionmaker in establishing policy and defining norms for that service. This norm-setting assignment asks more of courts attempting to apply the EAHCA than would the task of ensuring fairness in educational programming between the handicapped and nonhandicapped; these latter efforts do not define educational norms, but rather discover and apply them.

This is not a point about *how much* power either the federal government or state and local governments should have. In fact, it has been forceably argued that an increased federal presence in education does not necessarily weaken local authority, and may instead strengthen it.[200] It is, rather, a point about the nature and quality of the federal presence.[201] A federal presence that extends to guaranteeing a particular, albeit "minimal," level of educational services to the handicapped may intrude in an activity best left in our federal system to state and local government, while failing to perform its intended federal function of protecting disadvantaged individuals vis a vis the majority.

---

200. *See* Cohen, *Policy and Organization: The Impact of State and Federal Educational Policy on School Governance,* 52 Harv. Educ. Rev. 474, 489 (1982).

201. *See* A. Wise, *supra* note 165, at x-xi (1979) (the enforcement of particular educational standards creates a more intrusive, bureaucratic, and centralizing federal presence than the enforcement of equal educational opportunity); *cf.* Wise, *Legal Challenges to Public School Finance,* 82 School Rev. 1, 20 (1973) ("If the state seriously develops a prescription for minimal educational outputs, it may well become a more important partner in education than many would like to see happen.")

The notion of federally imposed minimums should be rejected even as a supplement to the concept of program parity. For some handicapped children it may seem that a guarantee of a minimal level of education may be necessary in addition to a guarantee of "equal" treatment. *See* Note, *Enforcing the Right, supra* note 8, at 1126 n.146. A severely handicapped child, whose first-rate educational program—placement in a residential institution—can bear no quality cuts if she is to gain any benefit, will not require, however, the protection of the minimum educational benefit standard. The concept of program parity guarantees programs that yield a comparable *opportunity* to experience comparable educational benefit. For those children for whom the high price of a first-rate program cannot be scaled down or compromised under this principle, greater imagination might be shown in spreading the costs of that program widely throughout society. *See* Moore, Walker & Holland, *supra* note 3, at 59-76. Currently, the level of funding from the federal government under the EAHCA does not vary depending upon the severity of the handicap or the cost of the child's educational program. *See* Barro, *supra* note 118, at 50-51; 20 U.S.C. § 1411 (1982). It is already common for other state agencies to assume some of the extraordinary costs associated with educating the handicapped, often through interagency agreements. *See* Moore, Walker & Holland, *supra* note 3, at 39-40. Jurisdictional disputes between state agencies often frustrate the authorization of programs for children with extraordinary needs. *See, e.g.,* North v. District of Columbia Bd. of Educ., 471 F. Supp. 136, 141 (D.D.C. 1979); Parks v. Illinois Dep't of Mental Health, 110 Ill. App. 3d 184, 187-89, 441 N.E.2d 1209, 1212 (1982); Kerr Center Parents Ass'n v. Charles, 572 F. Supp. 448, 454-55 (D. Or. 1983). These kinds of disputes are discussed at length in Mooney & Aronson, *supra* note 49, at 545-46. *See also* Stoppleworth, *Mooney & Aronson Revisited: A Less Than Solomon-Like Solution to the Problem of Residential Placement of Handicapped Children,* 15 Conn. L. Rev. 757, 764 (1983); Leviton & Shuger, *Maryland's Exchangeable Children: A Critique of Maryland's System of Providing Services to Mentally Handicapped Children,* 42 Md. L. Rev. 823 (1983).

E.   Program Parity and Cost-Benefit Analysis

Because program parity admits the relevance of cost and requires comparisons of quality between unlike programs, there may frequently arise the question of whether it is appropriate to engage in any kind of cost-benefit analysis in order to determine whether a particular program is required. As an initial matter, it would seem that the EAHCA does not permit any calculations of relative value or cost-effectiveness. A statement made by one court, speaking of the expenditures that may be required to allow severely handicapped children to make only slight progress, is typical of judicial attitudes on this point: "The language and the legislative history of the Act simply do not entertain the possibility that some children may be untrainable."[202] The conclusion that cost-effectiveness factors cannot enter into decisionmaking under the Act, however, bears closer analysis.

Cost-benefit calculations are of two types (at least). First, cost-benefit considerations could be used in choosing between alternative programs to achieve the same or similar results. This use of cost-effectiveness analysis,[203] focusing on the choice of means for attaining given goals, surely should be acceptable in education, even commendable. If a placement in a child's home district can meet the child's needs as well as a placement outside the district and is less expensive, the district should not be required to arrange the out-of-district placement for the child based upon the personal preference, whim, or convenience of the parents. Likewise, the school should not be required to invest in expensive experimental technology that has not demonstrated its effectiveness for a handicapped child.[204]

Other forms of cost-benefit analysis are more problematic. Consider the example of an aide who will increase, if only slightly, the likelihood that a mildly-retarded student could learn to read at an elementary level, but who can be afforded only at the expense of a classroom computer that could be profitably used to learn basic computer skills by twenty-five nonhandicapped children in a regular, third grade class. This aide may be justified under a cost-benefit analysis if the value to the child is greater than the expense of the aide. Alternatively, the aide may be said to be cost-beneficial if the benefit

---

202.   Kruelle v. New Castle County School Dist., 642 F.2d 687, 695 (3d Cir. 1981); *see also* Stark, *supra* note 2, at 497-98.

203.   For a discussion of the difference between cost-benefit and cost-effectiveness analysis, see Bangser, *An Inherent Role for Cost-Benefit Analysis in Judicial Review of Agency Decisions: A New Perspective on OSHA Rulemaking*, 10 B.C. ENVTL. AFF. L. REV. 365, 405 (1982).

An excellent comparison of the various legislative models of cost-benefit analysis, including the cost-effective and strict cost-benefit approaches, is given in Rodgers, *Benefits, Costs and Risks: Oversight of Health and Environmental Decisionmaking*, 4 HARV. ENVTL. L. REV. 191, 201-14 (1980). Rodgers also discusses an intermediate form of analysis which he calls the "cost-sensitive approach." Under this approach, decisionmakers are given authority to make decisions in consideration of such factors as feasibility and economic practicability. *Id.* at 206-10. Because this form of analysis permits cost-efficiency calculations, I refer to it here as cost-efficiency analysis.

204.   It is this kind of calculation that Bruce Ackerman may have had in mind in suggesting a modified cost-benefit analysis in choosing between various contestable alternatives that fall within the acceptable range of equivalent sacrifices. B. ACKERMAN, *supra* note 13, at 249-50.

received by the handicapped children is greater than the value of a computer to the nonhandicapped children.

The first determination, whether the benefit justifies the cost on its own terms, would seem an appropriate calculation in designing education programs.[205] Why should programs be financed by the school system when the expected benefit is not greater than the cost? This analysis must be conducted carefully, however, for judgments of value can be extremely subjective and can easily incorporate the biases upon which education was denied for so long to handicapped children. Will value be measured only in terms of future economic productivity? Or will it take proper account of the value to the individual of self-growth and dignity or of self-reliance? Although it is often argued that education of the handicapped is ultimately cost-effective because otherwise the handicapped children will become more dependent upon public assistance,[206] such a utilitarian or efficiency analysis, in focusing on economic factors, has some potential for corrupting the task.[207]

The second type of cost-benefit calculation is considerably more suspect. In asking whether some children can use resources more productively than others, decisionmakers may well value learning by the handicapped less highly than learning by the nonhandicapped. By making the benefits of learning relevant and by allowing comparisons between the benefits experienced by different children, this analysis treats some human pleasures as replaceable by the pleasures of others. This is unacceptable. As H. L. A. Hart explains, for "a single individual to sacrifice a present satisfaction or pleasure for a greater satisfaction later" is prudent and virtuous, but to require one individual to sacrifice in order for another to gain, "treats the division between persons as of no more moral significance than the division between times which separates one individual's earlier pleasure from his later pleasures, as if individuals were mere parts of a single persisting entity."[208] Thus, while efficiency analysis to evaluate whether a service for a handicapped child is "worth it" should

---

205. This type of cost-benefit analysis was approved in Roncker v. Walter, 700 F.2d 1058 (6th Cir.), *cert. denied*, 104 S. Ct. 196 (1983), when the court pointed out that "some handicapped children simply must be educated in segregated facilities . . . because any marginal benefits received from mainstreaming are far outweighed by the benefits gained from services which would not feasibly be provided in the non-segregated setting . . . ." *Id.* at 1063; *see also* MOORE, WALKER & HOLLAND, *supra* note 3, at 37-38, 40-43 (recommending modification of special education program and state reimbursement policies to encourage more cost-effective service practices).

206. *See* S. REP. No. 168, 94th Cong., 1st Sess. 9, *reprinted in* 1975 U.S. CODE CONG. & AD. NEWS 1425, 1433; 121 CONG. REC. 19,492 (1975) (remarks of Sen. Williams) ("providing appropriate educational services now means that many of these individuals will be able to become a contributing part of our society, and they will not have to depend on subsistence payments from public funds.") Note, *The Education for All Handicapped Children Act: Opening the Schoolhouse Door*, 6 N.Y.U. REV. L. & SOC. CHANGE 43, 58 (1976); MOORE, WALKER & HOLLAND, *supra* note 3, at 33-34; *see also In re* Downey, 72 Misc. 2d 772, 340 N.Y.S.2d 687, 690 (1973) (cost of education and transportation of handicapped child minimal in light of cost of institutionalization and value of loss of potentially productive adult); Murdock, *Civil Rights of the Mentally Retarded: Some Critical Issues*, 48 NOTRE DAME LAW. 133, 164-65 (1972); Comment, *Toward a Legal Theory of the Right to Education of the Mentally Retarded*, 34 OHIO ST. L.J. 554, 559-60 (1973); Levinson, *supra* note 191, at 271-72 (disproportionate number of learning disabled among high school dropouts, juvenile delinquents, and criminals).

207. *See* R. DWORKIN, TAKING RIGHTS SERIOUSLY 237, 275 (1977).

208. Hart, *Between Utility and Rights*, 79 COLUM. L. REV. 828, 831 (1979).

be allowed only if engaged in very carefully, cost-benefit comparisons between services for the handicapped and the nonhandicapped should be avoided altogether.

The program parity approach to the cost issue avoids some of the pitfalls of a cost-efficiency analysis by assuming that the educational goals of handicapped and nonhandicapped children are equally worthy. Under progam parity, goals set on the basis of the needs and abilities of each child are not compared or evaluated in light of other children's goals, as would be required under a strict cost-benefit analysis. Instead, they are treated as givens entitled to the same respect and the same degree of fulfillment.

V

THE PROCESS OF EDUCATIONAL DECISIONMAKING

As noted above and discussed by a number of other authors in this symposium issue, the EAHCA specifies detailed procedures to be followed in reviewing whether handicapped children have received the educational services to which they are entitled.[209] The purpose of this section is not to review or analyze these procedures fully—the basic model is assumed to be fair and reasonable and the reader is assumed to be familiar with the process—but to suggest implications that a program parity model might have in clarifying and improving the process so as to promote fair resolution of cases with difficult cost issues.

A.   Problems in Judicial Procedure Under the EAHCA

There are two process issues which bear on consideration of cost as a factor under the Act: 1) the allocation of burdens of proof on the various substantive issues that may arise (including the issue of cost); and 2) the level of deference, if any, that should be given to decisions made at the different levels of local and state authority under the Act.

Both the burden of proof and the judicial deference issues can be particularly important when decisionmaking involves difficult and close factual determinations.[210] Decisionmaking under the EAHCA entails such determinations. The assessment of potential educational needs and the design of an appropriate educational program often raise close questions of educational methodology and philosophy and difficult predictions about the success of techniques and materials on the future development of a child.[211] If program parity is pursued, the issue of whether resources have been fairly allocated also raises difficult issues of educational quality and program comparison.

The EAHCA is not specific about where the burdens of proof lie on the

---

209.   20 U.S.C. § 1415 (1982).

210.   *See* Texas Dep't of Community Affairs v. Burdine, 450 U.S. 248, 255 n.8 (1981).

211.   *See supra* note 78; *cf.* Addington v. Texas, 441 U.S. 418, 430 (1979) (psychiatric assessments based on nuances, uncertainties, and subjective factors).

various issues arising under the Act,[212] and courts have not been consistent in allocating these burdens. As to the most litigated issue under the EAHCA of whether an offered program is "appropriate," a number of courts have put the burden of proof on school districts to show that the educational services offered to a child are appropriate.[213] A few courts have put the burden of proof on the plaintiffs who are challenging the educational program offered to the handicapped child to show that the program is inappropriate.[214] Others put the burden of persuasion squarely on the party seeking a *change* in placement,[215] with some courts appearing to set the burden by reference to a decision made at one or another particular procedural level.[216] Although the

---

212. *See* Lang v. Braintree School Comm., 545 F. Supp. 1221, 1226 (D. Mass. 1982).

213. *See, e.g.*, Grymes v. Madden, 672 F.2d 321, 322 (3d. Cir. 1982); Davis v. District of Columbia Bd. of Educ., 530 F. Supp. 1209, 1211-12 (D.D.C. 1982) ("It is the school district's burden of proof to show that its proposal is indeed an appropriate one."); Lang v. Braintree School Comm., 545 F. Supp. 1221, 1228 (D. Mass. 1982) (school district must show appropriateness of IEP by preponderance of the evidence); In re Richard H., 1980-81 EDUC. HANDICAPPED L. REP. (CRR) 502:203, :204 (Ga. SEA 1980); Scott B. v. Harlingen Consol. Indep. School Dist., 1982-83 EDUC. HANDICAPPED L. REP. (CRR) 504:344, :349 (Tex. SEA 1983) (interpreting Board of Educ. v. Rowley, 458 U.S. 176 (1982), as placing burden on school district).

The burden of proof has also been placed on the school district to demonstrate that the program offered is the least restrictive alternative. *See* Roncker v. Walter, 700 F.2d 1058, 1061 (6th Cir.), *cert. denied*, 104 S. Ct. 196 (1983) (school district must prove that its proposed placement affords maximum appropriate contact with nonhandicapped). This requirement has also been placed on state education agencies. *See* Mallory v. Drake, 616 S.W.2d 124, 126 (Mo. App. 1981).; *cf.* Larry P. v. Riles, No. 80-4027, slip op. (9th Cir. Jan. 23, 1984) (available on LEXIS, Genfed library, Cir. file) (state has burden of proof under EAHCA in showing test and evaluation procedures free of racial and cultural bias).

214. *See, e.g.*, Bales v. Clarke, 523 F. Supp. 1366, 1370 (E.D. Va. 1981) ("Plaintiff bears the burden of establishing that the Regional School is inappropriate, that no other State facility is appropriate, and that Accotink Academy is appropriate."); Cothern v. Mallory, 565 F. Supp. 701, 705-08 (W.D. Mo. 1983) (parents failed to meet burden of proof on issue of inappropriateness of education or on issue of lack of compliance by school district with due process procedures). Tatro v. Texas, 703 F.2d 823, 830 (5th Cir. 1983) (school district has burden of showing IEP inappropriate), *aff'd in part, rev'd in part sub nom.* Irving Indep. School Dist.v. Tatro, 104 S. Ct. 3371 (1984); *see also* Zirkel, *supra* note 186, at 485 & nn.133-34. *Cf.* Fitz v. Intermediate Unit Number 29, 43 Pa. Commw. 370, 374, 403 A.2d 138, 140 (1979) (under state law, burden on petitioners to show inappropriateness of program).

215. Doe v. Brookline School Comm., 722 F.2d 910, 917 (1st Cir. 1983) (party wishing to depart from status quo should make motion for preliminary injunction). Some courts, in determining whether this burden is met, may be influenced by whether the child has made any progress in his current placement. *E.g.*, Norris v. Massachusetts Dep't of Educ., 529 F. Supp. 759, 767 (D. Mass. 1981); Gladys J. v. Pearland Indep. School Dist., 520 F. Supp. 869, 877-78 (S.D. Tex. 1981); San Francisco Unified School Dist. v. State, 131 Cal. App. 3d 54, 71, 182 Cal. Rptr. 525, 535-36 (1982); *see* Note, *Board of Education v. Rowley, supra* note 8, at 299 n.116. In the state of Washington, "academic progress" apparently will give rise to a presumption that a free and appropriate education has been provided by the school district. *See* Note, *Attack on the EHA, supra* note 161, at 207-08.

It has also been suggested that the Act places the burden of persuasion on the party which seeks to remove the child from the regular educational environment. Note, *Enforcing the Right, supra* note 8, at 1119, 1122; Colley, *supra* note 118, at 155 (1981) (burden on party advocating most restrictive environment).

216. *See, e.g.*, Tatro v. Texas, 703 F.2d 823, 830 (5th Cir. 1983), *aff'd in part rev'd in part sub nom.* Irving Indep. School Dist. v. Tatro, 104 S. Ct. 3371 (1984) (party attacking IEP bears burden to show inappropriateness); McKenzie v. Jefferson, 566 F. Supp. 404, 406 (D.D.C. 1983) (plaintiffs bear burden of establishing by a preponderance of evidence that *local hearing officer's* determination should be set aside); Pires v. Pennsylvania Dep't of Educ., 78 Pa. Commw. 127, 135, 467 A.2d 79, 82 (1983) (order of *state secretary of education* must be upheld unless shown to be unsupported by substantial evidence); Johnston v. Ann Arbor Pub. Schools, 569 F. Supp. 1502 (E.D. Mich. 1983) (deference to

allocation of the burden of proof appears to make a difference in the outcome of a case, [217] the burden of proof issue is sometimes ignored or finessed.[218]

The extent to which judicial deference should be given to state or local decisionmaking is only somewhat more clearly resolved. The Supreme Court, in *Board of Education v. Rowley*, acknowledging both the lack of expertise and experience by courts and the "primacy of States in the field of education,"[219] held that once a court determines that the requirements of the EAHCA have been met, questions of educational theory and methods are for resolution by the states.[220] There are some reasons for reserving deference only to *local* educators involved in formulating the individualized education plan (IEP). These professionals are comparable to the decisionmakers in *Youngberg v. Romeo*[221] and *Parham v. J.R.*,[222] to whom a presumption of correctness is owed when individuals facing institutionalization claim constitutional violations of their due process rights. More so than state review officers, the professionals responsible for drafting the IEP's are the experts who are closest to the facts of the individual case. Moreover, it is the local educational agency that receives the bulk of federal funds and to whom the job of providing educational services actually falls.[223] It might also make sense to extend deference to the decision of the local hearing officer who has heard all of the witnesses as well as the arguments of the parties.[224] Nevertheless, the EAHCA places ultimate responsibility for compliance on the state,[225] and the state is to provide a mechanism for de novo review.[226] Thus, under *Rowley* judicial defer-

---

findings of state officials); Cohen v. School Bd., 450 So.2d 1238, 1241 (Fla. App. 1984) (decision of hearing officer must be upheld unless no substantial evidence).

217. *Compare, e.g.*, Bales v. Clarke, 523 F. Supp. 1366 (E.D. Va. 1981) (burden of proof put on parents, who did not meet it) *and* Cothern v. Mallory, 585 F. Supp. 701 (W.D. Mo. 1983) (parents failed to meet burden) *with* Grymes v. Madden, 672 F.2d 321 (3d Cir. 1982) (burden put on school district, which did not meet it) *and* Mallory v. Drake, 616 S.W.2d 124 (Mo. 1981) (school district unable to meet burden). *But see* Lang v. Braintree School Comm., 545 F. Supp. 1221 (D. Mass. 1982) (school district meets its burden); McKenzie v. Jefferson, 566 F. Supp. 404 (D.D.C. 1983) (school district meets its burden); Pires v. Pennsylvania Dep't of Educ., 78 Pa. Commw. 127, 467 A.2d 79 (1983) (parents meet burden).

218. *See, e.g.*, Colin K. v. Schmidt, 536 F. Supp. 1375, 1386-87 (D.R.I. 1982), *aff'd*, 715 F.2d 1 (1st Cir. 1983) (proposed IEP "clearly inadequate" and evidence of disabilities "not sufficiently controverted by defendants' witnesses").

219. 458 U.S. 176, 208 (1982).

220. *Id.* at 207-08.

221. 457 U.S. 307 (1982).

222. 442 U.S. 584 (1979).

223. 20 U.S.C. §§ 1411(b), (d), 1420(a) (1982); *see* Note, *supra* note 206, at 49. In the state of Washington, school districts are aided at the state review level by a presumption affecting the burden of proof if their IEP procedures are correct and their experts are qualified and in agreement. *See* Note, *Attack on the EHA*, *supra* note 161 at 204-06.

224. *See* 34 C.F.R. §§ 300.506-.508(1984). A few cases have followed this approach. *See* McKenzie v. Jefferson, 566 F. Supp. 404, 406 (D.D.C. 1983); Cohen v. School Bd., 450 So. 2d 1238, 1241 (Fla. App. 1984).

225. 20 U.S.C. §§ 1412(1), (6), 1414(d) (1982); 34 C.F.R. §§ 300.134, .136, .600 (1984); *see also* Yaris v. Special School Dist. , 728 F.2d 1055, 1057 (8th Cir. 1984); Kruelle v. New Castle County School Dist., 642 F.2d 687, 696-98 (3d Cir. 1981); Kerr Center Parents Ass'n v. Charles, 572 F. Supp. 448, 458 (D. Or. 1983); North v. District of Columbia Bd. of Educ., 471 F. Supp. 136, 139-40 (D.D.C. 1979).

226. 20 U.S.C. § 1415(b)(2), (c) (1982).

ence is owed to the final outcome of the state review process.[227]

It is less clear whether deference is required on all issues or whether, as Judith Wegner suggests, deference is appropriate only as to matters of judgment about educational methodology, leaving the courts broad review power over questions of needs assessment and overall program effectiveness.[228] In providing that "[t]he primary responsibility for formulating the education to be accorded a handicapped child, and for choosing the educational method most suitable to the child's needs, was left by the Act to state and local educational agencies . . . ."[229] and that "due weight" should be given to the results of the state administrative proceedings,[230] the *Rowley* decision would seem to require deference on all issues. This view would conform to the *Youngberg* and *Parham* holdings that judicial review be limited to ensuring that professional judgment was in fact exercised.[231] On the other hand, in its recent decision in *Irving Independent School District v. Tatro,*[232] upholding an interpretation of the EAHCA to require clean intermittent catheterization for a spina bifida child as a "related service" under the Act, the Court, citing *Rowley,* noted the need for judicial review of the handicapped child's IEP to ensure that it conforms to the requirements of the EAHCA.[233]

Because the issues of burden of proof and judicial deference are critical ones, they require a clearer and more coherent resolution. I will reexamine these issues in the next section in light of the concept of program parity. This reexamination will focus primarily on local, rather than state, decisionmaking, for as a practical matter, how decisions by *local* school districts are treated will have the most significant impact upon how resources are allocated to handicapped children.

B. The Special Efforts Approach: A Program Parity Solution

It seems unlikely that Congress intended to reverse the neglect of handicapped children in public education by a set of procedures which leave up to the parents of those children the task of demonstrating that educational deci-

227. 458 U.S. at 206.
228. *See* Wegner, *supra* note 161, at 186-90.
229. *Rowley,* 458 U.S. at 207.
230. 458 U.S. at 206.
231. Youngberg v. Romeo, 457 U.S. 307, 321 (1982); Parham v. J.R., 442 U.S. 584, 606-16 (1979); *see* Monahan v. Nebraska, 687 F.2d 1164, 1171 (8th Cir. 1982) (decisions of state officials entitled to presumption of validity if professional judgment exercised).
232. 104 S. Ct. 3371 (1984).
233. *Id.* at 3376 n.6. Several courts before *Tatro,* especially in the First Circuit, adopted this interpretation. *See* Doe v. Anrig, 692 F.2d 800, 806 (1st Cir. 1982) (distinguishing between questions of educational policy, as to which deference is appropriate, and factual issues of effect of handicap on child's ability to benefit from an educational setting, as to which it is not); Abrahamson v. Hershman, 701 F.2d 223, 230 (1st Cir. 1983) (issues of whether particular program would serve handicapped child's needs and whether particular placement was "educational" within the scope of the Act were not matters of educational policy on which district court must defer to state administrative proceedings); Colin K. v. Schmidt, 536 F. Supp. 1375, 1385 (D.R.I. 1982) (court's role in EAHCA proceedings is to assess evidence independently), *aff'd,* 715 F.2d 1 (1st Cir. 1983). *But see* Karl v. Board of Educ., 736 F.2d 873, 877 (2d Cir. 1984) (courts must defer to state authorities on suitability of educational program).

sions by state and/or local educational agencies are inappropriate, especially if the procedures require deference to those agencies on all matters of educational theory, practice, or methodology. It also seems unlikely, however, that Congress intended to run roughshod over the tradition and practice of local and state decisionmaking or the custom of deference to professional decisionmakers in education. An ideal resolution of these issues would reconcile the affirmative goals of the EAHCA with the values and interests threatened by a single-minded adherence to these goals.

As an initial matter, it would seem that the burden of persuasion on whether an educational program offered to a handicapped child is appropriate (or otherwise meets the affirmative requirements of the EAHCA) should fall upon the defendant educational agency. Under the EAHCA, the school system is required to determine an appropriate educational program pursuant to detailed, specified procedures.[234] Because of this duty, the school district should have knowledge of the relevant facts upon which the decisions were made, as well as expertise about the issues, and superior access to the information. The school district is thus the most appropriate party to bear the burden on these issues.[235]

If the program parity approach is followed, it is not so clear who should bear the burden on the issue of parity. Nor is it clear whether, in determining if the school district's burden is met, deference should be accorded to school districts as to resource allocation decisions that may underlie the choice of an educational program. On the one hand, the legitimate business of public schools could be severely burdened if they had to meet a high burden of proof on every decision challenged for unfair resource allocation. On the other hand, the tradition of disregard of the handicapped in public schools suggests that without an effective check, these judgments will not give adequate recognition to the needs and interests of handicapped children. School districts can easily frustrate the policies of the EAHCA if they need not justify a placement decision, or if a minimal articulation of a rational basis will suffice.

To resolve this dilemma it is necessary to identify the factor that would justify a burden of proof rule either on policy grounds or because of its probative value. On both counts, the factor that seems most pertinent to whether a school district should be required to prove program parity is the degree of good faith or the level of commitment the district has demonstrated to the handicapped in its educational programs generally. This factor, which could be measured by a "special efforts" standard, has probative value and also provides a policy reason for allocating the burden of proof. If a school district has made special efforts on behalf of the handicapped, it would seem less likely that the district has disadvantaged a particular handicapped child with respect to others, and it would seem more fair, as a matter of policy, to place

---

234. 20 U.S.C. § 1415(b)(1)(A) (1982).

235. *Cf.* Allen, *Presumption, Inferences and Burden of Proof in Federal Civil Actions—An Anatomy of Unnecessary Ambiguity and a Proposal for Reform,* 76 Nw. U.L. Rev. 892, 899 (1982) (burdens of persuasion on issues "peculiarly within the knowledge" of a party frequently allocated to that party).

the risks of error upon a challenger to the school district's decision. On the other hand, if a school district has not made special efforts on behalf of the handicapped, there is some reason to assume that the district has not acted appropriately in a particular case, and it would be preferable on policy grounds to place the risks of error upon the district. Thus, whether the question of unequal or unfair treatment of a handicapped child is an affirmative defense to be proved by the school district or an element of the prima facie case to be proved by the parents of the child would turn upon the external criterion of whether the district has made "special efforts" toward educating the handicapped. If the district wants to benefit from the procedural advantages that accrue, it must first establish that special efforts have been made.

The same standard, though not helpful in resolving the question whether deference should be given to the outcome of the state hearing process, could also be used to determine whether to give deference to the programming decision of a school district. Deference to the professional educator in a decision that might have been influenced by cost considerations[236] should depend upon whether the school has demonstrated the level of commitment that warrants the assumption that those decisions have been made in good faith.

A rule that uses "special efforts" or some other measure of good faith as a basis upon which to allocate the burden of proof or to determine whether to give deference to the school district on certain issues would respect both the goals of the EAHCA and the potentially disruptive effects the EAHCA might have upon an educational system. It also provides an additional means for promoting a fair allocation of resources between the handicapped and the nonhandicapped. In requiring school districts that assert cost as a defense to claims for educational services by the handicapped to account for the relative assignment of resource shortfall between the handicapped and nonhandicapped, *procedural* weight will be given to actions of school districts that have some probative value as to the district's compliance and that permit a fair policy judgment on where the risks of error should fall. When the issue is raised as to whether something less than a first-rate program for the handicapped is justified, a showing of special efforts by a school district would be an appropriate basis upon which to excuse the district from the added burden of persuasion on the issue of whether the effects of resource limitations were being made to fall disproportionately upon the handicapped.

The special efforts standard is not offered as a test of substantive compliance with the EAHCA. Rather, it is a means of measuring the district's good faith, commitment, or intent, so as to effect the appropriate allocation of the parties' burdens of proof. This intent is not an element of the merits of the case itself but, instead, a factor in allocating the procedural burdens.

---

236. The question will arise under this standard whether a decision was in fact influenced by cost considerations, or whether it was an entirely professional judgment. I propose that where any colorable claim can be made that cost factors influenced the decision, the special efforts standard would come into play to determine whether the decision was presumptively a valid professional judgment.

The special efforts standard is analogous in the burden-shifting features of Title VII employment discrimination law and the Voting Rights Act. Under Title VII,[237] demonstration of a discriminatory pattern or practice of unlawful employment discrimination will give rise to a presumption that individual class members, who otherwise bear the burden of demonstrating unlawful discrimination,[238] have been the victims of discrimination.[239] The burden of persuasion then shifts to the defendant to prove that those individuals were not in fact victims of unlawful discrimination.[240]

Section 4 of the Voting Rights Act[241] similarly uses a threshold test to set the burdens of the parties. The statute provides an objective standard by which jurisdictions with a history of racial discrimination in voting are identified. If this standard is met, a voting district will have to obtain preclearance for change in a standard practice or procedure with respect to voting under section 5 of the Act.[242] External criteria are thus used as a measure of probability of noncompliance or lack of good faith in order to impose a burden on districts to which they would not otherwise be subject.[243]

An approach to the burden of proof issue consistent with a special efforts approach was followed by one court in *Lang v. Braintree School Committee.*[244] In *Lang,* the school district failed to comply with the procedural requirements of the EAHCA by not including the parents in the IEP planning process; on this basis, the court stated that "the burden must rest with the [defendant state and local educational agencies] to show, by a preponderance of the evidence, that Braintree's IEP provides [the child] with a 'free and appropriate public education.' "[245] Although no reasoning was given for this conclusion, and defendants in that case were able to meet the burden imposed upon them, the case exemplifies the use of an external criterion (compliance with mandated procedures) which are not legally relevant to the merits of the particular claim (whether the IEP provided a free and appropriate education) as a basis for allocating the burden of proof to a particular party. This approach takes account of policies ordinarily underlying the allocation of burdens of proof. The failure of the state and local educational agencies to comply with the clear, procedural requirements of the EAHCA reflects on the probability of the defendants acting properly in other regards under the EAHCA. This

---

237. Title VII of the Civil Rights Act of 1964, 42 U.S.C. § 2000e (1982).

238. United States Postal Serv. Bd. of Governors v. Aikens, 103 S. Ct. 1478 (1983); McDonnell Douglas Corp. v. Green, 411 U.S. 792, 802 (1973). Proof of a pattern and practice of discrimination will also justify class relief under Title VII, Franks v. Bowman Transp. Co., 424 U. S. 747 (1976), for which there is no analogy under the EAHCA.

239. Franks v. Bowman Transp. Co., 424 U.S. 747, 772 (1976); Cooper v. Federal Reserve Bank of Richmond, 104 S. Ct. 2794, 2799-2800 (1984).

240. Franks v. Bowman Transp. Co., 424 U.S. 747, 772 (1976).

241. 42 U.S.C. § 1973b (1982).

242. *Id.* § 1973c.

243. These external criteria are to be distinguished from the evidence of discriminatory effect of a voting practice which may be used to prove that discrimination was intentional. *See* Blumstein, *supra* note 83, at 649-50, 658-61; Rogers v. Lodge, 458 U.S. 613 (1982).

244. 545 F. Supp. 1221 (D. Mass. 1982).

245. *Id.* at 1228.

failure further suggests where, as a matter of policy, one might wish the risks of error to fall. Procedural defects could be a basis in addition to "special efforts," upon which to allocate the burden of proof on other issues as well, such as whether program parity has been achieved, or whether a "professional judgment" was influenced by resource considerations.[246]

Measuring special efforts, like measuring educational quality, would be difficult, and would depend upon rough measurements or approximations. Nevertheless, some lessons can be drawn from attempts to make similar judgments in other areas of law. Regulations promulgated under the Urban Mass Transit Act (UMTA), for example, define "special efforts" that are required in the planning and design of mass transportation facilities and services so that mass transportation can be effectively utilized by elderly and handicapped persons.[247] While the proposal I make in this paper is aimed at allocating procedural burdens rather than at determining compliance with the nondiscrimination provisions of a federal funding statute, UMTA regulations offer a few examples of special efforts and thus demonstrate how such a standard might be defined.

One illustration in the UMTA regulations defines a numerical percentage standard; the transit district satisfies the special efforts standard if it uses at least 3.5 percent of the financial assistance available under the UMTA for programs to serve wheelchair users and semiambulatory handicapped persons.[248] A similar percentage standard might be developed to measure the level of commitment by a school district to the handicapped. Under this standard, the percentage of the school district budget committed to services for the handicapped could be compared to the average percentages of other school districts, with an adjustment for differences in costs or needs by region, size of district, or other factors.[249] Quantification would be complicated due to local and state differences in methods of accounting and difficulties in determining how to allocate the costs of resources shared by both handicapped and nonhandicapped children. Nonetheless, records are kept so that it is now possible to accumulate statistics on the cost of educating the handicapped;[250] voluntary guidelines could be established which would enable school districts to check their level of commitment against national norms.

---

246. One student writer suggested in a 1979 note that a school's adherence to the procedural requirements should affect the weight given to its assertions on other legal issues. Note, *Enforcing the Right*, supra note 8, at 1111-13; *see also* Haggerty & Sacks, *supra* note 158, at 993 (urging that failure to identify handicapping conditions would give rise to a rebuttable presumption of the inadequacy of the services offered by the school). *But cf.* Davis v. Scherer, 104 S. Ct. 3012, 3019-20 & n. 12 (1984) (failure of defendant state official to follow state administrative regulations not relevant to whether qualified immunity for violation of plaintiff's constitutional rights was forfeited).

247. 49 U.S.C. § 1612 (1982); 49 C.F.R. § 27.77 (1984).

248. 49 C.F.R. pt. 27, subpt. D, app. A(1) (1984).

249. *See generally* KAKALIK, *supra* note 2; Miner, *supra* note 181, at 321-25.

250. *See generally* KAKALIK, *supra* note 2; MOORE, WALKER & HOLLAND, *supra* note 3; Jordan & Stultz, *supra* note 162. This task is complicated, of course, by differences in accounting systems, size and density of local school districts, cost of living factors, definitions and classifications of handicapping conditions, price differences within states, and other factors. *See,* MOORE, WALKER & HOLLAND, *supra* note 3, at 43-58.

The objection might be raised that a single numerical percentage standard would allow a school district's commitment to one group of handicapped children to camouflage its neglect of another group of handicapped children. For this reason, it might be advisable to develop separate percentage standards for different classifications of handicapped children. Alternatively, parents of a handicapped child who show a substantial disparity in commitment among the different groups of handicapped children served by the district could be given the benefit of a rebuttable presumption that resources have been unfairly allocated.

UMTA regulations also offer performance standards as an alternative measure of special efforts. For example, one UMTA standard measures performance by the purchase of equipment for use by the handicapped.[251] This standard helps to address the equity problems between categories of handicapped persons. Service unit or performance standards, measured in units of special classes, extra personnel, and other resources, could be used in special education to measure the special efforts made by the district to serve handicapped children.[252]

The special efforts approach adds an additional level of fact-finding to the review of local and state educational agency decisionmaking, inviting the criticism that this scheme will make due process under the EAHCA, which is already too legalistic,[253] even more burdensome. The additional factual issues also may open up the hearing to matters well beyond the individual whose educational program is at stake and to whom the issues of the hearing are ordinarily restricted. These are legitimate concerns, but not fatal ones. The data called for under either percentage or performance standards are the same type of data districts would need to determine for themselves whether educational programming decisions for handicapped children strike a fair balance between the needs of those children and the needs of others. Numerical spending standards and performance standards developed at the federal level could be useful to districts for evaluating their own priorities.

A special efforts standard affecting the allocation of burdens of proof and whether deference is given to local decisionmakers is consistent with the overall approach suggested by the program parity model. Program parity sets the focus on *proportional quality*. Like the special efforts standard, it puts alternative programs for the handicapped in perspective, helping to ensure that the interests of the handicapped are being taken into account *within the context of the needs and interests of the public education system*.

---

251. "Purchase of only wheelchair-accessible new fixed route equipment until one-half of the fleet is accessible . . . ." 49 C.F.R. pt. 27, subpt. D, app. A(2) (1984).

252. *See* KAKALIK, *supra* note 2 (study breaking down educational service units according to type of handicap and such factors as age of student, experience and educational level of teacher, instructional time, type of personnel, and others).

253. *See* Neal & Kirp, *supra* note 72.

VI

Conclusion

The future of special education suffers from the lack of a firm consensus on the nature and extent of the public obligation toward the handicapped. This lack of consensus is particularly troubling as resources available to public education continue to shrink in relation to the demand for them, and as pressures mount upon an education system increasingly evaluated in accordance with its success in educating the "normal" child.[254] The model of program parity provides one theoretical foundation for consensus. It seeks to bridge the gap opened by the necessary creation of particularized rights for members of one disadvantaged group, by interpreting those rights in light of the legitimate goals and values of the institution of public education within which those rights must be implemented.

Although program comparisons of the kind suggested in this article may seem unwieldy and impractical as a legal standard to resolve litigated cases, such cases are rare.[255] Rough comparisons by teachers and administrators who know their school system and its programs well may not be so difficult. School officials are accustomed to balancing priorities, setting goals, and making budgets with respect to numerous potentially conflicting interests. Within the broad flexibility of the substantive standard of the EAHCA and the *Board of Education v. Rowley* decision,[256] the understanding of the public educational obligation to the handicapped by these service providers is very important. Program parity defines this obligation in terms that are meaningful to schools. This concept maintains a special legal process for the handicapped that takes into account the special and individualized needs of the handicapped. It sets this process in a framework for decisionmaking that recognizes competing valuable interests and goals and mediates the tension between them. Handicapped children have individual, enforceable rights to education, but the program parity approach defines the content of these rights by reference to the collective decisions made for all others. Their educational programs are based on need, but the cost of those programs may be taken into account so as not to require unreasonable sacrifices by those seeking to progress according to their merits. A unitary federal standard is defined, but that standard relates not to content or level of education generally, but rather to the federal interest in parity of treatment.

Great flexibility in local educational systems is still allowed under this model—flexibility in the general level of education, in the choice of educational methods to be used, and in the opportunity for experimentation. This flexibility is subject to one substantive constraint, the constraint which most accurately reflects the limited nature of the legitimate federal concern for public education: that the handicapped should not be disadvantaged with

---

254. *See supra* note 7 and accompanying text.
255. Neal & Kirp, *supra* note 72, at 77.
256. 458 U.S. 176 (1982); *see* Note, *The Rowley Decision, supra* note 11, at 702-04.

respect to the nonhandicapped in their pursuit of an education of the highest possible quality.

In addition to providing a framework for resolving resource allocation issues in a way that reduces the tensions between the EAHCA and the public education system within which it must be implemented, the model of program parity provides incentives for local school personnel to adopt a broad equitable approach to program design. An approach that centers entirely on a case-by-case review of the educational programming of individual children whose parents dispute a programming decision encourages the squeaky wheel approach to educational programming, under which the most vocal parents obtain the best educational services for their children.[257] When the legal system demonstrates a respect for sound and equitable program-wide resource allocation/programming decisions, school administrators will be able to devote greater attention to overall program development and greater equity in programming decisions.[258]

In the final analysis, the concept of program parity is most important as a model for nonlegal decisionmaking by professional educators. Implementation of fair and equitable decisionmaking in education depends primarily upon a commitment by these personnel to certain ideals—ideals that are philosophical and political as well as educational. These ideals must be sufficiently clear and fair-minded to command respect. Program parity expresses one such set of ideals.

---

257. See Kirst & Bertken, *Due Process Hearings in Special Education: Some Early Findings from California*, in SPECIAL EDUCATION POLICIES 136, 154 (Chambers & Hartman eds. 1983) (showing key to receiving educational benefits under the EAHCA is willingness to contest school district decisions).

258. *Cf.* Clune, *A Political Mode of Implementation and Implications of the Model for Public Policy Research, and the Changing Roles of Law and Lawyers*, 69 IOWA L. REV. 47, 123 (1983) (role of legal rights created by "political law" is "to set the stage for creative and adaptive social programs").

I am grateful to Jack Nance, Director of Special Programs in the Wake County School System in North Carolina, for confirming this point at the February 24-25, 1984, conference held at Duke Law School in connection with this symposium issue.

7

BEYOND CONVENTIONAL EDUCATION: A DEFINITION OF EDUCATION UNDER THE EDUCATION FOR ALL HANDICAPPED CHILDREN ACT OF 1975

LAUREN A. LARSON

I

INTRODUCTION

Since the Education for All Handicapped Children Act (EAHCA)[1] was passed in 1975, courts and commentators have attempted to apply its provisions to a variety of children, all of them handicapped, each of them unique. The results have often been dissatisfying to both parents and school systems, due in large part to the definitional vagueness of the substantive provisions of the Act. Although the EAHCA requires states to provide a free and appropriate education to all handicapped children,[2] Congress was less than clear in defining that requirement.[3] This ambiguity has led interested parties to develop expectations and assumptions about what the state must provide to a handicapped child by way of education. Subsequently, courts often have rejected such beliefs as they attempt to interpret the intended meaning of "appropriate education."[4]

Both the judiciary and other observers have expressed opinions concerning such issues as the classification of services as "related services," the interpretation of the term "appropriate," and the categorization of the

---

1. 20 U.S.C. §§ 1400-1461 (1982).
2. In order to qualify for assistance, a state must have in effect "a policy that assures all handicapped children the right to a free appropriate public education." 20 U.S.C. § 1412(1) (1982); *see also id.* § 1400(c).
3. According to the EAHCA, free and appropriate public education is:
   special education and related services which (A) have been provided at public expense, under public supervision and direction, and without charge, (B) meet the standards of the State educational agency, (C) include an appropriate preschool, elementary, or secondary school education in the State involved, and (D) are provided in conformity with the individualized education program required under section 1414(a)(5) of this title.
20 U.S.C. § 1401(18) (1982).
4. Such lack of detail may have been necessary. Stated one court:
   Recognizing the broad range of special needs presented by handicapped children, the lack of agreement within the medical and educational professions on what constitutes an appropriate education, and the tradition of state and local control over educational matters, Congress refrained from mandating overly detailed programs.
Kruelle v. New Castle County School Dist., 642 F.2d 687, 691 (3d Cir. 1981).

reasons for residential placement as educational or other than educational.[5] Without a clear and uniform definition of education, however, any conclusions on these and other such issues are incomplete and likely to be inconsistent with each other and with legislative intent. For example, in order to determine if education is appropriate, logically one must first determine what education is. Likewise, if related services that enable a child to benefit from special education are to be provided, an initial determination must be made about what constitutes that education. Education is, after all, the noun to which the modifiers "appropriate" and "special" attach.

A clear definition of education is also crucial in the development of the handicapped child's individualized education program (IEP).[6] Teachers and parents must rely on their individual concepts of education when stating a child's level of educational performance or developing a child's educational goals. A widespread acceptance of a broad definition of education is evidenced by the fact that IEP's often include such activities as toilet training and dressing oneself.

Additionally, in residential placement decisions, the classification of a placement as educational or other than educational determines who will pay for the residential part of that placement.[7] Furthermore, under the narrower interpretations of education, some severely impaired children may be deemed "ineducable." As the costs of residential placements for handicapped children increase, so increases the significance of administrative and judicial distinctions among educational, psychological, custodial, and medical placements.

---

5. *See, e.g.,* Tokarcik v. Forest Hills School Dist., 665 F.2d 443 (3d Cir. 1981), *cert. denied,* 458 U.S. 1121 (1982) (holding catheterization to be a related service); Tatro v. Texas, 481 F. Supp. 1224 (N.D. Tex. 1979) (holding catheterization was not a related service), *vacated,* 625 F.2d 557 (5th Cir. 1980), *on remand,* 516 F. Supp. 968 (N.D. Tex. 1981) (holding catheterization to be a related service), *aff'd,* 703 F.2d 823 (5th Cir. 1983), *aff'd in part, rev'd in part sub nom.* Irving Indep. School Dist. v. Tatro, 104 S. Ct. 3371 (1984); Rettig v. Kent City School Dist., 539 F. Supp. 768 (N.D. Ohio 1981) (appropriate education), *aff'd in part, vacated in part,* 720 F.2d 463 (6th Cir. 1983), *cert. denied,* 104 S. Ct. 3581 (1984); Pinkerton v. Moye, 509 F. Supp. 107 (W.D. Va. 1981) (appropriate education); Mooney & Aronson, *Solomon Revisited: Separating Educational and Other than Educational Needs in Special Education Residential Placements,* 14 CONN. L. REV. 531 (1982); Stark, *Tragic Choices in Special Education: The Effect of Scarce Resources on the Implementation of Pub. L. No. 94-142,* 14 CONN. L. REV. 477 (1982); Stoppleworth, *Criteria for Making the Decision: Placement in Residence for Educational or Other than Educational Reasons,* 12 J.L. & EDUC. 77 (1983); Note, *Enforcing the Right to an "Appropriate" Education: The Education for All Handicapped Children Act of 1975,* 92 HARV. L. REV. 1103 (1979).

6. The EAHCA defines "individualized education program" as

a written statement for each handicapped child developed in any meeting by a representative of the local educational agency or an intermediate educational unit who shall be qualified to provide, or supervise the provision of, specially designed instruction to meet the unique needs of handicapped children, the teacher, the parents or guardian of such child, and whenever appropriate, such child, which statement shall include (A) a statement of the present levels of educational performance of such child, (B) a statement of annual goals, including short-term instructional objectives, (C) a statement of the specific educational services to be provided to such child, and the extent to which such child will be able to participate in regular educational programs.

20 U.S.C. § 1401(19) (1982).

7. "If placement in a public or private residential program is necessary to provide special education and related services to a handicapped child, the program, including non-medical care and room and board, must be at no cost to the parents of the child." 34 C.F.R. § 300.302 (1984).

This comment will offer the theory that education is a relative term. What may be education for one child may not be for another. Such a theory finds support in the legislative history of the EAHCA, in the relevant court decisions, and in the conclusions of authors and educators in the field of special education. The comment will present evidence to show that Congress relied upon this broad concept of education when it enacted the EAHCA. Every handicapped child, regardless of the nature or severity of the handicap, is included within the Act's mandate. Education under the EAHCA must, therefore, include even such basic processes as the acquisition of life skills, no matter how fundamental those skills may be.

In support of this theory, the educational setting and the legislative history of the EAHCA will be discussed. This comment also will focus on administrative and judicial standards developed for determining the educational requirements of the Act. Emphasis will be given to distinctions drawn by courts and educational agencies in determining whether a given activity is education. Such distinctions have been used to exclude from the Act's coverage some emotionally disturbed children and some children considered to be ineducable. Finally, the comment will recommend the acceptance of a uniform and flexible definition of education consistent with the EAHCA, recent court decisions, and traditional considerations.

II

BACKGROUND OF THE EAHCA

A.   Recent Developments in Education

The objectives of education are many-faceted and certainly more far-reaching than simple retention and usage of the "three R's." Social and moral development, expression of self and creativity, acquisition of knowledge, and attainment of skills and abilities needed in order to live in society are all settled goals of education for all children.[8]

According to Black's Law Dictionary,

[Education] comprehends not merely the instruction received at school or college, but the whole course of training[,] moral, religious, vocational, intellectual and physical. Education may be particularly directed to either the mental, moral, or physical powers and faculties, but in its broadest and best sense it relates to them all. [Education includes the] [a]cquisition of all knowledge tending to train and develop the individual.[9]

Forty-nine states now require either attendance at a public school or a state-approved private schooling experience. Such compulsory education is evidence of a commitment to the further goals of socialization, increased productivity, equal opportunity, and participation in democracy.[10] Paternalistic,

---

8.   See M. FROSTIG, EDUCATION FOR DIGNITY (1976); S. SARASON & J. DORIS, EDUCATIONAL HANDICAP, PUBLIC POLICY, AND SOCIAL HISTORY (1979).

9.   BLACK'S LAW DICTIONARY 461 (5th ed. 1979).

10.   See Sugarman & Kirp, *Rethinking Collective Responsibility for Education*, LAW & CONTEMP. PROBS., Summer 1975, at 144.

economic, humanitarian, and protectionist attitudes also have been satisfied by the imposition of compulsory education. Furthermore, as society has grown more complex, formal agencies of government have supplanted families in providing necessary training and education of children. Public schools, initially established solely for the purpose of teaching academics, now include in their curriculum such courses as sex education, vocational training, filmmaking, driver training, and other nonacademic subjects.[11] In addition, public schools receiving categorical aid under the Elementary and Secondary Education Act are obligated to develop programs for educationally deprived children[12] and for children whose native language is not English.[13]

The judiciary, like state and local legislatures, has recognized broader than academic purposes for education. In its 1954 opinion in *Brown v. Board of Education*,[14] the Supreme Court stated, "In these days, it is doubtful that any child may reasonably be expected to succeed in life if he is denied the opportunity of an education."[15] Almost two decades later, the Court, in *Wisconsin v. Yoder*,[16] recognized that education prepares individuals to be "self-reliant and self-sufficient participants in society,"[17] and assessed the value of that education in terms of its capacity to prepare a child for life.

During this same period, the courts began responding to parents' demands for meaningful specialized education for their handicapped children.[18] In the early 1970's, district courts in Pennsylvania and in the District of Columbia decided that their respective state or jurisdiction must provide free public education appropriate to each handicapped child's capabilities, regardless of the degree of impairment. In *Pennsylvania Association for Retarded Children v. Commonwealth*[19] (*PARC*) and *Mills v. Board of Education*,[20] the educational responsibility of the schools was defined to include instruction in the most basic of life skills—eating, toileting, and self care. Additionally, as part of a nationwide litigation campaign, lawsuits similar to these two landmark cases were decided in almost thirty states, drawing much attention to the ineq-

---

11. Bateman, *Prescriptive Teaching and Individualized Education Programs*, EDUCATING ALL HANDICAPPED CHILDREN 39 (R. Heinrich ed. 1979).

12. 20 U.S.C. § 2733 (1982).

13. *Id.* § 3222. *See also* Lau v. Nichols, 414 U.S. 563 (1974) (school system's failure to provide English language instruction to students of Chinese ancestry held a denial of a meaningful opportunity to participate in public education programs and therefore a violation of the Civil Rights Act of 1964).

14. 347 U.S. 483 (1954).

15. *Id.* at 493.

16. 406 U.S. 205 (1972).

17. *Id.* at 221.

18. Special education as it now exists is largely a product of the 1970's. Although special education was advocated early in the 1900's and especially once compulsory education became the norm, it was generally used as a means of excluding the severely impaired as ineducable and separating the mildly handicapped and disruptive into special schools where they were taught basic academic subjects, with appropriate adjustments, and such skills as sewing, weaving, basketry, and gymnastics. S. SARASON & J. DORIS, *supra* note 8, at 275-79.

19. 334 F. Supp. 1257 (E.D. Pa. 1971) (per curiam), 343 F. Supp. 279 (E.D. Pa. 1972)(amending consent agreement).

20. 348 F. Supp. 866 (D.D.C. 1972).

uitable and unacceptable educational treatment of handicapped children, and establishing their right to education.

The handicapped population was also fighting its battle against discrimination in institutions other than public schools. In response to demands for equal opportunity in the workplace and in life generally, Congress in 1973 enacted the Rehabilitation Act, a general civil rights act for the handicapped.[21] Section 504 of the Act[22] prohibits discrimination in any federally funded or assisted program or activity against an otherwise qualified handicapped person solely by reason of his or her handicap.

B. Legislative History

In the years preceding the enactment of the EAHCA, parents generally were expecting more from public schools, handicapped persons were calling for equality from all institutions, and parents of handicapped children were demanding special education from the public schools. These three social forces, the crunch of limited resources, and the *Mills* and *PARC* decisions convinced Congress to take a more active role in the education of handicapped children.

Congress initially added Title VI to the Elementary and Secondary Education Act in 1966 to assist in the education of handicapped children.[23] In 1970 Congress repealed Title VI and created the Education of the Handicapped Act, which authorized grants to the states for programs for the education of handicapped children.[24] Although the Education Amendments of 1974[25] incorporated the major principles of the right to education cases into federal law, limited resources continued to prevent implementation of many programs. The 94th Congress took its cue from the *Mills* and *PARC* decisions. The Senate Committee on Labor and Public Welfare recognized this shortage of resources when it reported that "[i]ncreased awareness of the educational needs of handicapped children and landmark court decisions establishing the right to education for handicapped children [point] to the necessity of an expanded Federal fiscal role."[26]

In 1975, to amend Title VI, to expand provisions enacted by the 93rd Congress, and to maximize benefits to handicapped children and their families, the 94th Congress enacted Public Law 94-142, the EAHCA.[27] The new Act mandated that states make available to all handicapped children a free and appropriate education consisting of special education[28] and related services[29]

---

21. Rehabilitation Act of 1973, Pub. L. No. 93-112, 87 Stat. 355 (1973) (codified as amended at 29 U.S.C. §§ 701-794 (1982)).

22. 29 U.S.C. § 794 (1982).

23. Pub. L. No. 89-750, tit. VI, 80 Stat. 1191, 1204-10 (1966).

24. Pub. L. No. 91-230, tit. VI, 84 Stat. 121, 175-88 (1970).

25. Pub. L. No. 93-380, 88 Stat. 489 (1974).

26. S. REP. No. 168, 94th Cong., 1st Sess. 5, *reprinted in* 1975 U.S. CODE CONG. & AD. NEWS 1425, 1429.

27. 89 Stat. 773 (codified at 20 U.S.C. §§ 1400-1461 (1982)).

28. The Act defines "special education" as:

specially designed instruction, at no cost to parents or guardians, to meet the unique needs of a

designed to meet their unique needs. Both the EAHCA itself and the implementing regulations require that each state establish a goal of providing full educational opportunity to all handicapped children.[30] Congress, however, failed to provide within the Act much guidance as to the specific activities which would satisfy such a goal. The legislative history, on the other hand, contains much evidence that Congress had in mind specific concepts of education when it drafted and passed the EAHCA.

The Senate Committee and the legislative sponsors expressed their intent that the Act enable each handicapped child to attain the self-sufficiency and independence necessary for that child to share in and contribute to society and, in many cases, to avoid institutionalization. The committee report stated:

> The long range implications of these statistics are that public agencies and taxpayers will spend billions of dollars over the lifetimes of these individuals to maintain such persons as dependents and in a minimally acceptable lifestyle. With proper education services, many would be able to become productive citizens, contributing to society instead of being forced to remain burdens. Others, through such services, would increase their independence, thus reducing their dependence on society.[31]

Congress envisioned future savings of institutionalization costs for some of these children who, through education, could eventually become self-sufficient, contributing citizens instead of dependents of the state. Senator Hathaway noted:

> Though the cost of providing such opportunities is substantial, this cost must be weighed against the cost to our society of people unable to utilize their talents fully, if at all, and of course, the direct financial cost involved in unnecessary institutional care which could be avoided if handicapped individuals were enabled to develop to their full potential.[32]

---

handicapped child, including classroom instruction, instruction in physical education, home instruction, and instruction in hospitals and institutions.
20 U.S.C. § 1401(16) (1982).
    29. "Related services" is defined under the Act as:
transportation, and such developmental, corrective, and other supportive services (including speech pathology and audiology, psychological services, physical and occupational therapy, recreation, and medical and counseling services, except that such medical services shall be for diagnostic and evaluation purposes only) as may be required to assist a handicapped child to benefit from special education, and includes the early identification and assessment of handicapping conditions in children.
20 U.S.C. § 1401(17) (1982).
    30. 20 U.S.C. § 1412(2)(a) (1982); 34 C.F.R. § 300.304(a) (1984).
    31. S. REP. No. 168, 94th Cong., 1st Sess. 9, *reprinted in* 1975 U.S. CODE CONG. & AD. NEWS 1425, 1433. *See also* H.R. REP. No. 332, 94th Cong., 1st Sess. 11 (1975).
Senator Williams expressed essentially the same concerns in floor debate when he said "providing appropriate educational services now means that many of these individuals will be able to become a contributing part of our society, and they will not have to depend on subsistence payments from public funds." 121 CONG. REC. 19,492 (1975). *See also id.* at 19,494 (remarks of Sen. Javits).
Congressman Brademas, cosponsor of the House bill and Chairman of the House Subcommittee on Select Education, maintained the same position. According to the Congressman:
    . . . [O]ver 50 percent of the handicapped children in this nation are being denied a fundamental educational opportunity which can help some of them become self-sufficient adults. . . .
    . . . This is a waste of one of our most valuable resources, our young people and the potential they possess to become contributing and self-sufficient members of this society.
Id. at 23,702-03.
    32. 121 CONG. REC. 37,420 (1975). *See also id.* at 37,419 (remarks of Sen. Beall).

Economic benefits to society from the contributions of these children were quite evidently perceived by Congress as a justification for the Act. According to one Senator:

> [O]ur failure to stimulate his or her potential can only lead to despair and dependence on the part of the handicapped individual, and this dependence will inevitably be funded by the American public. More important than this cost, however, is the resulting loss of the benefits that society might reap from the contributions these individuals could make.[33]

Humanitarian concerns for the emotional health and well-being of handicapped children also apparently influenced the decision of Congress to enact the EAHCA. Senator Williams, quoting first the Secretary of Health, Education and Welfare, stated:

> 'I think we all understand that the handicapped are faced with extraordinary circumstances, and for that reason, need extraordinary responses and attention to deal with their circumstances for the very reason you state—making them productive citizens, capable of contributing, and even more, capable of self-respect and pride which they so rightly deserve.'
>
> It is this goal and purpose which S.6 addresses. This legislation was designed to set forth a comprehensive program to meet the unmet needs of all handicapped children.[34]

Another compelling rationale expressed by supporters of the Act was equality of educational opportunity. Senator Stafford commented, "We can all agree that [the education of handicapped children] should be equivalent, at least, to the one those children who are not handicapped receive."[35] This rationale was reiterated by Senator Williams, who said, "[T]his measure fulfills the promise of the Constitution that there shall be equality of education for all people and that handicapped children no longer will be left out."[36]

In addition, some members of the House, including cosponsor Brademas, implied in early discussions that the purpose of the Act should be to help each handicapped child develop his or her maximum potential. "Individualized plans are of great importance in the education of the handicapped child in order to help them develop their full potential."[37]

For some or all of these purposes, the EAHCA was passed by a resounding majority in both the House and the Senate.[38]

It was the express intent of Congress that the goals of the Act be achieved

---

33. _Id._ at 19,505 (remarks of Sen. Beall); _see also_ H.R. REP. No. 332, 94th Cong., 1st Sess. 24 (1975).

34. 121 CONG. REC. 37,416 (1975); _see also id._ at 19,496 (remarks of Sen. Kennedy). ˙

35. _Id._ at 19,483.

36. _Id._ at 37,413; _see also id._ at 37,410 (remarks of Sen. Randolph); _id._ at 37,411 (remarks of Sen. Stafford).

37. _Id._ at 23,704; _see also_ H.R. REP. No. 332, 94th Cong., 1st Sess. 19 (1975); 121 CONG. REC. 37,029 (remarks of Sen. Minish).

38. The House vote was 404-7; the Senate vote, 87-7. Most of the postconference debate focused on disputes over the budget authorization. A number of congressmen opposed the authorizations section on the basis that it unfairly raised the hopes of the families of handicapped children, since Congress would never actually appropriate that amount to the EAHCA programs. _See generally_ 121 CONG. REC. 37,023-32 (1975) (House conference debate); _id._ at 37,409 (Senate conference debate).

through individualized education.[39] The requirement that special education be designed for the unique needs of the child is emphasized within the Act, especially in the provision which mandates the development of an IEP for each handicapped child.[40] An IEP is a written statement developed by a representative of the local educational agency, the teacher, the parents, and the child, which includes, inter alia, a statement of educational performance, annual goals, and specific educational services to be provided.[41] In the definition of an IEP, as in other definitions in the Act, Congress provided no indication whether the teaching of life skills should be included in the handicapped child's educational program.

Subsequently, however, courts and educational agencies have approved educational programs which include such activities as toilet training, dressing oneself, and feeding oneself.[42] The inclusion of such activities is justified in part by two express provisions of the EAHCA.

First are the priorities set forth in the Act for the provision of educational services. Top priority is accorded to those handicapped children who are not receiving any education; second priority is reserved for those who suffer from the most severe handicaps within each disability and who are currently receiving an inadequate education.[43] Many of the children singled out for priority treatment are those who have been excluded from public education because they cannot walk or think like normal children, and who have handicaps which make learning to tie a shoe a monumental task. If such children are to have first priority to EAHCA funds, then Congress must have intended that the funds be used to provide useful life services. Instruction in subjects which the child could never understand could not be considered "appropriate education."

The second EAHCA provision relevant to this concern requires that federal funds be used to provide services over and above those any normal student would receive. A handicapped child, according to the Senate Committee report, has "a right to physical education services, health screening, transportation services and all other services which are provided to children within the school system, and a right to as many options in curricula as are available to all children."[44] Local education agencies must satisfy the state educational agency that funds received under the EAHCA will be used for "excess

---

39. In H.R. REP. No. 332, 94th Cong., 1st Sess. 9 (1975), the committee stated, "The committee understands the importance of providing educational services to each handicapped child according to his or her individual needs." *See also* 121 CONG. REC. 19,483-84, 37,410 (1975) (remarks of Sen. Randolph); *id.* at 19,504 (remarks of Sen. Mondale); H.R. REP. No. 332, 94th Cong., 1st Sess. 13, 19 (1975); 121 CONG. REC. 23,704 (remarks of Rep. Brademas); 121 CONG. REC. 37,026 (remarks of Rep. Quie).

40. 20 U.S.C. § 1414(a)(5) (1982).

41. *See supra* note 6.

42. *See infra* section III B (discussion concerning the broad concept of education).

43. 20 U.S.C. § 1412(3) (1982); 34 C.F.R. § 300.320 (1984).

44. S. REP. No. 168, 94th Cong., 1st Sess. 12, *reprinted in* 1975 U.S. CODE CONG. & AD. NEWS 1425, 1436.

costs."[45] A public school has a commitment to spend the same amount of its general funds on each child. If the school were only required under the EAHCA to provide conventional education to handicapped children, it would have few "excess costs." The Act contemplates that the education of a handicapped child will be more expensive than that of a nonhandicapped child. Such "excess costs" would likely be the result of the provision of related services or the development of a special educational program uniquely suited to that child's needs and not available within the regular public school curriculum.

III

STANDARDS AND A DEFINITION

A. Judicial and Administrative Standards

After the EAHCA was enacted, the different courts set about developing various and often inconsistent standards to help them determine whether a school system was providing an "appropriate education" under the Act. Among the most popular of these standards were a self-sufficiency standard,[46] an equality standard which required the provision of educational opportunity commensurate with that given to nonhandicapped children,[47] a standard which required the maximization of a child's potential,[48] and a standard which required eliminating the effects of the handicap.[49] A few courts tried more unusual approaches, often borrowed from other areas of the law, including a best interests of the child standard developed by a former family court judge[50]

---

45. "Excess costs" is defined by the Act as:
> those costs which are in excess of the average annual per student expenditure in a local educational agency during the preceding school year for an elementary or secondary school student, as may be appropriate, and which shall be computed after deducting (A) amounts received under this subchapter or under title I [20 U.S.C. 2701 et seq.] or title VII [20 U.S.C. 3221 et seq.] of the Elementary and Secondary Education Act of 1965, and (B) any State or local funds expended for programs which would qualify for assistance under this subchapter or under such titles.

20 U.S.C. § 1401(20) (1982).

46. *E.g.*, Armstrong v. Kline, 476 F. Supp. 583, 603 (E.D. Pa. 1979), *remanded,* Battle v. Pennsylvania, 629 F.2d 269 (3d Cir. 1980), *cert. denied,* 452 U.S. 968 (1981); Matthews v. Campbell, 1979-80 EDUC. HANDICAPPED L. REP. (CRR) 551:264 (E.D. Va. 1979).

47. *E.g.*, Springdale School Dist. v. Grace, 656 F.2d 300, 304 (8th Cir. 1981), *vacated,* 458 U.S. 1118 (1982); Gladys J. v. Pearland Indep. School Dist., 520 F. Supp. 869, 875 (S.D. Tex. 1981); Rowley v. Board of Educ., 483 F. Supp. 528 (S.D.N.Y.), *aff'd,* 632 F.2d 945 (1980), *rev'd,* 458 U.S. 176 (1982).

48. *E.g.*, Rabinowitz v. New Jersey State Bd. of Educ., 550 F. Supp. 481 (1982); Age v. Bullitt County Pub. Schools, 1979-80 EDUC. HANDICAPPED L. REP. (CRR) 551:505 (W.D. Ky. 1980); *cf.* Bales v. Clarke, 523 F. Supp. 1366 (E.D. Va. 1981) (state is not required to provide a perfect education to any child); Springdale School Dist. v. Grace, 656 F.2d 300 (8th Cir.), *vacated,* 458 U.S. 1118 (1981) (state has no duty to provide the *best* education).

49. Harrell v. Wilson County Schools, 58 N.C. App. 260, 293 S.E.2d 687 (1982), *appeal dismissed,* 306 N.C. 740, 295 S.E.2d 759, *cert. denied,* 460 U.S. 1012 (1983). In that case the court said:
> We believe that our General Assembly "intended to eliminate the effects of the handicap, at least to the extent that the child will be given an equal opportunity to learn, if that is reasonably possible."

Id. at 264-65, 293 S.E.2d at 690 (quoting Board of Educ. v. Rowley, 458 U.S. 176, 215 (1982) (White, J., dissenting)).

50. Grkman v. Scanlon, 528 F. Supp. 1032, 1035 (W.D. Pa. 1981).

and a standard which required the balancing of interests.[51]

In 1982 the Supreme Court focused on the EAHCA for the first time in *Board of Education v. Rowley*[52] and either expressly or implicitly rejected all of these prior standards. The standard to be used for determining appropriate education, the Court held, was whether or not the child was receiving some educational benefit. The rationale set forth was as follows:

> Implicit in the congressional purpose of providing access to a "free appropriate public education" is the requirement that the education to which access is provided be sufficient to confer some educational benefit upon the handicapped child. It would do little good for Congress to spend millions of dollars in providing access to a public education only to have the handicapped child receive no benefit from that education . . . . We therefore conclude that the "basic floor of opportunity" provided by the Act consists of access to specialized instruction and related services which are individually designed to provide educational benefit to the handicapped child.[53]

Educational benefit in the case of Amy Rowley, a deaf child, meant she was performing better than the average child and advancing easily from grade to grade without the benefit of a sign language interpreter, although she understood less than she would have if not handicapped. The *Rowley* court relied considerably on the section of the EAHCA which requires the provision of related services necessary to permit the child to benefit from his instruction.[54]

The Court rejected the idea that self-sufficiency could be a standard in itself because it was at once an inadequate protection and an overly demanding requirement.[55] According to the majority opinion, the references in the legislative history to the attainment of self-sufficiency provided evidence of a congressional intent that the services provided to handicapped children be educationally beneficial, whatever the nature of their handicap.

Since maximization of a child's potential is not required of schools even in reference to nonhandicapped children, the Court saw no reason to impose such a standard in the case of handicapped children. The district court opinion in *Rowley* acknowledged that even the best public schools lack the resources to enable every child to achieve his full potential.[56]

Although the *Rowley* decision caused much consternation among commentators and advocates of education for the handicapped, who believed the Court was deviating from congressional intent, several factors reveal that it is, in fact, a decision consistent with the sort of standard Congress desired. The Court recognized that dramatic differences in ability exist from one handicapped child to the next and that one child may have little difficulty in an academic setting while another child may encounter great difficulty in

---

51. Pinkerton v. Moye, 509 F. Supp. 107, 112-13 (W.D. Va. 1981).
52. 458 U.S. 176 (1982).
53. *Id.* at 200-01.
54. *Id.*
55. This was so, according to the Court, because many mildly handicapped children will achieve self-sufficiency without state assistance while personal independence for the severely retarded may be an unrealistic goal. *Id.* at 201 n.23.
56. Rowley v. Board of Educ., 483 F. Supp. 528, 534 (S.D.N.Y. 1980).

acquiring even the most basic of self-maintenance skills.[57] Therefore, the Court confined its decision to cases in which a handicapped child is receiving substantial specialized instruction and related services and who is performing above average in the regular classrooms of a public school system. In doing so, the Court gave credence to the notion that the teaching of life skills may comprise education for some handicapped children who do not perform at that level. Indeed, the tone of the opinion is clearly consistent with the legislative concern that all handicapped children be served regardless of handicap and that priority be given to those not currently receiving an education. The Court, according to its reading of the legislative history and in light of scarce resources, considered children who were already receiving some benefits from public school education to be low on the list of congressional priorities, if covered at all, for they were receiving at least some education while others were not.[58]

It is an unfortunate result of the *Rowley* decision that the most capable handicapped children may bear the burdens of limited financial resources. One commentator has concluded that

> the expansive objectives of the Act are fundamentally at odds with the financial limitations that American public schools encounter in the 1980's. . . . As a result, states and localities are forced to make difficult triage decisions, sacrificing certain objectives to accomplish others. These triage decisions often have a disparate impact on different disability groups, pitting one group against another.[59]

The Supreme Court in *Rowley* could not blindly enforce the EAHCA mandate without regard for the realities of limited state educational resources. In arriving upon its decision, the Court was enforcing what it saw as the most explicit priorities of the Act, the education of the most severely handicapped children, and sacrificing the least handicapped children to financial limitations.

B. The Broad Concept of Education

It is necessary only to look at a sampling of EAHCA cases to discover that many courts, regardless of the standard used, have taken for granted what the *Rowley* court implied, the notion that a considerable range of activities and skills training ought to be considered education for handicapped children. Depending on the nature and severity of a child's handicap, a specific IEP might include any of a laundry list of basic life skills, such as using a fork and

---

57. The Court also stated, "It is clear that the benefits obtainable by children at one end of the spectrum will differ dramatically from those obtainable by children at the other end. . . ." *Rowley,* 458 U.S. 176, 202 (1982).

58. The Court reached this conclusion in part because of the manner in which Congress presented its statistics. Stated the Court:

> By characterizing the 3.9 million handicapped children who were "served" as children who were "receiving an appropriate education," the Senate and House Reports unmistakably disclose Congress' perception of the type of education required by the Act: an "appropriate education" is provided when personalized educational services are provided.

Id. at 196-97.

59. Stark, *supra* note 5, at 478-79.

sorting tableware, brushing teeth, washing hands, putting on pants, being mobile in the cafeteria line, walking independently from the bus, pouring milk, using a handkerchief,[60] developing communication skills (such as eye contact,[61] use of written and oral language, and integration of language skills[62]), bathing, cooking, cleaning, riding public transportation, learning basic prevocational skills,[63] or any mix of cognitive, academic, prevocational, and self-help skills.[64] One court has required the provision of a summer program consisting of noninstructional enrichment activities such as camping, field trips, swimming, other sports, playground and recreational activities, gardening, and work skills training.[65] According to another court, an IEP must focus on the acquisition of functional skills including daily living abilities, vocational activities, recreational activities, social and community adjustment, and the development of nonverbal communication skills.[66]

Instead of focusing on specific skills, a number of other courts have simply held that the concept of education is necessarily broad with respect to many profoundly and severely impaired children[67] and "embodies both academic instruction and a broad range of associated services traditionally grouped under the general rubric of 'treatment.' "[68] In *Kruelle v. New Castle County School District,*[69] for example, the Third Circuit used a broad concept of education to include within the EAHCA mandate the needs of 13-year-old Paul Kruelle, a profoundly retarded child suffering also from cerebral palsy. Paul had the social skills of a 6-month-old child and an IQ well below 30. He could not walk, dress himself, speak, or eat unaided, was not toilet trained, and had a low receptive communication level. Paul also had emotional problems which caused him to choke and induce vomiting when he was under stress.[70] Nevertheless, the court held that Paul was entitled to education under the EAHCA.

---

60.   Matthews v. Campbell, 1979-80 EDUC. HANDICAPPED L. REP. (CRR) 551:264, :265 (E.D. Va. 1979).

61.   Stacey G. v. Pasadena Indep. School Dist., 547 F. Supp. 61 (S.D. Tex. 1982).

62.   Matthews v. Ambach, 552 F. Supp. 1273 (W.D.N.Y. 1982).

63.   *In re* Alison I., 1979-80 EDUC. HANDICAPPED L. REP. (CRR) 501:257, :258 (Conn. SEA 1979).

64.   Adams Cent. School Dist. v. Deist, 214 Neb. 307, 334 N.W.2d 775 (1983), *cert. denied,* 104 S. Ct. 239 (1984).

65.   Birmingham School Dist. v. Superintendent of Pub. Instr., 120 Mich. App. 465, 328 N.W.2d 59 (1982).

66.   Campbell v. Talladega County Bd. of Educ., 518 F. Supp. 47, 55 (N.D. Ala. 1981).

67.   *See* definition of "profoundly retarded" and "severely retarded," *infra* text accompanying note 120.

68.   Tilton v. Jefferson County Bd. of Educ., 705 F.2d 800, 803 (6th Cir. 1983); *see* Abrahamson v. Hershman, 701 F.2d 223 (1st Cir. 1983); Kruelle v. New Castle County School Dist., 642 F.2d 687 (3d Cir. 1981).

In a case brought under the Developmentally Disabled Assistance and Bill of Rights Act against a state school, the Supreme Court recognized that "[t]here is a technical difference between treatment which applies to curable mental illness, and habilitation, which consists of education and training for those, such as the mentally retarded, who are not ill." Pennhurst State School v. Halderman, 451 U.S. 1, 7 n.2 (1981). While the Court recognized this technical difference, it declined to make that distinction for the purposes of the case.

69.   642 F.2d 687 (3d Cir. 1981).

70.   *Id.* at 688-89.

In such situations courts and educators may even conclude that academic achievement should be secondary to the acquisition of basic life skills if the EAHCA is to achieve its goals of self-sufficiency and educational benefit.[71] Courts often have based such decisions, at least in part, on the legislative emphasis on individualization.[72]

Other courts have noted that the establishment of a priority for the most severely handicapped children revealed congressional awareness of severely and profoundly impaired children and of the foundational nature of their education.[73] As one court observed, "It is not unusual for the [severely or profoundly retarded] child to enter the school system without such basic skills as toilet training, self-dressing and self-feeding. If this is the case, that is where the educator begins; the educational program will be designed to teach these skills."[74]

The idea that the education must fit the child was expressed by another court in the following manner:

> Placement of children with the intelligence of 2-year-olds in a program which emphasizes skills such as reading and writing would seem inadequate for their needs. The harmful consequences of denying plaintiffs an adequate education is underscored by the fact that mentally retarded children have greater need for formal education since they are less likely than ordinary children to learn and develop informally.[75]

The judicial acceptance of such theories becomes evident in cases where the courts have not even attempted to identify a concept of education but, nevertheless, have required the provision of special education services and residential placements to children who are absolutely incapable of benefitting from traditional public school training. In *Gladys J. v. Pearland Independent Schools*,[76] for example, a Texas district court, without attempting to define education, ordered residential placement for a 15-year-old schizophrenic and brain-damaged girl who was functioning at a prekindergarten level, was incapable of washing or dressing herself unaided, and could not maintain consistent toileting and eating skills. Similarily, the court in *Rabinowitz v. New Jersey Board of Education*[77] mandated educational services for an 11-year-old severely retarded child suffering from Down's Syndrome. Before entering school, Abby Rabinowitz had no speech, extremely limited fine and gross motor activities, and an IQ of 20. Her subsequent educational progress consisted of learning to feed and dress herself.

The provision of educational services in such cases is the result of the deciding courts' broad concept of education. If these courts did not believe

---

71. Rettig v. Kent City School Dist., 539 F. Supp. 768 (N.D. Ohio 1981), *aff'd in part and vacated in part*, 720 F.2d 463 (6th Cir. 1983), *cert. denied*, 104 S. Ct. 2379 (1984).

72. Crawford v. Pittman, 708 F.2d 1028 (5th Cir. 1983).

73. *E.g., Kruelle*, 642 F.2d 687 (3d Cir. 1981); Abrahamson v. Hershman, 701 F.2d 223 (1st Cir. 1983).

74. Armstrong v. Kline, 476 F. Supp. 583, 591 (E.D. Pa. 1979), *remanded sub nom.* Battle v. Pennsylvania, 629 F.2d 269 (3d Cir. 1980), *cert. denied*, 452 U.S. 968 (1981).

75. Fialkowski v. Shapp, 405 F. Supp. 946, 959 (E.D. Pa. 1975).

76. 520 F. Supp. 869 (S.D. Tex. 1981).

77. 550 F. Supp. 481 (D.N.J. 1982).

that life skills were a part of education, they would not prescribe educational services for children who were capable of learning little else.

IV

CONCEPTS IN CONTROVERSY

Not all courts have adopted such a broad concept of education for the purposes of the EAHCA, especially when the end result is residential placement. A great deal of the debate centers around the creation of a distinction between placements for educational purposes and placements for noneducational purposes.[78] This issue is divisible into two separate issues, both of which are significant in developing a practicable definition of education. First, a number of courts have purported to draw a line between psychological placements and educational placements. Second, some courts have decided that children with exceptionally severe handicaps are ineducable and therefore not included in the group to be served by the EAHCA.

A.   The Psychological/Educational Distinction

Placements for medical reasons are not considered educational placements under the EAHCA, and in such situtations, the school system is responsible only for the educational services rendered during the length of a child's hospitalization.[79] Some courts, and more educational agencies, have compared situations where a child is emotionally impaired with those where placement is necessary for medical reasons, and have reached similar results.[80]

In *McKenzie v. Jefferson*,[81] 11-year-old Alexandra McKenzie was determined by a hearing officer to be a seriously emotionally disturbed child. She had suddenly begun to experience feelings of grandiosity, depersonalization, and hallucinations of being Jesus. Later she started experiencing severe nightmares and depression, suffering severe pain with no organic basis, and exhibiting psychotic behavior. Nevertheless, the hearing officer refused to order the school district to pay for Alexandra's residential placement at a school for the learning disabled and emotionally disturbed. Instead he tried to place her at St. Elizabeth's Hospital which had no suitable program. The District of

---

78. The regulations read in part:

If placement in a public or private residential program is necessary to provide special education and related services to a handicapped child, the program, including non-medical care and room and board, must be at no cost to the parents of the child.

Comment. This requirement applies to placements which are made by public agencies for educational purposes, and includes placements in State-operated schools for the handicapped, such as a State school for the deaf or blind.

34 C.F.R. § 300.302 (1984).

79. *See supra* note 28 (definition of "special education" under the Act).

80. *E.g., In re* Bill D., 1980-81 EDUC. HANDICAPPED L. REP. (CRR) 502:259 (Conn. SEA 1981) (child with schizotypal personality disorder was denied residential placement because the curriculum of the residential school was the same as that of a normal high school with the addition of therapy); *In re* Edward K., 1979-80 EDUC. HANDICAPPED L. REP. (CRR) 501:315 (Conn. SEA 1979) (child's behavior and psychiatric problems influence and override educational needs).

81. 566 F. Supp. 404 (D.D.C. 1983).

Columbia Public Schools (DCPS) eventually placed her at a day school on the grounds of her residential school. The district court concurred with the argument of the DCPS that Alexandra was a very sick child whose illness directly caused her hospitalization for treatment and whose placement was therefore medically founded.[82] The court analogized her situation to that of a child who must be hospitalized for physical injury after an accident, and before receiving special education. Special education, concluded the court, referred to education as that term is commonly understood. It is " 'specially designed instruction.' . . . [T]he key word is instruction as it relates to education."[83]

Other courts have declined so to dichotomize educational and psychological needs. These courts may be separated roughly into two further categories: those who refuse to separate needs which are "intertwined," and those who perceive some differences between psychological and educational needs but consider psychological treatment obligatory on a related services basis.

The court in North v. District of Columbia Board of Education [84] was of the former persuasion. Ty North, a 16-year-old boy, was epileptic, emotionally disturbed, and learning disabled. When Ty was discharged from his original institutional placement, his parents refused to accept him and he was placed in a psychiatric treatment center. The Board of Education contended that Ty's educational needs could be met by a special education day program while his emotional difficulties admittedly required residential treatment. Therefore, the Board argued that the cost of residential placement should not be the responsibility of the public schools. The court disagreed and ordered the Board to provide an appropriate residential academic program with necessary psychiatric, psychological, and medical support and supervision.[85] All of Ty's needs were so intimately intertwined that it was not feasible to separate them.[86]

Since the North decision, other courts have seized this rationale to justify requiring state educational agencies to provide residential placement for schizophrenic and other emotionally and behaviorally disturbed children.[87] In Kruelle v. New Castle County School District,[88] the court combined a broad concept of education with this alleged inextricability of medical and educational needs and ordered residential placement as a necessary ingredient of Paul

---

82. Id. at 412.
83. Id. at 411.
84. 471 F. Supp. 136 (D.D.C. 1979).
85. Id. at 141-42.
86. Courts have often declined to decide matters of educational policy on the theory that courts lack sufficient expertise in such matters and educational policy decisions have traditionally been the responsibility of the state educational agencies. The North court added an interesting twist to that philosophy. While the court asserted its own inability to distinguish educational from other needs, it contemporaneously refused to allow state agencies to do the same. By so deciding, the court implied that matters concerning the scope of the EAHCA will not be decided by the individual state educational agencies but are the responsibility of the court.
87. E.g., Gladys J. v. Pearland Indep. Schools, 520 F. Supp. 869 (S.D. Tex. 1981); Erdman v. State, 1980-81 EDUC. HANDICAPPED L. REP. (CRR) 552:218 (D. Conn. 1980); Christopher T. v. San Francisco Unified School Dist., 553 F. Supp. 1107 (N.D. Cal. 1982).
88. 642 F.2d 687 (3d Cir. 1981); see also supra text accompanying notes 69-70.

Kruelle's learning. That court denied that its decision signaled an abdication of difficult decision making and claimed that the inseverability of such needs is the very basis for holding that the services are an essential prerequisite for learning.[89]

The *Kruelle* court also touched on a second theory used by courts unwilling to bifurcate psychological and educational needs completely, the classification of psychological treatment as related services. That theory states that even though psychotherapy and other psychiatric services might be related to mental health, such counseling also may be required before a child can benefit from an education. Psychological treatment, therefore, should be considered a related service in the same way that tutoring in sign language has been required as a related service, because it is necessary before a particular child can benefit from education.[90] Such a theory is supported further by the definition of related services in the EAHCA, which includes psychological services.[91]

In *In re "A" Family*,[92] the Montana Supreme Court ordered a school system to provide a residential placement, including an intensive psychotherapy program, to a mildly mentally retarded and schizophrenic child on the grounds that psychotherapy is not a medical service but a psychological service which is part of related services. Likewise, in *Papacoda v. Connecticut*,[93] all of the parties agreed that Cherie P., an 18-year-old seriously emotionally disturbed child, could not be educated without a residential placement which coordinated a therapy program with the teaching program. The court distinguished this type of placement from one solely for reasons of health, and ordered the school system to place Cherie in a proper facility which, in the court's opinion, was necessary in order to render her educable.[94] "The purpose of the Act is to provide education for handicapped children, no matter what the source or severity of their problems. . . . Placement in an educational institution designed to educate students with a particular handicap must be recognized as having an educational purpose."[95]

Even in situations similar to those in *Papacoda* and *North*, the courts refrain from holding that a residential placement will be considered to be for educational purposes in all situations where medical or emotional needs affect educational needs. For example, the *North* court noted that in some situations it may be possible "to ascertain and determine whether the social, emotional, medical, or educational problems are dominant and to assign responsibility

---

89. 642 F.2d at 693-95.
90. *E.g.*, Parks v. Pavkovic, 557 F. Supp. 1280 (N.D. Ill. 1983); Gary B. v. Cronin, 542 F. Supp. 102 (N.D. Ill. 1980). For good examples of related services cases, see Tatro v. Texas, 703 F.2d 823 (5th Cir. 1983), *aff'd in part, rev'd in part sub nom.* Irving Indep. School Dist. v. Tatro, 104 S. Ct. 3371 (1984), and Tokarcik v. Forest Hills School Dist., 665 F.2d 443 (3d Cir. 1981), *cert. denied,* 458 U.S. 1121 (1982).
91. *See supra* note 29 (definition of "related services" under the Act).
92. 184 Mont. 145, 602 P.2d 157 (1979).
93. 528 F. Supp. 68 (D. Conn. 1981).
94. *Id.* at 71.
95. *Id.* at 72.

for placement and treatment to the agency operating in the area of that problem."[96] This concept has subsequently been reiterated, by the courts in *Kruelle* and *Gladys J. v. Pearland Independent Schools,*[97] for example. Similarly, the court in *Papacoda* implied that a distinction existed between the placement of Cherie P. and a placement in which the need for education in an institution arises merely because the plaintiff must be institutionalized for psychiatric reasons, thus requiring educators to come to the hospital in order to reach the student.

The same distinction was drawn by the Pennsylvania state educational agency in *In re Carlisle Area School District*[98] when it considered the special education needs of Timothy L., a socially and emotionally disturbed child with a learning disability. The agency ordered a placement for Timothy which provided a more highly controlled and ordered educational program than anything available in the public schools.[99] According to the agency, a program is special education as long as it is designed to have an immediate and measurable impact on poor classroom performance which is the product of a student's handicap.[100] In any event, the agency continued, no substantial evidence appeared on the record to show that Timothy suffered from hallucinatory psychosis, autism, or any other extreme mental disorder. Such disorders would necessitate a child's placement in a psychological or health care institution for basic custodial or health needs rather than for the receipt of special education.[101] Judicial and agency statements like the preceding seem to reveal the belief that, in some subsequent case, the deciding court or agency would have the authority, if not the duty, to consider the placement of a seriously emotionally disturbed child a placement for other than educational purposes.

Certainly the EAHCA and its regulations do not mandate such results. The stated purpose of the Act is to assure that *all* handicapped children have available to them a free and appropriate public education, which emphasizes special education and related services designed to meet their particular needs.[102] The EAHCA expressly includes seriously emotionally disturbed children within its definition of handicapped children.[103] "Seriously emotionally disturbed" is defined in the EAHCA regulations as

a condition exhibiting one or more of the following characteristics over a long period of time and to a marked degree, which adversely affects educational performance:

---

96. 471 F. Supp. at 141.
97. 520 F. Supp. 869 (S.D. Tex. 1981); *see supra* text accompanying note 76.
98. 1982-83 EDUC. HANDICAPPED L. REP. (CRR) 504:194 (Pa. SEA 1982).
99. *Id.* at 504:198-99.
100. *Id.* at 504:196.
101. *Id.* at 504:197.
102. 20 U.S.C. § 1400(c) (1982).
103. The EAHCA definition of handicapped children reads as follows:
The term "handicapped children" means mentally retarded, hard of hearing, deaf, speech impaired, visually handicapped, seriously emotionally disturbed, orthopedically impaired, or other health impaired children with specific learning disabilities, who by reason thereof require special education and related services.
20 U.S.C. § 1401(1) (1982).

(A) An inability to learn which cannot be explained by intellectual, sensory, or health factors;

(B) An inability to build or maintain satisfactory interpersonal relationships with peers and teachers;

(C) Inappropriate types of behavior or feelings under normal circumstances;

(D) A general pervasive mood of unhappiness or depression; or

(E) A tendency to develop physical symptoms or fears associated with personal or school problems.

(ii) The term includes children who are schizophrenic. The term does not include children who are socially maladjusted, unless it is determined that they are seriously emotionally disturbed.[104]

Residential programs, including nonmedical care and room and board, must be provided at no cost to the parents of the child if a placement is necessary to provide special education and related services to a handicapped child.[105] The comment to the EAHCA regulations applies the foregoing requirement to "placements which are made by public agencies for educational purposes."[106] It remains possible that some courts may have viewed this comment as a limitation on the rights of handicapped children by interpreting educational purposes to mean only conventional education. To an emotionally disturbed child, however, the educational environment is a particularly important educational service. It is not uncommon for a seriously emotionally disturbed child's educational program to include psychotherapy or other programs designed to develop relationships with others, decrease inappropriate behavior, and increase appropriate behavior.[107] Such services are no less important to the education of a seriously emotionally disturbed child than clean intermittent catheterization is to the education of a spina bifida child, or learning to add before learning to multiply is to the education of a nonhandicapped child. Reading the comment to the regulations to impose narrow limitations on the meaning of education would prevent many seriously emotionally disturbed children from receiving the services necessary to their learning. Such an exclusion would be inconsistent with the federal mandate of providing education to all handicapped children, including the emotionally disturbed, regardless of the degree of handicap.

In addition, some courts may wrongly rely on the definition of "specific learning disability" in the regulations to exclude seriously emotionally disturbed children from the scope of the Act. That definition excludes from specific learning disabilities those learning problems which are primarily the result of visual, hearing, or motor handicaps, of mental retardation, of emotional disturbance, or of environmental, cultural, or economic disadvantage.[108] That phrase must be considered in context, however, by remembering that almost all of the handicaps listed, including emotional disturbance, are mentioned specifically in other provisions of the EAHCA. In

---

104. 34 C.F.R. § 300.5(b)(8)(ii) (1984).
105. Id. § 300.302.
106. Id.
107. Armstrong v. Kline, 476 F. Supp. 583, 591 (E.D. Pa. 1979).
108. 34 C.F.R. § 300.5(b)(9) (1984).

the learning disabilities section, Congress separated seriously emotionally disturbed children from those with learning problems resulting from environmental, cultural, or economic disadvantage. Clearly, the children excluded are not the emotionally disturbed children defined earlier in the Act, but are those children who have difficulty learning because of their home situations, cultural differences, or economic disadvantages. This section, according to the legislative history, is intended to exclude "slow learners."[109]

Courts have appeared more willing to impose the responsibility for residential programs on school systems when the emotionally disturbed children suffer from other physical or mental handicaps, when their emotional disturbance is congenital or organic, or when the child is adopted.[110] Such distinctions are probably the result of a widespread notion that emotional handicaps can be attributed to parental influences and a judicial view that courts should not force educational systems to pay for handicaps caused by poor parenting.[111] The idea that a serious emotional illness, such as that of Alexandra McKenzie,[112] is caused by a child's parents is speculative at best, especially in light of the inherent difficulty of tracing any emotional problems to their origins, and the lack of any detailed psychological knowledge or background.

Moreover, even if one could prove that the handicap was caused by a child's parents, the EAHCA does not allocate education based upon the origin of any child's handicap, but covers all children suffering from one or more of the handicapping conditions mentioned in the Act's virtually all-inclusive list.[113] The extreme result of such allocation could be the exclusion of broad categories of children whose handicaps were in some manner caused by their parents. For instance, a child with permanent physical injuries resulting from an accident caused by his father or a baby born with defects as a result of its mother's negligence during pregnancy might be excluded from special education programs because its parent caused its defect. No reasonable educational agency would consider making such exclusions. To differentiate among handicapped children would not only violate the equal education standards specifically endorsed by Congress in the legislative history of EAHCA, but it also would conflict with the pervading underlying philosophy of the Act. The EAHCA is a child-based statute, enacted to assist all handicapped children based on their own varied and individual special education needs. Nevertheless, many courts and educational agencies hold fast to their perception that residential placements for some seriously emotionally disturbed children are

---

109. S. REP. No. 168, 94th Cong., 1st Sess. 10, *reprinted in* 1975 U.S. CODE CONG. & AD. NEWS 1425, 1434.

110. For instance, the handicapped child in *Gladys J.* suffered from organic brain damage, the *Kruelle* and *North* children were both multiply handicapped, and the handicapped child in *In re "A" Family* had been adopted by the "A" family. Christopher T. v. San Francisco Unified School Dist., 553 F. Supp. 1107 (N.D. Cal. 1982), involved one child who was both schizophrenic and mentally retarded and another child who had been rejected by his family.

111. *See* Stark, *supra* note 5, at 521-23.

112. *See supra* text accompanying notes 81-83.

113. 20 U.S.C. § 1401(1) (1982); *see supra* note 103.

not the responsibility of the school system because their parents somehow caused their handicaps.

Some states have enacted statutes which separate medical, psychological, and institutional care or services from educational services.[114] In four of these states litigation infrequently arises over responsibility for residential placement costs because statutes mandate interagency cooperation in the delivery of special education services.[115] For use in one of these states, an observer has suggested the consideration of a modified "but for" test, which asks whether an educational program appropriate to meet the unique needs of the particular student is available and could be implemented but for the need for other than educational services, such as medical care or residential care outside of the home.[116] Noneducational placements might include placements made because of abusive or neglectful home conditions affecting the safety and health of the child. This practice of interagency cooperation is expressly permitted under the EAHCA.[117]

In states without such interagency cooperation statutes, another provision of the EAHCA, making the state educational agency responsible for assuring that all educational programs, including those administered by other agencies, are carried out according to state educational standards,[118] becomes relevant. In other words, the educational agency may divide costs with other agencies according to state definitions of educational and other than educational purposes. The educational agency, however, is responsible for assuring that all educational programs for all handicapped children within the EAHCA definition, including programs for the seriously emotionally disturbed, are provided without cost to the child's parents. Under the theory of education proposed in this discussion, education for seriously emotionally disturbed children includes instruction in whatever they are capable of learning, starting with fundamental skills, along with the related services they need in order to benefit from that education. It is presumed that residential care which provides the necessary environment for a child's education would be included. If a child can only learn in a residential placement, then that placement is for educational purposes and should be financed by the state.

---

114. Ariz. Rev. Stat. Ann. § 15-1015G (1981); Conn. Gen. Stat. § 10-76d(d) (West 1981 & Supp. 1983); Ill. Ann. Stat. ch. 122, § 14-7.02 (Smith-Hurd Supp. 1983); Mass. Gen. Laws Ann. ch. 71B, § 10 (West 1978 & Supp. 1983); Nev. Rev. Stat. § 395.050 (1983); S.C. Code Ann. § 59-33-90 (Law. Co-op Supp. 1983).

115. Ariz. Rev. Stat. Ann. § 15-1015G (1981); Conn. Gen. Stat. § 10-76g (West 1981 & Supp. 1983); Mass. Gen. Laws Ann. ch. 71B, § 10 (West 1978 & Supp. 1983).

116. See Mooney & Aronson, supra note 5, at 553.

117. According to 34 C.F.R. § 300.301(a) (1984):

Each State may use whatever State, local, Federal, and private sources of support are available in the State to meet the requirements of this part. For example, when it is necessary to place a handicapped child in a residential facility, a State could use joint agreements between the agencies involved for sharing the cost of that placement.

118. 20 U.S.C. § 1412(6) (1982).

B. The Educable/Ineducable Distinction

The educability of severely handicapped children is an even more hotly contested issue, largely because of the disproportionate cost-benefit ratio associated with educating the severely handicapped.[119] Since such decisions usually deal with the severely or profoundly retarded child, it may be helpful to define briefly the different classifications of mentally retarded children as outlined by the court in *Armstrong v. Kline.*[120]

A "mildly retarded" child has an IQ between 50 and 75. He or she may be able to read at a second or third grade level, do simple math, and function in society. Such children are often unidentifiable and can perform skilled and semiskilled work. The "moderately retarded" child has an IQ between 30 and 50 and frequently has physical impairments. He or she can learn simple arithmetic, basic vocabulary, and fundamental reading skills. Children with IQ's below 30 are considered "severely or profoundly impaired" (SPI). A "severely retarded" child usually will have a physical handicap, some difficulty in moving, and may lack many basic self-help and language skills. Though academically limited, a severely retarded child may learn to count, tell time, and identify a few words. "Profoundly retarded" children are likely to be nonambulatory, have no vocabulary, and possess minimal means of communication. They are much slower learners, forget those things learned more quickly than nonhandicapped children, and have great difficulty generalizing and transferring skills learned in one environment to another environment. These SPI children pose perhaps the greatest problems for interpreters of the EAHCA.

Of the five children involved in *Armstrong* two were SPI children. The other three children were seriously emotionally disturbed. One of the SPI children was Gary Armstrong, who was also hyperactive, partially deaf, and suffered from San Fillipo Syndrome, a fatal disease which caused him to have joint contractures and psychomotor seizures. The other was 17-year-old Natalie Bernard, who was also orthopedically impaired. She had acquired some reading and music skills, but few intellectual or social skills. Educators of the five children articulated their goals for four of the children as the attainment of each child's highest potential in terms of the highest degree of self-sufficiency. In Gary Armstrong's situation, the educational goal was to keep him mobile and at home as long as possible in order to increase his life expectancy. His program consisted of instruction in the following: sitting down

---

119. Note that one author stated:

> When funds are expended to provide an appropriate education for handicapped children, thereby rendering them capable of becoming productive members of society, few observers would object that the money is being wasted. When funds are diverted from the already scant resources allocated for the education of non-handicapped students in an attempt to educate children whom experts believe are incapable of ever functioning in society, however, the benefits may be outweighed by the costs.

Comment, *A Modern Wilderness—The Law of Education for the Handicapped*, 34 Mercer L. Rev. 1045, 1064 (1983).

120. 476 F. Supp. 583, 588 (E.D. Pa. 1979), *remanded sub nom.* Battle v. Pennsylvania, 629 F.2d 269 (3d Cir. 1980), *cert. denied*, 452 U.S. 968 (1981).

when asked, keeping his hands down, dressing, coming when called, feeding himself, toilet training, and sign language. All of this instruction was for the purpose of allowing him to be controlled at home. Natalie's program consisted of basic language, arithmetic, and living skills for the purpose of enabling her to live and work outside an institutional setting.

In striking down the school system's rigid policy of limiting instruction for all children to 180 days per year, the court considered the meaning of education for SPI children, many of whom enter the school system without basic life skills. The court stated that in such circumstances, the child's education begins with the teaching of those skills.[121] The court went on to express its conviction that Congress' intent in enacting the EAHCA was to provide for that education which would leave these children as self-sufficient as possible within the limits of their respective handicaps.[122] On appeal, the Third Circuit also struck down the rigid 180-day policy but it remanded the case for modification of the district court's orders.[123] According to the circuit court, the district court had acted improperly in focusing on the Act's provision of the particular educational goal of self-sufficiency, when such educational policy decisions should be left to the states.[124] The court of appeals disputed neither the facts nor the district court's determination that these children should be provided education. Rather, it repeated the lower court's perception that the point where formal education begins is where a handicapped child is lacking self-help and social skills.

This perception is not a new one. As long ago as 1908, advocates espoused special education as natural development, according to a general principle of special education commanding that education begin where the defect impeded the normal development of the child.[125] In 1979, Sally Smith[126] restated the same principle. In her book, Smith stated that no matter how difficult it may be to find an activity that a child can do independently, one must be found in order to offer him an opportunity for success. A child may need to be taught a whole spectrum of readiness skills before any attempt can be made to achieve his ultimate goals, because he may not have the foundations on which to begin.[127]

Such principles are premised on a belief that every child can learn or, conversely, that no child is ineducable. Not all courts and educational agencies,

---

121. *See supra* text accompanying note 73. For examples of other cases concerning the validity of the 180-day policy, see Crawford v. Pittman, 708 F.2d 1028 (5th Cir. 1983); Yaris v. Special School Dist., 558 F. Supp. 545 (E.D. Mo. 1983), *aff'd*, 728 F.2d 1055 (8th Cir. 1984); Georgia Ass'n of Retarded Citizens v. McDaniel, 511 F. Supp. 1263 (N.D. Ga. 1981), *aff'd*, 716 F.2d 1565 (11th Cir. 1983).

122. 476 F. Supp. at 604.

123. Battle v. Pennsylvania, 629 F.2d 269 (3d Cir. 1980), *cert. denied*, 452 U.S. 968 (1981).

124. *Id.* at 276.

125. *See* S. SARASON & J. DORIS, *supra* note 8, at 305.

126. S. SMITH, NO EASY ANSWERS: THE LEARNING DISABLED CHILD (1979). Sally Smith is an associate professor at American University and the founder and director of the Law School of the Kingsbury Center.

127. *Id.* at 113-14; *see also* Krass, *The Right to Public Education for Handicapped Children: A Primer for the New Advocate*, 1976 U. ILL. L.F. 1016, 1025 (1976).

however, are willing to concur in this belief. *Levine v. Institutions & Agencies Department* [128] involved two profoundly retarded children residing in a state institution for the mentally retarded. Nineteen-year-old Linda Guempel had an IQ between 14 and 35 and a mental and social age of 20 months. Her program emphasized the development of body awareness, sensorimotor skills, and rudimentary self-help skills. Max Levine was 10 years old and confined to a crib as a result of severe brain damage. A physician noted that Max, at age one, remained in a "frog position" with his hands clenched and no control over his head movements. In 1974 Max was admitted into the state institution with an estimated IQ of 1, the motor development of a one-month-old child, no vocalization or language skills, and extremely low adaptive behavior. Although Max had no regularly scheduled programming, as of March 1979 he was able to make sounds, follow objects, respond to noises, and demonstrate pleasure by smiling and moving his head toward the stimulation.

The New Jersey Supreme Court recognized that advances in the fields of education, medical science, and psychology created progressively more opportunities for greater numbers of children to benefit from education, and that some courts therefore might determine that a child such as Max was entitled to an appropriate education. Nevertheless, the court stated that

> the sad fact endures that there is a category of mentally disabled children so severely impaired as to be unable to absorb or benefit from education. It is neither realistic nor meaningful to equate the type of care and habilitation which such children require for their health and survival with 'education' in the sense that that term is used in the [New Jersey] [C]onstitution. [129]

According to the court, Max Levine and Linda Guempel were examples of this type of child.

Several possible rationales may explain the *Levine* decision. The case was decided under a clause in the New Jersey Constitution which requires a thorough and efficient public school system. The goal of that clause, according to the court, was not to provide care for the mentally handicapped, but to prepare children to function politically, economically, and socially in a democratic society. [130] Since profoundly retarded institutionalized children like Max and Linda would never be able to function in such a manner, the constitutional guarantee of education did not extend to them or to their habilitation programs. Futhermore, after noting that the parents of both children did not otherwise question their "moral or legal" obligation to support their children and that both sets of parents were fully capable of paying their share of support, the court found no reason to release them of the obligation. [131]

The *Levine* opinion has been fiercely criticized, beginning with a scathing

---

128. 84 N.J. 234, 418 A.2d 229 (1980).
129. *Id.* at 250, 418 A.2d at 237.
130. *Id.* at 244-49, 418 A.2d at 234-36.
131. Parental obligation for support was calculated on the basis of a statutory formula and reduced by an educational credit for educational expenses of teacher salaries and educational supplies and equipment. The final amount also took into account parental ability to pay. Any remaining costs were the responsibility of the state or the county of residence. *Id.* at 242-43, 418 A.2d at 233.

dissent by Justice Pashman in which he emphatically denounced the suggestion that any child is ineducable. The majority's opinion, according to the dissent, diminished the meaning of our common humanity and denied education its fundamental status by subordinating it to the ability to exercise the franchise or compete in the labor market. Justice Pashman continued:

> I have no quarrel with the majority that the education which children like Linda Guempel and Maxwell Levine can absorb is, even at their present ages, far less than that of the mentally average 5-year-old. Nevertheless, I cannot accept a definition of education which does not provide to each child the training and assistance necessary to function as best they can in whatever will be their environment—even if that environment will be insulated from the world of politics and economic competition . . . . The rudimentary level of their education does not render it unworthy of constitutional protection. We cannot ignore the intellect a child possesses because he possesses so little . . . .[132]

In addition to the criticism offered by Justice Pashman, commentators have found a number of faults in the *Levine* decision.[133] The decision has been criticized because of the speculative nature of differentiating between educable children and children incapable of education. The *Levine* court dismissed this concern on the basis that workable guidelines have been formulated to deal with the problem in the past. Although the court noted that advances in teaching technology might render more children educable, the decision does not account for such changes. Furthermore, the court did not propose any safeguards to ensure accurate prediction of ineducability. A child determined to be ineducable more than likely would be tucked away in a program where any hidden potential would remain undiscovered and unrealized. Given the difficulty of predicting the ability of any child to learn, this consequence is unjustly harsh. The court also failed to consider all of the previously stated purposes and objectives of education, other than the goal of self-sufficiency, which should apply to all children regardless of handicap.

A case like *Levine* arising under the EAHCA rather than a state constitution may have a different result. Several courts and commentators have observed that the EAHCA contains no exclusions for children suffering from exceptionally severe handicaps.[134] In *Matthews v. Campbell*[135] the court ordered residential placement at no cost to the parents despite "serious misgivings" about the ultimate efficacy of the placement, and a belief that attaining even a min-

---

132. *Levine*, 84 N.J. at 275, 418 A.2d at 250 (Pashman, J., dissenting) (footnote omitted).

133. *See* Rothstein, *Educational Rights of Severely and Profoundly Handicapped Children*, 61 NEB. L. REV. 586 (1982). This article also states the following:

> It should be noted that the New Jersey Standards on Public Institutions for the Division of Mental Retardation provide that educational services are "deliberate attempts to facilitate the intellectual, sensorimotor, and effective development of the individual . . . ." It is noteworthy that the head of the Adaptive Learning Center at Hunterdon School considered the following activities to fall within the "education program": increasing body control through motor skill development, increasing awareness through multisensory stimulation, developing self-help skills, developing social and emotional growth, developing receptive and expressive language, and developing visual and auditory skills.

Id. at 606 n.108 (citation omitted).

134. *See* Rothstein, *supra* note 133; Krass, *supra* note 127.

135. 1979-80 EDUC. HANDICAPPED L. REP. (CRR) 551:264 (E.D. Va. 1979).

imum level of self-sufficiency was an almost impossible goal. The *Matthews* court based its decision on the fact that "neither the language of the Act nor the legislative history appears to contemplate the possibility that some children may simply be untrainable."[136] Furthermore, Congress must certainly have set its priorities with these most seriously handicapped children in mind.

Actually, Congress' intent is not so clear. A reading of the legislative history suggests that Congress may have been primarily concerned with handicapped children who, despite their limitations, are capable in some ways of learning, being creative, and becoming productive. The Supreme Court's opinion in *Board of Education v. Rowley*[137] could certainly be read as envisioning that the recipients of educational services under the EAHCA would be children capable of benefiting from instruction. Such theories, however, fail to consider that Congress probably relied on a broad concept of education which differs considerably from traditional public school education.

The Fifth Circuit observed, in a 180-day-rule case, that "the Act requires the state to treat each child as an individual, a human whose unique qualities and needs can be evaluated and served only by a plan designed with wisdom, care and educational expertise."[138] Other commentators have concurred in this perception of education as a "humanization process," as well as a traditional learning process. One psychologist has stated:

> The process whereby an individual is helped to develop new behavior or to apply existing behavior, so as to equip him to cope more effectively with his total environment [is education]. It should be clear, therefore, that when we speak of education we do not limit ourselves to the so-called academics. We certainly include the development of basic self-help skills. Indeed, we include those very complex bits of behavior which help to define an individual as human. We include such skills as toilet training, dressing, grooming, communicating and so on.[139]

According to this humanization view of the EAHCA, "each child must be dealt with at his individual developmental level, and no failure to do so can be countenanced on the basis of the difficulty of a child's problems to treat, or the inadequacy of public resources."[140]

C. The Influence of Cost

Unfortunately, factors other than a child's ability to learn have had a substantial impact on the decisions of courts and educational agencies concerning the education of handicapped children. Because of inadequate resources, agencies and courts have relied on the cost of education to justify the exclusion of certain children, especially as the visible results of education

---

136. *Id.* at 551:266.

137. 458 U.S. 176 (1982); *see supra* notes 53-58 and accompanying text.

138. Crawford v. Pittman, 708 F.2d 1028 (5th Cir. 1983).

139. Roos, *Current Issues in the Education of Mentally Retarded Persons*, in PROCEEDINGS: CONFERENCE ON THE EDUCATION OF MENTALLY RETARDED PERSONS 2 (W. Cegelka ed. 1971), *quoted in* Rothstein, *supra* note 133, at 608.

140. Colley, *The Education for All Handicapped Children Act (EHA): A Statutory and Legal Analysis*, 10 J.L. & EDUC. 137, 160-61 (1981).

decrease.[141] Such reliance has sometimes led to discriminatory results, not only between handicapped and nonhandicapped children, but also among, and within, classes of handicapped children. The educational agency in *Levine v. Institutions & Agencies Department,*[142] for example, distinguished between children in residential programs and those in day programs who were receiving the same or similar services. Parents of the residentially placed children were responsible for a substantial part of their child's program costs, relieved only by an educational credit determined on the basis of teacher salaries and educational equipment. Day school children received an education at no cost to their parents. Furthermore, the educational credit given to the parents of the residential children was significantly lower than the cost of the day school program and did not account for related services.

The New Jersey court held that this variance did not deny equal protection of the laws and proposed several theories for its decision. The funding scheme, according to the court, encouraged mainstreaming by providing a financial disincentive to parents who place their children in residential institutions.[143] The flaw in this justification lies in its reliance on the fallacious belief that all handicapped children are better off living at home instead of in a residential facility. In reality, some handicapped children can benefit from an education only if they have 24-hour instruction and care and, thus, appropriate education for such children includes residential care. The use of generalizations to determine "appropriateness" violates the requirement of the EAHCA that each child be considered individually. Moreover, the funding scheme may, in some cases, provide incentive for families to place their handicapped child in an inappropriate educational setting.

The *Levine* court also considered significant the "unquestioned" moral obligations of parents to pay for the care of their children. Nothing in the EAHCA prohibits a school system from charging a parent for services other than educational care, or for a portion of the cost of residential placement when day care has been determined to be "appropriate education" for that child. A parent who chooses the residential placement route, however, should not be penalized for making that choice. Educational services provided free of charge to day school children should be equally available to similarly handicapped children in residential placements.

The *Levine* court found it relevant that the state statutory scheme challenged by the plaintiffs in that case took into account the parents' ability to pay.[144] The EAHCA, however, makes no exclusions on the basis of the parent's ability to pay. All handicapped children, regardless of the severity, cause, or cost of handicap, are entitled to a free and appropriate education under the EAHCA. Public school systems do not charge parents of nonhandi-

---

141. *See supra* note 115.

142. 84 N.J. 234, 418 A.2d 229 (1980); *see supra* notes 128-31 and accompanying text.

143. 84 N.J. at 263, 418 A.2d at 244.

144. The court conceded that the plaintiffs may be entitled to relief in relation to a determination of the amount of educational credit, especially in light of the EAHCA mandate of free public special education and related services. *Id.* at 264, 418 A.2d at 244.

capped children for the education of their children according to their ability to pay. To do so for parents of handicapped children would be directly opposed to the EAHCA mandate which calls for equality of educational opportunity. According to the legislative history, insufficiency of resources is no defense to unequal treatment. The Senate report stated the following principle:

> [A]vailable funds must be expended equitably in such a manner that no child is entirely excluded from a publicly supported education consistent with his needs and ability to benefit therefrom. The inadequacies of the . . . [s]ystem . . . certainly cannot be permitted to bear more heavily on the "exceptional" or handicapped child than on the normal child.[145]

Such a statement is evidence enough that, while Congress foresaw shortages of educational resources and deferred to the states as to the allocation of those resources, it also intended to forestall any attempt by a school system to differentiate among children based upon the cost of their respective educations. Nevertheless, it appears from recent EAHCA cases that courts and agencies have continued to consider cost-indicative factors when making determinations under the EAHCA.

A Uniform and Flexible Definition

If the EAHCA is to operate nondiscriminatorily, there must exist a uniform definition of education consistent with the goals of the EAHCA. According to the court in *Battle v. Pennsylvania,*[146] educational needs are necessarily determined in reference to goals. A child only needs certain programming in order to accomplish certain educational objectives. It seems, therefore, the definition of education provided by an individual judge, court, or agency determines not only what a handicapped child receives in educational services but also what that child needs.

It should now be clear that education should not be defined with reference to the cost of a program or to notions of parental fault. In addition, it is evident that Congress did not exclude severely or profoundly handicapped children from the Act's coverage. Congress very likely relied on the broad concept of education that was prevalent in the field of education in the 1970's. The legislative history acknowledges that Congress was greatly influenced by court cases in the early 1970's that established a right to free and appropriate education for all handicapped children.[147] Congress also must have been influenced to some extent by the prevailing attitudes of contemporary theorists and educators that no child is ineducable.

If Congress intended that education be provided to even the most severely

---

145. S. REP. No. 168, 94th Cong., 1st Sess. 23, *reprinted in* 1975 U.S. CODE CONG. & AD. NEWS 1425, 1447 (quoting Mills v. Board of Educ., 348 F. Supp. 866, 876 (D.D.C. 1972)).

146. 629 F.2d 269, 276 (3d Cir. 1980), *remanding* Armstrong v. Kline, 476 F. Supp. 583 (E.D. Pa. 1979), *cert. denied,* 452 U.S. 968 (1981).

147. Pennsylvania Ass'n for Retarded Children v. Commonwealth, 334 F. Supp. 1257 (E.D. Pa. 1971) (per curiam), 343 F. Supp. 279 (E.D. Pa. 1972); Mills v. Board of Educ., 348 F. Supp. 866 (D.D.C. 1972); *see supra* text accompanying notes 18-20.

handicapped children, then certainly that education must mean something beyond conventional education. In some cases, this type of education may mean something beyond even the attainment of basic life skills. Such a definition also includes the instruction given to a child with a serious emotional disturbance in order to assist him or her in learning and adjusting to the normal world.

The key concept underlying these definitions is that whatever a child can learn is education to that child. Education is a relative concept which begins wherever the normal course of development left off and follows a natural course.

This definition is intentionally flexible, adaptable to each child, and subject to change as a child's needs and abilities change. A child initially may have the educational goal of attaining basic self-help skills. If a child can achieve that goal, his or her definition of education will then take a somewhat higher form, perhaps learning simple arithmetic or learning to read. If a child cannot attain self-sufficiency, that child's education is measured by whatever it is he or she is able to learn. If a child is not entitled to the opportunity to maximize his or her potential, he or she is at least entitled to progress from simple tasks to more complex tasks, each building on the other, much as non-handicapped children are given the opportunity to progress from grade to grade.

A flexible definition has a number of advantages. It takes into account the varying degrees of ability of handicapped children and makes educational experience uniquely suited to each child's needs. It also is consistent with the Supreme Court's determination in *Board of Education v. Rowley*[148] that all handicapped children are entitled to some educational benefit. Such a definition excludes no handicapped children on the basis of cost, parental fault, or severity of handicap and, thus, avoids making arbitrary distinctions among handicapped children. It is based on notions of equality and individualization, consistent with legislative intent.

Opponents will criticize this definition for not taking into account the constraint of scarce resources. Admittedly, educational resources are currently limited. Clearly, however, Congress did not intend that scarce resources would deny education to any handicapped child. Instead, it intended to provide assistance to state educational agencies for the excess costs involved in educating all handicapped children. Furthermore, the cost of a program has no relevance in determining whether or not that program is education. Theoretically, a program which is considered education in a wealthy school district should still be considered education in a poor school district. Rather than permit states to slight handicapped children on the basis of scarce resources, Congress has required the states to provide certain programs regardless of cost. A fortunate consequence of such congressional prodding would arise if states were forced, as a result, to reconsider and increase their educational

---

148.   458 U.S. 176 (1982); *see supra* notes 53-58 and accompanying text.

budgets. In any event, allocation of resources must at least be equitable and must not weigh more heavily against the handicapped. Every handicapped child must receive some portion of the educational pie, even if that portion is instruction in the most fundamental of skills.

Such a definition of education is, in reality, a conglomeration of the more traditional definitions arranged on a sliding scale to be applied individually to the unique situation of each handicapped child. The novelty of this approach lies not in the definitions used, but in the use of the definitions.

V

CONCLUSION

Ideally, a flexible definition of education could be determined for all children, both handicapped and nonhandicapped, focusing on each child's individual needs and potential. It has even been suggested that IEP's be developed for all children.[149] Unfortunately, educational resources are often far too limited to provide such individualization. Under the EAHCA, however, Congress has selected one group of special children, the handicapped, who are most in need of individualized education, and has required special treatment for that group from the educational agencies. Education of these special children cannot be defined simply as conventional education. Rather, it must incorporate a broader concept of education and include whatever a handicapped child is able to learn in light of his or her unique needs and particular handicaps.

---

149. M. McCarthy & P. Deignan, What Legally Constitutes an Adequate Public Education? 86 (1983).

8

AGE APPROPRIATENESS AS A FACTOR IN EDUCATIONAL PLACEMENT DECISIONS

Evelyn M. Pursley

I

Introduction

Handicapped students are becoming integrated into the mainstream of public education as hundreds of thousands of exceptional children are now served in public schools at public expense[1] following the enactment of Public Law No. 94-142, the Education for All Handicapped Children Act of 1975[2] (EAHCA or Act) and section 504 of the Rehabilitation Act of 1973.[3] Enormous gains have been made toward achieving full educational opportunities for handicapped children. Now that the legislation appears to be successful in meeting its broad goals of providing access to an adequate public education for handicapped children, however, parents, school systems, and ultimately courts are grappling with many questions regarding specific placement decisions within the public school system—a particularly difficult task because the legislation gives little guidance regarding substantive requirements for the educational programs of handicapped children.[4]

One of these difficult questions will be addressed in this comment: should school districts be required to place children in an educational setting where they will have an opportunity to interact with chronological age peers, even if they are functioning academically at a different level? This question is not directly addressed by either of these statutes or their accompanying regulations, and few reported cases have even considered the question in making a placement decision—much less made it the determining factor. The issue, however, was recently litigated in the Durham (North Carolina) County School System when parents of an 18-year-old mentally retarded student challenged the placement of their son in a self-contained classroom for mentally handicapped students located in a junior high school because it was not "age appropriate." Instead, the parents requested the same academic program—a self-contained classroom for academic instruction with mainstreaming for physical education and extracurricular activities—but located at the high

---

1. Stark, *Tragic Choices in Special Education: The Effect of Scarce Resources on the Implementation of Pub. L. No. 94-142*, 14 Conn. L. Rev. 477, 478 (1982).
2. 89 Stat. 773 (codified as amended at 20 U.S.C. §§ 1401-1461 (1982)).
3. Pub. L. No. 93-112, 87 Stat. 394 (codified at 29 U.S.C. § 794 (1982)).
4. *See infra* note 24 and accompanying text.

school where the mainstreaming would be carried out with his chronological age peers. Although the parents lost on this issue at the due process hearing, and this decision was subsequently affirmed at the state hearing review level and in state court, the parties were not allowed to develop this issue fully at the first hearing.[5] Full development of the legal issues shows that consideration of chronological age appropriateness may be required as a factor in placement decisions for some children.

This comment will first describe the North Carolina case as an illustration of the issue of age-appropriate placement and then explore ways in which the two statutes and accompanying regulations may require consideration and implementation of chronological age-appropriate educational placement.

Second, it will develop the idea that education includes nonacademic benefits such as the development of social skills. Thus, age appropriateness should be considered in every placement decision as a method of providing socialization skills and may be required in cases where the child's individual program shows that he can function in and gain benefit from an age-appropriate environment. The comment will then show that the integration principle expressed by the least restrictive environment mandate also requires age-appropriate placement unless the handicapping condition requires removal from such a regular educational environment. Furthermore, it will assert that such a requirement does not infringe upon local autonomy in the field of public education as states have chosen to have their freedom of decisionmaking curbed to the extent necessary to comply with the statutory requirements for federal funding.

Finally, the comment will explore the idea that refusing to allow equal socialization benefits from participation in age-appropriate placements constitutes discrimination under section 504 of the Rehabilitation Act. It will also explore the suggestion that, in some situations, affirmative modification of programs may be required to avoid such discrimination.

II

POE CASE

A. Educational Placement

At the time of the hearing, Clint Poe was an 18-year-old moderately retarded student attending public school in the Durham County School System (hereinafter also referred to as the local educational agency or LEA or school system). He was classified as trainable mentally handicapped (TMH)[6]

---

5. Administrative Hearing Decision at 2 (Durham, N.C. 1982) [hereinafter cited as Hearing Decision]. The transcript of this hearing is recorded in three volumes, hereinafter cited as I, II or III Hearing Transcript.

6. Mental retardation is "a term referring to that group of conditions characterized by a) slow rate of maturation, b) reduced learning capacity, and c) inadequate social adjustment, present singly or in combination and associated with intellectual functioning which is below the average range. . . ." C. GOOD, DICTIONARY OF EDUCATION 499 (3d ed. 1973). Mentally retarded individuals are classified according to IQ range. Trainable mentally retarded individuals function in approxi-

and was functioning academically at approximately the first grade level.[7] The level of his social functioning was in dispute. The LEA contended that he was functioning at a pre-teen social level, while his parents and community acquaintances argued that he functioned well among persons of his own age and older.[8] Clint was receiving academic instruction in a self-contained classroom for TMH students located in a junior high school. Though he was not interacting with nonhandicapped students in the classroom, he did have an opportunity to do so at lunch time, between classes, and during field trips and other extracurricular activities.[9]

A survey of his placement history reveals that Clint was never placed in a school containing chronological age peers. Upon entering the Durham County School System in 1973 at age nine, he was placed in the TMH program which was then located at the Kindergarten Center.[10] He remained there through the 1975-76 school year when the school system established a second location for its TMH program. At age twelve, Clint moved with his class to a sixth grade center where he remained for three school years until age fifteen.[11]

In 1979, in response both to parental requests for age-appropriate placement for their retarded children and to a similar recommendation from its own TMR Study Committee, the LEA established a TMH class at the junior high school level.[12] Clint moved there at age fifteen and remained in that

---

mately the 40-60 IQ range and are capable of being trained "to perform some personally and socially useful operations, but . . . cannot acquire functional literacy." *Id.* at 362. Educable mentally retarded individuals fall within the 50-75 IQ range, "do not exhibit unusual or erratic behavior, are not necessarily marked by any special physical stigmata . . . are almost indistinguishable from the normal population," and may be expected to achieve literacy to the fourth or fifth grade level. *Id.*

Clint's psychological tests indicate that he did not fit the classical pattern for either TMH or EMH students. The parties, however, agreed that he functioned as a moderately retarded or TMH student.

7. Hearing Review Decision at 4 (Raleigh, N.C. 1982) [hereinafter cited as Hearing Review Decision].

8. *Id.*

9. Brief for Appellants at 7, Poe v. Durham County Schools, No. 82-2566 (N.C. Super. Ct. 1982) [hereinafter cited as Appellants' Brief].

10. Although Clint had begun his schooling in a TMH placement in another school system, upon first entering the Durham County System, his parents agreed to try placing Clint in an EMH program because he was testing at a mildly retarded level and because they considered the Kindergarten Center an undesirable location for the TMH class. However, Clint was not successful in the EMH program housed in a "regular" elementary school, and his parents agreed to return him to a TMH placement. Petitioners' Brief at 1, Administrative Hearing for Clint Poe (Durham, N.C. 1982) [hereinafter cited as Petitioners' Brief].

11. *Id.*

12. In fact, during the 1977-78 school year a group of concerned parents in the Durham City and Durham County School Systems studied the question of appropriate educational placement for retarded children. An early suggestion for a center for handicapped students segregated from both school systems eventually was rejected by the majority. Instead, based upon their studies of learning principles including role modeling, normalization, and least restrictive environment, 489 parents (184 parents of handicapped children and 305 parents of nonhandicapped children) endorsed a plan which called for "education in the least restrictive environment, placement of handicapped children in age appropriate settings, four levels of school placement (pre-school, elementary, junior high, and high school), a strong vocational program, and access to extracurricular and 'nonacademic' activities." Petitioners' Brief at 1.

After the plan was presented to both school systems in May 1978, the Durham County School

placement through the 1981-82 school year, when his due process LEA hearing was held. He was then eighteen years old.

The LEA argued that Clint could interact with chronological age peers even though placed at the junior high level because the school population included older nonhandicappped students. However, a study of the nonhandicapped junior high school population at Clint's school showed that, of the total 858 students attending:

- 600 were 14 years of age or younger
- 113 were 15
- 18 were 16
- 3 were 17
- 0 were 18 (Clint's age).[13]

Clint's teacher for 1981-82 suggested in the proposed 1982-83 individualized education program (IEP) developed for Clint that a high school placement would be preferred.[14] Durham County Schools did offer a program for mentally retarded students at the high school level, but it was designed for educable mentally handicapped (EMH) students and therefore was structurally different from a TMH program. The Durham program offered one to three class periods a day of academic work for EMH students in a separate classroom. The students joined nonhandicapped students for nonacademic classes and extracurricular activities.

Two TMH students who were functioning particularly well had moved into this program at the high school with some success, and such placement was offered to Clint. However, this program was not recommended for TMH students because it did not offer the necessary curriculum, structure, or pupil/teacher ratio for such students and the school system did not adapt the program to accommodate entering TMH students.[15] The Poes, therefore, refused such placement, requesting instead that an appropriate TMH program be established at the high school level so that Clint and other highschool-aged TMH students could be taught separately from EMH students in a self-contained classroom with appropriate vocational education,[16] yet could

---

System decided that it was not feasible to establish a joint program with the City Schools and set up its own TMR Study Committee. After conducting its own study which included visiting other school systems, the Committee reached the consensus that the system "should offer TMH classes in 'age-appropriate' settings with nonhandicapped students in at least three settings—elementary, junior high, and high school." Id.

13. Petitioners' Brief at 3.

14. Petitioners' Brief at 1, State Hearing Review (Raleigh, N.C. 1982).

15. Petitioners' Brief at 2; Appellants' Brief at 8.

16. The Poes requested in-school, hands-on vocational instruction for two hours daily to replace the introductory and exploratory courses which Clint was receiving for two hours every other week. They contended that the task training must be provided at the high school because of the programs and facilities available there. Although both hearing officers found that Clint did indeed need increased task training to prepare him for future employment and to allow him increased independence, the officers found that it was not necessary to provide this training at the high school because appropriate modifications could be made to his program at the junior high school. Hearing Decision at 7; Hearing Review Decision at 7.

be mainstreamed for lunch, assemblies, and school-wide events and possibly mainstreamed for nonacademic subjects.

B. The Poes' Challenge

When the Durham School System refused to establish such a program at the high school level, the Poes requested a hearing to determine whether the EAHCA required that an appropriate educational program for Clint include a high school placement with chronological age peers. In addition, they sought a determination of whether the failure to make accommodations for Clint to receive educational benefits and services in a high school with chronological age peers was a denial of equal educational opportunity in violation of section 504 of the Rehabilitation Act of 1973.

Although the hearing officer heard extensive testimony, much of which related to chronological age placement, she expressly declined to consider or determine the issue of whether chronological age placement was a necessary element of appropriate education for all trainable mentally retarded individuals. Because she believed the purpose of the hearing was to determine the appropriate placement for one individual, she did not allow the parties to fully develop the issue on the record; she considered only evidence and testimony specific to Clint's educational program, giving primary attention to his level of performance and his identified strengths and weaknesses.[17]

The hearing officer found that Clint's current placement in a self-contained class at the junior high level was appropriate[18] because no federal or state regulation required "a local school administrative unit to set up a particular type of class at each level within the educational system or . . . [indicated] that students, in order to receive an appropriate education, must be placed in a school with students of the same age."[19] She also found that section 504 only required that handicapped children have an opportunity to participate in nonacademic activities with nonhandicapped children—not necessarily nonhandicapped age mates.[20]

These factual and legal findings were affirmed by a State Hearing Review Officer. However, he specifically found that it was possible for a student "to benefit in social skills development from contact with other persons of approximately his chronological age," and that "the student could have increased access to such persons by placement at the senior high school level."[21] He also stated that he could not say that the parents' position was without merit because Clint and other high-school-aged TMH students might benefit from a self-contained class at the senior high school level and because the class might thrive with the support of the school system and the commu-

---

17. Hearing Decision at 2.
18. The Hearing Officer did require certain vocational training modifications to the current IEP. *See supra* note 16.
19. Hearing Decision at 6-7.
20. *Id.* at 7.
21. Hearing Review Decision at 5.

nity. The Hearing Review Officer suggested, however, that the local board of education would be the proper forum for requesting such a program, and that based upon the record of this case he could not order the requested placement.[22]

III

APPROPRIATE EDUCATION UNDER PUBLIC LAW NO. 94-142

The Poes' major argument under the EAHCA[23] was that Clint was not receiving the "appropriate" education which is required by the statute. To evaluate the validity of this argument, one must consider what is meant by "appropriate."

The EAHCA provides federal funds to assist state and local education agencies in educating their handicapped students. To qualify for such funds, a state must comply with the objectives and procedures established by the Act. The statute contains both procedural and substantive requirements. However, the procedural requirements far outweigh the substantive requirements in number, complexity, and specificity.[24] The goals, programs, and timetables of the state plan which must be submitted[25] and the methods for challenging the appropriateness of particular educational programs[26] are spelled out in great detail, whereas the major substantive requirement of the Act is merely that the state provide a "free appropriate public education" to handicapped children.[27] As one commentator noted, "in effect, the Act guarantees procedures whereby parents may challenge the appropriateness of their child's educational program, but provides only the most general guidelines for resolving the substantive questions such challenges may present."[28]

Because of the lack of substantive guidelines, most disputes have involved the meaning of "appropriate" education. Some commentators and courts concluded that Congress did not define the term because it intended that the

---

22. *Id.* at 17.
23. Pub. L. No. 94-142, 89 Stat. 773 (codified as amended at 20 U.S.C. §§ 1401-1461 (1982)).
24. In fact, one commentator noted that "it is difficult to find, in other Federal legislation concerning matters of such traditional local concern as education, a statute that is so prescriptive in its procedural obligations." *EHLR Analysis, What* Rowley *Means,* 1982-83 EDUC. HANDICAPPED L. REP. (CRR) SA-29, -34 (Supp. 84, Nov. 12, 1982).
There are good reasons for not creating specific substantive requirements for educational programs for the handicapped. Given the broad range of handicapping conditions covered by the statute, it would be virtually impossible to write generic requirements for educational programs without ignoring important differences among individuals. *See infra* Part III B. The lack of agreement among educators as to the most effective programs for certain handicapped students would also make Congress reluctant to adopt specific guidelines, especially since statutory adoption of certain methods would tend to stop potentially valuable experimentation at the local level. Furthermore, Congress is particularly wary of ordering specific programs because of the traditional notion that education is primarily a state and local concern. *See infra* part V; Note, *Enforcing the Right to an "Appropriate" Education: The Education for All Handicapped Children Act of 1975,* 92 HARV. L. REV. 1103, 1108-09 (1979).
25. 20 U.S.C. § 1413 (1982).
26. *Id.* § 1415(b), (e)(2).
27. *Id.* § 1412(1).
28. Note, *supra* note 24, at 1103.

courts and hearing officers should do so.[29] Although admitting that the definition "tends toward the cryptic rather than the comprehensive," the Supreme Court rejected this view in *Board of Education v. Rowley,*[30] finding that the Act does indeed define the term "appropriate education."[31] Based upon these statutory definitions, the majority stated a two-part standard[32] which may bear on the question of age- appropriate placement. A placement must both benefit the child educationally and provide the child with an individualized education program. This part of the comment addresses both of those elements.

A. Educational Benefits

At this point in our history there is little dispute that education and the benefits derived from education are not purely academic in nature. Education is also an instrument for socialization—both teaching cultural values and helping the child adjust to his environment. The Supreme Court accepted this notion in *Brown v. Board of Education*[33] when it found education to be a principal instrument in developing good citizenship and cultural values, preparing the child for later training, and helping him adjust normally to his environment.[34] In *Wisconsin v. Yoder,*[35] the Court further acknowledged the importance of public education in preparing individuals to be "self-reliant and self-sufficient participants in society" and accepted the view that the value

---

29. Stark, *supra* note 1, at 498 ("Nowhere does the EAHCA specify what is meant by an 'appropriate' education for handicapped children."); Rowley v. Board of Educ., 483 F. Supp. 528, 533 (S.D.N.Y.) ("[T]he Act itself does not define 'appropriate education' . . . it has been left entirely to the courts and the hearing officers to give content to the requirement of an appropriate education."), *aff'd*, 632 F.2d 945 (2d Cir. 1980), *rev'd*, 458 U.S. 176 (1982).

30. 458 U.S. 176, 188 (1982).

31. The Court stated:

The term "free appropriate public education" means *special education* and *related services* which (A) have been provided at public expense, under public supervision and direction, and without charge, (B) meet the standards of the State educational agency, (C) include an appropriate preschool, elementary, or secondary school education in the State involved, and (D) are provided in conformity with the individualized education program required under section 1414(a)(5) of this title.

Id. (citing 20 U.S.C. § 1401(18) (1982)) (emphasis added).

"Special education" is defined as "specially designed instruction, at no cost to parents or guardians, to meet the unique needs of a handicaapped child, including classroom instruction, instruction in physical education, home instruction, and instruction in hospitals and institutions." 20 U.S.C. § 1401(16) (1982). "Related services" are "transportation, and such developmental, corrective, and other supportive services . . . as may be required to assist a handicapped child to benefit from special education." 20 U.S.C. § 1401(17) (1982).

32. The Court stated:

Insofar as a State is required to provide a handicapped child with a "free appropriate public education," we hold that it satisfies this requirement by providing personalized instruction with sufficient support services to permit the child to benefit educationally from that instruction. Such instruction and services must be provided at public expense, must meet the State's educational standards, must approximate the grade levels used in the State's regular education, and must comport with the child's IEP.

458 U.S. at 203.

33. 347 U.S. 483 (1954).

34. *Id.* at 493.

35. 406 U.S. 205 (1972).

of all education must be assessed in terms of its capacity to prepare the child for life.[36] Thus, socialization, social skill development, and the development of self-sufficiency must be objectives of an appropriate education for every student.

Congress recognized that it is particularly important that such nonacademic components of education be offered to handicapped students; self-sufficiency and self-respect were major goals of the legislation. As expressed on the Senate floor, the goal and purpose of the statute was "to meet the unmet needs of all handicapped children" which included "making them productive citizens, capable of self-respect and pride which they rightly deserve."[37] Congress based these goals for the education of handicapped students at least partly on its assumption that spending the money to maximize the independence and self-sufficiency of handicapped students would ultimately relieve taxpayers of the burden of supporting unproductive members of society. Congress argued that "[w]ith proper education services, many [handicapped children] would be able to become productive citizens, contributing to society instead of being forced to remain burdens. Others, through such services, would increase their independence, thus reducing their dependence on society."[38]

Some courts in determining an appropriate education for handicapped students have considered whether a student was receiving necessary nonacademic educational benefits as part of his program. As a district court in Texas noted, "Full social interaction is an important part of today's educational curriculum and is even more vital to a child . . . who necessarily suffers a certain degree of isolation as a result of his handicap."[39] That court specifically found that depriving a handicapped child of an opportunity to interact fully with his peers constituted a deprivation of educational benefits.[40]

Advocates of age-appropriate placement argue that the handicapped student's social skills and self-respect are enhanced by such placement—in other words, that the student receives nonacademic educational benefits necessary to an appropriate education from the placement—while placement elsewhere deprives the student of proper, age-appropriate role models. In the Poe case,

---

36. *Id.* at 221.

37. 121 CONG. REC. 37,413 (1975) (statement of Sen. Williams).

38. S. REP. No. 168, 94th Cong., 1st Sess. 9, *reprinted in* 1975 U.S. CODE CONG. & AD. NEWS 1425, 1433.

39. Espino v. Besteiro, 520 F. Supp. 905, 913 (S.D. Tex. 1981) (granting motion for preliminary injunction based upon likelihood of success under EAHCA).

40. *Id.* The court went on to discuss the fact that the placement was not providing an opportunity for maximization of the student's social interaction skills commensurate with that provided other children in the class and that, in view of all the circumstances, he might be deprived of a full educational opportunity. These statements are very similar to the New York district court's definition of appropriate education—"an opportunity to achieve [her] full potential commensurate with the opportunity provided to other children"—which was later discredited by the Supreme Court in *Rowley.* 458 U.S. at 186. However, the *Rowley* decision should not be fatal to the holding in *Espino* that the child's placement was inappropriate since the court had specifically found that the student was receiving no educational benefits from the placement and that the placement might not be in conformity with his IEP. *Espino,* 520 F. Supp. at 913.

one expert witness testified that contact with chronological age peers would increase Clint's chance of modeling older students' behavior and allow him to profit from incidental learning—learning from his surroundings.[41] The Supreme Court seemed to approve of this type of learning in *Wisconsin v. Yoder* as a means of preparing the child for his adult role at least "during the crucial and formative adolescent period of life."[42] "During this period, the children must acquire Amish attitudes . . . and the specific skills needed to perform the adult role . . . . These traits, skills, and attitudes admittedly fall within the category of those best learned through example and 'doing' rather than in the classroom."[43]

In the special education context, providing the child with an opportunity to benefit from age-appropriate role models was a major reason for bringing handicapped children into the public schools. As several writers have argued, "With systematic instruction, many severely handicapped students can be taught to learn by imitating many of the appropriate actions of their chronological age peers. Interaction with nonhandicapped students thus provides the potential instructional advantage of having access to constructive models. . . ."[44] This "contact for normalization" was cited by the teacher of a high school EMH program in Durham County as the reason for including mainstreaming as one of the three components necessary for an appropriate TMH program.[45] In his opinion this would mean placing the program for high-school-aged students in or near the high school building so that students could have contact with others of the same age and size.[46] One of the experts testifying for Clint Poe succinctly stated the argument for moving the present TMH academic program to the high school: "Methods can be used anywhere and should be. Age-appropriate models are hard to provide outside of the place where age-appropriate models go to school."[47]

The importance of providing age-appropriate models as part of a handicapped child's educational program has been noted by several courts in determining the appropriateness of an educational placement. In *Campbell v. Talladega County Board of Education*,[48] the court ordered that the educational program of an 18-year-old severely retarded student include increased contact with nonhandicapped students based on the fact that "considerable evidence established that such interaction is essential to provide him with role

---

41. I Hearing Transcript at 48-50 (testimony of Kenneth Jens, Clinical Associate Professor of Special Education at the University of North Carolina).

42. 406 U.S. 205, 211 (1972).

43. *Id.*

44. Brown, Branston, Hamre-Nietupski, Johnson, Wilcox & Gruenewald, *A Rationale for Comprehensive Longitudinal Interactions Between Severely Handicapped Students and Nonhandicapped Students and Other Citizens,* AAESPH REV., Spring 1979, at 7.

45. III Hearing Transcript at 171 (testimony of Peter Hoyt, teacher of high school EMH program).

46. *Id.* at 174.

47. I Hearing Transcript at 48 (testimony of Kenneth Jens, Clinical Associate Professor of Special Education at the University of North Carolina).

48. 518 F. Supp. 47 (N.D. Ala. 1981).

models . . . ."[49] In reaching its decision, the court relied upon expert testimony that "considerable interaction between nonhandicapped and mentally handicapped children may be achieved when they are educated under the same roof and that such integration has been attained successfully in school districts across the country."[50]

Similarly, in *Mallory v. Drake,*[51] a Missouri state court upheld a hearing panel's decision that a severely handicapped student should be placed in a classroom with other severely handicapped children "located in a public school setting where she will have access to social interaction and modeling of less handicapped children."[52] And again, in *Hines v. Pitt County Board of Education,*[53] a federal district court in North Carolina, considering the proper residential placement for a 10-year-old emotionally handicapped student, specifically found that "an appropriate peer group for [the] plaintiff would be made up of children ages eight through ten."[54] The court then studied the ages of the student population in the student's current placement (which included no 10-year-olds, four 11-year-olds and nineteen children ranging from 12 to 17) and concluded that it was insufficient to meet his need for an appropriate peer group.[55] In reaching its decision, the court relied upon expert testimony that the age of the child's peer group was of primary importance.[56]

At the admininstrative hearing for Clint Poe, the school system countered the Poes' contention that Clint could benefit educationally from a high school placement by arguing that inclusion in the high school program actually would be harmful to Clint due to the risk that he would be ridiculed and would be unable to fit in.[57] It argued that TMH students in a self-contained classroom would be isolated from the rest of the students, that the greater tendency of high school students, as compared to junior high school students, is to operate as individuals rather than as part of a group, and that this tendency would make it harder for the TMH students to make friends and interact with nonhandicapped students.[58]

There was, however, contrary testimony that the tendency of high school students to make decisions as individuals rather than as part of a group, cou-

---

49. *Id.* at 55.
50. *Id.* at 50.
51. 616 S.W.2d 124 (Mo. App. 1981).
52. *Id.* at 127.
53. 497 F. Supp. 403, (E.D.N.C. 1980).
54. *Id.* at 407.
55. *Id.*
56. *Id.* at 408.
57. Respondent's Brief at 6, Administrative Hearing for Clint Poe (Durham, N.C. 1982) [hereinafter cited as Respondent's Brief].

The Durham County System also contended that this conclusion was based upon its unsuccessful experience with a self-contained classroom for retarded students located at one of its high schools during the late 1960's and early 1970's. It is undisputed, however, that this program was entirely self-contained for all school activities, both academic and nonacademic, and that the current program for EMH students which included appropriate mainstreaming for nonacademic instruction and other school activities was successful. Appellants' Brief at 15; Respondent's Brief at 10.

58. Respondent's Brief at 10-11.

pled with their greater maturity and volunteerism, would make them more likely to react positively to such a class.[59] The view that contact with age-appropriate peers was beneficial rather than harmful was also suported by actual experience within the Durham County School System. Clint's teacher observed an improvement in the social skills and behavior exhibited by him and others in his TMH class when they were moved from a sixth grade center to the junior high setting, a setting which, at the time, provided more age-appropriate peers.[60] Also, the teacher of the EMH program at the high school testified to behavioral gains and improved self-esteem achieved (though not without difficulty) by the two borderline EMH/TMH students who joined his program.[61] Further support for the view that such contact within a high school setting was beneficial to TMH students was provided by testimony that other school systems in North Carolina which were educating TMH students in age-appropriate high school settings reported successful educational programs, including observable improvements in the social behavior of handicapped students.[62]

The EAHCA clearly supports the argument that such interaction is beneficial, not harmful. As one hearing officer concluded:

> The statutes do not consider social interaction with peers to be harmful . . . . Rather, the statutes contemplate that interaction with similarly handicapped children or non-handicapped children will be a positive social experience for the child and that interaction with . . . children of approximately the same age will be socially beneficial to the child's development.[63]

The EAHCA also seems to contemplate that an appropriate education is to be provided at the proper chronological age level, as the definition of free appropriate public education "include[s] an appropriate preschool, elementary, or secondary school education in the State involved."[64] The *Rowley* Court included this requirement in its definitional checklist of items which must be satisfied, stating that the personalized instruction and supportive services provided the child must "approximate the grade levels used in the State's regular education."[65] Since many handicapped students, especially retarded students, will never be able to approximate the grade levels of a regular education academically, the statute must refer to placement of children in approximately the grade level that nonhandicapped children their age would attend. Most school systems allow this type of age placement for nonhandicapped children despite failure to meet grade level academic standards. The superintendent of the Durham County School System testified that placement

---

59. Petitioners' Brief at 4; Appellants' Brief at 15.

60. Appellants' Brief at 16.

61. III Hearing Transcript at 174-75 (testimony of Peter Hoyt, teacher of high school EMH program).

62. II Hearing Transcript at 125-27 (testimony of Lynn Whitley, Advocate, Governor's Advocacy Council for Persons with Disabilities); *see also* Appellants' Brief at 15-16.

63. *In re* Tracy, 1981-82 Educ. Handicapped L. Rep. (CRR) 503:297, :299 (Ill. SEA 1982) (hearing officer approved placement of 14-year-old girl in public school behaviorally disordered class despite parents' request for residential placement).

64. 20 U.S.C. § 1401(18)(C) (1982).

65. 458 U.S. at 189.

for nonhandicapped students was allowed in his system, at least through the tenth grade, on the basis of psychological considerations, academics, social skills, and other subjective criteria.[66] In accordance with the statute, then, this local practice should be followed for handicapped students as well.

The State Hearing Review Officer in the Poe case reached an interesting conclusion with respect to the requirement of approximating the grade levels of the state's regular education. He considered it arguable that the clear language of the statute required the TMH program to be provided both at the elementary and the secondary levels. State law defined elementary and secondary education; in North Carolina, elementary school included grades one through eight while grades nine through twelve made up secondary school. Local school systems, however, could choose to operate a junior high school including no more than grades seven through nine which would be a hybrid elementary/secondary school. Therefore, according to the hearing review officer, the Durham County School System arguably satisfied the specific mandate of the statute by providing education at both an elementary and secondary level by placing the program at a junior high.[67]

Following this logic, handicapped classes containing children from age 6 to 18 (approximately first grade through twelfth grade for nonhandicapped children) could be placed in such hybrid schools which would "arguably . . . provid[e] education both at the elementary and the secondary levels."[68] Such a situation would allow a significant departure from the congressional mandate that education be provided at regular educational levels.

The language of the EAHCA supports placement of handicapped children at regular educational levels. This preference reflects the general understanding that education includes nonacademic benefits such as the development of social skills and cultural values. Because the development of social skills and self-reliance was an important purpose of the EAHCA, some courts, in determining an appropriate education for handicapped children, have already considered age-appropriate placement as one method of helping handicapped children achieve these skills. Such nonacademic benefits should therefore be considered under the *Rowley* standard in determining the content of an appropriate education in every case. Whether such educational benefits are required for a particular handicapped child would be determined by his "unique needs" as identified in his individualized education program.

B. Individualization

Although the EAHCA as a whole has a broad goal—to provide a free appropriate public education for all handicapped children—it seeks to accomplish this goal by focusing on each individual handicapped student in order to identify and meet his specific educational needs. As one court pointed out, the Act "represents a clear national commitment to meet each handicapped

---

66. III Hearing Transcript at 19-23.
67. Hearing Review Decision at 17.
68. *Id.*

child's special needs in as integrated and complete a way as possible."[69]

Congress recognized that being handicapped is a complex, multidimensional condition[70] and therefore made no effort to establish educational programs or standards for each handicapping condition.[71] Instead, it provided that an individualized education program (IEP) must be developed for each handicapped child.[72] As one of the statute's supporters remarked during the House debate, "Because handicapped children are unique, setting up plans for each one makes good sense."[73]

The IEP prescribed by the Act is a written plan

> developed jointly by the local education agencies, a teacher involved with the specific education of the handicapped child, and his parents or guardian. The plan [includes] a statement of the child's present level of educational performance, a statement of the goals to be achieved, a statement of the specific services which will have to be provided, a projected date for initiation and duration of the services, and criteria and evaluation procedures for determining whether the objectives are being met.[74]

One of the Act's sponsors viewed the plan as an important means of achieving the goals of the statute: "Individualized plans are of great importance in the education of handicapped children in order to help them develop their full potential."[75]

In evaluating an educational program, hearing officers and courts must consider whether the program was designed to meet the unique needs of the handicapped child as developed in the IEP. As one court declared, "[T]here can be little doubt that by requiring attention to 'unique needs,' the Act demands that special education be tailored to the individual."[76] The court then took action to implement this requirement, holding that Pennsylvania could not inflexibly apply its absolute standard of a maximum 180-day school year to handicapped children because such a practice precluded consideration of individual needs.[77]

The United States Supreme Court recognized in *Rowley* that whether a handicapped child is benefiting educationally must also be determined by considering the child's unique abilities, needs, and related educational goals. The Court specifically stated that it was not attempting "to establish any one test for determining the adequacy of educational benefits conferred upon all children by the Act" because of the difficulty of answering this question for the broad spectrum of handicapping conditions.[78]

One commentator has suggested that the *Rowley* standard therefore calls

---

69. Lora v. Board of Educ., 456 F. Supp. 1211, 1226 (E.D.N.Y. 1978), *aff'd in part, vacated in part,* 623 F.2d 248 (2d Cir. 1980).
70. Krass, *The Right to Public Education for Handicapped Children: A Primer for the New Advocate,* 1976 U. ILL. L.F. 1016, 1065 [hereinafter cited as *Primer for the New Advocate*].
71. *See supra* note 24.
72. 20 U.S.C. §§ 1401(19), 1414(a)(5) (1982) (definition).
73. 121 CONG. REC. 23,707 (1975) (statement of Congressman Quie).
74. *Id.*
75. 121 CONG. REC. 23,705 (1975)(statement of Congressman Brademas).
76. Battle v. Pennsylvania, 629 F.2d 269, 280 (3d Cir. 1980), *cert. denied,* 452 U.S. 968 (1981).
77. *Id.*
78. 458 U.S. at 202.

for a two-pronged approach.[79] First, the child's abilities, needs, and objectives must be examined. Then the program must be examined to determine whether it benefits the child in terms of his or her uniqueness.[80] Such an analysis will focus even greater attention on the precise nature of the individual handicapped child's needs and abilities—"including needs for emotional as well as intellectual development"—in making and reviewing decisions.[81]

Social skill development may be included in the needs and goals described by an IEP. Indeed, it was identified as a primary educational goal for Clint Poe by several witnesses who cited lack of social skills as the main reason for vocational failure by the mentally retarded.[82] These witnesses considered this goal more important than many of the academic goals identified in Clint's IEP, an assertion which was uncontested by the school system.

Furthermore, in Clint's IEP, his teacher described him as "behaving socially in an age-appropriate manner, being well-liked by peers, and demonstrating 'normalized' social skills."[83] She therefore recommended in his IEP for 1981-82 that Clint be offered a high school program. This recommendation was supported by Clint's most recent psychological evaluation which stated that the lack of opportunity to interact with chronological age peers was one reason for his scoring at a pre-adolescent level in social development, and added that he would benefit from more contact with high school age peers.[84] Thus, Clint was being denied educational benefits necessary to meet his unique needs and objectives.

Although the importance of a chronological age peer group for meeting the socialization needs of a handicapped student has been litigated in few reported decisions, it has been a factor in several decisions. One California hearing considered an almost identical issue to the Poe question—whether for integration to be appropriate, it must be with nonhandicapped peers who are chronologically age equivalent rather than mentally age equivalent.[85] Although the California hearing officer felt that the addition of chronologically age-appropriate integration would make the educational program ideal, the lack of such integration did not make the program inappropriate.[86] In fact, the hearing officer opined that although the student might receive great

---

79. Wegner, *Variations on a Theme: The Concept of Equal Educational Opportunity and Programming Decisions under the Education for All Handicapped Children Act of 1975,* LAW AND CONTEMP. PROBS., Winter 1985, at 169, 186.
80. *Id.* at 186.
81. *Id.* at 187.
82. Petitioners' Brief at 23.
83. Appellants' Brief at 10.
84. Petitioners' Brief at 3.
85. *In re* Marin County Office of Educ., 1982-83 EDUC. HANDICAPPED L. REP. (CRR) 504:162 (Cal. SEA 1982).
86. 1982-83 EDUC. HANDICAPPED L. REP. at 504:165. Compare this finding with the statement by the Hearing Review Officer in the Clint Poe case that the Poes' position was not without merit because it could be that TMH students aged 16 to 18 would benefit from a class located at the high school and that the class might thrive, but that the evidence on the record did not show that it was required by the student. Hearing Review Decision at 17.

benefits from chronologically age equivalent nonhandicapped peer integration, it did not follow that integration with similarly functioning handicapped students would not bring its own unique benefits.[87]

This analysis seems to be based upon a "net benefits" determination. Under this approach, if the student is benefiting from the program in any way or if the student is receiving more benefit than harm, the educational program is deemed appropriate. Although it has been argued that this is the *Rowley* standard,[88] both the thrust of the statute towards individualization and the *Rowley* Court's recognition that a single benefits test cannot be articulated, suggest a benefits test which addresses the specific abilities, needs, and objectives of the individual. Thus, in determining whether a student is benefiting educationally from a placement, one should carefully scrutinize the student's needs and goals and ask whether they will be addressed in the particular placement. If all the student's needs cannot be met equally well in one placement, then one must determine the primary needs and meet those first and best.

Two other cases have analyzed the placement decision by considering the importance of the peer group in relation to the unique needs of the individual student. *In re Matthew S.*[89] involved a hearing to determine whether a profoundly deaf 7-year-old boy should continue in his placement at a learning center for the deaf or move to a public school's hearing impaired class which included students aged 6 to 8. The agency heard testimony that Matthew's paramount need at the time was "to strengthen his self-esteem, peer group identity, and social skills in the deaf community" where he could "find friends, competitors, and role models."[90] As in the Poe case, all agreed that the student could "learn his academics in either setting," so the hearing officer found that the question of his placement could not be dictated by his academic needs. Rather, the importance of socialization and peer group identity issues "made [the public school placement] inappropriate at this time."[91] Thus, in this case the student was not placed with age peers but with deaf peers. The placement points out the importance of determining with precision the socialization needs of the individual and meeting those needs in making a placement decision. For Matthew, it was determined that his need to socialize with other deaf students outweighed his need to interact with others in the community who could hear. The hearing officer was careful to note that this placement was necessary to meet his present socialization needs—the implication being that such needs may change over time as Matthew becomes adjusted to the deaf community. He then may need to move out into the hearing community, and this change in his needs would trigger a corresponding change in placement.

---

87. *Id.*
88. Wegner, *supra* note 79, at 186.
89. 1980-81 EDUC. HANDICAPPED L. REP. (CRR) 502:346 (Mass. SEA 1981).
90. *Id.* at 502:347.
91. *Id.*

In *Hines v. Pitt County Board of Education*,[92] a federal district court determined that placement of a 10-year-old emotionally handicapped student in a school with students aged 11 through 18 was inappropriate. Finding that "[f]or Brad, . . . the *most* important factor in that determination is his peer group," the court relied on "[t]he testimony of all the expert witnesses who pointed out that the age of the peer group was very important to Brad's further education, although they disagreed as to its relative importance vis-a-vis other desirable factors."[93] The court canvassed the population at his present placement and found that of the twenty-three children currently enrolled, there were no 10-year-old children and four 11-year-old children, with all other children ranging in age from 12 through 17. The court therefore found the current child population not appropriate to meet the unique needs of the plaintiff for a chronological age peer group and determined that he was appropriately placed in a program designed for pre-adolescent children.[94]

The Durham County School System argued that the junior high placement was appropriate to meet Clint's socialization needs based upon the presence of nonhandicapped high-school-aged students at the junior high school and the support of its SCREEN (placement) team decision for the junior high school placement.[95] The first contention, that chronological age peers were available at the junior high school, was belied by the kind of canvassing of the student population which the *Hines* court used. Of the nonhandicapped students among the 858 students at the junior high, none were 18; only 3 were 17 years old; 18 were 16 years old; 113 were 15 years old; and the vast majority were 14 years old and younger. Therefore, less than 3 percent of the student population was 16 or older.[96] The analysis of the *Hines* court, therefore, would lead to a finding that the junior high placement was inappropriate because it was insufficient to meet Clint's unique needs for an appropriate peer group.

The Durham County SCREEN team did recommend continued placement at the junior high school despite Clint's teacher's recommendation for high school placement in his IEP. However, testimony of SCREEN team members at the hearing indicated that they considered the junior high placement to be the best available and that they had, therefore, recommended it because they were unable to recommend any placement that was not currently available in

---

92. 497 F. Supp. 403 (E.D.N.C. 1980).

93. *Id.* at 408 (emphasis in original). *Cf.* Grkman v. Scanlon, 528 F. Supp. 1032, 1036 (W.D. Pa. 1981) (closeness in age to other pupils merely considered one advantage of continued placement at center for deaf students), *remanded*, 707 F.2d 1391 (3d Cir. 1982) (to be reconsidered in light of *Rowley*), *reh'g*, 563 F. Supp. 793 (W.D. Pa. 1983) (ordered current evaluation and IEP); *In re* Brockton Pub. Schools, 1982-83 EDUC. HANDICAPPED L. REP. (CRR) 504:128 (Mass. SEA 16, 1982) (lack of sufficient peer group because of age gap between 5-year-old handicapped student and other students aged 8, 10, and 12 considered as a factor in placement decision).

94. 497 F. Supp. at 407.

95. Petitioners' Brief at 3-4. The State Hearing Review Officer evidently accepted the argument that chronological age peers were available at the junior high school, because he specifically found that the LEA had provided the student with opportunities for contact with his chronological age peers. Conclusion of Law No. 12, Hearing Review Decision at 9.

96. Petitioners' Brief at 3.

the school system. Two of these witnesses stated that if a high school placement had been available it could have been considered appropriate for Clint.[97]

This limitation upon the SCREEN team's ability to make recommendations seems to bear out the fears of early commentators on the statute who felt that although the content of the appropriate education to meet each individual's needs was to be developed through the IEP, "it is perhaps more likely that the needs of the child will only be delineated in terms of the services actually available."[98] This type of limitation is totally inappropriate under the statute. For, as another commentator noted, "Congress has focused on the individual child's needs rather than those of the state as the standard by which the provision of educational benefits is to be measured."[99] Thus, although other factors which a school system takes into account, such as cost,[100] may be considered in an effort to weigh the needs of the individual nonhandicapped student against those of other handicapped and nonhandicapped students, this weighing should not take place until after the needs of the handicapped individual have been evaluated. Then, the system may consider existing resources (not programs) to decide how best to meet as many of the needs of all children in the system as possible.

IV

LEAST RESTRICTIVE ENVIRONMENT UNDER PUBLIC LAW NO. 94-142

Although the EAHCA does not specify the substantive content of an appropriate program, "[t]o direct placement decisions, it does include the requirement that handicapped children should be educated together with the nonhandicapped 'to the maximum extent appropriate.' "[101] Handicapped children should be removed from the regular educational environment only when the nature or severity of their handicap requires removal in order to provide a proper education. This requirement, popularly know as mainstreaming, is an integration principle distinct from the definition of the appropriate educational program, which states a preference for *where* educational services should be provided.[102] As such, it is "an antisegregation principle,

---

97. *Id.* at 4.
98. Haggerty & Sacks, *Education of the Handicapped: Towards a Definition of an Appropriate Education,* 50 TEMP. L.Q. 961, 989 (1977); *see also* Note, *supra* note 24, at 1109-10 ("Even assuming good faith on the part of school officials in dealing with the problems of handicapped children, budgetary constraints will inevitably color many decisions and restrict the range of alternatives offered in the formulation of individualized educational programs . . . . [L]ocal school administrators may focus on what is available within the school system rather than on what is most appropriate for an individual child.").
99. *Primer for the New Advocate, supra* note 70, at 1065.
100. *See, e.g.,* Pinkerton v. Moye, 509 F. Supp. 107, 112-13 (W.D. Va. 1981); *see infra* notes 122-25 and accompanying text.
101. Note, *supra* note 24, at 1106 (citing 20 U.S.C. § 1412(5)(B) (1976)). Indeed, one commentator sees this placement directive as the "only substantive requirement" of the Act. Stark, *supra* note 1, at 482.
102. *See* Roncker v. Walter, 700 F.2d 1058, 1062 (6th Cir. 1983), *cert. denied,* 104 S. Ct. 196 (1983) ("The use of 'appropriate' in the language of the Act, although by no means definitive, sug-

analogous to that established in *Brown v. Board of Educ[ation]*' designed to stop the automatic institutionalization and isolation of most handicapped children.[103] Congress was "concerned that children with handicapping conditions be educated in the most normal and least restrictive setting, for how else will they adapt to the world beyond the educational environment, and how else will the nonhandicapped adapt to them?"[104]

The regulations promulgated pursuant to the EAHCA add greater meaning to the requirement. In addition to repeating the requirement that separate schooling or removal from the regular educational environment occurs only when required by the nature or severity of the handicap,[105] the regulations require each agency to insure the availability of a continuum of alternative placements to meet the needs of all handicapped children.[106] The regulations also make clear that the least restrictive environment requirement applies to nonacademic services, including extracurricular services, meals, and recess periods.[107] In determining the placement for a specific handicapped child, the regulations require that the placement be based upon his IEP. Unless the IEP requires some other arrangement, the child must be educated in the school which he or she would attend if not handicapped.[108]

In the Poe case, the Hearing Review Officer found that because the least restrictive environment language referred only to contact with nonhandicapped persons, it did not require "age groupings."[109] The Poes argued that, although there may not be an absolute requirement of chronological age placement for every child, the language of the regulations does assume the least restrictive environment requirement normally will involve placement with age peers unless the individual's handicapping condition makes such placement impossible. First, the regulations state that removal from the regular educational environment is not preferred, but allowed only when ade-

---

gests that Congress used the word as much to prescribe the settings in which handicapped children should be educated as to prescribe the substantive content or supportive services of their education."). *Cf. Rowley*, 458 U.S. at 197 n.21. This statement supports the notion that setting is part of the definition of "appropriate" as discussed in part III rather than the idea that the least restrictive environment requirement is not a distinct integration principle which determines where the appropriate education will be provided.

103. Stark, *supra* note 1, at 482 n. 18.
104. 120 CONG. REC. 15,272 (1974) (statement of Sen. Stafford).
105. 34 C.F.R. § 300.550(b) (1984).
106. *Id.* § 300.551.
107. *Id.* §§ 300.306, .553.
108. *Id.* § 300.552(c).
109. Hearing Review Decision at 16. It is true that reported decisions generally refer to providing contact with nonhandicapped students without specifically considering age. *See, e.g.*, Campbell v. Talladega County Bd. of Educ., 518 F. Supp. 47 (N.D. Ala. 1981); Mallory v. Drake, 616 S.W.2d 124 (Mo. App. 1981); *In re* Educ. Assignment of Michael G., 1983-84 EDUC. HANDICAPPED L. REP. (CRR) 505:188 (Pa. SEA 1983); *cf. In re* Marin County Office of Educ., 1982-83 EDUC. HANDICAPPED L. REP. (CRR) 504:162 (Cal. SEA 1982).

Although the issue in *Marin County* was framed in terms of integration— whether for integration to be appropriate, it must be with chronological age equivalent nonhandicapped peers rather than mental age equivalent peers—the discussion and decision turned upon the "threshold question of appropriateness." *Id.* at 504:165.

quate education cannot be provided in regular classes.[110] Thus, the regular educational environment for nonhandicapped students is a classroom setting with others of his same age. Whether a handicapped student should be removed from this setting then depends upon the special needs imposed by his handicap as determined in his IEP.

Furthermore, the regulations require that the student be placed in the school he would attend if not handicapped—that is, with chronological age peers—unless the IEP requires something different.[111] Therefore, the student's IEP must include a statement describing the extent to which he will be able to take part in regular educational programs. These regulations emphasize the fact that Congress envisioned a combination of possible settings in a handicapped child's educational program.[112] For example, a student may be able to attend all regular classes with support services added, to attend special academic classes with mainstreaming for nonacademic classes, or to attend special classes with mainstreaming for lunch, recess, and extracurricular activities. Once the child's ability to learn in regular classes and activities is determined, "any adjustment made in the educational plan for a child because of a handicap must be scrutinized carefully to minimize the possibility that such a plan might encourage rather than reduce developmental discrepancies between that child and nonhandicapped students."[113]

"Only if a child cannot be educated 'satisfactorily' in the regular classroom either part of the time or all of the time should he or she be removed. Placement must then be in the next least restrictive setting."[114] The appropriate setting is determined by looking over the continuum of alternatives provided by the LEA and placing the child "in that environment which is consistent with his needs, yet does not restrict his freedom to associate with his normal peers [more] than is absolutely necessary."[115] As one court noted, this requirement is especially important for children whose educational needs necessitate their being solely with other handicapped children during most of each day.[116]

If these standards are applied to the Poe case, it is apparent that Clint's IEP did not require that he be removed from the regular age-appropriate school which he would normally attend; it merely required that he be placed in a self-contained classroom for academic instruction. In fact, as his IEP reflected, Clint's social goals would be better implemented in the high school

---

110. 34 C.F.R. § 300.550 (1984).

111. *Id.* § 300.552.

112. Comment, *The Least Restrictive Environment Section of the Education for All Handicapped Children Act of 1975: A Legislative History and an Analysis*, 13 GONZ. L. REV. 717 (1978).

113. Brown, Wilcox, Sontag, Vincent, Dodd & Gruenewald, *Toward the Realization of the Least Restrictive Educational Environments for Severely Handicapped Students*, AAESPH REV., Dec. 1977, at 195, 197 [hereinafter cited as *Least Restrictive Environments*].

114. Comment, *supra* note 112, at 776.

115. Goldgraber, *Educating Severely Handicapped Children in the Least Restrictive Environment*, 17 J. SPECIAL EDUCATORS 401, 407 (1981).

116. Campbell v. Talladega County Bd. of Educ., 518 F. Supp. 47, 53 (N.D. Ala. 1981) (quoting 34 C.F.R. § 104, app. A, subpart D, ¶ 24).

he would normally be attending. This placement would have provided the "most normal setting in which the pupil can function effectively"[117]—the goal of the least restrictive environment.

Educators also support the argument that the least restrictive environment mandate of the EAHCA requires placement with age-appropriate peers:

> Severely handicapped students should interact with nonhandicapped students of approximately the same chronological ages throughout their education. Placing secondary aged/young adult severely handicapped students in educational settings where there are no nonhandicapped students of the same age is not acceptable. For example, a wing serving severely handicapped students from ages five to twenty-five attached to an elementary school serving nonhandicapped students from ages five to twelve does not provide age appropriate peers for the severely handicapped students over age twelve. It is therefore unduly restrictive.[118]

Of course, individual needs may require removal from the regular school setting in which the child would normally function. A Michigan hearing officer found that a 20-year-old EMH student should remain at a center for the retarded rather than moving to the public high school as requested by parents because of specific findings that her directional and spatial difficulties would make close supervision and monitoring necessary to allow her to move around the large high school building.[119] The public high school was considered to be far more restrictive and destructive to the development of peer relationships than her present placement. Because of the finding that the unique needs of the student actually made the center the least restrictive environment, the hearing officer found it unnecessary to "compare the peer population of the [placement alternatives] desired for modeling purposes."[120]

Cost may also be a factor in deciding whether a particular placement is possible since excessive spending on one child may deprive other students, handicapped and nonhandicapped, of educational benefits.[121] At the Poe hearing, there was conflicting testimony regarding the feasibility of establishing a self-contained program at the high school based upon cost, potential transportation problems, and personnel reorganization. There was also a dispute as to whether all alternatives for the high school program, including those proposed by the Poes, had been explored by the school system. Furthermore, since the hearing was to determine an individual placement, the Hearing Officer did not consider the possibility that other high-school-aged TMH students might also be appropriately placed in the high school class if one were available, causing a change in personnel, transportation, and other cost-related factors.[122]

As one court pointed out, although cost is a proper factor to consider, it

---

117. Haggerty & Sacks, *supra* note 98, at 972.
118. *Least Restrictive Environments, supra* note 113, at 198.
119. Case No. H-487, 1979-80 EDUC. HANDICAPPED L. REP. (CRR) 501:174, :175-76 (Mich. SEA 1979).
120. *Id.* at 501:176.
121. Pinkerton v. Moye, 509 F. Supp. 102 (W.D. Va. 1981).
122. Hearing Review Decision at 5-6, 14-15; Appellants' Brief at 16-18. The Hearing Officer made no findings on the cost issue. The State Hearing Review Officer, however, accepted the evidence introduced by the school system regarding changes which would have to be implemented to

"is no defense . . . if the school district has failed to use its funds to provide a proper continuum of alternative placements for handicapped children."[123] Based upon the language of the regulations, it might be said that a "proper" continuum would include placement in an age-appropriate school unless the IEP required something different. The *Roncker* court pointed out that "provision of such alternative placements benefits all handicapped children."[124] This is even more likely in a system like Durham County where there are evidently a number of handicapped children who might benefit from age-appropriate placements were they available.[125]

Because of the cost factor and because of traditional judicial reluctance to invade local autonomy in the area of public education, some courts have declined to order a particular placement which might involve creation of new classes or programs (thus incidentally involving the court or officer in making funding allocation decisions); instead, the least restrictive environment requirement is stated as a mandate, and it is left to the schools to decide how it is to be implemented. For example, one hearing officer found that the law did not require the City of Cincinnati to recreate or duplicate its comprehensive TMR program in a regular elementary school building but did require that provisions be made for the handicapped child's interaction with nonhandicapped peers.[126] It was thus up to the school system to decide how to provide this interaction during the times it was appropriate for the student— lunch, recess, and during extracurricular activities. Under this approach, which represents one reasonable accommodation of the competing interests, if the Durham County School System did not place Clint's class at the high school, it would have to find another method to provide the requisite interaction during lunch and extracurricular activities.

V

DEFERENCE TO LOCAL AUTONOMY UNDER PUBLIC LAW NO. 94-142

At the Poe hearing, witnesses for the two parties expressed their beliefs regarding two different theories of social development. The Poes' expert witnesses believed that students of Clint's own chronological age would be role models for him and that he could benefit from incidental learning, or learning from his surroundings.[127] The school system argued that children learn social skills sequentially and the fact that Clint's social skills tested at a pre-adoles-

---

provide high school placement for Clint alone without considering the alternatives proposed by the Petitioners or the placement of other TMH students.

123. *Roncker,* 700 F.2d at 1063.

124. *Id.*

125. *See* Appellants' Brief at 8-9.

126. *In re* Cincinnati City School Dist., 1980-81 EDUC. HANDICAPPED L. REP. (CRR) 502:117, :120 (Ohio SEA 1979); *see also Roncker,* 700 F.2d at 1061 (Ohio State Board of Education found that academic instruction at a county school was appropriate but that provision should also be made to provide interaction with nonhandicapped students at lunch and recess).

127. I Hearing Transcript at 48-50 (testimony of Kenneth Jens, Clinical Associate Professor of Special Education at the University of North Carolina).

cent level meant that he had junior high level social skills still to learn, which could best be learned at the junior high school.[128]

The Hearing Officer did not consider this evidence in reaching her decision because it was her opinion that the purpose of the hearing was to determine the placement for one individual. She considered only evidence specific to Clint's program, concentrating on his level of performance and his demonstrated strengths and weaknesses.[129] The Hearing Review Officer did, however, make a specific finding that there is disagreement among educators concerning the process of social development. Educators are divided between the two theories argued by the Poes and by the school system, even though the two theories are not mutually exclusive.[130] This dispute points up a difficult problem in making placement decisions and determining educational programs: when there is disagreement over learning theories, how should a school system choose the method to be used for a particular handicapped student?

> The response to almost any interesting question concerning the education of the handicapped is either that the answer is unknown or that no generalizable beneficial effect of a given treatment can be demonstrated. This lack of knowledge, which is hardly peculiar to special education, makes it difficult to predict the consequences of any policy change.[131]

Congress chose not to establish specific substantive guidelines for appropriate educational programs for handicapped students. Among the reasons, evidently, was the difficulty of determining the best educational program for students with particular handicaps and the desire not to inhibit continued experimentation and innovation in the field of special education.[132] Recognizing the importance of experimentation and innovation in education, particularly special education, and the desirability of implementing the best available programs and techniques, Congress required the states to set up procedures to ensure that information produced by educational research is acquired and disseminated and that promising educational practices and materials developed by such research are adopted.[133]

The EAHCA does not, however, explain what qualifies as an educational theory or mandate when a state or LEA must adopt a promising educational practice. In other words, the statute does not provide specific guidelines for educational programs, nor does it give any guidance as to how school districts should decide which programs to use. The reason for the lack of specific mandates is probably that Congress felt constrained by its traditional deference

---

128. II Hearing Transcript at 154 (testimony of Jim Polk, Special Assistant to the Superintendent for Community Education and Social Services); *id.* at 204 (testimony of Genevieve Ortman, Director of Programs for Exceptional Children).

129. Hearing Decision at 2.

130. Finding of Fact No. 15, Hearing Review Decision at 5.

131. Kirp, Buss & Kuriloff, *Legal Reform of Special Education: Empirical Studies and Procedural Proposals,* 62 CAL. L. REV. 40, 47-48 (1974).

132. Note, *supra* note 24, at 1109.

133. 20 U.S.C. § 1413(a)(3) (1982). The *Rowley* Court saw this directive as additional evidence supporting the view that courts must show deference to the state's choice of an educational theory when reviewing a challenge to a program's appropriateness. 458 U.S. at 207-08.

towards state and local autonomy in the area of public education[134]—an area historically left to local discretion except in the face of overriding national policy concerns, such as racial integration. Thus, under the Act, state educational departments and local school boards "are given wide discretion to apply their expertise to devise the package of services appropriate to their locale and suited in some degree to each individual's capacities."[135]

Since the Act provides for judicial review of substantive questions regarding educational programs courts have also been cautioned to show deference to local decisionmakers.

> Because education generally reflects local values and interests, a court should bear in mind that its judgment may to some degree be viewed as second-guessing collective community wisdom. The importance of local control of education should encourage a court to exercise restraint in deciding cases under the Act.[136]

The *Rowley* opinion reiterated this view:

> In assuring that the requirements of the Act have been met, courts must be careful to avoid imposing their view of preferable educational methods upon the States. The primary responsibility for formulating the education to be accorded a handicapped child, and for choosing the educational method most suitable to the child's needs, was left by the Act to state and local educational agencies in cooperation with the parents or guardian of the child.[137]

Though realizing that states had the ultimate authority to choose educational methods, commentators hoped that "agencies and courts reviewing local schools' decisions as to appropriate education for the handicapped [would] require the schools to make a showing that the curriculum and teaching methods conform to a substantial body of expert opinion."[138] One court seemed to accept this view when it stated, albeit in dictum, that although a school system need not "experiment with every new teaching technique that may be suggested," it does have an obligation to keep abreast of changing educational strategies and implement them where success "may be demonstrated."[139]

This standard suggests that evidence of successful programs utilizing age-appropriate placement should be given substantial weight in making placement decisions. The Poes, for example, introduced expert testimony regarding a number of studies performed over a period of years which showed that placements such as the one suggested by the Poes were quite successful.[140] There was also testimony that such programs were operating

---

134. Note, *supra* note 24, at 1109.

135. Haggerty & Sacks, *supra* note 98, at 994; *see also*, Comment, *Self-Sufficiency Under the Education for All Handicapped Children Act: A Suggested Judicial Approach*, 1981 DUKE L.J. 516, 524 ("Aware of the Act's potentially destructive impact on local decision-making, the drafters of the Act were concerned that it reflect due regard for state and local sovereignty.").

136. Comment, *supra* note 135, at 529-30.

137. 458 U.S. at 207.

138. Haggerty & Sacks, *supra* note 98, at 994.

139. Rettig v. Kent County School Dist., 539 F. Supp. 768 (N.D. Ohio 1981), *aff'd in part, vacated in part*, 720 F.2d 463 (6th Cir. 1983), *cert. denied*, 104 S. Ct. 2379 (1984).

140. I Hearing Transcript at 48-49 (testimony of Kenneth Jens, Clinical Associate Professor of Special Education at the University of North Carolina).

successfully in other states[141] and, closer to home, that such high school programs for TMH students were operating successfully and bringing about improvements in the students' social behavior in other school districts in North Carolina.[142]

The question thus arises—would requiring the school system to accept a mainstreaming method successfully adopted elsewhere violate the requirement of local autonomy in determining educational policy? The *Rowley* Court recognized that courts lack the " 'specialized knowledge and experience' necessary to resolve 'persistent and difficult questions of educational policy.' "[143] On the other hand, the Court acknowledged that "once a court determines that the requirements of the Act have been met, questions of methodology are for resolution by the States."[144] In other words, courts have discretion to determine whether the requirements of the statute are being met, that is, whether a child's program provides an appropriate education and whether the child is being educated in the least restrictive environment. School systems may choose among teaching methods which meet these requirements. Thus, judicial acceptance of a particular method may be mandated by the substantive requirements of the Act if statutory requirements are being met through the use of that method.

Cases decided since *Rowley* have recognized its distinction between questions of methodology and factual determinations.[145] The First Circuit, while acknowledging that courts may not interfere with school authorities on issues of educational policy, held that judges may resolve difficult and complicated factual disputes regarding whether a child will benefit from a proposed placement. The court found that the dispute involved "not a choice of educational *policy*, but resolution of an individualized *factual* issue as to the effect of John's handicap on his ability to benefit from the proposed school setting. This falls within the scope of the question which *Rowley* says is for the court. . . ."[146] In resolving these "individualized factual issues," courts tend to rely upon the testimony of qualified witnesses; when a majority of such witnesses, especially teachers who have continuously worked with the child, support a particular program or service, their views usually convince the hearing officer or judge.[147] However, parties who demand a particular methodology without

---

141. *Id.* at 45 (witness had personal knowledge of thirteen to fourteen other programs in the nation where Clint would be in a high school setting).

142. II Hearing Transcript at 124-27 (testimony of Lynn Whitley, Advocate, Governor's Advocacy Council for Persons with Disabilities).

143. 458 U.S. at 208 (citing San Antonio Indep. School Dist. v. Rodriguez, 411 U.S. 1, 42 (1973)).

144. *Id.*

145. *EHLR Analysis, Application of* Rowley *by Courts and SEAs,* 1982-83 EDUC. HANDICAPPED L. REP. (CRR) SA-107, -112 to -13 (Supp. 93, Apr. 1, 1983) [hereinafter cited as *Application of* Rowley].

146. Doe v. Anrig, 692 F.2d 800, 806 (1st Cir. 1982) (emphasis in original).

147. *Application of* Rowley, *supra* note 145, at SA-108. Courts and Hearing Officers rely heavily upon the testimony of experts in the field of education including teachers and other school personnel who have worked closely with the child in determining programs. *See, e.g., In re* Campbell v. Talladega County Bd. of Educ., 518 F. Supp. 47, 55 (N.D. Ala. 1981) (expert testimony relied upon regarding successful programs in "school districts across the country"); Kruelle v. Biggs, 489 F.

presenting convincing expert testimony that it is needed by the child, tend to lose.[148]

The Sixth Circuit made the same distinction between a question of educational methodology, such as that involved in *Rowley*, and a factual determination as to whether a particular placement qualified as the least restrictive environment.[149] The court found that "the question is not one of methodology but rather involves a determination of whether the school district has satisfied the Act's requirement that handicapped children be educated alongside nonhandicapped children to the maximum extent appropriate . . . . Since Congress has decided that mainstreaming is appropriate, the states

---

Supp. 169 (D. Del. 1980) (school system recommendation refused and appropriate placement ordered on basis of expert testimony), *aff'd,* 642 F.2d 687 (3d Cir. 1981); Brockton Pub. Schools, 1982-83 EDUC. HANDICAPPED L. REP. (CRR) 504:128, :131 (Mass. SEA 1982) (finding that no professional who had worked with or evaluated the student recommended change of placement); *In re* West Brookfield Pub. Schools, 1982-83 EDUC. HANDICAPPED L. REP. (CRR) 504:166, :169 (Mass. SEA 1982) (abundant expert evidence heard in support of need for full-time aide).

The decisionmakers have also relied upon the insights and special knowledge of a child's abilities and needs which parents may impart. The wishes of the parents may be a factor to be considered in making a special education placement decision, *In re* Madison Metropolitan School Dist., 1981-82 EDUC. HANDICAPPED L. REP. (CRR) 503:125, :127 (Wis. SEA 1981), but will not be accepted as controlling absent other evidence or expert testimony regarding the issue. Johnston v. Ann Arbor Pub. Schools, 569 F. Supp. 1502, 1509 (E.D. Mich. 1983) (granting summary judgment to school district when no genuine issue of material fact was presented since plaintiff offered only opinion of her mother who is not an expert in field of special education); Frank v. Grover, 1982-83 EDUC. HANDICAPPED L. REP. (CRR) 554:148 (Wis. Cir. Ct. 1982) (expert testimony, including that of teacher, relied upon to uphold school's IEP and refuse parents' request for different educational method).

The Act encourages parental involvement in a number of ways, including requiring parents to be a part of the development of the IEP and allowing parents to file complaints challenging the educational program. *Rowley,* 458 U.S. at 182-83 n.6. The Comments to the EAHCA regulations make it clear that the parents are to have an active role as "equal participants" in developing the child's educational program. Comment, 34 C.F.R. § 300, app. C, at 65, 74 (1980). One court has seen the involvement of the parents in all significant decisions made by the LEA as necessary to justify the statutory deference accorded the state and local decisionmakers. Lang v. Braintree School Comm., 545 F. Supp. 1221, 1223 n.3 (D. Mass. 1982). As another court has noted,

Although the procedure established for formulation of these IEPs requires parental input, there is little doubt that the final decision rests with the local educational agency, a subdivision of the state. This fact is reflected in . . . the statutory appeal procedure which grants a right only to the parents to complain about the IEP, in contrast with the right to appeal decisions of the hearing examiner, which is granted to both the state and to the parents.

Battle v. Pennsylvania, 629 F.2d 269, 278 (3d Cir. 1980), *cert. denied,* 452 U.S. 968 (1981).

The placement of ultimate decisionmaking upon the state or local agency undoubtedly is based upon the fact that the agency is in a better position to weigh and balance the competing interests of *all* students within the system while parents' primary concern understandably will be the individual child.

In weighing these interests, however, school systems may make policy and budgetary decisions which unnecessarily limit the options available to the handicapped student before the parents ever are involved in the decisionmaking process through development of the IEP. *See* Sindelar, *How and Why the Law Has Failed: An Historical Analysis of Services for the Retarded in North Carolina and a Prescription for Change,* LAW. & CONTEMP. PROBS. Spring 1985, at 125. *See also supra* note 98 and accompanying text. One commentator has, therefore, proposed training parents to participate in the bureaucratic decisionmaking process. Sindelar, at 149-51. Such an undertaking should not only increase awareness of the needs of the handicapped on the part of the school system and public at large, but should also give parents of handicapped children greater insight into system-wide programs, priorities, and budgetary constraints.

148. *Application of* Rowley, *supra* note 145, at SA-109.

149. Roncker v. Walter, 700 F.2d 1058 (6th Cir. 1983), *cert. denied,* 104 S. Ct. 196 (1983).

must accept that decision if they desire federal funds."[150]

Even courts which have deferred to the LEA's choice of method have indicated that they did so after noting that the requirements of the Act had been met. For example, in Lang v. Braintree School Committee,[151] although the court stated that it would not interfere with a state's choice as long as it was a "minimally acceptable educational approach,"[152] it also specifically stated that "[i]nasmuch as the Braintree IEP relies on legitimate educational philosophy akin to the mainstreaming approach preferred by the Act, and will provide . . . what this court views as an education that benefits [the plaintiff] within the meaning of the Act, the IEP must be deemed satisfactory under the Act."[153] Decisions such as Lang indicate that courts are indeed attempting to balance concern for the individual child's welfare as defined by the statute against the principle of preserving local control over education decisions.[154]

VI

SECTION 504 OF THE REHABILITATION ACT

The Poes also challenged the school system's refusal to offer a chronologically age-appropriate placement at the high school as a violation of section 504 of the Rehabilitation Act of 1973[155] in that Clint and other high-school-aged TMH students were being excluded from programs and services to which they were entitled.

A. Requirement of Nondiscrimination

Section 504 is a broad requirement of nondiscrimination against the handicapped in all federally assisted programs—including public schools. It provides:

> No otherwise qualified handicapped individual in the United States, as defined in section 706(7) of this title, shall, solely by reason of his handicap, be excluded from the participation in, be denied the benefits of, or be subjected to discrimination under any program or activity receiving Federal financial assistance . . . .[156]

Regulations promulgated pursuant to section 504 add substance to its requirements.[157] The regulations provide that a recipient of federal funds may not:

---

150. *Id.* at 1062.
151. 545 F. Supp. 1221 (D. Mass. 1982).
152. *Id.* at 1227.
153. *Id.* at 1228; *see also* Silvio v. Commonwealth, 64 Pa. Commw. 192, 439 A.2d 893, 897-98 (1982) (court has no disposition to overturn conclusions of school district regarding "clash of philosophies among experts" when conclusion is based upon ample evidence and is in keeping with least restrictive environment requirement), *aff'd*, 500 Pa. 431, 456 A.2d 1366 (1983).
154. Comment, *supra* note 135, at 528.
155. Pub. L. No. 93-112, 87 Stat. 394 (codified at 29 U.S.C. § 794 (1982)).
156. *Id.* It was undisputed, and the State Hearing Officer concluded, that Clint Poe is a qualified handicapped person as defined in the statute and implementing regulations and that the Durham County School System is a recipient of federal funds and therefore subject to the requirements of the statute. Appellants' Brief at 40.
157. 34 C.F.R. §§ 104.1-104.61 (1984).

- deny a handicapped person the opportunity to participate in or benefit from an aid, service, or benefit provided by the local program;
- deny equal opportunities to a handicapped person to participate in or benefit from any aid, service, or benefit;
- provide an aid, service, or benefit to a handicapped person that is not as effective as that provided to others;
- provide different or separate aids, benefits, or services to handicapped persons unless necessary to make the program as effective as that offered to the nonhandicapped.[158]

As developed in part III of this comment, education involves more than academics. Thus, the aids, benefits, and services which a school must provide a student should include nonacademic elements of education because:

> school resources include both human and material elements that can influence achievement, social and cognitive development, and socialization. These resources may be highly motivated peers, specific socialization processes, counselors, or aspects of the curriculum and instructional program. By far the most important resource is interaction with nonhandicapped peers who provide entry into the normal life experiences of members of our society, such as going to dances, taking buses, shopping, dating and wearing fashionable clothes. Most of these normal life experiences can be obtained only within relationships with peers . . . .
>
> Experience with a broad range of peers is not a superficial luxury to be enjoyed by some students and not by others, but rather an absolute necessity for maximal achievement and healthy cognitive and social development.[159]

Thus, by failing to provide access to age-appropriate activities and peers and the benefits derived from such interaction, a school system precludes students from obtaining "system benefits," or at least benefits that were as effective as those realized by the nonhandicapped students in the system who do attend age appropriate schools. Such a practice may violate section 504.[160]

Part D of the section 504 regulations is directed at handicapped services offered by elementary and secondary schools. These regulations essentially parallel the substantive requirements of the EAHCA regulations, with some differences which seem to favor age-appropriate placement even more strongly. Relevant regulations include a requirement that a school system provide a free appropriate education to all handicapped students within the jurisdiction.[161] School systems must develop programs which meet the individual needs of handicapped students as adequately as the needs of nonhandicapped.[162] And to direct placement decisions, the regulations require that handicapped students be educated with nonhandicapped students "to the maximum extent appropriate to the needs of the handicapped person," placing him in the "regular educational environment operated by the recip-

---

158. *Id.* § 104.4.
159. Johnson & Johnson, *Integrating Handicapped Students into the Mainstream*, 47 EXCEPTIONAL CHILDREN 90 (1980).
160. New Mexico Ass'n for Retarded Citizens v. New Mexico, 678 F.2d 847, 853 (10th Cir. 1982).
161. 34 C.F.R. § 104.33(a) (1984).
162. *Id.* § 104.33(b).

ient unless it is demonstrated by the recipient" that education in that environment cannot be achieved satisfactorily, despite the provision of special services.[163] Under the regulations' mandate of the least restrictive educational environment, the student must be offered an equal opportunity to participate in nonacademic services such as physical education, athletics, and extracurricular activities.[164]

Note that this least restrictive environment requirement seems to be broader than its parallel regulation under the EAHCA. Its preference is not limited to regular classes but extends to the regular educational environment, which presumably could apply to a school facility as well as to a class. The burden is clearly placed upon the school system to show that the student's needs require his removal from the regular environment.

In the Poe case, the school system argued that social skills develop sequentially and that it would be inappropriate and perhaps harmful to place Clint at the high school while he was still testing at a pre-adolescent social skills level.[165] The superintendent of the system testified, however, that the school system had identified no specific social skill levels which all students must master in order to move to the high school,[166] that the activities, situations, and student behaviors at a high school were significantly different from those encountered in a junior high,[167] and that some nonhandicapped students were placed in grade levels (at least through the tenth grade) based upon subjective rather than academic considerations.[168] Thus, Clint was as qualified to attend the high school as these other students except for his handicap and was therefore excluded solely by reason of his handicap. To cure this problem, the system offered to place Clint at the high school in the EMH program, which everyone agreed was inappropriate to his needs, but refused to modify its existing program by providing a self-contained classroom for TMH students at the high school.[169]

B. Affirmative Modification

Although the Supreme Court has determined that the purpose of section 504 is to prohibit discrimination rather than to impose an affirmative action obligation,[170] the Court has also noted that the distinction between discrimination and affirmative action not taken is rather unclear and has conceded that in some situations refusal to modify an existing program might be discriminatory under section 504.[171] A number of courts have found a refusal to

163. Id. § 104.34(a).

164. Id. § 104.37.

165. Respondent's Brief at 5-6.

166. III Hearing Transcript at 38 (testimony of Dr. Yeager, Superintendent, Durham County Schools).

167. Id. at 10.

168. Id. at 19.

169. Id. at 38-39; Petitioners' Brief at 2.

170. Southeastern Community College v. Davis, 442 U.S. 397, 411-12 (1979).

171. Id. at 412-13.

make affirmative modifications to be a violation of section 504.[172] The courts have also stated, however, that they will not find a refusal to modify an educational program discriminatory under section 504 if the handicapped student could not realize the principal benefits of the program even after the accommodation was made since, as interpreted by the Supreme Court, "[S]ection 504 does not require 'substantial adjustments in existing programs beyond those necessary to eliminate discrimination against otherwise qualified individuals.' "[173] "Conversely, it is reasonable to conclude that refusal to accommodate a handicapped student in an educational program may constitute discrimination if the student could thereby realize and enjoy the program's benefits."[174]

Even in situations where the student could benefit from a modified program, the duty to modify is not unlimited. It is required only when it does not impose undue financial or admininstrative hardships.[175] Under this test, the school must show that modifying an existing program would cause sufficient hardship to justify its failure to take accommodating steps.[176] Thus, all alternatives and costs and administrative problems should be examined.[177] The Tenth Circuit has proposed a type of cost/benefit analysis, suggesting that "the greater the number of children needing the particular special education service, the more likely that failure to provide the service constitutes discrimination . . . because the more children in need of the service, the more the benefits of that service outweigh its cost."[178] In the Poe case, this type of analysis would require taking into account all other high school aged TMH students who might also benefit from a modification in the existing program.[179]

Although no cases were found which required a modification of existing programs based upon an age-appropriate placement mandate, the Office of Civil Rights did respond to a complaint from the Wake County (North Carolina) School District alleging that the educational settings of older TMH stu-

---

172. *See, e.g.*, Tatro v. Texas, 625 F.2d 557 (5th Cir. 1980) (failure to provide catheterization), *on remand*, 516 F. Supp. 968 (N.D. Tex. 1981), *aff'd*, 703 F.2d 823 (5th Cir. 1983), *aff'd in part, rev'd in part sub nom.* Irving Indep. School Dist. v. Tatro, 104 S. Ct. 3371 (1984) (because school district was liable to provide catheterization under EAHCA and § 504 is inapplicable when relief is available under EAHCA to remedy a denial of educational services, respondents would not be entitled to relief under § 504); Camenisch v. Univ. of Texas, 616 F.2d 127 (5th Cir. 1980) (granting preliminary injunction based upon likelihood of success on merits where university refused to provide interpreter for deaf students), *vacated and remanded on other grounds*, 451 U.S. 390 (1981); Lora v. Board of Educ., 456 F. Supp. 1211 (E.D.N.Y. 1978) (inadequate educational services in day schools for emotionally disturbed children), *aff'd in part, vacated in part*, 623 F.2d 248 (2d Cir. 1980).

173. Tatro v. Texas, 625 F.2d at 564 n.19 (quoting Southeastern Community College v. Davis, 442 U.S. 397, 410 (1979)).

174. New Mexico Ass'n for Retarded Citizens v. New Mexico, 678 F.2d 847, 854 (10th Cir. 1982).

175. *Id.*

176. Lynch v. Maher, 507 F. Supp. 1268, 1280 (D. Conn. 1981).

177. *See supra* notes 122-25 and accompanying text.

178. *New Mexico Ass'n for Retarded Citizens*, 678 F.2d at 854 (considering possible statewide violations of section 504).

179. *See supra* notes 122-25 and accompanying text.

dents were inappropriate because they were in schools where they had no contact with students their own age. The Office of Civil Rights found this to be a violation of the regulation mandating education in the least restrictive environment.[180]

VII

CONCLUSION

Handicapped students have been discriminated against and isolated from the rest of society for centuries. The EAHCA and section 504 of the Rehabilitation Act are attempts to rectify this situation; handicapped students have made tremendous gains within the public schools since their enactment. As the broad goals of bringing students into the public schools have been met, and hearing officers and judges begin to grapple with thorny questions "at the fringe" of the statutes, they should do so by carefully interpreting the statutes with an eye toward implementing their goals and purposes.

Chronologically appropriate placement is important to implement the goal of integration of the handicapped. For, as one commentator noted,

> The Supreme Court cases of *Brown v. Board of Education* and *Wisconsin v. Yoder* express the idea that education . . . is the primary social learning mechanism of society. To be deprived of an education is to be socially crippled; to be denied the opportunity to education in a particular milieu is to be cut off and alienated from that milieu . . . . [Children's] handicapped conditions, if *Brown* and *Yoder* are accepted, can only be aggravated by the additional injury that the lack of appropriate social interaction with the wider society causes.[181]

Thus, age-appropriate placement should be a factor to be considered in a placement decision under the EAHCA because it affords nonacademic socialization benefits which are part of an education. If a child's unique abilities and needs as developed in his individual program show that he can function in an age-appropriate environment and that he would obtain educational benefit from such an environment, he should be placed in that setting to implement both the goal of providing a free appropriate public education and of providing an education in the least restrictive environment. Such a requirement does not infringe upon local autonomy in the field of public education since

---

180. Wake County (N.C.) School Dist., Ref: Complaint No. 04-83-1006, 3 [§ 504 Rulings] EDUC. HANDICAPPED L. REP. (CRR) 257:432 (June 24, 1983).

No affirmative modification was required because the Wake County School District already had plans to provide age-appropriate placements.

In the Poe case, the Hearing Officer specifically found that the Office of Civil Rights has ruled that section 504 does not necessarily require that handicapped children of one age participate with non-handicapped age mates. Conclusion of Law No. 2, Hearing Decision at 7. Evidently, this finding was based upon an earlier conclusion of the Office of Civil Rights that an age inappropriate setting for a severely retarded child did not violate section 504. In the earlier decision, however, it was determined that the child did not interact with other children or distinguish people or environments. Thus, this situation is easily distinguishable from the Poe case since this child was evidently being denied the benefits of interaction due to the severity of her handicap, and placement by the schools made little difference. Petitioners' Brief at 10; Telephone Interview with Karen Sindelar, Attorney, North Carolina Protection and Advocacy System (March 19, 1984).

181. Colley, *The Education for All Handicapped Children Act (EHA): A Statutory and Legal Analysis,* 10 J.L. & EDUC. 137, 139-40 (1981).

the states have chosen to have their freedom of decisionmaking sharply curtailed to the extent necessary to meet the basic requirements of the Act in return for federal funds. Furthermore, refusing to allow equal participation and benefit from educational programs, including nonacademic activities and interaction with peers, to otherwise qualified handicapped individuals, constitutes discrimination under section 504 and may, in some situations, require rectification through affirmative modification of programs.

9

HOW AND WHY THE LAW HAS FAILED: AN HISTORICAL ANALYSIS OF SERVICES FOR THE RETARDED IN NORTH CAROLINA AND A PRESCRIPTION FOR CHANGE

KAREN SINDELAR*

I

INTRODUCTION

The Education for All Handicapped Children Act (EAHCA or the Act)[1] has resulted in widespread and relatively rapid implementation of a number of educational innovations, such as formulating individualized education programs (IEP's) for handicapped children, and affording parents an "impartial" hearing rather than a school board hearing when they disagree with a district's program. But whether the implementation of these innovations has improved the substantive education offered to handicapped children is debatable. Unfortunately, it seems that the progress school districts have made in complying with the law's many procedural requirements has obscured the lack of substantive progress in many areas of special education. Districts can achieve strict compliance with procedural requirements such as formulating IEP's,[2] giving parents notice,[3] and testing children before placement,[4] without making significant qualitative improvements in the programs offered handicapped children. The Act's substantive requirements—that children receive a "free appropriate public education"[5] in the "least restrictive environment"[6]—are ambiguous guarantees lacking objective criteria which can be used to measure compliance. As a result, any educational offering short of total exclusion can be termed "appropriate" and in the "least restrictive environment." Because compliance with these substantive mandates is so difficult to measure and so easily avoided, educational opportunities offered hand-

---

* Attorney for North Carolina Protection and Advocacy System, North Carolina Governor's Advocacy Council for Persons with Disabilities. The author also served as a State Hearing Officer for P.L. 94-142 appeals in 1979 and 1980.
  1. Pub. L. No. 94-142, 89 Stat. 773 (1975) (codified at 20 U.S.C. §§ 1400-1461 (1982)).
  2. 20 U.S.C. § 1414(a)(5) (1982); 34 C.F.R. § 300.342 (1984).
  3. 20 U.S.C. § 1415(b)(1)(C), (D) (1982); 34 C.F.R. § 300.504 (1984).
  4. 20 U.S.C. § 1412(5)(c) (1982); 34 C.F.R. § 300.531 (1984).
  5. 20 U.S.C. §§ 1401(18), 1412(1), 1414(a)(1)(C)(ii) (1982); 34 C.F.R. §§ 300.4, .121, .122, .300 (1984).
  6. 20 U.S.C. § 1412(5)(B) (1982); 34 C.F.R. §§ 300.550-.556 (1984).

icapped children are influenced far more by such factors as attitudes of key school personnel and fiscal incentives than they are by the Act itself.

This author, a practicing attorney who has advised both school districts and parents over the past five years, believes that policymakers and researchers have spent too much time assessing compliance with easily measurable procedural mandates of the law, and not enough on whether the substantive education offered handicapped children has improved. Policymakers need to analyze specific substantive education practices or areas of need that were considered problems prior to the EAHCA's passage and determine whether implementation of the law has resulted in improvements in those areas. If the Act has not had an impact, the causes for failure should be examined and federal efforts should be targeted at those causes.

This article attempts to identify some causes for the failure of the EAHCA to bring about changes in one area of special education. The author examines a specific problem area that existed prior to the passage of EAHCA —the inferior and segregated education offered to lower functioning retarded children. Both the status of services to these children prior to the Act's passage and current practices are discussed. The author then analyzes how certain factors have operated as barriers to change and have impeded progress in this problem area. In particular, historic practices, state fiscal policies, attitudes of key actors at the local level (including parents) and state and federal monitoring are examined. The author also looks at how some of the same factors have helped promote change in certain school districts. Based on this analysis, suggestions are offered concerning new federal incentive programs and regulatory changes that could bring about greater progress in this area of need.

The description, analysis, and conclusions drawn in this article are based on the author's own casework, observations, and discussions with teachers, parents, and administrators rather than on research or theories concerning institutional change. Although the author's experience has been limited to North Carolina, discussions with advocates in other states and recent court cases[7] challenging systemic inadequacies in services for the retarded indicate that this problem exists on a nationwide basis, even in states with well-funded special education programs. Also, the primary spokesperson on special education matters for the United States Department of Education has identified continuing unnecessary segregation as a national problem.[8]

This particular problem was selected because it illustrates how factors not

---

7. *See, e.g.*, Roncker v. Walter, 700 F.2d 1058 (6th Cir.), *cert. denied*, 104 S. Ct. 196 (1983) (challenge to Ohio's statewide system of educating the moderately retarded in segregated schools upheld in light of least restrictive environment mandate); St. Louis Developmental Disabilities Treatment Center Parents Ass'n v. Mallory, 591 F. Supp. 1416 (W.D. Mo. 1984) (challenge to Missouri's statewide system of educating the severely and profoundly retarded in segregated centers dismissed) [hereinafter cited as St. Louis Parents Assoc.].

8. Speech by Madeleine Will, Assistant Secretary for Special Education and Rehabilitative Service to the 62nd Annual Convention of the Council for Exceptional Children, *as reported in* Summary and Analysis, 1983-84 EDUC. HANDICAPPED L. REP. (CRR) SA:119-20 (Apr. 27, 1984) (states and local education agencies are not complying with the least restrictive environment requirement and

addressed by the EAHCA can frustrate its implementation. There are numerous other examples of failed implementation that similarly affect large numbers of handicapped children. Each of these problems is unique, with its own history and possible solutions. Factors that have impeded or promoted change in one problem area may be relatively insignificant in another. For example, whereas parental attitudes and pressure have been important in shaping services to retarded children, this factor has been relatively insignificant in a different problem area, the lack of adequate educational services for emotionally disturbed and behaviorally disordered children. For this reason, the author believes that meaningful progress will be made in improving the education of handicapped children only if problem areas are examined individually and solutions are carefully constructed.

II

IDENTIFICATION OF THE PROBLEM

A. Some Typical Cases

In North Carolina, most students who are more than mildly retarded are offered either inferior educational services and facilities or are segregated for their education, or are given an education that is both segregated and inferior. The number of retarded students involved is substantial. In North Carolina, of some 121,112 identified handicapped children[9] served by the public schools, 4,529[10] are identified as moderately retarded,[11] or having an IQ between 30 and 49, and 754[12] are identified as severely or profoundly retarded,[13] or having an IQ below 30. The following example illustrates both the functioning level of a hypothetical moderately retarded student, as well as the typical program options available to the moderately retarded in North Carolina.

John is a 16-year-old with Down's Syndrome and an IQ of 50. Physically he functions much like a nonhandicapped teenager, except that he is some-

---

have not developed standards for placement decisions, thus allowing unstructured and subjective decisionmaking).

9. December 1, 1983 Headcount of Children Receiving Special Education in North Carolina, (on file with the Division of Exceptional Children, N.C. Department of Public Instruction) [hereinafter December 1, 1983 Headcount, N.C.].

10. December 1, 1983 Headcount, N.C., *supra* note 9; October 1, 1983 Headcount for the Education Consolidation and Improvement Act, Chapter I Handicapped (on file with the Division for Exceptional Children, N.C. Department of Public Instruction) [hereinafter October 1, 1983 Headcount, N.C., Chapter I].

11. A mentally retarded student exhibits significantly subaverage general intellectual functioning, along with deficits in adaptive behavior — i.e., the ability to "adapt" to natural and social environmental demands. *See* 34 C.F.R. § 300.5(b)(4) (1984). In North Carolina, the moderately retarded, or trainable mentally handicapped student, is defined as having an IQ in the 30 to 49 range. NORTH CAROLINA RULES GOVERNING PROGRAMS AND SERVICES FOR CHILDREN WITH SPECIAL NEEDS, § .1509(3) (1984) (issued by the State Department of Public Instruction) [hereinafter cited as RULES].

12. December 1, 1983 Headcount, N.C., *supra* note 9; October 1, 1983 Headcount, N.C., Chapter I, *supra* note 10.

13. RULES, *supra* note 11, at § .1509(3)-(4). In addition to having an IQ below 30, the severely/profoundly retarded student may have a wide variety of handicapping conditions.

what less coordinated. However, he swims, bowls, plays basketball, and dances, though usually in groups of other retarded teenagers. Although his articulation is poor, he speaks in six or seven word sentences and he is capable of communicating about concrete things and simple abstract issues. Academically he functions at a first to second grade level. He writes his name, identifying information, and simple sentences, and can do simple arithmetic. Vocationally, John helps his father organize goods at his convenience store, does odd jobs around the house, and likes to help his father by identifying tools when his father is fixing small equipment. Socially, John has preteen interests and behaviors. He is interested in girls, sports, and motorcycles. He attends sports events and "hangs out" at the mall with his parents or brother. He interacts with nonhandicapped teenagers at church and in recreation programs. Although it is clear to everyone that he is significantly retarded, John acts appropriately in these social situations. He initiates conversation, responds to overtures from others, follows directions, and generally acts like those around him.

The education offered John varies considerably from district to district in North Carolina. In district A, John would attend a segregated school operated by the system especially for moderately retarded students. The school is old; it was used for black students when the system was segregated. The school serves sixty moderately retarded students from a number of school districts. Students at the segregated school receive physical education, art, and music once a week, less than they would receive in the district's other schools. The children also get one hour less education each day than their nonhandicapped peers; their bus routes are particularly long since they are bussed in from various parts of the district, and beyond. Despite these shortcomings, the principal and parents are proud of the school and consider it "a special place for special people."

District B offers John a cadillac version of the offerings in district A. Thus John would receive physical education, art, and music classes comparable to those given the nonhandicapped, speech therapy according to his needs, and an excellent hands-on vocational training program. The school, though segregated, is very modern. Students receive fewer hours of instruction than the nonhandicapped, however. As in district A, the necessity of transporting the moderately mentally handicapped kids around the district on a few "handicapped buses" leads to longer transportation times and fewer instructional hours. As in district A, John would have no regular contact with the nonhandicapped during the school day.

District C has contracted with a nearby "developmental center" to serve John. The center is part of a system of similar centers that are administered by the State's Department of Human Resources, rather than the state's public school system. The center serves moderately, severely, and profoundly retarded students as well as other students with severe handicaps. It does not offer traditional school services like music and art, except as part of a general recreation therapy program. Nor is there any vocational training in the school other than extremely low-level and repetitious training in sorting and ordering.

In district D, John would be placed in an elementary school with eleven other moderately retarded students aged five through twenty-one. None of the students receives art, music, or physical education classes. They are not considered part of the regular school program, and are the only class housed in the old wing of the school, which separates them from the other children. John would have no access to any vocational education since neither vocational courses nor equipment are normally available in an elementary school. However, an "occupational therapist" comes to the class twice a week for thirty minutes to teach students how to separate, sort and order.

Finally, in district E, John would be placed in a high school class for moderately retarded students. Art, music, and physical education are available to him on the same basis as they are to nonhandicapped students. However, the only vocational education offered to John is the opportunity to be bussed to a nearby "sheltered workshop," a segregated work training center for retarded, physically disabled and mentally ill adults.

B. Segregation and Unequal Opportunity: The Common Characteristics

The above examples typify the range of educational programs available to most moderately, severely, and profoundly retarded students in North Carolina. In forty-nine states, segregated schooling is the norm for the severely and profoundly retarded.[14] In a number of states it is the dominant service mode for the moderately handicapped as well. Segregated schooling takes many forms. In North Carolina, the predominant mode of service delivery for the severely and profoundly retarded is the segregated developmental center offered by district C in the example above. Moderately retarded students like John are also placed in developmental centers, but not as frequently. They are generally served directly by school districts, often in segregated schools or in separate buildings, wings, basements or trailers of regular schools. The degree of physical isolation and lack of regular daily contact with the nonhandicapped can be just as great in these settings as in segregated schools.

Services and facilities being equal, it is debatable whether segregation in separate schools denies educational opportunity. Since most retarded students can be offered the intensity of instruction and special services they need in self-contained classes in regular schools with their nonhandicapped peers, segregation is at least a technical violation of the least restrictive environment mandate of the EAHCA. Whether segregation goes beyond this and actually limits educational progress is still in doubt. Since controlled, empirical research concerning the effect of lack of exposure to nonhandicapped peers is virtually nonexistent,[15] the best available evidence appears to be teacher

---

14. St. Louis Parents Ass'n, 591 F. Supp. at 1464. (all states but Hawaii have separate education systems for the severely and profoundly retarded).

15. *Id.* at 1457-64 & n.80 (Plaintiffs' experts maintain that functional and social skills cannot be taught in a separate environment because of insufficient opportunities to intereact with nonhand-

observations. A sufficient number of school districts in North Carolina have implemented integrated age-appropriate programs for the moderately retarded in North Carolina for some conclusions to be drawn. Educators from these districts have uniformly reported that behavior, social skills, and self-esteem of the moderately retarded have improved as a result of placement with nonhandicapped peers.[16] If these reports are true, then placement in even the finest segregated facility deprives the moderately retarded student of potential behavioral, social and psychological gains. For the severely and profoundly handicapped, information is sparser; few integrated service models exist for these students in North Carolina or elsewhere. Advocates for these students maintain, however, that they also experience gains from a more integrated placement.[17]

Segregation is not the only problem retarded students face, as shown in the examples above. Whether retarded students are placed in segregated settings or in regular schools, they are commonly offered inferior facilities and are deprived of educational services that the nonhandicapped receive. They receive little effective hands-on vocational education, and fewer enrichment services such as art, music and physical education. Retarded students educated in regular schools are frequently placed in isolated, sometimes inferior sections of the school building. In addition, they are generally placed in age-inappropriate school settings serving students younger than they are.

The deprivations retarded students continue to face have been fully described in *St. Louis Developmental Disabilities Treatment Center Parents Association v. Mallory,*[18] the only major challenge of the 1980's to a statewide segregated system for the retarded. The plaintiffs, five advocacy organizations and thirteen individuals, alleged that Missouri's segregated system of special day schools and facilities for the severely and profoundly retarded violated the EAHCA, section 504 of the Rehabilitation Act of 1973,[19] and the United States Constitution. The court ruled against the plaintiffs on all grounds. Most of the state segregated day schools for the severely retarded in Missouri are relatively new, built since 1958 and specially equipped for the handicapped.[20] The extensive testimony from both sides in the case painted a pic-

---

icapped and poorer quality of instruction, but admit that research data does not exist to support their positions.).

16. *Age-Appropriate High School Programs for the Moderately Retarded,* in PRO-ACTION: A NEWSLETTER FROM THE N.C. GOVERNOR'S ADVOCACY COUNCIL FOR PERSONS WITH DISABILITIES, Special Issue (June 1982) [hereinafter cited as *N.C. Report on Age-Appropriate High School Programs*]. Reports from eight school districts in N.C. that have established integrated age-appropriate programs for high-school-aged moderately retarded students indicate uniformly positive experience and gains in students' social skills, behavior, and self-esteem.

17. *See supra* note 15. Other educators, however, claim that functional and social skills do not have to be learned through practice with the nonhandicapped in a regular education environment and, in fact, can be better learned if they are taught through intense instruction in a segregated setting with students then being taken out into the commmunity to practice skills. *Id.*

18. 591 F. Supp. 1416 (W.D. Mo. 1984).

19. Pub. L. No. 93-112, 87 Stat. 394 (codified as amended at 29 U.S.C. § 794 (1976)).

20. St. Louis Parents Ass'n, 591 F. Supp. at 1450. Eighty-five percent of the retarded students served in separate special schools in Missouri are in specially designed buildings.

ture of the continued deprivation suffered by retarded students who are supposedly "integrated" into local schools that was at least as striking as the alleged deprivation experienced by students in segregated settings. For the latter group, the primary discrimination proven was that they were offered only a five-hour school day, rather than the six hours that is standard in Missouri.[21] But the severely retarded students who had been accepted by their school systems for direct "integrated" service in local schools faced other problems. They were placed in segregated settings such as mobile units or rented buildings away from school grounds.[22] None of their classes had been located in age-appropriate settings.[23] Regular education administrators and teachers frequently were unaccommodating.[24]

Statistics that measure the number or the proportion of retarded students who are deprived of an important component of an education program—such as regular integration with the nonhandicapped, comparable enrichment services, or vocational education—do not appear to exist. The problem is difficult to measure, in part because degrees of handicap vary so substantially that it is impossible to say that all retarded students classified within a certain level of retardation would benefit from a particular educational component. Nationally, however, it has been estimated that only 3.3 percent of vocational education students are handicapped, though the percentage of handicapped students in the general school population is at least 12 percent.[25]

This author estimates that in North Carolina, over 90 percent of the severely and profoundly retarded are educated in segregated settings.[26] Virtually all severely and profoundly retarded students are deprived of enrichment services comparable to those received by the nonhandicapped and of effective, comparable hands-on vocational education. The educational offerings for the moderately retarded are more varied, as the examples offered above show. The author estimates approximately 40 percent of moderately retarded students receive an education in a segregated school or in an iso-

---

21. *Id.* at 1468 n.88. The denial of a full school day was the only deprivation the court indicated it would remedy, but plaintiffs declined as they were seeking a change in placement from special schools to local schools, not an increase in hours of education in the special schools.

22. *Id.* at 1451 n.73.

23. *Id.* at 1454 n.76.

24. *Id.*

25. Vocational Education Data System Statistics, compiled annually by the National Center for Education Statistics (NCES), U.S. Dep't of Educ. (unpublished data collected on a yearly basis through school year 1982-83, available on request from Mr. Arthur Podolsley, NCES) [hereinafter cited as Vocational Education Data Systems Study]. The last year in which statistics concerning handicapped participation were collected was 1980-81; the 3.3 percent figure is from that year.

26. The N.C. Department of Public Instruction reports that for 1983-84, 550 children aged 5 through 17 served in the special developmental day centers were subsidized with special legislative funding. The state does not keep statistics identifying the handicaps of these children, but most are severely and profoundly retarded. Memo to Karen Sindelar from Carolyn Perry, Division of Exceptional Children (Sept. 6, 1984). The total number of 6 to 17-year-old severely and profoundly handicapped school students both in and out of developmental centers was 663. December 1, 1983 Headcount, N.C., *supra* note 9; October 1, 1983 Headcount, N.C. Chapter I, *supra* note 10. From the author's observation, most of the severely and profoundly retarded students who are served directly by school systems rather than in developmental centers are also placed in segregated settings.

lated building, trailer, wing, or basement of a regular school.[27] Of those students integrated into regular schools, approximately 90 percent of retarded students age 12 and above are placed in age-inappropriate settings[28] and approximately 90 percent are denied a hands-on vocational program comparable in intensity and effectiveness to that offered the nonhandicapped.[29] Approximately 60 percent of all school-age retarded students are denied enrichment activities such as physical education, music, and art equivalent to those the nonhandicapped receive.[30] Overall, younger retarded students fare better than older retarded students since placement in elementary schools is age-appropriate for them and since they are not as much in need of vocational education as the older students. However, both young and old students are equally deprived of enrichment activities and speech therapy. In the case of John, the hypothetical moderately retarded student described previously, fewer than ten of North Carolina's 142 school districts would offer him an education in an integrated setting with age-appropriate peers, and vocational and enrichment opportunities comparable to those received by the nonhandicapped.

III

CAUSES OF THE SEGREGATED AND INADEQUATE SYSTEM

A combination of factors has contributed to the segregated and inadequate educational opportunities offered the retarded in North Carolina. These factors include: the existence of a segregated service system prior to the passage of the EAHCA and the perpetuation of this system through the state's fiscal policies; beliefs of poorly-educated school district personnel and parents that the retarded must be protected and that they are incapable of benefiting from occupational and enrichment courses available to the nonhandicapped; lack of leadership by the state; and the rigid, unaccommodating response of the state's vocational education system to the needs of handicapped students. These factors will be explored more fully below.

---

27. An incomplete survey by the N.C. Department of Public Instruction showed that 15 school districts maintain totally segregated facilities for the moderately retarded. Letter to Page McCullough from LaVerne Buchanan, Division for Exceptional Children (June 29, 1984) (on file with the N.C. Governor's Advocacy Council for Persons with Disabilities). Most of these facilities serve children from at least two school districts, and sometimes more, so it can be estimated that between 30 and 45 districts of 142 districts in North Carolina serve their moderately retarded children in totally separate schools. Of the remaining districts, a significant number use isolated areas—basements, trailers, and adjacent buildings—to serve the moderately retarded.

28. *N.C. Report on Age-Appropriate High School Programs, supra* note 16. An incomplete survey of N.C. school districts showed that eight of 142 had age-appropriate high school programs.

29. Vocational Education Data System Study, *supra* note 25. From the author's observation, the few handicapped students who are afforded comparable vocational education generally have milder handicaps, such as learning disabilities or mild mental retardation. The moderately and severely handicapped are either deprived of vocational education altogether, or are given special vocational instruction which is less effective than that offered the nonhandicapped, particularly because of the lack of access to vocational equipment and supplies available to nonhandicapped students in high schools.

30. This estimate is based on the author's observation and reports from parents around the state.

A. Fiscal Policies and Continued Service Outside the Schools for the Severely Retarded.

In North Carolina, fiscal incentives and attitudes concerning the desirability of segregating the retarded have reinforced and continued a system of educating many of the severely and profoundly retarded outside the public schools. Before the passage of the EAHCA, noninstitutionalized severely and profoundly retarded children were not considered educable. Many, however, received day services in separate "developmental" day centers funded and administered by the State Department of Human Resources. The moderately retarded, in comparison, have been educated in increasing numbers in the public schools since 1957. The state, in 1957, established a special funding system to reimburse local districts for the hiring of special teachers for the moderately retarded at a teacher-pupil ratio established by the state.[31] Services to the moderately retarded were, of course, discretionary. In districts that did not choose to apply to the state for funds, the moderately retarded were served in the developmental centers along with the more severely retarded.

When the EAHCA was passed, there was resistance to the possibility of closing the developmental centers. For a few years they continued to receive a substantial subsidy from the Department of Human Resources for the school-age children they served. With this subsidy they could contract with local school districts to serve the severely and profoundly retarded for less than it cost districts to serve such students themselves. For a number of reasons, most districts agreed to such contracts for the severely retarded without question despite the EAHCA's mandate for service in the least restrictive environment.

First, the Act's mandate for services in the least restrictive environment was as ambiguous as its requirement for appropriate services. There was no prohibition against serving children in separate schools; in fact, such schools were specifically mentioned in the EAHCA.[32] Neither the Act nor the regulations implementing it included any presumption that certain categories of handicapped children could generally be served in regular schools as opposed to separate schools which would have guided states and local districts in their interpretation of least restrictive environment. Thus, like most decisions made under the Act, the determination of a child's placement became a function of what service and placement options were already available in a district, rather than what current research or demonstration projects showed about

---

31. *See* Law of June 12, 1957, ch. 1369, 1957 N.C. Sess. Laws 1551.

32. 20 U.S.C. § 1412(5)(B) (1982). The section states that states must have "procedures to assure that, to the maximum extent appropriate, handicapped children, including children in public or private institutions or other care facilities, are educated with children who are not handicapped, and that special classes, separate schooling, or other removal of handicapped children from the regular education environment occurs only when the nature or severity of the handicap is such that education in regular classes with the use of supplementary aids and services cannot be achieved satisfactorily . . . ." By referring to separate schooling, institutions, and other care facilities, the Act clearly assumes the continued existence of these alternatives. *See* St. Louis Parents Ass'n, 591 F. Supp. at 1442-43.

the benefits of integration and normalization. The most prevalent and least expensive placement option that existed for the severely handicapped was the developmental center.

Second, in the initial years of the Act's implementation there was very little support for increased integration. Teachers in school systems had had no experience teaching the severely retarded and public school administrators knew nothing about educational possibilities for such students. Directors and personnel of developmental day centers who had been the primary service providers before the passage of the Act believed that they alone had the desire and the skills to teach the severely retarded. Parents generally agreed, since the developmental day centers were a known quantity that had successfully offered their children services in the past. Also, the State Department of Public Instruction neither trained local administrators about the benefits of educating the severely handicapped in the least restrictive environment nor discouraged the development day school placements through its monitoring activities. Since there were no attempts to reeducate service providers, financial subsidies favored developmental day placement, and there were no agents pushing for change in the existing system, the passage of the Act had little immediate impact on the segregation of severely and profoundly retarded children.

The situation for the moderately retarded was somewhat different. Since the moderately handicapped had been served in increasing numbers in the public schools in the 1950's and 1960's,[33] the idea of serving these students was not as foreign to the schools as was the concept of serving the severely handicapped. In addition, the state fully subsidized services for the moderately handicapped by providing teachers on the basis of the number of moderately retarded students a district served. This subsidy was not sufficient to provide enough teachers for the severely retarded. Thus, both attitudes and funding incentives favored direct service to the moderately retarded by the public schools. Passage of the EAHCA merely confirmed the right to an education in the public schools that most of the moderately retarded were already enjoying in North Carolina.

For the severely retarded, a situation had developed by 1979 that was ripe for change. Although most school districts had entered into contracts with nearby developmental centers to serve the severely retarded, the Department of Human Resources had, by this time, withdrawn its financial support for these school-age children in light of the public schools' legal responsibilities. Without the financial subsidy from the state, the developmental centers were increasing their charges to local districts. As a result, many districts were looking into the feasibility of serving the severely retarded directly in the

---

33. Number of Exceptional Children Served by Special Teachers, North Carolina Public Schools, Statistical Summary by School Year (Undated chart compiled by N.C. Department of Public Instruction) (on file with the N.C. Governor's Advocacy Council for Persons with Disabilities). In school year 1957-58 the state started funding special teachers for the moderately retarded. In that year, 391 students were served. The number increased substantially each year, with 2,049 moderately retarded students being served in 1968-69, 3,228 in 1971-72, and 4,424 in 1975-76.

public schools in hopes of decreasing costs. The actions that followed illustrate the important role that institutional interests seeking self-preservation play in impeding change. The developmental centers looked first to the State Department of Public Instruction for a direct subsidy. When the State Department refused to subsidize the centers, they approached the legislature through an organized association. Although the State Department of Public Instruction did not favor legislative funding, it did not fight the request. No opposition was voiced by any advocacy group, including the Association for Retarded Citizens. Thus, in 1979, the legislature initiated a direct subsidy to the centers which continues to date.[34] Although the subsidy is not sufficient to fully fund needed educational services, it enables school districts to continue to contract with the centers at substantially less cost than serving severely retarded children directly in the public schools.

The state also eliminated the old method of direct funding of teachers for the moderately retarded in 1980. With the change, districts received all of their special education funding according to the total pupil count (average daily membership) of both handicapped and nonhandicapped students. This money could be used by the local districts to serve any handicapped or gifted children. Unlike the old system of separate funding for teachers of different disability groups, the newer method provided no incentive to serve any high-cost children directly in the school if a cheaper nonpublic school alternative, such as the developmental day center, existed.

The importance that attitudes play in determining how children are served is illustrated by the fact that most moderately handicapped students continue to be served directly in the public schools even though a financial incentive— the state legislative subsidy—now exists to place them in segregated developmental centers along with the severely handicapped. Since 1980, only a handful of administrators have attempted to return moderately handicapped back to the developmental centers and take advantage of the state subsidy. This fact evidences the overwhelming acceptance that the idea of serving the moderately handicapped in public schools has achieved.

B. Effect of Attitudes, Failed Leadership and Funding Patterns on Service in the Schools

In contrast to the problem of the continued segregation of the severely retarded in nonpublic school settings, the treatment of the moderately and severely retarded students who are served directly by the public schools cannot be explained by state-level funding incentives. Attitudes based on the historic treatment of the retarded and the lack of state leadership in changing these attitudes have played major roles in continuing segregated placements for many of these students. These factors, as well as funding patterns, have

---

34. Interview with Jim Barden, Coordinator for Federal Title VI.B. State Plan, N.C. Dep't of Public Instruction, by Karen Sindelar (Oct. 31, 1984). The subsidy for fiscal year 1979-80 was $1,674,743. Interview with Henry Thomas, Director of Budget Development and Administration, N.C. Dep't of Public Instruction, by Karen Sindelar (Jan. 11, 1985).

combined to continue a system of inferior services for retarded students inside and outside segregated settings. Categorical special education funds have been insufficient to provide retarded students with services such as music and physical education which are normally provided from general funds for the education of all children, and special educators have been unable to gain access to general funds for these purposes. This section explores the attitudinal, leadership, and funding factors that have contributed to the continuing phenomena of segregated and inferior services for retarded students served directly in the public schools.

When the public schools in North Carolina began serving the moderately retarded in the 1950's, the segregated institutional service model was the norm. Administrators and educators knew little about educating the moderately retarded. These students were devalued, and were considered to be in need of protection and to be capable of only extremely limited progress. Placement in separate schools or in separate areas of regular schools that served elementary age students reflected the retarded students' devalued status and offered them the protection they were perceived to need. Parents supported this protective attitude toward their children as strongly as service providers did.

The model of segregated service and placement in age-inappropriate settings was continued as larger numbers of moderately retarded students entered the schools in the 1960's and 1970's. With larger numbers of students, many districts moved toward placing all their retarded students in separate schools. The schools chosen were often those determined to be no longer adequate for nonhandicapped students because of age or poor physical facilities; not surprisingly, some buildings were schools that had been used by black students during times of racial segregation. Despite their physical inferiority, the organizational separateness of these schools offered advantages. Having a principal and staff totally committed to serving retarded children helped foster feelings of institutional pride and loyalty among staff and parents. These feelings were, of course, even more pronounced in a few districts where totally new facilities for the retarded were built.

Attitudes also explain why, prior to the passage of the EAHCA, retarded students who were placed in regular schools received unequal services and facilities. As noted above, these students were generally placed in basements or separate wings in schools for much younger children, ostensibly for their own protection. The age differences between the retarded students and the rest of the students in these schools and the physical isolation of their classrooms made the retarded students the "stepchildren" of their schools. Often, they were not considered for programming in all the "extras"—music, art, and physical education—as regular students were. When they were considered, their devalued status often led principals to conclude that they could not benefit from these services. Vocational education was uncommon, as elementary schools lacked both the required personnel and facilities. Some communities, however, were large enough to support a "sheltered workshop," offering vocational training to handicapped adults. In the communities with workshops, older retarded students were sometimes bussed away from school for part-day placement in the workshop.

The passage of the EAHCA in 1975 and of the comparable North Carolina state law, the Creech Bill, in 1977,[35] did not bring about dramatic changes in any of these areas. Although there were many causes for this, three in particular were noticeable: lack of leadership at the state level, absence of parent advocacy, and lack of leadership at the local level.

In North Carolina the division within the State Department of Public Instruction that implements federal and state special education laws is the Division for Exceptional Children. In the decade since the EAHCA was first passed, the Division has generally maintained a passive posture concerning implementation of the Act. The Division did not initially support the Creech Bill. Similarly, the Division's leadership in controversial areas has been nonexistent. Instead, the Division's philosophy has been similar to that of the State Department as a whole, that is, to leave all decisions to local districts unless assistance is requested and, when rendering assistance, to refrain from establishing general guidelines applicable to all local districts. This approach, though certainly consonant with the American philosophy of local control over education, as well as with the political realities circumscribing the State Department's role in education, has not provided the leadership for major changes in local attitudes that were needed for successful implementation of a difficult law. Thus, although experience from the 1950's through the mid-1970's had shown that placement in segregated and age-inappropriate settings and the lack of adequate services and vocational education were problems that the moderately retarded faced statewide, there was no systematic attempt to address those issues on the state level. Instead, the State Department's efforts consisted of educating administrators about the procedural requirements of the EAHCA and regulations, and of providing consultants to assist local administrators and teachers in choosing curricula and special materials for the retarded.

The State Department was not alone in its failure to push for change. The one statewide advocacy group for the retarded, the Association for Retarded Citizens (ARC), neither raised the issues of segregation, age-inappropriate placement, and lack of services with the State Department nor attempted to focus the attention of local affiliates on these problems. Of course, the ARC's efforts were thinly spread and fragmented. As the primary voice for retarded persons and their parents and guardians, the ARC was concerned not only with education for children but also with institutional conditions, strengthening of sheltered workshops that trained adults for employment, establishment of group homes, and creation of day services for retarded adults in local communities. Voluntary citizen organizations are capable of only limited success without paid professional staff, and the staff of the state ARC consisted of

---

35. Creech Bill, 1977 N.C. Sess. Laws 927 (codified as amended at N.C. Gen. Stat. §§ 115C -106 to -115, -139 to -145 (1983)).

only two people. It is not surprising that, as a local ARC director stated, "We hoped and thought the law would do it for us."[36] Certainly the visible changes that occurred immediately after passage of the law—service to all retarded children and free bus transportation, which parents had generally had to provide themselves in prior years—were evidence that the EAHCA was making changes in key problem areas. The fact that retarded children were still not receiving comparable services or vocational training was not a pressing concern as long as the children were taken to school and kept there for an entire school day. With regard to placement, only a few parents had had exposure to information and training on "normalization," so most parents continued to support placement of their children in safe elementary schools and segregated centers.

At the local level, the special education directors were the persons most capable of improving services for retarded children. They had control of the funds made available by the state and federal governments for educating the handicapped. They also had been trained by the State Department concerning the Act's requirements, and had continuing contact with the State Department. However, these administrators were not familiar with "normalization" in education, so they provided little leadership in integrating retarded students. In the area of services, although they almost uniformly agreed that offering comparable services and facilities to the handicapped was desirable, they had neither the authority nor the funds to do so.

Few special education directors supported integration of the retarded into regular schools in age-appropriate settings. Drawn from the ranks of local school personnel, most had neither been trained in normalization principles nor seen them in practice. Many of these administrators had played instrumental roles as teachers or principals in the segregated schools established by local districts prior to the legal changes in the mid-1970's. They were advocates for children, but they had no reason to think that placing children in regular schools would improve their education. So with little leadership from the State Department, the directors generally continued the practices that had existed in their systems until the mid-1970's. Where segregated schools existed, they continued. Where they had never existed, retarded students continued to be housed in separate parts of schools serving younger students.

Administrators were more uniformly supportive of the need to upgrade facilities and services for the retarded, but limited funding and authority hindered their ability to make needed changes. The special education directors did have direct control over segregated schools, if their districts had such schools. Their budgets were not large enough, however, to justify using special education funds to finance major physical improvements in these inferior facilities. Moreover, superintendents and local school boards, with a few exceptions, usually had no desire to use local funds to improve facilities for

---

36. Interview with Jim Pritchard, Executive Director of the High Point Association for Retarded Citizens, by Karen Sindelar (June 7, 1984) (on file with the N.C. Governor's Advocacy Council for Persons with Disabilities).

the retarded. With regard to services such as physical education, music, and art, these activities were supposed to be funded through regular education dollars, given for the benefit of all students. Most of the segregated schools were small, serving thirty to eighty children, and did not have enough students to justify teachers in these areas from the regular education budget. The activities were thus unavailable because financing them out of special education dollars could not be justified when so many more basic needs, such as teacher aides, speech therapy, physical therapy, and occupational therapy, still had to be met.

The special education directors were also severely limited in their ability to improve services for students placed in regular schools. Unfortunately, passage of the EAHCA changed little in the politics or division of responsibilities in local school systems. Principals generally control such things as placement of classes in their schools and scheduling of classes for art, music, and physical education. Special education administrators control only the hiring of teachers for the handicapped and provision of related services from the special education funds which they directly administer. Since special education funding was insufficient to hire separate art, music, and physical education teachers for the retarded, the attitude of the principal generally determined the availability of these services for handicapped students served in integrated settings.

C. Vocational Education and the Retarded

Both fiscal and attitudinal factors explain the continued lack of vocational opportunities for the retarded. Vocational education developed as a separate field long before the EAHCA. Vocational education is expensive, partly because of the need for vocational facilities and equipment for hands-on training, and partly because of the small teacher-pupil ratio needed for hands-on instruction. New special education funds were sufficient to cover only basic services (such as teachers) for handicapped students. If retarded students were to receive vocational education, a substantial part of the financing would have to come from regular vocational education dollars. Fortunately, the federal government mandated that 10 percent of federal vocational education funds be used for handicapped students,[37] and required that a certain amount of state and local funds be spent as "matching" money. Overall, however, state and local funding made available for handicapped vocational education was miniscule, amounting to only 2 percent of the total state and local funds being spent for vocational education.[38] It was easy to ignore the retarded in this area, as most were placed in facilities where vocational educa-

---

37. 20 U.S.C. § 2310(a) (1982).

38. Vocational Education Data System Study, *supra* note 25. The statistics show that between 1978 and 1980, the federal government used approximately 8 percent of federal vocational education funds for handicapped education. However, state and local funds financed over 90 percent of vocational education and only 2 percent of these funds were used for the handicapped. Other observers have actually reported a decline in state and local support for handicapped vocational education. *See* Ognibene, *Preparing Individuals with Special Needs for Work-Related Placement in Cooperation*

tion was not normally offered, such as elementary schools or older segregated facilities.

Shifting service arrangements caused by the passage of the EAHCA also caused a decline in vocational education for retarded students. Prior to 1975, many retarded students aged 16 and older were given vocational training free of charge in local sheltered workshops. After the EAHCA was passed, most workshops requested contract money from school districts for services which were previously free. Most school districts refused and, as a result, many retarded students received no vocational training.

The State Department's vocational education curriculum presented additional barriers to retarded students who were placed at the junior high and high school level where vocational education was a normal offering. The curriculum was and is organized around a sequence of courses starting with general introductory courses that require substantial academic skills in reading and math. Retarded students cannot pass the introductory courses and therefore cannot gain entry to the hands-on training available only in advanced courses. In addition, vocational instructors generally had no experience working with handicapped students, and special educators had no experience in hands-on vocational education. These institutional barriers, illustrating again the failure of regular education to accommodate special education, demanded sustained and creative leadership from state and local special education directors to resolve. Unfortunately, such leadership was lacking at both the state and local levels.

In sum, attitudes based on historical practice, the failure of state leadership, and significant funding incentives have contributed to the maintenance of an entirely segregated nonpublic school system for the severely and profoundly retarded. Similar factors, with the exception of funding incentives, explain why moderately retarded students served directly by schools are often placed in segregated settings. Attitudes, the allocation of power within local districts, and the inadequacy of the special education budget to finance courses that should be financed from regular education funds and vocational funds explain the continued discrimination against the retarded in the provision of enrichment services and vocational training.

IV

ANALYSIS OF SUCCESSFUL CHANGE

It is instructive to examine how integrated educational programs which *do* provide comparable services, age-appropriate settings, or strong vocational programs came to be established. Although a single factor is rarely responsible for creating institutional change, a particular factor will often act as an impetus and set into motion other forces that in combination produce change. Some of the motivating factors that have had an impact on improving services

---

with Business and Industry, in INTERCHANGE: OFFICE OF CAREER DEVELOPMENT FOR SPECIAL POPULATIONS (College of Educ., Univ. of Ill., Jan. 1984).

for the retarded are examined in this section. In addition, the parameters and limitations of each of these agents of change are analyzed.

A. Financial Factors

Financial and pragmatic considerations have been strong enough in a few school districts to overcome longstanding attitudes about services to the moderately retarded. This effect is illustrated by the development of age-appropriate programs in a number of rural, relatively "backward" school districts. In a limited survey conducted in North Carolina in 1982, eight school districts in the state had developed age-appropriate high school programs for older retarded youth.[39] Most were large rural county districts not considered particularly progressive in their educational practices. The reason given by most of these districts for having developed their programs was the centralized location of the high school. Most of the districts had relatively small populations of older retarded students. Their most centralized schools were high schools; their elementary and middle schools were smaller and more scattered. It was more economical to serve older retarded students in one centralized high school than to serve them in scattered smaller groups.

Of course, in at least as many cases, financial and pragmatic considerations favor the maintenance of the status quo. Overall, however, it seems that financial factors neither significantly hinder nor promote change. For example, regarding the maintenance of segregated schools, the number of students in these facilities is usually not so large that they cannot be physically accommodated in regular schools. In many school districts individual school attendance boundaries are changed and students shifted from one attendance area to another with regularity, thus moving retarded students into regular schools would not present unusual administrative problems. Also, segregated facilities in many cases are old and in need of repair; the cost of transferring students is considerably less than the cost of extensive renovations. Similarly, there is no clear financial advantage in maintaining retarded students who are placed in regular schools in age-inappropriate settings or denying them comparable services. It costs no more to serve a child in an age-appropriate setting than in an age-inappropriate one. The savings gained from denying music, art, and physical education to retarded students are insignificant. In most cases, the students' needs could be taken care of through scheduling changes and a slight reallocation of existing teachers' times rather than through hiring additional teachers. Providing vocational education could present more of a problem as it is already perceived as a scarce resource for nonhandicapped students. However, at least some services from the regular education budget could be extended without great financial sacrifice.

Financial considerations may be a more critical factor with regard to transferring the severely retarded out of nonpublic placements and into the public schools. The legislative subsidy for children placed in the segregated devel-

---

39. *N.C. Report on Age-Appropriate High School Programs, supra* note 16.

opmental day centers is large—presently over $4,000 per year per child.[40]
This incentive has been strong enough to motivate a few school districts to
attempt to place their moderately retarded students back into the developmental centers. It is certainly an important enough factor to discourage districts from considering new ways to serve the severely retarded that could
result in considerable financial loss.

Since financial considerations in most cases have not been the deciding
factor in determining the location and extent of service for the moderately
retarded, the roles that various persons in the bureaucracy have played in
establishing progressive programs must also be examined.

B.   Leadership by Local Special Education Directors

Local special education directors, or their equivalents, possess the greatest
ability to promote systemic change in a school district. Although as a general
rule no systemic change comes without approval of the superintendent, local
education directors are in the best position to educate superintendents and
enlist their support for changes. Limitations on the powers of a local director
have already been partially explored. In North Carolina, the budgets they
control are not large enough to cover all handicapped children's needs
without funding some services from the general education budget. In addition, local special education directors have no direct control over school principals. The degree to which these factors limit the power of the director
depends on the model of organization and control used in a district and the
effectiveness of the local director.

Some school districts are operated on a model of centralized, hierarchical
control. Where it exists, substantial changes may be relatively easy to accomplish when the real decisionmaker concerning programs for handicapped children—either the superintendent or the local director—is convinced that such
changes should occur. Agreement from principals is not as important as it is
under other organizational forms. Thus, one district relocated six classes of
moderately retarded students of all ages to different schools between one
school year and the next because central directors had become convinced of
the educational advantages of age-appropriate education. Not surprisingly,
the district was an urban district with a well-organized and powerful central
bureaucracy. Pupil reassignments were also a regular occurrence because of
the previous consolidation of two systems, a continuing effort to maintain certain racial proportions, and development of "magnet" schools.

In contrast, principals in most districts wield greater power and frequent
reassignment of students is less common. In these districts, transferring students from one school to another may require the assent of various princi-

---

40. The amount given to school districts for each child placed in a developmental day center for
school year 1984-85 is $4,015 plus over $200 in federal money. This compares with $3,027 available
from all sources if the child is served directly by a school district. Interview with Carolyn Perry,
Consultant, Division of Exceptional Children, N.C. Dep't of Public Instruction, by Karen Sindelar
(Jan. 11, 1985).

pals, which demands greater political skill from the special education administration. Whatever the degree of centralized control in a district, the availability of enrichment courses and vocational education will most often depend on the principal since, as previously discussed, the special education budget is not large enough to fund these services separately for handicapped students.

Skilled special education administrators can have substantial influence over principals. In some districts, extensive services are uniformly offered to the retarded because principals have been cultivated and educated by special education administrators. Unfortunately, such leadership is the exception rather than the rule. The author has observed situations in which retarded students have been "dumped" into regular schools with no advance preparation or education of the principals by special education administrators. In one school, for example, relatively high-functioning moderately retarded students ate lunch separately from nonhandicapped students and received no physical education for an entire year because the principal, one of the most agreeable in the system, had been told by another principal that the students would be hurt by physical activity and contact with other students. The situation, which easily could have been prevented by the special education director, was rectified by a few interested parents.

In sum, although local special education directors generally do not directly control either placement of classes for the retarded or the extent to which they receive certain services, they can exert considerable influence over these issues through leadership. School districts in North Carolina that have the most integrated and extensive system of services for the retarded generally have directors who are effective leaders. Such directors keep abreast of developments in special education practices. They are "political," demonstrating an understanding of key administrators and of the internal allocation of power in their district, as well as an understanding of how to work with and sometimes manipulate parent groups. They are generally personable, persuasive, and energetic with a desire and ability to influence others.

C. Establishment of Programs by Individual Teachers

Strong advocacy by individual teachers with training or experience in high-quality programs has provided another avenue for change. Such teachers have independently convinced individual principals to give retarded students full access to enrichment services and have created successful hands-on vocational education programs by persuading and educating regular vocational teachers to work with handicapped children. The most successful and integrated high school program for moderately retarded students in North Carolina was created through the efforts of one teacher.[41]

---

41. *Handicapped Succeeding in High School*, ACCEPT: The Newsletter of the Advoc. Center for Children's Educ. and Parent Training, Aug. 1984, at 5. The program, located in Moore County, a mixed urban-rural school district, serves 22 moderately retarded students. The program is in a high school of 1,500 students. In addition to receiving special instructional services normally

Teachers, however, are more limited as agents of change than local directors. A teacher is forced to work with the principal of the school where he or she is located, unlike local directors who may exercise some choice in determining where to locate a new or controversial program. A teacher advocating educational reform may find it difficult to alter the position of a principal who has a negative attitude toward such reform. In addition, neither the interests nor authority of a teacher are likely to extend beyond his or her own program. If a successful program is replicated or expanded, it is generally because of the interest and leadership of the special education director. It is not uncommon, therefore, to find a well-integrated program with a full array of enrichment courses for moderately retarded students in one school, while a similar program in a nearby school languishes in the basement without extra services. This unevenness in program quality occurs frequently in districts where the local directors cannot replicate successful programs either because of their own attitudes or limited skills, or those of the superintendent.

D. Parents and Change

Parents, individually or in groups, may also be effective in motivating change. In one North Carolina district, an individual parent organized a parent group to successfully block the transfer to a segregated developmental center of moderately retarded children who for many years had been served directly by the schools. In another district, the local ARC successfully pressured the district to more completely integrate retarded children into a regular school from the isolated wing where they had been served. Its success in that district prompted the ARC to examine educational offerings to retarded children in all schools. In another district, an individual parent educated the local director about the benefits of normalization; the director then moved a number of classes for moderately retarded students out of a segregated school. Countless principals in North Carolina have been educated by parents about retarded students' potential and needs. In a number of districts, parent activism has brought improvements to individual programs in the form of new equipment, more services, additional teachers, or additional local money from the school board.

The role that an energetic parent or group of parents can play in bringing about change is virtually unlimited, as shown by the examples above. Parents can educate the professional educators, in particular, principals, local directors, and superintendents. Where change is blocked by a reluctant or obstinate bureaucrat at one level, parents can exert pressure at the next level, something employees within the system often cannot do. Parents can present issues and needs to the school board, a forum which is often off-limits to a special education director who must support the superintendent's budget priorities and public stands. And parents can use the media to publicize issues of

---

given the moderately retarded, the students attend regular vocational classes, work part-time, participate in clubs, go to lunch, and attend assemblies and other school functions. The program is unique for the degree of integration it has achieved.

concern, a tactic particularly effective for complaints about unequal services and one that is not available to local directors and special education teachers.

In light of the potential effectiveness of parents, it is unfortunate that there has not been more activism among parents. Much has been written about the failure of the EAHCA to bring about the effective parent involvement that was envisioned by its drafters.[42] It is not within the scope of this article to examine why parents of handicapped children have not become actively involved in their children's education programs. Lack of education, lack of experience and sophistication in negotiating with professionals, bureaucratic obfuscation and hostility, and parental deference to educators explain much of this general passivity. The issue of concern in this analysis is why parents of retarded children who are actively involved in the children's education have generally failed to advocate integration to improve their education. The reasons for this failure include the same lack of exposure to models of normalization that affects service providers, the nonexistence of local advocacy groups in many communities, the lack of both leadership and a political focus in local voluntary associations, and the limitations of due process as an avenue for systemic change.

There has been no systematic effort by the State Department to educate parents concerning the benefits of normalization. Parents' main sources of information are the service providers who educate their children and who are likewise unknowledgeable about the benefits of normalization. Where children are placed in segregated programs with adequate physical facilities, parents tend to be extremely supportive of the programs and resist efforts to merge them into regular schools. Parents with children in integrated programs are similarly supportive of their programs. Parents with a perspective independent from that of the local service model generally come from three groups: newcomers in a school district who have experienced the advantages of a different model elsewhere; parents whose children have been in a preschool program administered by a different public agency or private concern; and parents who are professionals in other fields such as mental health and mental retardation. In local districts using a segregated service model, these parents cannot single-handedly reorient both service providers and other parents supportive of the system. Thus, progressive parents who support integration resort to due process or, probably more frequently, move to a different district offering superior services.

A second reason that parents are not more effective in advocating change is the difficulty of organizing groups and using them effectively when they exist. The oldest parent and advocacy organization in North Carolina is the ARC, yet only thirty-five of one hundred counties in the state have local ARC chapters. Rural counties with a poor, undereducated, and dispersed population are particularly likely to lack such groups. Those local groups that do exist are generally overextended. Only the largest local chapters have a paid

---

42. *See* Clune & Van Pelt, *A Political Method of Evaluating the EAHCA and the Several Gaps of Gap Analysis*, LAW & CONTEMP. PROBS., Winter 1985, at 7.

staff, never consisting of more than one person, and most chapters are purely voluntary. Their concerns cover all agencies providing services—schools, sheltered workshops, mental health day programs, institutions, and group homes—as well as the frustrating gaps in the service system that the local chapters fill themselves through volunteer efforts or fundraising. The membership of these groups is often dominated by service providers who are interested in enlisting volunteers and support from parents rather than in conducting a critical examination of existing services and "old guard" parents who still remember the days when many retarded children were left totally uneducated. For these older parents, whose children are long past school age, the battles have already been fought and largely won. Their interest is now in development of community residential services so that their children can be cared for when the parents are gone. Existing ARC's, then, generally are not a strong factor in promoting educational change; they limit themselves primarily to enlisting general community support for projects which need funding. Hardnosed advocacy work comes, if at all, only in areas where services do not exist and need to be created. In the last four years, the author is aware of only a handful of ARC's that have given sustained attention to the quality and scope of local education opportunities for retarded children.

Group advocacy on education issues generally comes from new and often short-lived coalitions of parents and teachers that are sometimes loosely associated with, but rarely controlled by, an existing ARC. These groups form to deal with a particular problem and usually disband after the problem has been resolved. They are usually reactive rather than proactive. Most frequently, such groups have formed to resist a transfer from a segregated to a more integrated setting. As previously discussed, parents generally defend what they know and thus "radical" change, such as shutting down a segregated school, is usually resisted by parents and teachers who will be affected by the change. Because of the success of integrated programs and the legal preference (however weak) for placement in the least restrictive environment, it is rare for a district to attempt to resegregate retarded students once they have been integrated into the schools. However, in one case in the last four years in which such a move was attempted, parents successfully organized and resisted the change. Parents have only occasionally organized to improve existing programs through the addition of services or improvement of facilities, but where they have done so they have been uniformly successful. In part, this success comes about because these issues, unlike the segregation/integration controversy, unite parents and teachers and sometimes special education administrators. Also, when the issue of inferior facilities or inequitable services is directly raised it is difficult for administrators to defend. Such issues also have powerful media appeal.

Many parents are forced to use due process hearings to try to change the placement of the education programs that serve their retarded children. These parents choose due process hearings for a variety of reasons. Frequently, hearings are chosen because an advocacy group does not exist or cannot be persuaded to work for the needed changes. As noted, organized groups do not exist in many areas; where they do exist, they may resist supporting a challenge to an existing segregated school. Most parents who are unhappy with their children's education are not community organizers. They do not have the background, skills, time, or energy to organize a new group, or to educate or redirect the concerns of an existing group. In addition, legal assistance is more generally available than assistance in community organizing. Many parents have an exaggerated faith in the effectiveness of the more legalistic route of the due process hearing. At the same time, they distrust local political process and lack confidence in their ability to bring effective community pressure to bear on a problem. The due process hearing at least offers an "impartial" decisionmaker as a guarantor of some fairness in the process and result.

Unfortunately, hearings do not remedy systemic failures to implement the least restrictive environment or to offer services in age-appropriate settings. In systems that offer segregated services or age-inappropriate settings, age-appropriate alternative settings and integrated placements do not exist, and thus an individual child plaintiff cannot easily be moved to the desired setting. Hearing officers are reluctant to order remedies that would necessarily change the placement of other children. As a result, remedies for complaints concerning least restrictive environment or age-inappropriateness usually consist of ordering some slight accommodation to an existing program for children with a different disability. For example, a hearing officer may order that a moderately retarded child be moved to an existing integrated program for mildly retarded children rather than order a change in placement for a number of other moderately retarded children. Although such a remedy technically offers integration or age-appropriateness, it often does not provide an appropriate program for the individual child plaintiff.

Whether hearing officers would more readily make a decision that affects other children in cases involving lack of comparable services is a matter of conjecture. It certainly is not as invasive to order additional services for a group of similarly-situated retarded students as it is to move them to a different school. Technically, of course, the remedy would exceed a hearing officer's power, which is to provide an individual remedy for the complaining child. Interestingly, however, no due process hearings concerning inferior services for the retarded have been held in North Carolina. Few parents have become aroused over this issue. In the few cases where parents have made an issue of inferior services, improvements have been obtained prior to hearings through individual negotiation or community pressure.

V

A STRATEGY FOR CHANGE

To speed up the integration of retarded children into the American educational mainstream and eliminate the pervasive discrimination they suffer, a multifaceted strategy must be adopted. Different strategies should be used to address the problems of the severely retarded and the moderately retarded. This section discusses these strategies.

A. Federal Funding Incentive Program

The barriers to changing services for the severely retarded are more imposing than those faced by the moderately retarded. Major factors in this difference are the fiscal subsidies that support a largely segregated system for the severely retarded and the institutional interests committed to preserving these subsidies. As forty-nine states in this country have chosen largely segregated service models for serving their severely and profoundly retarded population,[43] it seems probable that funding patterns favoring continued segregation exist all over the country.[44] The lack of existing successful alternatives to segregated schools also militates against changes in the existing system. The possibility of amending federal law or regulations so as to absolutely prohibit segregated schools is politically unfeasible in the near future given the nearly unanimous resistance that would come from all states and from many parents. It seems, then, that the most feasible and effective method of starting to bring about change in this area would be a federal incentive program in which funds would be provided to states interested in desegregating their service system.

Precedent for such an effort exists in the Emergency School Aid Act which, prior to its termination, funded the transistion of school districts toward greater racial integration.[45] Although funding transitional efforts in all states would be ideal, the necessity of restricting costs would mandate a more limited effort. Since services for the severely and profoundly retarded are uniformly segregated throughout the United States and a strong catalyst for change is needed, at least two-thirds of the grants made available should go to states interested in desegregating services for this population; the remaining one-third should go to states which maintain segregated services for the moderately retarded on a state-wide level. Receiving states should be funded for a period of three years, primarily to effect a transition. As a condition for receipt of funds, states should have to assure that state funding for services to the retarded which was previously directed toward segregated centers would "follow the child" after integration. This would help ensure that services are not drastically reduced once integration is achieved. In states in which more than one agency funds segregated day services for the retarded, both agencies should have to maintain their funding during and after the transition.

Financing a change in even a small number of states would illustrate the feasibility of the integrated service model for severely and profoundly

---

43. See supra note 14.
44. For example, in Roncker v. Walter, 700 F.2d 1058 (6th Cir. 1983), cert. denied, 104 S. Ct. 196 (1983), funding patterns favoring continued segregated school placement for the moderately retarded in Ohio were described. Moderately retarded students in the special state schools received state funding not available to districts serving the retarded locally. Id. at 1060-61.
45. Emergency School Aid Act, 20 U.S.C. §§ 1601-1619 (1976), repealed by Education Amendments of 1978, P.L. No. 95-561, § 617(10)(b)(2), 92 Stat. 2268.

retarded students. Of course, promoting the integration of the severely retarded into regular school districts will not ensure that quality programs are established. To encourage the creation of adequate programs, the federal govenment should increase support for model programs which demonstrate significant quality and in which there is an intentional, planned approach toward integration of the handicapped with nonhandicapped.

Even with implementation of federal funding as suggested above, progress toward integration of the severely handicapped will probably be extremely slow. It is also questionable whether further integration of the severely and moderately retarded is desirable, given that the retarded who are presently in regular public school settings still face substantial discrimination. It seems, then, that concurrent with the federal initiative outlined above, a sustained effort should be undertaken to address the lack of equity and meaningful integration in existing public school programs for moderately retarded. A strategy to achieve progress in this area should focus primarily on the attitudinal and institutional barriers that have impeded change in the last decade in spite of the mandates of the EAHCA. In-depth leadership training for the various levels of education professionals as well as parents should be provided. These efforts should be accompanied by regulatory changes that would eliminate some of the ambiguity in present law and regulations. These suggestions are explored in greater depth below.

B. Leadership Training

Leadership training for local special education directors, principals, teachers, and parents would increase both the will and the capacity to create change at the local level. Teachers, with the support of principals, are able to create good programs in individual schools, and parent groups and special education directors are capable of creating systemic changes. Leadership training for all of these actors in the education system should be directed toward a number of goals. It should provide an education concerning the benefits of normalization and expose potential leaders to successful examples of integrated, age-appropriate programs in which retarded students receive a full array of services normally offered to the nonhandicapped. It should also provide skill training to enable these potential leaders to identify barriers to change, to persuade others concerning the benefits of change and to identify resources, such as persons outside of the bureaucracy, to provide support and help meet needs. Finally, the training should provide a mechanism by which key actors within each local system are brought together in a parent-professional partnership to support each other and maximize chances of success. In addition, training should provide professionals with new contacts from other nearby systems who can provide needed professional peer support.

Although the specifics of such a training program cannot be detailed in this paper, some guidelines can be offered. First, it appears that, at a minimum, four persons from every district should receive training—the local special education director, a principal, a teacher, and a parent. Although the selection of the administrator would be automatic, the selection of an appropriate principal, teacher, and parent would not be. The principal should be chosen by the local administrator, as the principals in a school district who have shown an interest in handicapped children's needs are easily identified by local directors. The teachers and parents should be chosen by local teacher groups and, where they exist, by parent groups so as to give these organizations knowledge about the goals of the training and an investment in its outcome. The identity of the trainers is also critical. In order to ensure the most generalized support for the program as well as broad perspective, the training group should include a state educational consultant, a local administrator, and a parent advocate from a recognized advocacy group, such as a federally funded parent training project, the State Protection and Advocacy System, or the state ARC.

A program that would target one-third of a state's school districts per year and provide at least two years of follow-up training for each school district would not be expensive. Based on parent training that has been done in North Carolina, an estimate of the cost in this state would be approximately $200,000 per year.[46] Providing a similar training program nationwide would cost less than $10 million per year, a relatively small sum when measured against the federal funds currently distributed under the EAHCA, an amount in excess of one billion dollars per year.[47]

The dual assumptions underlying the proposed training model are that educating different actors creates more possibilities for change, and that leadership can be strengthened, if not created. It is doubtful that a training program will have an immediate systemic impact in local districts in which the special education director has no leadership or administrative potential or has a strong personal bias against an integrated, normalized service model. Nonetheless, the training received by the other local actors in these districts could result in new pressures to force the director to take action, or to force a superintendent to bypass a passive or hostile director. In addition, even if systemic changes in such districts do not occur, changes in individual school programs may. In districts in which the local director is sympathetic to the desired change but has not previously been effective, the training will offer new allies at the local level, needed skill training, and peer support from outside the district. Involvement of the State Department of Public Instruc-

---

46. *See* DIVISION OF PERSONNEL PREPARATION AND TRAINING, FINAL REPORT OF THE PARENTS' EDUCATIONAL ADVOCACY CENTER (PEAC) 1981-83, Division of Personnel Preparation and Training (Oct. 17, 1983) (grant # G008101539) (on file with the U.S. Department of Education and the N.C. Governor's Advocacy Council for Persons with Disabilities, Raleigh, N.C.). The PEAC project was one of numerous parent training projects funded by the U.S. Department of Education, and cost approximately $200,000 over a two-year period ($120,000 the first year and $80,000 the second year). Among other things, the project gave intensive two-day training to a cadre of 62 parents of exceptional children statewide to function as trainers and technical assistants to other parents in the area of the EAHCA, and gave shorter training (six hours) to 746 parents and professionals in local workshops. It is estimated that approximately 200 administrators, parents, teachers, and principals could be given intensive two or three day training per year with the same amount of funds.

47. *See* Appropriations Act, 1985, Pub. L. No. 98-619, 98 Stat. 3324 (1984).

tion and a statewide advocacy group may also create or strengthen pressures from outside to create change locally, as well as generate publicity and awareness of changes that occur in other local districts.

Of course, it is probable that the leadership potential or interest of the various trainees in some districts will be so low that no change will occur either on a systemic or individual school level. Training programs never guarantee uniform results. The proposed program merely recognizes the importance of an area that has previously been ignored by the federal government, that of educating and reinforcing the actors at the local level who are instrumental in creating change.

C.   State Monitoring and the Need for Federal Pressure

The potential for vigorous state monitoring of segregated and inadequate services for the retarded already exists under the Act. The EAHCA and its implementing regulations require states to evaluate the effectiveness of programs provided the handicapped,[48] mandate state and local reporting of statistics concerning the different placements in which handicapped children are served,[49] and require that the state agency *ensure* that local districts place children in the least restrictive environment.[50] The regulations also authorize the states to use funds for training, personnel development, and public information and sharing of successful program models.[51] It is clear, then, that under current law states could, if they desired, drastically reduce segregated placements through strict monitoring and positive training of the type already described. Also, under their general monitoring authority states could collect information on age-appropriate placements, comparability of services, and provision of vocational education.

The failure of North Carolina and other states to monitor implementation of the least restrictive environment requirement and to collect information on other identified problem areas is, as discussed before, a reflection of the historic relationship between the state and local districts. The passive approach is politically safe. The state's failure to modify this approach can largely be attributed to the lack of strong federal pressure and leadership. For example, federal representatives conducting periodic monitoring visits to North Carolina have observed systems in which totally segregated facilities were the only available placement for moderately retarded students, and heard complaints from statewide advocacy groups concerning the state's failure to enforce use of the least restrictive environment. There has been no federal response to these issues in the past. Federal failure to monitor state enforcement of least restrictive environment has been amply documented by numerous national

---

48.   20 U.S.C. § 1413(a)(11) (1982); 34 C.F.R. § 300.146 (1984).

49.   20 U.S.C. § 1418(b)(2) (1982); 34 C.F.R. § 300.227 (1984).

50.   20 U.S.C. § 1412(5)(B) (1982); 34 C.F.R. § 330.550 (1984) (state agency must ensure local compliance with least restrictive environment (LRE)); *id.* § 300.555 (state must give technical assistance on LRE); *id.* § 300.556 (state agency must monitor LRE and take corrective action where there is noncompliance).

51.   34 C.F.R. §§ 300.370, .380-.387, 330.555.

advocacy groups.[52] Given the passive attitude of the federal government, there has been no incentive for North Carolina and other states to adopt a more aggressive posture and upset an established relationship between state and local authorities. Clearly, then, there is a need for a more aggressive federal approach to stimulate a more aggressive state approach.

How the state would respond to stronger federal pressure is a matter of conjecture. North Carolina has readily monitored local compliance with clear federal mandates, such as the procedural requirements of the EAHCA. It is probable that the state would also monitor compliance with the least restrictive environment mandate and the provision of comparable services and vocational education if the federal regulations in these areas were less ambiguous, or if strong federal policy statements concerning existing regulations were issued and made a part of the federal government's periodic monitoring of the states. Without a more aggressive federal posture, however, it seems certain that monitoring and leadership from state agencies in the area of least restrictive environment will remain weak.

D. The Federal Role: Clearly Articulating the Legal Requirements

The United States Department of Education could ensure greater integration of and equity in educational programs for retarded children by strengthening federal regulations or, at the least, by issuing policy statements defining existing regulations. The Department would also have to monitor these requirements in its periodic federal visits to state agencies. It does not seem necessary to rewrite the statutory language of either the EAHCA or section 504 of the Rehabilitation Act of 1973[53] in order to strengthen the administration of these acts. Although neither law specifically proscribes segregation or the failure to offer comparable services, both laws are broad enough to support regulatory language which adequately addresses these issues.

The current regulations implementing the EAHCA which address the requirement that handicapped students be educated in the least restrictive environment contain subjective language allowing significant professional dis-

---

52. *See, e.g.*, Report by the Education Advocates Coalition on Federal Compliance Activities to Implement the Education for All Handicapped Children Act (P.L. 94-142), 4-23 & app. 4 (Apr. 16, 1980) (unpublished manuscript) (on file with the N.C. Governor's Advocacy Council for Persons with Disabilities). The Coalition is a nationwide coalition of advocacy groups including state-based advocacy groups working in eleven different states and national groups such as the Children's Defense Fund, Mental Health Law Project, and National Center for Youth Law. In its report, the culmination of six months of investigation, the coalition determined that ten critical areas were being ignored by states and by the Department of Education in its monitoring activities. Continued unnecessary segregation was one of the ten problem areas. Other issues included lack of services for institutionalized children, illegal suspension and expulsion of handicapped children, and denial of necessary related services. The coalition report documents that the Department of Education has (1) consistently relied on state assurances of compliance with the least restrictive environment mandate, (2) failed to collect needed data from the states, and (3) failed to analyze data that has been provided. The Department has also consistently failed to take action when advocates shared data concerning least restrictive environment violations. In some of these cases, law suits eventually had to be filed to correct problems previously brought to the attention of the federal government. *See id.* at app. 4.

53. 20 U.S.C. § 794 (1982).

cretion, thereby making it easy to continue whatever service arrangements happen to exist in a district. One regulation does nothing more than repeat the vague statutory language of the EAHCA mandating contact with the nonhandicapped "to the maximum extent *appropriate*".[54] Similar qualifying language is utilized in the regulation concerning the provision of nonacademic services.[55] The directive that districts offer a "continuum" of services[56] appears to ensure that every handicapped student have available an array of services options; however, there is no mandate that the required continuum be offered for each individual disability category. As a result, some systems which routinely segregate their severely and profoundly retarded, or even moderately retarded, students by placement in segregated schools claim to fulfill the continuum requirement by offering special classes for more mildly retarded students in regular schools. In fact, these special classes are not useful or appropriate for the more substantially handicapped who may realistically have only one service option—the segregated school.

The regulation which sets forth considerations to be used in placing a child under the EAHCA[57] is also easy to circumvent. Although there is a preference for placement in the child's home school, a district can easily structure a child's individualized education program to show a need for placement in a different school by including services not available in the home school. One subsection, stating that districts may consider the harmful effect of a less restrictive placement on the child or on the quality of services available, seems to be a license for districts to routinely continue placing children in segregated settings with concentrated services.[58]

Regulations promulgated under section 504 of the Rehabilitation Act are scarcely clearer. Both the general provisions and those specifically for preschool, elementary, and secondary education discourage separate services, but allow them where necessary to provide the handicapped student with effective services, or where the student cannot be "satisfactorily" educated in the regular education environment even with the use of supplementary aids or services.[59] The regulations also clearly recognize the existence of separate facilities for the handicapped.[60] Under these regulations, recipients who wish to concentrate special educators and related services personnel in one facility may do so in reliance on the argument that they are only able to offer effective services in this setting.

---

54. 34 C.F.R. § 300.550 (1984) (emphasis added). *Compare* 20 U.S.C. § 1412(5)(B) (1982).

55. 34 C.F.R. § 300.553 (1984). The regulation provides that the handicapped shall participate with the nonhandicapped in nonacademic and extra curricular services such as meals, recess, counseling, athletics, transportation, health services, recreational activities, clubs, and employment assistance "to the maximum extent appropriate." *See also id.* § 300.306.

56. *Id.* § 300.551. The continuum includes regular classes, resource rooms, special classes, special schools, home instruction, instruction in hospitals and institutions, and itinerant instruction.

57. *Id.* § 300.552 (1984). Placement should be determined annually, be based on the child's IEP, be as close to the child's home as possible, and be in the child's home school unless the IEP "requires some other arrangement."

58. *Id.* § 300.552(d).

59. *Id.* §§ 104.4(b)(1)(iv), (b)(2)(b), (b)(3), 104.34(a), (b), 104.37(c).

60. *Id.* §§ 104.4(b)(3), 104.34(a), (c).

On the other hand, section 504 regulations are clear in their requirement that the disabled be offered both facilities and services that are equal and comparable to those provided the nonhandicapped.[61] Surprisingly, the EAHCA regulations are less clear. They guarantee that handicapped students receive a "variety" of program options[62] and that physical education be made "available."[63] However, they do not guarantee that services be equivalent in amount. An equivalence requirement should be added to the EAHCA regulations to provide a more clear-cut mandate. This is especially important since the Supreme Court held in *Smith v. Robinson* that claims covered by the EAHCA must be brought under that statute rather than under section 504.[64]

It does not seem possible, however, to end segregated schooling entirely through regulation. Segregated schooling is recognized in the EAHCA; its elimination would contradict congressional intent. There is also considerable disagreement concerning the advantages of segregated schooling for particular subgroups such as the deaf and the severely and profoundly retarded. The political resistance to any such move would probably be considerable and prevent any dramatic change.

A more realizable goal would be to make more modest changes that can be used by proponents of reform as they challenge local practices or uniformly segregated state systems. One possibility would be to require every local district to make a regular school placement available to every handicapped student who requests it, with provision in the regular setting of all instructional, related, and support services offered to similar students in a segregated setting. Essentially, this would require every system that segregates the more substantially handicapped to create and fund a dual system of services upon parents' request. The expense of supporting a dual system would be an incentive for districts to move towards a fully integrated service model. In addition, parents wishing to avail themselves of less restrictive placements could avoid the current necessity of due process hearings since their right to a less restrictive alternative would be absolute.[65] Although such an amendment would undoubtedly be resisted by administrators, it would be less controversial among parents, advocacy groups, and educators than other alternatives since it would not prohibit segregation, but would assure the availability of more placement options.

---

61. 34 C.F.R. § 104.4(b)(ii)-(iii) (services for handicapped must be equal to those provided non-handicapped and as effective); *id.* § 104.34(c) (services and activities in separate facilities must be comparable to those provided the nonhandicapped).

62. *Id.* § 300.305 ("Each public agency shall take steps to insure that its handicapped children have available to them the variety of educational programs and services available to nonhandicapped children . . . including art, music, industrial arts, consumer and homemaking education, and vocational education."); *id.* § 300.306 (guaranteeing handicapped children an "equal opportunity" to participate in nonacademic and extracurricular activities).

63. *Id.* § 300.307(a) ("physical education services, specially designed if necessary, must be *made available* to every handicapped child receiving a free appropriate public education.") (emphasis added).

64. Smith v. Robinson, 104 S. Ct. 3457, 3473-74 & n.22 (1984) (where § 504 and the EAHCA are the same or similar in substantive requirements, plaintiff must pursue claim under the EAHCA).

65. *Cf.* 34 C.F.R. § 300.550(b)(2) (1984).

Regulatory revisions will result in little change unless there is a concerted effort at the federal level to enforce these regulations through federal monitoring of the states. Fortunately, in 1984 there were some indications that the federal government is interested in enforcing the least restrictive environment requirement after years of virtually total passivity.[66] Whether the new federal rhetoric will be followed up in its compliance visits to the states will probably determine whether federal attention to this area has an impact.

The strategy for change outlined above will be most effective if action occurs on all fronts. Leadership training at the local level clearly will have little impact if state fiscal policies continue subsidization of statewide segregated schools for the moderately and severely retarded. And desegregation through a federal incentive program or stricter federal and state monitoring could be harmful rather than helpful to the retarded if the will and capacity of leaders at the local level to provide good integrated programs is not increased. Regulatory change will have little impact alone unless accompanied by stronger monitoring. Clearer regulations could also help attorneys and advocates for the retarded in challenging segregated systems or integrated systems offering inferior and unequal services. Such challenges, however, have been infrequent in the last five years because of continuing controversies over the advantages of segregation and integration and the high cost of undertaking major class action litigation. Given the Supreme Court's ruling in *Smith v. Robinson*,[67] denying attorney fees in EAHCA cases, major systemic challenges will be even rarer. Certainly they cannot be relied on to fulfill the federal and state governments' enforcement roles in this area.

VI

Conclusion

Using North Carolina as an example the author has explored why services to moderately, severely, and profoundly retarded students remain inadequate and unduly segregated despite the guarantees of the EAHCA and section 504 of the Rehabilitation Act. Public attitudes toward the retarded, established service arrangements, and lack of leadership from state and local administrators and advocacy groups have contributed to the lack of change. In addition, for the severely and profoundly retarded population, fiscal subsidies established by the state legislature in response to lobbying by institutional interests have created disincentives for the development of integrated services. Legal remedies are not adequate to force change.

A coordinated approach in which a sustained program of leadership training at the local level is accompanied by clearer legal definition and stronger monitoring of the least restrictive environment and comparability of services requirements is needed. Such efforts should especially be directed

---

66. Will, *supra* note 8. Interestingly, Mrs. Will in this speech strongly critized states for not enforcing least restrictive environment, but did not recognize the total absence of federal enforcement in this area that has existed in the past.

67. 104 S. Ct. 3457 (1984) (attorney fees not available for EAHCA claims).

toward the moderately handicapped as there is presently greater promise for improvement in services to this group. In addition, for states in which a state-wide segregated system of services for either the moderately or severely and profoundly retarded exists, a new federal desegregation incentive grant program is proposed. The author also recommends regulatory changes that would strengthen requirements that the handicapped receive services equivalent to those received by the nonhandicapped and would give parents an absolute right to services in a regular school if desired. In the author's opinion, the proposed changes are all politically feasible and are not unduly expensive, especially compared to total federal funding under the EAHCA. Without a new multi-pronged approach to the specific problems retarded students continue to face, progress toward both integration and equality of services will be spotty and halting and will proceed no faster than it has in the past decade.

10

LEARNING TO LIVE WITH THE DILEMMA OF DIFFERENCE: BILINGUAL AND SPECIAL EDUCATION

Martha Minow*

I

Introduction

Bilingual education and special education initially appear to be different solutions to different problems. Bilingual education offers instruction to children whose primary language is not English; special education offers instruction to children with physical or emotional handicaps. What the two programs share seems quite superficial: they attend to the needs and interests of some identifiable subset of the student population, both have sparked political controversy, and sometimes they overlap or deal with the same children.[1] At this superficial level, comparing the two programs hardly seems likely to reveal anything that is not already apparent about each one.

This article suggests, however, that a comparison of the programs yields important insights into why each one has been controversial and what may be at stake in the construction and implementation of the programs. In so doing, this article argues that the two programs actually encounter the same problem, which can be cast as the question: how can schools deal with children defined as "different" without stigmatizing them on that basis? For a glimpse of the shared problem, consider this curiosity: during the past few decades, educational policymakers switched allegiance to bilingual programs, pulling students at least part-time from the mainstream classroom, while at the same time educators have sponsored special education programs integrating exceptional students into the mainstream classroom. This changing-of-the-guard on integration suggests an initial version of the dilemma encountered by bilingual and special education. Are the stigma and unequal treatment encountered by minority groups better remedied by separation or by integration of such groups with others? Either remedy risks reinforcing the stigma associated with assigned difference by either ignoring it or focusing on it. This double-edged risk is the "difference dilemma."

---

* Assistant Professor, Harvard University Law School. The author would like to thank Katharine Bartlett, William Clune, Clare Dalton, Christopher Edley, Jr., Richard Fallon, Gunter Frankenberg, Gerald Frug, Louis Kaplow, David Kennedy, Duncan Kennedy, Frank Michelman, Kathleen Sullivan, and Judith Wegner for their comments on an earlier version of this article.
    1. *See generally* L. Baca & H. Cervantes, The Bilingual Special Education Interface (1984) (examining programs treating children who qualify for special education and also for whom English is a second language).

One seeming way out of the dilemma would be to focus on the means to achieve chosen ends. On examination, however, this route yields no escape from the difference dilemma. Constructing measures to achieve the ends of schooling is always a problematic enterprise. Unintended consequences and counterproductive results often occur, and a particular implementation problem arises in response to the desired goal of preventing the stigmatization of children who are identified as different from the rest of the students. In a powerful sense, the dilemma of difference reappears as decisionmakers consider whether the school should be structured to replicate the larger community in terms of population mix and cultural mores, or instead should create an enclave away from that larger community. Which approach, for example, would better prepare a student to deal with the adult community? Which approach would better prepare a minority group to overcome discrimination in the larger community? Are the ends of schooling better attained by designing a microcosm of the world inside the school to give students practice with it, or by designing different environments tailored to support students and accommodate their differences? This design problem arises as much for those who wish to use the schools to preserve existing social arrangements as for those who wish to use schools for social change, or for some combination of these goals. Whatever position on change and stability educators and parents select, whether the school is more likely to achieve that position by replicating the larger community or by serving as an enclave away from it is still open for debate.[2]

Another seeming way out of the dilemma would address techniques for constraining the power of the school which may otherwise stigmatize some children. Yet this approach also fails to escape the difference dilemma. As programs mandated by law are subject to litigation, bilingual and special education expose to scrutiny the nature of the school power deployed to deal with children who are considered different. Should the school personnel and programs assume a relationship to students modeled on a parent-child relationship or modeled on a state-citizen relationship? Different procedures, methods, and directions in school programming follow from this choice, and different legal frameworks for school activities would also result. There is no clear choice between parental and state models of school power given the public school's status as both protector and promoter of youth and as a state-run institution wielding state power. In the context of the dilemma of difference, addressing the legal shape of school power hardly solves the problem of limiting state stigmatization of students; rather, it recasts the dilemma as a choice between sharply contrasting but equally plausible procedural models. An examination of bilingual education and special education exposes the difference dilemma and its recurrence in decisions over the means and ends of schooling and the legal conceptions of school power.

---

2. This debate includes the issue: can the school be treated solely as a means, preparing students for the world beyond, or must it also be understood as itself a community, whether constructed to resemble the larger community or assuming a structure and climate of its own?

The difference dilemma and its reappearance in debates over means and ends and over constraining school power should not be surprising; these issues appear in varied forms in the history of American education. Indeed, the problems' very conventional quality—conventionally understood to exist and to resist resolution—may dull our awareness of them and nonetheless cabin debates over bilingual and special education. By highlighting the dilemma of difference and its reappearance in other forms, this article does not claim to offer a solution. Instead, it suggests that heightened awareness may permit a new stance toward the dilemma and new approaches toward living with it.[3] Thus, this article is written with the commitment that self-conscious reflection about the ways we think about our problems may offer new possibilities in continuing efforts to deal with those problems.[4] Budgetary and bureaucratic problems will not disappear in the face of new conceptual understandings; however, new attitudes and strategies for dealing with these very problems could emerge. In short, we cannot change our world simply by thinking about it differently, nor can we change it unless we think differently enough to see where we are, and, with this sight, act differently.

This article first describes the difference dilemma and its expression within the histories, laws, and programs of bilingual and special education. The reoccurrence of the difference dilemma in the problems of designing educational programs and constraining school power is examined next. Finally, the article offers an alternative approach to the difference dilemma and some examples of problem-solving using this approach.

II

THE DIFFERENCE DILEMMA

This nation is committed to both pluralism and equality, yet it also bears a history of prejudice against people whom the dominant group calls different. Indeed, differences in race, gender, and ethnicity have spelled determinate positions on its social hierarchy. But nonrecognition of difference leaves in place a faulty neutrality, constructed so as to advance the dominant group and hinder those who are different. No wonder people caught in the dilemma

---

3. *Cf.* A. WHEELIS, How PEOPLE CHANGE 17, 100 (1973) (describing psychotherapy: therapeutic insight does not produce change but is instrumental to it; suffering does not disappear without a change in underlying conflict which connects to changes in how one lives, feels, and reacts).
4. *See* S. CAVELL, PURSUITS OF HAPPINESS: THE HOLLYWOOD COMEDY OF REMARRIAGE 10-12 (1981) (describing philosophic commitment to "being guided by our experience but not dictated to by it" and "to educate your experience sufficiently that it is worthy of trust"); R. HOWARD, THREE FACES OF HERMENEUTICS (1982) (philosophic traditions converging in study of knowledge and deliberate efforts to uncover role of the interpreter in interpretation); J. SARTRE, SEARCH FOR A METHOD 180 (H. Barnes trans. 2d ed. 1968) (freedom grasped as condition of human limits through self knowledge). *See generally* R. RIEFF, FELLOW TEACHERS 23 (1973) (psychotherapy as "the social procedure of release from the authority of the past" but not rejecting the pre-existing world); P. RIEFF, FREUD: THE MIND OF THE MORALIST 65-101 (1975) (psychoanalytic uncovering of the hidden self bearing some relationship to freedom); Taylor, *Interpretation and the Science of Man*, in KNOWLEDGE AND VALUES IN SOCIAL AND EDUCATIONAL RESEARCH 153, 177-78 (E. Bredo & W. Feinberg eds. 1982) (interpretation searches for subjective and shared meanings); A. WHEELIS, *supra* note 3, at 113 (freedom depends on awareness but does not necessarily follow awareness).

experience an impossibility of movement, for movement in any direction creates risks of recreating the dilemma.

Identification or acknowledgment of a trait of difference, associated by the dominant group with minority identity, risks recreating occasions for majority discrimination based on that trait. Nonidentification or nonacknowledgment, however, risks recreating occasions for discrimination based on majority practices, such as tests, norms, and judgments forged without regard for difference, or with regard solely for the perspective, needs, and interests of the dominant group. Because minority differences have been made to carry implications for a person's worth and status a minority member may be reluctant to expose or emphasize such difference. Yet nonexposure can subject the minority to evaluation by allegedly neutral criteria that in fact implement the majority values and view.

Similarly, separation or segregation of a minority group risks promoting distrust and misunderstandings based on group differences, and yet integration risks perpetuating chafing expressions of hostility between dominant and minority groups. Separation reinforces stigma and feelings of inferiority by the group historically encountering discrimination. Separation may also permit inequalities in resources as the majority allocates differentially to minority groups, sharing with itself its special access to resources and leaving the minority to struggle with less. Separation in the short run may promote the association of difference with inferiority by perpetuating group misunderstandings, minority feelings of inferiority, and majority feelings of superiority.

Yet integration also risks perpetuating hierarchy. It may deny minority members a safe place to develop themselves by isolating them as individuals amid the dominant group. By depriving minority group members of opportunities to develop group identity and strength, integration can imply or reinforce the inferiority of that minority identity. Patterns of difference are set in motion by inequalities of experience, of access to resources, and of self-esteem upon entry into the integrated setting, while the commitment to avoid reiterating difference in that setting can leave these patterns in place. A history of assigned difference and infirmity can be frozen, then, by a current commitment to stop assigning difference; both focusing on and ignoring difference risk recreating it. This is the dilemma of difference.

The dilemma is not a model nor a theoretical scheme, but a felt experience and pattern of social practice. This rather stark statement of the dilemma needs shading and context. The example of race and schooling helps ground the difference dilemma and helps locate it in a context more familiar to many than the subjects of bilingual and special education, to which the article then turns.

A.   The Example of Racial Desegregation

The dilemma of difference should be familiar to students of the civil rights movement, for the efforts leading to and following *Brown v. Board of Education*[5] demonstrate this dilemma—and the impossibility of avoiding its choice of undesirable alternatives.[6] The situation of Linda Brown, who as a child had been involved in the landmark *Brown* case, offers a glimpse of the dilemma. Her childhood was indelibly marked by that historic case, itself a culmination of twenty years of legal struggle for the decision forbidding racial segregation in the schools. When she became a young mother, Linda Brown faced deteriorating public schools technically desegregated but effectively racially segregated, with more than half of the black grade-school children concentrated in six of the thirty-four elementary schools, four of which were at least 60 percent black. Both black and white parents, however, joined in opposition to city-wide busing to desegregate the schools.[7]

This development points to the historical movement after *Brown* in which groups working for desegregation chose community control as their watchword.[8] Frustrated and disappointed with the tardy and controversial implementation of *Brown*, parents and civil rights leaders turned toward community control of basically segregated schools. Unraveling this historical journey reveals the persistent tension between the search for equality through integration and the search for equality through segregation. This tension is not the product of isolated historical actions but has appeared continuously in the search for equality.

The NAACP picked schools as the focal point of its attack on the Court's approval of Jim Crow laws in *Plessy v. Ferguson*.[9] Indeed, the Court had supported the "separate but equal" principle upheld in *Plessy* in the context of railroads in part by reference to a Massachusetts state decision approving segregated schools.[10] In *Plessy* the Court expressed awareness of the issue of how separation affected status and attributed inferiority. The Court reasoned,

> [L]aws permitting, and even requiring, [racial] separation in places where [the races] are liable to be brought into contact do not necessarily imply the inferiority of either race to the other, and have been generally, if not universally, recognized as within the competency of the state legislatures in the exercise of their police power.[11]

So long as the accommodations provided were equal, continued the Court,

---

5. 347 U.S. 483 (1954).

6. The dilemma also occupies feminist discussions. *See* Eisenstein, *Introduction* to THE FUTURE OF DIFFERENCE at xv, xvii-xviii (H. Eisenstein & A. Jardin eds. 1980); Jardin, *Prelude: The Future of Difference*, in THE FUTURE OF DIFFERENCE, *supra*, at xxv, xxvi. *See generally* THE FUTURE OF DIFFERENCE, *supra*.

7. *See* R. KLUGER, SIMPLE JUSTICE 777-78 (1976).

8. *See generally* M. FANTINI, M. GITTELL & R. MAGAT, COMMUNITY CONTROL AND THE URBAN SCHOOL (1970) (failures of integration and compensatory education led to demands for community control by less powerful parent groups); D. RAVITCH, THE GREAT SCHOOL WARS (1974); Comment, *Alternative Schools for Minority Students: The Constitution, the Civil Rights Act and the Berkeley Experiment*, 61 CALIF. L. REV. 858, 899 (1973) (arguing in favor of racially homogeneous community schools).

9. 163 U.S. 537 (1896).

10. *See id.* at 544 (citing Roberts v. City of Boston, 59 Mass. (5 Cush.) 198, 206 (1849)). The Massachusetts precedent had itself been superseded by state legislation requiring integrated schools just six years after the *Roberts* decision—long before *Plessy*.

11. *Id.*

separation of the races itself carried no stigma.[12]

The NAACP in large measure took the Court at its word and challenged the equality of separate facilities rather than the principle of separate but equal. The litigation strategy conducted by the NAACP thus started with graduate level public universities and colleges, where separate facilities for blacks were either nonexistent or a sham. A string of victories required integration of law schools where no state supported legal education was available for blacks,[13] integration of law schools where separate (but tangibly inferior) legal education was provided for blacks,[14] and integration of graduate schools.[15] Then the NAACP turned to the elementary schools with the same argument that the facilities for blacks are unequal. But the NAACP also hoped to assault at this point the "separate but equal" principle itself. The NAACP lawyers took advantage of evolving social science teachings which attacked traditional theories of racial victimization, and worked with social psychologist Kenneth Clark who developed studies of the low-self image of black children.[16] Social science data became the basis for the controversial footnote 11 in *Brown* which was used to bolster the Court's reasoning that segregated education undermined the black child's self-esteem and motivation to learn, and its conclusion that, in the field of public education, "[s]eparate education facilities are inherently unequal."[17]

The social science basis for this conclusion immediately triggered debate,[18] and the desegregation remedies produced frustration and disappointment with the supposed link between integration and equality. White resistance in the form of violence, white flight, and continued stigmatization of blacks in integrated schools made segregation no longer the obvious target. Resenting their continued degradation and powerlessness, a new generation of black leaders started the Black Power movement and favored community control of local, segregated schools. They vocally rejected assimilation as a threat to black culture and black self-consciousness and sought to raise their group status through self-governance.[19]

Courts and scholars soon sensed these demands for community control and developed new schemes to remedy race discrimination with an emphasis on black empowerment and redistributed authority over schooling. The Atlanta Plan, often cited as a model, emphasized the hiring of blacks to fill administrative posts in the school system—including the job of the superin-

---

12. *See id.* at 551-52.
13. *See, e.g.,* Missouri *ex rel.* Gaines v. Canada, 305 U.S. 337 (1938).
14. Sweatt v. Painter, 339 U.S. 629 (1950).
15. McLaurin v. Oklahoma State Regents for Higher Educ., 339 U.S. 637 (1950).
16. *See* R. KLUGER, *supra* note 7, at 315-45.
17. Brown v. Board of Educ., 347 U.S. 483, 494-95 nn.10-11 (1954).
18. *See, e.g.,* Cahn, *Jurisprudence,* 30 N.Y.U. L. REV. 150, 153-54 (1955); Honnold, Book Review, 33 IND. L.J. 612, 614-15 (1958).
19. Ravitch, *The Evolution of School Desegregation Policy, 1964-1979,* in RACE AND SCHOOLING IN THE CITY 9, 15 (1981); *see also* R. BLUMBERG, CIVIL RIGHTS: THE 1960's FREEDOM STRUGGLE 117-37 (1984) (Black Power movement).

tendent.[20] Scholars like Derrick A. Bell, Jr. campaigned for judicial remedies addressing the quality of education rather than racial integration.[21]

Kenneth Clark reflected on these developments and warned that:

[Community control] may further isolate the poor and the minority groups from the majority society and bring the customary consequences of racial and class isolation—eroded facilities, inadequate teaching and administrative staffs, and minimum resources. . . .

Community control, therefore, requires a commitment of the city as a whole, genuine delegation of power, and continued efforts to relate the community to the larger society. Perhaps paradoxically, the lower-status community will never have genuine power until its isolation is ended.[22]

The paradox, indeed, expresses the dilemma of difference: continued powerlessness for blacks could emerge from even self-chosen segregation, but powerlessness could also emerge from efforts to integrate with a larger community still assigning a lower status to blacks. Separation might permit the assertion of minority group identity and strength, but without acceptance and empowerment by the majority, the minority will continue to suffer from the associations between racial difference and social and political status.

This dilemma which arises in the treatment of racial difference was not, however, a new discovery in the post-*Brown* era. W.E.B. Dubois and Booker T. Washington had carried on a similar debate more than half a century before. In particular they debated the issue of whether reform efforts should seek to integrate blacks within the ideology and social patterns created by the dominant culture or should attempt to alter that culture by celebrating the separate heritage and culture of the minority group.[23] Each position received periodic acclaim followed by blame as a cause of continuing racial oppression. Debate over these positions etched the shape of the difference dilemma. Continued attachment to a separate racial identity—complete with separate schools and cultural socialization—could perpetuate rather than alter the historic degradation of blacks; integration aimed at assimilation could do the same or even accentuate black student difference without equipping them with a supporting community backed by their own parents.

Assimilation continues to be criticized as either impossible or undesirable;

---

20. *See* Jackson, *Urban School Desegregation from a Black Perspective,* in RACE AND SCHOOLING IN THE CITY 204, 209-11 (1981).

21. *See* Bell, *Brown v. Board of Education and the Interest-Convergence Dilemma,* 93 HARV. L. REV. 518 (1980); Bell, *Waiting on the Promise of* Brown, LAW & CONTEMP. PROBS., Spring 1975, at 341; *see also* Bell, *Serving Two Masters: Integration Ideals and Client Interests in School Desegregation Litigation,* 85 YALE L.J. 470 (1976) (describing black opposition to school busing plans and criticizing public interest lawyers for failing to recognize minority group desires). *See generally* Hawley, *The New Mythology of School Desegregation,* LAW & CONTEMP. PROBS., Autumn 1978, at 214 (criticizing scholarly disenchantment with desegregation).

22. Clark, *Introduction* to M. FANTINI, M. GITTELL & R. MAGAT, *supra* note 8, at xi.

23. *See* M. CURTI, THE SOCIAL IDEAS OF AMERICAN EDUCATORS 288-309 (1959) (comparing Washington and Dubois); R. KLUGER, *supra* note 7, at 91-100 (same); *see also* W.E.B. DUBOIS, THE SOULS OF BLACK FOLK (1916) (describing richness of black heritage deserving preservation); B. WASHINGTON, UP FROM SLAVERY (1970) (describing his own education and conception of education for blacks).

attributed differences continue to stigmatize. As one black parent told a white psychologist in the 1970's:

> The goal, I think, is not that people have to get to the point of being colorblind. No one needs to tell me you're white, and no one needs to tell you I'm black. . . . The goal is simpler than that. You get to know our family, we get to know you and your family. That they aren't equal, well, that's what we're all going to have to live with. Maybe together we'll change it.[24]

Ignoring differences could reproduce them, even when well-intentioned people prescribe reforms. The prospect of learning new ways to live with the experience of difference may be what study of the dilemma offers.

B. Bilingual Education and Special Education: Historical Preoccupations with Difference

Historically, school programs for children who are not native English speakers have sometimes ignored their difference, but more recently they have emphasized it. Historically, school programs for children with handicaps have sometimes emphasized their differences, but more recently they have emphasized their similarities. Both types of programs continue to struggle with the dilemma of difference. A brief review of the histories of these programs,[25] followed by an examination of their legal and programmatic structures, demonstrates this preoccupation.

1. *Bilingual Education.* Educators, lawyers, and historians frequently depict the history of bilingual education as a political struggle ultimately yielding recognition of native language as an important differentiating characteristic of students—a characteristic deserving accommodation by the public schools. This history begins with the presentation of this nation as a country peopled by immigrants who supplanted the language and culture of indigenous peoples. English became the dominant language in this country's public life. English is the language of the legislatures and courts, the marketplace, and the public schools.[26]

The supplanting of languages other than English in the schools did not, however, go uncontested. Subcommunities which maintained the language of their home country through local newspapers, cultural entertainment, and religious activities periodically pushed for recognition of their language and culture within the schools. Indeed, in some pockets, politically sophisticated immigrants successfully elected school boards which in turn implemented bilingual educational programs, preserving the ethnic language of the group while also instructing the children in English.[27] Opposition to the use of for-

---

24. T. COTTLE, BLACK CHILDREN, WHITE DREAMS 53 (1974).

25. This synthesis of the histories offered in textbooks and monographs does not attempt to uncover competing versions of the historical events that future scholarship may develop in response to shifting political attitudes about the programs.

26. *See* Edelman, *Basic American*, 6 NOLPE SCH. L.J. 83, 88 & n.47 (1976) (majority of states have statutes requiring English to be primarily used in the public schools and allowing foreign languages to be used only to aid in the mastery of English) (listing statutes).

27. D. TYACK, THE ONE BEST SYSTEM 106-09 (1974) (discussing German programs in Cincinnati

eign languages in the schools, however, mounted; this sentiment motivated the enactment of statutes forbidding the teaching of any non-English language even in a private school to students below the eighth grade. One Court ruled that such a statute violated the Constitution's guarantee of liberty and due process. In *Meyer v. Nebraska*, even though the Court recognized the state's power to "foster a homogeneous people with American ideals, prepared readily to understand current discussions of civic matters," the Court concluded that the legislative means selected violated the Constitution.[28] The decision in *Meyer*, then, became an important milestone in the nation's commitment to pluralism—but that decision did not place foreign languages on an equal footing with English. Nor did it entitle children to instruction in foreign language; it simply forbade rules proscribing such instruction. The case stands in the history of bilingual education as a reminder of longstanding local struggles over non-English instruction, marked by escalating opposition in the name of patriotism during wartime.[29]

Instruction in languages other than English became unpopular during and after the First World War, except as elective courses for students already proficient in English.[30] Developments after World War II paved the way for the instruction in their mother tongue for children not proficient in English; mounting immigration, Cold War competition with the Soviet Union, and the civil rights movement all supplied bases for compensatory educational programs, including instruction for students whose native language was not English.[31] Ethnic pride movements figured importantly in the call for combining language instruction with cultural awareness programs. The history of bilingual education usually concludes with a comparison of the experiences of immigrants who, earlier in the nation's history, had to or chose to abandon their ethnic heritage in contrast to contemporary groups who reject homogenization and nurture cultural difference.

This frequently depicted history of bilingual education is a story of the growing recognition of language and cultural differences and of the harm children experienced when such differences were not recognized. This story, then, manifests one half of the difference dilemma: nonacknowledgment of difference reiterates difference, given a social world making difference matter. Leonard Covello, the first New York City public school principal of Italian

---

and St. Louis, 1840-1890). *See generally* H. KLOSS, THE AMERICAN BILINGUAL TRADITION (1977) (describing bilingual patterns in the 19th century).

28. 262 U.S. 390, 402 (1923).

29. *See, e.g.,* Wagner, *The Historical Background of Bilingualism and Biculturalism in the United States,* in THE NEW BILINGUALISM: AN AMERICAN DILEMMA 29, 42 (M. Ridge ed. 1981) ("We cannot tolerate any attempt to oppose or supplant the language and culture that has come down to us from the builders of this republic with the language and culture of any European country. The greatness of this nation depends on the swift assimilation of the aliens she welcomes to her shores.") (quoting Theodore Roosevelt).

30. T. ANDERSON & M. BOYER, BILINGUAL SCHOOLING IN THE UNITED STATES 21-22 (2d ed. 1978); P. CAFFERTY & C. RIVERA-MARTINEZ, THE POLITICS OF LANGUAGE: THE DILEMMA OF BILINGUAL EDUCATION FOR PUERTO RICANS 4, 14-15 (1981).

31. *See* Bilingual Education Act, Pub. L. No. 90-247, tit. VII, §§ 701-708, 81 Stat. 783 (1968) (current version at 20 U.S.C. §§ 3221-3261 (1982)).

heritage, recalled his experience in the public schools at the turn of the century:

> During this period the Italian language was completely ignored in the American schools. In fact, throughout my whole elementary school career, I do not recall one mention of Italy or the Italian language or what famous Italians had done in the world, with the possible exception of Columbus. . . . We soon got the idea that "Italian" meant something inferior, and a barrier was erected between children of Italian origin and their parents. This was the accepted process of Americanization. We were becoming Americans by learning how to be ashamed of our parents.[32]

Advocates of bilingual education link this shame about family, ethnicity, and ultimately self, to the poor academic achievement of many children for whom English is a second language. The advocates contend that it is worse than cruel, in fact it is devastating to a child's self-respect, when a child is forced to give up a family language while attending school. This denigrates not only the mother tongue but also the value system of the home culture. It is little wonder such children do poorly in school. Educating children in part in the language of their homes—at least until they have mastered it—is as important as learning English. This, it is argued, will create a spirit of self-respect and self-confidence in students.[33]

Author Richard Rodriguez offered a different assessment of his parochial school education, where his native Spanish was not used or acknowledged:

> Without question, it would have pleased me to hear my teachers address me in Spanish when I entered the classroom. I would have felt much less afraid. I would have trusted them and responded with ease. But I would have delayed—for how long postponed?—having to learn the language of public society. I would have evaded—and for how long could I have afforded to delay?—learning the great lesson of school, that I had a public identity. And, [w]hat I needed to learn in school was that I had the right—and the obligation—to speak the public language of *los gringos.*[34]

Here then is the other side of the dilemma; acknowledgment of difference can create barriers to important aspects of the school experience and delay or derail successful entry into the society that continues to make that difference matter. Both sides of the dilemma appear and reappear in the history of education for students who are not native English speakers.

2. *Special Education.* A contrasting history appears for education for the handicapped, but here, too, the dilemma of difference appears and reappears. As frequently told, this history emphasizes the exclusion of exceptional chil-

---

32. SILBERMAN, CRISIS IN THE CLASSROOM 58 (1970) (quoting Leonard Covello).

33. Ridge, *The New Bilingualism: An American Dilemma,* in THE NEW BILINGUALISM: AN AMERICAN DILEMMA 259, 260 (M. Ridge ed. 1981). A Hispanic school administrator explained, "You tell the child: 'Your language is second-rate and you shouldn't speak it. Your culture is second-rate and you need to be something else. . . .' What you are in fact saying to the kids is '*You* are second-rate.'" Lanier, *Teaching with Subtitles,* CHI. MAG. at 163, 191 (June 1984) (quoting Jose Gonzales, Associate Superintendant of Chicago Board of Education).

34. R. RODRIGUEZ, HUNGER OF MEMORY: THE EDUCATION OF RICHARD RODRIQUEZ 19 (1982) (emphasis in original). Even though they differ in their views on bilingual education, both Covello and Rodriguez understand schooling as a process of transferring loyalties and transforming identities.

dren from mainstream classrooms or from schooling altogether.[35] This history is complicated by the broad, ambiguous, and shifting conception of handicap; exceptional children can include children with developmental disabilities, emotional disturbances, learning or perceptual disabilities, sensory deficits, mobility impairments, and each of these definitional categories has shifted over time. Nonetheless, a general historical picture of the educational opportunities for exceptional children depicts the gradual but steady progress toward recognizing what these children share with other children, rather than emphasizing their differences. It is thus a story of expanding humanitarianism and increasing inclusion of handicapped children in the worlds of education, training, and social life.

The story begins before schooling was compulsory, when local authorities had discretion to exclude children from public education on the grounds of ineducability, and communities tended to consider handicaps as barriers to adult responsibilities. As a result, until the Civil War, children with special needs were usually hidden in poorhouses. Humanitarian reforms, led by physicians in both Europe and the United States, produced special institutions for the deaf and for the blind during the early part of the nineteenth century.[36] Local policies segregated the disabled in institutions removed from the community.[37]

After the Civil War, as many communities adopted compulsory education laws and then began to enforce them, exceptional children began to present themselves in increasing numbers to public schools. Educators responded with separate day schools—and separate classes within existing schools—for the deaf, the mentally retarded, the crippled, and other groups of children identified with the handicap labels of that time. Previously consigned to institutions or locked away at home, during this later period children with special needs at least had a place, and a chance for some education and attention.[38] Some recent versions of this history emphasize the interaction between proliferating separate classes for special children and the influx of new immigrants to the community and the community schools.[39] This isolation of minority groups in special education classes drew attention to the similarities between special education and education segregated by race or ethnicity.[40] At the

---

35. *See, e.g.*, Stark, *Tragic Choices in Special Education: The Effect of Scarce Resources on the Implementation of Pub. L. No. 94-142*, 14 CONN. L. REV. 477, 479-80 (1982).

36. Reformers established in Hartford, Connecticut, a residential institution offering training and a protective environment for the deaf in 1817. Schools for the blind were established around the same era; by the time of the Civil War, such institutions were common. S. KIRK & J. GALLAGHER, EDUCATING EXCEPTIONAL CHILDREN 4-5 (3d ed. 1979).

37. F. HEWETT & S. FORNESS, EDUCATION OF EXCEPTIONAL LEARNERS 32-41 (1974).

38. *E.g.*, S. SARASON & J. DORIS, EDUCATIONAL HANDICAP, PUBLIC POLICY, AND SOCIAL HISTORY 232 (1978); Cruickshank, *The Development of Education for Exceptional Children*, in EDUCATION OF EXCEPTIONAL CHILDREN AND YOUTH 11-12 (W. Cruickshank & P. Xurland 3d ed. 1975); Tyack, *Ways of Seeing: An Essay in the History of Compulsory Schooling*, 46 HARV. EDUC. REV. 355 (1976).

39. S. SARASON & J. DORIS, *supra* note 38, at 245.

40. *See* Hobson v. Hansen, 269 F. Supp. 401 (D.D.C. 1967), *aff'd sub nom.* Smuck v. Hobson, 408 F.2d 175 (D.C. Cir. 1969) (en banc); Larry P. v. Riles, 343 F. Supp. 1306, 1309 (N.D. Cal. 1972), *aff'd*, 502 F.2d 963 (9th Cir. 1974).

same time, social scientists uncovered the psychological detriment to a child from being labeled as different and inferior.[41] The harmful effects of separate treatment became the focus of the culminating chapter in this story of the progressive inclusion of handicapped children.

During the 1970's, law reformers pushed for both expanding the services for special education and educating the exceptional child with his or her "normal peers to whatever extent is compatible with potential for the fullest development."[42] Two landmark federal district court cases produced stipulated relief to this effect,[43] and state and federal legislation between 1970 and 1978 incorporated these mainstreaming goals.[44] What happened during the intervening decades to yield this trend toward integrating or "mainstreaming" exceptional children? Building on the civil rights movement and *Brown v. Board of Education*,[45] educational reformers sensitized the legal community to the stigma of separate treatment, the risks of misclassification and labeling in creating stigma and low self-esteem, and the abusive use of separate classes to perpetuate discrimination against racial and ethnic minorities.[46] Legal reformers in turn adopted a due process tack to promote accountability by public decisionmakers and individualized consideration of students, just as the due process doctrine had previously been used to help recipients of public benefits. In the special education context, litigators and legislators used the due process doctrines to structure procedural and substantive protections for handicapped children who were excluded from public schooling.[47] These legal frameworks provided a rhetoric for treating excep-

---

41. Stigma from segregation, of course, emerged as a psychological detriment in the context of racial desegregation. *See* Brown v. Board of Educ., 347 U.S. 483, 494 n.11 (1954). *But cf.* Levin & Moise, *School Desegregation Litigation in the Seventies and the Use of Social Science Evidence: An Annotated Guide*, LAW & CONTEMP. PROBS., Winter 1975, at 50, 53-56 (since *Brown*, courts have questioned use of social science research in regard to the question of whether a constitutional violation occurred, but have used them to fashion remedies); Yudof, *School Desegregation: Legal Realism, Reasoned Elaboration, and Social Science Research in the Supreme Court*, LAW & CONTEMP. PROBS., Autumn 1978, at 57, 69-71 (noting limitations of social science methodology applied in Brown v. Board of Educ.). The relationship between handicap labeling and stigma became a major issue in social services during the 1970's. *See* J. MERCER, LABELING THE MENTALLY RETARDED: CLINICAL AND SOCIAL SYSTEM PERSPECTIVES ON MENTAL RETARDATION 31, 82 (1973) (service providers should be aware of links between social systems, status, and handicap labels); J. SHRYBMAN, DUE PROCESS IN SPECIAL EDUCATION 6 (1982) (due process concerns about reputational interest threatened by labeling).

42. S. KIRK & J. GALLAGHER, EDUCATING EXCEPTIONAL CHILDREN 7 (1979).

43. Mills v. Board of Educ., 348 F. Supp. 866 (D.D.C. 1972) (court-ordered remedy, including order for comprehensive plan by defendants); Pennsylvania Ass'n for Retarded Children (PARC) v. Pennsylvania, 343 F. Supp. 279 (E.D. Pa. 1972) (consent agreement).

44. *See* Zettel & Abeson, *The Right to a Free Appropriate Public Education*, in THE COURTS AND EDUCATION 188, 198-99 (C. Hooker ed. 1978) (77th Yearbook of the National Society for the Study of Education) (describing legislative developments).

45. 347 U.S. 483 (1954).

46. Hobson v. Hansen, 269 F. Supp. 401 (D.D.C. 1967), *aff'd sub nom.* Smuck v. Hobson, 408 F.2d 175 (D.C. Cir. 1969) (en banc) (illicit use of tracking to perpetuate racial segregation); *see, e.g.*, Kirp, Buss, & Kuriloff, *Legal Reform of Special Education: Empirical Studies and Procedural Proposals*, 62 CALIF. L. REV. 40, 46 (1974) (misclassification).

47. *See* Pennsylvania Ass'n for Retarded Children (PARC) v. Pennsylvania, 334 F. Supp. 1257 (E.D. Pa. 1971) (per curiam) (injunction and consent agreement), 343 F. Supp. 279 (E.D. Pa. 1972) (injunction and amended consent agreement); Mills v. Board of Educ. 348 F. Supp. 866 (D.D.C. 1972).

tional children as, first and foremost, persons entitled to legal and educational rights. The rhetoric could also advance their inclusion, at least conceptually, in the larger community.

The history of special education thus depicts increasing faith in the educability of special needs children and growing commitment to grant them entry to the social life of other children. Yet the dilemma of difference recurs. On the one hand, ever more sophisticated methods to recognize varieties of handicapping conditions identify increasing numbers of children as different and therefore entitled to some specialized instruction. On the other hand, increasing commitment to treat special needs children like other children cautions against this very result, or argues for creating facsimiles of the mainstream classroom in special schools or in classes for those with special needs. Making difference matter recreates difference and its associated hierarchy of status; making difference not matter, though, may cause the same result. Even given their contrasting histories, both bilingual and special education highlight this dilemma.

C. Legal and Programmatic Structures

As a result of federal and state litigation and legislation during the past several decades, a welter of legal authorities have emerged to construct and define the programs known as bilingual and special education. In addition, competing program types have emerged in both areas. These legal and programmatic structures share complexity, but diverge in shape and content. Nonetheless, the underlying difference dilemma can help explain points of confusion and contention in these programmatic structures.

1. *Bilingual Education: Legal Framework and the Difference Dilemma.* When the Supreme Court decided *Lau v. Nichols*[48] in 1974, it accepted the claim of non-English speaking Chinese students that instruction solely in English denied them "a meaningful opportunity to participate in the educational program," and it construed Title VI of the Civil Rights Act of 1964 to supply a legal basis for demanding special instruction for language minority students in schools receiving federal financial assistance. The Court thereby linked affirmative obligations to provide language instruction to the statutory requirement that "[n]o person in the United States shall, on the ground of race, color, or national origin, be excluded from participation in, be denied benefits of, or be subjected to discrimination under any program or activity receiving Federal financial assistance."[49] The Court refrained, however, from detailing the form such language instruction must or should take. Indeed, the Court noted that no particular remedy was requested by the plaintiffs: "[t]eaching English to the students of Chinese ancestry who do not speak the language is one choice. Giving instruction to this group in Chinese is another. There may be

---

48.   414 U.S. 563 (1974).
49.   Title VI of the Civil Rights Act of 1964, 42 U.S.C. § 2000d (1982).

others."[50]

It could be argued that anything but immersion in the mainstream classroom violates the plain language of Title VI; what made *Lau* an impressive
decision was the Court's recognition of an experiential context in which such
mainstreaming, with no attention to language and cultural differences, constituted, for the Chinese-speaking plaintiffs, exclusion, denied benefits and discrimination. In this respect, the *Lau* decision resembles the Court's opinion
in *Loving v. Virginia*,[51] where the social meaning of majority-minority differences was a factor in the Court's rejection of a miscegenation statute. The
Court concluded that although the miscegenation law equally forbade blacks
and whites from marrying each other, in the context of a national history of
discrimination against nonwhites, this law reinforced the stigma against the
minority race and thus unconstitutionally discriminated. In *Loving*, a straightforward legal rejection of the miscegenation statute did not recreate the difference dilemma in the construction of a legal remedy,[52] yet the *Lau* decision
could not avoid this dilemma in developing legal alternatives. State decisions
remain to be made about how to treat minority language children in the
public schools. The generality of the language adopted in the Civil Rights
Act—undoubtedly without the *Lau* problem in mind—is commodious enough
to support contrasting remedial alternatives, any of which may well continue
to stigmatize the children who are different. The dilemma of difference, then,
remains for decisions based on the reasoning of *Lau*.

The second legal framework for bilingual education, the Bilingual Education Act, as amended by the Equal Educational Opportunity Act,[53] also
presents the difference dilemma. The Bilingual Education Act acknowledges
the need for both English language and native language instruction, but
obscures the critical choice between integration and segregation and between
English usage and native language usage by directing that the mix of languages "shall, to the extent necessary, be in all courses or subjects of study
which will allow a child to progress effectively through the educational

---

50.   414 U.S. at 564-65.

51.   388 U.S. 1 (1967).

52.   The Court in *Loving* did not need to craft a new law; it just struck down the law under
challenge. Yet even though the Court could escape the difference dilemma, eliminating the law
against miscegenation hardly eliminates the difference dilemma for an interracial couple contem-
plating marriage in some contemporary American communities. Their marriage, premised on their
belief that their racial differences should not matter, may expose both them and their children to the
risks of stigma. *Cf.* Palmore v. Sidoti, 426 So. 2d 34 (Fla. Dist. Ct. App. 1982) (affirming without
opinion trial court's holding that change of custody for white daughter was warranted where white
mother married black man since children of interracial marriage would be stigmatized), *rev'd*, 104 S.
Ct. 1879 (1984) (acknowledging risks to the child from custody with interracial couple but rejecting
this as basis for state imposed change in custody). However, a decision on their part not to marry
surely just as much reconfirms the stigmatizing, discriminatory dimensions of difference as it has
come to have social meaning. *See also* M.P. v. S.P., 169 N.J. Super. 425, 438, 404 A.2d 1256, 1263
(1979) (judge explains that removing children from custody of lesbian mother to protect them from
community disapproval would teach them to leave their problems and to believe that loved ones
should be abandoned if others dislike them).

53.   20 U.S.C. §§ 3221-3261 (1982).

system."[54] The critical choices, then, are to be resolved with reference to undefined terms such as "to the extent necessary," and "to progress effectively through the educational system"—where the meanings of "necessary" and "effective progress" may be themselves changed by the introduction of bilingual education. Similarly, the Equal Educational Opportunity Act leaves critical terms undefined and thereby preserves the difference dilemma; depending on terms like "appropriate," and "equal participation,"[55] the Act preserves the dilemma about whether to avoid discrimination by constructing special and separate programs or by pushing the different child into participation in the mainstream class.

2. *Bilingual Programs and the Difference Dilemma.* In the face of this remedial ambiguity, federal courts and agencies developed a range of possible programs. As implemented by local school boards and school staff, varied programs abound.[56] Grouping the programs into two major kinds of programs can serve to highlight this variety and also to underscore the continuing remedial ambiguity in legal developments since *Lau.*

a. *Types of Bilingual Programs.* The first type of program, called "English as a Second Language Instruction" (ESL), has been defined by the federal government as "[a] structured language acquisition program designed to teach English to students whose native language is not English."[57] Typically, ESL provides intensive instruction in English, with the goal of enabling the student to speak and understand English as soon as possible, and employs the "pull out" method: the language minority student spends most of the school day in the regular class without language assistance, and the student is pulled out of the mainstream class during part of the day for ESL instruction. ESL does not, then, use native language instruction to conduct substantive classes in, say, math or social studies, while the student is gaining mastery of English;

---

54. 20 U.S.C. § 3223(a)(4)(A)(i) (1982).

55. "No state shall deny equal educational opportunity to an individual on account of his or her race, color, sex, or national origin by. . .(f) the failure by an educational agency to take appropriate action to overcome language barriers that impede equal participation by its students in its instructional programs." 20 U.S.C. § 1703 (1982).

56. *See* Baker & de Kanter, *Federal Policy and the Effectiveness of Bilingual Education,* in BILINGUAL EDUCATION: A REAPPRAISAL OF FEDERAL POLICY 33, 34-35 (K. Baker & A. de Kanter eds. 1983) (describing English as a second language (ESL), structured immersion, and transitional bilingual education); Carpenter-Huffman & Samulon, *Case Studies of Delivery and Cost of Bilingual Education,* in BILINGUAL EDUCATION: A REAPPRAISAL OF FEDERAL POLICY, *supra,* at 141, 145-50 (describing variety of instructional methods and choices among self-contained classrooms and pull-out programs); *see also* S. GOLDSTEIN & E. GEE, LAW AND PUBLIC EDUCATION: CASES AND MATERIALS 801 (1980) (describing 1) segregation of non-English speaking students in classrooms where instructors use English and their own language; 2) segregated students taught in their own language and instructed in English as a second language; 3) integrated classroom where both English and other language are used; and 4) English as a second language, placing minority students in mainstream classroom with supplementary English instruction). Thus, programs may differ in both the mix of services they combine and the setting in which the services are offered.

57. OFFICE FOR CIVIL RIGHTS, U.S. DEP'T OF HEALTH, EDUCATION AND WELFARE, TASK FORCE FINDINGS SPECIFYING REMEDIES FOR ELIMINATING PAST EDUCATIONAL PRACTICES RULED UNLAWFUL UNDER *LAU V. NICHOLS* (1975), *reprinted in* BILINGUAL EDUCATION: A REAPPRAISAL OF FEDERAL POLICY 213, 221 (1983) [hereinafter cited as LAU GUIDELINES].

nor does ESL expose the English-speaking students to the language or culture of the non-English-speaking students.[58]

A variant on this model, called "transitional bilingual education," also aims for transition from special treatment to total integration in the regular classroom. Under this approach, subject matter instruction may temporarily be conducted in the children's home language until their proficiency in English improves enough to enable participation in the regular classroom.[59] Because both the transitional variation and ESL seek to integrate the minority language student in mainstream classes, any segregation under these programs is intended to be temporary. Nonetheless, segregated instruction often stretches longer than planned since the child may have fallen behind the mainstream class in other subjects or may perform less successfully because of the prior language barrier.

The second major type of program, commonly called bilingual-bicultural education, combines native language instruction in substantive courses, ESL training, and instruction in the culture and history of both America and the nation or group associated with the student's native language. Programs are additionally distinguishable by whether their cultural emphasis addresses "surface" culture, such as crafts and music, or "deep" culture, such as attitudes about family, health, and sex roles.[60] In 1975, the U.S. Commission on Civil Rights identified six objectives in this kind of program: (1) fostering the student's healthy self-image; (2) developing cognitive powers; (3) creating an atmosphere not totally alien to the child's familiar environment; (4) developing reading skills; (5) teaching language skills systematically; and (6) improving English skills.[61] Although the Supreme Court did not specify a preference for bilingual-bicultural programs, the Department of Health, Education and Welfare did so after *Lau* in advisory form.[62] Subsequent legal developments, however, complicated both federal and state postures on this issue.

b. *Post-Lau Legal Developments.* Shortly after *Lau,* the Supreme Court decided *Regents of the University of California v. Bakke,*[63] which reopened the issue of what affirmative obligations public educational institutions might have to minorities; *Bakke* required demonstration of discriminatory intent before affirmative remedies could be ordered by school authorities. Next, Congress itself increased federal support for bilingual programs; building on

---

58. *See* S. GOLDSTEIN & E. GEE, *supra* note 56, at 801.

59. Birman & Ginsberg, *Addressing the Needs of Language-Minority Children,* in BILINGUAL EDUCATION: A REAPPRAISAL OF FEDERAL POLICY xi-xii (1983). *See also* LAU GUIDELINES, *supra* note 57, at 221. The task force report particularly opposed ESL for elementary school students unless modified through the transitional method. *Id.* at 215.

60. Gonzales, *Reinforcing Culture in Three Bilingual Education Programs,* in EARLY CHILDHOOD BILINGUAL EDUCATION: A HISPANIC PERSPECTIVE 93, 96-99 (T. Escobedo ed. 1983).

61. U.S. COMMISSION ON CIVIL RIGHTS, BILINGUAL-BICULTURAL EDUCATION: A BETTER CHANCE TO LEARN 1, 29-30 (Clearinghouse Publication 51, 1975).

62. LAU GUIDELINES, *supra* note 57, at 215-18.

63. 438 U.S. 265 (1978).

the 1968 amendment to the Elementary and Secondary Education Act, Congress adopted amendments in 1974 and in 1978 which expanded the target population for federally-aided services.[64] Congress did not oblige local school authorities to adopt bilingual-bicultural programs in implementing equal opportunity requirements; instead, the statutes preserved local school discretion on this issue.[65] The statutory definition of "program of bilingual education" employed the flexible language of "to the extent necessary" regarding both the use of the child's native language and the integration of bicultural materials with other subjects.[66] Although some have argued that the federal commitment continued to favor bilingual-bicultural programs,[67] the legislative and administrative record itself is unclear. Federal judicial interpretation of these statutes has also produced ambiguous results.[68] The legal ambiguity, which may have emerged from political conflict, promotes continued political battles among interest groups over which of the permitted types of programs for minority language students should be used.[69]

---

64.   *See* Bilingual Education Act of 1968, Pub. L. No. 90-247, tit. VII, §§ 701-708, 81 Stat. 783; Act of Nov. 1, 1978, Pub. L. No. 95-561, tit. 7, § 702, 92 Stat. 2143 (amendment expanding services to students with limited proficiency in reading, writing, and speaking English); Act of Aug. 21, 1974, Pub. L. No. 93-380, tit. 7, § 702, 81 Stat. 484 (expanding services beyond low income children) (current version at 20 U.S.C. §§ 3221-3261 (1982)); *see also* Morales v. Shannon, 516 F.2d 411, 415 (5th Cir. 1975), *cert. denied*, 423 U.S. 1034 (1975) (unlawful educational practice to fail to take appropriate action to overcome language barriers); Equal Educational Opportunity Act, 20 U.S.C. § 1703(f) (1982) (prohibiting "failure by an educational agency to take appropriate action to overcome language barriers that impede equal participation").

65.   *See* 20 U.S.C. § 3222 (1982) (federal grants program). State legislation also generally does not specify which form of bilingual program schools must use. *See e.g.,* TEX. EDUC. CODE ANN., § 21.451; (Vernon Supp. 1973) (requiring bilingual instruction). *But see* MASS. ANN. LAWS ch. 71A, §§ 1-9 (Law. Co-op. 1978) (requiring transitional program but including instruction in history and culture of native language speakers).

66.   Thus, the statute defines a "program of bilingual education" in elementary and secondary schools as a program where "there is instruction given in, and study of, English and, to the extent necessary to allow the child to achieve competence in the English language, the native language of the children of limited English proficiency, and such instruction is given with appreciation for the cultural heritage of such children, and of other children in American society, and, with respect to elementary and secondary school instruction, such instruction shall, to the extent necessary, be in all courses or subjects of study which will allow a child to progress effectively through the educational system . . . ." 20 U.S.C. § 3223 (a)(4)(A)(i) (1982).

67.   *See* N.Y. Times, May 14, 1983, at 22, col. 1 (editorial page) (criticizing federal "blessing" for native language maintenance programs). The regulations proposed but never implemented under the Carter administration would have required bilingual instruction for eligible students instead of ESL, 45 Fed. Reg. 52,052 (1980) (proposed regulation), but as the Secretary of Education later described, these regulations were intended "to require school districts to teach non-English proficient youngsters English as quickly as possible, and, while the children were learning English, to give them instruction in required courses in a language they could understand." Hufstedler, *Is America Over-Lawyered?*, 31 CLEV. ST. L. REV. 371, 380 (1982); *see also* Haft, *Assuring Equal Educational Opportunity for Language-Minority Students: Bilingual Education and the Equal Educational Opportunity Act of 1974*, 18 COLUM. J.L. & SOC. PROBS. 209, 258-63 (1983) (arguing that Congressional and administrative authority favored bilingual programs).

68.   *Compare* Cintron v. Brentwood Union Free School Dist., 455 F. Supp. 57, 62-64 (E.D.N.Y. 1978) (requiring bilingual and bicultural instructional methods) *with* Rios v. Read, 480 F. Supp. 14, 22 (E.D.N.Y. 1978) (requiring temporary bilingual instruction) *and* Guadalupe Org., Inc. v. Tempe Elementary School Dist., 587 F.2d 1022, 1030 (9th Cir. 1978) (approving nonbilingual-bicultural program to meet the needs of language-minority students).

69.   *See* Hufstedler, *supra* note 67, at 380-81 (discussing public debate over federal regulations); Daley, *Panel Asks Stress on English Studies*, N.Y. Times, May 6, 1983, at 1, col. 1 (debate among Hispanic

The contrast between ESL instruction and bilingual-bicultural instruction illustrates the most obvious contrast between the different solutions to the dilemma; the continuing debate between the two models demonstrates how the dilemma structures common understandings. ESL proposes short-term segregation during part of the school day, and long-term integration, with an abandonment of minority identity, in the school context. Its critics argue that the program reconfirms the association of difference with inferiority by refusing to recognize the positive experiences of minority difference and by failing to instruct either minority or majority children in the minority language and culture. Bilingual-bicultural programs attempt to meet this criticism, but in turn encounter the other side of the dilemma. By reinforcing minority difference and prolonging separation, such programs risk reconfirming the identification of difference with alien and inferior status and also risk failing to prepare their students for a society that makes mastery of English language and American culture a precondition for success.

3. *Special Education Law and the Difference Dilemma.* The legal framework for special education combines a general ban on discrimination to protect the handicapped in any program receiving federal funds and a categorical assistance grant program which conditions the grants on statewide compliance with substantive and procedural requirements to educate exceptional children. The general antidiscrimination ban, section 504 of the Rehabilitation Act of 1973,[70] follows the model of the Civil Rights Act of 1964,[71] which supplied the basis for the *Lau v. Nichols* decision and which forbids exclusion from or denial of benefits due to an individual's race, color or national origin. Section 504 in part borrows the same structure—forbidding exclusion of or denial of benefits to a member of the protected group, here handicapped persons, by any program receiving federal support. Section 504 also adds the requirement that the protected minority group member, here a handicapped person, be "otherwise qualified" for the program or benefits before the provisions of the law may apply.[72] Thus, section 504 describes with considerable ambiguity the group it actually protects; the statute does not clearly indicate whether it covers persons qualified except for their handicap or persons qualified even given their handicap. *Southeastern Community College v. Davis*[73] presented this definitional ambiguity, and the Supreme Court found that section 504 did not require the school to undertake affirmative steps to accommodate the needs

---

and education communites over programs for English proficiency.); Lopez, *Bilingual Schooling Comes Under Review*, The Sunday Record, Jan. 31, 1982, at 1, col. 6 (Bergen/Passaic/Hudson Counties, New Jersey) (state legislation debated to alter bilingual programs developed under federal law).

70. 29 U.S.C. § 794 (1982): "No otherwise qualified handicapped individual in the United Sates . . . shall, solely by reason of his handicap, be excluded from participation in, be denied the benefits of, or be subjected to discrimination under any program or activity receiving Federal financial assistance . . . ."

71. Pub. L. No. 88-352, 78 Stat. 241 (codified as amended at 42 U.S.C. §§ 2000a to 2000h-6 (1982)).

72. *See supra* note 70.

73. 442 U.S. 397, 407, 413 (1979).

of a deaf student in a college nursing program. The case did not, however, resolve the issue of the coverage of the section in any more general fashion. The Court concluded that "[a]n otherwise qualified person is one who is able to meet all of a program's requirements in spite of his handicap,"[74] but also reasoned that a refusal to modify an existing program to accommodate a handicapped person could amount to illegal discrimination.[75] The Court's decision left case-by-case analysis as the likely mode for interpreting the law.[76]

The second federal statute framing special education policy is commonly known as the Education for All Handicapped Children Act (EAHCA).[77] Its complicated terms produce programmatic choices for local authorities which deserve some elaboration. The difference dilemma highlights both the statutory commitments and the programmatic choices.

As a state or local activity, public education receives major funding from state and local sources. Through the EAHCA, however, the federal government provides financial incentives for state provision of special services for handicapped children.[78] To obtain grants under the Act, an applicant state must submit a plan on a yearly basis which details how the state intends to meet the Act's objectives; the federal objectives, then, are adopted by the state in exchange for accepting federal assistance. The Act's objectives include (1) identifying all handicapped children needing special education and related services;[79] (2) protecting rights of children and their parents to nondiscrimination in the evaluation and placement process and confidentiality in the handling of personally identifiable data;[80] and (3) mainstreaming, or integrating

---

74. *Id.* at 406.

75. *Id.* at 411-12.

76. See Note, *Employment Discrimination Against the Handicapped and Section 504 of the Rehabilitation Act: An Essay on Legal Evasiveness,* 97 HARV. L. REV. 997, 1009 (1984). *See generally* Wegner, *The Antidiscrimination Model Reconsidered: Ensuring Equal Opportunity Without Respect to Handicap Under Section 504 of the Rehabilitation Act of 1973,* 69 CORNELL L. REV. 401, 452-58 (1984) (discussing Southeastern Community College v. Davis, 442 U.S. 397 (1979)).

77. Pub. L. No. 94-142, 89 Stat. 773 (1975) (codified as amended at 20 U.S.C. §§ 1400-1461 (1982)). *See generally* Stark, *Tragic Choices in Special Education: The Effect of Scarce Resources on the Implementation of Pub. L. No. 94-142,* 14 CONN. L. REV. 447, 479-84 (1982) (describes how EAHCA works); Note, *Enforcing the Right to an "Appropriate" Education: The Education for All Handicapped Children Act of 1975,* 92 HARV. L. REV. 1103, 1104-08 (1979) (discusses history of EAHCA and statutory framework).

78. 20 U.S.C. §§ 1411-1420 (1982) (grant programs). Also, the Act defines "handicap" broadly; and its interpretive regulations focus on whether a child has an impairment and because of that impairment needs special education and related services. 34 C.F.R. § 300.5(a) (1984). Aside from such defined impairments as deafness and mental retardation, the regulations also identify "other health impaired" conditions that "adversely affects a child's educational performance." *Id.* § 300.5(a)(7); *see also id.* § 300.5(a)(8)(i) ("seriously emotionally disturbed" conditions defined as one or more characteristics "which adversely affect educational performance").

79. "Related services" are noneducational services that may be essential if a handicapped student is to benefit from education; such services can include transportation, speech pathology, psychological services, physical therapy, and diagnostic medical services. 20 U.S.C. § 1401(17) (1982); 34 C.F.R. § 300.13 (1984). Litigation over the definition of "related services" under the Act has been extensive. *See, e.g.,* Irving Indep. School Dist. v. Tatro, 104 S. Ct. 2379 (1984) (heart catheterization is covered); *In re* San Mateo County Sup't of Schools, 1980-81 EDUC. HANDICAPPED L. REP. (CRR) 502:199 (Cal. SEA 1980) (sign language instruction for child's parents covered).

80. 20 U.S.C. § 1412(5)(C) (1982) (testing and evaluation procedures not to be racially or cul-

handicapped children with nonhandicapped.[81] While the federal government leaves to each participating state the task of detailing the actual programs it will use to achieve these goals, the EAHCA specifies a set of substantive and procedural rights that each participating state must endorse. Substantively, each participating state must guarantee every handicapped child a "free appropriate public education"[82] and an education in the "least restrictive environment" possible—which means mainstreaming the child in a classroom with nonhandicapped children if possible, or if not, then the closest approximation that can serve the child's needs.[83] Exactly what these substantive requirements mean for individual children has emerged as a legal battleground.[84]

Such disputes become comprehensible as expressions of the difference dilemma. Whether and how much to mainstream an exceptional child clearly presents the issue of whether to respond to difference by separation or by integration. The problem is whether in order to overcome stigma, social isolation, and inter-group misunderstanding, a child with a severe hearing impairment should be enrolled in a mainstream classroom[85] or instead in a special class or school for deaf children. As with analogous issues in bilingual education, the dilemma truly presents two sides: a deaf student may experience the pain of attributed inferiority and isolation amid a class of hearing

---

turally discriminatory); 20 U.S.C. § 1417(c) (1982) (protection of rights and privacy of parents and students).

81. 20 U.S.C. § 1412(5)(B) (1982). *See* J. SHRYBMAN, *supra* note 41, at 13-14 (discussing statutory purposes).

82. 20 U.S.C. § 1401(18) (1982): "The term "free appropriate public education" means special education and related services which (A) have been provided at public expense, under public supervision and direction, and without charge; (B) meet the standards of the state educational agency; (C) include an appropriate preschool, elementary, and secondary school education in the state involved; and (D) are provided in conformity with the individualized education program required under section 1414(a)(5) of this title."

83. To qualify for federal financial assistance, a state should demonstrate that it established "procedures to assure that, to the maximum extent appropriate, handicapped children, including children in public or private institutions or other care facilities, are educated with children who are not handicapped, and that special classes, separate schooling, or other removal of handicapped children from the regular educational environment occurs only when the nature or severity of the handicap is such that education in regular classes with the use of supplementary aids and services cannot be achieved satisfactorily." 20 U.S.C. § 1412(5)(B) (1982). As with bilingual programming, programs may differ in both the mix of services provided, and the setting where the services are offered; the requirement of "appropriate" education may refer to both the setting and the mix of services, while the requirement of the "least restrictive" placement refers to the setting—but may influence the mix of services and their delivery.

84. *See* Board of Educ. v. Rowley, 458 U.S. 176 (1982); Armstrong v. Kline, 476 F. Supp. 583 (E.D. Pa. 1979), *remanded on other grounds*, Battle v. Pennsylvania, 629 F.2d 269 (3d Cir. 1980), *cert. denied*, 452 U.S. 968 (1981) (self-sufficiency education). *See generally* Comment, *Self-Sufficiency Under the Education of All Handicapped Children Act: A Suggested Approach*, 1981 DUKE L.J. 516, 519-27 (1981) (discussing varied interpretations of statute's substantive requirements); Neal & Kirp, *The Allure of Legalization Reconsidered: The Case of Special Education*, LAW & CONTEMP. PROBS., Winter 1985, at 63, 71-72 (substance of rights for handicapped children unspecified by law; elaboration depends on individual education plan); Note, *Legal Remedies for the Misclassification or Wrongful Placement of Educationally Handicapped Children*, 14 COLUM. J.L. & SOC. PROBS. 389 (1979) (discussing litigation challenging over-classification and under-classification affecting placement and services).

85. This option could involve some special instruction during part of the school day. *See infra* notes 135-43 and accompanying text (discussing Board of Educ. v. Rowley, 458 U.S. 176 (1982)).

children, but he or she may have a similar experience of stigma and alienation from segregation in the separate class for deaf children. Although the statutory commitment to the "least restrictive" placement might support the mainstream classroom placement, the statutory commitment to the "appropriate" educational placement could be used to support an alternative, and the language of the statute itself does not resolve this choice.[86]

Cost concerns, of course, are likely to influence the placement choices. Although the requirement of the least restrictive alternative was endorsed by Congress to overcome the detriment[87] and isolation experienced by children in such placements, least restrictive placements may be pushed in practice by the school departments confronting budgetary constraints. The administration thus may favor "mainstreaming" or providing some other placement that is cheaper than totally separate instruction. In that case, the placements may fail to provide the benefits of an education appropriate to the particular child's needs, as required by the Act. An extreme case arises with residential schooling, perhaps the most restrictive alternative and the most expensive placement option, and yet conceivably the appropriate placement for some severely disabled children. Regulations promulgated to implement the EAHCA mandate that when residential placement is "necessary to provide special education and related services to a handicapped child, the program, including non-medical care and room and board, must be provided at no cost to the parents. . . ."[88] Parents who prefer a residential placement for their children even when the placement process yields a nonresidential placement must assume the costs of the placement themselves. With such considerable sums of money involved, it is not surprising that residential programming issues are the most frequently litigated topic in special education.[89] Parents favoring residential placements have prevailed or obtained opportunities for reconsideration of adverse school decisions in cases where the school system committed procedural errors in the placement process[90] and where the resi-

---

86. If the statute had included only one of the terms—appropriate or least restrictive—the ambiguity would remain because both terms can be used to support contrasting placements. The statute's inclusion of both terms exposes on the surface of the law the tension between mainstreaming goals and tailor-made education responding to the "different" student.

87. One possible detriment, asserted by some critics, is that programs for disabled people may create the disability alleged. *See* S. SARASON & J. DORIS, *supra* note 38, at 42 (describing "iatrogenic retardation—a form of intellectual retardation that is induced by the very system designed to foster intellectual development"). *See generally* AN ALTERNATE TEXTBOOK IN SPECIAL EDUCATION (1977) (criticizing creation of inequality based on assumed disabilities). One special education teacher described the instance of a misdiagnosed child who manifested the symptoms associated with the diagnosis—and whose parents reinforced and expected those symptoms in the child. "She had been in a classroom with a lot of kids who had cerebral palsy. When we started changing that, the parents took her out of the program. Because 'You're changing our daughter!' They didn't like that at all." K. HOWELL, INSIDE SPECIAL EDUCATION 27 (1984).

88. 34 C.F.R. § 300.302 (1984).

89. *See* Mooney & Aronson, *Solomon Revisited: Separating Educational and Other Than Educational Needs in Special Education Residential Placements*, 14 CONN. L. REV. 531 (1982).

90. *See, e.g.*, Lang v. Braintree School Comm., 545 F. Supp. 1221, 1228 (D. Mass. 1982) (failure to include parents in IEP planning process); Matthews v. Ambach, 552 F. Supp. 1273, 1278-79 (W.D.N.Y. 1982) (deaf child permitted to sue for monetary damages after delay in school placement decision).

dential placement preserved the status quo or educational progress of the child.[91] School systems have prevailed by demonstrating that day-school placements are appropriate even if, on a comparative basis, they are less appropriate than residential placements.[92] The statutory framework itself structures this set of arguments, while the cost concerns propel the schools, and the desire to maximize services motivates the parents.

Where less restrictive placements, like special classes, are at issue for students with behavioral or learning problems, the teacher's interests may counter the school administration's desire to provide a cheaper placement than the "appropriate" one authorized by statute. In this context, teachers may push for an "appropriate" placement outside the mainstream classroom.[93] This very rhetoric of "appropriate" placements may, in use, conflict with the statute's simultaneous commitment to the least restrictive placement. After all, the commitment to the least restrictive alternative was devised in part to combat this very reluctance of the classroom teacher to deal with the unusual or more difficult child. One special education teacher explained that some teachers

> think these kids really don't belong in the classroom or in the school, for that matter. They just basically refuse to teach them. . . . Teacher contracts don't stipulate certain kinds of kids—they just stipulate that you *will* teach a certain subject matter or grade level. It is not right that some teachers decide not to do their job because a kid isn't behaving the way the teacher prefers. I think we've gotten to the point now where we select out the LD [learning disabled] kids and send them off to LD classrooms, the EH [emotionally handicapped] kids go to EH classrooms, the hearing-handicapped go to hearing-handicapped classrooms, visually-impaired go to visually-impaired classrooms, and the physically handicapped go off somewhere else, and the gifted go off to Europe and study paintings, or whatever the hell they do. By the time you pull them all out, you've got this little core group of average WASPs, and that's kind of frightening to me . . . [so] I do a lot of reinforcement of the regular classroom teachers who are willing to work, or at least attempt to work with the kids that I phase back in the regular classes.[94]

The teachers' expectations, then, can lead them to define as different many student subgroups by reference to the statutory commitment to serving individual student's needs. Again, the ambiguity preserved by the statutory commitments to both the "least restrictive" and the "appropriate" education permit the incentives of teachers, the desires of parents, and the pressures of budgets to give content to the law. The statutory ambiguity itself preserves

---

91. *See, e.g.,* Lang v. Braintree School Comm., 545 F. Supp. 1221, 1228 (D. Mass. 1982); Appel v. Ambach, 1982-83 EDUC. HANDICAPPED L. REP. 554:236 (S.D.N.Y. 1982) (emotionally-disturbed child; case remanded for completion of IEP).

92. *See, e.g.,* Hessler v. Board of Educ., 700 F.2d 134 (4th Cir. 1983) (also by demonstrating that parents failed to pursue administrative remedies); Cain v. Yukon Pub. Schools, 556 F. Supp. 605 (W.D. Ok. 1983).

93. *See* MASSACHUSETTS DEP'T OF EDUC., FINAL REPORT: IMPLEMENTING MASSACHUSETTS' SPECIAL EDUCATION LAW: A STATEWIDE ASSESSMENT 56 (1982) (prepared by James McGarray) [hereinafter cited as MASS. REPORT]. Of course, budgetary and bureaucratic constraints may produce simple noncompliance with even the procedural dimensions of the statute, COURT MONITOR'S REPORT, SUFFOLK SUPERIOR COURT 23-25 (1982) (30 percent of Boston schools' noncompliance with court order results from failure to implement IEP requirement).

94. K. HOWELL, *supra* note 87, at 81 (quoting Win Chadwick).

for the implementation stage the dilemma of difference; placement and programmatic decisions receive little guidance about when to favor the "least restrictive" placement and when to find "appropriate" some more restrictive alternative, and these choices express the simultaneous concerns about making student difference matter and not matter.

Another statutory ambiguity becomes understandable in light of the difference dilemma: specifically, the statute is unclear about which children shall be included within the reach of its guarantees and this ambiguity expresses well the pros and cons of identifying difference. Given the guarantee of individual assessments and diagnoses, the Act on its face would authorize the evaluation of any and every child in a state system; given the concern to meet the needs of all children who, because of impairments, need special education, conceivably any child could claim entitlement to benefits under the Act. Yet the procedural dimensions of the EAHCA, which supply the motor and structure for the operating programs, assure protection against labeling a child as handicapped without diagnostic testing.[95] These procedural dimensions express the statute's contrasting commitment to guard against the negative effects of being labeled as "different." This tension between restricting and enabling labeling actually occurs within the procedural mechanisms themselves. The procedural requirements not only guard against unjustified labeling, they also link diagnosis to entitlements: if the testing identifies special needs, the child then is entitled to an Individualized Education Plan (IEP)[96] that specifies the type of services the child needs, who will provide those services, the educational objectives for the individual child, and plans to evaluate the child's progress.[97] The Act further details procedural rights for the child's parents during the evaluation process, including rights to challenge educational placement decisions within the school administrative structure and ultimately before a state appellate court or federal district court.[98]

An evaluative study concluded that the EAHCA encourages lawsuits and gives parents and children leverage to obtain favorable settlements from school systems, but minimally affects the court workload.[99] If this is the case, the procedural dimensions of the special education programs constitute a

---

95. 20 U.S.C. § 1412(5)(C) (1982).
96. Id. § 1412(4).
97. See id. §§ 1401(19), 1412(2)-(6).
98. Id. § 1415(e)(2). Parents also are entitled to written notice of any education decision adopted by the school, id. § 1415(b)(1)(C); they are entitled to access to all records that the school maintains on the child, id. § 1415(b)(1)(A); and to participate in educational decisions made by placement teams, id. § 1414(a)(1)(C)(iii). In these respects the Act implements a traditional conception of due process, complete with notice, participation and impartial review elements. These procedural dimensions can also be conceived as implementing a medical model, which begins with diagnosis and evaluation, and culminates in treatment and review, with opportunities for obtaining second, and even third opinions. Cf. Minow & Kraft, Deinstitutionalization of the Chronically Mentally Ill (Dec. 8, 1982) (unpublished manuscript). The prevalence of a medical model in the special education literature is compatible with the individualized assessment dimension of the due process framework.
99. MASS. REPORT, supra note 93, at 9-11, 27-28; see also Handler, Special Education and Cooperative Decision-Making, in THE DISCRETIONARY DECISION (1984) (procedural rights give parents bargaining power). Some school personnel have concluded that the procedural requirements divert educators' attention from substantive educational questions. P. HILL & D. MADEY, EDUCATIONAL POLICY MAKING

major reallocation of power to parents in the assignment of educational resources and placements. The substantive dimensions of the program remain ambiguous, however, especially regarding what kind of special needs should entitle the child to special placements or services. In the context of this substantive ambiguity, the procedural mechanisms may empower parents to demand an evaluation of the child, and to pursue educational services responsive to his or her needs even where the child in previous times would not have been considered handicapped.

This hypothetical problem is a genuine issue raised by the category of "learning disabilities." Increasing recognition by educators of perceptual and psychological conditions which impair learning can be used to identify handicapping conditions of increasing numbers of students; this category of learning disabilities already includes the largest number of students served by special education.[100] One expert observed that the incidence of learning disabilities in the school-aged population has been estimated as anywhere from one to ten percent, and he noted further that "[a]n outstanding elementary school principal stated to this writer that 83 percent of her center-city elementary school pupils functioned as if they were perceptually handicapped."[101] Although labeling a child as handicapped can carry a stigma, categorization under the Act also carries educational benefits, and parents may seek to use this route to obtain extra services and attention for children who once would have been called slow learners.[102] The attraction of labeling, then, for the purpose of getting services may produce more attribution of "difference" than before the statute, and it is not clear what the stigmatizing effects will be.

Nor is it clear what the labels mean, given these conflicting pressures to assign and to avoid assigning them. One administrator commented:

> You guys at the university teach about *the characteristics of MR* [mental retardation] as if MR is real. It may be real in a laboratory but in the classroom MR is whatever *I* give out money for. The teachers think they are teaching kids with recognizable handicaps resulting from chromosomes or brain damage or parenting. That's a crock. . . . The kids in handicapped programs are in those programs because they made it through a chain of policy and procedure. . . . Funding procedures are the primary cause of

---

THROUGH THE CIVIL JUSTICE SYSTEM 5 (Rand Institute for Civil Justice 1983) (reporting results of study of school superintendants).

100. DIVISION OF EDUCATIONAL SERVICES SPECIAL EDUCATION PROGRAMS, U.S. DEP'T OF EDUCATION, U.S. OFFICE OF SPECIAL EDUCATION AND REHABILITATIVE SERVICES, FOURTH ANNUAL REPORT TO CONGRESS ON THE IMPLEMENTATION OF PUBLIC LAW 94-142: THE EDUCATION FOR ALL HANDICAPPED CHILDREN ACT 103 (1982); STATE PROGRAM IMPLEMENTATION STUDIES BRANCH, OFFICE OF SPECIAL EDUCATION AND REHABILITATION SERVICES, SECOND ANNUAL REPORT TO CONGRESS ON THE IMPLEMENTATION OF PUBLIC LAW 94-142: THE EDUCATION FOR ALL HANDICAPPED CHILDREN ACT, 161 (1980); *see also* CHILDREN'S HOSPITAL-BOSTON, REPORT OF FINDINGS FROM THE COLLABORATIVE STUDY OF CHILDREN WITH SPECIAL NEEDS: ROCHESTER CITY SCHOOL DIST. 19 (May 1984) (learning problems cited for over 70 percent of the children).

101. Cruickshank, *Myths and Realities in Learning Disabilities,* 10 J. LEARNING DISABILITIES 51 (1977), *reprinted in* EDUCATING EXCEPTIONAL CHILDREN 148, 151 (Annual Editions 79/80).

102. Parents may also seek to invoke the statute to deal with a difficult child, and the result may be a battle of experts over whether the child's difficulties are due to "severe emotional disturbance" or simply "characterological" or personality traits—with services following the first label and not the second. *See* In the Matter of Peggy, Fairoaks County Public Schools, Hearing Officer's Decision, (May 12, 1980), *reprinted in* J. SHRYBMAN, *supra* note 41, at 425-45.

handicapping conditions. . . . The point is that a kid isn't officially handicapped unless he's labeled. The labeling process is designed to secure funding.[103]

The service and program benefits available through labeling alter the stigma issue, and parents or teachers may push to label a child in order to obtain extra educational resources. This phenomenon can be called "magnet labeling" and can be understood as the consequences of both increasing knowledge about and programs for learning disabled children. School systems currently struggle to develop definitions of learning disabilities to contain this demand for services and to limit the students covered by the Act, yet nothing within the Act itself provides a basis for these limitations.

Aside from the budgetary and administrative burdens posed by this struggle, the use of special education procedures to make entitlements available for more children presents a new version of the difference dilemma. Inclusion within the programs for handicapped children can bear two consequences, one for each side of the difference dilemma. Identification as handicapped entitles the child to individualized educational planning and special services, but also labels the child as handicapped and may expose the child to attributions of inferiority for this labeling with the attendant risks of stigma, isolation, and reduced self-esteem. Nonidentification frees the child from such labeling risks but also denies the child the specialized attention and services.[104] As school districts encounter parents clamoring for services for their children despite the labeling problem, the procedural dimensions of the EAHCA give parents leverage to express their concern for whatever individualized attention or special programs their children can receive. The stigma issue, then, may be practically overshadowed by real benefits or effectively avoided by converting a minority of labeled, special needs kids into a growing and specially privileged category.

Thus the individualized focus and special benefits of the EAHCA offer a double-barreled version of the difference dilemma: nonidentification of a special need may result in forgone special benefits and yet identification of a special need may produce a stigmatizing label; at the same time, identification of increasing numbers of children as having special needs may overcome the risks of stigma and isolation, but by converting minority to majority, threaten the definitional and budgetary constraints on serving the handicapped. Thus, the legal framework for special education expresses the difference dilemma. The EAHCA embodies an express tension between its two substantive commitments to the "appropriate education" and to the "least restrictive alternative." This tension invokes the choice between specialized services and some degree of separate treatment on the one side and minimized labeling and minimized segregation on the other. Both substantive commitments critically depend on undisclosed delimiters that would give content to the key terms of

---

103. K. HOWELL, *supra* note 87, at 280-81 (emphasis in original).

104. *Cf.* Liebman, *The Definition of Disability in Social Security and Supplemental Security Income: Drawing the Bounds of the Welfare Estates*, 89 HARV. L. REV. 833, 854-55 (1976) (denial of benefits can undermine security and status even where benefits depend on finding of total disability).

"least," "appropriate," and "to the extent feasible." The procedural protections express both a concern to restrict stigmatizing labels and mechanisms to press for those labels as a way to secure entitlements.

The other governing statute, section 504 of the Rehabilitation Act, utilizes a straightforward ban against discrimination and does not designate which programmatic alternatives are discriminatory: does discrimination result from mainstreaming or separate classes, from identification, labeling and specialized services or nonidentification, nonlabeling, and no services? The search for answers to these open questions resurrects the difference dilemma. Are there any ways out of the dilemma? The next section identifies some possibilities, but finds them wanting.

III

FALSE LEADS OUT OF THE DIFFERENCE DILEMMA

Conceptual approaches to bilingual and special education may initially suggest routes out of the difference dilemma, but that dilemma reappears even in such alternative approaches. Thus, at first it may seem fruitful to focus on the relationship between means and ends in these educational programs in order to avoid the problem of recreating difference through ignoring it or through focusing upon it. Similarly, it may at first seem useful to address frameworks for constraining the power of the school so that it does not recreate difference. Yet, upon examination, these alternatives reopen the difference dilemma, and indeed, draw connections between this problem and other problems in the legal and programmatic construction of schooling.

A. Designing Means for Chosen Ends

Finding the right means for desired ends is a familiar implementation problem in social policy. Attending to this design problem, some would argue, may be as or more important than the initial policy commitment.[105] Some means/ends problems take the general form of unintended consequences from chosen means that may undermine desired ends. Indeed, a standard criticism of schools emphasizes the lack of fit between the means

---

105. *See, e.g.,* J. PRESSMAN & A. WILDASKY, IMPLEMENTATION (1973); E. QUADE, ANALYSIS FOR PUBLIC DECISIONS 259-63 (1975). Here, the design problem refers to the selection of strategies in the initial design of the program rather than the mastery of political, organizational, and psychological constraints and resistences to change. For effective studies of this latter concern with implementation, *see* Clune & Van Pelt, *A Political Method of Evaluating the EAHCA and the Several Gaps of Gap Analysis,* LAW & CONTEMP. PROBS., Winter 1985, at 7 (implementation of special education programs affected by political adjustment among competing interests); Kuriloff, *Is Justice Served by Due Process?: Affecting the Outcome of Special Education Hearings in Pennsylvania,* LAW & CONTEMP. PROBS., Winter 1985, at 89; Neal & Kirp, *The Allure of Legalization Reconsidered: The Case of Special Education,* LAW & CONTEMP. PROBS., Winter 1985, at 63; Weatherly & Lipsky, *Street-Level Bureaucrats and Institutional Innovation: Implementing Special-Education Reform,* 47 HARV. EDUC. REV. 171 (1977). The particular concern here is instead with the choice between program designs aimed at creating enclaves different from the dominant community and programs aimed at reflecting the dominant community. *See infra* notes 108-33 and accompanying text.

schools use and the ends they seek. John Holt dramatizes this criticism while telling of the student who handed in the ink copy of her written composition:

> Our rule is that on the ink copy there must be no more than three mistakes per page, or the page must be copied again. I checked her paper, and on the first page found five mistakes. I showed them to her, and told her, as gently as I could, that she had to copy it again, and urged her to be more careful—typical teacher's advice. She looked at me, heaved a sigh, and went back to her desk. She is left-handed, and doesn't manage a pen very well. I could see her frowning with concentration as she worked and struggled. Back she came after a while with the second copy. This time the first page had seven mistakes, and the handwriting was noticeably worse. I told her to copy it again. Another bigger sigh, and she went back to her desk. In time the third copy arrived, looking much worse than the second, and with even more mistakes.[106]

On reflection, Holt commented,

> In schools—but where isn't it so?—we so easily fall into the same trap: the means to an end becomes an end in itself. I had on my hands this three-mistake rule meant to serve the ends of careful work and neat compositions. By applying it rigidly was I getting more careful work and neater compositions? No; I was getting a child who was so worried about having to recopy her paper that she could not concentrate on doing it, and hence did it worse and worse, and would probably do the next papers badly as well.[107]

The connections between means and ends in bilingual and special education are more complicated than the governing statutes imply. The laws governing both bilingual and special education rely at key points on undefined terms, such as "appropriate," "to the maximum extent feasible," "to the extent necessary," and "to progress effectively." Such terms on their face imply that there are known or uncontroversial connections between the means called for by the law and the ends endorsed by it—or that reasonable decisionmakers could agree about what means will be appropriate, necessary, and so forth. Of course, it is more likely that legislators and judges adopt such terms to hold off for another day debates over the meaning of such delimiters. The question of how to connect means to ends in bilingual and special education, not surprisingly, triggers renewed controversy. But it may be surprising to see the difference dilemma reappearing in these controversies.

1. *The Design Dilemma and Bilingual Education.* The problem of connecting means to ends was left open in *Lau v. Nichols*:[108] what programs should be designed to remedy the functional exclusion of students without English proficiency in regular classes taught in English? This design problem is especially tricky for two reasons. First, the term "exclusion" appeared in the governing civil rights statute framed with racial segregation in mind,[109] but the "exclusion" of the non-English-proficient students was not due to segregation, but to the lack of fit between the school program and the students' own backgrounds. The remedy obviously could not simply be to integrate such stu-

---

106. J. HOLT, HOW CHILDREN FAIL 133-34 (1964).
107. *Id.*
108. 414 U.S. 563, 564-65 (1974); *see supra* text accompanying notes 48-52.
109. Civil Rights Act of 1964, § 601, 78 Stat. 252 (codified at 42 U.S.C. § 2000d (1982)).

dents into existing classrooms, for it was in such classrooms that these students were effectively excluded from the educational benefits.

Secondly, and also growing from experience with racial segregation of school children, the concern for student self-esteem as a key element in equal educational opportunity complicates the design of bilingual programs. As one observer of the federal legislative process on the subject observed:

> Arguments about the degree to which assimilation process assaulted a child's sense of self-worth led in one programmatic direction, while contentions about the Hispanic level of academic achievement and school dropout rate,[110] had they been the most compelling, would have led in quite another. That is, concern solely about the academic record of children of limited-English-speaking ability would have led to unequivocal support for the establishment of transitional programs aimed at giving those children an equal educational start. But concern about the psychological harm of forced assimilation lent legitimacy to the establishment of programs which aimed to promote not scholastic achievement but a greater sense of self-worth by means of linguistic and cultural maintenance. They lent legitimacy to schools within schools, to ethnic educational enclaves run for and by ethnic groups.[111]

It is important to clarify that the concern for students' senses of self-worth marks debates over the means, not the ends, of schooling. Few if any supporters of bilingual-bicultural education dispute that a major goal of such programs is to develop the students' proficiency in English.[112] To some extent, the choice among different types of means to achieve this end may be resolved with reference to empirical studies of the effectiveness of contrasting programs. But such studies are currently inconclusive, and the debate focuses not on effectiveness but on the issue of stigmatizing cultural difference.[113]

The design problem thus juxtaposes preoccupation with English-language proficiency against preoccupation with creating environments within schools that are more hospitable to children who feel alien there. The first preoccupation would focus on academic skills and English language acquisition; the second would address the cultural contrasts between child and school. Designing programs solely responsive to either one of these concerns could exacerbate the children's educational problems.[114] The difference dilemma, in short, reappears at this point: how to address the needs of students who

---

110. Much of the debate over bilingual education focuses on the Hispanic experience.

111. *Implications of Bilingualism: Education,* in THE NEW BILINGUALISM: AN AMERICAN DILEMMA 155-56 (M. Ridge ed. 1981) (quoting Abigail Thernstrom) (proceedings of a conference sponsored by the Center for Study of the American Experience, The Annenberg School of Communications, University of Southern California, May 1980).

112. *See* Lanier, *Teaching with Subtitles,* CHI. MAG., June 1984, at 163.

113. There are unresolved debates over the effectiveness of different programs simply in terms of producing English proficiency. *See* L. BACA & H. CERVANTES, THE BILINGUAL SPECIAL EDUCATION INTERFACE 332-33 (1984) (reviewing debate over effectiveness of bilingual programs); Baker & de Kanter, *supra* note 56, at 33 (reviewing studies); Carpenter-Huffman & Samulon, *supra* note 56, at 141, 147, 169 (students in self-contained classrooms at the elementary level receive more language-assistance instruction than children in pull-out programs). The debate at this point occurs even at the level of social science measures. *See* A. COHEN, M. BRUCK, F. RODRIGUEZ-BROWN, BILINGUAL EDUCATION SERIES 6 (Center for Applied Linguistics 1982) (methodological debates).

114. *Compare* Serna v. Portales Mun. Schools, 499 F.2d 1147, 1150 (10th Cir. 1974) ("[New Mexico teacher] testified that 'until a child developed a good self image not even teaching English as a second language would be successful. If a child can be made to feel worthwhile in school then he will learn even with a poor English program'.") *with* Glazer, *Pluralism and Ethnicity,* in THE NEW BILIN-

are considered different without stigmatizing them or undermining their identity becomes a salient concern in crafting programs for children whose primary language is not English.

This link between the difference dilemma and the problem of designing means and ends in bilingual education is highlighted by two early bilingual cases which made use of intelligence testing (IQ scores) to arrive at contrasting conceptions of how to implement the mandate of bilingual education. In *Serna v. Portales Municipal Schools*,[115] the district court found that IQ test scores for Spanish-surnamed children were different from those of the "average" child in the same school system.[116] The court concluded that, compared with the performance of the other students, the performance of the Spanish-surnamed children was not what it should have been. The court added that "[c]oupled with the testimony of educational experts regarding the negative impact upon Spanish-surnamed children when they are placed in a school atmosphere which does not adequately reflect the educational needs of this minority," the evidence established a legal violation.[117] In affirming, the Court of Appeals for the Tenth Circuit observed that "[i]ntelligence quotient tests show that Lindsey students fall further behind as they move from the first to the fifth grade."[118] The district court ordered a curriculum plan to implement bilingual training and bicultural outlook programs and also directed that a special effort be made to recruit and hire bilingual teachers.[119]

In contrast, in *Otero v. Mesa County Valley School District No. 51*,[120] the district court accepted the school department's theory that differentials in student abilities, rather than linguistic deficiencies, explained the educational problems of Mexican-American students.[121] The court then rejected the plaintiffs' claim that poor school performance by Chicano students occurs because the school district

> has created a school system oriented for middle class Anglo children, has staffed that system with non-Chicano personnel who do not understand and cannot relate with Chicano students who are linguistically and culturally different, to the extent that the Chicano students and their parents do not feel that School District 51 is "their" school.[122]

GUALISM: AN AMERICAN DILEMMA 55, 62-63 (M. Ridge ed. 1981) (pragmatic advantages to assimilation, given public school control of access to higher education).

115. 351 F. Supp. 1279 (D.N.M. 1972), *aff'd*, 499 F.2d 1147 (10th Cir. 1974).

116. *Id.* at 1281-82.

117. *Id.* at 1282. The district court relied on the equal protection clause of the Constitution. *Id.* The court of appeals affirmed, but relied on Lau v. Nichols. *See* 499 F.2d at 1153.

118. 499 F.2d at 1150.

119. Serna v. Portales Mun. Schools, 351 F. Supp. 1279, 1283 (D.N.M. 1972), *aff'd*, 499 F.2d 1147, 1154 (10th Cir. 1974) (expressing approval of district courts' plan).

120. 408 F. Supp. 162 (D. Colo. 1975), *remanded*, 568 F.2d 1312 (10th Cir. 1977), *on remand*, 470 F. Supp. 326 (D. Colo. 1979), *aff'd*, 628 F.2d 1271 (10th Cir. 1980). A useful case study of the suit appears in M. REBELL & A. BLOCK, EDUCATIONAL POLICY MAKING AND THE COURTS: AN EMPIRICAL STUDY OF JUDICIAL ACTIVISM 147-74 (1982).

121. M. REBELL & A. BLOCK, *supra* note 120, at 162-63, 173-74. The case study explains more explicitly than does the opinion itself the use of IQ tests. The court also relied on achievement tests, and on studies of the use of Spanish in the students' homes. 408 F. Supp. at 165-66.

122. Plaintiffs' Opening Statement, quoted in *Otero*, 408 F. Supp. 162, 164 (D. Colo. 1975). Plantiffs also explained that their case would show that "[t]he cultural and linguistic makeup of Chi-

The district court rejected the plaintiffs' request for bilingual-bicultural instruction[123] and the hiring of more bilingual teachers.[124] The court concluded that relatively few students had no English proficiency, and the transitional English instruction already offered them by the school district was an adequate means for dealing with any legal obligation the school had to eliminate inequality.[125] Thus, the *Otero* court relied on IQ tests—the very measure used in *Serna* to identify a language barrier requiring a remedy—to rule out the need to remedy a language barrier.[126]

What explains this inconsistent use of IQ scores? What different conceptions of the remedy for inequality may be at work here? In *Serna*, the scores are treated as "outcome" measures, capturing the effect of schooling and therefore measuring what happens when schools make the error of ignoring student difference. According to this view, the school systems' failure to create an environment hospitable to the different cultural, ethnic, and language experiences of the Spanish-surnamed children produced the discrepancy in IQ scores and justified the remedy of bilingual and bicultural programming, as well as the hiring of bilingual teachers. Here, then, liability is founded on the error of ignoring difference where it exists.

Otero, in contrast, used the IQ scores without assuming any pre-existing difference between Mexican-American students and other students. The difference in their IQ scores, then, could be used to explain their different experiences in school, and to rule out the claim for curricular and staff changes to address the identity and self-esteem of the Mexican-American studies. This use of the IQ scores relied on a conception of the right means to achieve the ends of bilingual education: the right means should alter the educational system as little as possible, and deploy short-term intensive English instruction for the few students unable to function in the mainstream classroom.

cano students has posed an educational incompatibility between District 51's educational program and the learning style of these students to the degree that they do not effectively and equally benefit from the school's program as compared to Anglo students." *Id.* at 163-64.

123.   The court may have been influenced by the Tenth Circuit's decision in Keyes v. School Dist. No. 1, 521 F.2d 465, 480 (10th Cir. 1975), *cert. denied*, 423 U.S. 1066 (1976), which rejected a bilingual education plan designed by the same expert used in *Otero;* both the appellate court in *Keyes* and the district court in *Otero* emphasized the importance of state and local control rather than judicial intervention for dealing with the problem of minority students. *See id.* at 482; *Otero*, 408 F. Supp. at 171-72; *see also* Teitelbaum & Hiller, *Bilingual Education: The Legal Mandate*, 47 HARV. EDUC. REV. 138, 151 (1977) (discussing *Keyes* and *Otero*.)

124.   Plaintiffs argued that the school district's hiring practices produced an environment alien to the Chicano children; plaintiffs couched their claim as an employment discrimination issue. The district court initially rejected plaintiffs' employment discrimination claim on the grounds that they lacked standing to assert it; on remand from the court of appeals, the district court concluded that the plaintiffs failed to establish discriminatory intent in the school district's employment practices, and also accepted the school board's nondiscriminatory reasons for statistical evidence of discrimination against Chicano job applicants. Otero v. Mesa County Valley School Dist. No. 51, 470 F. Supp. 326, 327 (D. Colo. 1979), *aff'd*, 628 F.2d 1271 (10th Cir. 1980).

125.   408 F. Supp. at 168-70. Plaintiffs' claims were couched in constitutional terms; the court found no constitutional violation and compliance with state and federal statutes.

126.   The *Otero* court similarly relied on standardized English proficiency tests, 408 F. Supp. at 165-66.

The link between the use of the IQ scores and the implicit choice of means for bilingual education becomes apparent in critiques of this testing method. These critiques further expose the difference dilemma, even at this level of technical debate about testing. The *Otero* court's reliance on IQ scores could be challenged for failure to acknowledge the cultural and linguistic bias of the tests themselves.[127] In a sense, relying on tests of "intelligence" to explain why students without English proficiency perform less well in school than other students confirms a tautology, because intelligence is defined in terms of mastery of English language skills. Some commentators have observed that the math scores of Chicano students more closely approximate the scores of Anglo students; this implies that the greater disparity in the language arts scores reflects difficulty with the verbal content of the tests.[128] Thus, it is possible to criticize the *Otero* court for its failure to understand how ignoring pre-existing differences can recreate them.

It is equally important, however, to consider the other side of the difference dilemma: does focusing on difference also re-establish it? In particular, starting with the premise that IQ tests do not test innate ability, the tests nonetheless may accurately identify those students who are not likely to do well in the classroom designed for Anglo children.[129] So long as those measures of classroom success are not being challenged as discriminatory, disparities in the IQ scores support educational programming geared toward those traditional classroom success measures, not toward the language and cultural identities of Mexican-American children.[130]

Thus, the *Otero* court may well have applied a tautology by using IQ scores to explain the school problems of Mexican-American students, but the design of means to solve the discrimination problem must take into account the real likelihood that the same Anglo measures of success will be applied to the Mexican-American children at each point throughout the school system, and

---

127. To the extent that plaintiffs raised this issue at trial, it was rebutted by the defense expert who claimed his methodology compensated for any alleged bias. M. REBELL & A. BLOCK, *supra* note 120, at 163-64.

128. M. REBELL & A. BLOCK, *supra* note 120, at 163-64; *cf.* Hobson v. Hansen, 269 F. Supp. 401 (D.D.C. 1967), *aff'd in part and appeal dismissed in part, sub nom.* Smuck v. Hobson, 408 F.2d 175 (D.C. Cir. 1969) (en banc) (rejecting use of scholastic aptitude tests in assigning students to tracks due to racial and socio-economic impact); Light & Smith, *Social Allocation Models of Intelligence: A Methodological Inquiry*, 39 HARV. EDUC. REV. 484 (1969) (bias problems in intelligence testing). *See generally* S. GOULD, THE MISMEASURE OF MAN (1981) (racial, class, and sex bias historically expressed in theories and testing of intelligence); Kirp, *Schools as Sorters: The Constitutional and Policy Implications of Student Classification*, 121 U. PA. L. REV. 705, 726-30 (1973) (reviewing research on student classification).

129. *See* Blatt & Garfunkel, *Psycho-Educational Assessment, Curriculum Development, and Clinical Research with the 'Different Child'*, in AN ALTERNATIVE TEXTBOOK IN SPECIAL EDUCATION 277, 288 (1977) (IQ as good predictor of academic success, and generally used as such); Goodman, *De Facto School Segregation: A Constitutional and Empirical Analysis*, 60 CALIF. L. REV. 275, 434-35 (1972) (IQ tests reflect endowment and experience and accurately identify those students unlikely to do well in mainstream classroom).

130. Success measures that vary from the traditional ones need not undercut the commitment to English proficiency. *See supra* note 112 and accompanying text (discussing importance of learning English to supporters of bilingual-bicultural education).

beyond. English language and American culture will continue to measure the students' success and future opportunities. Nathan Glazer put it this way:

> One will never do as well in the United States living in Spanish, or French, or Yiddish, or Chinese, as one will do living, learning, and working in English. . . . [it] is therefore a naive argument to say that putting bilingual/bicultural education into the public school curriculum will make a significant difference in affecting the general respect in which a given culture and language are held.[131]

Failing to acknowledge the way in which all children in this sense are similarly situated to the school criteria for success could produce programming that reinforces the differences of the already stigmatized groups. The two sides of the difference dilemma, accordingly, may take on competing conceptions of means and ends. Should we create an enclave of Chicano language and culture within the school to bolster the student's self-esteem and ability to perform well in school? The enclave would include more teachers with a background in the language and culture, and more curricular attention to and acknowledgment of that cultural identity, even in the development of English-language skills. Or should we instead create limited, transitional programs to give Chicano students basic language skills and then incorporate them as soon as possible within the classroom designed for the rest of the students?

Arguments for and against replicating the larger community within the school as the best means of preparation are met by arguments for and against creating an alternative, tailored environment within the school to support individual student development. Replicating the larger social order within the school would involve creating the school as a community where English is the dominant language and proficiency in it is not only expected, but is sought through immersion or intensive instruction; the medium is the message, and the school's own commitment to English as the dominant language is expressed through its required use of English in the classroom, hallways, and life of the school. There are problems with this approach, however. It may actually not produce English proficiency among non-English native speakers.[132] It may undermine such students by depriving them of a sense of self-respect and identification with school culture. Imposing a dominant English approach in the school may reproduce the patterns of economic and social inequality which are present in the outside community rather than offering an enclave away from those hierarchies. Such an enclave would be a safe terrain where each child would have a chance to succeed.

Constructing the school as an enclave, in contrast, would deploy bilingual-bicultural programs designed to create the same combination of comfort with the familiar and introduction to the unfamiliar that the majority-language student typically encounters in public school.[133] This approach, however, could

---

131. Glazer, *supra* note 114, at 55, 63.

132. *See supra* note 113 and accompanying text (discussing studies of effectiveness of different programs).

133. Many excellent schools are viewed by their staff and students as enclaves of one sort or another. *See* S. LIGHTFOOT, THE GOOD HIGH SCHOOL: PORTRAITS OF CHARACTER AND CULTURE 321-22 (1983) (discussing Milton academy and parochial schools); *cf.* Cover, *The Supreme Court, 1982*

impede the minority-language child's fluency in English. It might also shore up values and attitudes that compete with the culture dominant in the larger community and create painful ambivalence in the child.

The tension over means, then, may reveal genuine underlying tension over the ends of schooling. Some wish to use the school to transform the society so that different kinds of adults can function or succeed within it, not just to transform the individual child into an adult capable of functioning in that society. Clarity or unanimity on goals would not resolve the means/ends dilemma. Designing the best preparation for a child entering any given vision of the larger community still involves the dilemma of choice between replicating that vision in the school design, or designing some other protective environment. Which route gives the child better opportunities for growth, development of skills, and the equipment for success in whatever society will greet her or him?

2. *The Design Dilemma and Special Education.* As with bilingual education, education for the handicapped could take the form of giving special students experience with an unaccommodating, untransformed world—minimizing special treatment, mixing students with special needs in with other students, and exposing each group to one another as they would be outside the school. Alternatively, the school can be designed to include measures tailored for the handicapped child, ranging from specialized instruction within the mainstream classroom to separate classrooms or individualized schooling and evaluations. Both routes run the risk of not preparing the child with special needs for the waiting world.[134]

The case of Amy Rowley, which was reviewed by the Supreme Court,[135] illustrates this problem. The case presented the Court with the following statutory interpretation questions: What is the meaning of the EAHCA term "free appropriate public education", and what means would achieve the ends of the Act to give content to the term "appropriate"? The Court concluded that challenges to a school placement brought under this statutory requirement should be assessed according to whether (a) the state complied with the procedures established in the statute,[136] and (b) "the individualized educational program developed through the Act's procedures [is] reasonably calculated to enable the child to receive educational benefits."[137]

Behind this language was the problem of devising an educational program for Amy Rowley, a prelingually deaf child who attended regular classrooms from kindergarten on. The individual educational plan developed by the

---

Term—Foreword: NOMOS and Narrative, 97 HARV. L. REV. 4, 31-33 (1983) (subgroup may develop a normative world and seek associational rights for self-realization in normative terms).

134. *See* J. HANDLER, THE DISCRETIONARY DECISION 34 (1984).

135. Board of Educ. v. Rowley, 458 U.S. 176 (1982).

136. *Id.* at 207.

137. *Id.* at 206-07. The Court emphasized the nature of the Act as a grant with conditions agreed upon by participating states, and that if the state has complied with the obligations imposed by Congress "the courts can require no more." *Id.* at 207.

school while Amy attended first grade provided that her education should be supplemented by instruction from a tutor one hour each day and from a speech therapist for three hours a week.[138] Amy's parents objected that this plan failed to provide an "appropriate" education; they believed that she should also be provided with a qualified sign language interpreter in all of her classes. The school countered that Amy did not need such an interpreter because she was "achieving educationally, academically, and socially" without such assistance. Her parents maintained that without an interpreter, Amy understood a maximum of fifty-eight to fifty-nine percent of oral communications, but with an interpreter, her comprehension of oral communication was 100 percent.[139]

Obviously, a major difference in cost to the school would follow from the positions taken by the school officials and by the child's parents. In addition, their positions reflected contrasting concepts of the means to achieve the ends of her education. The school's position looked to the child's achievement and, as endorsed by the Supreme Court, asked whether the educational program was designed by the school to enable the child to receive educational benefits. Because Amy's achievement levels were above average, and she was easily able to advance from grade to grade in mainstream classrooms, the school and the Court concluded that her educational program was appropriate.[140] The parents, in contrast, were committed to a method of communication for the deaf called "total communication," which involved not only lip reading and speech development, but also sign language, fingerspelling, touching, and visual cues.[141] Without such complete assistance, they maintained, she was not provided the same opportunity as other children to receive oral communications in the classroom, or to succeed in life.[142]

Fundamentally, the parents wanted to create a special environment for Amy that would adjust fully for her disability and use the special measure of a sign-language interpreter to provide as much of the educational "inputs" as the school provided other students, although it would be unlikely that the child would have a sign language interpreter with her for the rest of her life. The school wanted to provide educational services which would allow Amy to function and achieve in the classroom setting and develop her self-sufficiency, meaning self-sufficiency in a world not likely to accommodate her special needs.[143]

---

138.   *Id.* at 184. The plan also provided for use of an FM hearing aid which could amplify words spoken into a receiver. Amy had the ability to hear sounds in low frequencies, and very diminished ability to hear sounds in the frequencies of human speech. Brief for Respondents, at 11-12.

139.   The Rowleys relied on tests administered by a speech and hearing expert for these percentages. Rowley v. Board of Educ., 483 F. Supp. 528, 532 (S.D.N.Y. 1980), *aff'd*, 632 F.2d 945 (2d Cir. 1980), *rev'd*, 458 U.S. 176 (1982).

140.   Board of Educ. v. Rowley, 458 U.S. 176, 209-10 (1982).

141.   Brief for Respondents, at 2-3.

142.   *Id.* at 10-11, 20.

143.   *See* Brief for Petitioners, at 66 (discussing legislative history of EAHCA). In further contrast, the district court had reasoned that an "appropriate education" meant an opportunity for each handicapped child "to achieve his full potential commensurate with the opportunity provided to other children," Rowley v. Board of Educ., 483 F. Supp. 528, 534 (S.D.N.Y. 1980); thus the shortfall

Amy Rowley's situation does not seem so dire because, as a gifted child, she was able to perform adequately within the terms set by the mainstream classroom. Nonetheless, the conflicting conceptions of her educational alternatives highlight the risks of each possible means of educating her: without an interpreter she would miss some of the educational opportunities afforded her classmates, and, as a result, miss the chance to develop as fully as she might; but with an interpreter she would not be forced to develop the ability to function well without support in preparation for the day when such support would be unavailable.

In response to these kinds of risks for other children with special needs, some experts emphasize educational services for handicapped students which are specifically designed to help them become competent in daily adult life.[144] Another strategy would supplement the special needs student's experience in the mainstream classroom with sign language interpretation, special learning materials, or weekly tutoring.[145] Different educational strategies have emerged for severely and mildly handicapped children, but risks remain for any child with either technique: the student may be stigmatized by specialized instruction,[146] or subjected to a self-confirming labeling process.[147] It is also possible that the student may be burdened by special services.[148] The student

---

from the handicapped students' potential should not be greater than the shortfall from the non-handicapped students' potential in their educational achievement. The difficulties in measuring either student potential or the shortfall from it doomed this standard, even though it acknowledged the possibility that Amy Rowley's school achievements despite her handicap reflected potential for even greater achievement.

144. I. Amary, The Rights of the Mentally Retarded-Developmentally Disabled to Treatment and Education 71 (1980) (urging social relations, personal grooming, personal safety, and transportation curriculum for developmentally disabled).

145. See J. Handler, supra note 134, at 3-4, 9-10 (special education programs supplementing classroom instruction with remedial help, resource rooms, and consulting experts). Massachusetts, for example, developed ten "prototype" placements based on the degree to which modifications of the mainstream classroom program are made. Thus, the prototypes are: (1) regular classroom instruction with some modifications; (2) an educational program at the regular school with no more than 25 percent of the time spent in special education classes; (3) an educational program at the regular school with no more than 60 percent of the time in special education classes; (4) a special class placement within the regular school setting but mostly separate from the regular educational programming; (5) a special private day school program; (6) teaching or treatment at home or (7) in a hospital; (8) occupational training in a public school; (9) teaching or treatment in a residential school; and (10) combinations of the previous possibilities. See Massachusetts Advocacy Center, Making School Work: An Education Handbook for Students, Parent and Professionals 48 (rev. ed. 1975); see also J. Shrybman, supra note 41, at 26-129 (describing continuum of educational services ranging from least to most restrictive).

146. Kirp, Buss & Kuriloff, supra note 46, at 45-46.

147. See Bogdan & Taylor, The Judged, Not the Judges: An Insider's View of Mental Retardation, in An Alternative Textbook in Special Education 217, 228, 230-31 (1977) (mentally retarded individual describes impact of label on his sense of his own abilities). This problem may be particularly acute for the doubly different child who is a member of both a racial or ethnic minority and a handicapped or special education subgroup: "When a child from a deprived background is treated as if he is uneducable because he has a low test score, he becomes uneducable and the low test score is thereby reinforced." Hobson v. Hansen 269 F. Supp. 401, 484 (D.D.C. 1967) (quoting Kenneth Clark).

148. One child reportedly progessed better academically and socially when psychological services and tutoring were suspended and the academic lessons were programmed for his level and graded less strictly. Sarason, Levine, Goldenberg, Cherlin & Bennett, Translating Psychological Concepts into Action, in An Alternative Textbook in Special Education 233, 252-53 (1977).

may also fail to learn how to function effectively outside the setting of a specially designed school. Consider this episode: An instructor in a residential
school for blind children points out the mantel of a fireplace to a child who is
about to bang his head on it. The child says, "Why don't you put some padding on it? This is a school for the blind, we could hurt ourselves." The
instructor replies, "There won't be padding outside the school when you
leave here."[149] Not padding the mantelpiece at the school for the blind may
train the blind students to be wary about such hazards; it may also permit
accidents within the school.

Nevertheless, designing programs that do not tailor the school environment or educational plans to the special needs of the students could similarly
perpetuate their disabilities. The student may fail to develop the ability to
function, with or without special assistance. Also, integration into a mainstream classroom may produce less sensitivity to individual student needs.[150]
In this light, some thoughtful observers have urged that classification and
placement decisions should explicitly address "facts concerning possible disadvantages resulting from special classification" as well as student needs and
school system resources.[151] The risks of stigmatization from special services
and continual reliance on special assistance arise if negative attitudes toward
handicaps persist in the larger community, and if the adult worlds of employment, housing, and transportation fail to accommodate people with special
needs. Yet the dilemma of how best to achieve preparation for adulthood
remains, whatever vision of the evolving society underlies the means selected.

3. *Designing Means and Ends: Minorities and the Difference Dilemma.* The following episodes further illustrate the design problem in the treatment of
varied minority groups by educational institutions:

—In an all-black urban school, one teacher advises another not to bring up
slavery while discussing the cotton gin. She said, without malice and only with
an expression of the most intense and honest affection for the children in the
class: " 'I don't want these children to have to think back on this year later on
and to have to remember that we were the ones who told them they were
Negro.' "[152]

---

149. An exchange like this occurs in a children's book about a boy who becomes blind. J. GAR-
FIELD, FOLLOW MY LEADER (1957); *see also Unwanted Help*, N.Y. Times, Sept. 16, 1984, at 49, col. 1
(Association for the Blind oppose university developed electronic guidance system because the
system would discourage blind students from developing their own senses).

150. Blatt, *The Integration-Segregation Issue: Some Questions, Assumptions, and Facts*, in AN ALTERNA-
TIVE TEXTBOOK IN SPECIAL EDUCATION 128-29 (1977) (describing this view and lack of evidence on
either side).

151. Kirp, Buss & Kuriloff, *supra* note 46, at 137.

152. J. KOZOL, DEATH AT AN EARLY AGE: THE DESTRUCTION OF THE HEARTS AND MINDS OF NEGRO
CHILDREN IN THE BOSTON PUBLIC SCHOOLS 68 (1968). Kozol continues:

The amount of difficulty involved in telling children they are Negro, of course, is proportional to
the degree of ugliness which is attached to that word within a person's mind . . . What she was
afraid of was to be remembered as the one who told them that they were what they *are* . . . . To
be taught by a teacher who felt that it would be wrong to let them know it must have left a silent
and deeply working scar. The extension to children of the fears and evasions of a teacher is
probably not very uncommon, and at times the harm it does is probably trivial. But when it

—A rehabilitation program for drug addicts creates a supportive, structured residential setting, emphasizing honesty, affection, consistency, and respect for self and others. Students in the program develop skills in honest communication, empathy, and collaboration. On entering the workplace, the students discover that these skills are not rewarded and may even hinder success. Frank conversation and cooperative concern for others collide with workplace values separating public and private life and emphasizing competition and individual success. Moreover, taking cues from others at the workplace, the program's students resort back to escapist and destructive ways of dealing with their emotions—such as drug use.[153]

As these episodes suggest, constructing an environment to prepare students for success outside of it poses risks of failure within the training environment and failure outside of it. Steps to avoid failure within the learning environment may increase chances of failure outside, but recreating the outside environment for the purpose of training increases the risks inside. Not confronting race issues within the school may protect the students from some discomfort during the school hours, but will not prepare them for the hostility about race they will encounter outside the school. Creating an alternative environment of support and honesty within a drug rehabilitation program may strengthen participants so that they can enter the job world, but their new-found strength may depend on support and honesty which is absent and even rejected at the workplace.

Shielding a minority child from community dislike may allow her to develop a sense of self-esteem but disable her from recognizing hostility when it comes her way. In her autobiography, the black poet Audre Lorde recalls racial tension on the streets of New York when she was growing up:

> As a very little girl, I remember shrinking from a particular sound, a hoarsely sharp, guttural rasp, because it often meant a nasty glob of grey spittle upon my coat or shoe an instant later. My mother wiped it off with the little pieces of newspaper she always carried in her purse. Sometimes she fussed about low-class people who had no better sense nor manners than to spit into the wind no matter where they went, impressing upon me that this humiliation was totally random. It never occurred to me to doubt her. It was not until years later once in conversation I said to her: "Have you noticed people don't spit into the wind so much the way they used to?" And the look on my mother's face told me that I had blundered into one of those secret places of pain that must never be spoken of again.[154]

Professor Catherine MacKinnon commented on this incident: "Which is worse: to protect the child from knowing that she is the object of degradation by some members of the community, or to alert her and prepare her to deal with that attitude when it comes her way?"[155] But these problems arise not

---

comes to a matter of denying to a class of children the color of their skin and of the very word that designates them, then I think that it takes on the proportions of a madness. *Id.* at 68-69 (emphasis in original).

153. Bookbinder, *Educational Goals and Schooling in a Therapeutic Community*, 45 HARV. EDUC. REV. 71, 80-83 (1975).

154. A. LORDE, ZAMI: A NEW SPELLING OF MY NAME 17-18 (1982).

155. Lecture by Professor Catherine MacKinnon at Harvard Law School (January 1983). Of course, experience with community hostility may itself be the best educator, but this too could work

just for children who are in some way different from other children. The means/ends problem, and its relation to the dilemma of difference, recurs in more general questions about treating all children, as the following examples of first amendment issues in public schools indicate.

4. *The First Amendment and Schooling.* In the context of free speech and freedom of expression issues, the courts rely on a view of the school's mission as preparing students for participation in a political community committed to freedom of expression and wide ranging exchange of views. The courts, however, also embrace a view of the school's special function, clientele, and problems that may be incompatible with free expression and a wide ranging exchange of views within the school itself. Judicial ambivalence about the reach of first amendment protections within the school displays the dilemma over how to design the means of schooling to advance its ends. Thus, the Supreme Court has declared that students do not "shed their constitutional rights to freedom of speech . . . at the schoolhouse gate,"[156] and "[t]he classroom is peculiarly the 'marketplace of ideas'."[157] According to this view, there is an identity between means and ends; "[t]hat [school boards] are educating the young for citizenship is reason for scrupulous protection of Constitutional freedoms of the individual, if we are not to strangle the free mind at its source and teach youth to discount important principles of our government as mere platitudes."[158]

At the same time, the Supreme Court has expressed solicitude for the special vulnerabilities of children and the "special characteristics of the school environment."[159] According to this view, schools should be authorized to socialize young people, to inculcate habits of good citizenship and values associated with the democratic political system. Free expression issues should be treated differently in the schools than in the larger community; student and teacher speech may need to be restricted, curricula may be constructed to select ideas and values to accomplish the task of socialization. The means, then, for preparing young people to participate in the open debate in the adult community could recreate the same open debate in the schools or arrange a more restricted and controlled exchange of ideas framed by the

---

the other way. This issue has arisen in the context of challenges to the custody of a child by a lesbian mother; some argue that the experience of community intolerance will injure the child. *E.g.*, Townend v. Townend, 1 FAM. L. REP. (BNA) 2830, 2831 (Ohio Ct. Com. Pleas, 1975). Others suggest that the experience itself could strengthen the children:

> It is just as reasonable to expect that they will emerge better equipped to search out their own standards of right and wrong, better able to perceive that the majority is not always correct in its moral judgments, and better able to understand the importance of conforming their beliefs to the requirements of reason and tested knowledge, not the constraints of currently popular sentiment or prejudice.

M.P. v. S.P., 169 N.J. Super. 425, 438, 404 A.2d 1256, 1263 (1979).

156. Tinker v. Des Moines Indep. Community School Dist., 393 U.S. 503, 506 (1969).

157. Keyishian v. Board of Regents, 385 U.S. 589, 603 (1967).

158. West Virginia State Bd. of Educ. v. Barnette, 319 U.S. 624, 637 (1943).

159. *See* Board of Educ. v. Pico, 457 U.S. 853, 868 (1982) (opinion of Justice Brennan) (quoting *Tinker*); Tinker v. Des Moines Indep. Community School Dist., 393 U.S. 503, 506 (1969).

school officials and guarding against disorder within the school.[160] The judiciary wants to allow school officials to arrange a protected environment and yet it also wants to avoid the apparent restrictions on first amendment activities within the school that this protected enclave notion would implement.

The Supreme Court's consideration of this subject in *Board of Education v. Pico*,[161] reveals persistent disagreement on these issues; the seven separate opinions diverge on this means/ends question. Some members of the Court seem to endorse the view that the better means for preparing students for the adult community is to have them experience the marketplace of ideas in the school setting; other members of the Court favor inculcation of norms and values by the school in a setting protected from expression which school boards find objectionable.[162]

This first amendment problem suggests the complications in devising means to ends in schooling; creating a sheltered environment may not prepare students to handle the range of expression they will encounter as adults, but students may not be ready to handle some expression permitted in the adult world. In a sense, then, the problem of schooling is itself a problem of designing means for the end of preparing students for what awaits them. The creation of either an enclave or a microcosm of the awaiting world carries risks. This problem of design derives from the dilemma of difference: it is because children are considered different from adults that the need for a special environment arises, but it is because they are also not to be excluded ultimately from the world of adults that they need some experience with the world awaiting them. The problem highlights ambivalent attitudes about whether children are already more like or more unlike adults with respect to either their abilities to handle free expression or their entitlement to enjoy and learn from it. They are, at the same time, different and similar to us, and on the route to becoming like us.

Conceiving of children as potential adults does not resolve the ambivalence because this conception could support either denying children the free expression rights of adults until they become adults, or granting children those rights in deference to what they will become. A child's potential to become like an adult may seem less problematic than the potential of the

---

160. *See* Tinker v. Des Moines Indep. Community School Dist., 393 U.S. 503, 509, 524 (1969) (Black, J., dissenting) (modify first amendment protections in light of risks of school disruption).
161. 457 U.S. 853 (1982).
162. *Compare id.* at 863-68 (opinion of Justice Brennan, joined by Justice Marshall and Justice Stevens) *with id.* at 879-80 (opinion of Justice Blackmun) *and id.* at 886-93 (dissenting opinion of Chief Justice Burger, joined by Justices Powell, Rehnquist and O'Connor) *and id.* at 894-85 (dissenting opinion of Justice Powell) *and id.* at 908-10 (dissenting opinion of Justice Rehnquist, joined by Chief Justice Burger and Justice Powell). Although all the opinions make reference to both the students' first amendment rights and the school board's legitimate socialization function, the identification of a "right to receive" ideas by Justice Brennan's opinion marks a commitment to access within the school context to ideas expressed in the larger community; the rejection of this idea by the other opinions marks a contrasting view of the school as a more protected enclave. For general discussions of the tensions between the socialization and free expression issues in schooling, see S. ARONS, COMPELLING BELIEF: THE CULTURE OF AMERICAN SCHOOLING 65-74 (1983); van Geel, *The Search for Constitutional Limits on Governmental Authority to Inculcate Youth*, 62 TEX. L. REV. 197 (1983).

handicapped or non-English-proficient child to become like the nonhandicapped or English-proficient child. But in a real sense, the debate over means and ends in schooling suggests that the dilemma of difference arises for all of them. It is a very similar problem in each case: does treating the different one as though he or she were not different promote sameness or confirm difference? Focusing on means and ends deepens rather than avoids this problem.

B. Constraining School Power: The Difference Dilemma Recurs

Another possible approach to the difference dilemma would seek legal constraints to curb school power and guard against the risk that the school may cause or exacerbate stigma for "different" students. Two related strategies for constraining school power arise in the contexts of bilingual and special education: (1) using other agencies (courts, school departments, state and federal agencies) to check the exercise of school power, and (2) according students and their parents procedural rights to participate in schooling decisions. Such strategies have commonly been identified as the "legalization" of school problems.[163]

1. *External Checks on School Power.* The first strategy underlies the pioneering litigation in *Lau, Mills,* and *PARC,*[164] in seeking judicial supervision of school treatment of non-English speaking and handicapped children. Federal and state legislative efforts led to further external review of school decisions. Thus, the federal Justice Department and state departments of education become involved in local school treatment of special children by promulgating regulations and developing programs. This very strategy of external regulation of schools, however, puts in issue the allocation of power over educational policy and programming. Discussions of this power allocation question appear in judicial opinions about bilingual education.

In *Otero,* for example, the district court bolstered its denial of the plaintiffs' request for bilingual programs by express deference to the school district, which the court felt was "making a real effort."[165] The judge added that: "I could do no better, and I do not believe that a federal judge should step in where the school board and the school officials are doing their best and are doing a good job."[166]

The Tenth Circuit reasoned similarly in *Keyes v. School District No. 1,* although it was the state legislature, as well as the local schools, that received the court's deference:

---

163. *See* Neal & Kirp, *supra* note 105; Yudof, *Legalization of Dispute Resolution, Distrust of Authority, and Organization Theory: Implementing Due Process for Students in the Public Schools,* 1981 Wis. L. Rev. 891, 894-98; *see also* Kirp, *Proceduralism and Bureaucracy: Due Process in the School Setting,* 28 Stan. L. Rev. 841, 859-76 (1976) (discussing proceduralism).

164. *See supra,* notes 47-48 and accompanying text (discussing Lau v. Nichols, Mills v. Board of Educ., and Pennsylvania Ass'n for Retarded Children v. Commonwealth).

165. Otero v. Mesa County Valley School Dist. No. 51, 408 F. Supp. 162, 171 (D. Colo. 1975), *vacated,* 568 F.2d 1312 (10th Cir. 1977).

166. *Id.*

The policy of the state of Colorado is to encourage local school districts to develop bilingual skills and to assist in the transition of non-English-speaking students to English. The state legislature has established a comprehensive program for the education of children of migrant workers and has mandated the teaching of minority group history and culture in all public schools. . . . We believe that the district court's adoption [of a different plan] would unjustifiably interfere with such state and local attempts to deal with the myriad economic, social, and philosophical problems connected with the education of minority students.[167]

In contrast, other courts prescribed bilingual programs and reviewed the implementation of programs mandated by statute.[168]

Of course, both in the cases where courts approve school board decisions and those where they supplant them, the problems of constructing programs which do not create or recreate stigma for the "different" student remain. One court acknowledged the complexity:

[l]ittle could be more clear to the Court than the need . . . for special education consideration to be given to the Mexican-American students in assisting them in adjusting to those parts of their new school environment which present a cultural and linguistic shock. Equally clear, however, is the need to avoid the creation of a stigma of inferiority akin to the "badges and indicia of slavery". . . .[169]

The court called upon the Anglo-American students "to adjust to their Mexican-American classmates, and to learn to understand and appreciate their different linguistic and cultural attributes."[170] But there is nothing about the court's power, compared with the school's power, that would make this adjustment less problematic. The injection of the power allocation problem — between federal and state governments, and between school boards and other entities — thus can become an issue in legal arguments, but not a replacement for the choices presented by the difference dilemma.[171]

---

167. Keyes v. School Dist. No. 1, 521 F.2d 465, 482 (10th Cir. 1975), *cert. denied*, 423 U.S. 1066 (1976). Special education triggers similar discussion by courts, but the structure of the EAHCA as a federal grants program with stipulations accepted by participating states frames these discussions. *See, e.g.*, Board of Educ. v. Rowley, 458 U.S. 176, 203, 208-09 (1982).

168. Serna v. Portales Mun. Schools, 499 F.2d 1147 (10th Cir. 1974) (approving district court's detailed plan); United States v. Texas, 342 F. Supp. 24 (E.D. Tex. 1971), *aff'd*, 466 F.2d 518 (5th Cir. 1972) (detailing comprehensive plan for curriculum, instructional methodology, and staff treatment); *see also* Martin Luther King Jr. Elementary School Children v. Ann Arbor School Dist., 473 F. Supp. 1371 (E.D. Mich. 1979) (requiring school board to take steps to help teachers recognize students used to "Black English").

169. United States v. Texas, 342 F. Supp. at 28.

170. *Id.*

171. The state and federal governments, including the judiciary, legislative, and executive branches of the governments at these two levels, have become involved with bilingual and special education. Justicial decrees, administrative rules, and legislative enactments each contribute to the legal complexity in bilingual and special education programming. This governmental complexity may serve to modulate change through the existing structures of power, checking each other and balancing competing conceptions of program directions. The results divert attention from substance to the battle for control, but the legal rhetoric effectively frames policy debates in terms of a government designed to have limited power and intended to provide for orderly change. This legal structure thus resembles the central devices of the Constitution which divide power in order to create processes of decisionmaking which will prevent tyranny; thus, the Constitution contemplates a two-tiered federal and state government and also separated but shared powers among the branches at each level. Protecting these structures of divided power sets in motion a rhetoric of decisionmaking such that controversial matters involve different centers of authority, contributing their perspectives to the problem and preventing any other center of authority from having the sole word. The Constitution's commitment to due process, as interpreted by the Supreme Court, similarly engages govern-

2. *Due Process Checks on School Power.* The second strategy for constraining the power of the school grants students and parents procedural rights to participate in schooling decisions and to invoke review by higher state or federal authorities. This strategy notably characterizes special education.[172] To some extent, this due process solution to the difference dilemma stems from a conviction that granting students and their parents opportunities for participation can reduce or obviate the risks of stigmatization in the assessment of educational needs and assignment of educational placements. According to this view, the opportunities for children and parents to check the school's decision, and simply to be acknowledged in the decisional process mitigate the danger that the school's decision will create or exacerbate stigma either by noting or failing to note the child's special needs. This procedural solution does not entirely eliminate this danger; the substance of the educational placement still will pose these risks.

To some extent, reliance on procedures, like hearings, paper submissions, and bureaucratic review, may divert the attention of teachers, parents, and policymakers from substance to procedure. In terms of the statutory framework of special education, the substantive dimensions are overshadowed by the rigor of its procedural requirements. Once a special education case progresses to a courtroom, the focus will likely emphasize procedure: the Supreme Court so prescribed in reasoning that:

> [t]he congressional emphasis upon full participation of concerned parties throughout the development of the IEP, as well as the requirements that state and local plans be submitted to the Secretary for approval, demonstrates the legislative conviction that adequate compliance with the procedures prescribed would in most cases assure much if not all of what Congress wished in the way of substantive content in an IEP.[173]

Further, the use of procedural due process in special education may expose another version of the difference dilemma. The hearing and appeal structure introduces an adversarial mode to the educational placement decision. This can cast the child and the child's parents in the roles of outsiders or complainers—stigmatized roles—even as they seek to use the process to challenge an educational placement or to seek additional benefits. Once in the legal mode, school personnel may respond with legalistic maneuvers.[174] Of course, not invoking the procedural protections could leave parents and

---

mental actors in processes of decisionmaking that take time, require participation by different actors, and occasion review by other officials.

172. This marks a significant point of contrast between special education, which makes the placement decision on an individualized basis, and bilingual education, which usually makes educational programming decisions on the classroom or school-wide level. This contrast may be important for many purposes, but neither route is more effective in avoiding or resolving the dilemma of difference.

173. Board of Educ. v. Rowley, 458 U.S. 176, 206 (1982). In a sense, the procedural emphasis of the governing statute converts school districts into veritable jurisdictions that promulgate rules, conduct hearings, and participate in the elaborate process of review—and this legal framework incorporates the school into the governmental structure and culture that connects local, state, and federal legal institutions.

174. *See* M. BUDOFF & A. ORENSTEIN, SPECIAL EDUCATION APPEALS HEARINGS: THEIR FORM, AND THE RESPONSE TO THEIR PARTICIPANTS (1979); *see also* Kirp, Buss & Kuriloff, *supra* note 46, at 128-36 (legal procedures and possibility that school personnel view parents as burden).

child with an undesirable placement decision or with a failure by the school to undertake an assessment and select a placement. Again, inattention by the school could create a problem, but attention by the school could also create a problem for the child.

It is also possible, however, that school personnel will take advantage of the legally-mandated procedures to include parents and children in a collaborative process that builds trust over time.[175] Nothing in the adoption of procedural due process, however, assures or even promotes this result. Indeed, the use of procedural due process presents a governmental norm in contrast to a trusting and caretaking norm that may otherwise dominate school personnel's conceptions of their power. The tension between these two kinds of norms can be identified as the tension between models of state power and family power. It is a tension that has occupied other efforts to check the power of schools. Schematically, legal conceptions of family power presume that the persons in power, parents, act with love, focus on the individual needs of actual persons, and depend on mutual trust and continuity. State power, in contrast, is clothed in neutrality, generality, and equal treatment regardless of individual identity, is dependent on official earmarks of authority, and is exercised with restraint and distance. As one scholar put the prevailing wisdom:

> [A] government succeeds when it acts dispassionately, avoids nepotism, and treats all citizens in the same way. Conversely, a family succeeds when it acts lovingly, favors its own, and accepts each member without reservation. The one institution, then, provides justice, while the second offers acceptance.[176]

In short, the power exercised by the parent is presumed to be committed to the interest of the child; the parent's and child's positions toward the world are presumptively compatible and mutually beneficial. The power exercised by the state, however, is presumed to be contrary to the interests of the private individual and must be justified, limited, and bounded. Accordingly, different legal constraints apply when parents act and when the state acts; the state is constrained by the requirements of due process and equal protection, while the parents are restrained only by the state's own concern that parents love and not abuse their children.

When constraining school power is the issue, the contrast between the family and state models of power comes to the fore. In the space of two years, the Supreme Court adopted first the model of state power and then the model of parental power in constraining the nature and limits of school disciplinary power. In *Goss v. Lopez*,[177] the Court concluded that when a public school seeks to discipline a child by suspension from school, constitutional rules

---

175. J. HANDLER, *supra* note 134, at ch. 4 (study of Madison, Wisconsin special education experience). Handler describes a collaborative decisionmaking process in which conflict is treated as an occasion for sharing information. Handler also notes that the roots of this process antedate the introduction of procedural due process by the legal initiatives in special education.

176. Stiehm, *Government and the Family: Justice and Acceptance*, in CHANGING IMAGES OF THE FAMILY 361, 362 (1979).

177. 419 U.S. 565 (1975).

which constrain state withdrawals of entitlements apply, and therefore the suspension must be accompanied by a due process hearing.[178] Here the Court viewed the school's power as state power:

> The authority possessed by the State to prescribe and enforce standards of conduct in its schools, although concededly very broad, must be exercised consistently with constitutional safeguards. Among other things, the State is constrained to recognize a student's legitimate entitlement to a public education as a property interest which is protected by the Due Process Clause and which may not be taken away for misconduct without adherence to the minimum procedures required by that Clause.[179]

Thus the Court ordered adherence to the devices constructed by the Constitution for restraining arbitrary governmental activity and for affording individuals confronted with adverse governmental decisions with opportunities to be heard and to present a defense.[180]

Two years later, in *Ingraham v. Wright,*[181] the Court considered the application of the due process clause to school discipline accomplished by paddling students,[182] and opted for the parental conception of school power. The Court identified a common law privilege entitling public schools to use of corporal punishment, even though the Court acknowledged that the child retained the liberty interests identified in *Goss.*[183] The Court concluded that the cost of interposing due process hearing opportunities between student and teacher outweighed the value of the use of corporal punishment unhindered by such procedures. The Court also relied on the availability of subsequent tort actions such as suing the school authorities over punishment "later found to have been excessive—not reasonably believed at the time to be necessary for the child's discipline or training . . . ."[184] In so concluding, the Court effectively adopted a conception of the school's power as parental power. Parents, too, enjoy a common law privilege to physically punish their children; parents, too, need not comply with due process requirements in meting out such punishment; and parents, too, may be held liable in subsequent actions for damages where the punishment was excessive.[185]

---

178. *See id.* at 574 (suspension could damage child's reputation and interest in the educational benefits, so some process is due preferably before or within a reasonable time following suspension; formal adversarial hearing, however, not required).

179. *Id.*. The Court also considered the claim that due process was required to protect the child's liberty interest and reputation.

180. The Court did suggest that this approach can and should be made compatible with the teaching process:

> further formalizing the suspension process and escalating its formality and adversary nature may not only make it too costly as a regular disciplinary tool but also destroy its effectiveness as part of the teaching process.

Id. at 583. This apparently was a large concern for the dissenters. They viewed the teacher as at times a "parent-substitute" and discipline as an educational lesson, and rejected due process guarantees as a challenge to the teacher's authority. The dissent also conceived of the classroom as "the laboratory in which this lesson of life is best learned;" thus conceiving of the means of schooling as both like the larger community and different from it. *Id.* at 594.

181. 430 U.S. 651 (1977).

182. The plaintiff also raised an eighth amendment claim. *Id.* at 658.

183. *Id.* at 676.

184. *Id.* at 677.

185. *See, e.g.,* Gillett v. Gillett, 168 Cal. App. 2d 102, 104-07, 335 P.2d 736, 737-39 (1959) (parent civilly liable for willful tort of battery of child); RESTATEMENT (SECOND) OF TORTS §§ 147,

The dissenters in *Ingraham* argued that this decision departed from the usual rules that apply to state power and state threatened deprivations of liberty in such areas as traffic regulations and prisons.[186] However, it was this notion that school power is like state power in other contexts that was rejected by the majority.

Accentuated by the short time lapse between the two opinions, the disagreement over school discipline dramatizes the tension between competing concepts of what constraints there should be on power when the public schools act.[187] In a sense, the model of state power, requiring due process, implies that the child is in opposition to the school and in need of the fullest set of governmental rules to guard against undue exercises of governmental power. The alternate model of parental power implies that the child is not in opposition to the school but on the same side, and governmental rules to constrain the school's power are only needed in exceptional circumstances.[188]

Both models conceive of the disciplinary problem as with the individual child, rather than in the relationship between the child and other children or the school staff.[189] The judicial ambivalence about which conception should govern in the schools resembles the treatment of first amendment issues. Again, the special status of children as potential adults—but not yet adults—seems to complicate their legal treatment. As both like us and unlike us, children pose a discomfiting problem. We may treat them as though they were adults in designing disciplinary procedures in school, but their compulsory presence in school signals our view that they are unlike adults. At the same time, denying children the kinds of treatment adults would deserve if threatened with punishment also sits uncomfortably. The unsettled choice

---

150-55 (1966) (parents privileged to use reasonable force to control or educate child, but excessive punishment that is unnecessarily degrading or inflicts serious or permanent harm is not privileged); *see also* Salten, *Statutes of Limitations in Civil Incest Suits: Preserving the Victim's Remedy*, 7 HARV. WOMEN'S L.J. 189, 189-90 (1984) (discussing child's tort remedies for incest). The state may seek criminal sanctions against the abusive parent, again as a legal measure taken after the fact of parental action. *See, e.g.*, CAL. PENAL CODE § 273a(2) (West 1970 & Supp. 1985) (child abuse as misdemeanor when committed by any person); CAL. WELF. & INST. CODE § 300 (West Supp. 1984) (court may adjudge child to be dependent of the court if parents unwilling or incapable of providing care or control or if home unfit due to parents' abuse or neglect).

186.   See 430 U.S. at 696 (White, J., dissenting). The Supreme Court split the difference in its recent decision that students do enjoy fourth amendment protections against searches by school officials, but this constitutional constraint may be satisfied by the lower standard of "reasonableness" rather than probable cause. New Jersey v. T.L.O., 53 U.S.L.W. 4083, 4086-88 (U.S. Jan. 15, 1985).

187.   The same dilemma underlies the historical rise and fall of a specialized juvenile court over the course of the last 80 years. Progressive era reformers advanced *parens patriae*—the state as parent—as the theory to support a specialized court to deal with juvenile delinquency, child abuse and neglect, and other legal problems of children. The juvenile court was freed from due process and other constitutional constraints. Over time it became the object of resounding criticism for the abuses of power administered without such constraints, and modern reforms reintroduced procedural rights for children in juvenile court. *See* A. PLATT, THE CHILD SAVERS: THE INVENTION OF DELINQUENCY (1969); E. RYERSON, THE BEST LAID PLANS: AMERICA'S JUVENILE COURT EXPERIMENT (1978).

188.   The parental and state conceptions of power do not exhaust the possible forms power may take, and the development of a positive alternative to traditional state power that is not modeled on the parental role remains an important intellectual and political challenge.

189.   For a contrasting view see *infra* note 210 and accompanying text.

between the two conceptions makes the procedural techniques for constraining school power unlikely to solve the dilemma that disobedient children may be stigmatized among their peers if singled out for treatment with due process or stigmatized even if not accorded procedural rights. This version of the difference dilemma arises in the very legal strategy devised to curb coercive state power. Rather than seeking conceptual escapes from such dilemmas, we need to learn to live with the tension between differing concepts of power and the tension between varying responses to difference in the particular institutional settings we arrange. Thinking about such tensions differently, however, can help us learn to live with them, and it is in that spirit that the article next offers a different stance toward the difference dilemma.

IV

A DIFFERENT STANCE TOWARD DIFFERENCE

The dilemma of altering the treatment of "different" children without reiterating those lines of difference cannot be avoided by focusing on the means to achieve the end of eliminating stigma, nor by seeking to check the power of schools through other institutions or due process rights. To the extent that educators and policymakers debate the relationship between means and ends, the problem of difference recurs, and it does not become more simple. Further, to the extent that bilingual and special education law and programs adopt the legal solutions of institutional checks and procedural due process, they follow a well-trodden route of legal problem solving in this culture. These solutions, however, at best forestall the difference dilemma, or move it to another point of decisionmaking or implementation. Reimmersion in the dilemma, rather than avoidance of it, can yield a more vivid understanding. In offering a reexamination, a different stance toward the difference dilemma is suggested here, not with the hope of solution, but with the hope of a more productive struggle.

A. Restating the Dilemma

The dilemma of difference is the risk of reiterating the stigma associated with assigned difference either by focusing on it or by ignoring it. Both the handicapped child and the non-English-proficient child may be stigmatized by segregated or specialized schooling based on their perceived differences from other students; yet not acknowledging their differences, and not developing programs for their needs, may make their differences continue to matter and mark them apart, in both identity and accomplishment, from other students. There are several dimensions of this dilemma, however, that contribute to its construction but have not come to light thus far.

First, the connections between difference and stigma, on the one hand, and sameness and equality on the other, must be unearthed. Indeed, equality itself can be understood as founded on the belief that people are fundamentally the same or interchangeable. As J.R. Pole has explained, constitutional notions of equality in America rest on the idea that people are equal because they could all take each others' places in work, intellectual exchange, or political power if they were dissociated from their contexts of family, religion, class, or race, and if they had the same opportunities and experiences.[190] The problem with this concept of equality is that it makes the recognition of differences a threat to the premise behind equality. If to be equal you must be the same, then to be different is to be unequal. Indeed, as some have noted, to be different is to be deviant.[191] In view of the risk that difference will mean deviance or inequality, stigmatization from identified difference is not surprising. Nor is it surprising that stigmatization results from differences which are denied or ignored (but reappears for the child perceived as different from his or her peers) or for the child who is tested as different by testing instruments designed without taking his or her characteristics into account.

This concept of equality, which links equality and sameness, and inequality and difference, is also unsatisfactory because it obscures the possibility that equality can apply to people who are different—with their differences acknowledged—and thereby obviates the need to relate across differences, rather than through the myth of interchangeability or sameness.[192] At the same time, the connection between inequality and difference treats the particular categories of difference used to assign positions of equality and inequality as permanent, and, indeed, treats people as subject to categorization rather than as manifesting multitudes of characteristics.[193] Categories that take the form of dichotomies—same and different, normal and handicapped, English proficient and not English proficient—especially obscure the variety and range of characteristics that more aptly describe experience.

The tendency to construct simplifying categories to make sense of the

---

190. J. POLE, THE PURSUIT OF EQUALITY IN AMERICAN HISTORY 293-94 (1978). An influential version of this view appears in the work of John Rawls, who posits the hypothetical original position, in which individuals abstracted from actual identities and situations choose from a position of equality the first principle of justice. *See* J. RAWLS, A THEORY OF JUSTICE 12-13 (1974); *see also id.* at 72-74, 123-24 (individuals to be treated as equal because luck, not desert, explains difference). The notion of the self, freed from differentiating circumstances, experiences, and involvements with others, has come under recent criticism from many quarters. *See* J. ELSHTAIN, PUBLIC MAN, PRIVATE WOMAN 344-45 (1981)(analysis of class rather than individualism may produce equality); M. SANDEL, LIBERALISM AND THE LIMITS OF JUSTICE 171-74 (1982) (self is constituted in part by family and community membership); M. WALZER, SPHERES OF JUSTICE 255-62, 271-80 (1983) (criticizing Rawls).

191. Gilligan, *In a Different Voice: Women's Conceptions of Self and of Morality,* 47 HARV. EDUC. REV. 481, 482 (1977); A. LORDE, *Age, Race, Class and Sex: Women Redefining Difference,* in SISTER OUTSIDER: ESSAYS AND SPEECHES 114, 116 (1984).

192. Some recent psychological work identifies the theory of personality development as a root to this problem of equality and difference. In particular, the development of the child's sense of self in opposition to the mother has undergirded earlier studies of personality development, and supported an idea of individual identity as preoccupied with differentiation from the mother. *See* N. CHODOROW, THE REPRODUCTION OF MOTHERING; PSYCHOANALYSIS AND THE SOCIOLOGY OF GENDER 67-91, 99-129 (1978); Chodorow, *Gender, Relation, and Difference in Psychoanlaytic Perspective,* in THE FUTURE OF DIFFERENCE, *supra* note 6, at 3, 7-8, 13; Benjamin, *The Bonds of Love: Rational Violence and Erotic Domination,* in THE FUTURE OF DIFFERENCE, *supra* note 6, at 41, 46-47. A promising line of inquiry would explore how the sameness supporting equality could be understood as each individual's potential to differ from others, and indeed, to differ from earlier versions of himself or herself.

193. *See* G. ALLPORT, THE NATURE OF PREJUDICE 19-27 (1958) (prejudice founded on categorical thinking and overgeneralization).

complicated world may well be inevitable,[194] but treating the categories as though they existed and as though they defined a person's identity and worth is another matter. Treating the individual as handicapped or English-language deficient runs the risk of assigning to that individual, as an internal limit, the category of difference that carries the message of inequality.[195] This is not inevitable, for the categories of handicap and language proficiency are not the sum total of those individuals, nor are they indications of those individuals' potential or worth. Stephen Jay Gould put it this way:

> Few tragedies can be more extensive than the stunting of life, few injustices deeper than the denial of opportunity to strive or even to hope, by a limit imposed from without, but falsely identified as lying within. . . . We inhabit a world of human differences and predilections, but the extrapolation of these facts to theories of rigid limits is ideology.[196]

Ideology is the concern here because expressions of power, approval and disapproval are at work in the links between categories of sameness and difference and the values of equality and inequality.

A second dimension of the difference problem emerges from the following conception of equality and difference: for there to be an assignment of deviancy, it must be from the vantage point of some claimed normality; for there to be a position of inequality, there must be a contrasting position, not of equality, but of superiority. In short, the idea of difference depends on the establishment of a relationship between the one assigned the label of "different" and the one used as the counterexample.[197] Once noted as a concept forged in relationship, difference no longer belongs to the one child who is called "different," but instead to the relationship between the two children under comparison. They are both different from each other, whatever the proficiencies or deficiencies used to characterize each.

Two insights can be drawn from this notion of difference as dependent upon or created by a relationship. First, there is no "normal" person or position which is itself free from being different: even as a hearing-disabled child is defined as different in terms of the child without hearing impairments, the

---

194. *See* Bruner, *Art as a Mode of Knowing*, in ON KNOWING; ESSAYS FOR THE LEFT HAND 59, 69 (1979):

> There is, perhaps, one universal truth about all forms of human cognition: the ability to deal with knowledge is hugely exceeded by the potential knowledge contained in man's environment. To cope with this diversity, man's perception, his memory, and his thought processes early become governed by strategies for protecting his limited capacities from the confusion of overloading. We tend to perceive things schematically, for example, rather than in detail, or we represent a class of diverse things by some sort of averaged 'typical instance.'

Id.

195. The flexible, individualized approach to special education embodied in the individualized education plan required by the EAHCA helps to identify the variety of deficits and strengths of each child, but the placement process used by the school may recreate categorical treatment, given limits on the school's placement options. *See supra* note 145 and accompanying text.

196. S. GOULD, *supra* note 128, at 28-29.

197. Psychological theories that locate the development of personality link the construction of a separate identity within the relationship between parents and child, which has its own dynamic of power. *See* E. BECKER, THE BIRTH AND DEATH OF MEANING 21-53 (1971); N. CHODOROW, *supra* note 192; R. KEGAN, THE EVOLVING SELF 76-110 (1982); Winnicott, *Mirror-role of Mother and Family in Child Development*, in PLAYING AND REALITY 130 (1982).

latter child is also a "different" child, different from the hearing-impaired child.[198] Both children are situated within a matrix of difference which we use to describe them; their relationship constructs what we mean by difference. Indeed, the "normal" child depends on the existence of the "different" child for the label of normal; it is the relationship, again, that constructs the difference.[199]

But if this point emphasizes the role of the "normal" child in the definition of difference, the second point emphasizes the participation of the "different" child in that relationship. The "different" child may actively participate in the construction and retention of the attributed difference. One educational researcher described an example of this. Rosa is a child whose native language is Spanish and who is at the bottom of her English reading group in first grade. After filming Rosa's interaction with her teacher and classmates, the researcher concluded that Rosa

> conspires with the teacher in not getting a turn to read. Although she often requests a turn to read, she does so in unusual ways: she checks to see what pages the other children are reading, turns to a different page, and then calls for a turn; she waits for the teacher to start to call on another child and then quickly calls for a turn; or she calls for a turn while looking away from the teacher. . . . The teacher organizes the turn taking in the group randomly, so that Rosa never has to be asked to read as she would if the teacher called on children in order around the table . . . . Rosa spends her time avoiding a turn to read.[200]

The researcher concluded that

> Rosa's actions make sense when one considers her beginning reading skills, the competitive pressures of the classroom, and the teacher's organizational methods. The teacher's behavior makes sense given her task—teaching a child to read while keeping a whole roomful of children busy at other tasks. Together, they behave sensibly in relation to each other and appear to be doing their best. But together they do not achieve trusting relations. Rosa and the teacher do not understand each other's behavior as directed to the best interest of what they are trying to do together, namely, to get Rosa organized for learning how to read.[201]

This may be an extreme case of a child's collusion in the construction of difference; it suggests her belief that exposing her difference by seeking a reading turn would be more painful than retaining that difference.

The difference dilemma, then, depends on the relationship constructed to define "different" and "normal," and on the association of equality with sameness and of deviance with difference. These conceptual associations are in conflict with the mission of schools, which aim to help all students, and which carry an ethos of possibility and future equality for all. As noted in the discussion of first amendment issues in the schools, the commitment to con-

---

198. This is a separate point from the real possibility that this child has still other impairments or strengths not relevant to the question of hearing.

199. Hegel's master/slave discussion elaborates this point: the master needs the slave for the master to be recognized as master, and therefore constructs a relationship of dominance and submission rather than negating or destroying the slave. G. HEGEL, PHENOMENOLOGY OF SPIRIT 141-50 (1952).

200. McDermott, *Social Relations as Contexts for Learning in School*, in KNOWLEDGE AND VALUES IN SOCIAL AND EDUCATIONAL RESEARCH 252, 257-58 (E. Bredo & W. Feinberg eds. 1982).

201. *Id.*

sider all children as potential participants in the adult community, however far from that they currently may seem, challenges the association of the child's difference from the adult with deviance, and urges efforts to prepare the child for adulthood. How can this set of values in schooling survive the difference dilemma? Other than describing as vividly as possible the nature of this dilemma, what strategies for dealing with it might reduce the risks of recreating stigma by either ignoring or focusing upon it?

B. Toward a Different Stance

Understanding that stigma is a likely risk so long as "difference" means "deviance" rather than equality exposes the following problem: how can equality be achieved given the acknowledgment of difference? In a sense, this is the problem buried within the difference dilemma: the fear of reiterating difference, whether by acknowledgment or nonacknowledgement, arises as long as difference carries stigma and precludes equality. Locating difference in the relationship rather than in the person or group called "different" may permit a new stance toward the problem of stigma. Focusing on the relationship or matrix in which difference is created may offer people the chance to acknowledge difference and not locate it in another who then is unequal, but instead in the relationship used to define that "difference." More simply, this set of rather abstract arguments can justify looking at the problem of difference as a shared problem of relationships and contexts—a problem requiring a collaborative solution to change the very matrix of difference. The goal is not to pretend that differences are not noticed, nor that all students are the same, nor to focus on the students who are "different" as the problem, but instead to identify as the problem the shared context in which difference appears. The dilemma of difference will not disappear, but struggles with it may prove more fruitful from this shifted stance toward the shared problem of difference.[202]

C. Some Examples and Some Continuing Problems

1. *Parents of Special Education Students.* An initial example of a school system's shift in stance on the issue of difference appears in Joel Handler's study of special education in Madison, Wisconsin.[203] The focus in this study is on the parents of students in special education, rather than on the students themselves. Parents of children with special needs can be made to feel different from other parents, at odds with the school and obstacles in the

---

202. Who shares the power to make decisions about educational programs which deal with difference is bound to be an issue. If decisional power is held only by people who assign the difference problem to others, who have no decisional power, a shift in stance is unlikely. This article does not address who should be included in the planning decisions or in the definitions of the problems to be addressed by those decisions, but it may be important to include in educational planning teachers and administrators, parents, and students who "have" the characteristics of "difference" to give the planners themselves the chance to grapple with their own involvement in the construction of difference.

203. J. HANDLER, *supra* note 134, ch. 4.

school's response to their children, and stigmatized for having failed or otherwise earned blame. But parents with children in the Madison program describe a different experience. Handler explains that the culture and ideology of the Madison program made special education part of general education, and special education services part of a continuum of all educational services.[204] Also, because all parents are treated as an important part of regular education, parents whose children receive special education services are also considered to have important roles in their children's education. As one school administrator reported, " 'Parents with handicapped children are made more like other parents rather than being differentiated. Parents and kids build their identity first as members of the school district rather than as a handicapped child or a parent of a handicapped child.' "[205] By including parents early on in the planning process for their child's special education program, the parents develop a stake in the outcome.[206] Even with the framework of due process rights and potential adversarial hearings, the school's stance brings the parents on the same side of the problem as the school; both are part of the solution.

However, there are real shortcomings with this approach: parents may be co-opted or moved to a position of passivity in the face of the school's attitude and expertise.[207] Further, community attitudes stigmatizing students may well remain untouched. Again, this example concerns only the treatment of parents of students in special education; when the students themselves are involved, a shift in stance must somehow locate all the students on the same side of the problem, as part of the solution.

2. *A Classroom and a Hearing-Impaired Student.* Imagine a teacher facing a mainstream second grade class which included a severely hearing-impaired child like Amy Rowley. Initially, the choices seem to be to obtain a full-time sign language interpreter in the mainstream classroom or simply to include Amy in the regular classroom instruction, supplemented by some separate instruction for her during part of the day.[208] Both of these approaches treat the problem of difference as located in the hearing-impaired child, and equality as conditioned on sameness. Either a special instructor has to be secured just for her, or else she is to be treated for the most part just like any other student. Any special treatment again singles her out, reiterating the assignment of difference to Amy. A different stance toward the problem would conceive of all the students as part of the problem. The individual teacher would ask herself what approach to the problem would work to the educational benefit of every student in the classroom.

---

204. *Id.* at 21.
205. *Id.* at 22. How children actually feel is not examined in detail in the study.
206. *Id.* at 36.
207. *Id.* at 63-64, 79.
208. *See supra* notes 135-43 and accompanying text (discussing Board of Educ. v. Rowley, 458 U.S. 176 (1982)). Another option would be to send the child to a class specially for the hearing-impaired. Cost factors may, of course, operate quite powerfully in the assessment of the alternatives.

One approach she might take would be to instruct all the students in sign language, and run the class in both spoken and sign language simultaneously. This approach would engage all the students in the difficult and educational issues of how to communicate across traditional lines of difference, how to struggle with the difficulties of translation, how to understand all language as arrangements of signs, how to employ group action to improve the situation of an individual, and how to turn the authority of the teacher into the compassion of the group. This approach affords a different stance toward the dilemma of difference: making the hearing-impaired child's difference no longer signify stigma or isolation while still responding to that difference as an issue for the entire community. It also could bring the means of education close to the ends of individual and community responsibility for problem solving and enhanced individual knowledge. This solution also involves the exercise of school power in a way which resembles love while achieving the legal demands of equal treatment.

Again, this example is hardly a model for all classrooms, or even for many. There is no promise that the non-hearing-impaired students will happily respond to this approach, or that their parents will not reject it as a waste of their children's time.[209] Moreover, an analogous approach to bilingual education, such as having each child learn the languages other children use at home, would be unwieldy and likely to provoke massive opposition. Nonetheless, the learning value of the experience for all the children could be defended. Struggling to be understood in a language that feels foreign would provide an important lesson to each child about their shared problems and about the abilities and disabilities of each student. Once located, the problem of difference in this shared context could alleviate the risk of stigma, while deepening each child's sense of what it means to live in a social world.

An analogous stance toward the problem of the unmanageable child already contributes to educational programs. The unmanageable child can disrupt an entire class, but rather than simply placing the child in isolation outside the classroom, one alternative is to pair two teachers who may send an unmanageable child to each other's classroom. Significantly, the procedure is introduced to the entire class in a group discussion so that the defiant child is not singled out, and when that child returns to the original classroom,

> the excluding teacher reviews the situation with her class, emphasizing the reasons behind the relevant rules and alternative ways in which the excluded child might have acted. Whenever possible her remarks are channeled into a group discussion that can be used to marshal the support of the class in helping the excluded child. Once children have expressed their expected bitterness toward the defiant child in such discussions, the teacher can elicit more sympathetic interest from them in helping him,

---

209. The identification of many different kinds of special needs expressed by other students could complicate the program considerably. How would a blind or a cerebral palsied student participate? Yet these and other practical problems could be worked out within a specific school context. After this article was written, it came to the author's attention that a local school responded to the enrollment of a hearing-impaired child with sign language instruction for classmates, much like the suggestion made here. Telephone communication with Clare Dalton (Dec. 16, 1984) (describing Cambridge Friends School).

especially when she points out that she needs help from the class in teaching the excluded child to follow class rules.[210]

Here, too, the entire class is included in the problem as well as another class. The issue of discipline itself becomes an educational process involving all of the students. The problem, then, is not located solely in the "different" child, but in the demands of the society of the classroom for managing behavior and following rules.

3. *Schooling, Not Schools.* At a more macro level, another kind of inquiry would pursue the features of schooling that could be altered to ease the dilemma of difference. One such feature is the confinement of the schooling process to a given school setting.[211] This feature exacerbates the difference dilemma by making the removal of any individual child from the established school setting carry stigmatizing and isolating consequences. Because that child is treated differently from other children, the association of inequality follows, and the "difference" is deposited on the child rather than on the school setting itself.

Consider as an alternative the creation of supplemental schooling environments so that students spend different days or portions of different days in different settings, with different mixes of children and teachers. Experiments of this nature may be costly or difficult to administer. The idea is worth some attention, however, because at least it provides a different stance toward the difference dilemma in bilingual and special education. Making "pull-outs" and movement in and out of the standard classroom the norm rather than the exception could cut the link between stigmatizing difference and special educational programming. No student or subset of students would be considered "different" simply because of classes or programs outside the regular classroom; the regular classroom itself would cease to be the "norm" against which "difference" is established. Students would undoubtedly take little time in establishing who is leaving the classroom for an enrichment science class, and who is leaving for remedial speech therapy.[212] Nonetheless, a real mix of special classes could modulate the implicit hierarchy of such extra classes, and diminish the implication that difference resides in the unusual student rather than in all the students.

One strategy would pull each student out for instruction in a language in which he or she is not proficient—and make use of that language instruction in the mainstream social studies class for those studying Spanish as well as those studying English. This could diffuse the status issue associated with each language problem, and enrich the social studies class as well. Engaging

---

210. S. SARASON, THE CULTURE OF THE SCHOOL AND THE PROBLEM OF CHANGE 138 (1971) (quoting member of Yale Psycho-Educational Clinic who described procedure implemented in an inner-city school).

211. *But see* L. CREMIN, AMERICAN EDUCATION: THE NATIONAL EXPERIENCE 1783-1876 163-71 (1980) (education historically conducted in settings outside of schools: families, churches, job settings).

212. *Cf.* S. LIGHTFOOT, *supra* note 133, at 358 (students sensitive to curricular divisions as expressions of class hierarchy).

in multiple educational strategies could avoid the elevation of any given means to the ends of schooling. Diffusing power through different relationships within the life of the school, rather than through different governmental power centers directing school programs, could provide openings for more individualized attention, and create trusting relationships between adults and students.

V

CONCLUSION

The dilemma of difference is unlikely to disappear in the near future. The patterns of debate and legal response to the dilemma fail to uncover the ways in which difference is created in relationships and inequality is associated with difference. The choice between programs that create enclaves of bilingual and special education and programs that create a microcosm of the larger community in each classroom does not offer a way out of the dilemma. Developing methods to check school power through institutional review or through due process similarly does not resolve the problem. This article has tried to describe the hold that the difference dilemma seems to have in legal and policy debates over bilingual and special education. In part, this explicit and at times anecdotal depiction of the dilemma is intended to make it more apparent, and less likely to catch us unaware.

The article has also suggested an alternate stance toward the problem. This different stance locates the problem of difference in the relationships that define it, and the problem of stigma in the association of sameness with equality and of difference with inequality. This stance bears a resemblance to the new stances developed by philosophers of science and social science toward the problem of knowledge. There, too, the problem of difference has been highlighted, but in the form of the distinction between the observer and the observed. The scientist-observer, according to recent theorists, is not separate nor totally different from the subject under observation, but participates in the creation of knowledge and in the construction of what is to be known.[213] Similar ideas animate developments in psychology. Not only is the relationship between the therapist and the client a focus for psychotherapy, each individual's construction of relationships to her or his social world and the interactions that occur is attended to by psychology. The development of

---

213. R. BERNSTEIN, BEYOND OBJECTIVISM AND RELATIVISM: SCIENCE, HERMENEUTICS, AND PRAXIS 71-108 (1983) (role of choice and judgment in scientific knowledge, challenging distinction between objectivity and relativism); S. LIGHTFOOT, *supra* note 133, at 376-78 (researcher using portraiture exchanges and engages with the subject, and directly touches them); M. POLANYI, PERSONAL KNOWLEDGE: TOWARDS A POST-CRITICAL PHILOSOPHY (1958) (tacit participation of observer in knowledge); C. WILSON, THE NEW EXISTENTIALISM 39, 49 (1966) (phenomenology rejects positivism's assumption that the mind can be taken for granted in the study of the world); Flax, *Mother-Daughter Relationships: Psychodynamics, Politics, and Philosophy,* in THE FUTURE OF DIFFERENCE 20, 21 (1980) (criticizing view from "empiricism and many forms of rationalism, the subject is considered totally different, substance and process, from the object"); Taylor, *Interpretation and the Science of Man,* in KNOWLEDGE AND VALUES IN SOCIAL AND EDUCATIONAL RESEARCH 153, 177-78 (1982) (subjective meanings and shared meanings constitute study, not just brute facts).

categories to explain mental disturbances is linked to the development of categories to explain "normal" development, and the potential for both normal and abnormal development, for anyone, is the basic message.[214]

Each of these intellectual moves may carry real consequences for moral conduct, for they each speak to the problem of how one person should approach another. As Walter Kaufman put it:

> Nothing Freud has done, and little that anyone else has done, is more relevant to ethics than his success in breaking down the wall between the normal and abnormal, the respectable and the criminal, the good and the evil. Freud gave, as it were, a new answer to the gospel query, "Who is my neighbor?" The mentally troubled, depressed, hysterical, and insane are not possessed by the devil but essentially "as thyself."[215]

Perhaps these intellectual developments can sustain practical efforts not to escape the dilemma of difference, but to locate it as the context for all children, regardless of how we adults may describe their impairments or strengths, cultural backgrounds or language proficiencies. Perhaps then we can hope to act on the conflicting but sincere commitments to the children involved.

---

214. *See* M. Edelson, The Idea of a Mental Illness 105-36 (1971) (shared human symbolic processes the subject of therapy in relationship between patient and therapist); R. Kegan, *supra* note 197, at 76-110 (the construction of the self in relationship to others); S. Minuchin, Families and Family Therapy 4-15 (1974) (interaction between individual and social context is site of pathology and subject of therapy); Freud, *Psychoanalysis*, in Character and Culture 230-52 (P. Rieff ed. 1963) (1922 essay describing elements of psychoanalysis).

215. W. Kaufman, From Shakespeare to Existentialism: An Original Study 337 (1960).

11

EQUAL EDUCATIONAL OPPORTUNITY FOR CHILDREN WITH SPECIAL NEEDS: THE FEDERAL ROLE IN AUSTRALIA

BETSY LEVIN*

I

INTRODUCTION

Starting in the mid-1960's, the national governments in both the United States and Australia significantly increased their level of involvement in elementary and secondary education, despite the fact that in both systems there is no direct constitutional responsibility for education at the federal level. Among the primary concerns of both governments has been the enhancement of equal educational opportunity for children with special needs. Initiatives in this area have created tensions and strains in the federal systems of both nations. State education authorities (and, in the United States, local authorities as well) resent federal intrusion upon what has traditionally been their prerogative and seek more flexible guidelines and more state autonomy. On the other hand, interest groups representing special pupil populations (such as the poor, minorities, linguistic minorities, and the handicapped) press for tighter federal guidelines to ensure that federal funds are spent for the purposes specified and to ensure that those who have been excluded by educational institutions or given less than an equal opportunity are adequately protected.

There are many similarities between the United States and Australia that make such a comparison between the two countries useful.[1] They are both

---

* Dean and Professor of Law, University of Colorado; LL.B. Yale University. The author wishes to acknowledge the very able and conscientious research assistance of James Scott Needham, a third-year law student at the University of Colorado School of Law. Special thanks are due to Dr. I.F.K. Birch, Head, Department of Education, University of Western Australia, both for providing the opportunity for undertaking the research on which this article is based and for sharing his insights on the topic.

1. When an occasion arose to explore the federal role in education in Australia and its constitutional underpinnings, it seemed to be an ideal opportunity to get some comparative perspective on the federal approach to providing equal educational opportunity for special pupil populations. I was invited to be a Visiting Fellow at the University of Western Australia, in Perth, in the summer of 1983. The all-too-brief time spent there gave me, at best, merely a superficial impression of the role that the Commonwealth government plays in education and issues of federalism in Australia. I met with officials from the Commonwealth Schools Commission, the Commonwealth Department of Education, State Education Departments of Western Australia (Perth) and New South Wales (Sydney), the Department of Education of the Australian Capital Territory (ACT), the Catholic Education Commission of New South Wales, and the Goldfield Region District of Western Australia. I also met

modern, industrialized nations which developed from former British colonies.[2] Their language, laws, systems of government, political, economic, and social customs and traditions reflect their predominantly English origins.

The governmental systems of the two countries have much in common. They are both federations with written constitutions[3] and judicial review.[4] Both countries, prior to unification by federation, consisted of collections of self-governing Crown colonies. Each colony was independent of the others, sometimes very much so.[5] Both countries adopted a political system that

---

with Justice Lionel Murphy of the High Court of Australia, several federal judges, a number of lawyers, and members of the education and law faculties at several universities; I visited several elementary and secondary schools and teachers. I am extremely grateful to all those who gave so generously of their time to try to enlighten me. The errors and misunderstandings that undoubtedly have crept into this article are my own—surely due, in part, to the sensory overload I experienced in the six short weeks I was in Australia.

Although I understand that some legislative or other changes in programs may have occurred during the past year, this article, written in Spring 1984, is based on information obtained during the summer of 1983.

2. Australia may owe its existence to the United States. The establishment on the island continent of New South Wales as an English colony was precipitated by the successful struggle of the thirteen American colonies for independence, since Great Britain needed an alternative location to which to transport convicts.

3. A comparison of the language of the Australian and U.S. constitutions reveals striking similarities. Indeed, the U.S. Constitution was the model for the Australian Constitution, although the most obvious model for the federal union of a contiguous group of British colonies would seem to have been the Canadian Constitution. The Australians were concerned, however, with the dominant position assigned to the central government in the Canadian Constitution (in particular, the power of the federal government in Canada to veto provincial legislation). *See* J. LA NAUZE, THE MAKING OF THE AUSTRALIAN CONSTITUTION 16-17 (1972).

At a conference on federation, held in Melbourne in 1891, a draft constitution was introduced, drawing heavily on the U.S. Constitution. However, it was "put by" (tabled) for six years. *Id.* at 87. When the Constitutional Convention reassembled in Adelaide in 1897, various committees of the Convention worked from the chapters of the 1891 draft. *Id.* at 123. The original 1891 draft had provided for the possibility of a system of "inferior" federal courts like that of the United States. These courts, together with the Supreme Court, would exercise the whole of federal jurisdiction. The committee, however, modified the 1891 draft to provide for the possibility of investing state courts with federal jurisdiction. *Id.* at 130-31.

The drafters also relied on American legal precedents. For example, as has been noted with regard to commerce:

> [I]t was abundantly clear from American precedents that the general federal power to regulate trade and commerce with other countries and among the States amply covered the use of navigable rivers as highways for commerce. There was no need to name specific rivers, and indeed to do so would inevitably invite restrictive interpretation of the power.

Id. at 210.

Even more striking than the parallels in language are the parallels in structure. In the Australian document, as in that of the United States, many national powers are specifically listed. *Compare* AUSTL. CONST. § 51 *with* U.S. CONST. art. I, § 8. Residual powers remain with the states. *Compare* AUSTL. CONST. §§ 106-108 *with* U.S. CONST. amend. X. Although a few powers are exclusive grants to the Commonwealth, most are concurrent. The Australian supremacy clause provides that when State and Commonwealth laws conflict, those of the Commonwealth prevail. *Compare* AUSTL. CONST. § 109 *with* U.S. CONST. art. VI, § 2.

However, the Australian Constitution contains no guarantees of individual liberties and rights comparable to those enshrined in the Bill of Rights and the fourteenth amendment to the U.S. Constitution. *See infra* text accompanying note 32.

4. "[I]n our system the principle of *Marbury v. Madison* is accepted as axiomatic." Australian Communist Party v. Commonwealth (The Communist Party Case), 83 C.L.R. 1, 262 (Austl. 1951) (Fullager, J.).

5. In Australia, the colonial legislatures were considerably more independent in domestic matters than were the American colonies.

would preserve most of the advantages and powers that had been enjoyed by the colony-states as separate entities, yet would also result in a unified nation.[6] Within this federal structure, powers and responsibilities are divided between central (or federal) and state governments.[7] Jurisdictional disputes and conflicts about authority are commonplace in both countries.

The two countries have many demographic similarities. Both are essentially urban, industrialized societies[8] with densely populated cities and suburbs. Despite the concentration of population in the urban areas, however, both countries have recent rural origins and still have strong rural interests that play a more powerful role in economic, political and social life than the size of the rural populations appears to warrant. Moreover, because the countries are large and contain within their borders a number of different geographical regions, there are in both countries wide divergences in population density and cultural characteristics that may have substantial influence on educational policy.

The ethnic backgrounds of the two countries also are similar. In both the United States and Australia, there were indigenous people whose cultures and social structure fell victim to white settlers' prejudice and ignorance. The Australians have now recognized, as have the Americans, that addressing the problems these people currently face has a national priority. The difficult issue is how to preserve what remains of their cultures while allowing them to enter with full dignity into the mainstream of society.

Despite their predominantly English origins, both countries are comprised of immigrant stock from many European cultures. Australia, however, had a much more recent European immigration and now a very heavy Asian immigration. In the United States, European immigration waves not only occurred somewhat earlier than in Australia, but also from a greater variety of European countries. Both countries until recently espoused the melting-pot philosophy and adopted policies with respect to immigrants which attempted to discourage or submerge the subcultures of their citizens in order to promote national unity.[9] The educational system was the principal means for integrating immigrants into the British culture.[10] Both countries have only recently begun to question the validity of assimilationist policies and to explore the value of cultural pluralism, and the role that the educational system should play.

In the field of education policy, there are also some common aspects. Both countries have highly developed educational systems which extend from

---

6. *See* P. HAY & R. ROTUNDA, THE UNITED STATES FEDERAL SYSTEM 1-25 (1982); J. MCMILLAN, G. EVANS, & H. STOREY, AUSTRALIA'S CONSTITUTION: TIME FOR CHANGE? 39-48 (1983).

7. *See generally* P. HAY & R. ROTUNDA, *supra* note 6; Hutley, *The Legal Traditions of Australia as Contrasted with those of the United States*, 55 AUSTL. L.J. 63, 70 (1983). In the case of the United States, major responsibilities and powers are also delegated by the states to local authorities.

8. Australia, of course, is not nearly as industrialized as the United States.

9. *See generally* D. TYACK, TURNING POINTS IN AMERICAN EDUCATIONAL HISTORY 123-24, 228-63 (1967).

10. *Id.*

preschool through higher education. In both countries, although public education constitutes the major sector, private schools are an important part of the educational pattern.[11] Indeed, there is some evidence in both countries of an upward trend in private school enrollments.

Both countries divide responsibility for education between state and federal governments, as a result of constitutional provisions and other legal and administrative requirements. Both are attempting to implement the goal of equality of educational opportunity while also seeking to ensure freedom of choice, the attainment of appropriate standards, and the promotion of social cohesion. In seeking to achieve these goals, the two countries must deal with federal-state political and fiscal relationships, sharply declining birthrates, large ethnic minority groups, and the fact that education no longer has as high a priority as other public needs.[12]

Finally, the pattern of intervention in education on the part of the federal government has been similar in the two countries.[13] Both countries relatively recently increased the federal role in education even though the states have the constitutional responsibility for education. For the first half of the twentieth century, there were only sporadic, incremental federal aid-to-education programs in both countries, and there were no federal civil rights mandates in either country. Sputnik was the impetus in Australia as well as in the United States for the first major aid-to-education program. Sputnik triggered the National Defense Education Act of 1958 in the United States.[14] It took Australia a little while longer, but in 1964 the Science Laboratories Act, which was to provide federal funds for improving science education and training (as did the NDEA), was passed.[15]

In 1965, the United States enacted a multibillion dollar act, the Elementary and Secondary Education Act,[16] which along with other measures provided funds for compensatory education for disadvantaged children[17] and for school libraries.[18] Similarly, in Australia, a significant federal aid-to-education act, the States Grants (Schools) Act 1973, provided funds for disadvantaged children and for school libraries along with other specific purpose

---

11. A higher proportion of students go to private schools in Australia than in the United States and "nongovernment" schools (both religious and secular) receive public funds.

12. *See* Levin, *Equal Educational Opportunity for Special Pupil Populations and the Federal Role*, 85 W. VA. L. REV. 159, 183 (1983). *But see* NAT'L COMM'N ON EXCELLENCE, A NATION AT RISK: THE IMPERATIVE FOR EDUCATIONAL REFORM (1983).

13. When the Labor government came to power in 1972 in Australia, education was split off from the Department of Science and Education and a new Department of Education was created. Interview with Kim Beazley, former Minister of Education (June 1980); Interview with Kenneth Jones (June 1980). Similarly, the U.S. Department of Education was separated from the Department of Health, Education & Welfare (now the Department of Health and Human Services) in 1979. *See* Department of Education Organization Act of 1979, Pub. L. No. 96-88, 93 Stat. 668 (codified as amended at 20 U.S.C. §§ 3401-3510 (1982)).

14. Pub. L. 85-864, 72 Stat. 1580 (1958) (codified as amended at 20 U.S.C. §§ 401-589 (1982)).

15. States Grants (Science Laboratories and Technical Training) Act 1964, 1964 Austl. Acts 246.

16. Pub. L. No. 89-10, 79 Stat. 27 (1965) (codified as amended in scattered sections of 20 U.S.C.).

17. *Id.* tit. I, 79 Stat. at 27-36 (codified as amended at 20 U.S.C. §§ 2701-2854 (1982)).

18. *Id.* tit. II, 79 Stat. at 36-39 (codified as amended at 20 U.S.C. §§ 2881-2887 (1982)).

grants.[19]

Despite these similarities, there are also significant differences between Australia and the United States and these differences must be kept in mind in comparing the federal role in education in the two countries. They differ vastly in the size of their population — Australia's population of fourteen million is in stark contrast to the 236 million of the United States — and in number of political divisions — Australia has only six states[20] and two territories.[21] Moreover, in Australia, a local government system with only limited powers evolved and thus there is no locally organized educational system. The original settlements were at the coastal ports, and most of the population remains along the coast today. The tremendous number of local authorities and special districts, each with its own taxing authority, that are found in the United States—school districts, fire districts, water districts, and mosquito abatement districts, for example, as well as counties, cities, and townships—does not exist in Australia.

The population in the United States is not only much larger, it is also much more diverse.[22] Thus the United States has both greater complexity in its governmental structure and more diverse special interests. This greater diversity and complexity has, in large part, been responsible for the proliferation of categorical programs at both state and federal levels, in contrast to what has occurred in Australia.

Both Australia and the United States have written constitutions. Despite similarities both in documentary language and in the structure of government set up in these constitutions,[23] however, there are some fundamental differ-

---

19. States Grants (Schools) Act 1973, 1973 Austl. Acts 1407. Australia's act went beyond categorical funding, however, and included funds for general operating and capital expenses, for both public *and* private schools. *See infra* text accompanying notes 96-97.

20. An act of the British Parliament brought the Commonwealth of Australia into being on January 1, 1901, as a federation of six self-governing British colonies: New South Wales (capital: Sydney), Victoria (capital: Melbourne), South Australia (capital: Adelaide), Queensland (capital: Brisbane), Tasmania (capital: Hobart), and Western Australia (capital: Perth). Commonwealth of Australia Constitution Act, 1900, 63 & 64 Vict., ch. 12.

21. The Northern Territory remains a territory administered by the Commonwealth. Australian Capital Territory (ACT) is the area in which the Australian capital, Canberra, is located. The Australian Constitution provides that "[t]he seat of Government of the Commonwealth shall be determined by the Parliament . . . ." AUSTL. CONST. § 125. In 1908 a 911 square mile area now known as the Australian Capital Territory was chosen for this purpose; it was transferred to the Commonwealth by the State of New South Wales in 1911. Administered by the federal government, the Territory contains large areas of land set aside for parks, natural reserves, and other public purposes, as well as Canberra, the national capital.

22. The lack of racial and ethnic diversity has its origins in the "white Australia" policy. With the exception of its small aboriginal population, Australia at the time of federation was more than 98 percent white. One of the first statutes enacted by the Parliament of the new Commonwealth, the Immigration Restriction Act 1901, 1901-2 Austl. Acts 252 (repealed 1958), helped ensure that Australia remained so. Section 3(a) of the Act excluded "[a]ny person who when asked to do so by an officer fails to write out at dictation and sign in the presence of the officer a passage of fifty words in length in an [sic] European language directed by the officer." This test remained in effect until 1958. It has been pointed out that no unwanted immigrant could satisfy the dictation test, as "all an officer had to do was select a language that the applicant did not know." W. MURPHY & J. TANENHAUS, COMPARATIVE CONSTITUTIONAL LAW: CASES AND COMMENTARIES 69 (1977). This test was used to keep out southern Europeans as well as Asians, Africans, and Middle Easterners. *Id.*.

23. *See supra* text accompanying notes 3-4.

ences. The Australian Constitution contains no such guarantees of fundamental rights and individual freedoms as appear in the U.S. Constitution's Bill of Rights and fourteenth amendment. Moreover, the structure of government established in the Australian Constitution is that of a parliamentary system. The possibility of an independently elected executive and the marked separation of the executive and the legislative branches found in the American system are absent from the Australian Constitution, which requires that all Commonwealth ministers be elected members of the Senate or House of Representatives.[24]

There are a number of important differences between the two legal systems which may be explained in part by the physical differences between the two countries and in part by the way in which the two countries gained independence. The United States had seemingly limitless expanses of rich, arable land and inexhaustible supplies of valuable natural resources. On the other hand, "[i]n Australia, the law bears the imprint of the limitless expanse of the land, but also of the poverty of the soil, the arid climate, and the absence of resources except minerals."[25] Although the country (an island continent actually) is about the size of the United States, excluding Alaska, it is "the driest, flattest and most barren land of comparable size on earth."[26] The population was sparse prior to federation and remains so today. The sparseness of the population meant that there were no local institutions, and that governance — under one system of laws — was centralized at the state level.[27]

Moreover, Australia is a country that "obtained the advantages of independence without having to fight for it."[28] Its isolation meant that there was no danger of external enemies, and the Aboriginal population presented no serious obstacle to white settlers. There was no necessity to formulate an ideology to rally forces, as was needed in the United States to fight Great Britain and later to fight for the preservation of the Union. Thus, the United States appears to have more of an "ideological" constitution and an "ideological" legal system than is evident in Australia.[29]

For this reason, one of the major differences between the two countries lies in the role that the constitution plays. Although the justices of the High Court of Australia from time to time emphasize that the document they are construing is a constitution,[30] it has also been said that they construe the con-

---

24. AUSTL. CONST. § 64.
25. Hutley, *supra* note 7, at 63.
26. *Id.*
27. *See id.* at 63-64.
28. *Id.* at 65.
29. *See id.* The Commonwealth that emerged in 1901, after ten years of consultation and hard bargaining, "was no Phoenix arising from the ashes of revolution or disaster; it was begotten of no great surge of political idealism; it was in fact the child of as hard-headed a *mariage de convenance* as was ever raised in the *salons* of France." Anderson, *The States and Relations with the Commonwealth*, in ESSAYS ON THE AUSTRALIAN CONSTITUTION 93 (R. Else-Mitchell 2d ed. 1961).
30. "[I]t is a Constitution we are interpreting, an instrument of government meant to endure and conferring powers expressed in general propositions wide enough to be capable of flexible application to changing circumstances." Australian Nat'l Airways Proprietary, Ltd. v. Commonwealth, 71 C.L.R. 29, 81 (Austl. 1945) (Dixon, J.).

stitution exactly as they would a will.[31] Treating the constitution as an ordinary British statute means that it has not acquired the sacred aura which surrounds the American Constitution; it does not enunciate any moral principles. Partly for this reason, the Australian Constitution contains no guarantee of rights analogous to those articulated in the U.S. Bill of Rights.[32]

Another fundamental difference between Australia and the United States is the relatively greater homogeneity of Australian law. In Australia the states, when they entered the Federation, had already adopted English law, while some states in the United States[33] had a different system of law in existence when they became part of the Union. One factor lessening the diversity of law among the Australian states is the dominance of English traditions in the training of lawyers and organization of the legal profession. Another factor is the possibility of appeal to the Privy Council of Great Britain from Australian state courts in state matters; until very recently, appeals could also be taken

---

31. Hutley, *supra* note 7, at 65; *see also* W. MURPHY & J. TANENHAUS, *supra* note 22, at 77-78.

32. This omission is the result of a conscious decision by the framers of the Australian Constitution, who, in drafting their own document, had before them the American Constitution but deliberately excised substantially all of the Bill of Rights. *See* Hutley, *supra* note 7, at 65. An Australian Chief Justice, Sir Owen Dixon, explained to an American audience that "this silence . . . reflected the firm confidence of the framers in the traditions and institutions of Parliamentary democracy." J. LA NAUZE, *supra* note 3, at 227. "Why, asked the Australian democrats, should doubt be thrown on the wisdom and safety of entrusting to the chosen representatives of the people sitting either in the federal Parliament or in the State Parliaments all legislative power, substantially without fetter or restriction?" O. Dixon, *Two Constitutions Compared,* in JESTING PILATE 100, 102 (1965), *quoted in* J. LA NAUZE, *supra* note 3, at 227. This explanation may "account for the absence of such American guarantees as those against the quartering of soldiers in private houses in time of peace, and against unusual and cruel punishments: these and other such relics of the eighteenth century were (as it seemed in the 1890s) forever obsolete." J. LA NAUZE, *supra* note 3, at 227. It does not, however, account for the absence of some of the other American guarantees such as equal protection.

The 1891 draft had included the following clause, adopted without debate: "[a] State shall not make or enforce any law abridging any privileges of citizens of other States, nor shall a State deny to any person within its jurisdiction the equal protections of the laws." *Id.* at 230. This was clearly based on the fourteenth amendment to the U.S. Constitution, though it omitted "due process of law"; it also resembled art. IV, section 2 "in referring to citizens of States rather than of the federation." In the end, however, proposals to include such provisions were defeated. *Id.* In part, the proposals' defeat resulted from an opponent pointing out that the equivalent phrases in the U.S. Constitution had been provided mainly to protect emancipated Negroes after the Civil War, and could be very difficult to interpret. Later in the debate, the issue was raised again by pointing to lower court decisions in the United States which were by no means confined to those involving Negroes. A debate ensued on the meaning and definition of "citizens of the Commonwealth" and finally, section 117 was adopted, reflecting only the privileges and immunities clauses of the U.S. Constitution. *See* U.S. CONST. art. IV, § 2; *id.* amend. XIV, § 2. Section 117 has had no discernible constitutional significance in the ensuing years. J. LA NAUZE, *supra* note 3, at 229.

There were other, less generous, reasons for rejecting references to "equal protection." One was a concern about the validity of state legislation that discriminated against nonwhites. For example, the State of Victoria had factory laws that discriminated against the Chinese and the State of Western Australia had laws prohibiting Asian or African aliens from mining gold. These examples were raised by a number of delegates and soon other apprehensions about interference with state legislation began to appear. One of the delegates to the Constitutional Convention has been quoted as follows: "[W]e want, as I understand it, to prohibit any discrimination which is based upon false principle . . . we want a discrimination based on colour." Statement of Henry Bournes Higgins, *quoted in* Evans, *The Most Dangerous Branch? The High Court and the Constitution in a Changing Society,* in AUSTRALIAN LAWYERS AND SOCIAL CHANGE 13, 17 (D. Hambly & J. Goldring eds. 1976).

33. · *E.g.,* California, Louisiana, and Texas.

from the High Court to the Privy Council.[34] One of the objectives of the Privy Council was to promote the uniformity of law throughout the British Empire. The Privy Council said in *Trimble v. Hill*,[35] an 1879 case on appeal from the Supreme Court of New South Wales, that "it is of the utmost importance that in all parts of the empire where English law prevails, the interpretation of that law by the Courts should be as nearly as possible the same."[36] The High Court of Australia accepted this principle and, on a number of occasions, reversed its own previous decisions to bring them into line with decisions of the Privy Council.[37]

Also affecting the lack of diversity in Australian law is the fact that the High Court is the final court of appeal for all state courts, even on state matters,[38] as well as for the new system of federal courts.[39] The High Court is therefore the final court of appeal on all legal questions in Australia, subject only to the remnants of power still vested in the Privy Council. Thus there is no limit on the jurisdiction of the High Court equivalent to the limitations imposed on the U.S. Supreme Court by article III of the U.S. Constitution.[40]

---

34. The Privy Council (Appeals from the High Court) Act 1975, 1975 Austl. Acts 225, abolished all appeals from the High Court.

35. 5 App. Cas. 342 (P.C. 1879).

36. *Id.* at 345.

37. *See* Hutley, *supra* note 7, at 68 (and cases cited therein).

38. Although the section of the Australian Constitution dealing with judicial power is modeled after article III of the U.S. Constitution, there are considerable differences. Section 71 of the Australian Constitution provides: "The judicial power of the Commonwealth shall be vested in a Federal Supreme Court, to be called the High Court of Australia, and in such other federal courts as the Parliament creates, and in such other courts as it invests with federal jurisdiction." Section 77(iii) authorizes Parliament to make laws "[i]nvesting any court of a State with federal jurisdiction." Thus, rather than creating a comprehensive system of federal courts, as in the United States, the Judiciary Act 1903 established only one federal tribunal, the High Court. Judiciary Act 1903, § 4, 1903 Austl. Acts 8, 9 (amended 1976). Sweeping federal jurisdiction was then granted to the state court systems. With the exception of the specialized federal tribunals, established in 1976, *see infra* note 39, this situation continues today.

39. Judiciary Act 1903, 1903 Austl. Acts 8, *as amended by* Judiciary Amendment Act 1976, 1976 Austl. Acts 1378. The Federal Court of Australia was established by the Federal Court of Australia Act 1976, 1976 Austl. Acts 1323. This Act confers *original* jurisdiction in "matters arising under laws made by Parliament." *Id.* § 19(1), 1976 Austl. Acts at 1330. The Industrial Division of the Federal Court handles labor questions such as conciliation and arbitration, while the General Division of the Federal Court handles matters involving bankruptcy, copyright, administrative law, consumer protection, restrictive trade practices, and price justification (i.e., antitrust cases). There is also a separate federal Family Court, created in 1975 and given exclusive jurisdiction to handle cases arising under the Commonwealth Family Law Act, with a direct appeal by special leave to the High Court. The Federal Court has *appellate* jurisdiction in three kinds of cases: (1) appeals from the judgments, decrees, or orders and sentences of a single federal judge, Federal Court of Australia Act 1976, § 24(1)(a), 1976 Austl. Acts at 1331; (2) general appeals, civil and criminal, from a supreme court of a *territory, id.* § 24(1)(b), 1976 Austl. Acts at 1331; and (3) appeals, pursuant to a specific provision of an act of Parliament, from a single-judge state supreme court exercising federal jurisdiction, *id.* § 24(1)(c), 1976 Austl. Acts at 1331. Crawford, *The New Structure of Australian Courts,* 6 ADELAIDE L. REV. 201 (1978). *See generally* Lane, *The New Federal Jurisdiction,* 54 AUSTL. L.J. 11 (1980).

40. The High Court's procedures are somewhat different from those of the U.S. Supreme Court. The justices do not normally sit *en banc,* but in panels which, in cases arising under the Court's appellate jurisdiction, must consist of two or more justices. (In cases coming to the Court under its original jurisdiction, a single justice sits as trial judge. His findings are then referred to the full court—which may be as few as two justices—which then proceeds as in other appeals.) Normally, three members hear routine private-law appeals, but five to seven members sit in more important litigation and, when there is a constitutional case of significance, the court tries to sit *en banc.* Inter-

Finally, and of most importance in understanding the differences between the two countries with respect to the federal role in education, the Australian federal constitution addresses itself much more to the mechanics of government than to checks and balances at the federal level. Rather than a concern for the balance of power among the three branches of the federal government, the emphasis in Australia is on an appropriate balance between the Commonwealth and the states.[41]

II

THE PRESENT FEDERAL ROLE IN EDUCATION IN AUSTRALIA

A.   The Historical Role of the Commonwealth in Education

In Australia, the states existed before the establishment of the Commonwealth in 1901,[42] and thus the state constitutions predate the Commonwealth constitution. The state constitutions empower their legislatures to provide for "peace, order, and good government,"[43] thus giving the states authority

---

view with Mr. Justice Lionel Murphy (July 8, 1983) (memorandum on file with the author). Since Section 23(i) of the Judiciary Act requires at least three justices to concur in a decision (but not an opinion) settling a question involving the Commonwealth's constitutional powers, at least five justices must participate in constitutional cases. *See* Judiciary Act 1903, § 23(i), 1903 Austl. Acts 8, 12 (amended 1976).

Cases are presented almost entirely through oral argument; written briefs are not submitted. Oral argument is unlimited; for example, Commonwealth v. Tasmania (The Tasmanian Dam Case), 46 Austl. L.R. 625 (1983) (discussed *infra*, text accompanying notes 161-206) took 8 days to argue. *Id.* at 625; Interview with Mr. Justice Murphy, *supra*. The *Communist Party Case*, Australian Communist Party v. Commonwealth, 83 C.L.R. 1 (Austl. 1951), took 24 days. Even routine cases take half a day. Determining the *ratio decidendi* for any particular judgment is extremely difficult, since each justice generally writes his own separate opinion. According to Justice Murphy, the justices did not meet to vote on the cases. Although each justice writes his own opinion, they do, of course, see copies of their colleagues' opinions before they are released to the public. However, the justices sometimes may not know the outcome of the case until the pro and con opinions are counted up. Interview with Mr. Justice Murphy, *supra*.

In accordance with section 35 of the Judiciary Act 1903, *as amended by* Judiciary Amendment Act 1976, 1976 Austl. Acts 1378, 1379-80, there is an appeal as of right from state supreme courts only with respect to judgments of a full state supreme court involving at least $20,000 or a matter of constitutional interpretation. All other appeals, including those from a single-judge state supreme court, require special leave. Special leave is granted only under "exceptional circumstances." *Cf.* Mason, *Where Now?*, 49 AUSTL. L.J. 570, 576 (1975). In addition, cases can be removed to the High Court in two circumstances: (1) in constitutional cases, before judgment by a lower appellate court, on application of a state or Commonwealth Attorney-General or, at the discretion of the High Court, on application and a showing of special cause by a party, Judiciary Act 1903, § 40(1), *as amended by* Judiciary Amendment Act 1976, 1976 Austl. Acts 1378, 1380; or (2) in nonconstitutional cases involving the exercise of federal jurisdiction (identified in Sections 75 and 76 of the constitution), *id.* § 40(2)(b), *as amended by* Judiciary Amendment Act 1976, 1976 Austl. Acts at 1381. In nonconstitutional cases, removal is always a matter for High Court discretion and requires the consent of all parties. *Id.* § 40(4), *as amended by* Judiciary Amendment Act 1976, 1976 Austl. Acts at 1381.

41.   The federal system in Australia, like that in the United States, is a limited government, having only those powers that are specifically enumerated. Section 107 of the Australian Constitution is similar to the U.S. Constitution's tenth amendment, differing, however, in its use of the words "unless. . . *exclusively* vested in the Parliament of the Commonwealth or withdrawn from the Parliament of the State." AUSTL. CONST. § 107 (emphasis added).

42.   The last state to be established was Western Australia in 1890.

43.   *See, e.g.*, N.S.W. CONST. § 5 (enacted by Constitution Act 1902, 2 N.S.W. PUB. ACTS 340, 342 (1938)).

over all social services. Relying on such provisions, the states have enacted public instruction acts.[44] Like the U.S. Constitution, the Australian Constitution contains no education provision. Since section 106 of the Australian Constitution saves the states' constitutions at the time of federation,[45] and sections 107 and 108 save the laws and powers of the state governments,[46] education appears to have been a matter constitutionally left to the states.

Educational policy is still determined primarily by the states, though the delegation of authority within each state differs. The determination of school policy and authority to disburse funds may be formally or legally granted to the State Minister of Education, the Director-General,[47] or the Governor. While there are also various national committees and commissions with differing roles, virtually all school policy is determined at the state level. There is no counterpart to the local education agencies or school boards found in the United States[48] nor, at the other end of the spectrum, was there until recently any significant effort on the part of the Commonwealth to exert influence over educational policy.

One such attempted exercise of power by the Commonwealth government was based on the defense power,[49] resulting in a High Court decision declaring that the states had responsibility for education in the Australian federal system.[50] In that case, an applicant had met all the requirements for university matriculation and admission to either the faculty of medicine or the faculty of dentistry. The plaintiff's application for admission was denied pur-

---

44. *See, e.g.*, Public Instruction Act of 1880, 9 N.S.W. PUB. ACTS 390 (1957) (amended 1979); Education Act 1928-1981, 19 Geo. 5, no. xxxiii, 5 W. AUSTL. REPR. ACTS 1 (1982).

45. "The Constitution of each State of the Commonwealth shall, subject to this Constitution, continue as at the establishment of the Commonwealth, or as at the admission or establishment of the State, as the case may be, until altered in accordance with the Constitution of the State." AUSTL. CONST. § 106.

46. Every power of the Parliament of a Colony which has become or becomes a State, shall, unless it is by this Constitution exclusively vested in the Parliament of the Commonwealth or withdrawn from the Parliament of the State, continue as at the establishment of the Commonwealth, or as at the admission or establishment of the State, as the case may be. AUSTL. CONST. § 107.

Every law in force in a Colony which has become or becomes a State, and relating to any matter within the powers of the Parliament of the Commonwealth, shall, subject to this Constitution, continue in force in the State; and, until provision is made in that behalf by the Parliament of the Commonwealth, the Parliament of the State shall have such powers of alteration and of repeal in respect of any such law as the Parliament of the Colony had until the Colony became a State. AUSTL. CONST. § 108.

47. The Director-General is the permanent head of the state education department. The position is equivalent to that of a state commissioner or superintendent of education in the United States, although it is never an elected position. It is different, however, in that the state Minister of Education establishes policy, and the Director-General implements it — although in many cases, a Director-General is quite influential in the development of major educational policy changes. Educational policies are approved by the Minister but often shaped by the Director-General. Interview with Dr. Robert Vickery, Director-General of the Department of Education of Western Australia (July 5, 1983) (memorandum on file with the author).

48. Victoria has recently established local school boards or councils that are elected. However, there is no local responsibility for revenue raising or for the hiring and promotion of teachers. Interview with Dr. Robert Vickery, Director-General of the Department of Education of Western Australia (July 12, 1983) (memorandum on file with author).

49. AUSTL. CONST. § 51(vi).

50. The King v. University of Sydney, 67 C.L.R. 95 (Austl. 1943).

suant to national security regulations which gave power to the Commonwealth to "regulate, restrict or enlarge the number of students who may be enrolled in any faculty or course of study at that University."[51] The regulations were promulgated under the authority of the National Security Act which provided that appropriate regulations could be enacted "for securing the public safety and the defense of the Commonwealth" or "for prescribing all matters which are necessary or convenient to be prescribed, for the effectual prosecution" of the war.[52] A quota had been established, and the seats had already been filled when the plaintiff applied. A majority of the High Court found the regulation to be an invalid exercise of Commonwealth power, related not to defense but to education, which the Court said was a function of the states.

In 1946, the Commonwealth Constitution was amended to permit the Commonwealth Parliament "to make laws . . . with respect to . . . benefits to students."[53] This provision gives the federal government some authority over education; however, the policy has still been to leave primary authority to the states.

One major difference between the United States and Australia, historically, has been the way in which education is financed. Although the Australian states play the principal role in policy setting and decisionmaking in the Australian schools, the Commonwealth has the primary powers of revenue raising. This revenue is partially directed back to the states, with discretion in spending left to the states.

Based on section 51(ii) (the taxing power) and the section 96 power to

---

51. Regulation 16(2)(a), National Security (Universities Commission) Regulations, 1943 Austl. Stat. R. 28, at 773, 777.

52. National Security Act 1939-40, § 5(l), 1940 Austl. Acts 78, 79 (repealed 1950).

53. AUSTL. CONST. § 51(xxiiiA). After the High Court's decision in the *Pharmaceutical Benefits Case*, Attorney-General for Victoria *ex rel.* Dale v. Commonwealth, 71 C.L.R. 237 (Austl. 1945), which significantly restricted the scope of the Commonwealth's power under section 81 to appropriate funds "for the purpose of the Commonwealth," the constitutional validity of all direct federal spending programs not authorized by a particular fount of Commonwealth legislative power was in question. Among the statutes thought questionable in whole or in part under the *Pharmaceutical Benefits* decision was the Education Act 1945, 1945 Austl. Acts 423 (intended "to establish a Commonwealth Office of Education and a Universities Commission, to provide for [schooling for veterans and financial aid to university students], and for other purposes"). The Constitution Alteration (Social Services) Act 1946, 1946 Austl. Acts 273, introduced to guarantee the validity of future federal welfare programs and to enable the Commonwealth to administer them, resulted in approval of section 51(xxiiiA) by national referendum in 1946 and subsequent amendment of the constitution. *See* Sackville, *Social Welfare in Australia: The Constitutional Framework*, 5 FED. L. REV. 248, 256-57 (1973). Federal Council of the British Medical Ass'n in Australia v. Commonwealth (The B.M.A. Case), 79 C.L.R. 201 (Austl. 1949) is the principal case interpreting section 51(xxiiiA). In that case, the word "benefits" was given an expansive reading, to cover "provisions made to meet needs arising from special conditions with a recognized incidence in communities or from particular situations or pursuits such as that of a student, whether the provision takes the form of money payments or the supply of things or services." *The B.M.A. Case*, 79 C.L.R. at 260 (Dixon, J.). The *B.M.A.* decision indicated that the Commonwealth, in providing benefits, could impose whatever conditions it chose, and that the section 51(xxiiiA) power is "limited to the provision of the specified benefits *by the Commonwealth itself*," Sackville, *supra* at 260 (emphasis in original), and does not extend to legislation dealing with benefits provided, for example, by the states, "public bodies," and trading corporations. *Id.*

make conditional grants, the Uniform Tax Scheme was introduced by the Commonwealth in 1942. Up until that time, both the Commonwealth and the states had taxed income, but there were significant variations among the states in tax structure and rates. The Uniform Tax Scheme[54] altered this arrangement.[55] A Commonwealth income tax was levied at a rate that would yield the same amount as that previously raised by the Commonwealth and the states combined; taxpayers were required to pay the Commonwealth income tax before any state income tax. If a state refrained from imposing a state income tax, it would receive from the Commonwealth an annual amount equal to that which it had previously collected in income tax. If a state levied any income tax at all, it would not get any portion of the Commonwealth's income tax revenue.

Financial assistance was thus granted to a state on condition that it abstain from exercising its own power to tax income. The effect was to force the states to cede their power to tax income to the federal government. In effect, Australia developed an extensive revenue-sharing program that has remained in existence ever since.[56] "The proportion of total tax revenue collected by the Commonwealth is about 80 per cent,"[57] and it distributes about 30 per-

---

54. The Uniform Tax Scheme was based on four statutes. States Grants (Income Tax Reimbursement) Act 1942, 1942 Austl. Acts 46 (repealed 1946); Income Tax (War-Time Arrangements) Act 1942, 1942 Austl. Acts 48; Income Tax Assessment Act 1942, 1942 Austl. Acts 52 (amended 1973); Income Tax Act 1942, 1942 Austl. Acts 64.

55. See J. MCMILLAN, G. EVANS, & H. STOREY, supra note 6, at 108-09.

56. Although the scheme was a wartime measure, it has been continued to the present day. The states challenged its validity twice. In the principal case, South Australia v. Commonwealth, 65 C.L.R. 373 (First Uniform Tax Case) (Austl. 1942), a majority of the High Court upheld the Uniform Tax Scheme. The states had argued that sections 106 and 107′ of the constitution prohibited either the Commonwealth or the states from usurping or undermining the functions or constitution of the other. Since taxation is an essential sovereign function, they argued, and principles of federalism require limiting the scope of Commonwealth powers that are exercised in derogation of such functions, the scheme was unconstitutional. A majority of the High Court found that since the scheme neither repealed state tax legislation nor required or compelled a state to abandon its taxing activities, but merely offered an inducement not to exercise power conceded to continue to exist, it was constitutional. Chief Justice Latham noted that the fact that in reality the states could not refuse to take the Commonwealth grants and thus were forced to give up their taxing power was not dispositive of the constitutional issue: "temptation is not compulsion." 65 C.L.R. at 417. Chief Justice Latham quotes from Justice Cardozo's majority opinion in Steward Machine Co. v. Davis, 301 U.S. 548, 589-90 (1936): "Every rebate . . . is in some measure a temptation. But to hold that motive or temptation is equivalent to coercion is to plunge the law in endless difficulties." South Australia v. Commonwealth, 65 C.L.R. at 418. The interpretation of sections 106 and 107 appears to be like that of the tenth amendment to the U.S. Constitution, in that these sections merely make clear that the Commonwealth is a government of limited powers. These sections do not limit or restrict those powers (such as taxation) granted to the Commonwealth.

The states challenged the validity of the Uniform Tax Scheme again in 1957. Victoria v. Commonwealth, 99 C.L.R. 575 (Second Uniform Tax Case) (Austl. 1957). In response to this challenge, the High Court ruled invalid the priority given to the Commonwealth income tax, but the remaining elements of the scheme were upheld and those elements provided a sufficient basis for the Commonwealth to retain supremacy in the area of income tax. See J. MCMILLAN, G. EVANS & H. STOREY, supra note 6, at 109. The states had also sought to invalidate the portion of the Uniform Tax Scheme which, enacted pursuant to section 96, provided for financial assistance to those states that did not collect state income tax. All members of the High Court concurred in giving section 96 the widest possible scope: the Commonwealth can grant financial assistance to any state or to all and on whatever terms or conditions it sees fit. 99 C.L.R. at 575.

57. J. MCMILLAN, G. EVANS & H. STOREY, supra note 6, at 109. In effect, the States' capacity to

cent of these revenues to the states, principally through tax reimbursement grants but also using special equalization grants,[58] specific purpose grants, and miscellaneous grants. The 30 percent distributed to the states constitutes about two-thirds of the states' total revenue.[59]

Thus, funds for education are substantially derived from consolidated revenues which are dispersed to the states as Parliament thinks "fit."[60] The Commonwealth government provides financial assistance grants[61] to the states in a lump sum (as untied funds), and education is financed primarily out of these tax reimbursements. This means that the financing inequities that exist in the United States (both among states and among school districts within each state) do not exist in Australia.

In addition to what might be called general revenue sharing, additional Commonwealth funds specifically for education are distributed through specific purpose grants. Because inequities are relatively insignificant, this special federal funding for education actually operates to supplement or "top up" the basic educational program. By contrast, in the United States, federal funds for education often do not achieve this "topping up" effect because of fiscal disparities between school districts and among states.[62]

B. Constitutional Power for Intervention in Education, the Role of the Courts and of the Executive

1. *Constitutional Authority.* Most of the Commonwealth's express legislative powers are enumerated in section 51 of the constitution.[63] Section 51 includes forty express legislative powers with the following preamble to the list of powers: "The Parliament shall, subject to this Constitution, have power to make laws for the peace, order, and good government of the Commonwealth with respect to . . . ." These enumerated legislative powers are concurrent, that is, the fact that these specific grants of power have been made to the Commonwealth does not subtract anything from the states' general powers to make laws for the peace, order, and good government of the states.[64]

---

raise revenues independently is confined to such minor taxes as the payroll tax, automobile tax, stamp duties, probate and inheritance taxes, land tax, gambling tax, and liquor tax. *Id.* at 108.

58. *See id.* at 115-16.

59. *Id.* at 117.

60. AUSTL. CONST. § 96 (although section 81 is sometimes also relied upon).

61. "In 1959 the Commonwealth introduced a system of financial assistance grants in place of the tax reimbursement arrangements. Under [this] system, grants increased not merely by reference to changes in population and wages, but also in accordance with something called a 'betterment' factor." J. MCMILLAN, G. EVANS & H. STOREY, *supra* note 6, at 122. Under the current scheme, introduced in 1982-83, the states share in a grant based on a fixed percentage, about 20 percent, of total (not just income tax) Commonwealth taxation collections. *Id.* at 123.

62. For a discussion of the patterns of allocation of federal aid to education in the United States, see generally J. BERKE & M. KIRST, FEDERAL AID TO EDUCATION: WHO BENEFITS? WHO GOVERNS? (1972); Berke & Kirst, *The Federal Role in American School Finance: A Fiscal and Administrative Analysis,* 61 GEO. L.J. 927 (1973).

63. *Compare* U.S. CONST. art. I, § 8.

64. Some of the legislative powers in section 51 are, of course, exclusive to the Commonwealth because their subject matter is inherently beyond the competence of the states or because other parts

As noted above, the only provision expressly referring to education is the amendment adopted by referendum[65] in 1946, permitting the Commonwealth Parliament to "make laws . . . with respect to . . . benefits to students."[66] This provision, however, does not appear to lend itself to a broad interpretation of the extent of Commonwealth power over education, or at least it has not been so interpreted. Thus, with the almost total absence of express constitutional authority for federal intervention in education, coupled with the absence of an Australian equivalent to the equal protection clause[67] from which such authority might be implied, there appears to be no constitutional basis for the Commonwealth's imposing on the states unfunded mandates analogous to such U.S. statutes as Title VI of the Civil Rights Act of 1964, Title IX of the Education Amendments of 1972, or section 504 of the Rehabilitation Act of 1973, and their implementing regulations.[68]

One possible source of constitutional authority, however, may lie in the external affairs power,[69] discussed in part III of this article. Another is section 96 of the Australian Constitution, similar to the taxing and spending clause of the U.S. Constitution[70] which provides authority in this country for federal grants-in-aid to education. The U.S. statutes frequently include extensive conditions that operate similarly to some of the civil rights mandates.[71] The U.S. Supreme Court has repeatedly taken a broad view with respect to the

---

of the constitution exclude the states from acting in the area. *See* J. McMillan, G. Evans & H. Storey, *supra* note 6, at 42-43. *See generally id.* at 39-67.

Section 51 concludes with a provision that is similar to the "necessary and proper" clause in the U.S. Constitution, U.S. Const. art. I, § 8, cl. 18. The Australian provision states that Parliament shall have power to make laws with respect to "matters incidental to the execution of any power vested by this Constitution in the Parliament or in either House thereof, or in the Government of the Commonwealth, or in the Federal Judicature, or in any department or officer of the Commonwealth." Austl. Const. § 51(xxxix).

65. The principal mechanism for amending the Australian Constitution is by referendum under section 128 of the constitution. That section provides that the proposed law for amending the constitution be passed by a majority of each house of the Parliament. Not less than two or more than six months after its passage through both houses, the proposed law is to be submitted in each state to the electors qualified to vote in that state for the election of members of the House of Representatives. A proposed law must be approved both by a majority of all the electorate voting and also by a majority of the electors voting in a majority of the states. Austl. Const. § 128. Those requirements have proved very hard to satisfy. Since federation, only eight of thirty-six such proposed amendments have been approved. J. McMillan, G. Evans & H. Storey, *supra* note 6, at 359.

66. Austl. Const. § 51 (xxiiiA). The full provision covers a range of social services. Parliament may legislate with respect to "the provision of maternity allowances, widows' pensions, child endowment, unemployment, pharmaceutical, sickness and hospital benefits, medical and dental services (but not so as to authorize any form of civil conscription), benefits to students and family allowances." Austl. Const. § 51 (xxiiiA). *See* discussion *supra* note 53.

67. *See* discussion *supra* note 32.

68. Civil Rights Act of 1964, tit. VI, 42 U.S.C. §§ 2000d to 2000d-4 (1982); 34 C.F.R. §§ 75, 76, 100, 222, 700 (1984); Education Amendments of 1972, tit. IX, 20 U.S.C. §§ 1681-1686 (1982); 34 C.F.R. §§ 106, 122 (1984); Rehabilitation Act of 1973, § 504, 29 U.S.C § 794 (1982); 34 C.F.R. §§ 104, 222, 300 (1984). Since these statutes withhold other federal funds when their provisions are violated, the authority for these statutes may also lie in the taxing and spending power of article I, section 8, clause 1 of the U.S. Constitution, as well as in section 5 of the fourteenth amendment.

69. Austl. Const. § 51 (xxix).

70. U.S. Const. art. I, § 8, cl. 1.

71. *See, e.g.,* Education for All Handicapped Children Act of 1975, 20 U.S.C. §§ 1232, 1401, 1405-1406, 1411-1420, 1453 (1982).

scope of Congress' power to condition the receipt of federal grants enacted pursuant to the spending clause.[72] Although the Australian provision *explicitly* says any federal grant can be conditioned[73] whereas the U.S. approach has been developed through court interpretation, there has been in Australia little reliance on section 96 as a basis for extensive conditioning of specific purpose grants,[74] and Australia imposes relatively few conditions on those grants, at least compared with the United States. Whether section 96 could be used as authority for conditions such as those included in the Education for All Handicapped Children Act or Title I of the Elementary and Secondary Education Act will be discussed in part IV of this article.

2. *The Role of the Courts.* The policymaking role of courts in Australia is very different from that of courts in the United States. At about the same time that the legislative and executive branches of the federal government were expanding their involvement in education, the U.S. federal courts began to assume a significant policymaking role in the field of education beginning with *Brown v. Board of Education.*[75] Following *Brown,* for the remainder of the 1950's, the courts were primarily concerned with implementing the constitutional requirement that no student be denied an equal educational opportu-

---

72. In King v. Smith, 392 U.S. 309 (1968), where the Court upheld a condition of the Aid to Families with Dependent Children program against state regulations which would have diminished its effectiveness, the Court stated: "There is of course no question that the Federal Government, unless barred by some controlling constitutional provision, may impose the terms and conditions upon which its money allotments to the States shall be disbursed . . . ." *Id.* at 333 n.34. Similar statements have been made with respect to conditions imposed on federally funded construction projects, *see* Fullilove v. Klutznick, 448 U.S. 448, 474 (1980) (10 percent of funds for public works project required to be used to procure services or supplies from "minority business enterprises"); requirements under Title VI of the Civil Rights Act of 1964 banning discrimination in "any program or activity receiving Federal financial assistance," *see* Lau v. Nichols, 414 U.S. 563, 569 (1974) (failure of school district to provide affirmative language assistance to students of Chinese ancestry who spoke little or no English); and legislation providing that no state official employed "in connection with any activities . . . financed in whole or in part by [federal funds] shall . . . take any active part in political management or in political campaigns," *see* Oklahoma v. United States Civil Serv. Comm'n, 330 U.S. 127, 143-44 (1947) (under Section 12(a) of the Hatch Act, 54 Stat. 767 (1940) (current version at 5 U.S.C. §§ 1501(4), 1502 (1982)), agency may withhold funds in an amount equaling two years' salary); *see also, e.g.,* Pennhurst State School v. Halderman, 451 U.S. 1, 17-18 (1981) (reaffirming power to condition funds but finding no effective condition imposed). Although the Court has announced that the power is not without limits, its attempts to articulate the content of those limits are remarkably vague. *See Pennhurst,* 451 U.S. at 17 n.13 (and cases cited therein). "Requiring States to honor the obligations voluntarily assumed as a condition of federal funding . . . simply does not intrude on their sovereignty. . . . If the conditions were valid, the State had no sovereign right to retain funds without complying with those conditions." Bell v. New Jersey, 103 S. Ct. 2187, 2197 (1983). National League of Cities v. Usery, 426 U.S. 833 (1976), left open the question whether grant conditions that intrude upon state sovereignty with respect to "integral operations of state governments" would be upheld. *Id.* at 852 n.17. The D.C. Circuit has recently noted that the most diligent inquiry will not "uncover any instance in which a court has invalidated a funding condition." Oklahoma v. Schweiker, 655 F.2d 401, 406 (1981); *see also* cases cited *id.* at 406 n.9.

For a general description of specific grant conditions enacted pursuant to the spending clause, see P. HAY & R. ROTUNDA, *supra* note 6, at 173-81.

73. "During a period of ten years after the establishment of the Commonwealth and thereafter until the Parliament otherwise provides, the Parliament may grant financial assistance to any State on such terms and conditions as the Parliament thinks fit." AUSTL. CONST. § 96.

74. *See* discussion *infra* at text accompanying notes 287-305.

75. 347 U.S. 483 (1954).

nity because of his or her race. While their involvement in the dismantling of dual school systems has continued unabated,[76] the U.S. courts have also become involved in other areas which long had been the prerogative of school authorities.[77] In the last 15 years, the U.S. Supreme Court has reviewed cases involving nearly every major area of educational policy: school curriculum questions,[78] student rights of free expression and of nondisruptive protest,[79] exemptions from state compulsory school attendance laws,[80] school finance reform,[81] gender discrimination,[82] discrimination against handicapped students,[83] bilingual or English-language instruction for those with limited English skills,[84] school personnel policies,[85] student discipline,[86] and liability of school officials for violating the civil rights of students.[87] The involvement of the lower federal courts and of state courts in educational issues has been even more pervasive, including such areas as the tracking and classification of students[88] and minimal competency testing.[89]

There is no such tradition of court intervention in educational policy issues in Australia. The federal courts are only 6 years old and do not have a general "arising under" jurisdiction.[90] Since the federal courts have a narrow jurisdiction, most cases that might involve education would come up through the state courts and then be appealed to the High Court. Most cases, how-

---

76. *See e.g.*, Washington v. Seattle School Dist. No. 1, 455 U.S. 934 (1982); Crawford v. Board of Educ., 455 U.S. 904 (1982); Columbus Bd. of Educ. v. Penick, 443 U.S. 449 (1979).

77. *See generally* M. YUDOF, D. KIRP, T. VAN GEEL & B. LEVIN, EDUCATIONAL POLICY AND THE LAW (2d ed. 1984); Levin, *The Courts, Congress, and Educational Adequacy: The Equal Protection Predicament*, 39 MD. L. REV. 187 (1979).

78. *See, e.g.*, Board of Educ. v. Pico, 457 U.S. 853 (1982); Milliken v. Bradley, 433 U.S. 267 (1977); Epperson v. Arkansas, 393 U.S. 97 (1968).

79. Tinker v. Des Moines Indep. Community School Dist., 393 U.S. 503 (1969).

80. Wisconsin v. Yoder, 406 U.S. 205 (1972).

81. San Antonio Indep. School Dist. v. Rodriguez, 411 U.S. 1 (1973).

82. Mississippi Univ. for Women v. Hogan, 458 U.S. 718 (1982).

83. *See, e.g.*, Irving Indep. School Dist. v. Tatro, 104 S. Ct. 3371 (1984); Board of Educ. v. Rowley, 458 U.S. 176 (1982); Southeastern Community College v. Davis, 442 U.S. 397 (1979).

84. Lau v. Nichols, 414 U.S. 563 (1974).

85. *See, e.g.*, Perry Educ. Ass'n v. Perry Local Educators' Ass'n, 460 U.S. 37 (1983); Hortonville Joint School Dist. No. 1 v. Hortonville Educ. Ass'n, 426 U.S. 482 (1976); Cleveland Bd. of Educ. v. La Fleur, 414 U.S. 632 (1974).

86. Goss v. Lopez, 419 U.S. 565 (1975); Ingraham v. Wright, 430 U.S. 651 (1977).

87. Wood v. Strickland, 420 U.S. 308 (1975).

88. *See, e.g.*, Larry P. v. Riles, 502 F.2d 963 (9th Cir. 1974).

89. *See, e.g.*, Debra P. v. Turlington, 730 F.2d 1405 (11th Cir. 1984).

The constitutional rights of teachers also expanded during the period of the sixties and early seventies—encompassing such diverse areas as free speech, *see, e.g.*, Givhan v. Western Line Consol. School Dist., 439 U.S. 410 (1979); Mount Healthy City School Dist. Bd. of Educ. v. Doyle, 429 U.S. 274 (1977); Pickering v. Bd. of Educ., 391 U.S. 563 (1968), and the ways in which teachers are certified, *see, e.g.*, United States v. North Carolina, 400 F. Supp. 343 (E.D.N.C. 1975), *vacated*, 425 F. Supp. 789 (E.D.N.C. 1977), as well as issues involving the right to bargain collectively, *see, e.g.*, McLaughlin v. Tilendis, 398 F.2d 287 (7th Cir. 1968); National Educ. Ass'n v. Board of Educ., 212 Kan. 741, 512 P.2d 426 (1973); *cf.* Abood v. Detroit Bd. of Educ., 431 U.S. 209 (1977), and to strike or apply other sanctions, *see, e.g.*, School Dist. v. Holland Educ. Ass'n, 380 Mich. 314, 157 N.W. 2d 206 (1968), and the right to bargain about various aspects of educational policy, *see, e.g.*, City of Beloit v. Wisconsin Employment Relations Comm'n, 73 Wis. 2d 43, 242 N.W. 2d 231 (1976); San Mateo City School Dist. v. Public Employment Relations Bd., 33 Cal. 3d 850, 663, P.2d 523, 191 Cal. Rptr. 800 (1983). *See generally*, Edwards, *The Emerging Duty to Bargain in the Public Sector*, 71 MICH. L. REV. 885 (1973).

90. *See supra* note 39.

ever, are not heard by the High Court as a matter of right.[91] Moreover, even if Australia had a tradition of court intervention in education, the results would be very different there than in the United States, since the constitutional issues involving education that arise under the first, fourth, and fourteenth amendments in the United States would not arise in Australia.

3. *The Role of the Executive.* The federal structure for governing education in Australia is headed by a Minister of Education, who is appointed by the party in power and has a seat in Parliament. The Minister will change as the party in control changes. There is also a Secretary of Education, a top civil servant, who is the permanent head of the Department of Education.[92] The Secretary of Education is responsible for administering funds for student aid, policymaking, and providing advice to the Minister.[93]

Labor government reforms in 1972 created a Schools Commission whose four full-time and six part-time members dispensed almost all specific purpose Commonwealth funds for elementary and secondary education, including funds for nongovernment schools (with the principal exception of funds for student aid).[94] Although the Commission has separate statutory authority, it submits its budget to the Department of Education and to the Secretary of Education.[95]

C. The Schools Commission's Statutory Authority

The States Grants (Schools) Act 1973 originated financial assistance to

---

91. *See supra* note 40.

92. When there has been a party change as a result of an election, if the incoming government wishes to remove the Secretary of Education, it can only be done by transferring him to another secretarial position in another department or by making him an ambassador to a foreign country, since Department Secretaries carry ambassadorial rank. Interview with Peter Tannock (July 9, 1983); Interview with Dr. Peter Wilenski (July 8, 1983) (memorandum on file with author).

93. Interview with Dr. Peter Wilenski, *supra* note 92. The major function of the Commonwealth Education Department appears to be to process and handle applications for student assistance. The Department provides assistance to students in secondary education who are 16-years-old and older (about $16 per week, given to the student's parent). This stipend is to encourage students to stay in school for the last few years and to encourage the parents not to rely on their children's earnings. There is also a program of assistance to students enrolled in tertiary (higher) education. Since tertiary education is free, these grants are for living expenses; tertiary students receive the funds directly. The major financial aid programs for youth are all strictly income-tested (need-based). *Id.*

The Department administers the Youth-to-Work Transition grants program, but the remaining specific purpose grants programs are administered by the Commonwealth Schools Commission. *See infra* text accompanying notes 94-95.

Although responsibility for running the schools in the Northern Territory was recently transferred from the Commonwealth to the Northern Territory, the Australian Capital Territory (ACT) schools and those in other nonstate areas are run by the Commonwealth government, as are the schools on the government aboriginal reserves.

94. In 1972, the Labor Party appointed the interim Committee for the Australian Schools Commission. This Committee resulted in a report in 1973 (The Karmel Report—so named for Peter Karmel, the Chair of the Committee) that led to the passage of the States Grants (Schools) Act 1973, 1973 Austl. Acts 1407, and the Schools Commission Act 1973, 1973 Austl. Acts 1398.

95. There is also a Tertiary Education Commission that gives out all Commonwealth higher education money. Currently, all institutions of higher education are wholly supported by federal funds.

Australia's schools through specific purpose grants.[96] Special federal program funds for education were divided into seven categories, the first two being essentially block grants:

(1) general building grants (capital costs);
(2) general recurrent expenditures (operating expenses);
(3) grants for school library projects;
(4) grants for both capital and operating expenses for disadvantaged schools;
(5) grants for special schools for the handicapped;
(6) grants for teacher development; and
(7) grants for special experimental projects designed to promote innovation or change.[97]

These specific purpose funds are paid to the states with minimal conditions. The funds must be used by the state for the specified purposes, such as building projects or recurring expenses in connection with government or nongovernment primary and secondary schools in the state.[98] The state must also furnish the Minister evidence, within six months after the end of the year in which the payment is made, that the funds were spent for the designated purpose. If the state fails to meet these two conditions, the state must repay an amount equal to the payment it received. In addition, the state must report statistical and other information with respect to its schools. Even for the more narrowly focused grants, such as libraries or disadvantaged schools, there appear to be no conditions other than that the funds be spent for the particular purpose (e.g., librarian training courses), and that there be some fiscal accounting to the Commonwealth at the end of the grant period.

A federal policy which has only seven specific target areas (two of which are essentially block grants for capital and operating expenses) is very different from the often complex federal education legislation in the United States.[99] Moreover, the bulk of Australian expenditures for education are financed by the states from the general revenue sharing funds returned to the states by the Commonwealth under the 1942 Uniform Tax Scheme.[100] The remainder comes from financial assistance provided by the Schools Commission under the States Grants (Schools) Act.[101] The Schools Commission paid

---

96. States Grants (Schools) Act 1973, 1973 Austl. Acts 1407.
97. *Id.* §§ 17-25, 1973 Austl. Acts at 1426-33.
98. *See id.* § 4(1), 1973 Austl. Acts at 1415. As noted earlier, recipients of specific purpose funds include both public schools (called government schools in Australia) and nonpublic or parochial schools (called nongovernment schools). Another condition is that the Commonwealth may not fund a building project whose sole or principal object is either to increase the maximum number of students that may be provided for at government primary or secondary schools in the state, or to provide housing for teaching or other staff in any capital city. *Id.* § 5(1)(a)(i)-(ii), 1973 Austl. Acts at 1415.
99. Compare the statutory conditions attached to grants for disadvantaged schools in the States Grants (Schools) Act 1973, § 27, 1973 Austl. Acts 1407, 1414, with the conditions in Title I of the Elementary and Secondary Education Act of 1965, 20 U.S.C. §§ 2701-2854 (1982). In Australia, grants to the states for operating and capital expenses supplement the funds provided through consolidated revenues (these latter funds are not restricted to specific uses: states can decide what proportion to spend on highways, on education, and so forth).
100. *See supra* notes 54-61 and accompanying text.
101. A percentage of both the state funds (whose sources are partly Commonwealth revenue, partly state revenue) and the Commonwealth specific purpose funds for education go to nongovern-

about 50 percent of the states' total capital budget in 1983 (the usual figure is closer to 30 percent) and 10 percent of the states' operating budget. This 10 percent is broken down into 7 percent for the "block grants" for general operating costs in the States Grants (School Assistance) Act, known as "recurrent expenditure," and 3 percent for the five special purpose grants enumerated above.[102] And, as already noted, there are only a limited number of objectives or conditions for these grants, primarily having to do with fiscal reporting.

Since the 1973 Act, Australia has only added two categories of functions receiving specific purpose grants. One is migrant education, comprised of English-as-a-Second-Language (ESL) programs and part-time ethnic education programs designed to teach a language other than English "that is the first language of peoples who have migrated to Australia."[103] The other is multicultural education, which provides programs "designed to take account of the culture of Aboriginal or immigrant peoples."[104] The current Commonwealth grants programs will be discussed in part IV of this article.

III

THE EXTERNAL AFFAIRS POWER

As the previous section indicated, Australia has not used its section 96 power significantly to condition specific purpose grants to protect special pupil populations, at least when compared with some of the U.S. statutes.[105] More important, the Australian Constitution has no guarantees of individual rights and liberties, such as those that appear in the U.S. Constitution's Bill of Rights and the fourteenth amendment,[106] that would provide the authority for

---

ment schools, including sectarian schools. *See* States Grants (Schools) Act 1973, scheds. 1-6, 1973 Austl. Acts 1407, 1456-59.

102. Interview with members of Commonwealth Schools Commission (July 8, 1983) (memorandum on file with author). For tables showing the disbursement of funds to the states, see States Grants (Schools Assistance) Amendment Act 1982, 1982 Austl. Acts 276; States Grants (Schools) Act 1973, 1973 Austl. Acts 1407, 1456-59. Total funding for specific purpose education grants disbursed by the Schools Commission doubled in the ten-year period since the passage of the initial act. *Compare* States Grants (Schools) Act 1973, 1973 Austl. Acts 1407, 1456-59 *with* States Grants (Schools Assistance) Amendment Act 1982, 1982 Austl. Acts 276.

103. States Grants (Schools Assistance) Act 1982, § 3(1), 1982 Austl. Acts 1745, 1754.

104. *Id.,* 1982 Austl. Acts at 1752.

105. *Compare* States Grants (Schools) Act 1973, §§ 35-42, 1973 Austl. Acts 1407, 1438-44 (Grants in Respect of Special Schools for Handicapped Children) *with* Education for All Handicapped Children Act, 20 U.S.C. §§ 1400-1461 (1982); *compare* States Grants (Schools) Act 1973, §§ 26-34, 1973 Austl. Acts 1407, 1433-38 (Grants for Disadvantaged Schools) *with* Title I of the Elementary and Secondary Education Act of 1965, 20 U.S.C. §§ 2701-2854 (1982).

106. *See supra* note 32 and accompanying text. For various reasons, discussed *supra* note 32, the founding fathers rejected the need to include in the Australian Constitution anything like the Bill of Rights. Only a few guarantees, which have been narrowly interpreted, appear in the Australian Constitution. For example, AUSTL. CONST. § 51(xxxi) requires that the taking of property by the Commonwealth be on "just terms." *Compare* U.S. CONST. amend. V ("Private property [shall not] be taken for public use, without just compensation"). Section 80 guarantees a trial by jury for any person charged with an indictable Commonwealth offense. (This requirement has frequently been avoided by providing that an offense can be tried summarily rather than by indictment.) Section 116 provides that the Commonwealth "shall not make any law for establishing any religion, or for imposing any religious observance, or for prohibiting the free exercise of any religion . . . ." This has been inter-

civil rights statutes.

The only attempt in Australia to establish broad-based human rights guarantees was made in 1973 by the Labor government. A human rights bill was introduced in the Senate that would have invalidated Commonwealth and state laws and practices that infringed a wide variety of fundamental rights and freedoms.[107] The authority for the human rights bill was said to be the external affairs power, section 51(xxix). The bill, however, was not voted on in Parliament.[108]

Several recent cases, however, have indicated that the external affairs power, section 51(xxix), may be the source of constitutional authority for a greater Commonwealth role in education, particularly in the civil rights area. The two major cases dealing with the external affairs power are *Koowarta v. Bjelke-Petersen*[109] and *Commonwealth v. Tasmania* (the *Tasmanian Dam Case*).[110] These cases drew upon the precedents developed in several earlier cases.

A. Early Cases

The principal precedent case is *The King v. Burgess*,[111] which reviewed the conviction of a pilot who flew intrastate[112] without a federal license in violation of regulations requiring such a license. The regulations were promulgated pursuant to an act implementing an international air navigation convention. The High Court held that the Commonwealth could regulate flights occurring wholly within a state since, as a signatory to the Paris Air

---

preted, however, to permit Commonwealth financial assistance to go to sectarian schools. *See* Victoria *ex rel.* Black v. Commonwealth, 146 C.L.R. 559 (Austl. 1980). *See generally* I. Birch, State-Aid at the Bar: of DOGS and a Bone (Nov. 18, 1982) (unpublished manuscript) ("DOGS" refers to Defense of Government Schools, the plaintiff organization in *Victoria ex rel Black.*). Moreover, since there is no fourteenth amendment, the states are not similarly barred from interfering with the free exercise of any religion or from establishing any religion. *See* Birch, *Non-Public Education in the U.S. and Australia,* in CONTEMPORARY ISSUES IN EDUCATIONAL POLICY 203 (1983). Finally, section 117, paralleling the privileges and immunities clauses both of article IV, section 2 and of section 1 of the fourteenth amendment of the U.S. Constitution, provides that "a subject of the Queen, resident in any State, shall not be subject in any other State to any disability or discrimination which would not be equally applicable to him if he were a subject of the Queen resident in such other State."

This does not mean that Australia does not protect individual rights. There is heavy reliance on various accepted practices and on the doctrine of natural justice which, for example, operates to entitle an individual to notice and a hearing before being deprived of any right, liberty, or property. J. MCMILLAN, G. EVANS & H. STOREY, *supra* note 6, at 320-21.

107. J. MCMILLAN, G. EVANS & H. STOREY, *supra* note 6, at 320.

108. In 1981, a Human Rights Commission was established by statute, Human Rights Commission Act 1981, 1981 Austl. Acts 254, based on the United Nations International Covenant on Civil and Political Rights, *opened for signature* Dec. 19, 1966, Annex to G.A. Res. 2200, 21 U.N. GAOR Supp. (No. 16) at 52, U.N. Doc. A/6316 (1966). The Commission conducts research and educational activities, advises whether Commonwealth legislation is compatible with the U.N. Covenant, and investigates complaints of human rights violations. The Human Rights Commissioner, however, has no enforcement powers. *See also* Racial Discrimination Act 1975, 1975 Austl. Acts 347, discussed *infra* text accompanying notes 129-34.

109. 39 Austl. L.R. 417 (1982).

110. 46 Austl. L.R. 625 (1983).

111. 55 C.L.R. 608 (Austl. 1936).

112. Goya Henry was an eccentric stunt flyer who flew paying passengers in an ancient aircraft over city areas. One story has it that he flew his plane under Sydney Harbour Bridge. *See* J. MCMILLAN, G. EVANS & H. STOREY, *supra* note 6, at 59.

Convention, the Commonwealth was obligated to control all domestic airspace.

This case required the Court to examine the scope of section 51(xxix). A majority of the justices viewed that section as providing broad, independent legislative power potentially reaching any subject matter that could be the object of international agreement and limited only by express constitutional prohibitions. Two justices would have extended the power beyond the implementation of an international agreement to reach "matters of concern to Australia as a member of the family of nations."[113] At the other end of the spectrum, one justice would have limited the scope of the section 51(xxix) power to legislation implementing only those international agreements which bound the Commonwealth in reference to some matter "indisputably international in character".[114] Another justice strongly implied that he would require a treaty to be of "sufficient significance" to be a "legitimate" subject of international concern, arguing that the section 51(xxix) power was limited by implied as well as express constitutional prohibitions.[115]

While the High Court in *Burgess* apparently endorsed the Commonwealth's authorization to enact legislation pursuant to section 51(xxix), it reversed the defendant's conviction: four of the five justices required that there be fairly strict congruence between the statute (and regulations) and the objectives of the international agreement. The regulations in question were held invalid as too incidental to the reach of the agreement. The dissenting justice on this point, however, argued that once an act of Parliament was found to be within the section 51(xxix) power, its implementation should be liberally construed to include incidental subjects.[116]

The *Burgess* case laid the groundwork for the use of the external affairs power domestically. After *Burgess*, the major questions addressed in subsequent litigation have been (1) whether the subject matter of an international agreement is an external affair and (2) to what extent the agreement can be implemented domestically (how strict a congruence is required between the international agreement and the domestic legislation).[117]

Airlines of N.S.W. Proprietary, Ltd. v. New South Wales[118] upheld regulations governing intrastate aviation that were enacted to implement the Chicago Convention on International Civil Aviation of 1944. The Court found these regulations "appropriate and adapted"[119] to the ends of the treaty, even though the treaty itself did not specifically mention intrastate aviation. The decision contains statements by a number of justices expressly recognizing Commonwealth power under section 51(xxix) to legislate in areas normally

---

113. 55 C.L.R. 687 (Austl. 1936) (Evatt & McTiernan, JJ.).
114. *Id.* at 669 (Dixon, J.).
115. *Id.* at 658 (Stark, J.).
116. *Id.* at 659-60 (Stark, J.).
117. Van Son, *The Australian Constitution: The External Affairs Power and Federalism*, 12 CAL. W. INT'L L.J. 46, 54-55 (1982).
118. 113 C.L.R. 54 (1965).
119. *Id.* at 86 (Barwick, C.J.).

reserved to the states.[120]

In *The King v. Sharkey*,[121] involving the conviction of a Communist leader in Australia for seditious acts directed not at Australia but at a member of the Dominion, Chief Justice Latham apparently went further. He indicated that the existence of a treaty or convention was not a prerequisite to the exercise of the section 51(xxix) power.[122] Australia's desire to maintain "friendly relations with other dominions," he found, was a sufficient basis for legislation authorized under that section.[123] It should be noted, however, that the case involved a Crown Statute, later adopted by Australia, rather than original Commonwealth legislation.[124]

B.   The *Koowarta* Case

Koowarta v. Bjelke-Petersen,[125] which upheld the Racial Discrimination Act 1975, arose when Koowarta, an Aborigine from Queensland, sought on behalf of himself and members of his tribe to obtain a Crown leasehold on land in Queensland. Negotiations led to a contract for the purchase of the lease. Under both the contract and a Queensland law, sale or transfer of this lease was subject to approval by the Queensland Minister of Lands. The Minister denied approval because the request came within the declared policy of the Queensland Cabinet: "The Queensland Government does not view favourably proposals to acquire large areas of additional freehold or leasehold land for development by Aborigines or aboriginal groups in isolation."[126]

Koowarta claimed that the Queensland Minister of Lands had acted unlawfully under the Racial Discrimination Act 1975, passed by the Commonwealth to implement the International Convention on the Elimination of All Forms of Racial Discrimination,[127] to which Australia was a signatory. Article 2(*l*) of the Convention requires States Parties to "pursue by all appropriate means" a policy of eliminating racial discrimination by any persons, groups, or organizations, "including legislation as required by circumstances."[128] Article V of the Convention provides that

States Parties undertake to prohibit and to eliminate racial discrimination in all its

---

120.   *See, e.g., id.* at 82 (Barwick, C.J.), 115 (Kitto, J.), 125-26 (Taylor, J.). A related case was New South Wales v. Commonwealth (the Submerged Lands Case), 135 C.L.R. 337 (Austl. 1975). In this case, a Commonwealth act (enacted pursuant to an international convention) claimed Commonwealth jurisdiction of contiguous marine areas. The majority upheld the act against the states' claim that if the subject matter is geographically external to Australia, there need not be any reciprocity of international interests.

121.   79 C.L.R. 121 (Austl. 1949).

122.   *Id.* at 135-38.

123.   *Id.* at 137. A second justice agreed with this point. *Id.* at 163.

124.   In an earlier case, Ffrost v. Stevenson, 58 C.L.R. 528 (Austl. 1937), two of five justices would have upheld legislation providing for extradition of fugitives from New Guinea under section 51(xxix). That legislation was based on a Crown act later adopted by Australia.

125.   39 Austl. L.R. 417 (1982).

126.   Decision of September 1972, *quoted in Koowarta,* 39 Austl. L.R. at 420 (Gibbs, C.J.).

127.   *Opened for signature* March 7, 1966, 660 U.N.T.S. 195, G.A. Res. 2106, 20 U.N. GAOR Supp. (No. 14) at 47, U.N. Doc. A/6104 (1965) (hereinafter cited as International Convention on the Elimination of All Forms of Racial Discrimination).

128.   *Id.* art. 2(1).

forms and to guarantee the right of everyone, without distinction as to race, colour, or national or ethnic origin, to equality before the law, notably in the enjoyment of the following rights: . . . the right to own property alone as well as in association with others . . . .[129]

Section 9 of the Racial Discrimination Act 1975 declares that it is

unlawful for a person to do any act involving a distinction, exclusion, restriction or preference based on race, colour, descent or national or ethnic origin which has the purpose or effect of nullifying or impairing the recognition, enjoyment or exercise, on an equal footing, of any human right or fundamental freedom . . . .[130].

The Act adds that the reference to "a human right or fundamental freedom" includes a reference to any right found in article V of the Convention.[131] Section 12(1) of the Act specifically forbids discrimination in the sale or disposition of property.[132] The Act also created a right of action for a "person aggrieved"[133] and provided remedies, including injunction and damages.[134]

Koowarta brought suit under the Racial Discrimination Act. The defendants argued that the Act was unconstitutional, with the Court limiting argument to the validity of sections 9 and 12 of the Act under section 51(xxix) of the constitution.[135]

The *Koowarta* case is significant because the Commonwealth legislation dealt with purely domestic acts in the context of moral commitments found appropriate by international agreement. Previous cases had dealt with less abstract subject matter, such as internationally shared air or sea space or crimes committed against or in other states.[136] The issue was thus more clearly drawn in *Koowarta*: whether the Commonwealth, under section 51(xxix), could enact laws to implement any treaty on any subject matter, despite express constitutional limitations on Commonwealth powers in relation to state powers.

The issue whether sections 9 and 12 of the Racial Discrimination Act were

---

129. *Id.* art. 5.
130. Racial Discrimination Act 1975, § 9(1), 1975 Austl. Acts 347, 352.
131. *Id.* § 9(2), 1975 Austl. Acts at 352.
132. Section 12(1) of the Act, 1975 Austl. Acts at 353, provides:
It is unlawful for a person, whether as a principal or agent—
    (a) to refuse or fail to dispose of any estate or interest in land, or any residential or business accommodation, to a second person;
    (b) to dispose of such an estate or interest or such accommodation to a second person on less favorable terms and conditions than those which are or would otherwise be offered;
    (c) to treat a second person who is seeking to acquire or has acquired such an estate or interest or such accommodation less favorably than other persons in the same circumstances;
    (d) to refuse to permit a second person to occupy any land or any residential or business accommodation; or
    (e) to terminate any estate or interest in land of a second person or the right of a second person to occupy any land or any residential or business accommodation,
by reason of the race, colour or national or ethnic origin of that second person or of any relative or associate of that second person.
133. *Id.* § 24(1), 1975 Austl. Acts at 357.
134. *Id.* § 25, 1975 Austl. Acts at 358.
135. Section 51(xxvi), which grants the Commonwealth legislative powers with respect to "the people of any race for whom it is deemed necessary to make special laws," was also involved.
136. *See supra* text accompanying notes 111-18.

valid under the external affairs power had to be analyzed in two steps. First, was the subject matter within the concept "external affairs"? Second, if so, was the scope of the challenged legislation reasonably appropriately designed to effectuate the obligation incurred? The State of Queensland conceded that sections 9 and 12 conformed to the terms of the Convention. Thus the only question was whether the subject matter fell within the concept of external affairs. By a narrow three-to-four majority, the High Court held that the Racial Discrimination Act 1975 was properly a law with respect to external affairs.

The High Court majority consisted of Justices Mason, Murphy, Brennan and Stephen. The first three took a broad view of what constituted an "external affair." A subject matter, in their view, becomes an "external affair" upon becoming the object of a treaty. Justice Mason held that any treaty obligation, if not entered into solely in order to be able to utilize the authority in section 51(xxix), is an external affair, although exercise of that authority is limited by any express or implied constitutional restrictions.[137] The fact that a power is normally reserved to the state, however, is *not* such a restriction. According to Justice Mason, "[i]t is very difficult to see why [an implementing] law would not be a law with respect to an external affair, once it is accepted that the treaty is an external affair."[138] The concept of "external affairs" is fixed and unchanging. However, recent expansion in international cooperation raises the potential for Commonwealth activity in new legislative areas, since "it is a Constitution we are interpreting."[139]

Justice Mason seemed to go further, however, in maintaining that the existence of "international concern" over a topic would create an "external affair" within the meaning of section 51(xxix) even if Australia were not a party to a treaty with respect to the topic. For him, as for Justice Murphy, the existence of a treaty is *not* a necessary prerequisite to the exercise of the section 51(xxix) power. "[A] matter which is of external concern to Australia having become the topic of international debate, discussion and negotiation constitutes an external affair before Australia enters into a treaty relating to it."[140] Any expansion of Commonwealth power into areas usually reserved to the states is justified to the extent necessary to allow Australia to participate in the international community. The rationale is that if Australia failed to meet its obligations, it would become the object of international discussion, disapproval, and perhaps even enforcement action by international bodies.[141]

Having once determined that the subject matter is within the purview of section 51(xxix), Justice Mason takes the view that the power to enact imple-

---

137. *Koowarta,* 39 Austl. L.R. at 460.

138. *Id.* at 459.

139. *Id.* at 462 (*quoting* Australian Nat'l Airways Proprietary, Ltd. v. Commonwealth, 71 C.L.R. 29, 81 (Austl. 1945) (Dixon, J.)). This is obviously reminiscent of Chief Justice Marshall's statement "it is a *constitution* we are expounding." McCulloch v. Maryland, 17 U.S. (4 Wheat.) 316, 407 (1819) (emphasis in original).

140. *Koowarta,* 39 Austl. L.R. at 466-67.

141. *Id.* at 468.

menting legislation is broad and discretionary. As long as the legislation is appropriate and adapted to the enforcement of the Convention, rather than repugnant to it, the legislation should be upheld.[142]

Justice Murphy, who also took a very broad approach, shared Justice Mason's opinion that the existence of a treaty is not prerequisite to invoking section 51(xxix) authorization. In his view, any act relating to matters of international concern such as "observance in Australia of international standards of human rights"[143] would provide the basis for laws reaching purely domestic matters even if there is no international agreement. With regard to racial discrimination, Justice Murphy noted that this century had seen the "greatest recognition of and also the greatest denial of human rights in all history."[144] Moreover, various U.N. agencies, declarations, and conventions had evidenced a great degree of international concern about the persistence of racial discrimination.[145] Certainly, the concern of the Commonwealth with discrimination in Australia is related to its concern about discrimination elsewhere. "In the practical realm of international politics it would be futile for Australia to criticize racial discrimination or other human rights violations in other countries if it were to tolerate such discrimination within Australia."[146] Like Justice Mason, Justice Murphy would not require precise congruence between the implementing act under section 51(xxix) and the terms of the international agreement.[147]

Justice Brennan's opinion was somewhat more constrained, but he found that "[i]f Australia, in the conduct of its relations with other nations, accepts a treaty obligation with respect to an aspect of Australia's internal legal order, the subject of the obligation thereby becomes . . . an external affair and a law with respect to that subject [is within section 51(xxix)]."[148]

The opinions of these three justices in *Koowarta* support a broad interpretation of the section 51(xxix) power. However, Justice Stephen, whose vote was necessary for a majority in favor of an interpretation of section 51(xxix) that permits legislation to reach domestic matters, heavily qualified his agreement with the plurality, and agreed with the dissenters that mere entry into an international agreement does not generate an external affair. To come within section 51(xxix), it is not enough that a law effectuate a treaty obligation. A "matter of international concern" must be involved, one which displays "the capacity to affect a country's relations with other nations . . . ."[149] Thus, in his view, though "external affairs" is a fixed concept, its content "lies very much in the hands of the community of nations of which Australia forms a

---

142. *See id.* at 458, 465.
143. *Id.* at 473.
144. *Id.* at 470.
145. *Id.* at 471.
146. *Id.*
147. *See id.* at 472.
148. *Id.* at 487.
149. *Id.* at 453.

part."[150] The prohibition of racial discrimination is clearly part of that content. Although it would appear that the Racial Discrimination Act is a Commonwealth intrusion into a legislative area previously exclusively left to the states, this was not, according to Justice Stephen, a redistribution in the federal balance, but only a growth in the content of "external affairs" reflecting "the new global concern for human rights and the international acknowledgment of the need for universally recognized norms of conduct. . . ."[151] In his view, the subject matter must have to do with "such of the public business of the national government as relates to other nations or other things or circumstances outside Australia,"[152] and any such legislation should receive intense scrutiny to assure "general international concern" or "especial concern to the relationship between Australia and [another] country."[153]

Chief Justice Gibbs led the dissent,[154] taking the view that Commonwealth laws implementing international agreements were invalid *unless* the provisions to which they gave effect specifically addressed external affairs. According to Justice Gibbs and the other dissenters, "external affairs" required that the subject matter of the provision involve a relationship with other countries or with persons or things outside Australia. The term "external affairs" as used in section 51(xxix) thus was not coextensive with the treatymaking power. In this view, earlier cases, such as *The King v. Burgess,*[155] *Airlines of N.S.W. Proprietary, Ltd. v. New South Wales*[156] and *New South Wales v. Commonwealth* (the *Submerged Lands Case*)[157] "had, in themselves, an international element; they affected the relations between Australia and other countries in some direct way."[158]

The *Koowarta* case presented a different issue: whether Parliament can, under section 51(xxix), effectuate "a treaty which deals with a matter that is entirely domestic and affects only Australians within Australia, and their relations to each other, and does not involve any trelationship [sic] between Australia or Australians and other countries or their citizens."[159] The only way in which international obligations could be given domestic effect, under the constitution, would be by state law unless the subject matter is within express grants of Commonwealth power elsewhere in the constitution. It could not, however, be done through the external affairs power alone. Thus, as Justice Wilson added in his dissenting opinion, the provisions of the Racial Discrimination Act 1975 lacked the necessary external aspect, since the conduct those

150. *Id.* at 454.
151. *Id.*
152. *Id.* at 449.
153. *Id.* at 453.
154. *Id.* at 419-45. Justice Aicken concurred in the dissent with no separate opinion, *see id.* at 417-19, and Justice Wilson also joined in the dissent, to which he added "supplementary remarks." *Id.* at 475-82.
155. 55 C.L.R. 608 (Austl. 1936); *see supra* text accompanying notes 111-17.
156. 113 C.L.R. 54 (Austl. 1965); *see supra* text accompanying notes 118-20.
157. 135 C.L.R. 337 (Austl. 1975); *see supra* note 120.
158. *Koowarta*, 39 Austl. L.R. at 433.
159. *Id.* at 434.

sections proscribed would only take place in the day-to-day interaction among persons within Australia.[160]

C. The *Tasmanian Dam Case*

In 1983, the High Court, again by a four-to-three vote, handed down its decision in the *Tasmanian Dam Case.*[161] That case involved actions stemming from a convention that Australia had ratified in 1974, the Convention for the Protection of the World Cultural and Natural Heritage.[162] The object of the Convention was to establish "an effective system of collective protection of the cultural and natural heritage of outstanding universal value."[163] Under the terms of the Convention, a World Heritage Committee was established.[164] The Committee was to establish criteria for inclusion of properties on a World Heritage List and a List of World Heritage in Danger.[165] States Parties were required to make contributions to a World Heritage Fund to finance assistance with respect to included (or potentially suitable) properties approved by the Committee.[166]

Various articles of the Convention established obligations on the part of States Parties, primarily to protect and conserve property designated as a natural heritage situated on its territory.[167] The Australian National Parks and Wildlife Conservation Act 1975,[168] adopted pursuant to this Convention, authorized the Governor-General of Australia to "make regulations for and in relation to giving effect" to the Convention for the Protection of the World Cultural and Natural Heritage.[169] In September of 1981, the Premier of the State of Tasmania wrote to Commonwealth Prime Minister Malcolm Fraser requesting that several national parks in Tasmania be nominated for inclusion on the World Heritage List, including the Gordon River-Below-Franklin Dam area. In April 1982, the Prime Minister submitted his nomination of these parks to the World Heritage Committee.

In June of that same year, a statute was enacted by the parliament of the State of Tasmania authorizing construction of a dam, a power generating sta-

---

160. *See id.* at 477-78.

161. Commonwealth v. Tasmania, 46 Austl. L.R. 625 (1983).

162. Convention for the Protection of the World Cultural and Natural Heritage, *done* Nov. 23, 1972, 27 U.S.T. 37, T.I.A.S. No. 8226.

163. *Id.* preamble.

164. *Id.* art. 8.

165. *Id.* art. 11(5).

166. *Id.* art. 16.

167. Under article 4, States Parties recognize a "duty of ensuring the identification, protection, conservation, presentation and transmission to future generations of the cultural and natural heritage [as defined by articles 1 and 2] and situated on its territory . . . ." Article 5 provides that each State Party "shall endeavor, in so far as possible, and as appropriate for each country" to take specified measures in pursuit of that duty. Under article 6, States Parties "undertake . . . to give their help in the identification, protection, conservation and preservation of . . . cultural and natural heritage . . . [and] not to take any deliberate measures which might damage [it] directly or indirectly . . . ."

168. National Parks and Wildlife Conservation Act 1975, 1975 Austl. Acts 103.

169. *Id.* § 69, 1975 Austl. Acts at 128.

tion, and other associated works on the Gordon River.[170] At the time that the authorization was adopted, the Premier of Tasmania (not the same Premier who recommended that the area be listed as one of the World Heritage areas) requested that Prime Minister Fraser withdraw the World Heritage nomination. Despite the fact that Fraser refused to withdraw the nomination, construction on the dam began. Areas of land were excised from the Franklin-Lower Gordon Wild Rivers National Park by the state and vested in the Hydro-Electric Commission of Tasmania.

In December 1982, the World Heritage Committee, listing the three parks as natural heritages, expressed concern at the possible destruction of national and cultural features in the region as a result of the dam project. Extensive flooding of both wilderness land and archeological sites was feared. The Committee suggested that the property be placed on the World Heritage in Danger list until the question of the construction of the dam was resolved.

When the Labor Party came to power in March 1983, it proceeded to enact legislation and regulations with respect to the dam, putting the Commonwealth in direct confrontation with the State of Tasmania. One regulation, pursuant to section 69 of the 1975 Act, forbade inter alia "construction of a dam or associated works [or] . . . any act in the course of, or for the purpose of," such construction; excavation; erection of buildings "or other substantial structure[s];" killing or damaging any trees; or "carry[ing] out any other works" without the consent of a Commonwealth Minister.[171] The second section of that regulation went further and forbade any act "that is likely adversely to affect the conservation or preservation of that area as part of the world cultural heritage or natural heritage."[172] A 1983 Commonwealth statute[173] identified specific properties, including the Franklin Dam area, as subject to essentially the same prohibitions, noting that protection or conservation of the properties was "a matter of international obligation"; "necessary or desirable for the purpose of giving effect to a treaty . . . or obtaining for Australia any . . . benefit under a treaty"; and "a matter of international concern (whether or not it is also a matter of domestic concern)," because failure to conserve or protect "would, or would be likely to, prejudice Australia's relations with other countries."[174]

The State of Tasmania challenged both the regulations and the Act as ultra vires and invalid. The validity of the regulations depended upon whether section 69 of the 1975 Act was valid as an exercise of the external affairs power and whether the regulations themselves were "regulations for and in relation to giving effect to the Convention."[175] The validity of sections 6 and 9 of the

---

170. Gordon River Hydro-Electric Power Development Act 1982, 1982 [Pt. 1] Tasm. Sess. Stat. 3.
171. Regulation 5(1), World Heritage (Western Tasmania Wilderness) Regulations (modified March 1983), cited in The Tasmanian Dam Case, 46 AUSTL. L.R. at 640-41.
172. Id. Regulation 5(2), cited in The Tasmanian Dam Case, 46 Austl. L.R. at 641.
173. World Heritage Properties Conservation Act 1983, 1983 Austl. Acts — (unavailable at publication).
174. See id. §§ 6, 9.
175. The Tasmanian Dam Case, 46 Austl. L.R. at 675.

1983 Act also depended upon whether they were valid exercises of the external affairs power.[176]

The High Court upheld section 69 of the 1975 Act by a four-to-three vote, but it found the regulations invalid. A four-person majority also upheld section 6 and part of section 9 of the 1983 Commonwealth Act, as well as the regulations and proclamations made in accordance with those sections, although the remainder of section 9 was found to be invalid. The net result was to support the exercise of Commonwealth power over the State of Tasmania as within the external affairs power of section 51(xxix), permitting the prohibition of the dam project despite state legislation authorizing the construction of the dam.

The four-person majority included three members of the *Koowarta v. Bjelke-Petersen*[177] majority: Justices Mason, Murphy, and Brennan. They were joined by Justice Deane.[178] All of the justices in the majority were in agreement that the existence of an international agreement on any subject matter supports implementing laws, and that there is virtually no limit to the range of possible subject matter. Thus, in the majority view, the section 51(xxix) power is, in effect, coextensive with the executive treatymaking power as implemented by the Parliament of the Commonwealth, subject only to a limited number of express prohibitions contained elsewhere in the constitution. The mere fact that the power was one generally reserved to the states would not prevent the Commonwealth from enacting legislation concerning that subject matter area.

Justice Mason's opinion[179] asserted that all that is required to justify legislation under the external affairs power is mutuality of interest between international parties or some benefit resulting from observance of the treaty. The Court had to defer to Parliament on this issue. Because the law in question was directed to the protection and conservation of the region, it was valid even though its "impact on Tasmania's capacity to control development is severe."[180] Justice Murphy agreed with Justice Mason and added that it was the electorate, not the Court, that should control any exercise of power in this regard.[181] If a matter was one of international concern, that fact alone would bring it within the definition of "external affairs."[182]

Justice Brennan's opinion[183] was not quite so broad. If a treaty did not clearly impose an obligation, to justify Commonwealth legislation it must at least evidence international concern over its subject matter. That is, the sub-

---

176. Tasmania raised several other arguments under various provisions of the constitution that are not discussed in this article.
177. 39 Austl. L.R. 417 (1982); *see supra* notes 125-60 and accompanying text.
178. Justice Stephen had left the High Court to become Australia's Governor-General in 1982.
179. The Tasmanian Dam Case, 46 Austl. L.R. at 688-720.
180. *Id.* at 702. The case came at a time of economic recession in Australia, felt most acutely in Tasmania. The Franklin River Dam was seen as a way of reducing the cost of power and employing vast numbers of people in its building and related industries. Thus it was thought that this decision's economic impact on Tasmania would be severe.
181. *Id.* at 728.
182. *See id.* at 729-30.
183. *Id.* at 760-97.

ject must affect or be likely to affect Australia's relations with international persons.[184] Implementing laws must actually be conducive to the international convention, however.[185] When the convention permits discretion, the test for the Court would be whether any part of the implementing law is not reasonably considered as appropriate to the treaty's goals.[186] Here, of course, Justice Brennan felt that the Commonwealth act in question was appropriate.

Justice Deane, the new member of the majority, interpreted the external affairs power very broadly.[187] In his view, "responsible conduct of external affairs . . . [requires] observance of the spirit as well as the letter of international agreements . . . [in] pursuit of international objectives which cannot be measured in terms of binding obligation."[188] A treaty with a broad purpose would permit wide discretion in implementing legislation. As long as the laws were reasonably appropriate to the purposes of such agreements, they should be upheld.[189]

As they had been in *Koowarta*, the dissenters were led by Chief Justice Gibbs.[190] They emphasized that a majority of the *Koowarta* Court had rejected the notion that mere entry into a treaty will support the exercise of the section 51(xxix) power. Because Justice Stephen's opinion in *Koowarta* had been the swing position, they contended that the High Court was required by notions of precedent to formulate and apply an acceptable articulation of the "international in character" criterion set forth in his opinion.[191] The dissenters felt that the preservation and conservation of natural and cultural heritage were not nearly so important morally or politically as the elimination of racial discrimination, with which the *Koowarta* case had been concerned.[192] Moreover, failure to meet the obligations of the Convention was not likely to affect Australia's relations with other nations.[193] The dissenters also argued that the fact that the Convention vested so much discretion in States Parties to determine how they would perform was an indication that international concern was not that intense.[194] Justice Gibbs interpreted Justice Stephen's position in the *Koowarta* case as requiring consideration of the *degree* to which a treaty affects Australia's relations with other nations and the extent to which it embodies international intentions to act.[195] Finally, the Convention, in its operative articles,[196] created no binding obligations; rather, it expressed a

---

184. *Id.* at 777. Justice Brennan said that in this case, unless Australia wished to "attribute hypocrisy and cynicism to the international community," such relations would indeed be affected.
185. *Id.* at 782.
186. *Id.*
187. *Id.* at 798-834.
188. *Id.* at 805.
189. *See id.* at 805-06.
190. *Id.* at 633-87.
191. *See supra* text accompanying notes 149-53.
192. The Tasmanian Dam Case, 46 Austl. L.R. at 670.
193. *Id.* at 671.
194. *Id.*
195. *Id.* at 670.
196. Convention for the Protection of World Cultural and Natural Heritage, *supra* note 162, arts. 4-5.

consensus as to aspirations. The dissenters argued that the earlier cases of *The King v. Burgess*[197] and *Airlines of N.S.W. Proprietary, Ltd. v. New South Wales*[198] strongly suggest that if no obligation is imposed on the Commonwealth by the treaty, no obligations can be imposed on the states by the Commonwealth.[199]

Justice Gibbs went on to note that even if the treaty in this case were considered to represent an "external affair," the Commonwealth's implementing legislation did not give effect to the international convention, that is, it did not "perform the obligations or secure the benefits" that the international convention imposed or conferred.[200] If there is no obligation created, the Commonwealth can only attempt to persuade the states to pursue the goals of the agreement. The Commonwealth, in his view, could not mandate protective measures such as these because they went beyond the terms of the agreement and were ultra vires under the *Burgess* case.[201]

All members of the court in the *Tasmanian Dam Case* purported to apply the "congruence" test.[202] The difference in result on the question whether the legislation is congruent with the obligations of the treaty depends on how the "obligation" is characterized. The dissenting Justices, Gibbs, Wilson, and Dawson, recognized no obligation.[203] Justices Deane and Brennan, two members of the majority, required some degree of closeness of fit between the obligation and the exercise of the section 51(xxix) power.[204] Justice Mason was satisfied that the obligation was that of instituting a "regime of control" with respect to protection and conservation of cultural and natural heritage and that all operative provisions were "appropriate and adapted to the desired end."[205] Justice Murphy merely stated that the operative sections were "reasonably appropriate to implementation of the Convention."[206]

State officials and other commentators were highly critical of the *Tasmanian Dam* decision. Premier Gray of Tasmania said that "decisions which have such far-reaching effects on the constitution of this country should at least be decided unanimously by the High Court and not be a majority decision."[207]

---

197. 55 C.L.R. 608 (Austl. 1936); *see supra* text accompanying notes 111-17.
198. 113 C.L.R. 54 (Austl. 1965); *see supra* text accompanying notes 118-120.
199. The Tasmanian Dam Case, 46 Austl. L.R. at 671-75.
200. *Id.* at 671.
201. In *Airlines of N.S.W. Proprietary, Ltd.*, Chief Justice Barwick said, in an often-quoted passage:
    But where a law is to be justified under the external affairs power by reference to the existence of a treaty or a convention, the limits of the exercise of the power will be set by the terms of that treaty or convention, that is to say, the Commonwealth will be limited to making laws to perform the obligations, or to secure the benefits which the treaty imposes or confers on Australia. Whilst the choice of the legislative means by which the treaty or convention shall be implemented is for the legislative authority, it is for this Court to determine whether particular provisions, when challenged, are appropriate and adapted to that end. The Court will closely scrutinize the challenged provisions to ensure that what is proposed to be done substantially falls within the power.
ll3 C.L.R. at 86.
202. *See id.*
203. The Tasmanian Dam Case, 46 Austl. L.R. at 674, 745-49, 849.
204. *Id.* at 770-72, 801-06.
205. *Id.* at 702-03.
206. *Id.* at 736.
207. The Weekend Australian, July 2-3, 1983, at 1.

Premier Bjelke-Petersen of Queensland stated that the decision marked "the end of Federation and shows the first crack in the Commonwealth."[208] Another Queensland politician was quoted as saying that "the rights of each state are imperilled if the Commonwealth uses its UN treaties as a stick with which to beat the states into submission."[209] A Queensland legal expert said "the States are now virtually subject to the whim of Canberra, which can make international agreements and bind itself to overrule the States."[210] One newspaper editorial commented that "the judgment has created the most fundamental constitutional change since Federation, in a way that was probably never envisaged by its founders."[211] Another editorial noted that "control over the basic principles of Australia's system of government has been taken out of the hands of the people and delivered to judges not answerable to any electorate," and that the federal government's "legal victory has saved a river but has sacrificed one of the safeguards of our democratic system."[212] A Liberal Party spokesman said that the decision would have such a "profound effect on the division of powers between the Commonwealth and the States . . . that the system as we have known it could virtually cease to exist."[213]

D. The External Affairs Power After the *Tasmanian Dam Case*

The decision in the *Tasmanian Dam Case* supports the broader view of the external affairs power: Parliament can implement any treaty made by the Commonwealth, no matter what its subject matter, provided it does not contravene a specific constitutional prohibition and is not a treaty artifically entered into in order to usurp legislative power for the Commonwealth that otherwise had not been given it. The decision rejects the narrow view that some limitation must be placed on the Commonwealth's power to implement treaties in order to maintain the careful balance between state and Commonwealth powers incorporated in the constitution. The dissenting view, that Parliament's power is confined to implementing treaties truly international in character, was also rejected.

Although the broad, expansive view of the section 51(xxix) power prevails, even some members of the *Tasmanian Dam* majority emphasized that the legislation in question must be clearly designed to implement the treaty. Whether the test articulated by some, that the legislation be "reasonably appropriate" to implementing the treaty or convention, is so broad as to impose virtually no limit on legislation, remains to be seen. At least the High Court, in both *Koowarta v. Bjelke-Petersen*[214] and the *Tasmanian Dam Case*, has upheld use of the external affairs power to reach subjects normally reserved to the states by the

---

208. *Id.* at 8, col. 2.
209. *Id.* at 8, col. 3.
210. *Id.* at 1.
211. *Id.* at 10, cols. 1-2.
212. The Australian, July 7, 1983, at 1, cols. 2-3.
213. Statement of Senator Peter Durack, *quoted in* The Weekend Australian, July 2-3, 1983, at 1 (Senator Durack is the opposition's spokesman on attorney general matters.).
214. 39 Austl. L.R. 417 (1982); *see supra* notes 125-60 and accompanying text.

constitution and tradition. Admittedly, however, the vote in each case was extremely close.

To what extent might future Commonwealth legislation on education be authorized by the external affairs power, particularly with regard to unfunded civil rights mandates like those of such U.S. statutes as Title VI of the Civil Rights Act of 1964,[215] Title IX of the Education Amendments of 1972,[216] and section 504 of the Rehabilitation Act of 1973?[217] Justice Wilson, in his dissenting opinion in *Koowarta*, expressed concern that the emerging "sophisticated network of international arrangements directed to the personal, economic, social and cultural development of all human beings," would mean that if section 51(xxix) were interpreted as vesting Parliament with power in all of these areas, the effect "would be to transfer to the Commonwealth virtually unlimited power in almost every conceivable aspect of life in Australia, including . . . education."[218] Justice Gibbs also was concerned that if section 51(xxix) were interpreted to empower Parliament to make laws to carry into effect within Australia "any treaty which the Governor-General may make," Parliament would, in effect, be empowered to make laws on any subject, thus destroying the federal balance achieved by the constitution.[219] "[The executive] could, for example, by making an appropriate treaty, obtain for the Parliament powers *to control education*, to regulate the use of land, to fix the conditions of trading and employment, to censor the press or to determine the basis of criminal responsibility."[220] Thus, at least two of the dissenters believed that the majority's opinion in *Koowarta* would give the Commonwealth power over education if it could be related to treaties, international agreements, or covenants.

IV

THE EFFECTS OF A BROAD INTERPRETATION OF SECTIONS 51(XXIX) AND 96 ON THE COMMONWEALTH'S ROLE IN EDUCATION

A. International Agreements to Which Australia is a Party

One recent commentator has pointed out that education today clearly is an international concern, and he notes that many international organizations of which Australia is a member consider education to be an important objective

---

215. 42 U.S.C. §§ 2000d to 2000d-4 (1982).

216. 20 U.S.C. §§ 1681-1686 (1982).

217. 29 U.S.C. § 794 (1982). As previously noted, AUSTL. CONST. § 96 permits the Commonwealth to provide financial assistance to any State on such terms and conditions as the Parliament thinks fit, and therefore might support a grant-in-aid statute for education with the kinds of conditions which are found, for example, in the Education for All Handicapped Children Act of 1975. *See infra* text accompanying notes 336-40. In addition, section 51(xxiiiA) gives Parliament the power "to make laws for the peace, order, and good government of the Commonwealth with respect to . . . [t]he provision of . . . benefits to students . . . ." This section thus provides authorization for financial aid directly to students. It might also authorize a much broader exercise of power in the area of educational policy, although it has not been so interpreted to date.

218. *Koowarta*, 39 Austl. L.R. at 481.

219. *Id.* at 438.

220. *Id.* (emphasis added).

for them or even their principal focus.[221] These organizations include the United Nations Organization, the United Nations Educational, Scientific, and Cultural Organization, the International Labor Organization, and the Organization for Economic Cooperation and Development. Moreover, Australia has participated in educational programs through its membership in the Commonwealth Education Conference, the Colombo Plan, the Southeast Asia Treaty Organization, and the Asian and Pacific Council. He argues that conventions signed or agreements made on issues involving education by Australia as a member of these international organizations would attract the operation of the external affairs power and thus permit the Commonwealth to enact legislation dealing with education.[222]

There are five major conventions or covenants which deal with education, at least in part. The first is the International Convention on the Elimination of All Forms of Racial Discrimination.[223] This Convention was relied upon by Parliament when it enacted the Racial Discrimination Act 1975,[224] challenged by the State of Queensland in *Koowarta v. Bjelke-Petersen.* [225] In that Convention, the States Parties undertake to prohibit all forms of discrimination wherever found. Article 5, in particular, provides in part:

> States Parties undertake to prohibit and eliminate racial discrimination in all its forms and to guarantee the right of everyone, without distinction as to race, colour or national or ethnic origin, to equality before the law, notably in the enjoyment of the following rights:
>
>   . . . .
>
> (e) Economic, social and cultural rights, in particular:
>
>   . . . .
>
> (v) The right to education and training; . . . .[226]

In article 6, the States Parties undertake to "assure . . . effective protection and remedies" against any violations of the Convention.[227]

The International Convention on the Elimination of All Forms of Discrimination Against Women[228] was adopted by the United Nations General Assembly in December 1979. Article 10 of that Convention reads:

> States Parties shall take all appropriate measures to eliminate discrimination against

---

221. Birch, *Education and the External Affairs Power: Implications for the Governance of Australian Schools,* 27 AUSTL. J. EDUC. 234, 240-42 (1983). Following Koowarta v.Bjelke-Petersen, 39 Austl. L.R. 417 (1982), *see supra* notes 125-60 and accompanying text, other authors also suggested that the Commonwealth could legislate in the field of human rights to implement international agreements, and that such legislation could override any state or Commonwealth laws that were inconsistent with human rights guarantees. *See* J. MCMILLAN, G. EVANS & H. STOREY, *supra* note 6, at 95.

222. Birch, *supra* note 221, at 240.

223. *Supra* note 127. The Convention was adopted by the General Assembly of the United Nations on December 21, 1965. Australia signed the Convention on October 13, 1966 and ratified it on September 30, 1975. The Convention entered into force January 4, 1969.

224. 1975 Austl. Acts 347.

225. 39 Austl. L.R. 417 (1982); *see supra* notes 125-60 and accompanying text.

226. International Convention on the Elimination of All Forms of Racial Discrimination, *supra* note 127, art. 5.

227. *Id.* art. 6.

228. *Opened for signature* March 1, 1980, G.A. Res. 180, 34 U.N. GAOR Supp. (No. 46) at 193, U.N. Doc. A/RES/34/180. The Convention was signed by Australia on July 17, 1980, and entered into force on September 3, 1981.

women in order to ensure to them equal rights with men in the field of education and in particular to ensure, on a basis of equality of men and women:

    (a) The same conditions for career and vocational guidance, for access to studies and for the achievement of diplomas in educational establishments of all categories . . . ;

    (b) Access to the same curricula, the same examinations, teaching staff with qualifications of the same standard and school premises and equipment of the same quality;

    (c) The elimination of any stereotyped concept of the roles of men and women at all levels and in all forms of education . . . in particular, by the revision of textbooks and school programmes and the adaptation of teaching methods . . . ;

. . . .

    (e) The same opportunities for access to programmes of continuing education . . . ;

. . . .

    (g) The same opportunities to participate actively in sports and physical education . . . .[229]

In article 2, States Parties specifically undertake "to adopt appropriate legislative and other measures, including sanctions where appropriate, prohibiting all discrimination against women . . . ."[230] Finally, article 4 permits, but does not require, States Parties to adopt affirmative action measures to "accelerat[e] *de facto* equality between men and women."[231]

The International Covenant on Economic, Social and Cultural Rights[232] specifically notes that States Parties "recognize the right of everyone to education."[233] Article 2(2) notes that the States Parties undertake to guarantee that the rights in the Covenant, including the right to education, "will be exercised without discrimination of any kind as to race, colour, sex, language, religion, political or other opinion, national or social origin, property, birth or other status."[234] In this Covenant, however, the obligations are not fully guaranteed immediately. Article 2(1) says that each State Party undertakes to take steps "to the maximum of its available resources, with a view to achieving progressively the full realization of the rights recognized in the present Covenant by all appropriate means, including particularly the adoption of legislative measures."[235] One might call this the "all deliberate speed" provision.

There is also an international agreement that is concerned solely with education. The United Nations Educational, Scientific, and Cultural Organization (UNESCO) adopted the Convention Against Discrimination in Education on December 14, 1960.[236] The preamble to the Convention notes that UNESCO

---

229. *Id.* art. 10.

230. *Id.* art. 2(b).

231. *Id.* art. 4(1).

232. *Opened for signature* Dec. 19, 1966, Annex to G.A. Res. 2200, 21 U.N. GAOR Supp. (No. 16) at 49, U.N. Doc. A/6316 (1966) (hereinafter cited as International Covenant on Economic, Social and Cultural Rights). The Covenant was adopted by the U.N. General Assembly on December 16, 1966; signed by Australia on December 18, 1972, and ratified on December 10, 1975; and entered into force on January 3, 1976.

233. *Id.* art. 13(1).

234. *Id.* art. 2(2).

235. *Id.* art. 2(1).

236. Annex I to U.N. Doc. E/CN.4/Sub.2/210 (1961) (hereinafter cited as Convention Against Discrimination in Education). The Convention was ratified by Australia in August 1974 and entered into force in November 1974.

"has the duty not only to proscribe any form of discrimination in education but also to promote equality of opportunity and treatment for all in education . . . ."[237] Article 1 of the Convention defines the term "discrimination" to include:

> any distinction, exclusion, limitation or preference which, being based on race, colour, sex, language, religion, political or other opinion, national or social origin, economic condition or birth, has the purpose or effect of nullifying or impairing equality of treatment in education and in particular:
> (a) Of depriving any person or group of persons of access to education of any type or at any level;
> (b) Of limiting any person or group of persons to education of an inferior standard;
> (c) Subject to the provisions of Article 2 of this Convention, of establishing or maintaining separate educational systems or institutions for persons or groups of persons; . . . .[238]

The establishment or the maintenance of separate educational systems or institutions on the basis of sex is permitted, however, "if these systems or institutions offer equivalent access to education, provide a teaching staff of qualifications of the same standard as well as school premises and equipment of the same quality, and afford the opportunity to take the same or equivalent courses of study."[239]

Under this Convention, States Parties undertake to repeal statutory provisions or discontinue administrative practices that involve discrimination in education and "to ensure, by legislation where necessary, that there is no discrimination in the admission of pupils to educational institutions."[240] Furthermore, the States Parties undertake to "formulate, develop and apply a national policy which . . . will tend to promote equality of opportunity and of treatment in the matter of education . . . . "[241]

Finally, while the International Covenant on Civil and Political Rights[242] does not specifically deal with education, it purports to protect individual civil and political rights, as well as economic, social and cultural rights. Article 26 of that Covenant provides:

> All persons are equal before the law and are entitled without any discrimination to the equal protection of the law. In this respect, the law shall prohibit any discrimination and guarantee to all persons equal and effective protection against discrimination on any ground such as race, colour, sex, language, religion, political or other opinion, national or social origin, property, birth or other status.[243]

---

237. *Id.* preamble.
238. *Id.* art. 1.
239. *Id.* art. 2(a). Article 2 also permits separate schools for "religious or linguistic reasons," as long as attendance at such institutions is optional, *id.* art. 2(b), and the establishment or maintenance of private educational institutions as long as the purpose "is not to secure the exclusion of any group," *id.* art. 2(c).
240. *Id.* art. 3(a)-(b).
241. *Id.* art. 4.
242. *Supra* note 108. The Covenant was adopted by the General Assembly of the United Nations on Dec. 16, 1966; signed by Australia on December 18, 1972, and ratified on August 13, 1980; and entered into force on March 23, 1976. The latter date does not apply to article 41, which entered into force on March 28, 1979.
243. *Id.* art 26.

A State Party undertakes "to take the necessary steps, in accordance with its constitutional processes . . . to adopt such legislative or other measures as may be necessary to give effect to the rights recognized in the . . . Covenant."[244] In addition, States Parties must provide effective remedies to any person whose rights or freedoms recognized in the Covenant are violated.[245] The provisions of the Covenant apply to "all parts of federal states" as well as to nations.[246] Australia signed the treaty with reservations,[247] including one which related to this last provision. The reservation indicated that implementation of the provisions of the Covenant which were the responsibility of the federal authorities, as assigned by Australia's constitution, was to be a matter for those authorities, but that implementation of those provisions of the Covenant over whose subject matter the states were assigned authority by the constitution would be a matter for the states.[248] This reservation also applied to the adoption of legislation to give effect to the rights recognized in the Covenant.[249]

The question of the significance of Australia's reservation to the Covenant would appear to be mooted by the current state of section 51(xxix) doctrine. The effect of the reservation, if valid, was to leave implementation of the Covenant with respect to matters of state law to the states. The effect of *Koowarta v. Bjelke-Petersen*[250] and the *Tasmanian Dam Case*,[251] however, is to make the subject matter of any treaty to which Australia is a signatory a matter for Com-

---

244. *Id.* art. 2(2).
245. *Id.* art. 2(3).
246. *Id.* art. 50.
247. A reservation is "a unilateral statement, however phrased or named, made by a State, when signing, ratifying, accepting, approving or acceding to a treaty, whereby it purports to exclude or modify the legal effect of certain provisions of the treaty in their application to that State. . . ." Vienna Convention on the Law of Treaties, art. 2(1)(d), *opened for signature* May 23, 1969, U.N. Doc. A/CONF. 39/27/Corr. 1, *reprinted in* 63 AM. J. INT'L L. 875 (1969); *see* Triggs, *Australia's Ratification of the International Covenant on Civil and Political Rights: Endorsement or Repudiation?*, 31 INT'L & COMP. L. Q. 278, 280-84 (1982). A reservation to a multilateral treaty becomes effective when another state accepts it. Vienna Convention on the Law of Treaties, *supra,* art. 20(4)(a). Failure to object to a reservation within twelve months of notification waives any rights to object to the legal effects it creates. *Id.* art. 20(5). A reservation may be invalid per se, however, if it is found to be "incompatible with the object and purpose of the treaty." Triggs, *supra,* at 283. There exist no reliable criteria for resolving this question but authorities have isolated several factors which guide the inquiry. *See id.* at 284 & nn.31-32.
248. The reservation specifically states:

Australia advises that, the people having united as one people in a Federal Commonwealth under the Crown, it has a federal constitutional system . . . . It enters a general reservation that article 2, paragraphs 2 and 3, and article 50 shall be given effect consistently with and subject to the provisions in article 2, paragraph 2.
. . . .
In particular, in relation to the Australian States the implementation of those provisions of the Covenant over whose subject matter the federal authorities exercise legislative, executive and judicial jurisdiction will be a matter for those authorities; and the implementation of those provisions of the Covenant over whose subject matter the authorities of the constituent States exercise legislative, executive and judicial jurisdiction will be a matter for those authorities; and where a provision has both federal and State aspects, its implementation will accordingly be a matter for the respective constitutionally appropriate authorities . . . .
[M]ultilateral Treaties Deposited with the Secretary-General 118, U.N. Doc. St/LEG/SER.E/1 (1982).
249. *See supra* text accompanying note 244.
250. 39 Austl. L.R. 417 (1982); *see supra* notes 125-60 and accompanying text.

monwealth legislative power, even if the subject matter was otherwise constitutionally committed to the states.

B. The Significance of These Agreements for Civil Rights Mandates

The question now to be explored is whether the foregoing covenants and
conventions, when coupled with the external affairs power of section 51(xxix),
provide the Commonwealth with the authority to enact civil rights laws similar
in nature to Title VI of the Civil Rights Act of 1964,[252] Title IX of the Education Amendments of 1972,[253] section 504 of the Rehabilitation Act of 1973,[254]
and their implementing regulations.

The broad language of each of the convenants and conventions discussed
above, together with the expansive reading given to the section 51(xxix)
power by the majority in both *Koowarta* and the *Tasmanian Dam Case*, arguably
gives the Commonwealth authority to pass legislation similar to Title VI.
Article 5 of the International Convention on the Elimination of All Forms of
Racial Discrimination[255] and article 2(2) of the International Covenant on
Economic, Social and Cultural Rights[256] would seem to provide such
authority. Even the International Covenant on Civil and Political Rights,
although it does not specifically mention education, in providing for "equal
protection of the law" in article 26[257] would seem to authorize legislation
comparable to Title VI.

The broad view of the external affairs power taken by the *Koowarta* and
Tasmanian Dam cases[258] — that the existence of an international agreement on
virtually any subject will support Commonwealth legislation implementing the
obligations of the agreement[259]—would permit legislation related to the
above-mentioned Conventions. The second question, whether legislation
patterned after Title VI would be congruent with the obligations of the international agreements,[260] also should be answered in the affirmative in view of
the majority position that laws and regulations need only be reasonably
related to accomplishing the obligation undertaken in the agreement.[261]

---

251. Commonwealth v. Tasmania, 46 Austl. L.R. 625 (1983); *see supra* notes 161-213 and accompanying text.

252. "No person in the United States shall, on the ground of race, color, or national origin, be
excluded from participation in, be denied the benefits of, or be subjected to discrimination under any
program or activity receiving Federal financial assistance." 42 U.S.C. § 2000d (1982); *see also id.*
§§ 2000d-1 to 2000d-5.

253. "No person in the United States shall, on the basis of sex, be excluded from participation
in, be denied the benefits of, or be subjected to discrimination under any education program or
activity receiving Federal financial assistance . . . ." 20 U.S.C. § 1681(a) (1982).

254. "No otherwise qualified handicapped individual . . . shall, solely by reason of his handicap,
be excluded from participation in, be denied the benefits of, or be subjected to discrimination under
any program or activity receiving Federal financial assistance." 29 U.S.C. § 794 (1982).

255. *See supra* text accompanying notes 223-26.

256. *See supra* text accompanying note 234.

257. *See supra* text accompanying notes 242-43.

258. *See supra* section III D.

259. *See supra* text accompanying notes 179-89.

260. *See supra* text accompanying note 117.

261. While two members of the majority in the *Tasmanian Dam Case,* Justices Deane and

The "all deliberate speed" provision[262] in the International Covenant on Economic, Social and Cultural Rights permits the argument to be made that equality of education is aspirational only, and thus not of sufficient international concern to permit Commonwealth legislation in an area committed to the states. This kind of argument clearly failed in the *Tasmanian Dam Case*, however.[263]

One of the interesting questions is whether the terms "national or ethnic origin" in the Convention on the Elimination of All Forms of Racial Discrimination,[264] and "language" and "national origin" in the Covenant on Civil and Political Rights,[265] the Covenant on Economic, Social and Cultural Rights,[266] and the Convention Against Discrimination in Education[267] would be interpreted in the same manner as the term "national origin" in Title VI[268] has been interpreted. The U.S. Department of Education, following policy originally established by the Department of Health, Education and Welfare (HEW), has interpreted this language to require affirmative assistance to children with limited English proficiency.[269] This interpretation was upheld by the Supreme Court in *Lau v. Nichols*.[270] At one point, the Department of Education went so far as to promulgate regulations that interpreted affirmative assistance to require, in certain circumstances, the provision of bilingual education.[271] Failure to do so would be a violation of Title VI.[272] Similar interpretation in Australia of the relevant provisions of these conventions and covenants could permit the Commonwealth to view failure on the part of school authorities to provide affirmative assistance (including bilingual education) to language minority children as discrimination on the basis of "language," "ethnic origin," or "national origin."

Looking at the language of the Convention on the Elimination of All Forms of Discrimination Against Women, it is not unlikely that a majority of

---

Brennan, would require some degree of closeness of fit between the obligation and the implementing legislation, 46 Austl. L.R. at 770-72, 801-06; *see supra* text accompanying notes 202-04, Title VI-type legislation would clearly pass the test. Justices Murphy and Mason would require only that the legislation be "reasonably appropriate." 46 Austl. L.R. at 702-03, 736; *see supra* text accompanying notes 205-06.

262. *See supra* text accompanying note 235.

263. *See supra* text accompanying notes 191-99.

264. International Convention on The Elimination of All Forms of Racial Discrimination, *supra* note 127, art. 1(l).

265. United Nations International Covenant on Civil and Political Rights, *supra* note 108, art. 2(1).

266. International Covenant on Economic, Social and Cultural Rights, *supra* note 232, art. 2(2).

267. Convention Against Discrimination in Education, *supra* note 236, art. 1.

268. 42 U.S.C. § 2000d (1982).

269. *See* 35 Fed. Reg. 11,595 (1970).

270. 414 U.S. 563 (1974).

271. Proposed Rules (Nondiscrimination Under Programs Receiving Federal Assistance Through the Department of Education), 45 Fed. Reg. 52,052, 52,055-59 (1980) (proposed Aug. 5, 1980).

272. *Id.* The regulations did not become final, however. *See* Levin, *An Analysis of the Federal Attempt to Regulate Bilingual Education: Protecting Civil Rights or Controlling Curriculum?*, 12 J.L. & EDUC. 29 (1983).

the High Court would also find legislation similar to Title IX[273] to be congruent with the obligation undertaken by Australia as one of the States Parties. This conclusion would apply as well to the other three conventions and covenants which bar discrimination on the basis of sex.[274]

Article 10(c) of the Convention,[275] promoting elimination of gender stereotypes through revision of textbooks and teaching methods, raises an interesting question. In drafting regulations to implement Title IX, HEW took the position that it would exclude textbooks and curricular content from the scope of administrative purview,[276] out of concern that federal intervention in such matters "would thrust the Department into the role of Federal censor" and might possibly violate the first amendment.[277] Since Australia does not have a constitutional equivalent to the U.S. Constitution's first amendment, there might be no equivalent difficulty for the Commonwealth in introducing a legislative or regulatory provision dealing with the subject matter of article 10(c) of the Convention.

The real question is whether legislation similar to section 504 of the Rehabilitation Act could be enacted in Australia under any of these covenants or conventions. Would either the term "birth" or the term "other status" be considered broad enough to include the handicapped as a protected group? Nowhere else in the covenants and conventions are the handicapped specifically mentioned. In both the Covenant on Civil and Political Rights and the Covenant on Economic, Social and Cultural Rights, discrimination on the ground of "birth or other status" is prohibited.[278] The Convention Against Discrimination in Education prohibits discrimination on the ground of "birth."[279] However, the term "other status" is not included in that Convention, and it is by no means evident that discrimination against the handicapped was meant to be included.[280]

---

273. Title IX has some of the same exceptions as the Convention: in regard to admissions, elementary and secondary schools, whether public or private, are exempt as are private institutions of undergraduate higher education and public institutions of undergraduate higher education that have traditionally been single-sex; military institutions are exempt; and religious institutions are exempt if Title IX would be inconsistent with their religious tenets. 20 U.S.C. § 1681 (1982).

274. International Covenant on Economic, Social and Cultural Rights, *supra* note 232; Convention Against Discrimination in Education, *supra* note 236; International Covenant on Civil and Political Rights, *supra* note 108.

275. *See supra* text accompanying note 228.

276. 34 C.F.R. § 106.42 (1984).

277. 40 Fed. Reg. 24,135 (1975).

278. International Covenant on Civil and Political Rights, *supra* note 108, art. 2(1); International Covenant on Economic, Social and Cultural Rights, *supra* note 232, art. 2(2).

279. Convention Against Discrimination in Education, *supra* note 236, art. 1.

280. There are several U.N. General Assembly declarations which touch on issues of educational opportunity for the handicapped. One is the Declaration of the Rights of the Child, G.A. Res. 1386, 14 U.N. GAOR Supp. (No. 16) at 19, U.N. Doc. A/4354 (1959). Principle 5 of the Declaration states that "[t]he child who is physically, mentally or socially handicapped shall be given the special . . . education . . . required by his particular condition." The second is the Declaration on the Rights of Mentally Retarded Persons, G.A. Res. 2856, 26 U.N. GAOR Supp. (No. 29) at 93, U.N. Doc. A/8588 (1971). It "calls for national and international action" to ensure that the Declaration will be a "frame of reference" for the protection of several listed rights, including "a right . . . to such education, training, rehabilitation and guidance as will enable him to develop his ability and maximum potential." The third is the Declaration on the Rights of Disabled Persons, G.A. Res. 3447, 30

The remaining issue for a Commonwealth Parliament wishing to enact civil rights mandates in education under its section 51(xxix) power is that of enforcement. In the United States, Title VI, Title IX, and section 504 are all enforced by the termination of federal funds going to any "program or activity" in which discrimination occurs. The phrase "program or activity" has recently been given a narrow interpretation by the U.S. Supreme Court.[281] An expansive interpretation in Australia could have an over-whelming impact, particularly if not only the specific purpose grants but also the revenue sharing or tax reimbursement grants are considered to be federal or Commonwealth funds which can be cut off if discrimination occurs.

C. Section 96 Authority

As noted above, the international covenants and conventions discussed in this section do not provide clear and convincing support for equal educational opportunity for the handicapped. Thus a statute similar to U.S. section 504 might not be found to be within the Commonwealth's section 51(xxix) power. Similarly, it is not clear that an affirmative duty to provide special assistance to the economically disadvantaged could be based on any of the agreements, although the Covenant on Civil and Political Rights and the Covenant on Economic, Social and Cultural Rights prohibit discrimination on the basis of "social origin,"[282] and the Convention Against Discrimination in Education prohibits discrimination on the basis of "social origin" and "economic condition."[283] Nevertheless, grant-in-aid statutes could contain conditions, similar to those found in the Education for All Handicapped Children Act[284] and in Title I (now Chapter 1) of the Elementary and Secondary Education Act of 1965,[285] designed to ensure benefits to the economically disadvantaged.

The authority, in other words, need not lie in international conventions or covenants, coupled with the exercise of section 51(xxix) power, but in a broader application of section 96 than has hitherto been followed. The question here would be whether section 96 could be read that expansively. The role that section 96 power played in enabling the Commonwealth to introduce

---

U.N. GAOR Supp. (No. 34) at 88, U.N. Doc. A/10284/Add.1 (1975). It is similar to the Declaration on the Rights of Mentally Retarded Persons, and includes "the right to . . . education, vocational training and rehabilitation, aid, counseling . . . and other services which will enable them to develop their capabilities and skills to the maximum and will hasten the process of their social integration or reintegration." Such Declarations do not ordinarily carry the same weight as international treaties or agreements. As discussed above, *see supra* text accompanying notes 140-41, only two High Court Justices, Murphy and Mason, might find that the existence of a treaty is not a necessary prerequisite to the exercise of the section 51(xxix) power. For them, it is sufficient that the legislation relate to a matter of international "concern" or to "observance in Australia of international standards of human rights," Koowarta v. Bjelke-Petersen, 39 Austl. L.R. 417, 473 (1982) (Murphy, J.), even if there is no international agreement.

281. Grove City College v. Bell, 104 S. Ct. 1211 (1984).
282. International Covenant on Civil and Political Rights, *supra* note 108, art. 2(1); International Covenant on Economic, Social and Cultural Rights, *supra* note 232, art. 2(2).
283. Convention Against Discrimination in Education, *supra* note 236, art. 1.
284. 20 U.S.C. § 1412 (1982).
285. 20 U.S.C. § 236 (1982).

and carry out the Uniform Tax Scheme has already been outlined.[286] Although the section 81 power to appropriate money for "the purposes of the Commonwealth" has been used from time to time, it has not been a broadly used power and so the primary vehicle for the distribution of federal funds has been, and continues to be, section 96.[287]

As has been previously pointed out, section 96 grants can be made without any conditions at all. These are the general revenue grants made under the tax reimbursement or financial assistance grants programs in accordance with the 1942 Uniform Tax Scheme. The only "condition" presently imposed on these programs is that the States refrain from imposing their own income taxes. There are also specific purpose grants, which are made with specific conditions attached. Conditional grants are made in areas where the Commonwealth does not normally have legislative power, as illustrated by the States Grants (Schools) Act.[288] Most commentators believe that section 96 can be construed to permit the Commonwealth to grant financial assistance to any state on such terms and conditions as it sees fit.[289]

In 1926, the High Court was presented with a case challenging the constitutionality of the Federal Aid Roads Act of 1926.[290] This was "[t]he first specific purpose grant enacted in Australia for a purpose not within the Commonwealth legislative power."[291] Under this Act, the Commonwealth was to enter into agreements with the various states, and provide funds to the states, based on these agreements, to enable them to construct and maintain roads. It was argued on behalf of the States of Victoria and South Australia that the law was invalid because it was a law relating to roadmaking rather than a law for granting financial aid to the states. Thus, it was not authorized under either section 96 or section 51 of the constitution. The States argued that, under section 96, Parliament could not attach as conditions to its grant any conditions which were, in effect, the exercise of legislative power not within section 51. In this case, since the principal purpose of the Act was road construction, it was not authorized by section 96. Indeed, the plaintiffs went so far as to argue that section 96 applied only to loans for temporary purposes and that grant conditions could only be those of a kind customarily imposed to secure repayment of such loans.

The High Court, in what must be one of its briefest opinions, said simply that the Federal Aid Roads Act was a valid enactment, "plainly warranted by the provisions of Section 96 of the Constitution," and proceeded to dimiss the action.[292]

---

286. *See supra* text accompanying notes 54-56.

287. *See* J. MCMILLAN, G. EVANS & H. STOREY, *supra* note 6, at 84, 117.

288. 1973 Austl. Acts 1407; *see supra* text accompanying notes 96-98.

289. *See, e.g.,* J. MCMILLAN, G. EVANS & H. STOREY, *supra* note 6, at 120.

290. Victoria v. Commonwealth (The Federal Roads Case), 38 C.L.R. 399 (Austl. 1926) (per curiam).

291. Saunders, *The Development of the Commonwealth Spending Power,* 11 MELB. U.L. REV. 369, 386 (1978).

292. The Federal Roads Case, 38 C.L.R. at 406.

Section 81 of the Australian Constitution authorizes the legislature to appropriate funds for "the purposes of the Commonwealth," and it is generally accepted that this power extends to the making of grants to the States. There is still some doubt whether the phrase "purposes of the Commonwealth" is limited to those matters over which the Commonwealth Parliament has legislative or executive power under the constitution (primarily those powers given to it in section 51).[293] Limitations on the scope of the appropriations power, however, have not acted as a constraint on grants to the states, inasmuch as the Commonwealth Parliament can use the grants power in section 96. The section 96 power has been interpreted, however, as requiring that the grants be made through the state governments rather than directly by the Commonwealth.[294]

It was not until the Labor Party gained power in 1972 that resort to conditional grants under section 96 of the constitution was extensively used to implement policies in areas that went beyond the legislative powers given to the Commonwealth by the constitution. Prime Minister Whitlam said that the Commonwealth would be expected

> to be involved in the planning of the function in which we are financially involved. We believe that it would be irresponsible for the national Government to content itself with simply providing funds without being involved in the process by which priorities are met, and by which expenditures are planned and by which standards are met.[295]

Expansion through the use of the section 96 power into many areas, including education, was slowed by the change of government following the December 1975 elections. The Liberal-Country Party indicated that it would end the specific purpose grants under section 96 and transfer the funds now going to such programs to general purpose revenue reimbursement. In a comment reminiscent of those of the present U.S. administration (and also the Nixon administration), Prime Minister Fraser, shortly after the elections, said:

> [T]here are some programs . . . which represent areas of expenditure which clearly deserve continuing Commonwealth support but in which there is no obvious need that my Government can see for the Commonwealth to be involved in a specific way. There are matters in respect of which priorities should appropriately be left to the States and their authorities to determine.
>
> In such cases, some form of absorption of specific purpose funds into general purpose funds would be appropriate.[296]

Despite such rhetoric, the number of specific purpose grants did not significantly diminish after the 1975 elections. Certainly grants for education continued and were even expanded to cover additional specific purposes.[297]

---

293. Else-Mitchell, *The Australia Federal Grants System and Its Impact on Fiscal Relations of the Federal Government with State and Local Government*, 54 AUSTL. L.J. 480, 481 (1980).

294. *Id.*

295. *Id.* at 484.

296. *Id.* at 485.

297. For examples of specific purpose grants under the States Grants (Schools) Act 1973, 1973 Austl. Acts 1407, see *supra* text accompanying notes 96-98.

The *Federal Roads Case*[298] and subsequent statutes enacted by both political parties indicate that specific purpose grants can be enacted in Australia for purposes not otherwise within the legislative power of the Commonwealth under the authority of section 96. The question, then, is whether anything in section 96 or elsewhere limits the extent or nature of the conditions the Commonwealth may attach to such grants.[299]

In upholding the validity of the Federal Aid Roads Act 1926, the High Court rejected the argument that the terms and conditions attached to a grant pursuant to section 96 must be restricted to financial terms and conditions "analogous to the terms and conditions of a mortgage, which are imposed to secure repayment of the loan."[300] The conditions attached to the grants in that statute were clearly regulatory conditions, specifying, among other things, the types of roads to be built, details of construction, and standards for future road maintenance. The grants were also conditioned on the states' providing matching sums.

The scope of section 96 was further clarified by *Deputy Federal Commissioner of Taxation v. W.R. Moran Proprietary, Ltd.*[301] which indicated that section 96 power is not necessarily restricted by other provisions of the constitution. Chief Justice Latham noted in that case that "the remedy for any abuse of the power conferred by Section 96 is political and not legal in character."[302] In light of these cases, as well as the *Uniform Tax Cases*,[303] the broad extent of section 96 power seemed to be a settled matter.

Theoretically, it would seem that the Commonwealth Parliament has the same extensive power to condition grants under section 96 as the U.S. courts have held Congress to have under article I, section 8, clause 1 of the U.S. Constitution.[304] As we have already seen, however, the conditions actually imposed on specific purpose grants, in the States Grants (Schools) Act 1973 and subsequent annual appropriations acts, have been almost non-existent compared to those attached to U.S. grant-in-aid statutes.[305]

---

298. Victoria v. Commonwealth, 38 C.L.R. 399 (Austl. 1926); *see supra* text accompanying notes 290-92.

299. *See supra* note 72, indicating that there are no significant limits on the nature and extent of the conditions that can be imposed on grants-in-aid statutes enacted under U.S. CONST. art. I, § 8, cl. 1.

300. The Federal Roads Case, 38 C.L.R. at 405. The argument was made on behalf of the state of South Australia. *Id.*

301. 61 C.L.R. 735 (Austl. 1939).

302. *Id.* at 764.

303. South Australia v. Commonwealth (First Uniform Tax Case), 65 C.L.R. 373 (Austl. 1942); Victoria v. Commonwealth (Second Uniform Tax Case), 99 C.L.R. 575 (Austl. 1957). *See supra* note 56.

One recent commentator has noted that, in view of this series of cases, "[i]t is now settled that the nature and extent of the conditions attached to grants depend solely on political rather than legal considerations. In the case of specific purpose grants the most relevant political consideration is the philosophy of the current federal government." Saunders, *supra* note 291, at 395.

304. *See supra* notes 70-72 and accompanying text.

305. *See supra* text accompanying note 98.

V

AUSTRALIA'S CURRENT EDUCATIONAL GRANT PROGRAMS UNDER SECTION 96

A. Language Minority Programs

The principal grant-in-aid program for language minority children in the United States is the Bilingual Education Act,[306] passed in 1968 as part of the amendments to the Elementary and Secondary Education Act. Under the original statute, a limited amount of funding was made available to school districts which submitted proposals. Among the programs to be funded were "bilingual education programs" and "programs designed to impart to students a knowledge of the history and culture associated with their languages."[307]

In 1974, Congress amended the Act,[308] noting that the purpose was "to encourage the establishment and operation, where appropriate, of educational programs using bilingual educational practices, techniques, and methods."[309] Bilingual education was defined as the giving of instruction in English "and to the extent necessary to allow a child to progress effectively through the educational system, the native language of the children of limited English-speaking ability."[310] The Bilingual Education Act provides fiscal incentives to school districts committed to assisting children with limited English proficiency, in contrast to the federal government's interpretation of Title VI of the Civil Rights Act of 1964[311] as imposing an affirmative duty on school officials to provide special assistance to such children. Title VI, of course, does not provide any fiscal assistance, and the sanction for non-compliance with Title VI is the cutoff of *all* federal funds received by the school district.

Despite the discretionary nature of programs funded under the Bilingual Education Act, there are a number of conditions that clearly control what the schools may do if they receive the funds. For example, "to prevent the segregation of children on the basis of national origin" in programs supported under the Bilingual Education Act, "and in order to broaden the understanding of children about languages and cultural heritages other than their own, a program of bilingual instruction may include the participation of children whose language is English, but in no event shall the percentage of such children exceed 40 percent."[312] Moreover, in such courses as art, music, and physical education, children with limited proficiency in English must participate in regular classes rather than in separate classes.[313] There are other con-

---

306. Bilingual Education Act, Pub. L. No. 90-247, §§ 701-706, 81 Stat. 783, 816-21 (1968) (codified as amended at 20 U.S.C. §§ 3381-3382, 3384 (1982)).

307. *Id.* § 704(c)(1)-(2), 81 Stat. at 817 (repealed 1972).

308. Bilingual Education Act, Pub. L. No. 93-380, tit. I, § 105(a)(l)-(b), 88 Stat. 484, 503-12 (1974) (codified as amended at 20 U.S.C. §§ 3221-3261 (1982)).

309. *Id.* § 702(a)(A), 88 Stat. at 503 (codified as amended at 20 U.S.C. § 3222(a)).

310. *Id.* § 703(4)(i), 88 Stat. at 504-05 (codified as amended at 20 U.S.C. § 3223(a)(4)(A)(i)).

311. 42 U.S.C. §§ 2000d to 2000d-4 (1982).

312. 20 U.S.C. § 3223(a)(4)(B) (1982).

313. *Id.* § 3223(a)(4)(C).

ditions governing application for funds for a program of bilingual education, including limitations on what the funds can be used for and who may apply for the funds, a requirement that the proposal be developed in consultation with an advisory council of stipulated composition, and other criteria governing approval of the application.[314] There are also detailed fiscal criteria to ensure that federal funds "supplement the level of State and local funds that, in the absence of those Federal funds, would have been expended for special programs for children of limited English proficiency and in no case to supplant such State and local funds."[315] The regulations promulgated to implement this statute occupy fifty-nine pages in the Code of Federal Regulations.

As recently as 1978, nothing much had been done at the federal level in Australia either in English as a Second Language or in multicultural curricula. In 1978, a commission was established which then made recommendations to the Commonwealth government. As a result of these recommendations, the Schools Commission was authorized to make grants to the states for programs in these areas.

1. *ESL Programs.* In Australia, there are few conditions attached to funds for language minority children, and most of these are related to fiscal accounting. Grants for the English-as-a-Second-Language (ESL) Program had two elements in 1983. The larger share of funds was allocated for general support to government and nongovernment schools to provide services directed "at improving the English language competence of students from non-English-speaking backgrounds."[316] The States Grants (Schools Assistance) Act 1982[317] requires only that the state ensure that the money be spent for that general purpose, that it submit a statement to the Commonwealth summarizing how the money was spent, and that it furnish the Commonwealth with a private accountant's certification that the funds have been spent as intended.[318] There are no enforceable regulations implementing the statute. There are guidelines, but these merely suggest how the funds might be used:

- the employment of specialist teachers, including bilingual teachers, to teach English as a second language, and their use in a variety of situations, including, but not restricted to intensive and part-time withdrawal situations, and assistance to regular teachers to enable them to attend more adequately to English language development across the curriculum for second language learners;
- the employment of advisory staff, interpreters, translators, bilingual welfare officers, teacher aides and school-community liaison workers; and
- curriculum development and the provision of learning materials.[319]

---

314. *See id.* §§ 3223(a)(4)(E), 3231.

315. *Id.* § 3231(b)(3)(G).

316. COMMONWEALTH SCHOOLS COMMISSION, PROGRAM GUIDELINES 1983, at 39 (1983) [hereinafter cited as GUIDELINES]. The total amount available was $55,377,000, with $16,463,000 of that amount going to nongovernment (including sectarian) schools. *Id.* at 41. (The amounts are given in Australian dollars.)

317. 1982 Austl. Acts 1745.

318. *See id.* § 17, 1982 Austl. Acts at 1765.

319. GUIDELINES, *supra* note 316, § 6.5, at 39-40.

The remaining ESL funds are to be used for "intensive English language programs for non-English-speaking students who are newly arrived in Australia."[320] An "eligible new arrival" is defined in the statute as a person from a country other than Australia whose first language is a language other than English and who arrived in Australia the previous year.[321] The intensive instruction is separate from the regular education program and is designed to prepare children for entry into primary or secondary education at either a government or nongovernment school.[322] The guidelines again suggest the variety of purposes for which funds might be used and state that a per capita grant of $833[323] will be made for each eligible student enrolled in a program of intensive English language instruction.[324]

In the State of Western Australia, the ESL program consists of the new-arrivals program for immigrants or refugees and a different ESL program in the regular schools.[325] Every 3 months, the Department of Education for the State of Western Australia notifies the Commonwealth how many new arrivals they have who will be attending an Australian school for the first time. The $833 per child received from the Commonwealth is the only funding for the ESL program. A child may spend from 3 to 6 months in the program before being placed in a regular school. For the newly arrived non-English speaker, there are four intensive centers in the State—two primary school and two secondary school age programs—located near where the immigrants enter the country or where they are likely to settle first. In the more rural areas, there are not enough such children to warrant a center. Thus immigrant children who come into the oil-producing, mining, or agricultural areas enter a regular school and are given only "withdrawal" assistance, consisting of ESL instruction away from the regular classroom for 30 minutes a day, 5 days a week. If there are fewer than six or eight such children in a school, the State provides only an advisory teacher from the capital, who visits the school from time to time to consult with regular teachers.

The intensive centers provide programs in three stages: (1) an intensive program in survival English—basic language skills children might need "on the street"; (2) a transition program in which they begin to learn the language of subjects they will be studying in school; and (3) a "withdrawal program" providing supplementary help to those who have recently entered the public schools.[326]

The teachers in the intensive centers are drawn from the best ESL teachers

---

320. *Id.* § 6.3, at 39.
321. States Grants (Schools Assistance) Act 1982, § 3(1), 1982 Austl. Acts 1745, 1751; GUIDELINES, *supra* note 316, §§ 6.17-6.20, at 42-43.
322. States Grants (Schools Assistance) Act 1982, § 12(2)(b), 1982 Austl. Acts 1745, 1762.
323. All monetary figures are given in Australian dollars.
324. Compare with the Immigration and Nationality Act, 8 U.S.C. § 1522(d) (1982), authorizing English language instruction in the schools for refugee children.
325. Interview with Dr. Harry Pearson, Director of Child Migrant Education and Multicultural Education, Department of Education, Western Australia (July 12, 1983) (memorandum on file with author).
326. *Id.*

in the regular schools.[327] There is, however, very little training for teachers of English as a Second Language, at least in Western Australia. What training there is consists of a short program of in-service training: 5 days in intensive study and then 5 additional Fridays.[328]

In New South Wales, there is pressure for bilingual education that could be termed language maintenance rather than transitional education. The major ethnic organizations pushing for a community languages program provided by the school system include Greek, Italian, Turkish, Arabic, and Yugoslav organizations.[329] The Labor Party, which has only recently been elected to office, has apparently made promises that it would provide bilingual education where there were concentrations of ethnic groups. As a result, some recent observers have predicted that the issue of bilingual education will become a much more significant issue in Australia as the Labor Party attempts to deliver on its promise.[330]

2. *Ethnic Schools Program.* Funds for ethnic education programs under the statute are to be spent on joint government and nongovernment school programs administered by a nongovernmental authority. The ethnic education grants require only that the state ensure that the funds received for ethnic education will be paid to a nongovernmental school authority, that the nongovernmental school authority furnish the Commonwealth with a private accountant's certification that funds have been applied as intended, and, as is generally the case when monies are to be administered by a nongovernment school authority, that there be a formal agreement between the state and the nongovernment school authority.

The Commonwealth Minister of Education must designate a body as an approved ethnic schools authority before it can receive funds from the Commonwealth. Funds are approved only if it is shown that the program will be open to all, regardless of ethnic origin, and that no other financial assistance will be provided by the Commonwealth toward the program. The Guidelines state that the program is to "help maintain the languages of people from non-English-speaking backgrounds."[331] Ethnic schools authorities are eligible for assistance under the Guidelines, if their programs are:

- designed to teach a community language (which may or may not be accompanied by cultural instruction) and where religious instruction does not form a predominant part of the program;
  . . . .
- open to students from any ethnic background . . . ;
- and not supported by other financial assistance provided by the Commonwealth towards any recurrent expenditure.

---

327. *Id.*
328. *Id.*
329. Interview with Dr. Douglas Swan, Director-General, and staff members, Department of Education, New South Wales (July 22, 1983) (memorandum on file with author). Dr. Swan noted that he was stressing "organizations," not parents.
330. Interview with members of the Commonwealth Schools Commission (July 8, 1983) (memorandum on file with author).
331. GUIDELINES, *supra* note 316, at 47.

Funding will not be available to ethnic schools which are regarded as serving political instruction purposes.[332]

In the State of Western Australia, ethnic schools meet after school or on Saturday mornings in government school buildings. The Commonwealth provides $30 per child per year for a 2-hour language and culture program. The particular ethnic community involved provides the teachers. Children who go to the ethnic schools also attend the regular schools during the regular school day.

3. *Multicultural Programs.* Multicultural education is defined as:

> education . . . that is provided for students attending government or non-government schools and that is designed to take account of the culture of peoples of the Aboriginal race of Australia or of peoples who have migrated to Australia, including . . . education that is provided by way of instruction in languages (other than the English language) spoken by those peoples.[333]

The Commonwealth Schools Commission funds the multicultural program in its entirety. Funds may be spent on a variety of activities, *excluding* the teaching of English as a Second Language.[334] The eastern states purportedly have better programs of multicultural education because of the larger proportion of immigrants. The nature and quality of the programs vary considerably from state to state as there are no conditions, other than fiscal reporting, attached to the federal funding. The Western Australia Department of Education staff members assigned to develop these programs feel they are struggling in an environment in which the programs are not deemed very important. There are limited resources and limited support. Multicultural education also tends to be limited to European cultures; Asian and Aboriginal cultures are generally excluded. In parts of Western Australia distant from Perth, there is even less interest in multicultural education. Several school officials have indicated that the money is used in non-productive ways. Teachers are not really interested in taking on yet another program. Moreover, no great pressure for change appears to be coming from parent or community groups.[335]

It is apparent from the foregoing that, perhaps because there are no particular requirements imposed by the federal government as a condition for receipt of grants, the extent of programs for language minority children may be greater in some states than in others.

---

332. *Id.* at 48. Funds can only be used for "educational purposes of a recurrent nature" and not for capital expenses, although use of federal funds for the rental of premises is permitted. *Id.* at 49

333. States Grants (Schools Assistance) Act 1982, § 3(1), 1982 Austl. Acts 1745, 1752.

334. GUIDELINES, *supra* note 316, at 44.

335. Interviews with Dr. Harry Pearson, Director of Child Migrant Education and Multicultural Education, Department of Education, Western Australia (July 12, 1983); with staff members, Multicultural Affairs, Department of Education, Western Australia (June 29, 1983); and with William McKenzie, Educational Officer, Goldfield Region District, Kalgoorlie, Western Australia (July 15 1983) (memoranda on file with author).

B. Programs for the Handicapped

As is well known, section 504 of the Rehabilitation Act of 1973,[336] with its comprehensive set of regulations, imposes upon school authorities in the United States stringent requirements regarding educational opportunities for the handicapped. In addition, the Education for All Handicapped Children Act (EAHCA)[337] is an extremely prescriptive grant-in-aid statute; many of the conditions look to the provision of procedural safeguards rather than substantive requirements. Under the EAHCA, a handicapped child is *entitled* to 'a "free appropriate public education" which includes those "related services" necessary to enable the handicapped child to benefit from special education.[338] States and school districts are required to identify and locate all unserved handicapped children.[339] Special education and related services are to be provided in accordance with an individualized education program (IEP).[340]

An "appropriate" education is one that takes place in the least restrictive educational setting.[341] If the regular educational setting is inappropriate for academic subjects, handicapped students must at least participate with non-handicapped students in nonacademic and extracurricular activities. Congress has thus mandated "mainstreaming" or "integration" (the term more frequently used in Australia) of the handicapped. The burden is put on the educational system to show that the child could not be educated satisfactorily in a regular classroom; that is, Congress has imposed an affirmative duty on state and local authorities to provide special aids, services and other resources to enable handicapped children to overcome the barriers to an equal educational opportunity imposed by their handicap. There are also extensive procedural requirements and safeguards for handicapped children and their parents.[342] To meet the requirements of the federal statute, states and school districts must make substantial expenditures from their own resources, as the federal funds do not begin to cover the needs of the handicapped.

By contrast, the federal program for the handicapped in Australia is quite limited. For school-age children, special education is defined in the States Grants (Schools Assistance) Act 1982 as "education under special programs designed specifically for handicapped children that is provided in classes conducted at schools, or in classes conducted at centres other than schools . . . ."[343] Financial aid is provided to the states "for the purpose of meeting recurrent expenditures . . . in connection with special education provided at

---

336.   29 U.S.C. § 794 (1982).
337.   20 U.S.C. §§ 1400-1461 (1982).
338.   *Id.* §§ 1400(c), 1401(17).
339.   *Id.* § 1414(a)(1)(A).
340.   *Id.* § 1414(a)(5).
341.   "A recipient shall place a handicapped person in the regular educational environment . . . unless it is demonstrated by the recipient that the education of the person in the regular environment with the use of supplementary aids and services cannot be achieved satisfactorily." 34 C.F.R. § 104.34(a) (1984).
342.   20 U.S.C. § 1415 (1982).
343.   States Grants (Schools Assistance) Act 1982, § 3(1), 1982 Austl. Acts 1745, 1755.

or in connection with government schools or government centres in the State."[344] Funds also go to nongovernment schools for expenditures in connection with special education.[345]

The states must ensure that the amount of the grant they receive is spent for this purpose, and that a portion of the grant is "applied in connection with integration activities conducted at government schools in the State or places of education approved by the Minister . . . ."[346] For example, in the 1982 Act, Western Australia received $103,000 for "government integration activities" out of a total of $1,876,000 for special education.[347] "Integration activities" are defined as: "activities the purpose of which is to integrate handicapped children into schools, or other places of education approved by the Minister . . . , at which education is provided for children other than handicapped children . . . ."[348] Fiscal reporting requirements include certification by an authorized person that the funds have been spent for the designated purpose and a statement indicating for what the money was spent.[349]

In Australia, there are no extensive conditions attached to the receipt of funds for special education comparable to those in the EAHCA. "Integration" is not prescribed as "mainstreaming" is in the United States. Nor are there the other kinds of requirements seen in the EAHCA, such as the requirement to provide supplementary aids or services for the integrated handicapped students.[350] In some areas in the State of Western Australia, for example, there are special education classes only for the primary grades. Therefore, once students complete the primary grades, they are "integrated" into the regular classes in the secondary school without any supplementary aids or services.[351]

The Schools Commission's Guidelines for special education grants provide: "[F]unds are allocated according to priorities determined by the States in meeting the special needs of handicapped children. These needs will vary from school to school according to the type of handicap being catered for."[352] With regard to integration of the handicapped, in contrast to the stringent requirements of the EAHCA, the Guidelines note that "there are differences in the extent to which integration has been achieved and . . . variations in State and Territory policies concerning the ways in which it should be undertaken."[353] The Guidelines also give examples of the use to which integration

---

344. *Id.* § 15(2), 1982 Austl. Acts at 1763.
345. *Id.* § 32(2), 1982 Austl. Acts at 1782.
346. *Id.* § 15(2), 1982 Austl. Acts at 1763.
347. *Id.* sched. 4, 1982 Austl. Acts at 1800.
348. *Id.* § 3(1), 1982 Austl. Acts at 1752.
349. *Id.* § 17, 1982 Austl. Acts at 1765.
350. 20 U.S.C. § 1414(a)(1)(C)(iv) (1982).
351. Interview with Derrick Tomlinson, Director of the National Centre for Research on Rural Education, University of Western Australia (June 28, 1983) (memorandum on file with author).
352. GUIDELINES, *supra* note 316, at 22.
353. *Id.* at 26. The Commission, however, *recommends* that funds be applied in accordance with the following priorities:
——The movement of handicapped children from special to regular schools;

funds may be put, which include in-service training of teachers, equipment, development of curricular materials, speech therapy, excursions, teacher salaries, transportation, and minor building projects such as installation of handrails and ramps and widening of doorways.[354]

Some of the members of the Commonwealth Schools Commission have expressed concern about what is happening to the funds for the handicapped because there are no meaningful conditions and no mechanism for enforcement of the Guidelines. Many schools use the money to buy equipment, but there is a dearth of programs, particularly programs for the mentally handicapped. It has also been suggested that, because of the strong teachers' union in Australia, pressures for integration of the handicapped might lead to teacher demands for smaller class sizes. Consequently, the issue of integration has received little attention.[355]

Although requirements at the federal level are limited, a number of the states have legislation for the handicapped. Under Western Australia's statute, if the parents disagree with the placement of the child, an assessment panel can be convened. The panel makes recommendations to the Minister, and once the Minister has issued a "direction," the burden shifts to the parent to show that the Minister's direction is incorrect. If the parents do not agree with the "Minister's direction," they have 30 days within which to go to the children's court.[356] The state's guideline with regard to integration is "the maximum useful association in the best interests of all children."[357]

The Commonwealth Schools Commission's funds are primarily spent for salaries and special equipment in Western Australia.[358] There is no requirement at either the state or the Commonwealth level that the school system identify unserved and underserved handicapped children.[359]

In one region of Western Australia outside of the capital city area,[360] even fewer services are provided to the handicapped than in Perth. The decision whether to place a child in a special class within a regular school rather than in a special school is made by the educational psychologist for the district, often

---

    ——the provision of services to enable isolated handicapped children to attend neighborhood schools;
    ——facilitating enrollment into regular primary schools of handicapped children who are beginning their formal schooling;
    ——the funding of activities to assist in the education of handicapped children already fully or partially integrated into regular schools; and
    ——facilitating enrollment into regular pre-schools of handicapped children below school age.
Id. at 26-27.

354. *Id.* at 27-28.

355. Interview with members of the Commonwealth Schools Commission (July 8, 1983) (memorandum on file with author).

356. Interview with Dr. Robert Weiland, Superintendent for Special Education, Department of Education, Western Australia (July 12, 1983) (memorandum on file with author).

357. Compare this with the EAHCA's requirement of the "least restrictive environment." 20 U.S.C. § 1418(f)(2)(E) (1982).

358. Interview with Dr. Robert Weiland, *supra* note 356.

359. *Id.* Compare this with 20 U.S.C. § 1414(a)(1)(A) (1982). *See supra* text accompanying note 339.

360. Kalgoorlie, Western Australia is a mining town of about 20,000.

based on whether the child can follow instructions, sit still at a desk, and so forth. In other words, children are sent by the educational psychologist to a special education class in the regular school if they have "appropriate adaptive behavior." There they get instruction, but at a reduced level. Others are sent to special schools for the handicapped. In addition, Aboriginal children who come into the school system at older ages (nine or ten) without any prior education are put in special education classes. Since these children will not be up to their age level in math or reading, there is no place to put them other than in a special education class.[361]

If the regular school is one which schedules "softer" courses such as arts and crafts or music in the afternoon, some of the special students may join classes of regular students. However, children who cannot "adjust to the regular classroom" or who "aren't accepted" in the regular classroom remain separate even for the "softer" courses. In this district, when children are "integrated" into the "softer" classes, the regular teacher is given no special assistance or guidance. There are no teacher aides, supplementary services, or other resources.[362] Indeed, outside the capital city, at least, special education classes are often assigned to novice or inexperienced teachers. There is no significant special training or degree in special education in Western Australia.[363]

It is really the school principals who decide whether there will be special education classes in their schools and how they are to be operated. If they do not want the handicapped to mingle with other children, no mingling will occur. Under the handicapped law in Western Australia, however, a principal cannot place a child in a special education class without an assessment by the educational psychologist or by the guidance counselor, and an assessment cannot be undertaken without the written permission of the parent. It is also up to individual teachers to determine whether the children will interact on the playground. Only if the school is organized conveniently, with academic subjects in the morning and arts and crafts or music in the afternoon, can there be integration in nonacademic subjects as well.[364]

In New South Wales, there is no state legislation for the handicapped, although such legislation was being proposed in 1983. Under the then existing system parents could reject the placement of their child in a separate institution and demand that the child be integrated, but it was still up to school principals to decide whether a school would admit the child or not. A parent could appeal the principal's decision to the Director-General of the State Education Department. Under the proposed legislation, an independent panel would be established for the appeal.[365]

---

361. Interviews with school officials in the Goldfield Region District, Western Australia (which includes Kalgoorlie and several smaller towns) (July 15, 1983) (memoranda on file with author).
362. *Id.*
363. *Id.*; *see also* interview with Dr. Robert Weiland, *supra* note 356.
364. Interviews with school officials in the Goldfield Region District, *supra* note 361.
365. Interview with Dr. Douglas Swan, *supra* note 329.

C. Programs for the Economically Disadvantaged

The Australian Disadvantaged Schools Program is somewhat comparable in *purpose* to Title I of the Elementary and Secondary Education Act in the United States, although the statutes operate very differently.[366] Conditions for receipt of Title I funding are extensive, occupying many pages of the statute. For example, in order to receive funds, a local educational agency (LEA) must use the funds "in school attendance areas having high concentrations of children from low-income families," and if the funds are insufficient to provide programs for all educationally deprived children in the eligible areas, the LEA must rank its school attendance areas from highest to lowest, in accordance with the degree of concentration of children from low-income families.[367] Funds are available only if an LEA makes "an assessment of educational need each year."[368] This assessment must "identify [the] educationally deprived children in the eligible attendance areas and . . . select those educationally deprived children who have the greatest need for special assistance"; identify the instructional areas for the program; and determine the "special educational needs" of the children who will participate in the program.[369] The funds received by an LEA may only be used for programs "which are of sufficient size, scope, and quality to give reasonable promise of substantial progress toward meeting the special educational needs of the children being served.[370]

LEA's may receive funds only if they adopt effective procedures for evaluating the effectiveness of the programs "in meeting the special educational needs of the educationally deprived children."[371] LEA's may not receive funds unless teachers, school boards, and parents of children participating in the programs are involved in the planning of the programs.[372] There must be an advisory council for the entire school district and the composition of that advisory council is specified in the statute. It must include members elected by the school advisory councils, representatives of children and schools eligible for Title I programs but not participating in those programs (these rep-

---

366. Pub. L. No. 89-10, 79 Stat. 27 (1965), later amended by Act of Nov. 1, 1978, Pub. L. No. 95-561, 92 Stat. 2143, 2152-201. This Act was repealed in 1981 and has now become chapter I of the Education Consolidation and Improvement Act, Pub. L. No. 97-35, tit. V, subtit. D, 95 Stat. 463 (1981) (codified in scattered sections of 20 U.S.C.), which is comparable in scope and character. Title I's preamble sets forth its purpose:

In recognition of the special educational needs of children of low-income families and the impact that concentrations of low-income families have on the ability of local educational agencies to support adequate educational programs, the Congress hereby declares it to be the policy of the United States to provide financial assistance . . . to local educational agencies serving areas with concentrations of children from low-income families to expand and improve their educational programs by various means (including pre-school programs) which contribute particularly to meeting the special educational needs of educationally deprived children.

20 U.S.C. § 2701 (1982); *see also id.* § 3801.
367. *Id.* § 2732(a)(1).
368. *Id.* § 2734(b).
369. *Id.*
370. *Id.* § 2734(d). Ordinarily, no project may be less than $2,500. *Id.*
371. *Id.* § 2734(g)(1).
372. *Id.* § 2734(i)-(j).

resentatives must be elected by the parents in such areas), and a majority of its members must be parents of children to be served by Title I projects.[373] In addition, each project area or school must also have an advisory council, and a majority of its members also must be parents of children to be served by the programs. Members must be elected by the parents in the project area.[374] School districts are required to provide a program for training the members of advisory councils.[375]

With regard to fiscal requirements, LEA's are required to maintain their level of spending from state and local funds in order to receive federal funds under Title I ("maintenance of effort");[376] funds may only be used to cover those program costs which exceed the average per pupil expenditure for pupils in the LEA ("excess costs");[377] and funds may be used only "to supplement and, to the extent practical, increase the level of funds that would, in the absence of such Federal funds, be made available from regular non-Federal sources . . . , and in no case may such funds be so used as to supplant such funds from such non-Federal sources."[378] There are also "comparability requirements": an LEA may receive funds "only if State and local funds will be used . . . to provide services in project areas which, taken as a whole, are at least comparable to services being provided in areas in such district which are not receiving [Title I] funds."[379] Detailed recordkeeping is required by each school district and extensive reports are required to be filed annually.[380]

In contrast, the requirements for Australia's Disadvantaged Schools Program are quite minimal. In the States Grants (Schools Assistance) Act 1982, a disadvantaged school is defined as a school "that should, in the opinion of the State Education Minister, be treated as a disadvantaged school."[381] In the States Grants (Schools) Act 1973, a disadvantaged school was defined more precisely as a school

> (a) the students at which, or a substantial portion of the students at which, are members of a community which, for social, economic, ethnic, geographic, cultural, lingual or any similar reason, has a lower than average ability to take advantage of educational facilities; and (b) which requires special facilities (whether in the form of buildings, equipment, teaching staff or in some other form) for the purpose of enabling the school to provide adequate educational opportunities for students at the school.[382]

Disadvantaged schools can be government or nongovernment schools. The only statutory conditions for receipt of the funds are the usual fiscal reporting requirements.[383] In the Schools Commission's Guidelines, "school communities," as a condition of funding, "are required to review their objec-

---

373. *Id.* § 2735.
374. *Id.* § 2735(a).
375. *Id.* § 2735(d).
376. *Id.* § 2736(a).
377. *Id.* § 2736(b).
378. *Id.* § 2736(c).
379. *Id.* § 2736(e).
380. *Id.* § 2737(a)-(b).
381. States Grants (Schools Assistance) Act 1982, § 3(1), 1982 Austl. Acts 1745, 1751.
382. States Grants (Schools) Act 1973, § 3(1), 1973 Austl. Acts 1407, 1411-12.
383. *See supra* text accompanying note 98.

tives and operations, to draw up proposals designed to improve learning outcomes, to relate the curriculum more closely to the life experiences of the children enrolled, and to bring about a closer association between parents and the school."[384] Almost anything can be supported under the rubric of a "Disadvantaged Schools Program": curriculum innovation, basic skills programs, or programs for promoting interaction with the community.[385] Most programs, however, are concerned with promoting the involvement of the community in the school. Funds are supposed to be allocated in response to proposals formulated at the school level. Although the Commission Guidelines state that parents and teachers *should* participate in the formulation of these proposals,[386] such participation is not required; even if it were, there is no mechanism for enforcing such a requirement. State education ministers are responsible for determining which schools are to be declared disadvantaged schools.

Although the federal grants are supposed to supplement or "top up" what the states are providing through their general funds, there is concern that there may be a good deal of substitution rather than supplementation, because there are no requirements such as the "maintainance of effort" and "supplement, not supplant" provisions of Title I.[387] Indeed, although the Disadvantaged Schools Program has been in existence for 10 years, there is no comprehensive and systematic way of determining what the impact of the program has been. The Schools Commission itself has undertaken no evaluations and there has been no other objective evaluation.

In many states the Disadvantaged Schools Program operates through a joint committee for disadvantaged schools which has representatives from the Catholic Education Commission, the independent schools, and the State Department of Education.[388] These committees are supposed to follow the Guidelines, but there is currently no mechanism for the Commonwealth to determine whether they are being followed. The Disadvantaged Schools Program differs from Title I in that it provides aid for disadvantaged *schools* rather than disadvantaged children; there are, accordingly, some schools that have severely disadvantaged children, but not enough to meet the criteria for receiving funds. Other schools may have a sizeable minority of non-disadvantaged children, yet program aid is used to benefit the entire school. A second problem, from the perspective of some state administrators, is that in many cases funds are not spent usefully, often going for equipment.[389]

In New South Wales, there are now 418 disadvantaged schools, most of which have been "on the list" for at least 3 years, and many for much longer, even though the character of the student population may have changed in the

---

384. GUIDELINES, *supra* note 316, at 17.
385. *Id.* at 17-18.
386. *Id.* at 18.
387. 20 U.S.C. § 2736(a)-(c), (e) (1982); *see supra* text accompanying notes 376-79.
388. Interview with Dr. Robert Vickery, Director-General, Department of Education, Western Australia, and other State Department officials (July 12, 1983) (memorandum on file with author).
389. *Id.*

meantime. The Disadvantaged Schools Program does not provide much money. There are only about 130,000 children attending the disadvantaged schools in New South Wales, which receives about $70 per capita from the Commonwealth to support the program.[390]

State Education Department officials in New South Wales consider that the impact of the Disadvantaged Schools Program has been on the *general* system. For example, the community is supposed to be involved in developing funding proposals. Therefore, many schools, whether disadvantaged or not, have now established in-school planning committees. Although some schools there have misused funds for equipment,[391] most of the money received probably goes for instruction. One concern, however, is that the high level of community involvement might protect the program even if it is not as effective as other possible programs would be.

D.   Summary of Australia's Grant Programs for Special Pupil Populations

As the foregoing analysis has indicated, the Commonwealth has not conditioned any of its specific purpose grants on the establishment of significant substantive or programmatic requirements or procedural safeguards for the target pupil populations. Thus Australia's current approach has been very different from that taken by the federal government in the United States.

One problem with the federal role in education as it has developed in the United States is the increasing number of federal requirements that have been enacted in the last 20 years, beginning with Title VI of the Civil Rights Act of 1964,[392] followed by Title I, and further complicated by various statutes and regulations prohibiting discrimination based on gender, handicap, and national origin. In addition, federal aid for the handicapped, and for students with limited English proficiency, has been extensively conditioned on both procedural and substantive requirements.

It has been difficult for states, school districts, and schools to adjust to this proliferation of programs and requirements. Each new federal program or mandate has been established and administered separately from previous programs and requirements. School districts and states, therefore, tend to create separate administrative structures for the various programs. It is at the school level, however, that the combined effects of these requirements are felt. The reporting requirements are extensive and require a good deal of paperwork for both teachers and administrators. In the case of teachers, one of the principal concerns is that the considerable administrative burdens may take time away from actual classroom instruction. The fiscal reporting requirements have also encouraged the use of "pull out" programs ("withdrawal" programs in Australia), removing children from regular classrooms for special treatment.

---

390.   Interview with Dr. Douglas Swan, *supra* note 329.

391.   One example given was of a school which used program funds to purchase six tables for table tennis. *Id.*

392.   42 U.S.C. §§ 2000d to 2000d-4 (1982).

With so many proliferating categorical programs, schools have often taken an uncoordinated approach to the child who falls into more than one category. The educational problems of such children are compartmentalized in response to federal accounting requirements rather than being classified according to the children's educational needs. Thus the tendency has been to organize the delivery of educational services to special pupil populations in accordance with federal funding categories rather than along functional lines.

Another problem is that many requirements, unfunded mandates as well as conditions to grants-in-aid, must be financed from state and local revenues at a time when school districts have come under increasingly severe financial restraints. Moreover, the enforcement of civil rights requirements has been complicated by the fact that the principal remedy for noncompliance is the termination of federal funds, a draconian measure that the federal government is reluctant to use because it punishes the very children that the laws are designed to help.

The system in Australia avoids many of these problems either by taking a school-based approach for programs such as the Disadvantaged Schools Program, or by not imposing burdensome requirements that create undue amounts of paperwork or limit the ability to adapt to the needs of a particular community. There are, however, other problems with the Australian system which have been pointed out previously.

There are significant differences between Title I programs and the Disadvantaged Schools Program as they are actually implemented. Largely as a result of detailed federal regulation, Title I programs generally take the form of supplementary instruction in the basic skills. The Disadvantaged Schools Program in Australia is much broader and thus permits a greater variety of programs not necessarily addressed to cognitive skills alone. Also, since the program is school-based, rather than confined to specific targeted students, the "pull out" problem is avoided. The difference in the size of the programs — 14,000 school districts (and multiple schools within many of those districts) receiving Title I funds, in contrast to about 1,000 schools in the Disadvantaged Schools Program — may explain, in part, the need for extensive regulation in Title I programs.

Owing to disparities in per pupil expenditures among school districts, Title I funds are not always a means of getting more than average resources to disadvantaged pupils. In many cases, particularly in rural and impoverished urban districts, Title I funds help bring resources up toward the average in low-spending districts.[393] By contrast, the Disadvantaged Schools Program does provide greater than average resources to the schools selected. The funds are so minimal for this program, however,—amounting to only about $50 per pupil nationally—that they hardly constitute a significant increase over regular per pupil expenditures. Using these funds to supplement the

---

393. On the other hand, the Title I program has done much to eliminate intradistrict disparities in state and local funding. Thus as between Title I and non-Title I schools within a school district, the funds can be a significant increment.

teaching of basic skills would accomplish little. A program which fosters school-based experimentation and community involvement with the school may be better suited to the limited nature of the funding and the limited number of schools participating. Thus the U.S. program seeks to attack directly low achievement in specific pupils; the Australian program seeks to improve schooling in schools where there has been the least pupil success.

The Australian program neither identifies the problem nor specifies an approach to addressing it. There is no way to measure the effectiveness of programs that are developed in individual schools, or to disseminate knowledge about what works and what does not. Thus it is unclear whether the Disadvantaged Schools Program has had any significant impact on the target children, and whether the funds are being effectively used to address academic and related needs.

Programs for language minority children in Australia have primarily been directed toward new arrivals (children whose language is other than English and who have not yet entered an Australian school), with intensive instruction to prepare them to enter a regular school. The Commonwealth cannot ensure that a state does much more than that. ESL training for teachers is rudimentary, and "withdrawal" programs are for minimal periods during the school week. Nothing is done for second or third generation children with limited English proficiency, although such children exist in Australia as well as in the United States. Affirmative language assistance programs are much better developed in the United States and apply to a wider group of children than in Australia.

In the area of aid to the handicapped, the situation in Australia appears to be similar to that in the United States prior to the first major lawsuit establishing the rights of the handicapped, *Pennsylvania Association for Retarded Children v. Pennsylvania*.[394] In Australia, neither parents nor the children themselves enjoy significant procedural or substantive guarantees of an equal educational opportunity for handicapped children. Individual school principals retain a good deal of autonomy in this area. In the United States, the EAHCA, without dictating educational content, establishes the right to a free appropriate public education guaranteed through procedural safeguards, permitting parents to participate in developing the child's individualized education plan and in determining appropriate placement for the child. In Australia, by contrast, no state except Western Australia[395] has passed legislation providing for parental involvement in decisions regarding the education and placement of a handicapped child. No such requirements are attached to the receipt of Commonwealth funds, and parents do not enjoy a right of appeal.

---

394. 343 F. Supp. 279 (E.D. Pa. 1972) (consent decree); *see also* Mills v. Board of Educ., 348 F. Supp. 866 (D.D.C. 1972).

395. Western Australian legislation gives parents a right to participate in a planning conference and a right of appeal from decisions of the Minister, Education Act 1928-1981, 19 Geo. 5, no. xxxiii, § 20E, 5 W. Austl. Repr. Acts 1, 33 (1982), but this has not had a significant impact on parental involvement in placement decisions. *See supra* text accompanying note 356.

VI

CONCLUSION

The High Court decisions in *Koowarta v. Bjelke-Petersen*[396] and the *Tasmanian Dam Case*[397] indicate that the Australian Parliament, using its external affairs power, could enact federal legislation guaranteeing equal educational opportunity for various special pupil populations. Existing international covenants and agreements on human rights provide a sufficient nexus for such domestic legislation. In addition, the Parliament has broad power under section 96 of the Australian constitution to condition its specific purpose grants for education so as to protect the interests of children with special needs, much in the same way as the U.S. Congress has done in Title I of the Elementary and Secondary Education Act,[398] the EAHCA,[399] and the Bilingual Education Act.[400]

Although the Parliament would seem to have the constitutional authority to enact civil rights mandates in the area of education and to condition its aid to education programs on similar requirements, the question is whether Australia's traditions and political/legal culture will permit this authority to be exercised. Australia's educational system is basically paternalistic: the power of educational decisionmaking is entrusted to the professional. The political/legal culture of the United States, fostered by the Bill of Rights and its tradition of protecting the individual, makes parents more ready to assert their rights against the professional and courts more ready to enforce those rights than is evident in Australia.

In light of the strong Australian preference for "states' rights" rather than a strong national government, combined with a tradition of deferring to professionals,[401] it would not be suprising if there is, in the future, little change in

---

396. 39 Austl. L.R. 417 (1982); *see supra* notes 125-60 and accompanying text.

397. Commonwealth v. Tasmania, 46 Austl. L.R. 625 (1983); *see supra* notes 161-213 and accompanying text.

398. Pub. L. No. 89-10, tit. I, 79 Stat. 27, 27-36 (1965) (codified as amended in scattered sections of 20 U.S.C.); *see supra* note 366.

399. 20 U.S.C. §§ 1400-1461 (1982); *see supra* text accompanying notes 337-42.

400. *Id.* §§ 3221-3261; *see supra* text accompanying notes 306-15.

401. Despite the much less intrusive nature of the federal programs in Australia, the tensions between the state departments of education and the Commonwealth are reminiscent of those in the United States. Consider the following:

The role of the Director-General of Education as an instrument of State Government policy is complicated by the increasing prevalence of education policy dictates from the Commonwealth Government. The increasing use of specific purpose grants under Section 96 of the Commonwealth Constitution, has enabled the Commonwealth Government to impose its own educational priorities by making grants available for special purposes such as Aboriginal education, multicultural education, community involvement in schools, choice and diversity in schools, professional development, school-based curriculum development, transition education, and English as a second language. These priorities may or may not conform with the priorities of State Governments which consider themselves more able than a national government to accurately assess the needs of students . . . .

The Commonwealth's priorities . . . have been pursued by . . . the Schools Commission . . . . Inevitably with the extension of the national educational bureaucracy, questions of power and personality impinged on the deeper philosophical and educational issues . . . . [T]he determination of specific priorities is the prerogative of State Governments . . . .

the status quo.[402] It seems likely that some civil rights protections related to education will be introduced by the Labor Government, but they are unlikely to contain the kinds of sanctions, or to be implemented with the kind of detailed regulations, found in the United States. It also seems unlikely that the Government will use its section 96 power to attach extensive conditions on its federal aid to education.

In sum, there is constitutional authority for significant changes in the current system, but the political/legal culture of Australia will inhibit such changes, at least in the near future. The seeds have been planted, however, and perhaps a model may yet develop that includes some of the "rights" focus of the U.S. legislation, while retaining some of the flexibility and cooperative nature of the current Australian approach.

Vickery, The Practising Administrator: Dilemmas and Strategies of a State Department of Education, (July 1983) (unpublished paper).

402. *But see* Buss, *Special Education in England and Wales*, LAW & CONTEMP. PROBS., Winter 1985, at 119 (indicating that Great Britain has begun to alter the status quo with regard to the rights of handicapped children to an equal educational opportunity).

12

NOTE

STATE RESPONSE TO THE EDUCATION FOR ALL HANDICAPPED CHILDREN ACT OF 1975

I

INTRODUCTION

Efforts to establish a strong federal policy for educating handicapped children in the United States culminated in 1975 in the Education for All Handicapped Children Act (hereinafter "EAHCA" or the "Act").[1] This Act, which is designed to supplement existing state programs for the delivery of special education services, offers fiscal incentives to states which choose to meet the standards of the EAHCA. The Act requires participating states to establish policies and to submit plans which assure all handicapped children the right to a "free appropriate public education." Consistent with Congress' belief that the participation of concerned parties, combined with the use of due process guarantees, would best ensure the provision of educational services appropriate to the needs of the individual child, the requirements of the Act are more procedural than substantive.[2]

The Act is designed to leave many of the policymaking and substantive decisions with state and local educational agencies. This design is consistent with the nation's traditional policy of decentralizing the responsibility for education to the greatest extent practicable. This approach also allows states to experiment and innovate in devising ways to deliver a free appropriate education to handicapped children.

This note was conceived with the purpose of surveying state responses to the EAHCA to determine whether the federal act has produced the intended experimentation. The authors looked in particular for variation among the states in several substantive areas, as well as in certain funding policies. The survey also looked at whether the states have obligated themselves to provide services above and beyond those required by the EAHCA. This survey was intended to be restricted to an examination of *state* statutory and decisional law and of state educational agency decisions rendered thereunder. Limiting the scope of the survey in this manner turned out to be much more difficult than contemplated since the vast majority of claims relating to special educa-

---

1. 20 U.S.C. §§ 1400-1461 (1982). For a summary of the Act, see Lora v. Board of Educ., 456 F. Supp. 1211 (E.D.N.Y. 1978), *vacated,* 623 F.2d 248 (2d Cir. 1980).
2. *See* S. REP. No. 168, 94th Cong., 1st Sess. 11-12, *reprinted in* 1975 U.S. CODE CONG. & AD. NEWS 1425, 1435-36.

tion have been brought and decided under the federal act. Many decisions, while recognizing the existence of applicable state law, virtually ignore the state law as grounds for decision because of (1) its substantial similarity to the federal mandate and (2) the decisionmaker's recognition that the federal act supersedes any conflicting state law. Consequently, in a few areas the authors have had to refer to cases decided solely under the EAHCA.

The findings herein indicate a high degree of uniformity among the states in most substantive areas, such as the provision of transportation and other related services, homebound and year-round services, and reimbursements for unilateral placements. With respect to the range of each state's coverage, some variations are found in eligibility ages and in the length of time services will be provided. This variation may be attributable to the fact that while the federal act *mandates* the provision of services only to children aged 6 to 18, it also *permits* and subsidizes services to children aged 3 to 5 and 18 to 21 if consistent with state law.[3] Only a few states purport to guarantee something more than an "appropriate" education, such as the "best" or "most appropriate" education.[4]

Several possible explanations exist for these essentially uniform results. Perhaps the federal act has hit upon the most efficacious standard; to provide anything more than an "appropriate" education may bring only marginal returns not commensurate with the additional cost of attaining a higher standard. Furthermore, since the cost of providing special education and related services is already extremely high, the states may not be able to afford to go beyond the minimum requirements. Finally, the availability of the federal court system to parties who wish to appeal a state agency decision has resulted in the creation of certain substantive standards which are applied consistently across federal districts and even circuits throughout the United States.

Only New Mexico has chosen not to participate in the EAHCA. However, because New Mexico's educational institutions receive federal funds under other programs, the state has been required to comply with the regulations promulgated under section 504 of the Rehabilitation Act.[5] Section 504 prohibits discrimination against handicapped individuals by any program receiving federal financial assistance and has been interpreted to apply in the educational and vocational contexts, as well as in many other areas.[6] Many of the regulations promulgated under section 504 are substantially similar to those under the EAHCA.[7] Thus, although it may not have to meet the same due process requirements as states receiving grants directly under the EAHCA, New Mexico is still required to provide a free appropriate public

---

3. 20 U.S.C. § 1412(2)(B) (1982).

4. *See infra* note 48.

5. 29 U.S.C. § 794 (1982). *See* New Mexico Ass'n for Retarded Citizens v. New Mexico, 495 F. Supp. 391 (D.N.M. 1980), *rev'd on other grounds,* 678 F.2d 847 (10th Cir. 1982).

6. *See* Lora v. Board of Educ., 456 F. Supp. 1211, 1228 (E.D.N.Y. 1978).

7. *Compare* 34 C.F.R. §§ 300.1-.754 (1984) (promulgated under EAHCA) *with* 45 C.F.R. §§ 84.1-.61 (1984) *and particularly* 45 C.F.R. §§ 84.31-.40 (1984) (promulgated under § 504 of the Rehabilitation Act; requires provision of free appropriate public education to qualified handicapped person).

education.[8]

II
ELIGIBILITY UNDER STATE STATUTES

Before a child can request a special placement or other services related to special education, he must establish that he qualifies under the relevant state statute. Most jurisdictions speak in terms of "exceptional children;"[9] however, some statutes refer to "children requiring special education,"[10] while others speak of "handicapped children"[11] or those with "special needs."[12]

Factors such as age, handicapping condition, and the extent of a handicap are woven into the definitions of "eligible" children. Special considerations are also made, in some cases, for pregnant or gifted and talented children. While all of the above definitions and descriptive factors are basically within the scope of the EAHCA, some variations from state to state may be noted.

A. Age

At a minimum, all states follow EAHCA requirements by providing special education services to children aged 6 to 18.[13] Many state acts raise the upper limit, with the most common maximum age (in twenty-one states) being 21,[14] although six states discontinue coverage at age 20.[15] Even those states which do not mandate coverage to the age of 21 often permit local agencies that are able to do so to provide services.[16]

The most common minimum ages (in twenty-six states) for coverage under state statutes are 6[17] and 5.[18] In some states, the age at which the right to

---

8. New Mexico Ass'n for Retarded Citizens v. New Mexico, 495 F. Supp. 391, 397-98 (D.N.M. 1980).

9. *See, e.g.,* ALA. CODE § 16-39-2(1) (1977); ALASKA STAT. § 14.30.180 (1982); ARIZ. REV. STAT. ANN. § 15-761(2) (1982); ARK. STAT. ANN. § 80-2102 (1980); CAL. EDUC. CODE § 56000 (West Supp. 1984); CONN. GEN. STAT. ANN. § 10-76a(c) (West Supp. 1983); DEL. CODE ANN. tit. 14, § 3101(1) (1981); HAWAII REV. STAT. § 301-21 (Supp. 1983); IDAHO CODE § 33-2002 (1981); KAN. STAT. ANN. § 72-962(f) (Supp. 1982); KY. REV. STAT. ANN. § 157.200(1) (Baldwin 1981).

10. *See, e.g.,* IOWA CODE ANN. § 281.2(1) (West Supp. 1983); N.M. STAT. ANN. § 22-8-2(N) (Supp. 1984).

11. *See, e.g.,* MD. EDUC. CODE ANN. § 8-401(a)(2) (Supp. 1983); MINN. STAT. ANN. § 120.03 (West 1960 & Supp. 1984); MO. ANN. STAT. § 162.675(2) (Vernon Supp. 1984); N.J. STAT. ANN. § 18A:46-1 (West Supp. 1984); OR. REV. STAT. § 343.035(2) (1983); WASH. REV. CODE ANN. § 28A.13.010 (1982).

12. *See, e.g.,* MASS. ANN. LAWS ch. 71B, § 1 (Law. Co-op. Supp. 1983); N.C. GEN. STAT. § 115C-106(b) (1983).

13. 20 U.S.C. § 1412(2)(b) (1982).

14. *See, e.g.,* ILL. ANN. STAT. ch. 122, § 14-1.02 (Smith-Hurd Supp. 1983); MASS. ANN. LAWS ch. 71B, § 1 (Law. Co-op. Supp. 1983); TENN. CODE ANN. § 49-10-102(1) (Supp. 1983); UTAH CODE ANN. § 53-18-3 (1981).

15. *See, e.g.,* CONN. GEN. STAT. ANN. § 10-76a(b) (West 1977); HAWAII REV. STAT. § 301-21 (1976 & Supp. 1983); KY. REV. STAT. ANN. § 157.200(1) (Baldwin 1983); MO. ANN. STAT. § 162.670 (Vernon Supp. 1984); N.Y. EDUC. LAW § 4401 (McKinney 1981).

16. *See, e.g.,* MONT. CODE ANN. § 20-7-412(a) (1983).

17. *See, e.g.,* ALA. CODE § 16-39-2(1) (Supp. 1983); ARK. STAT. ANN. § 80-2124 (1980); MISS. CODE ANN. § 37-23-69(b) (Supp. 1983).

18. *See, e.g.,* MO. ANN. STAT. § 162.700(1) (Vernon Supp. 1984); NEV. REV. STAT. § 388.490

special education accrues depends on whether kindergarten is offered.[19] Minimum ages in other states range from four to birth, although many states condition inclusion of these preschool age children upon their ability to benefit from special education or upon the possibility of their handicap worsening without it.[20] As with the maximum ages, some states make the extended limits mandatory while others merely permit coverage of preschool age children.[21]

B. Handicapping Condition

Assuming that a child has been able to satisfy the bright-line age requirements, he must still establish that he suffers from what qualifies as a handicapping condition under the applicable state statute. Even though the states' eligibility criteria are all clustered within the requirements of the EAHCA, some variation does exist from state to state. For example, certain learning disabilities will qualify a child for special education under the EAHCA and all state statutes.[22] In other cases, especially those involving emotional handicaps, the outcome will be neither clear in particular states nor consistent among the states.

What is a state's obligation to a child whose educational performance is above average despite his handicap? Is that child really handicapped within the meaning of the statute? Some states say yes and provide special education.[23] In fact, one state specifically provides that the handicap need not have any impact on schoolwork.[24] On the other hand, some states look at subpar academic performance as a key determinant.[25] Connecticut provides an

---

(1981) (with exceptions for specified handicaps); S.C. CODE ANN. § 59-63-20 (Law Co-op. Supp. 1983).

19. *See, e.g.,* ARK. STAT. ANN. § 80-2124 (1980); ARIZ. REV. STAT. ANN. § 15-822 (Special Pamphlet 1983); FLA. STAT. ANN. § 232.01 (West Supp. 1984); 22 PA. ADMIN. CODE § 13.1 (1984).

20. *See, e.g.,* IOWA CODE ANN. § 281.2(2) (West Supp. 1984) (younger than 5 included if it will help education process when child reaches 5); LA. REV. STAT. ANN. § 17:1943(4) (West 1982) (younger than 3 included if handicap could be greatly compounded by time child reaches school age); N.H. REV. STAT. ANN. § 186-C:2 (Supp. 1983) (minimum age of 3); S.D. CODIFIED LAWS ANN. § 13-37-1 (1982) (no minimum age).

21. *See, e.g.,* N.J. STAT. ANN. § 18A:46-6, -6.2 (West Supp. 1984) (mandatory for children ages 3-5; programs for children under age 3 available through Department of Health and Human Services).

22. *See, e.g.,* 20 U.S.C. § 1401(15) (1982); ARIZ. REV. STAT. ANN. § 15-761(4)(d) (1982); CAL. EDUC. CODE § 56337 (West Supp. 1984).

23. *See, e.g.,* Pitts v. Board. of Educ., 568 S.W.2d 595, 597 (Mo. App. 1978) (dictum) (where high I.Q. predicted high academic standing but only average performance was realized due to minimal brain dysfunction, special education was required since child had not developed to maximum capacity); *In re* Burton Valley School Dist., 1981-82 EDUC. HANDICAPPED L. REP. (CRR) 503:256, :258 (Cal. SEA 1982) (special education provided above average student if behavior problems may lead to expulsion and resulting decrease in education).

24. *In re* Cranston School Dept., 1981-82 EDUC. HANDICAPPED L. REP. (CRR) 503:287, :288 (R.I. SEA 1982) (applying Board of Regents Regulations).

25. *See, e.g.,* Diane K. v. West Jefferson Hills School Dist., 1979-80 EDUC. HANDICAPPED L. REP. (CRR) 501:227, :228 (Pa. SEA 1979) (asthmatic child performing well academically held not "exceptional"); *In re* Beaverton School Dist., 1979-80 EDUC. HANDICAPPED L. REP. (CRR) 501:375, :376-77 (Or. SEA 1979) (where child was teased by classmates regarding eye condition but academic performance was satisfactory, child was not entitled to special education); *In re* Gore Pub. Schools, 1981-82 EDUC. HANDICAPPED L. REP. (CRR) 503:179, :180-81 (Okla. SEA 1981) (child not entitled to special education program without showing of significant severe discrepancy between achievement and ability).

excellent illustration of how a conservative definition of handicap may limit the obligation to provide special education. In that state, average academic performance generally precludes a student from receiving special education services.[26]

Academic progress notwithstanding, another definitional problem is found in the characterization of behavioral and disciplinary problems. California, taking a generous approach, has found an obligation to provide special education to alcoholic truants,[27] students who did satisfactorily at school but were involved with drugs at home,[28] students who assaulted classmates,[29] and students whose parents failed to provide a proper home environment.[30] There is also some authority that convicted felons may be eligible for special education in at least one state.[31]

Less generous states require a close nexus between the handicap and the learning process itself. In Illinois, for example, problems in the home environment must be related to educational needs in order to qualify as a handicapping condition.[32] Other states have rejected claims based on a child's need for peer group influence[33] or on a desire to keep a child out of a Youth Correctional Center.[34] In order to qualify for special education in many states, a child must demonstrate that he can benefit from that special education even if he is clearly below average academically because of a handicapping condition.[35]

While it is clear that an underlying purpose of the state and federal special education statutes is to extend education to those children who were histori-

---

26. *See* S.P., 1980-81 EDUC. HANDICAPPED L. REP. (CRR) 502:258, :259 (Conn. SEA 1981) (math whiz with emotional problems not entitled to transportation for college level course); M.N., 1980-81 EDUC. HANDICAPPED L. REP. (CRR) 502:331, :335 (Conn. SEA 1981); B., 1980-81 EDUC. HANDICAPPED L. REP. (CRR) 502:286 (Conn. SEA 1981) (*M.N.* and *B.* held that where residential placement was for nonacademic reasons, board's obligation was limited to costs of special education). *But see* O.T., 1980-81 EDUC. HANDICAPPED L. REP. (CRR) 502:292, :294 (Conn. SEA 1981) (suicidal child who was rejected by mother found to have "intertwined" educational and emotional problems and therefore was handicapped).

27. *In re* Capistrano USD, 1980-81 EDUC. HANDICAPPED L. REP. (CRR) 502:129 (Cal. SEA 1980).

28. *In re* Los Angeles Unified School Dist., 1980-81 EDUC. HANDICAPPED L. REP. (CRR) 502:364 (Cal. SEA 1981).

29. *In re* Santa Ana Unified School Dist., 1982-83 EDUC. HANDICAPPED L. REP. (CRR) 504:151, :152 (Cal. SEA 1982) (reasoning that if expelled, the student would suffer loss of special educational services).

30. *In re* San Marcos Unified School Dist., 1983-84 EDUC. HANDICAPPED L. REP. (CRR) 505:105, :107 (Cal. SEA 1983) (children have right to education regardless of parents' failures).

31. *See, e.g.,* Green v. Johnson, 513 F. Supp. 965, 974 (D. Mass. 1981).

32. Case No. SE-61-82, 1982-83 EDUC. HANDICAPPED L. REP. (CRR) 504:297, :298 (Ill. SEA 1983) (suicidal 14-year-old girl who assaulted mother ineligible); Jeffrey K. v. Concord Carlisle High School, 1979-80 EDUC. HANDICAPPED. L. REP. (CRR) 501:205, :207 (Mass. SEA 1979) (special education and related services to be provided students with emotional problems when a nexus between the disturbance and inability to make progress in a regular education program is established).

33. *In re* R.C., 1981-82 EDUC. HANDICAPPED L. REP. (CRR) 503:114, :119-20 (Conn. SEA 1981) (Board responsible only for special education costs where residential placement made for noneducational reasons).

34. *In re* Madison County School Dist., 1981-82 EDUC. HANDICAPPED L. REP. (CRR) 503:130, :132 (Ga. SEA 1981).

35. *See, e.g.,* 72 Op. Att'y Gen. 652 (Iowa 1982); KAN. STAT. ANN. § 72-976 (1980).

cally ostracized because of their handicaps,[36] some statutes extend the definition of a handicapping condition beyond any literal interpretation. For example, although most states make gifted and talented special education discretionary with the local education agency,[37] some statutes mandate special education for gifted or talented children.[38] Pregnancy is similarly treated as a handicapping condition in some states.[39]

A review of the statutes and cases indicates that the sine qua non of special education is that the handicap have some sort of impact on classroom performance; however, almost anything in the life of a child may affect his academic progress. For example, a drawn-out custody battle between a child's parents might be reflected in poor performance in school. The variation among the states (and indeed from case to case within a state) may be attributable to the willingness or reluctance of an educational agency to find a nexus and accept responsibility for dealing with a problem that, even though reflected in school work, really is far removed from education. Statutes which are, by necessity, vaguely worded do not provide bright-line guidance as to what is a handicapping condition and, in turn, contribute to the problem of inconsistent coverage.

III

LEVEL OF STATE COMMITMENT

Once a state accepts the obligation to provide special education, there remains the question of how far that obligation extends. The federal standard[40] notwithstanding, the states vary in the level of assistance they provide to handicapped children.

The most common obligation that states have undertaken is to provide an "appropriate" education.[41] Some states interpret appropriate in terms relative to the handicapped child's needs.[42] Other interpretations of appropriate education include terms such as "competent,"[43] "suitable,"[44] or "meaningful" education.[45] Other states set out their obligations in terms of the

---

36. 20 U.S.C. § 1400 (1982); S. REP. No. 168, 94th Cong., 1st Sess. 7-9, *reprinted in* 1975 U.S. CODE CONG. & AD. NEWS, 1425, 1431-33.

37. *See, e.g.,* HAWAII REV. STAT. § 301-33 (Supp. 1983); MD. EDUC. CODE ANN. § 8-203 (1978); WASH. REV. CODE ANN. § 28A.16.030 (1982).

38. *See, e.g.,* 24 PA. CONS. STAT. ANN. § 13-1372(3) (Purdon Supp. 1983); S.D. CODIFIED LAWS ANN. § 13-37-25 (1982).

39. *See, e.g.,* TEX. EDUC. CODE ANN. § 16.16(b)(1) (Vernon 1972); WIS. STAT. ANN. § 115.76(3)(h) (West Supp. 1983).

40. *See* Board of Educ. v. Rowley, 458 U.S. 176 (1982).

41. *See, e.g.,* ALA. CODE § 16-39-3 (1977); CAL. EDUC. CODE § 56000 (West Supp. 1984); MD. EDUC. CODE ANN. § 8-401(3) (Supp. 1983); N.H. REV. STAT. ANN. § 186-C:1 (Supp. 1983); OHIO REV. CODE ANN. §§ 3323.01, .02 (Page Supp. 1983); S.C. CODE ANN. § 59-33-10 (Law. Co-op. 1977); VA. CODE § 22.1-214-A (Supp. 1984).

42. *See, e.g.,* ARK. STAT. ANN. § 80-2117 (1980); N.M. STAT. ANN. § 22-13-5 (1984); WASH. REV. CODE ANN. § 28A.13.010 (1982); 22 PA. ADMIN. CODE § 13.1 (1984).

43. *See, e.g.,* ALASKA STAT. § 14.30.180 (1982); ARK. STAT. ANN. § 80-2101 (1980); MISS. CODE ANN. § 37-23-1 (Supp. 1983).

44. *See, e.g.,* N.J. STAT. ANN. § 18A:46-13 (West Supp. 1984).

45. *See, e.g.,* NEB. REV. STAT. § 43-641 (1978).

potential or capabilities of handicapped children,[46] while some states take a quasi-equal-protection position, directing their education agencies to provide equivalent opportunities to handicapped and nonhandicapped children.[47] A few states, in providing for the maximum or "best" education, imply a commitment to exceed the federal mandate.[48] It is clear, however, that no state is obligated to provide a utopian educational program.[49] Notwithstanding these facially varying levels of commitment, no clear difference can be found among the states in the actual provision of day-to-day services.[50]

Of course, vague definitions and policies are not in themselves very important to handicapped children. What is important to these children is the degree of special education that they receive. Various provisions for related services, mainstreaming, year-round placements, homebound instruction, and unilateral placements reflect this concern.

A. Related Services

While all states provide the related services required by the EAHCA,[51] some states exceed the minimum standards. The general eligibility test inquires into the extent to which a related service will help the child benefit

---

46. *See, e.g.,* KAN. STAT. ANN. § 72-962(f) (Supp. 1983) (enable them to progress toward maximum of abilities); MASS. ANN. LAWS ch. 71B § 2 (Law. Co-op. Supp. 1983) (maximum possible development); MICH. COMP. LAWS ANN. § 380.1701(a) (West Supp. 1983) (maximum potential); Mo. ANN. STAT. § 162.670 (Vernon Supp. 1983) (maximize capabilities); TENN. CODE ANN. § 49-10-101 (Supp. 1983) (maximize capabilities).

47. *See, e.g.,* IOWA CODE ANN. § 281.2(2) (West Supp. 1984) (commensurate with nonhandicapped children); ME. REV. STAT. ANN. tit. 20A, § 7201(1) (1983); NEV. REV. STAT. § 388.450 (1983) (reasonably equal educational opportunity).

48. *See* IOWA CODE ANN. § 281.2 (West Supp. 1984) (special education opportunities sufficient to meet the needs and maximize the capabilities of children); MICH. COMP. LAWS ANN. § 380.1701 (West Supp. 1984-85) (to develop the maximum potential of every handicapped person); Mo. ANN. STAT. §§ 162.670, .675(4) (Vernon Supp. 1984) (to meet the needs and maximize the capabilities of handicapped children); R.I. GEN. LAWS § 16-24-1 (1981) (special education that will *best* satisfy the needs of the handicapped child). *See also* Geis v. Board of Educ., 589 F. Supp. 269 (D.N.J. 1984) (standard in New Jersey regulations requires provision of services according to how the pupil can *best* achieve educational success); *In re* Traverse Bay Intermediate School Dist., 1982-83 EDUC. HANDICAPPED L. REP. (CRR) 504:140, :142 (Mich. SEA 1982) (to develop maximum potential); Finn, *Advocating for the Most Misunderstood Minority: Securing Compliance with Special Education Laws,* 14 SUFFOLK U.L. REV. 505, 517 (1980) (examining Rhode Island law); Note, *Damages Actions for Denials of Equal Educational Opportunities,* 45 Mo. L. REV. 281, 297 (1980) (Missouri law requires development to maximum capacity).

49. *See, e.g.,* Lang v. Braintree School Comm., 545 F. Supp. 1221, 1227 (D. Mass. 1982) (this court may not interfere where the state is providing the child with an education that is of some benefit and is utilizing a minimally acceptable educational approach, citing *Rowley*); Bales v. Clarke, 523 F. Supp. 1366, 1370-71 (E.D. Va. 1981) (an "appropriate" education is not synonymous with the best possible education); Case No. SE-99-80, 1982-83 EDUC. HANDICAPPED L. REP. (CRR) 504:267, :268 (Ill. SEA 1983); Victoria P. v. Springfield School Dist., 1980-81 EDUC. HANDICAPPED L. REP. (CRR) 502:174, :175 (Pa. SEA 1980) (school district's duty is to provide an appropriate education, not one which affords plaintiff an opportunity to "achieve her utmost potential").

50. *See, e.g.,* Case No. H-0152, 1982-83 EDUC. HANDICAPPED L. REP. (CRR) 504:368, :369 (Mich. SEA 1983) ("If the maximum potential standard is reachable, it will be achieved only after a program has been designed to meet the unique educational needs of the handicapped child.").

51. *See* 20 U.S.C. §§ 1401(17), 1412(2) (1982); *see also* ALA. CODE § 16-39-2(6) (1977); CAL. EDUC. CODE § 56031(g) (West 1978); N.C. GEN. STAT. § 115C-108 (1983).

from special education.[52] The test results in different outcomes depending on the jurisdiction. Numerous examples of these varying outcomes exist. For instance, while psychological and counseling services are provided in some states[53] (even for parents[54]), others find the connection between education and psychological treatment tenuous and do not provide psychotherapy.[55] Likewise, school boards usually have only a limited responsibility to provide medical care.[56] Some states, however, provide medical care where essential to school attendance.[57]

Residential placements provide another example of how states implement federal policy. Whether a child receives a residential placement is a function of his needs.[58] Although many states provide funding for room and board,[59] at least one state does not recognize an obligation to pay for the cost of raw food.[60] In other circumstances, the obligation to provide related services has been found to mandate music therapy[61] and vocational training[62] but not a

---

52. See, e.g., In re E.F., 1981-82 EDUC. HANDICAPPED L. REP. (CRR) 503:300, :304 (Conn. SEA 1982); Lorrie v. Natick Pub. Schools, 1979-80 EDUC. HANDICAPPED L. REP. (CRR) 501:366, :367 (Mass. SEA 1980) (service directly related to success of IEP).

53. See, e.g., In re Palm Springs Unified School Dist., 1980-81 EDUC. HANDICAPPED L. REP. (CRR) 502:279 (Cal. SEA 1981). Several states' statutes include psychological, counseling, and/or social work services among those related services provided to handicapped children when appropriate. See, e.g., COLO. REV. STAT. § 22-20-114(b)(III) (Supp. 1983) (reimbursable costs include consultation and evaluation services by psychiatrists, psychologists, and social workers); IDAHO CODE § 33-2002A (1981); KY. REV. STAT. ANN. § 157.200(4) (1981); LA. REV. STAT. ANN. § 17:1943(3) (1982); OHIO REV. CODE ANN. § 3323.01 (Page Supp. 1983).

54. See, e.g., Lorrie v. Natick Pub. Schools, 1979-80 EDUC. HANDICAPPED L. REP. (CRR) 501:366, :367 (Mass. SEA 1979) (test for including psychotherapy in IEP is directness of relationship of the services to success of the IEP). There are several states which provide for counseling, social work, or training services for a handicapped child's parent or guardian as well as for the child. See, e.g., CONN. GEN. STAT. ANN. § 10-76a(h) (West Supp. 1983); MASS. ANN. Laws ch. 71B, § 3 (Law. Co-op. Supp. 1984); MO. ANN. STAT. § 162.675(4) (Vernon Supp. 1984); N.C. GEN. STAT. § 115C-108 (1983); WIS. STAT. ANN. § 115.83(3) (West Supp. 1983-84).

55. See, e.g., In re "A" Family, 184 Mont. 145, 159, 602 P.2d 157, 166 (1979) (finding that state statute would not provide therapy; therefore federal act, which would, applies); Case No. SE-14-83, 1982-83 EDUC. HANDICAPPED L. REP. (CRR) 504:363, :365 (Ill. SEA 1983); see also Wegner, Variations on a Theme—The Concept of Equal Educational Opportunity and Programming Decisions Under the Education for All Handicapped Children Act of 1975, LAW & CONTEMP. PROBS., Winter 1985, at 169.

56. See 20 U.S.C. § 1412 (1982); see, e.g., In re Tredyffrin-Eastown School Dist., 1981-82 EDUC. HANDICAPPED L. REP. (CRR) 503:245, :246-47 (Pa. SEA 1982) (public school not responsible for medical care); CAL. EDUC. CODE § 56345.5 (West Supp. 1984) (prescription of health care not authorized); IND. CODE ANN. § 20-1-6-8 (Bobbs-Merrill 1975) (health care is responsibility of family physician or Department of Public Welfare).

57. See, e.g., Department of Educ. v. Katherine D., 531 F. Supp. 517 (D. Hawaii 1982) (tracheotomy cleaning required even where teachers grieved under contract that they were not required to provide such service), modified 727 F.2d 809 (9th Cir. 1984); cf. Tatro v. Texas, 703 F.2d 823 (5th Cir. 1983), aff'd in part, rev'd in part sub nom. Irving Indep. School Dist. v. Tatro, 104 S. Ct. 3371 (1984) (must provide catheterization, which is not a medical service).

58. Compare Bill D., 1980-81 EDUC. HANDICAPPED L. REP. (CRR) 502:259, :262 (Conn. SEA 1981) (residential placement not for educational reasons) with San Francisco Unified School Dist. v. State Dep't of Educ., 131 Cal. App. 3d 54, 71, 182 Cal. Rptr. 525, 536 (1982) and In re Palo Alto City Unified School Dist., 1980-81 EDUC. HANDICAPPED L. REP. (CRR) 502:186, :187 (Cal. SEA 1980) (residential placement for educational reasons).

59. See, e.g., DEL. CODE ANN. tit. 14, § 3124(c)(1) (1981).

60. 62 Op. Att'y Gen. 353 (Md. 1977).

61. In re Cambridge Public Schools, 1981-82 EDUC. HANDICAPPED L. REP. (CRR) 503:136 (Mass.

place on the wrestling team.[63]

B.   Mainstreaming

In accordance with the EAHCA requirement, all of the states have obligated themselves to provide handicapped children an education in the least restrictive environment (LRE) possible.[64] The most common statutory language directs regular classroom placement unless, even with supplemental services, special education cannot be satisfactorily provided in that setting.[65] Other states simply mandate the use of least restrictive environments, or placement with nonhandicapped children, to the maximum extent possible.[66] However, the LRE placement need not be the one nearest the student's home,[67] nor does it necessarily require placement with children of the same age.[68]

While it is clear that an LRE is part of an appropriate education,[69] there are countervailing considerations which affect placement.[70] For example, placement in a classroom with nonhandicapped students may require a handicapped child to forego the better facilities and specially trained staff available in a separate special education classroom or school. Some states therefore allow mainstreaming in nonacademic activities where academic mainstreaming is not possible,[71] and no state allows students to be endangered by mainstreaming.[72] Given such complications, it is not surprising that the federal standard has been difficult to implement with anything approaching uniformity.

SEA 1981) (although hearing officer did not find music therapy appropriate in this case, officer notes it has been used for other handicapped children).

62. See, e.g., Brindisi v. Passave Valley Regular High School, 1983-84 EDUC. HANDICAPPED L. REP. (CRR) 505:192, :194 (N.J. SEA 1983); CAL. EDUC. CODE § 56345(b)(2) (West Supp. 1984).

63. Poole v. South Plainfield Bd. of Educ., 490 F. Supp. 948 (D.N.J. 1980) (decided under federal law).

64. 20 U.S.C. § 1412(5)(B) (1982). See, e.g., In re Katherine, 1979-80 EDUC. HANDICAPPED L. REP. (CRR) 501:237, :239 (Md. SEA 1979); Janet H. v. School Dist., 1979-80 EDUC. HANDICAPPED L. REP. (CRR) 501:163 (Neb. SEA 1979); ALA. CODE § 16-39-8 (1976); S.D. CODIFIED LAWS ANN. § 13-37-2 (1982); WIS. STAT. ANN. § 115.85(2)(d) (West Supp. 1983).

65. See, e.g., ARIZ. REV. STAT. ANN. § 15-764(A)(3) (1982); ARK. STAT. ANN. § 80-2118 (1980); CAL. EDUC. CODE § 56345(b)(6) (West Supp. 1984); COLO. REV. STAT. § 22-10-103(5.5) (1982); IOWA CODE ANN. § 281.2(2) (West Supp. 1984); LA. REV. STAT. ANN. § 17:1946B (West 1982); ME. REV. STAT. ANN. tit. 20A, § 7201(2) (1983); MINN. STAT. ANN. § 120.17, subd. 3a (West Supp. 1984).

66. See, e.g., ILL. ANN. STAT. ch. 122, § 14-8.02(c) (Smith-Hurd Supp. 1984-85); MO. ANN. STAT. § 162.680 (Vernon Supp. 1983); OHIO REV. CODE ANN. § 3323.04 (Page Supp. 1984); TENN. CODE ANN. § 49-10-103(c) (1983).

67. In re Cabarrus County Schools, 1980-81 EDUC. HANDICAPPED L. REP. (CRR) 502:218, :220 (N.C. SEA 1980).

68. In re Marin County Office of Educ., 1982-83 EDUC. HANDICAPPED L. REP. (CRR) 504:162, :165 (Cal. SEA 1982).

69. See 20 U.S.C. §§ 1401(18), 1401(19), 1412(5) (1982).

70. See, e.g., In re Mathew S., 1980-81 EDUC. HANDICAPPED L. REP. (CRR) 502:346 (Mass. SEA 1981) (need for deaf role models found more important than mainstreaming).

71. See, e.g., Cincinnati City School Dist., 1980-81 EDUC. HANDICAPPED L. REP. (CRR) 502:117, :119-20 (Ohio SEA 1979) (mainstream in nonacademic activities where handicap warrants removal from ordinary academic environment).

72. See, e.g., A.M.M. v. Board. of Educ., 1979-80 EDUC. HANDICAPPED L. REP. 501:304 (N.J. SEA 1979).

C. Year-Round Services

The question whether local school districts can be required to provide educational services for exceptional children for more than the traditional 180-day school year has been the subject of much litigation. As a result of a federal court decision interpreting requirements under the EAHCA, the response from states has been fairly uniform. *Battle v. Pennsylvania*[73] held that Pennsylvania's policy of refusing to provide or fund education for more than 180 days per year for any child, whether handicapped or nonhandicapped, violated the federal act. The court focused on the Act's requirement of a free appropriate public education designed to meet the unique needs of a handicapped child.[74] The court of appeals acknowledged the district court's finding that because of regression and the length of time required to recoup lost skills and behaviors, interruptions in programming brought about by the 180-day rule render it impossible or unlikely that mentally retarded children will attain the objectives of their individualized education programs.[75] Pennsylvania's categorical refusal to consider the needs of each individual student therefore violated federal policy.[76] Similar categorical refusals to consider providing more than 180 days of service have been found invalid in other states under the EAHCA.[77]

As a result of the above decisions, it appears that all states must provide more than 180 days of educational services where the unique needs of a child require such instruction as part of a free appropriate public education. To this end, several state codes allow the provision of year-round services where required.[78] Other states have expressly complied with the federal policy either through case law or through administrative decisions.[79]

Most courts apply a "substantial regression" standard to determine which exceptional students are entitled to a year-round program, holding that the handicapped child is not entitled to a summer placement at the school district's expense unless his parents can demonstrate that the child would regress substantially without such a program.[80] Some of these courts have

---

73. 629 F.2d 269 (3d Cir. 1980), *cert. denied,* 452 U.S. 968 (1981).
74. *Id.* at 276.
75. *Id.* at 275.
76. *Id.* at 280.
77. *See* Crawford v. Pittman, 708 F.2d 1028 (5th Cir. 1983) (Mississippi); Yaris v. Special School Dist., 558 F. Supp. 545 (E.D. Mo. 1983); Georgia Ass'n of Retarded Citizens v. McDaniel, 511 F. Supp. 1263 (N.D. Ga. 1981), *aff'd,* 716 F.2d 1565 (11th Cir. 1983).
78. *See, e.g.,* ALASKA STAT. § 14.30.350(2) (1982); MINN. STAT. ANN. § 120.17, subd. 5a (West Supp. 1984) N.H. REV. STAT. ANN. § 186-C:15 (Supp. 1983) (if interruption of program would result in severe and substantial harm and regression); N.D. CENT. CODE § 15-59-02.1 (1981) (if required in child's individualized education program (IEP) and interruption would cause regression); OKLA. STAT. ANN. tit. 70, § 13-101 (Supp. 1983-84) (extension not to exceed 40 days in summer months and only if for severely or profoundly multiple-handicapped student whose IEP states need for continuing program); WIS. STAT. ANN. § 115.83(4) (West Supp. 1983) (may include summer program).
79. *See* cases cited *infra* notes 80-84. These cases were decided pursuant to both state and federal law unless otherwise noted.
80. *See, e.g.,* Rettig v. Kent City School Dist., 539 F. Supp. 768, 778-79 (N.D. Ohio 1981), *aff'd in part and vacated in part,* 720 F.2d 463 (6th Cir.), *cert. denied,* 104 S. Ct. 2379 (1984) (federal act only); Bales v. Clarke, 523 F. Supp. 1366 (E.D. Va. 1981) (irreparable loss of progress); *In re* S., 1980-81

also considered an additional "recoupment" component, examining whether the child requires inordinately more time than nonhandicapped children to regain lost skills.[81] Following *Battle v. Pennsylvania* and its interpretation of the EAHCA, many states have fashioned similar standards for determining a handicapped child's eligibility for summer educational services. These standards acknowledge the state's obligation to provide an appropriate education which meets a student's individual needs, including year-round educational services where necessary.[82]

New York has a unique dual system for providing educational services to exceptional children beyond the regular school year. While the school district ordinarily is required to provide services for only the traditional 10-month school year, parents may petition the family court for an order to provide educational services during the summer months.[83] One drawback is that the parent or guardian in New York is inconvenienced by the necessity of petitioning both the commissioner of education and the family court each year.[84]

D. Homebound Services

One useful measure of a state's compliance with the federal act is its willingness to provide services for exceptional children who are homebound. The majority of states give a passing acknowledgment to homebound instruction by incorporating homebound and hospital instructional services into their definition of special education, as is done in the EAHCA.[85] Several states go a step further and include homebound instruction by visiting teachers in their statutory listing of alternative services, placements, or means for delivering services.[86] Those few jurisdictions which attempt to define the circumstances under which homebound services may be provided generally

EDUC. HANDICAPPED L. REP. (CRR) 502:362, :363-64 (Conn. SEA 1981); *In re* Jay R., 1983-84; EDUC. HANDICAPPED L. REP. (CRR) 505:123, :126 (Mass. SEA 1983); *In re* Canton Pub. Schools, 1981-82 EDUC. HANDICAPPED L. REP.; 503:235 (Mass. SEA 1982) (cases decided under state statutes and regulations); *see also* Anderson v. Thompson, 495 F. Supp. 1256, 1265 (E.D. Wis. 1980), *aff'd*, 658 F.2d 1205 (7th Cir. 1981).

81. *See* cases cited *supra* note 80; N.D. CENT. CODE § 15-59-02.1 (1981).

82. *See, e.g.*, Birmingham School Dist. v. Superintendent of Pub. Instruction, 120 Mich. App. 465, 474-76, 328 N.W.2d 59, 63 (1982); Mahoney v. Admin. School Dist. No. 1, 42 Or. App. 665, 670, 601 P.2d 826, 828 (1979); *In re* J.B., 1981-82 EDUC. HANDICAPPED L. REP. (CRR) 503:289, :290 (Nev. SEA 1980); *In re* Lake Oswego School Dist., 1979-80 EDUC. HANDICAPPED L. REP. (CRR) 501:344, :345 (Or. SEA 1980).

83. *In re* Frank G., 98 Misc. 2d 837, 842, 414 N.Y.S.2d 851, 855 (N.Y. Fam. Ct. 1979); N.Y. EDUC. LAW §§ 4401-4409 (McKinney 1981).

84. *In re* Dwella P., 98 Misc. 2d 869, 414 N.Y.S.2d 878 (N.Y. Fam. Ct. 1979).

85. 20 U.S.C. § 1401(16) (1982); *see, e.g.*, ALA. CODE § 16-39-7 (1977); MONT. CODE ANN. § 20-7-401(12) (1983); N.Y. EDUC. LAW § 4401 (McKinney 1981 & Supp. 1983); S.C. CODE ANN. § 59-33-20(c) (Law. Co-op. 1977); VA. CODE § 22.1-213.2 (Supp. 1984).

86. *See* NEB. REV. STAT. § 43-607(3) (1978 & Cum. Supp. 1982); OKLA. STAT. ANN. tit. 70, § 13-103 (West 1972) (when exceptional or pregnant child is unable to attend any school or class in the district); 24 PA. CONS. STAT. ANN. § 13-1372(3) (Purdon Supp. 1983) (the regulations promulgated hereunder specify homebound instruction as being within a school district's special educational program, 22 PA. ADMIN. CODE § 13.11(d) (1984)); VT. STAT. ANN. tit. 16, § 2944(a) (1982) (for those temporarily or permanently homebound or hospitalized when private instruction will best serve the interest of such persons).

require that a child be physically unable to attend any school[87] and that a physician so certify.[88]

The current lack of specific statutory limitations on the provision of homebound services may be attributable to the fact that there has been little litigation on the subject. Since a child's home is one of the most restrictive environments in which services can be provided, homebound services presumably are used only as a last resort or as a temporary placement while the school district seeks a more appropriate permanent placement. The few cases which do discuss homebound services recognize this situation and impose conditions similar to those found in the statutory law.[89]

E.   Unilateral Placement

The heart of the EAHCA is in the section delineating procedural safeguards.[90] Rather than defining an "appropriate education" in the abstract, the Act ensures that the content of a free appropriate public education is decided upon in a particular case through the participation of the child's parents, the local educational agency, and educational and medical experts.[91] Accordingly, parents and school districts are required to follow strict procedural rules throughout the placement process.[92] Failure to abide by these rules may result in shifting the financial responsibility for an educational placement from the school district to the parents, or vice versa. This shifting of costs frequently arises as a result of "unilateral placements" made by the child's parents or guardian. A unilateral placement occurs when the parent places the child in an educational facility or environment which has not been approved by the local educational agency.

Due to the mandatory nature of the federal procedural safeguards, judicial responses to unilateral placements are fairly uniform across the nation. One well-established point is that a local school district will not be liable for the

---

87.   OHIO REV. CODE § 3323.12 (1980 & Supp. 1983) (for handicapped children of compulsory school age who are unable to attend school, even with the help of special transportation).

88.   W. VA. CODE § 18-20-1 (1984) (to be provided after July, 1983 for children who are homebound due to injury or who for any other reason as certified by a licensed physician are homebound for a period of more than 3 weeks); WIS. STAT ANN. § 115.85(2)(e) (West Supp. 1983) (placement at child's home or residence if there is a physician's statement in writing that the child is unable to attend school); see also ARIZ. REV. STAT. ANN. § 15-761(c) (1983 Special Pamphlet) (defining "homebound" child).

89.   Case No. SE-17-83, 1982-83 EDUC. HANDICAPPED L. REP. (CRR) 504:353, :354 (Ill. SEA 1983) (citing the following state regulatory criteria for homebound services: 1) absence from school for 2 weeks to 6 months; 2) certification by a licensed medical doctor that the student has a health or physical impairment which will require such absence; and 3) determination by school personnel that student can benefit from services); In re Stoneham Pub. Schools, 1981-82 EDUC. HANDICAPPED L. REP. (CRR) 503:207 (Mass. SEA 1982) (requiring that severely multiple-handicapped child be provided occupational, physical, and speech therapy in home pursuant to physician's judgment that placement in hospital program was threatening to child's health).

90.   20 U.S.C. § 1415 (1982).

91.   See, e.g., Lora v. Board of Educ., 456 F. Supp. 1211, 1227, 1234-42 (E.D.N.Y. 1978), vacated, 623 F.2d 248 (2d Cir. 1980); Case No. 25, 1979-80 EDUC. HANDICAPPED L. REP. (CRR) 501:110, :111 (Wis. SEA 1979).

92.   See 20 U.S.C. § 1415 (1982); 34 C.F.R. §§ 300.500 - .589 (1984).

costs of a unilateral placement when the school district first attempts in good faith to provide an appropriate placement and services for a handicapped child.[93] A school district has no legal obligation to reimburse parents if it offers an appropriate publicly provided placement which the parents refuse.[94] A parent may also be denied reimbursement if he places the child without ever requesting a placement from the local education agency.[95]

Many unilateral placement cases are tied closely to the "status quo" provision of the federal act.[96] This provision requires that a child remain in his *then* current educational placement during the pendency of any due process proceedings unless the state or local educational agency and the parents or guardian agree otherwise.[97] Thus, parents generally are not entitled to reimbursement if they change the child's placement, either without the school district's consent during the pendency of the proceedings,[98] or without first pursuing the appropriate administrative procedures.[99] Correspondingly, a school district which changes a handicapped child's placement in violation of the status quo provision *will* be liable for the costs incurred by the parents'

---

93. *See, e.g.,* Flavin v. Connecticut State Bd. of Educ., 553 F. Supp. 827, 832-33 (D. Conn. 1982) (federal law only); Lux v. Connecticut State Bd. of Educ., 34 Conn. Supp. 257, 386 A.2d 644, 647 (Conn. Super. Ct. 1982); *In re* Newport Mesa Unified School Dist., 1981-82 EDUC. HANDICAPPED L. REP. (CRR) 503:186, :187 (Cal. SEA 1982); Case No. 36-82, 1982-83 EDUC. HANDICAPPED L. REP. (CRR) 504:250, :253 (Ill. SEA 1982). Note that the cases cited *infra* notes 94-106, were decided under either state law or both state and federal law unless otherwise noted.

94. *See, e.g,* Stacey G. v. Pasadena Indep. School Dist., 695 F.2d 949, 954 (5th Cir. 1983) (also discusses state regulation comparable to federal "status quo" provision); Fitz v. Intermediate Unit #29, 43 Pa. Commw. 370, 403 A.2d 138, 141 (1979) (absent showing that placement was inappropriate, state secretary of education justified in denying tuition reimbursement for unilateral placement); Case No. 9953, 1979-80 EDUC. HANDICAPPED L. REP. (CRR) 501:120, :121 (N.Y. SEA 1979); Scott B. v. Harlingen Consol. Indep. School Dist., 1982-83 EDUC. HANDICAPPED L. REP. (CRR) 504:344, :349 (Tex. SEA 1983); *In re* Todd B., 1979-80 EDUC. HANDICAPPED L. REP. (CRR) 501:165 (Wash. SEA 1979) (affirming local hearing officer's finding that school had offered four appropriate program alternatives and denying private placement at public expense).

95. *See, e.g.,* Welsch v. Commonwealth, 42 Pa. Commw. 41, 44, 400 A.2d 234, 235 (1979); *In re* New York City School Dist., 1982-83 EDUC. HANDICAPPED L. REP. (CRR) 504:178, :178-79 (N.Y. SEA 1982).

96. *See infra* notes 98-100.

97. 20 U.S.C. § 1415(e)(3) (1982).

98. *See* Mt. View-Los Altos Union High School Dist. v. Sharon B.H., 1983-84 EDUC. HANDICAPPED L. REP. (CRR) 555:113 (9th Cir. 1983) (federal law only); Stemple v. Board of Educ., 623 F.2d 893 (4th Cir. 1980), *cert. denied,* 450 U.S. 911 (1981) (federal law); Cain v. Yukon Pub. Schools, 556 F. Supp. 605 (W.D. Okla. 1983) (federal law); Lillian S. v. Ambach, 92 A.D.2d 979, 461 N.Y.S.2d 501 (1983); Newport-Mesa Union School Dist. v. Hubert, 132 Cal. App. 3d 724, 730, 183 Cal. Rptr. 334, 338 (1982); Case No. 82-162, 1982-83 EDUC. HANDICAPPED L. REP. (CRR) 504:133 (Cal. SEA 1982). *But cf.* Doe v. Anrig, 561 F. Supp. 121 (D. Mass. 1983), *aff'd,* 728 F.2d 30 (1st Cir. 1984) (ordering reimbursement where court upheld parent's unilateral placement decision); Doe v. Brookline School Comm., 722 F.2d 910 (1st Cir. 1983) (holding reimbursement available to the prevailing party under authority of 20 U.S.C. § 1415(e)(2)). For a discussion of the challenges to the *Doe v. Brookline* interpretation of the status quo provision, see generally Osborne, *Reimbursement Under the EAHCA for Unilaterally Obtained Private Schooling: The Implications of Doe v. Brookline,* 19 EDUC. L. REP. 469 (West 1984).

99. *See In re* Los Angeles Unified School Dist., 1980-81 EDUC. HANDICAPPED L. REP. (CRR) 502:381, :382 (Cal. SEA 1981) (no reimbursement, absent irreparable harm or unreasonable delay, if parents have not exhausted administrative remedies); Case No. 10686, 1981-82 EDUC. HANDICAPPED L. REP. (CRR) 503:124 (N.Y. SEA 1981) (parents not entitled to reimbursement for unilateral placement without first pursuing the appropriate administrative procedures).

subsequent unilateral placement.[100]

A handicapped child's parents are also entitled to reimbursement for a unilateral placement that was necessitated by an educational agency's conscious failure or refusal to provide a free appropriate public education[101] or by other procedural violations, such as an unreasonable delay in providing services.[102] Some courts have also held that a parent who takes action to protect his child's physical health from a threatening situation may be entitled to damages or reimbursement.[103] Likewise, if the school district places a child inappropriately, the district may have to bear the expense of a unilateral placement by the parents.[104] On the other hand, parents who make a unilateral placement take the risk of making an inappropriate choice themselves and thereby assume the risk of being reimbursed only partially or not at all.[105]

F. Graduation

A recurring point of contention concerns whether handicapped children are entitled to a diploma upon completion of their education. Receiving a diploma is a particularly compelling concern for many of the less severely handicapped because it affects their prospects for obtaining employment after they leave school. A few states have enacted statutes that authorize school boards to issue a diploma or certificate of graduation to exceptional children.[106] For the most part, these statutes merely empower the school district

---

100. *In re* Ramsey County School Dist., 1981-82 EDUC. HANDICAPPED L. REP. (CRR) 503:304, :305 (Minn. SEA 1981) (dropping handicapped child from high school membership rolls constituted a change in placement); Deist v. Adams Cent. School Dist. No. 090, 1980-81 EDUC. HANDICAPPED L. REP. (CRR) 502:241 (Neb. SEA 1980).

101. *See, e.g.,* Adams Cent. School Dist. v. Deist, 214 Neb. 307, 334 N.W.2d 775, 785 (1983) (school district which fails to provide a free appropriate public education is liable to reimburse parent who does obtain such services); New York City Bd. of Educ. v. Ambach, 88 A.D.2d 1075, 1076, 452 N.Y.S.2d 731, 733 (1980); *In re* Board of Educ., 1983-84 EDUC. HANDICAPPED L. REP. (CRR) 505:142, :144 (N.Y. SEA 1983).

102. *See, e.g.,* New York City Bd. of Educ. v. Ambach, 88 A.D.2d 1075, 452 N.Y.S.2d 731, 734 (N.Y. App. Div. 1982) (ordering reimbursement where content and time requirements for formal notice of rejection not met); Jose P. v. Ambach, 1981-82 EDUC. HANDICAPPED L. REP. (CRR) 553:298 (E.D.N.Y. 1982) (upholding 1977 order of Commissioner of Education that permits parents unilaterally to place children who have not been placed within 60 days of referral for evaluation and requires New York City to bear expense); *In re* Worcester Pub. Schools, 1981-82 EDUC. HANDICAPPED L. REP. (CRR) 503:166, :169 (Mass. SEA 1981) (failure to offer timely appropriate placement).

103. *See* Anderson v. Thompson, 658 F.2d 1205, 1214 (7th Cir. 1981) (federal law only); Walker v. Cronin, 107 Ill. App. 3d 1053, 1059 , 438 N.E.2d 582, 587 (1982).

104. Amherst-Pelham Regional School Comm. v. Department of Educ., 376 Mass. 480, 493, 381 N.E.2d 922, 931 (1978).

105. *See, e.g.,* Blomstrom v. Massachusetts Dep't of Educ., 532 F. Supp. 707, 713 (D. Mass. 1982) (school district obligated to pay for only day portion of residential placement; court says dispute is governed by federal law); Board of Educ. v. Connecticut Bd. of Educ., 179 Conn. 694, 7C3, 427 A.2d 846, 851 (1980); *In re* Worcester Pub. Schools, 1981-82 EDUC. HANDICAPPED L. REP. (CRR) 503:166, :169 (Mass. SEA 1981).

106. ILL. ANN. STAT. ch. 122, § 14-6.01 (Smith-Hurd Supp. 1983) (no handicapped child may be denied promotion, graduation, or a general diploma on the basis of failing minimal competency test when failure of such test directly related to handicapping condition); IND. CODE ANN. § 20-1-6-17 (Michie Bobbs-Merrill Supp. 1984) (authorized to issue to handicapped child completing special education program); 22 PA. ADMIN. CODE § 13.15 (1984) (under state law, exceptional child who satisfactorily completes special education program is entitled to a high school diploma, except trainable or profoundly mentally retarded, who are entitled to a certificate of graduation).

to issue a diploma or certificate, leaving the decision whether to do so to the discretion of the school.[107] This discretion has been held to be permissible, since the denial of a high school diploma to handicapped children does not violate the EAHCA[108] or section 504 of the Rehabilitation Act.[109] While the federal acts ensure that a student is provided access to an appropriate education, they do not guarantee that the student will successfully reach the level of academic achievement necessary for the award of a diploma. In addition, courts have observed that a state has a legitimate interest in restricting the issuance of diplomas to ensure the value of the diplomas in the community and to improve the general quality of education.[110] In cases where a handicapped child is not given sufficient advance notice of the requirements for obtaining a diploma, however, a school district violates the child's right to due process.[111]

In some states, a school district may terminate educational services when the handicapped child becomes eligible for graduation from high school or reaches a certain age, whichever occurs first.[112] Although these states do not specifically address the question of eligibility for a diploma, they do imply, through their criteria for determining when special education services will be terminated, that exceptional students may receive a diploma or other certification of graduation from high school.

A related question concerns the time at which a school district may terminate special education services and programs for exceptional children. As noted above, in some states educational services may be terminated when a handicapped student either becomes eligible to graduate from high school or

107.   See In re Peoria School Dist. #150, 1980-81 EDUC. HANDICAPPED L. REP. (CRR) 502:299 (Ill. SEA 1981).

108.   Brookhart v. Illinois State Bd. of Educ., 697 F.2d 179 (7th Cir. 1983).

109.   29 U.S.C. § 794 (1982); Board of Educ. v. Ambach, 107 Misc. 2d 830, 436 N.Y.S.2d 564 (Sup. Ct. 1981), modified, 90 A.D.2d 227, 458 N.Y.S.2d 680 (1982), aff'd, 60 N.Y.2d 758, 457 N.E.2d 775 (1983) (both acts); In re Peoria School Dist. #150, 1980-81 EDUC. HANDICAPPED L. REP. (CRR) 502:299 (Ill. SEA 1981) (both acts).

110.   Board of Educ. v. Ambach, 107 Misc. 2d 830, 835, 436 N.Y.S.2d 564, 569, modified, 90 A.D.2d 227, 458 N.Y.S.2d 680 (1982), aff'd, 60 N.Y.2d 758, 457 N.E.2d 775 (1983).

111.   See Brookhart v. Illinois State Bd. of Educ., 697 F.2d 179, 187-88 (7th Cir. 1983) (constitutionally inadequate notice); Board of Educ. v. Ambach, 107 Misc. 2d 830, 844-45, 436 N.Y.S.2d 564, 574-75, modified, 90 A.D.2d 227, 458 N.Y.S.2d 680 (1982), aff'd, 60 N.Y.2d 758, 457 N.E.2d 775 (1983). But cf. Case No. SE-55-82, 1982-83 EDUC. HANDICAPPED L. REP. (CRR) 504:300 (Ill. SEA 1983) (child should graduate even though IEP did not contain specific criteria for determining that he had satisfactorily completed program).

112.   Alycia C., 1980-81 EDUC. HANDICAPPED L. REP. (CRR) 502:140 (Conn. SEA 1980); In re Steven, 1980-81 EDUC. HANDICAPPED L. REP. (CRR) 502:143 (Md. SEA 1980); B.J.M. v. Perth-Amboy Bd. of Educ., 1982-83 EDUC. HANDICAPPED L. REP. (CRR) 504:334 (N.J. SEA 1983); In re New Trier Township High School Dist No. 203, 1982-83 EDUC. HANDICAPPED L. REP. (CRR) 504:255, :257 (Ill. SEA 1982) (eligible for services in Illinois until age 21 or successful completion of secondary program); In re Windsor Cent. High School, 1980-81 EDUC. HANDICAPPED L. REP. (CRR) 502:268 (N.Y. SEA 1981); CONN. GEN. STAT. ANN. § 10-76d(b)(1) (West 1981) (obligation terminates at high school graduation or age 21); N.J. REV. STAT. ANN. § 18A:46-14 (West Supp. 1984) (may furnish special education to any person over 20 who does not hold a high school diploma); N.Y. EDUC. LAW § 4402(1)(b) (McKinney 1981 & Supp. 1983) (services do not continue after age 21 or receipt of high school diploma); 1979 Op. Att'y Gen. 126 (S.C.) (neither EAHCA nor South Carolina law requires a local school district to provide a FAPE for a handicapped child who has graduated from high school or completed the program provided in his IEP).

reaches a specified age.[113] Other states declare that their obligation to provide special education services terminates when the child completes the program set forth in his individualized education program (IEP) or reaches a designated age, whichever occurs first.[114] Oklahoma has chosen simply to establish a minimum number of years of service to which an exceptional child is legally entitled, while permitting continuation up to age 21.[115] In addition, there are a few state agencies that are more lenient toward the continuation of special education services after the child meets requirements for graduation or completion in individual cases where such continuation appears necessary for an appropriate and adequate education.[116]

IV

FINANCIAL RESPONSIBILITY

A. Compensatory Education

In the last few years there has arisen a question whether a handicapped child is ever entitled to educational services beyond age 21.[117] A small number of cases have held that a school district may be required to provide compensatory educational services when it has deprived a handicapped child of a free appropriate public education because of violations of procedural safeguards and/or because of an inappropriate placement.[118] These cases, however, have arisen primarily under the federal act and have not relied upon

---

113. See supra note 112.

114. See In re Lincoln Consol. Schools, 1982-83 EDUC. HANDICAPPED L. REP. (CRR) 504:232, :234 (Mich. SEA 1982); CAL. EDUC. CODE § 56001(a) (West Supp. 1984) (until completion of child's prescribed course or child meets proficiency standards); Op. Att'y Gen. No. I 79-265 (Ariz. 1979) (must provide special education until child meets IEP objectives or is 22 years old).

115. In re Broken Arrow Pub. Schools, 1982-83 EDUC. HANDICAPPED L. REP. (CRR) 504:208 (Okla. SEA 1982); OKLA. STAT. ANN. tit. 70, § 13-102 (1972).

116. See, e.g., Wayne S. v. Framingham Pub. Schools, 1980-81 EDUC. HANDICAPPED L. REP. (CRR) 502:238, :239 (Mass. SEA 1981) (eligibility age extended to 22 to improve reading ability); Geraldine M. v. Ashland Pub. Schools, 1979-80 EDUC. HANDICAPPED L. REP. (CRR) 501:265, :268 (Mass. SEA 1979); In re Michigan School for the Deaf, 1982-83 EDUC. HANDICAPPED L. REP. (CRR) 504:143 (Mich. SEA 1982) (student lacking minimum competency skills after meeting graduation requirements); see also In re J.R., 1981-82 EDUC. HANDICAPPED L. REP. (CRR) 503:291 (Nev. SEA 1981) (since district provides education to nonhandicapped students over age 18 in certain circumstances to meet graduation or completion requirements, it must do the same for handicapped students).

117. The question arises because the federal mandate in the EAHCA requires provision of special educational services through age 18 and permits an extension to age 21 if consistent with state law. 20 U.S.C. § 1412(2)(B) (1982).

118. Campbell v. Talladega County Bd. of Educ., 1980-81 EDUC. HANDICAPPED L. REP. (CRR) 552:472, :478 (N.D. Ala. 1981); In re Davis County Community School Dist., 1981-82 EDUC. HANDICAPPED L. REP. (CRR) 503:273 (Iowa SEA 1981); In re New Bedford Pub. Schools, 1982-83 EDUC. HANDICAPPED L. REP. (CRR) 504:122 (Mass. SEA 1982) (setting forth eligibility criteria to establish prima facie case for compensatory education); Lane v. Arnold Pub. School Dist. #89, 1980-81 EDUC. HANDICAPPED L. REP. (CRR) 502:366, :368 (Neb. SEA 1981). Contra Adams Cent. School Dist. v. Deist, 214 Neb. 307, 334 N.W.2d 775 (1983) (state not obligated under either EAHCA or state law to provide a free appropriate public education beyond child's 21st birthday); In re City of Yonkers, 1979-80 EDUC. HANDICAPPED L. REP. (CRR) 501:241 (N.Y. SEA 1979) (there is no statutory or regulatory provision in state or federal law entitling petitioner to compensatory special education services). All cases cited infra notes 120-30, were decided primarily under federal law.

any interpretation of state law or obligations.[119]

A recent line of cases in the federal courts suggests that the remedy of compensatory educational services may soon become obsolete. In *Anderson v. Thompson*,[120] the Court of Appeals for the Seventh Circuit held that monetary damages may be allowed under the EAHCA only in the following exceptional circumstances: (1) when a parent secures services which should have been provided by the school district to protect the physical health of the child; and (2) when the school district acts in bad faith by failing in an egregious fashion to comply with procedural provisions of the EAHCA.[121] While no claim for compensatory education was made in *Anderson*, the court denied an award of money damages necessary to recompense the parents for cost of a unilateral placement.[122] The Eighth Circuit also has held that relief under the EAHCA is usually restricted to injunctive relief and that money damages are appropriate, if at all, only under the most exceptional circumstances.[123]

In *Timms v. Metropolitan School District*,[124] the court cited *Anderson* in holding that compensatory education is not recoverable under the EAHCA where school officials have made good faith, though incorrect, placement decisions, since such relief would be punitive. The court also held that the EAHCA provides the exclusive basis through which procedural noncompliance with the Act may be challenged; claims under section 504 of the Rehabilitation Act[125] and under the Civil Rights Act of 1871[126] would not be heard.[127]

In *Max M. v. Thompson*,[128] remedial education was denied even though the school district had failed to provide psychotherapy services recommended in its own evaluation of the child. The plaintiffs in this case alleged violations of the Illinois School Code, as well as of the EAHCA. The court found that the school code was merely a "reflection of the EAHCA on the state level" and could confer no greater rights than the federal act itself.[129] The remedy of compensatory education was unavailable against either the state or the intermediate and local school defendants since monetary relief is limited to reimbursement.[130] Consequently, compensatory education apparently is not an appropriate remedy for violations of a handicapped child's procedural (and therefore substantive) rights unless the state creates such a remedy by statute.

---

119. *But see* MD. EDUC. CODE ANN. § 8-101.1 (Supp. 1983). This provision of the Maryland Code prescribes up to 2 years of compensatory special education services for handicapped individuals who were deprived of appropriate educational services due to health reasons or to state or local school system violations. The programs under this section were to terminate in 1983.
120. 658 F.2d 1205 (7th Cir. 1981).
121. *Id.* at 1214.
122. *Id.*
123. Miener v. Missouri, 673 F.2d 969 (8th Cir.), *cert. denied*, 459 U.S. 909 (1982).
124. 718 F.2d 212, 216 (7th Cir.), *aff'd as modified*, 722 F.2d 1310 (7th Cir. 1983).
125. 29 U.S.C. § 794 (1982).
126. 42 U.S.C. § 1983 (1982).
127. 718 F.2d at 216.
128. 566 F. Supp. 1330 (N.D. Ill. 1983).
129. *Id.* at 1338.
130. *Id.* at 1336-37 (citing Anderson v. Thompson, 658 F.2d 1205 (7th Cir. 1981) and Miener v. Missouri, 673 F.2d 969 (8th Cir.), *cert. denied*, 459 U.S. 909 (1982)).

Compensatory education is almost certainly barred as a remedy against state defendants because compensatory educational services are, like money damages, retrospective in nature; they are intended to remedy a past deprivation of educational services. Thus, as with money damages, the eleventh amendment bars an award of compensatory education against state defendants.[131]

B. Parental and Third Party Contributions

The EAHCA defines a free appropriate public education as "special education and related services which (A) have been provided at public expense, under public supervision and direction, and without charge. . . ."[132] Accordingly, many states guarantee a special education free of charge. Nonetheless, a few states have attempted to impose some costs on the parent or guardian of the handicapped child. Such attempts have resulted in litigation over whose responsibility it is to provide or to fund various related services.[133] The courts have held consistently that neither school districts nor states may charge a handicapped child or his responsible relatives for education-related services,[134] though the parents or guardians may be required to assume such costs and expenses for a handicapped child as they would be obliged to pay if the child were not handicapped.[135]

A few states have attempted to charge parents indirectly by requiring the application of family insurance or other third party payors' obligations towards related services.[136] The courts have given mixed reviews to this approach. One case arose when the New York Commissioner of Education decided that the parents of an exceptional child could be required to apply voluntarily acquired insurance benefits to the cost of providing physical and occupational therapy for their child.[137] The parents petitioned the Office for Civil Rights for Region II (which includes New York) which declared that such a requirement violated section 504 of the Rehabilitation Act because payment for a portion of a public education was being sought solely from the

---

131. Miener v. Missouri, 673 F.2d 969, 982 (8th Cir.), *cert. denied,* 459 U.S. 909 (1982).

132. 20 U.S.C. § 1401(18) (1982).

133. *See supra* notes 51-63 and accompanying text.

134. *See, e.g.,* Parks v. Pavkovic, 557 F. Supp. 1280 (N.D. Ill. 1983).

135. 34 C.F.R. § 300.14(b)(1) (1984). *See also* N.D. CENT. CODE § 15-59-02.1 (1981).

136. *See* CAL. EDUC. CODE § 56363.5 (West Supp. 1984) (school district may seek reimbursement from insurance companies either directly or through the pupil's parents); MASS. ANN. LAWS ch. 71B, § 5 (Law. Co-op. Supp. 1983) (school committee is not required to pay for medically necessary treatment which would be covered by a third party payor but for child's eligibility for goods and services under this chapter); ILL. ANN. STAT. ch. 122, § 14-7.02 (Smith-Hurd Supp. 1983) (State's liability for funding of these tuition costs never to begin until after the legal obligations of third party payors have been subtracted from such costs); N.D. CENT. CODE § 15-59-02.1 (1981) (requiring use of insurance or third party payments when determining school district's responsibility for providing special education resulting from a child's medically related handicapping condition). Each of these statutes provides that the school district must assume costs not covered by such payments.

137. *In re* Three Village Cent. School Dist., 1979-80 EDUC. HANDICAPPED L. REP. (CRR) 501:320 (N.Y. SEA 1979).

parents of handicapped pupils.[138] The New York Commissioner of Education then annulled his first decision and followed the pronouncement of the Office of Civil Rights.[139] While following the law of his region, the Commissioner's second ruling observed that the Office of Civil Rights for Region V had found that the State of Illinois *could* compel the use of insurance benefits to cover educational expenses.[140]

Given the current split among jurisdictions, one can probably anticipate further litigation in this area. In some respects, the EAHCA does seem to allow the requirement of third party contributions. Its policy of leaving primary control of substantive matters and the bulk of funding in the hands of the state and local school districts indicates an intent to give the states free rein over such matters.[141] Moreover, a federal regulation regarding methods of payment for a free appropriate public education states that "[n]othing in this part relieves an insurer or similar third party from an otherwise valid obligation to provide or pay for services provided to a handicapped child."[142] In addition, the Department of Education issued an interpretation of Part B of the EAHCA and section 504 of the Rehabilitation Act[143] in December, 1980. The Department stated:

> Both Part B and Section 504 prohibit a public agency from requiring parents, *where they would incur a financial cost*, to use insurance proceeds to pay for services that must be provided to a handicapped child under the "free appropriate public education" requirements of these statutes. The use of parents' insurance proceeds to pay for services in these circumstances must be voluntary on the part of the parents.[144]

Thus, parents may be asked to apply insurance benefits to their handicapped child's education if they will suffer no financial loss by filing a claim.[145]

On the other hand, insofar as the parents have paid the insurance premiums and insofar as both their ability to obtain insurance in the future and their insurance rates are affected by the required use of such benefits to pay for education-related services, these handicapped children are not receiving services without charge. In addition, such a requirement may discriminate unlawfully between the parents of handicapped and nonhandicapped chil-

---

138. *See In re* Three Village Cent. School Dist., 1980-81 EDUC. HANDICAPPED L. REP. (CRR) 502:141, :142 (N.Y. SEA 1980).

139. *Id.*

140. *Id.*; Illinois Bd. of Educ., 2 [EHA Decisions] EDUC. HANDICAPPED L. REP. (CRR) 257:82 (Ill. OCR 1980). *But see* School Dist. #220, 2 [EHA Decisions] EDUC. HANDICAPPED L. REP. (CRR) 257:200, :202 (Ill. OCR 1981) (parents may no longer be required to use private insurance to pay for residential programs, including nonmedical care and room and board). See also comments on the Illinois statute in Kula, *The Right to Special Education in Illinois — Something Old and Something New,* 55 CHI.-KENT L. REV. 649, 679-81 (1979).

141. *See* 20 U.S.C. §§ 1400-1461 (1982).

142. 34 C.F.R. § 300.301(b) (1984).

143. 29 U.S.C. § 794 (1982).

144. 45 Fed. Reg. 86,390 (1980) (emphasis added).

145. The Department's interpretation states that financial losses include, but are not limited to: "(1) A decrease in available lifetime coverage or any other benefit under an insurance policy; (2) An increase in the premiums or the discontinuation of the policy; or (3) An out-of-pocket expense such as the payment of a deductible amount incurred in filing a claim." 45 Fed. Reg. 86,390 (1980). "Financial losses do not include incidental costs such as the time needed to file an insurance claim or the postage needed to mail the claim." *Id.*

dren, or between the parents of handicapped children who do and those who do not have insurance benefits that will cover these expenses.[146]

V

CONCLUSION

While statutory language as well as case law regarding handicapped education is not totally consistent among the states, this investigation of the various state responses to the EAHCA revealed very few, if any, remarkable contrasts or differences among jurisdictions. Obviously no state can provide all things to all people, whether handicapped or not. Some educational requests are clearly outside of what any jurisdiction has undertaken an obligation to meet, and are consequently likely to be denied in almost every case. Conversely, the failure to provide for other more basic needs would be tantamount to totally ignoring the EAHCA, and no state has so failed.

Cases in the gray areas are the ones that ought to provide an indication of any appreciable variations among states. Although the "hard" cases exist, no distinguishing trends appear. The reasons for this relate to the very nature of the problem. Because the EAHCA so pervades the legislative background and case law of the states, it is difficult to separate decisions based on state law from those based either solely on federal law or on a combination of state and federal law. In addition, each child has unique problems and potential, so that no case is truly on "all fours" with any other. Therefore, comparing and distinguishing cases in the special education area is less instructive than such analysis in other more doctrinal areas of the law. Moreover, statutory terms such as "appropriate education" are by their very nature vague. As a result, agencies and courts are applying vague standards to highly fact-dependent cases. Apparent consistency is a victim of such circumstances.

The fact that the "hard" cases are not totally consistent from state to state, or even within states, ought not give rise to concern, given the structure of the EAHCA. Indeed, uniformity in the clear cases along with fluctuations at the borderlines is to be expected in a system which provides federal funding to help meet the national goal of providing a free appropriate education to all handicapped children, while leaving implementation decisions with those state and local authorities which have traditionally been responsible for education.

---

146. *See In re* Three Village Cent. School Dist., 1980-81 EDUC. HANDICAPPED L. REP. (CRR) 502:141 (N.Y. SEA 1980); 45 Fed. Reg. 86,390 (1980) (will not require parents to contribute insurance benefits where they would suffer a financial loss not incurred by similarly situated parents of nonhandicapped parents).